Major Problems in
the History of
American Sexuality

MAJOR PROBLEMS IN AMERICAN HISTORY SERIES

GENERAL EDITOR
THOMAS G. PATERSON

Major Problems in the History of American Sexuality

DOCUMENTS AND ESSAYS

EDITED BY

KATHY PEISS

UNIVERSITY OF PENNSYLVANIA

WADSWORTH
CENGAGE Learning

Australia • Brazil • Japan • Korea • Mexico • Singapore • Spain • United Kingdom • United States

Major Problems in the History of American Sexuality: Documents and Essays
Kathy Peiss

Editor in Chief: Jean L. Woy

Senior Development Editor: Frances Gay

Project Editor: Carla Thompson

Editorial Assistant: Christian Downey

Associate Production/Design Coordinator: Christine Gervais

Senior Manufacturing Coordinator: Priscilla Bailey

Marketing Manager: Sandra McGuire

Cover Image: Beatrice Cuming, *Saturday Night, New London,* c. 1939. Lyman Allyn Art Museum at Connecticut College, New London, Connecticut.

For product information and technology assistance, contact us at **Cengage Learning Customer & Sales Support, 1-800-354-9706**

For permission to use material from this text or product, submit all requests online at **www.cengage.com/permissions** Further permissions questions can be emailed to **permissionrequest@cengage.com**

Library of Congress Control Number: 9971959

ISBN-13: 978-0-395-90384-1

ISBN-10: 0-395-90384-X

Wadsworth
20 Channel Center Street
Boston, MA 02210
USA

Cengage Learning is a leading provider of customized learning solutions with office locations around the globe, including Singapore, the United Kingdom, Australia, Mexico, Brazil, and Japan. Locate your local office at **www.cengage.com/global**

Cengage Learning products are represented in Canada by Nelson Education, Ltd.

To learn more about Wadsworth, visit **www.cengage.com/wadsworth**

Purchase any of our products at your local college store or at our preferred online store **www.CengageBrain.com**

Printed in the United States of America
7 8 9 10 11   19 18 17 16 15

IN MEMORY OF
ROSE AGREE
vital spirit

Contents

C H A P T E R   6
Love and Intimacy in Nineteenth-Century America
Page 187

C H A P T E R   7
Free Love, Free Speech, and Sex Censorship
Page 238

CHAPTER 14
Sexual Identities, Family Matters, and Border Crossings in Contemporary America
Page 484

Preface

In a 1964 Supreme Court ruling on obscenity, Justice Potter Stewart famously said of hard-core pornography, I know it when I see it. The same might be said of sexuality: Everyone knows what *it* is, and yet *it* is, in fact, nearly impossible to define. The dictionary definition the condition of being characterized and distinguished by sex is circular. Indeed, what simple definition could capture the tangle of bodily sensations, feelings, thoughts, and interactions that are conjured up by the word sexuality ? Showing how sexuality s meaning has changed over time, this anthology makes the case that a historical perspective is crucial to a better understanding of this subject.

Born in the late 1960s, the history of sexuality is still an emergent field of inquiry. In those years of social turmoil and sexual revolution, the feminist and gay liberation movements brought sexuality into the political arena. Activists believed that understanding the sexual past indeed uncovering it from beneath years of suppression and denial was a profoundly political act. Knowledge of history strengthened collective identity and the struggle for sexual freedom and rights. Moreover, if sexuality had a history if it was neither merely instinctual nor simply an innate biological process then change might occur in the way Americans perceived and organized the erotic realm.

Since the 1960s, historians have developed the field by unearthing primary source materials, writing path-breaking books, and teaching exciting new courses. Although its legitimacy was initially questioned many universities were reluctant to hire scholars in this field the history of sexuality is now more firmly established. The *Journal of the History of Sexuality* began publication in 1990, and the leading journals, such as the *Journal of American History*, regularly carry articles examining sexuality s past. Still, if the history of sexuality has become more respectable in the academy, it continues to be animated by the sexual politics and culture of the present day. The documents and articles selected for this book explore many of the key concerns and debates among historians of sexuality.

One of the major issues debated by historians of sexuality is the relationship of power to sex. How have different authorities in American society colonial governors, religious leaders, anti-vice moralists, sexologists, the Federal Bureau of Investigation regulated sexual behavior and beliefs? To what ends? In what historical contexts has opposition to such regulation arisen, and who have been the opponents? What makes for periods of sexual reform and revolution? How are the politics of sexuality related to other political and social developments?

A theory of power and sexuality presented by French philosopher Michel Foucault in *The History of Sexuality: An Introduction* has influenced many of the historians whose work appears in this collection (see, for example, essays in Chapters 2, 3, 11, and 13). Power over sexuality has been exercised not only through repressive actions courts jailing pederasts, mobs lynching black men cohabiting with white women. Power has also been put into play by *discourses* specific terminologies and ways of conceptualizing that construct sexuality in particular frames. For instance, medicine and psychology in the late nineteenth century conceptualized a diverse set of behaviors as coherent and deviant identities: the invert, the homosexual. The prevalence of this discourse regulated sexual behavior even as it solidified the authority of medical experts and psychologists among the wider public: increasingly, ordinary people came to understand their own sexuality in scientific terms. In the view of Foucault and historians inspired by his work, sexuality is *produced* in the intimate relationship between knowledge and power.

Other historians in this volume are more concerned with the experience of erotic life in the past (see, for example, essays in Chapters 6, 8, and 14). They uphold a fundamental insight of history: that the past really *is* different from the present, and we must be careful and self-aware about imposing our sexual categories and moral values on our ancestors. (The same might be said about present-day attitudes toward sexual minorities.) The relation between physical contact and emotional intimacy, notions of the sexed body, same-sex and male-female bonds, pornography and sexual imagery, sexual violence, concepts of marriage, love, friendship, and family: these all have distinctive histories with their own meaning and significance.

Historical interpretations of sexuality have rested primarily on a broad social analysis that encourages the exploration of gender, race, ethnicity, class, and region, the approach reflected in these selections. These social histories acknowledge how such differences have fostered distinct sexual cultures and show how sexuality has marked different social and political identities: under racial slavery, for instance, notions of white women s purity underwrote white men s sexual access to black women, who were disparaged as licentious and wanton ; at the same time, black people asserted their own beliefs about sexual respectability and marriage, in ways that often diverged from the ideals of white society. At the present time, most historians focus more on women than men; white and black Americans are more widely written about than Latino/as, Asians, and other peoples of color. Nevertheless, scholars are increasingly documenting through primary sources and historical analysis the rich diversity of our sexual past. Even more important, the work collected here begins to suggest how the relationships *between* different groups their cultural encounters, political conflicts, and struggles over images and ideas shape the history of sexuality.

As with other books in this series, each chapter examines a particular problem or theme, in this case, those questions central to the history of sexuality. An introduction in each chapter presents its theme or problem and provides historical context, and brief introductions precede each document and essay section to identify the selections. Primary documents of the period court records, diary entries, letters, government investigations, political tracts, poems, and the like introduce the key questions, convey a flavor of the times, and allow us to see how Americans in the past wrestled with the issue of sexuality in their lives. Two and sometimes three essays show how historians read historical documents in different ways, come to different and sometimes opposing interpretations, or choose to focus on different aspects of an issue. Finally, each chapter closes with suggestions for further reading.

The documents and essays in this collection challenge us to think hard about the nature of both sexuality and history. Excavating the past is never easy, but this is especially true when it comes to sex, a subject often surrounded by silence, shame, distortion, and bravado. The documents must be read mindfully: imagine the circumstances in which they were created, the events they record, the people represented by their words, the thoughts left unsaid or censored. Then consider the perspectives of the historians in their essays, test their explanations against the primary evidence, and determine your own conclusions, using evidence and logic to support your viewpoint. History is a discipline that simultaneously *connects* and *distances* us from its subject. It takes the long view, puts in context, reconstructs from fragments, and makes coherent the seemingly chaotic, but it does not do this from a position of objective or pure knowledge even as it aspires to. History is the relationship between present and past. Thus the history of sexuality also illuminates *ourselves* and contributes a significant perspective to contemporary debates about sexual matters.

The good advice and generous assistance of many people helped me meet the challenge of preparing a volume on such a new field, and I gratefully acknowledge them here. My thanks go foremost to Grey Osterud, whose clarity of mind, historical expertise, and editorial skills rescued me from occasional befuddlement. I am grateful for the guidance of historians who reviewed the project: Sharon Block, University of California at Irvine; Richard Godbeer, University of California at Riverside; Kathryn M. Tomasek, Wheaton College; Andrea L. Volpe, Colby College. As always, Peter Agree s discriminating eye, word magic, and loving support made all the difference.

Glendyne Wergland and Jane Berger heroically tracked down documents and made helpful suggestions along the way. I thank the gallant Interlibrary Loan librarians at the University of Massachusetts; archivist Brenda Marston, the Human Sexuality Collection, Cornell University; the Sophia Smith Collection and College Archives, Smith College; Mari Jo Buhle, Brown University; and Nancy Carnevale and Maria Galetta for a superb translation. I appreciate the editorial suggestions of Thomas Paterson, the series editor, and thank Jean Woy, Fran Gay, Carla Thompson, Mary Dalton-Hoffman, and Jay Boggis at Cengage Learning for their exceptional work producing this book.

My undergraduate students not only gave me important feedback on these selections but also discovered several documents that appear here. I thank them and the generation of scholars who created this field against the odds for their work, insight, and inspiration. I welcome suggestions and comments from readers as well. Please send your comments to me at www.cengage.com/history.

K. P.

*Major Problems in
the History of
American Sexuality*

C H A P T E R

1

Sexuality in History

*Only in recent decades has sexuality become a subject of historical inquiry.
How has the experience and meaning of sexuality changed over time, and why?
How have different discourses—based, for instance, in theology, medicine, or
psychology—fashioned sexual identities and shaped erotic encounters in the past?
When has sexuality become a site of political conflict and an expression of power
relations? These questions and others have sparked a flourishing new scholarship.*

*Unlike more traditional fields of history, the history of sexuality has been shaped
by present-day political concerns. In the last thirty years, feminism, gay liberation,
and New Right conservatism have placed sexual issues—gay rights, rape, sexual
harassment, abortion—in the public eye; historians of sexuality frequently highlight
the political implications of their research. Disputes over theory also mark this field:
Is sexuality socially constructed? In what ways? Is there a "core" or "essential" dimension to sexuality that we must consider, and if so, how should historians account for
it? French philosopher Michel Foucault, in his influential* History of Sexuality: An
Introduction, *has inspired many historians to examine the relationship between
sexual knowledge, discourses, and the deployment of power in a given society.*

*In addition to the debates over politics and theory is the sheer problem of his-
torical evidence. Of all human activities, sexuality is perhaps the most unsettling,
concealed, and mysterious.Evidence of sexual activity has often been destroyed,
censored, or denied. In many cases, it may never have been recorded. How can we
interpret the history of sexuality from the fragments and traces of the past?*

E S S A Y S

The idea that sexuality is socially constructed—produced in social relationships and
institutions, and articulated in culture—has been a guiding framework in the history of
sexuality. Jeffrey Weeks, Professor of Sociology and Dean of Humanities and Social
Science at South Bank University in London and a pioneering British historian in the
field, explains the social constructionist approach in this excerpt from his 1986 book
Sexuality. Some scholars have begun to point out the shortcomings of this approach.
Rictor Norton, an independent editor and scholar in Great Britain, makes a case for
"essentialism"—that there is a transhistorical core of desire—and that historians
must explore the organic growth and continuities in sexual cultures, homosexual or
"queer" culture in particular. In a different perspective on historical interpretation,

John D. Wrathall, an independent scholar and historian of the YMCA, raises the question of evidence in the archives. Looking at the correspondence of a YMCA leader in the late nineteenth century, he emphasizes the importance—and the difficulty—of reading the silences and gaps in the documents of the past.

Week 2

The Social Construction of Sexuality

JEFFREY WEEKS

The more expert we become in talking about sexuality, the greater the difficulties we seem to encounter in trying to understand it. Despite sustained attempts over many years to "demystify" sex, and several decades of much proclaimed—or condemned—"liberalism" and "permissiveness," the erotic still arouses acute moral anxiety and confusion. This is not because sex is intrinsically "naughty," as a sensitive commentator has rightly remarked, but "because it is a focus for powerful feelings." The strong emotions it undoubtedly arouses [give] to the world of sexuality a seismic sensitivity making it a transmission belt for a wide variety of needs and desires: for love and anger, tenderness and aggression, intimacy and adventure, romance and predatoriness, pleasure and pain, empathy and power. We experience sex very subjectively.

At the same time, the very mobility of sexuality, its chameleon-like ability to take many guises and forms, so that what for one might be a source of warmth and attraction, for another might be one of fear and hate, makes it a peculiarly sensitive conductor of cultural influences, and hence of social and political divisions. Not surprisingly, therefore, especially during the past century, sexuality has become the focus of fierce ethical and political divisions: between traditional moralists (of various religious hues, or of none) and liberals, between the high priests of sexual restraint and the advocates of sexual liberation, between the defenders of male privilege and those such as feminists who challenged it, and between the forces of moral regulation and a host of radical sexual oppositions, some of whom attack each other as much as they oppose sexual orthodoxy.

In the past such debates might have been regarded as marginal to the mainstream of political life, whatever their importance for those closely involved. Increasingly over the past decades, however, sexual issues have moved closer to the centre of political concerns. . . . [T]he increasing politicization of sex in the past century offers new possibilities and consequent challenges: not just of moral control, and its inevitable converse, sexual deviance, but of political analysis, opposition and of change. This makes it all the more necessary that we know what we are talking about when we speak of sexuality, that we clarify the meaning (or more accurately meanings) of this complex phenomenon. We need to know what it has been and is, before we can rationally decide what it should, or could, be.

This is an easy aim to proclaim. It is a notoriously more hazardous task to carry out. All of us have so much invested in our own concept of what is the true sex that we find it difficult enough to understand dispassionately the sexual needs and

Jeffrey Weeks, "The Social Construction of Sexuality," excerpted from *Sexuality* (London: Routledge, 1986), 11–18, 23–25, 27–31. Reprinted by permission of Taylor & Francis Books Ltd.

behaviour of our closest contemporaries, let alone the infinitely more ambiguous desires of our predecessors. The mists of time and the various disguises of prejudice conveniently obscure other ways of living a sexual life. This resilient will-not-to-know is backed up by an assumption which is deeply embedded in our culture: that our sexuality is the most spontaneously natural thing about us. It is the basis for some of our most passionate feelings and commitments. Through it, we experience ourselves as real people; it gives us our identities, our sense of self, as men and women, as heterosexual and homosexual, "normal" or "abnormal," "natural" or "unnatural." Sex has become, as the French philosopher Michel Foucault famously put it, "the truth of our being." But what is this "truth"? And on what basis can we call something "natural" or "unnatural"? Who has the right to lay down the laws of sex? Sex may be "spontaneous" and "natural." But it has not stopped an endless barrage of advice on how best to do it.

Let us start with the term "sex" and its common uses. Its very ambiguity signals the difficulty. We learn very early on from many sources that "natural" sex is what takes place with members of the "opposite sex." "Sex" between people of the "same sex" is therefore, by definition, "unnatural." So much is taken for granted. But the multiple meanings of the word "sex" in these last few sentences should alert us to the real complexity of the question. The term refers both to an act and to a category of person, to a practice and to a gender. Modern culture has assumed an intimate connection between the fact of being biologically male or female (that is, having appropriate sex organs and reproductive potentialities) and the correct form of erotic behaviour (usually genital intercourse between men and women). The earliest usage of the term "sex," in the sixteenth century, referred precisely to the division of humanity into the male section and the female section (that is, to differences of gender). The dominant meaning today, however, and one current since the early nineteenth century, refers to physical relations between the sexes, "to have sex." The extension of the meanings of these words indicates a shift in the way that "sexuality" (the abstract noun referring to the quality of being "sexual") is understood in our culture.

The social processes through which this has taken place are complex. But the implications are clear, for they are ones we still live with. In the first place, there is an assumption of a sharp distinction between "the sexes," a dichotomy of interests, even an antagonism ("the battle of the sexes") which can only be precariously bridged. Men are men and women women—and rarely the twain shall meet. But secondly, there is a belief that "sex" is an overpowering natural force, a "biological imperative" mysteriously located in the genitals (especially the wayward male organs) that sweeps all before it (at least if you are male) like hamlets before an avalanche and that somehow bridges this divide, like a rainbow over a chasm. Thirdly, this gives rise to a pyramidical model of sex, to a sexual hierarchy stretching downwards from the apparently Nature-endowed correctness of heterosexual genital intercourse to the bizarre manifestations of "the perverse" hopefully safely buried at the base but unfortunately always erupting in dubious places.

This view of the world of sex is deeply embedded in our culture, part of the air we breathe. It provides an ideological justification for uncontrollable male lust, and even, therefore, for the fact of rape, for the downgrading of female sexual autonomy, and for the way we treat those sexual minorities who are different from ourselves, as well as for the more acceptable verities of love, relationships and security. Since the late nineteenth century, moreover, this approach has had the ostensibly scientific endorsement of the broad tradition known as sexology, the "science of desire." Sexologists such as Krafft-Ebing, Havelock Ellis, August Forel, Magnus Hirschfeld, Sigmund Freud and many others, sought to discover the true meaning of sex by exploring its various guises: the experience of infantile sexuality, relations between the sexes, the influence of the "germ plasm," the hormones and chromosomes, the nature of the "sexual instinct," and the causes of sexual perversions. They often disagreed with one another; they frequently contradicted themselves. In the end, even the most dedicated had to admit to a certain defeat. . . .

Sexology has had important positive effects in extending our knowledge of sexual behaviours and I have no desire to denigrate its real achievements. Without it we would be enslaved to an even greater extent than we are to myths and nostrums. On the other hand, in its search for the "true" meaning of sex, in its intense interrogation of sexual difference, and in its obsessive categorization of sexual perversities it has contributed to the codification of a "sexual tradition," a more or less coherent body of assumptions, beliefs, prejudices, rules, methods of investigation and forms of moral regulation, which still shape the way we live our sexualities. Is sex threatening and dangerous? If we want to believe that then we can find justification not only in a particular Christian tradition but in the writings also of the founding father of sexology, Krafft-Ebing, and in many of his scientific successors. Is sex, on the other hand, a source of potential freedom, whose liberatory power is only blocked by the regressive force of a corrupt civilization . . . ? If so, then justification can be found in works of polemicists and "scientists" from the nineteenth century to the present, embracing not only socialist pioneers such as Charles Fourier and Edward Carpenter, Freudo-Marxists like Wilhelm Reich and Herbert Marcuse, but also more ostensibly sober-suited "social bookkeepers" like Alfred Kinsey. Whatever our moral and political values, it has been difficult to escape the naturalistic fallacy that the key to our sex lies somewhere in the recesses of "Nature," and that sexual science provides the best means of access to it. . . .

Against the certainties of this tradition I . . . offer an alternative way of understanding sexuality. This involves seeing it not as a primordially "natural" phenomenon but rather as a product of social and historical forces. "Sexuality," I shall argue, is a "fictional unity," that once did not exist, and at some time in the future may not exist again. It is an invention of the human mind. As Carole S. Vance has suggested, "the most important organ in humans is located between the ears."

This does not mean we can simply ignore the massive edifice of sexuality which envelops us. . . . Of course sexuality exists as a palpable social presence, shaping our personal and public lives. But I am suggesting that what we define as "sexuality" is an historical construction, which brings together a host of different biological and mental possibilities—gender identity, bodily differences, reproductive capacities, needs, desires and fantasies—which need not be linked together, and in other cultures have not been. All the constituent elements of sexuality have their source either in the body or the mind, and I am not attempting to deny the limits posed by biology or mental processes. But the capacities of the body and the psyche are given meaning only in social relations. . . .

. . . [T]he meanings we give to "sexuality" are socially organized, sustained by a variety of languages, which seek to tell us what sex is, what it ought to be—and what it could be. Existing languages of sex, embedded in moral treatises, laws, educational practices, psychological theories, medical definitions, social rituals, pornographic or romantic fictions, popular music, and commonsense assumptions (most of which disagree) set the horizon of the possible. They all present themselves up as true representations of our intimate needs and desires. The difficulty lies in their contradictory appeals, in the babel of voices they bring forth. In order to make sense of them, and perhaps to go beyond the current limits on the possible, we need to learn to translate these languages—and to develop new ones. This has been one of the tasks of those who have sought, in recent years, to "deconstruct" the apparent unity of this world of sexuality. Together they have provided the elements of a non-essentialist concept of "sexuality."

From social anthropology, sociology and post-Kinsey sex research there has come a growing awareness of the vast range of sexualities that exist in other cultures and within our own culture. Other cultures, Ruth Benedict noted, act as laboratories "in which we may study the diversity of human institutions." . . .

The legacy of Freud and his theory of the dynamic unconscious is another major source of the new sexual theory. From the tradition of psychoanalysis that he initiated has emerged a recognition that what goes on in the unconscious mind often contradicts the apparent certainties of conscious life. The life of the mind—of fantasies above all—reveals a diversity of desires to which the human being is heir. It unsettles the apparent solidities of gender, of sexual need, of identity. . . .

Alongside these developments, the "new social history" of recent years, with its emphasis on the history of populations and of "mentalities," the experiences and beliefs of the downtrodden and oppressed as much as the powerful, has posed new questions about what we mean by "the present" as well as about the "history of the past." *The History of Sexuality* by Michel Foucault has had a spectacular influence on modern thinking about sex because it grew out of, as well as contributed to, this fertile development of our historical understanding. Foucault, like Freud two generations earlier, stands at a crossroads of sexual thought, important as much for the questions he raises as for the answers he provides.

Finally, and most powerfully of all, the emergence of new social movements concerned with sex—modern feminism, the gay and lesbian and other radical sexual movements—ha[s] challenged many of the certainties of the "sexual tradition," and ha[s] offered new insights into the intricate forms of power and domination that shape our sexual lives. The politics of homosexuality have placed on the agenda questions about sexual preference, identity, and choice. The women's movement has forced a recognition of the multiple forms of female sexual subordination, from endemic male violence and misogyny to sexual harassment and a pervasive language of sexual denigration and abuse. It has demanded a recognition of women's rights over their own bodies by re-posing questions about consent and reproductive rights, desire and pleasure. Again there are as many questions posed as answers given. Differences have emerged between men and women, homosexuals and heterosexuals, black and white. No acceptable codes of appropriate behaviour have been elaborated despite all the heated debates. But something much more valuable has happened. We are being forced to rethink what we understand by sexuality because of a growing awareness of the tangled web of influences and forces—economics, race, gender, morals—that shape our emotions, needs, desires and relationships. . . .

In practice, most writers on our sexual past assume that sex is an irresistible natural energy barely held in check by a thin crust of civilization. . . .

These approaches assume that sex offers a basic "biological mandate" which presses against and must be restrained by the cultural matrix. This is what I mean by an essentialist approach to sexuality. It takes many forms. Liberatory theorists such as Reich and Marcuse tend to see sex as a beneficent force which is repressed by a corrupt civilization. Contemporary sociobiologists on the other hand see all social forms as in some unspecified way emanations of basic genetic material. Yet they all see a world of nature which provides the raw material we must use for the understanding of the social. Against all these arguments I want to stress that sexuality is shaped by social forces. And far from being the most natural element in social life, the most resistant to cultural [molding], it is perhaps one of the most susceptible to organization. Indeed I would go so far as to say that sexuality only exists through its social forms and social organization. Moreover, the forces that shape and mould the erotic possibilities of the body vary from society to society. "Sexual socialization," Ellen Ross and Rayn[a] Rapp have written, "is no less specific to each culture than is socialization to ritual, dress or cuisine." This puts the emphasis firmly where it should belong, on society and social relations rather than on nature.

I do not wish to deny the importance of biology. The physiology and morphology of the body provide the preconditions for human sexuality. Biology conditions and limits what is possible. But it does not cause the patterns of sexual life. We cannot reduce human behaviour to the mysterious workings of the DNA or what two contemporary writers have recently called "the dance of the chromosomes." I prefer to see in biology a set of potentialities which are transformed and given meaning only in social relationships. Human consciousness and human history are very complex phenomena.

This theoretical stance has many roots: in the sociology and anthropology of sex, in the revolution in psychoanalysis and in the new social history. But despite these disparate starting points, it coheres around a number of common assumptions. First, there is a general rejection of sex as an autonomous realm, a natural domain with specific effects, a rebellious energy that the social controls. We can no longer set "sex" against "society" as if they were separate domains. Secondly, there is a widespread recognition of the social variability of sexual forms, beliefs, ideologies and behaviour. Sexuality has a history, or more realistically, many histories, each of which needs to be understood both in its uniqueness and as part of an intricate pattern. Thirdly, we must abandon the idea that we can fruitfully understand the history of sexuality in terms of a dichotomy of pressure and release, repression and liberation. Sexuality is not a head of steam that must be capped lest it destroy us; nor is it a life force we must release to save our civilization. Instead we must learn to see that sexuality is something which society produces in complex ways. It is a result of diverse social practices that give meaning to human activities, of social definitions and self-definitions, of struggles between those who have power to define and regulate, and those who resist. Sexuality is not given, it is a product of negotiation, struggle and human agency. . . .

Five broad areas stand out as being particularly crucial in the social organization of sexuality: kinship and family systems, economic and social organization, social regulation, political interventions, and the development of "cultures of resistance."

(1) Kinship and family systems

These *appear* as the most basic and unchanging forms of all—preeminently the "natural" focus of sexual socialization and experience. The taboo on incest, that is the prohibition of sexual involvement within certain degrees of relationship, seems to be a universal law, marking the passage, it has been often argued, from a state of nature to human society: it is constitutive of culture. (It is also the basis for our most enduring myth—that of Oedipus.) Yet the forms of the taboo vary enormously. In the Christian traditions of the Middle Ages, marriage to the seventh degree of relationship was prohibited. Today, marriage to first cousins is allowed. In the Egypt of the Pharoahs, sibling marriages were permitted, and in some cases so were father–daughter marriages, in the interests of preserving the purity of the royal line. The existence of the incest taboo illustrates the need of all societies to regulate sex—but not how it is done. Even "blood relationships" have to be interpreted through the grid of culture.

The truth is that kin ties are not *natural* links of blood but are social relations between groups, often based on residential affinities and hostile to genetic affinities. . . . Who we decide are kin and what we describe as "the family" are clearly dependent on a range of historical factors. There are many different family forms especially within highly industrialized, Western societies—between different classes, and different geographic, religious, racial and ethnic groups. Family patterns are shaped and re-shaped by economic factors, by rules of inheritance, by state interventions to regulate marriage and divorce or to support the family by social welfare or taxation policies. All these affect the likely patterns of sexual life: by encouraging or discouraging the rate of marriage, age of marriage, incidence of reproduction, attitudes to non-procreative or non-heterosexual sex, the relative power of men over women, and so on. These factors are important in themselves. They are doubly important because the family is the arena in which most of us in Western culture gain some sense of our individual sexual needs and identities, and if we follow psychoanalysis, it is the arena where our desires are organized from a very early stage indeed. So to understand sexuality we have to understand much more than sex: we have to understand the relationships in which most of it takes place.

(2) Economic and social organization

As I have suggested, families themselves are not autonomous, natural entities. They themselves are shaped by wider social relations. Domestic patterns can be changed by economic forces, by the class divisions to which economic change gives rise, by the degree of urbanization and of rapid industrial and social change. In the past, and probably also in the present, labour migrations have affected patterns of courtship and have helped dictate the incidence of illegitimacy rates. . . . Work conditions can shape sexual lives. A good example of this is provided by the evidence for the 1920s and 1930s that women who worked in factories tended to be much more familiar with methods of artificial birth control, and thus to limit their family size to a greater degree than women who worked solely in the home or in domestic service.

The relations between men and women are constantly affected by changes in economic conditions. The growing involvement of married women in the paid workforce in the 1950s and 1960s inevitably affected the patterns of domestic life.

It also fuelled a consumer boom which provided one of the preconditions for a proliferation of new markets for sexual commodities in the past generation. Sexuality
is not *determined* by the mode of production, but the rhythms of economic life provide the basic preconditions and ultimate limits for the organization of sexual life.

(3) Social regulation

If economic life establishes some of the fundamental rhythms, the actual forms of
regulation of sexuality have a considerable autonomy. Formal methods of regulating
sexual life vary from time to time depending on the significance of religion, the
changing role of the state, the existence or not of a moral consensus which regulate
marriage patterns, divorce rates and incidence of sexual unorthodoxy. One of the critical shifts of the last hundred years has been the move away from moral regulation by
the churches to a more secular mode of organization through medicine, education,
psychology, social work and welfare practices. It is also important to recognize that
the effects of these interventions are not necessarily pre-ordained. As often as not
sexual life is altered by the unintended consequences of social action as much as the
intention of the authors. Laws banning obscene publications more often than not give
rise to court cases that publicize them. . . . [L]aws designed to control the behaviour
of certain groups of people can actually give rise to an enhanced sense of identity and
cohesion amongst them. This certainly seems to be the case with the refinement of
the laws relating to male homosexuality in the late nineteenth century.

But it is not only formal methods which shape sexuality; there are many informal
and customary patterns which are equally important. The traditional forms of regulation of adolescen[t] courtship can be [a] critical means of social control. It is very
difficult to break with the consensus of one's village or one's peer group in school,
and this is as much true today as it was in the pre-industrial societies. A language of
sexual abuse ("slags" and "sluts") works to keep girls in line, and to enforce conventional distinctions between girls who do and girls who don't. Such informal methods
enforced by strictly adhered to rules often produce, by contemporary standards, various bizarre manifestations of sexual behaviour. One such example is provided by the
traditional form of courtship . . . up to the nineteenth century known as "bundling,"
which involved intimate but fully clothed rituals of sex play in bed. Closer to the
present, we can find the equally exotic phenomenon of petting, which is dependent
on the belief that while intercourse in public is tabooed, other forms of play, because
they are not defined as *the* sex act, may be intimately engaged in. . . . Implicit in such
phenomena are intricate though only semiconscious rules which limit what can and
cannot be done. Informal methods of regulation like these can have important social
effects—in limiting, for example, illegitimate conceptions. They have often been enforced in the past by customary patterns of public shaming, rituals of humiliation and
public mocking . . . which serve to reinforce the norms of the community.

(4) Political interventions

These formal and informal methods of control exist within a changing political
framework. The balance of political forces at any particular time can determine
the degree of legislative control or moral intervention in sexual life. The general

social climate provides the context in which some issues take on a greater significance than others. The existence of skilled "moral entrepreneurs" able to articulate and call up inchoate currents of opinion can be decisive in enforcing existing legislation or in conjuring up new. The recent success of the New Right in America in establishing an agenda for sexual conservatism by mobilizing against sexual liberals and/or sexual deviants underlines the possibilities of political mobilization around sex.

(5) Cultures of resistance

But the history of sexuality is not a simple history of control, it is also a history of opposition and resistance to moral codes. Forms of moral regulation give rise to cultures of resistance. A prime example of these is provided by the female networks of knowledge about methods of birth control[,] especially abortion. . . .

Other examples of cultural resistance come from the emergence of the subcultures and networks established by sexual minorities. There is a long history of subcultures of male homosexuality throughout the history of the West, manifest for instance in Italian towns of the late Middle Ages, and in England from the late seventeenth century. These have been critical for the emergence of modern homosexual identities which have been largely formed in these wider social networks. More recently, over the last hundred years or so, there have been series of explicit oppositional political movements organized around sexuality and sexual issues. The classic example is that of feminism. But in addition recent historical work has demonstrated the longstanding existence of sex reform movements often closely linked to campaigns for homosexual rights: the modern gay and lesbian movements have antecedents going back to the nineteenth century in countries like Germany and Britain.

What we so confidently know as "sexuality" is, then, a product of many influences and social interventions. It does not exist outside history but is a historical product. This is what we mean by the "social construction" of sexuality.

So what does a non-essentialist theory of sexuality mean for the politics of sexuality and for sexual ethics? These . . . topics . . . pose perhaps the most difficult challenges of all. The "sexual tradition" assumed that your sex was your fate or destiny: what you desired was what you were. Sexuality pinned you down like a butterfly to the table. If you break with this tradition, if you reject the idea that sexuality embodies its own values and goals, then you are faced with complex problems of alignment and choice. Confronted by such uncertainties, it is all too easy to retreat into moral or political absolutes, to reassert again, against all the odds, against all the evidence, that there is a true sexuality that we must find at all costs. The aim of this essay is to challenge such absolutes without falling into the trap of saying no values are possible, "anything goes." "Sexuality" is a deeply problematic concept, and there are no easy answers to the challenges it poses. But if we begin to ask the correct questions then we might find the way through the maze. We shall not find at the end of the journey a prescription for correct behaviour. But we might find a framework which allows us to come to terms with diversity—and to re-find, in sexuality, new opportunities for creative relationships, agency and choice.

Essentialism and Queer History

RICTOR NORTON

During the past half-generation the history of homosexuality has been dominated by social constructionist dogma. . . .

. . . Jeffrey Weeks and other social constructionists have stressed "the vital importance of distinguishing between behaviour, role, and identity in any sociological or historical approach to the subject of homosexuality." On the contrary, I believe it is vital to recognize the integrity, unity and ambiguity of the [queer] experience that is falsified by over-intellectual analysis.

One of the reasons why many contemporary lesbian and gay theorists fail to appreciate that homosexuals existed before 1869 [when the term "homosexual" was invented] is the politically correct view that terms such as "queer," "faggot" and "queen" are not nice, and especially since the late 1960s people have endeavoured to use the phrase "gay and lesbian" wherever possible. There are certain men who lived before 1869 whom I would feel uneasy to call "gay" or "homophile," but I would not hesitate to call them queer or even silly old queens. Many of the mollies of the early eighteenth century were undoubtedly queens, whose interests and behaviour are virtually indistinguishable from queens I have known in the early 1960s (and later). I use the word "queer" in such a way as to subsume the meanings of words such as homosexual, homophile, homoerotic and homosocial— all of which I think involve false distinctions rather than continuity (homosociality is little more than homosexuality with a fig leaf)—within the meanings of queer, faggot, dyke and gay, which more accurately reflect the working-class reality which formed gay (sub)cultures, whose authenticity middle-class lesbians and gays began denying in the 1950s and 1970s. My emphasis will be upon ethnic autonomy rather than assimilation (reflecting the separatist stance of contemporary "queers"). "Gay and lesbian" is perfectly acceptable for life since the 1960s, but most of my focus is upon the earlier past. "Queer" was the word of preference for homosexuals as well as homophobes for the first half of the twentieth century, and of course is being reclaimed today in defiant rather than defensive postures. In English during the eighteenth and most of the nineteenth century the words of preference were "molly" and "sapphist," for which good modern equivalents are "queer" and "dyke." During the seventeenth century and earlier the commonest terms were "sodomite" and "tribade," for which, again, precise modern equivalents are "queer" and "dyke." In ancient and indigenous and premodern cultures the nearest modern equivalents are "queer" and "tomboy." And the nearest modern equivalent for the nineteenth-century term "homosexual" is: queer. . . .

The absence of historical underpinning to social constructionist theory can be readily demonstrated. "The most vulnerable claim [of the constructionists] is that the notion of the homosexual as a distinct 'species' originated only about a hundred years ago, an invention of the medical profession or the product of capitalist urbanization," [writes David F. Greenberg]; the materials gathered by Greenberg's exhaustive review of research

> make abundantly clear that the world was neither conceptually nor behaviorally poly-morphously perverse prior to the Industrial Revolution. . . . [Michel] Foucault, who held a chair in the history of ideas, assumed too readily that intellectuals are the sole repository of conceptual invention and simply imposed a new hegemonic discourse on passive recipients.

On the whole, a strictly social constructionist strategy has ended up throwing the baby out with the bath water. . . .

[Colin] Spencer rightly rejects Foucault's position that "The sensuality of those who did not like the opposite sex was hardly noticed in the past." Rather than the end of the nineteenth century, Spencer, with a much better survey of the available histori-cal evidence, places a noticeable shift at the beginning of the medieval period:

> the concept of bisexuality was discarded from the consciousness of society, [and] a polarity began to establish itself between the Other (what is repressed) and the Self (which is publicly acknowledged); between that which will later be called homosexual, which must be hidden, and the status quo, the heterosexual, which needs to be publicly enhanced. Human sexual nature, in the way it was considered socially, was divided into two parts, homosexual and heterosexual, as if they were mutually exclusive.

This itself is not a very satisfactory "grand theory," for there are many examples prior to the thirteenth century that show an awareness of a predominantly homo-sexual orientation, and, equally, many contemporary queers who do not regard themselves as being exclusively homosexual.

. . . The myth that the homosexual was born circa 1869 is easily demolished, but beyond that I aim to show that the social constructionist emperor has no clothes. I will argue that a typology of queer personalities and relationships and the characteristic features of a queer culture arise from a core of queer desire and are not wholly configured by the regulation of that desire. Queer history properly con-sidered is the attempt to recover the authentic voice of queer experience rather than simply to document suppression or oppression.

My position is sited within the essentialist camp, and I hope to expose some of the fallacies of social constructionist theory, which I see as the main impediment to the understanding of queer history. The history of ideas (and ideologies) is enormously interesting and valuable, but it is tragic that homosexuals have been subsumed *totally* under the idea of the homosexual. The result is little better than intellectual ethnic cleansing. In the social constructionist view, knowledge is constructed, deconstructed and reconstructed through ideological discourse. In my essentialist view, knowledge is discovered, repressed, suppressed and recovered through history and experience. Social constructionism emphasizes revolutionary development (the dialectic); I see evolutionary development, cultural growth and permutation, and sometimes mere change in fashion. Rather than the word "con-struct," which implies building from scratch according to an arbitrarily chosen blue-print, I prefer "consolidate" or "forge," implying that the basic material already exists but can be subjected to shaping and polishing.

"Cultural constructs" are sometimes set up in opposition to "universal truths" in an effort to force essentialists into an impossibly idealistic corner, but "culture" is a concept that can be claimed by essentialists as well as by social constructionists. The essentialist position is that queer culture is organic rather than artificial. Social constructionists see culture as a construct whose arbitrary foundation is determined by the builder; I see culture as the cultivation of a root, and I shall be developing the ethnic view that queer culture grows naturally from personal queer identity and experience and is self-cultivated by queers rather than by the ideology and labels of straight society. I have no objection if critics wish to call me an "essentialist" pure and simple, because I believe that homosexuals are born and not made. However, I also believe that queers fashion their own culture (using their own resources rather than being imposed upon by society), and that will be a significant focus of my own version of essentialism, which might be called "queer cultural essentialism." I take the view that there is a core of queer desire that is transcultural, transnational and transhistorical, a queer essence that is innate, congenital, constitutional, stable or fixed in its basic pattern. However, I distinguish between queer persons, queer sexual acts and behaviour, and queer social interactions, and try not to confuse the constancy of the desire with the variability of its expression. Personal queer identity arises from within, and is then consolidated along lines suggested by the collective identity of the queer (sub)culture. . . .

I have no problem in reconciling the view that queer desire is innate but that it also expresses itself in sexual or social actions and (sub)cultures that may reflect to a greater of lesser degree the time and place in which they occur. Self-presentation can be carefully constructed while being founded upon an innate self-conception. There should be no difficulty in recognizing, for example, that modern British gay consciousness was well in place before American styles of presenting gayness were deliberately imported into Britain. . . . The specific sexual custom of fistfucking appeared first in America and was exported to Europe and Japan, probably in the year 1971, but it is not likely that an entirely new *mentalité* arose in that year, or even that decade.

Beneath a (fairly limited) variety of customs that differ from culture to culture lies the phenomenon of queer desire. That desire need not necessarily be expressed through sexual acts: queer culture and queer "sexuality" go beyond genital sexuality. Henry James, as he walked along the river in Oxford in 1869, seeing the punts full of "the mighty lads of England, clad in white flannel and blue, immense, fair-haired, magnificent in their youths," felt that his heart "would crack with the fullness of satisfied desire." This kind of diffuse homoerotic passion for golden lads or lasses is a central feature of gay and lesbian culture, whether or not it reflects the sexual longing and nostalgia that can arise from "sublimation," and even though its avenues of expression are often restricted and controlled by society in ways specific to each society. Homosexuality is a broad stream which continues to run despite being dammed up and channelled off by social control. The evidence of history points to repression rather than construction as the shaping force of queer identity and culture. The opportunities for expressing queer desire have been increasingly restricted in modern times, but the desire remains the same. The inner drive has simply been repressed or liberated to varying degrees from one era and culture to another. . . .

Historical research tends to support the essentialist position that queer desire is congenital and then constituted into a meaningful queer identity during childhood.

The message of abundant personal testimony on the subject, in a wide range of sources, from fifteenth-century Italy to late twentieth-century Thailand, from biographies and autobiographies to novels, is that *queerness dawns* around the age of 7, or, if it comes later, that it is something that has lain dormant in the personality, but was always there. Chosen as the spokesperson for the 1988 World Expo in Australia because she was the only one living who had attended the 1888 Expo, E. M. "Monte" Punshon, who died in 1989 at the age of 106, revealed to the media that "she had known she was a lesbian for nearly a century—since the age of six." . . .

Most queers are as recognizable for their characteristic speech, mannerisms and bearing as are Jamaicans, Italians, Pakistanis or any other ethnic group. . . .

"Do queers walk funny?" is a question still half-seriously debated in Internet queer newsgroups, the general consensus being that the walk imitates female prostitutes. But men who lived in the 1930s and 1940s when swishing was especially noticeable felt that the real construct was the exaggeratedly masculine walk of heterosexual men. . . . [English writer] Quentin Crisp remarked upon the Dilly boys in the 1920s:

> A passer-by would have to be very innocent indeed not to catch the meaning of the mannequin walk and the stance in which the hip was only prevented from total dislocation by the hand placed upon it. . . . The strange thing about "camp" is that it has become fossilized. The mannerisms have never changed. If I were now to see a woman sitting with her knees clamped together, one hand on her hip and the other lightly touching her back hair, I should think, "Either she scored her last social triumph in 1926 or it is a man in drag."

However, "camp stylization" can be traced much further back than the 1920s. [Judy] Grahn points out that not all "femme" faggotry imitates female mannerisms:

> Some of it is an independent Gay cultural tradition . . . handed along from faggot to faggot. . . . It is commonly supposed that faggots lisp in imitation of women. Modern women, however, do not lisp. . . . But the sweet sibilant faggot speech is peculiar to Gay men, and completely distinctive. For the most part faggots learn their particular manner of speaking from each other. . . .

. . . The queer gaze is immediately recognizable, whether one participates in it or just observes; as a man who cruised Leicester Square during the Second World War explained, "The eyes, the eyes, they're a dead giveaway. . . . If someone looks at you with a lingering look, and looks away, and then looks at you again." Like countless others, I can recognize a gay man at fifty feet, by sight or by sound. I can tell if a man is gay by the way he walks, by the inflections in his voice, by the way he steps out of a car. It is not simply a matter of being effeminate or even camp; as Donald Webster Cory said in the 1950s, there are signs "neither masculine nor feminine, but specifically and peculiarly homosexual." When these features are exaggerated they become the mincing gait, the high-pitched, haughty or ironic voice and lisp, the self-conscious display of the body and the flutter of the fingers. "The special language of a queen, or even an ordinary garden-variety faggot, is so distinct I find I can distinguish it even in a crowd of men in a restaurant or on the street, far from any Gay scene," [says Grahn]. To assert that various queer gestures and signs are "culturally specific" is to ignore the evidence that a quite limited number of gestures and signs marks out the effeminate/camp man and the butch woman across a very wide range of cultures and across several thousand years. A "third sex" category is almost universally discernible even while the "manly" and "feminine" elements that go into that category differ. . . .

. . . The idea that sexual identity is "malleable" to the degree that social constructionists believe seems to me absurd. Abundant evidence demonstrates that sexual orientation cannot be changed even for men who are strongly motivated to change and who have voluntarily undergone extensive psychiatric therapies, involving the use of drugs and hormone injections, behaviour modification techniques, electric shock therapy, etc., in an effort to turn straight. The main result has been to make many therapists rich while shattering the lives of countless homosexuals. The widespread failure of such therapies has led to their virtual abandonment except by psychiatric institutions supported by the radical religious right in America. Most therapists now advise their clients to accept themselves and concentrate on *managing* their identities in a positive fashion; it is recognized, in effect, that their queerness is part of their essential nature and cannot be changed. . . .

The cultural relativism observed by the social constructionists has been very much exaggerated. The essentialist does not reject the notion that there are "homosexualities" rather than a single monolithic homosexuality. It is obvious that the ways of being homosexual sometimes vary in different historical periods and in different cultures. But they are not infinitely different; in fact the differences are not very wide (perhaps there are not even so many as a dozen different homosexualities). . . .

The assertion that there are an infinite number of homosexualities is a political statement rather than an observable fact. Not only have a very limited number of homosexual paradigms been observed throughout history and throughout different cultures, but they are very often found concurrently in a single culture. These models display more similarities to one another than do individual cultures, and it is remarkable that queer (sub)cultures have more in common with each other than with the larger cultures of which they are a part. Empirical research has not borne out the universal-polymorphous hypothesis, nor has it discovered a very wide range of configurations of erotic pleasure. . . .

Most social constructionists, taking their cue from Weeks and Foucault, concentrate on the "discourse" of homosexuality, namely the discussion and investigation of homosexuality by professional sexologists and physicians, and ignore the evidence that falls outside that discourse. But if anything suggests that experiential reality exists outside of discourse, it is the feeling of thousands of homosexuals of a desire *for which they have no name.* Even when we examine the professional discourse, repeatedly we find instances of a dawning awareness among heterosexuals (especially the middle classes) of the existence of a world of homosexuals (especially among the working classes) which homosexuals have known about for decades and even centuries. . . . [British writer John Addington] Symonds, for example, in the 1870s, was actively engaged in the discourse [of homosexuality] before he discovered the reality with a Guardsman; the truth dawned for him not as a result of discourse, but after seeing "a rude *graffito* scrawled with slate-pencil upon slate. It was of so concentrated, so stimulative, so penetrative a character—so thoroughly the voice of vice and passion in the proletariat—that it pierced the very marrow of my soul. 'Prick to prick, so sweet.'" There are also many cases in which the authorities, those who supposedly define and create the homosexual construct, began an investigation which suddenly revealed to their astonishment a large underworld, which becomes so threatening that it put a halt to the inquiry. The investigation of the gay subculture at the Newport Naval Training Station led to the arrest of twenty sailors and sixteen civilians in 1919, at which point the chairman of the court ordered the chief investigator to curtail the investigation, warning, "If your men [the decoys] do not knock off, they will hang the whole state of Rhode Island." So even within the discourse what we are often dealing with is social *discovery* rather than social *construction*. A key feature of the homosexual "discourse" during the 1950s and early 1960s consisted of ordinary homosexuals successfully persuading the sociologists to recognize them and to begin basing their theories on the majority of homosexuals who had never consulted psychiatrists or been arrested. It was this line of sociological enquiry, by the likes of Evelyn Hooker, whose pool was drawn from acquaintances of her ordinary gay friends, which successfully began to deconstruct the models constructed by psychiatry and the law.

. . . As far as I am concerned, [historical] "watersheds," "shifts" and "ruptures" have very little to do with queers themselves, and much to do with the education of heterosexuals, who gradually became less naive as sexologists and the more outrageous queens made clear what queers have always known. . . .

In the history of camp, including camp in public and in the movies, we can see that naivety is the only possible explanation for why such things were not immediately understood the moment they were uttered or imagined. There was a thriving American queer/fairy subculture in the 1910s and 1920s, quite safe and secure due, as one man said, to "the ignorance and naïveté of the American public." . . .

. . . The main difference in historical changes of perception is that the heterosexual public at large has gradually become more sophisticated in recognizing queer semiotics. It is not that "modern perception" has changed, but that modern straight perception has belatedly incorporated queer perception. This is not a conceptual "rupture," merely straight time-lag. Not even the time-lag itself is modern: for many centuries queers have felt themselves to be sophisticated and cosmopolitan, in contrast to provincial rustics. . . .

Social constructionism violates common-sense in its insistence that "sexuality" did not exist until modern times. Of course sexuality has cultural meaning, but it does not therefore follow that sexuality "represents the *appropriation* of the human body and of its physiological capacities by an ideological discourse," nor does it follow that "'sexuality' seems indeed to be a uniquely modern, Western, even bourgeois production" [as David Halperin has argued]. Note Halperin's pre-emptive use of the Marxist term "production" rather than something more neutral such as "phenomenon." Halperin's employment of concepts such as "the production of desire" obviously mirrors the Marxist theory of production and distribution:

> Instead of concentrating our attention specifically on the history of sexuality, then, we need to define and refine a new, and radical, historical sociology of psychology, an intellectual discipline designed to analyze the cultural poetics of desire, by which I mean the processes whereby sexual desires are constructed, mass-produced, and distributed among the various members of human living-groups.

His theory of "modes of construction" is an echo of "means of production," part of the socialist subtext of nearly all social constructionist theory. Theorists who adopt the cultural emphasis of the theory often seem unaware of its fundamental premise that a sexual construct is an economic product. . . .

It may be perfectly reasonable to analyse the structures of power and status to which sexual relations—heterosexual and homosexual—are linked, but that is not all there is to be said about sexual relations: we still need to deal with precisely what makes them specifically *sexual* and distinguishes them from non-sexual power relations. The history of homosexuality as power is not coterminous with the history of homosexuality as desire. . . .

A theory that is politically useful may be either true or false: its political value does not depend upon its accuracy, but upon its power of persuasion or coercion. Social constructionism is politically useful for undermining mechanisms of social control and oppression. Essentialism is politically useful for empowering minority groups by a sense of solidarity grounded upon an awareness of identity. An effective gay rights movement might well employ strategies suggested by both schools of thought, exploiting each approach according to circumstances, without regard to consistency; the fundamental contradiction between them can be mitigated by arguing that homophobia is a construct while homosexuality is innate.

It is naive to think that one theory or the other will inevitably affect the predominantly negative attitudes of modern Western society, and societies influenced by the West.

Reading the Silences Around Sexuality

JOHN D. WRATHALL

In April 1886 W. W. Vanarsdale of the Chicago Young Men's Christian Association (Y.M.C.A.) was arranging a fiftieth birthday celebration for Robert Weidensall of the International Committee of the Y.M.C.A. He solicited testimonials from Weidensall's co-workers. From the Reverend John B. Brandt, a long-time Y.M.C.A. leader, he received a letter containing the following passage:

> Weidensall is fifty is he? Just think of it. It seems but yesterday when we all thought we were boys. Isn't there some mistake? Why he is not even married yet. It is very unlike Robert to "put himself forward" or in any manner claim what does not belong to him. Yet here he comes and says he is fifty and this important business of life is not yet attended to. It ought to have been done at least twenty five years ago. I am sure you will agree that we would not have thought this of one so conscientious and devoted to every known duty as this dear Brother of ours has always shown himself to be. But here is another sad example of the influence of Associates. If in the early days of our association work we could have kept Weidensall away from Morse & McBurney and altogether under good wholesome western influence all this might have been different. It is some encouragement that Morse has seen his error repented and is now trying to undo the mischief of nearly a life time. But McBurney seems to be obdurate as ever. Here he is right along side of Weidensall. Fifty years and no wife yet. I think some of you Chicago

John D. Wrathall, "Provenance as Text: Reading the Silences Around Sexuality in Manuscript Collections," *Journal of American History* 79 (June 1992): 165-178. Reprinted by permission of the Organization of American Historians.

Brethren ought to lay aside all other matters for a year if necessary and teach these boys a thing or two. These young gentlemen should be shown up in their true light. They will be the ruin of the country if they are not stopped. Just see already how Cree, Orr, Mather and many of our brightest and best are going in the same wretched way. Cannot something be done.

This startling passage and the collection that contains it suggest some of the archival issues that confront historians of sexuality.

. . . Scholars in . . . [the history of sexuality], perhaps more than those in any other, have to contend with the problem of silences: silences created by the censorship of archival and educational institutions, silences created by historians' refusal to acknowledge the sexualities of the individuals they study, and silences created by the authors of the documents historians use to reconstruct the past. Problems of censorship may diminish as individuals challenge the norms that made silence seem acceptable. But silences within historical documents will always pose a problem of analysis and interpretation. To read around such silences, historians have explored the broadest possible context in which sexuality was given meaning. Rather than focusing on discrete sexual acts, they have examined sexual mores and beliefs about the body, religious rites of passage, social institutions like marriage, kinship, and friendship, and the ways discourse about sexuality has been shaped or silenced. . . .

This article . . . [explores] what it means to use a collection's provenance as a historical source. It attempts to read the collection itself as a unit in order to illuminate the meaning of silences, particularly when one is studying the history of sexuality. Since any discussion of methodology and theory is best done in the concrete, indeed, since my conclusions about method have emerged from my experience processing manuscripts at the YMCA of the USA Archives at the University of Minnesota, I have framed this discussion as an analysis of a collection in those archives. The Robert Weidensall Papers lend themselves particularly to such analysis, because more than most collections received by archivists, this one was extensively processed by its donor. Furthermore, it contains documents discussing that processing. The passage above, from the Weidensall Papers, draws attention to the problem of censorship and the processing of manuscript collections and sheds light on the history of sexuality and gender in the nineteenth-century United States.

The way in which the Brandt letter appears in the Weidensall Papers suggests that its preservation was an accident, the result of an oversight. The cited passage comes near the beginning of a six-page, handwritten letter in which Brandt discusses his work and relationship with Weidensall. Scrawled in a different pen in the margin next to almost the entire passage is a bracket and the word "omit." Later in the collection there appears a typewritten version of the letter, with the offensive passage gone, and without ellipsis or other marks to indicate that anything had been removed. The missing portion of text begins with "Why he is not even married yet" so that the edited version of the letter reads: "Weidensall is fifty is he? Just think of it. It seems but yesterday when we all thought we were boys. Isn't there some mistake?" It then continues with Brandt's recollections of his early work with Weidensall. The editing makes Brandt's comments on Weidensall's age sound like friendly and nostalgic reminiscing on the passage of time, when in fact in the initial and full statement Brandt was setting the stage for a rude salvo expressing dismay over what he regarded as a severe moral shortcoming.

Why was the letter edited in this way? Is it possible that Weidensall wished to retain the letter for historical purposes, but intended to create a sanitized version to replace the original? Perhaps the typewritten version was intended for use at the birthday celebration, where testimonials were read out loud. According to the account of the celebration in the *Watchman,* an official Y.M.C.A. publication, an excerpt from Brandt's letter was recited there. But other edited versions of letters used at the celebration were clearly labeled as excerpts. Evidence in the collection indicates that Weidensall, who began supervising the intensive processing of his papers around 1904, had many other letters copied in typewritten format and then destroyed the originals. It seems likely that the original Brandt letter, with its offensive passage, survives as an oversight, that its destruction was intended but accidentally never accomplished. One is left, of course, wondering what did not survive.

The essential historical context of the passage, its statements and its silences, is the Y.M.C.A. of the nineteenth and early twentieth centuries. The passage itself links Weidensall's unmarried state to influences within the Y.M.C.A. The passage was written by a Y.M.C.A. leader as part of a testimonial solicited by another Y.M.C.A. leader for a celebration of Weidensall's birthday as an official Y.M.C.A. event. And the survival of the document and its availability to researchers was a probably unintended result of very deliberate efforts to preserve the history of the Y.M.C.A.

The Y.M.C.A., an assertively all-male organization, provides an ideal context for studying homoerotic ties and male identity in a time of crucial shifts in American attitudes toward gender and sexuality. Y.M.C.A. leaders in the nineteenth century frequently referred to their association as a "movement" of young men, of Evangelical Christian laity. Starting in 1851 in Boston and Montreal, partly following the example of associations organized in the United Kingdom since 1844, Y.M.C.A.'s sprang up in many North American cities. Y.M.C.A.'s typically consisted of Bible study groups and prayer circles. They also frequently helped young men who had recently arrived in a city find respectable lodging and employment. In 1854 the United States and Canadian associations formed a loose confederation for mutual encouragement. After the Civil War, they created a centralized International Committee and began hiring full-time "secretaries" to coordinate outreach and offer aid and guidance to struggling local associations. Local associations in major cities such as Boston, New York, Washington, and Chicago had already begun employing "general secretaries" to perform administrative work. Weidensall was the first full-time paid field secretary of the International Committee of the Y.M.C.A. Brandt, the general secretary of the Indianapolis association, collaborated with Weidensall in the 1870s to form the International Association of General Secretaries of the Y.M.C.A. W. W. Vanarsdale was a former general secretary of the Chicago Y.M.C.A., and at the time Brandt wrote him in 1886, editor of the *Watchman.*

The Y.M.C.A. was primarily concerned with leading young men to Jesus Christ as Lord and Savior. As the Y.M.C.A. evolved, some local associations included working-class men and men of other age groups; some included women. Y.M.C.A.'s also developed social service and general mission work programs. Weidensall and others sought to rein in these tendencies, insisting that the Y.M.C.A. keep strictly to its Evangelical basis and that it remain an association for young men only. As the first cohort of secretaries aged, there was concern that the organization was falling away from its earlier expectation that young men would supply the leadership, but the perseverance of the postbellum leadership into the early twentieth century created a sense of intergenerational continuity and perpetuated the association's fraternal ethos and organizational structure. Weidensall, for instance, in the 1890s became a mentor to John Lake and John R. Boardman. In letters to Weidensall, Luther D. Wishard acknowledged that it was the loving concern and personal warmth Weidensall had shown him that drew him into the Y.M.C.A.'s student work.

Philosophies of "Christian manhood" and of "manly Christianity" eventually developed within the Y.M.C.A., and many associations adopted a "fourfold program" for the spiritual, social, mental, and physical development of young men. Along with its distinctive ideals and spirituality, the Y.M.C.A. fostered a way of life that united men in intense shared commitments. In framing questions about that way of life, about Brandt's strictures against some of its aspects, and about the surrounding silences, one can draw on recent work in the history of sexuality. That work has drawn attention to the non–biologically determined—the "socially constructed"— aspects of sexuality. As long as sexuality was understood to be entirely determined by biology, one could at most write a history of attitudes toward sexuality. Sexuality itself was assumed to remain constant and therefore to have no history. The other major achievement of this new literature has been to challenge the assumption of universal heterosexuality and to highlight the social and political ramifications of systems of sexual morality, sexual economy, and sexual relationships.

The study of the history of sexuality has posed unique epistemological problems. A sort of common wisdom has assumed that taboos in Western culture have suppressed or silenced frank discussions of sexual behavior. This is true in the sense that many of our questions regarding the history of sexuality cannot be answered because individuals in the past could not or would not speak about sexuality in the way we do today. But a more sophisticated understanding of the problem, according to Michel Foucault, recognizes that knowledge of sexuality is framed in the terms of certain kinds of "discourse"—popular, familial, theological, legal, medical, and psychiatric. As people change the categories they use to discuss sexuality, or as they talk about sexuality in different contexts, the kinds of things they can and cannot say (indeed, even think it possible to say) about sexuality change. From this point of view, the misunderstandings arise, not so much from historical censorship or suppression of sources (although, as this case shows, this can be a problem), as from the historian's tendency to bring to the study of the history of sexuality questions framed in her or his own categories and not in the categories of the societies or eras being studied. Indeed, one might argue that the field of the history of sexuality has not existed until now, not because of any prudery or puritanism in Western culture, but because the categories have not existed that would have allowed anyone even to conceive of a history of sexuality.

For example, historians have shown that until the late nineteenth century public discourse about sexuality occurred primarily in theological and legal contexts. But in the United States in the 1880s and 1890s, sexuality increasingly became a concern of the rising medical and psychiatric professions. The kinds of questions that doctors and psychiatrists brought to the study of sexuality were considerably different from those posed by priests, pastors, theologians, and legislators.

In the nineteenth century, Anthony E. Rotundo has argued, expressions of male-male intimacy and affection were considered normal parts of a boy's maturation into manhood. The Y.M.C.A. differed from the norm described by Rotundo in that intense emotional ties between men in the organization were nurtured into adulthood and even into old age. But Rotundo's research certainly indicates a social and discursive environment where love could be openly expressed even between adult men and not be viewed as deviant or sick. George Chauncey, Jr., documents a considerable change in attitude by 1919, however, when United States Navy trials in Newport, Rhode Island, implicated in a homosexual scandal an Episcopal priest who worked at the Y.M.C.A. and a Y.M.C.A. lay volunteer. Chauncey documents participants' (somewhat distorted) awareness of medical literature on homosexuality. He further argues that by then, male-male affection had become suspect, at least in the eyes of navy investigators and prosecutors; the new mood of suspicion caused considerable anxiety to Y.M.C.A. workers and clergy. Brandt's accusation and Weidensall's later attempt to cover it up must be seen in the context of the changing discourse on sexuality and the anxiety it caused for men.

Awareness of shifts in discourse permits a new perspective on the problem of silences in the historical record regarding sexuality. As Eve Kosofsky Sedgwick has shown "silence" on the subject of sexuality far from being a "lack" or an "absence" of discourse is, at least in the twentieth century, itself constructed. This has implications for the interpretation of such silences. Sedgwick argues that homosexuality became constructed in the late nineteenth century as an "open secret," as something about which one might know, but about which one was simultaneously supposed to know nothing. Particularly important was the invention of "bachelorhood," which obscured the existence of gay men and provided important camouflage for the modern homosexual "closet."

Brandt's letter of April 14, 1886, to W. W. Vanarsdale startles because it is effectively an ominous, accusing finger pointing right at the closet door, demanding that it be opened and that the closet be cleaned out. By calling into question the innocence of singleness and by drawing attention to the disproportionate number of Y.M.C.A. secretaries who were "going in the same wretched way," Brandt threatened to expose a secret that an unspoken consensus agreed was better left unexposed. He was violating the rule that would become the norm in the twentieth century regarding interrogations about the meaning of male singleness: "Don't ask."

For the most part, the singleness of many Y.M.C.A. secretaries assumed the form of this "open secret." Ignoring singleness was fairly easy in an organization where women were virtually absent and invisible even when they were present. In biographical sketches of Y.M.C.A. leaders, little attention was paid to marital status and whether or not they had children. Typical in this regard was Richard C. Morse, one of the men cited in Brandt's letter as an unwholesome influence on Weidensall and other young men, and of whom Brandt noted, "It is some encouragement that [he] has seen his error repented and is now trying to undo the mischief of nearly a life time [by marrying at the late age of forty-five]." . . .

It is hardly surprising that there is no record of any response to Brandt's call for the "Chicago brethren" to look into the problem of single secretaries. Open confrontation was not the style of an organization that, more than most, sought to minimize differences and promote unity. Furthermore, by 1886 Weidensall was already revered throughout Canada and the United States as a pioneer of the movement. Vanarsdale was probably appalled and embarrassed by Brandt's accusations, and he undoubtedly responded simply by filing the letter away and ignoring it, even as he quoted other parts of it in the *Watchman* as a testimonial to Weidensall's faithful service. But Weidensall's apparent attempt to censor the letter for the historical record draws attention to his role many years later in the processing of the collection.

For Weidensall, putting his historical papers in order was a life work that formed part of his commitment to the Y.M.C.A. He began the task in 1904 or 1905 and likely continued at it virtually until his death in 1922. . . .

The work involved sorting through the letters one by one, removing letters that Weidensall deemed to have no historical worth and with the aid of the stenographer copying letters that he deemed of historical worth but that required editing. Anyone sorting through the Robert Weidensall Papers sees his caring hand throughout: Almost every letter has a note scrawled on it in Weidensall's hand (for example, "important" and "keep this"); there are occasional comments on the significance of a particular individual or event and, as noted above, even directions for the omission of passages.

Just as letters in the collection give clues as to how the donor initially processed it, they reveal the logic underlying his decisions about what was "historically relevant" and what was "of no worth." Weidensall, like many other Y.M.C.A. leaders, used history to endow his work with a sacred aura. . . .

Early histories of the Y.M.C.A. and biographical sketches of Weidensall characterized him as a "prophet," a "pioneer," and a "pathfinder." This fit Weidensall's own view of his mission. In 1902 he implied that one purpose of his historical papers was to demonstrate his ability to foresee the path that the Y.M.C.A. eventually followed. . . . The letters demonstrate that Robert Weidensall believed the Y.M.C.A to be "the single most efficient" work of God for young men in the history of the world, that he saw himself as a founder and prophet of that work, and that he intended his historical papers to document both of these facts.

The structure of the collection lends insight into the categories through which Weidensall went about making sense of the Y.M.C.A. and of his life work. It is likely that the current arrangement of the papers reflects Weidensall's original arrangement. The bulk of the material is divided into two categories: "business" and "personal." . . . Within each series, Weidensall's papers are arranged in chronological order. The division of materials into business and personal is reminiscent of the distinction between "public" and "private," about which so much has been written in the field of women's history. Another, perhaps related, distinction is that between "public" and "secret." The latter would be important to understanding historical censorship or suppression.

The existence of business and personal categories indicates that Weidensall distinguished a realm of public activity and relationships from a realm of the private. This is not remarkable; many manuscript collections before and since have been similarly organized. Of interest, however, are the kinds of material that Weidensall filed, under each category. . . .

Many letters in the business series document personal relationships that Weidensall had with other men but that were established and nurtured in the public sphere of his Y.M.C.A. business. An example is a document clearly labeled as an extract from a 1915 letter of Luther D. Wishard, a leader in the Y.M.C.A. student movement. The labeling indicates that Weidensall intended it for public consumption, even though the feelings expressed in the letter seem very intimate and personal. Wishard writes of the "peculiar pleasure" it gives him to write to an "old and well-tried friend," and of his inability adequately to express his feelings "on earth." But he promises Weidensall that

> there will be a time in the not very distant future when we can talk together after the work is done and can enter into a full appreciation of its results. Then I shall appreciate your relationship to men on earth more than ever, and then I can express the appreciation better.

He closes his letter "with the same old love."

Correspondence and documents relating to Weidensall's Y.M.C.A. career, his voluntary service to his congregation and his denomination, and personal relationships and events that he shared with Y.M.C.A. associates could all be placed under the category of business. This arrangement implies that Weidensall saw faith and religious service as part of a public realm; that friendship and intimate relationships, when formed and sustained in the context of such religious service are part of that public realm; and that the fostering of love and faith in God *was* his business.

Weidensall categorized as personal correspondence with family members, hometown neighbors, and a comrade from his service in the United States Construction Corps during the Civil War. Weidensall did not define his military service and subsequent work on a railroad as business but as part of a life that predated his real career as a Y.M.C.A. secretary. Autobiographical notes by Weidensall offer clues to the significance of his category of the personal. In almost formulaic fashion, these notes offer an account of his Christian upbringing. . . .

. . . For Weidensall, what was historically important from the category of the personal was what established his development as a man of faith and prepared him for his public ministry. Thus his army days and his work on the railroad are bracketed as trials and tribulations through which his faith fortunately passed intact. The personal is not identical with Weidensall's love life or his domestic life, about which almost nothing is known. What survives is a comment implying that Weidensall's failure to marry was immoral and could be attributed to the bad "influence of associates." And we have evidence of Weidensall's attempt to suppress, rather than rebut, this comment.

It is clear from other letters in the YMCA archives announcing romance and the intention to marry (the Weidensall Papers, for instance, contain one such letter from Wishard) that a man's love life, as it related to the fulfillment of a Christian duty to marry, was an acceptable—indeed, expected—part of public discourse. From this, one might draw one of two conclusions regarding the subjective sphere of romance and feelings of love in the lives of unmarried Evangelical men. Either it did not exist, or the one that did exist could not be spoken of.

When I first began reading Weidensall's personal correspondence, I had hoped to answer several questions: Why did he never marry? Did he ever make an attempt to marry? Did he ever court anyone? Were there ever any female loves in his life? Given the Evangelical Protestant context in which Weidensall lived and worked, these questions seemed important. Brandt's letter confirmed that it mattered to Evangelical ministers whether men in positions of religious leadership, such as Robert Weidensall, Richard Morse, and Robert R. McBurney, were married or not.

But the search for direct evidence about why Weidensall had not married was disappointing. For Weidensall, personal correspondence meant family correspondence that established the sincerity and the reality of a public life of faith. Of love, except for the public love of friendship fostered in the context of the association, there was nothing—or rather only a locked closet door with the key thrown away.

But how could Weidensall justify deliberately falsifying the historical record? The distinction between public and secret was probably less analogous in Weidensall's mind to the distinction between business and personal than it was to the distinction between historically valuable and historically irrelevant. In fact, Weidensall considered virtually all the materials in the Weidensall Papers, both business and personal, to be public or historically valuable. One would surmise that most material Weidensall considered secret or historically irrelevant is not available in the collection. The papers include few such items, which apparently survived through accident or oversight: the Brandt letter, a few notes on financial matters, and some letters labeled "confidential" that detailed problems with staff members. Only in the case of the Brandt letter is there evidence of an attempt to censor material. One can reasonably assume that any *other* material that Weidensall wanted to censor no longer exists.

Weidensall was undoubtedly offended by the passage, especially since it cast aspersions on his sterling record of service. "I am sure you will agree that we would not have thought this of one so conscientious and devoted to every known duty as this dear Brother of ours has always shown himself to be." These words must have had a particular sting for a man as preoccupied with his public and historical image as Weidensall. I am certain that Weidensall could justify suppressing this passage because he saw his marital status as beyond the realm of discussion. His particular construction of the category of the personal included only the parts of his home and family life that contributed to a public life of faith. Weidensall effectively constructed a silence around such matters as his unmarried state. In doing so, he was not unique.

I can offer one final observation regarding the quality of this silence. The popular image of the late nineteenth-century "bachelor," corresponding as it did to the eighteenth-century "rake," was obviously not a model for Y.M.C.A. leaders. That image might explain the apparent alarm in Brandt's letter. There were models for "celibate" Christian service, most obviously the Roman Catholic priesthood, but given the general discomfort among nineteenth-century Protestants with anything smelling of incense or papal benediction, it would not have worked for the Y.M.C.A. . . .

The most convincing answer to the question "Why did so many Y.M.C.A. secretaries never marry?" is because of their love for and attraction to young men, expressed in a desire to serve them in a Christian context. One anonymous biographer wrote of McBurney, "without father and mother, brother or sister, *wife or child* . . . he also unselfishly denied himself to social and all other calls, keeping himself only unto 'this work for Christ among young men.'" Weidensall in an 1876 letter compared his work to that of Ignatius of Loyola and drew parallels between the task of training Y.M.C.A. leaders and the work of a religious order. Characteristically, Weidensall noted, "Of course we don't want to follow the evils of Jesuitism but ought to imitate their good [practices]." What he specifically meant by "good practices" was the example Loyola set as a young man who had "gathered around him young men and trained them." In the last years of his life, Weidensall devoted himself to the volunteer extension work, which, as he defined it in 1898, involved "selecting a band of young men—hand-picked young men—spirit called young men" and personally disciplining them. His emphasis was on a close relationship between the trainer and the disciples: they were to remain in intense contact for an extended time, and the group was to consist of not more than twelve, perhaps as few as two or three. In 1912 he wrote to a co-worker that he needed time to "qualify myself for [this] last work which probably the Lord will give me to do."

In this essay, I argue that the provenance and organizational structure of manuscript collections can be used as historical sources. Doing so illuminates documents in them, especially when one is trying to evaluate the significance of silences within collections. I have assumed that all silences, as Eve Kosofsky Sedgwick has pointed out, are not the same, that they hide different meanings, and that something of what they hide can be deducted from the context in which they exist and the purpose for which they were produced. In few fields is evaluating silences as important as in the history of sexuality, where, in modern American culture in particular, the forces of shame and punishment have hedged discourse and determined what could and could not be expressed.

FURTHER READING

Paula Gunn Allen, "Lesbians in Native American Culture," *The Sacred Hoop* (1986), 106–117.

John Boswell, "Towards the Long View: Revolutions, Universal and Sexual Categories," *Salmagundi* 58–59 (Fall 1982–Winter 1983): 89–113.

Ann Ducille, "Othered Matters: Reconceptualizing Dominance and Difference in the History of Sexuality in America," *Journal of the History of Sexuality* 1 (1990): 102–127.

John D'Emilio and Estelle Freedman, *Intimate Matters: A History of Sexuality in America* (1988).

Martin Duberman et al., eds., *Hidden from History: Reclaiming the Gay and Lesbian Past* (1989).

Stephen Epstein, "Gay Politics, Ethnic Identity: The Limits of Social Constructionism," *Socialist Review* 93/94 (May–August 1987): 9–54.

Michel Foucault, *The History of Sexuality, Vol. 1: An Introduction* (1978).

Estelle Freedman, "'The Burning of Letters Continues': Elusive Identities and the Historical Construction of Sexuality," *Journal of Women's History* 9 (Winter 1998): 181–200.

David F. Greenberg, *The Construction of Homosexuality* (1988).

Evelyn M. Hammonds, "Toward a Genealogy of Black Female Sexuality: The Problematic of Silence," in M. Jacqui Alexander and Chandra Talpade Mohanty, eds., *Feminist Genealogies, Colonial Legacies, and Democratic Futures* (1997).

Elizabeth Lapovsky Kennedy, "Telling Tales: Oral History and the Construction of Pre-Stonewall Lesbian History," *Radical History Review* 62 (Spring 1995): 58–79.

Thomas Laqueur, *Making Sex: Body and Gender from the Greeks to Freud* (1990).

Robert Padgug, "Sexual Matters: On Conceptualizing Sexuality in History," *Radical History Review* 20 (1979): 3–33.

Richard G. Parker and John H. Gagnon, eds., *Conceiving Sexuality* (1995).

Donna Penn, "Queer: Theorizing Politics and History," *Radical History Review* 62 (Spring 1995): 24–43.

Gayle Rubin, "Thinking Sex: Notes for a Radical Theory of the Politics of Sexuality," in Carole S. Vance, ed., *Pleasure and Danger* (1984), 267–319.

Eve Kosofsky Sedgwick, *Epistemology of the Closet* (1990).

Judith Shapiro, "Transsexualism: Reflections on the Persistence of Gender and the Mutability of Sex," in Julia Epstein and Kristina Straub, eds., *Body Guards* (1991), 248–279.

Martha M. Umphrey, "The Trouble with Harry Thaw," *Radical History Review* 62 (Spring 1995): 8–23.

Carole S. Vance, "Social Construction Theory: Problems in the History of Sexuality," in International Conference on Gay and Lesbian Studies, *Homosexuality, Which Homosexuality?* (1989), 13–33.

Martha Vicinus, " 'They Wonder to Which Sex I Belong': The Historical Roots of the Modern Lesbian Identity," *Feminist Studies* 18 (1992): 467–497.

CHAPTER
2

Sexual Cultures and Encounters
in the New World

During the early colonization of North America, European observers of indigenous peoples were struck by the diversity of their sexual practices and by the profound differences between Native American and European sexual cultures. Written descriptions of early cross-cultural encounters came, almost without exception, from the pens of European men; we must first understand their world-view and assumptions in order to analyze these documents. Nor was their perspective a unified one: Different religions, military cultures, and governing systems in France, England, and Spain affected their perceptions of Native sexual beliefs and behavior.

The most detailed observations were made by Jesuit priests, who ventured into woodland villages well in advance of French fur traders and soldiers. Priests studied Native practices and beliefs carefully, seeking to elevate what they found praiseworthy and to reform what they found reprehensible by teaching Christian morality. Other men's observations were also shaped by their interests, for example, as fur traders. Perplexed by the sexual variety they observed, European men interpreted indigenous cultures in relation to their own. All assumed that pagan and barbarous people were inferior to Christian and civilized ones. Some chroniclers compared Native Americans favorably to ancient Greeks and Romans; others associated them with humanity's evil animal impulses. A few commentators used Native American cultures to criticize their own society's failure to practice Christian ideals of chastity.

In reading these texts, it is difficult to sort out Europeans' misperceptions from the variations among Native American cultures. Nonetheless, some common features of indigenous sexuality are visible in the records: the absence of rape or sexual abuse; voluntary marriage and divorce; deliberate control of reproduction; the centrality of kinship to identity; diversity in patterns of descent and residence; and the possibility of cross-gender roles and same-sex attachments for both women and men.

Sexual relationships between Europeans and Native Americans were shaped by the dynamics of power between their societies. Rape and other forms of sexual abuse were most frequent where European men sought to control and exploit Native Americans' bodies and land. Indeed, some historians argue that sexual violence was a key instrument of European conquest. In some circumstances, however, marriages and informal alliances between European men and Native women were tacitly approved; in fur-trading societies, for instance, economic advantages could be gained through such relationships.

DOCUMENTS

Catholic priests, English fur traders, and French aristocrats all observed and reported on Native American sexual practices. Historians need to interpret these documents with care. What viewpoints do they represent? Why were they written? How reliable are they as records of the sexuality of indigenous people?

In Document 1, Baron Lahontan, writing in 1703, noted several fundamental features of Huron sexual practices and compared them to European ways; interestingly, he praises Native peoples' sexual self-control and lack of possessiveness, even as he expresses outrage over women's sexual autonomy. John Lawson's 1709 account of the Native people of the Carolinas, in Document 2, reflects his own economic and sexual interests: As a trader, he recognized the economic advantages obtained through sexual relationships with indigenous women. How do these interests lead him to misconstrue Native life? Europeans were also intrigued by the cross-gender roles and same-sex attraction they witnessed in many Native American societies. In Document 3, written in 1733, missionary Joseph François Lafitau compared the friendships among Iroquois men to those of the ancient Greeks. Although Lafitau saw these relationships as virtuous, most missionaries assumed that they involved sexual intimacy and sought to suppress them.

One of the most powerful records of the sexual abuse of indigenous women by Spanish soldiers appears in Document 4, written in 1772 by Father Luis Jayme, a Franciscan missionary. He recounts cases of rape that traumatized entire Native communities. Jayme distinguished priests from soldiers, but California Natives often did not, perceiving missionaries to be agents of colonialism accountable for Spanish crimes. In 1775, Father Jayme was killed, in a deliberate act of retribution, during a mass uprising in San Diego.

1. Baron Lahontan Describes Love and Marriage Among the Hurons, 1703

It may be justly said, That the Men are as cold and indifferent as the Girls are passionate and warm. The former love nothing but War and Hunting, and their utmost Ambition reaches no farther. When they are at home, and have nothing to do, they run with the Match; that is, they are Night-walkers. The Young Men do not marry till they are Thirty Years of Age, for they pretend that the Enjoyment of Women does so enervate 'em, that they have not the same measur of Strength to undergo great Fatigues, and that their Hams are too weak for long Marches, or quick Pursuits. . . . But after all, we must not imagine that they live chaste till that Age; for they pretend

Louis Armand de Lom d'Arce, Baron de Lahontan, *New Voyages to North-America*, ed. Reuben Gold Thwaites (English ed. 1703; Chicago: A. C. McClurg & Co., 1905), vol. 2, 451–458, 460–464.

that Excessive Continence occasions Vapours, Disorders of the Kidneys, and a Suppression of Urine; so that 'tis necessary for their Health to have a Run once a Week.

If the Savages were capable of being subjected to the Empire of Love, they must needs have an Extraordinary Command of themselves to disguise the Just Jealousie they might have of their Mistresses, and at the same time to carry it fair with their Rivals. I know the Humour of the Savages better than a great many *French* People that have liv'd among 'em all their Life-time; for I study'd their Customs so narrowly and exactly, that all their Conduct of Life is as perfectly well known to me, as if I had been among 'em all my Life-time: And 'tis this Exact Knowledge that prompts me to say, That they are altogether Strangers to that Blind Fury which we call Love. They content themselves with a Tender Friendship, that is not liable to all the Extravagancies that the Passion of Love raises in such Breasts as harbour it: In a word, they live with such Tranquility, that one may call their Love Simple Goodwill, and their Discretion upon that Head is unimaginable. Their Friendship is firm, but free of Transport; for they are very careful in preserving the Liberty and Freedom of their Heart, which they look upon as the most valuable Treasure upon Earth: From whence I conclude that they are not altogether so savage as we are.

The Savages never quarrel among themselves, neither do they reproach or affront one another; One man among them is as good as another, for all are upon the same Level. They have no Disorders occasion'd by a Girl or a Wife, for the Women are Wise, and so are their Husbands: The Girls indeed are a little foolish, and the Young Men play the fool with them not unfrequently: But then you must consider that a Young Woman is allow'd to do what she pleases; let her Conduct be what it will, neither Father nor Mother, Brother nor Sister can pretend to controul her. A Young Woman, say they, is Master of her own Body, and by her Natural Right of Liberty is free to do what she pleases. But on the other hand the Married Women being allow'd the Priviledge of quitting their Husbands when they please, had as good be dead as be guilty of Adultery. In like manner, the Husbands being entituled to the same Priviledge, would look upon themselves as infamous, if they were faithless to their Wives.

Nothing of Intrigue or Courtship must be mention'd to the Savage Ladies in the Day time, for they will not hear it; they'll tell you the Night-time is the most proper season for that. . . . [W]hoever designs to win the Affection of a Girl, must speak to her in the Day-time, of things that lie remote from the Intrigues of Love. One may converse with them privately as long as he will, and talk of a thousand Adventures that happen every minute, upon which they make their Replies very pleasantly; for you cannot imagine what a Gay and Jovial Temper they are of; they are very apt to laugh, and that with a very engaging Air. 'Tis at these Private Interviews that the Savages smell out the Young Womens Thoughts; for though the Subject of their Discourse is of an Indifferent Strain, yet they talk over nicer Subjects in the Language of their Eyes. After a Young Man has paid two or three Visits to his Mistress, and fancies that she has look'd upon him with a favourable Eye, he takes the following Course to know the Truth of the Matter.

You must take notice, that forasmuch as the Savages are Strangers to *Meum and Tuum* [mine and thine], to Superiority and Subordination; and live in a State of Equality pursuant to the Principles of Nature; they are under no apprehension of Robbers or Secret Enemies, so that their Huts are open Night and Day. . . . 'Tis then that the Young Savage comes well wrapt up to his Mistress's Hut, and lights a sort of a Match at the Fire; after which he opens the Door of his Mistresses Apartment, and makes up to her Bed: If she blows out the Light, he lies down by her; but if she pulls her Covering over her Face, he retires; that being a Sign that she will not receive him. The Young Women drink the Juice of certain Roots, which prevents their Conception, or kills the Fruit of the Womb; for if a Girl proves with Child, she'll never get a Husband. They'll suffer any body to sit upon the Foot of their Bed, only to have a little Chat; and if another comes an hour after, that they like, they do not stand to grant him their last Favours. As to this Custom, which indeed is singular, the most sensible Savages gave this Reason for it, That they will not depend upon their Lovers, but remove all ground of Suspicion both from the one and the other, that so they may act as they please.

The Savage Women like the *French* better than their own Countreymen, by reason that the former are more prodigal of their Vigour, and mind a Woman's Business more closely. In the mean time the Jesuits use all Efforts to prevent their keeping Company with the *French:* They have Superannuated Fellows placed in all the Huts, who, like Faithful Spies, give an Account of all that they see or hear. The *French* who have the Misfortune to be discover'd, are publickly nam'd in the Pulpit, complain'd of to the Bishop and the Governor General, excommunicated, and treated as Transgressors of the Law: But after all the Artifices and Opposition of the Good Fathers, a great many Intrigues are carried on in the Villages, that they know nothing of. The Jesuits never offer to check the Young Savages for keeping company with Girls; for if they offer'd to censure their Conduct, and use 'em with the same liberty as they do the *French,* they would tell 'em roundly, that they're sorry the Fathers have a mind to their Mistresses. This was the Answer that a Young *Huron* spoke aloud one day in the Church, when a Jesuit addressing himself to him, was preaching down the Night-Rambles of the Savages with an Apostolical Freedom.

This People cannot conceive that the *Europeans,* who value themselves upon their Sense and Knowledge, should be so blind and so ignorant as not to know that Marriage in their way is a source of Trouble and Uneasiness. To be ingag'd for one's Life time, to them is matter of Wonder and Surprise. They look upon it as a monstrous thing to be tied one to another without any hopes of being able to unite or break the Knot. In fine, in spite of all the Reasons and Arguments that that Subject affords, they lay down this for a firm and unmoveable Truth, that we *Eropeans* are born in Slavery, and deserve no other Condition than that of Servitude.

In our Country, their state of Marriage would be justly look'd upon as a Criminal way of Conversation. A Savage (for Instance) that has signalis'd himself several times in the Field, and acquir'd the Reputation of a brave Warrior, hath a mind to Marry by the means of a Contract, or rather a Lease of Thirty Years, with the hopes of seeing in his old Age a Family descended of himself, that shall provide for him. This Hero looks out for an agreeable Girle, and after he and she have settled the matter, they reveal their Design to their Relations, who at the same time cannot oppose it, but are oblig'd to consent, and to assist at the Ceremony. They meet together in the Hut of the ancientest Relation or Parent, where a Feast is prepar'd on a Day fix'd for that purpose. Upon such Occasions that Company is very numerous, and the Table is cover'd with all manner of Dainties in a very prodigal manner; and those who assist at the Festival, Dance and Sing, and perform the other Diversions of the Country. After the Feasting and Merry-making is over, all the Relations of the Bridegroom retire, excepting four of the oldest, after which the Bride, accompany'd with four of her ancientest Female Relations, appears at one of the Doors of the Hut, and is receiv'd by the most decrepit Man of the Bridegroom's Company, who conducts her to the Bridegroom at a certain place, where the two Parties stand upright upon a fine Mat, holding a Rod between them, while the old Men pronounce some short Harangues. In this Posture do the two married Persons Harangue one after another, and Dance together, singing all the while, and holding the Rod in their Hands, which they afterwards break into as many pieces as there are Witnesses to the Ceremony, in order to be distributed among them. This done, the Bride is reconducted out of the Hut, where the young Women stay for her to accompany her to her Father's Apartment, and the Bridegroom or married Man is oblig'd to go there to find her when he has a mind to her Company, till such time as she brings forth a Child; then, indeed, she conveys her Cloaths to her Husbands Apartment, and continues with him till the Marriage is dissolv'd.

'Tis allowable both for the Man and the Woman to part when they please. Commonly they give one another eight Days Warning; sometimes they offer Reasons to justifie their Conduct, but for the most part the usual Plea is, that they are sick and out of order, and that Repose is more proper for them than the fatigue of a married Life. Then the little pieces of the Rod that were distributed among the Relations of the married Persons, are brought into that Hut in which the Marriage was Solemniz'd, and burnt in their Presence. You must observe that this Separation is accomplish'd without any Dispute or Quarrel. Both the Men and the Women thus unmarried may be marry'd again to whom they please: But commonly they lie bye three or six Months before they consummate their second Marriage. When this Separation happens the Children are divided equally between them, for the Children are the Treasure of the Savages. If their number be odd the Woman hath the better half. . . .

These Savages are uncapable of Jealousy; that is a Passion they know nothing of. They jeer the *Europeans* upon that head; and brand a man's distrust of his Wife, for a piece of manifest Folly; as if, say they, we were not certain that 'tis impossible for so weak an Animal to be true to its promises. . . . I am fully convinced that a Savage would chuse rather to suffer Mutilation than to Embrace his Neighbours Wife. Nor is the Chastity of the she Savages less nice, for I do not believe that in the space of Fifty Years there has been one Instance among 'em of the Invasion of another Man's Bed. 'Tis true the *French,* being uncapable to distinguish between the Married and Unmarried Women, sometimes make their Address to the former, when they find them alone in the Woods, or when they walk out into the Fields; but upon such occasions they always receive this Answer; *The Fiend which is before mine Eyes hinders me to see thee.*

. . . Some Savages continue Batchelours to their Dying day, and never appear either at Hunting or in Warlike Expeditions, as being either Lunatick of Sickly: But at the same time they are as much esteem'd as the Bravest and Hailest Men in the Country, or at least if they rally upon 'em, 'tis never done where they are present. Among the *Illinese* there are several Hermaphrodites, who go in a Woman's Habit, but frequent the Company of both Sexes. These *Illinese* are strangely given to Sodomy, as well as the other Savages that live near the River *Missisipi.*

This, Sir, is all that I could learn of the way of Marriage and the Amours of the *Americans;* who are so far from giving a full loose to their Venerial Appetite, that they always act with a command over themselves, being very moderate in their Adventures with Women, whom they make use of only for the Propagation of their Families and the Preservation of their Health. Their Conduct upon this Head may serve for a just Reprimand to the *Europeans.*

I observ'd before, that if once a Girle proves with Child, she never gets a Husband; but I ought to have added that some young Women will not hear of a Husband, through a principle of Debauchery. That sort of Women are call'd *Ickoue ne Kioussa,* i.e. *Hunting Women:* for they commonly accompany the Huntsmen in their Diversions. To justify their Conduct, they alledge that they find themselves to be of too indifferent a temper to brook the Conjugal yoak, to be too careless for the bringing up of Children, and too impatient to bear the passing of the whole Winter in the Villages. Thus it is, that they cover and disguise their Lewdness. Their Parents or Relations dare not censure their Vicious Conduct; on the contrary they seem to approve of it, in declaring, as I said before, that their Daughters have the command of their own Bodies and may dispose of their Persons as they think fit; they being at their liberty to do what they please. In short, the Children of these Common Women are accounted a Lawful Issue, and intitled to all the Privileges of other Children; abateing for one thing, namely, that the noted Warriours or Counsellours will not accept of 'em for their Sons in Law, and that they cannot enter into Alliance with certain Ancient Families; though at the same time these Families are not possessed of any peculiar Right or Preheminence. The *Jesuits* do their utmost to prevent the Lewd Practices of these Whores, by Preaching to their Parents that their Indulgence is very disagreeable to the Great Spirit, that they must answer before God for not confineing their Children to the measures of Continency and Chastity, and that a Fire is Kindled in the other World to Torment 'em for ever, unless they take more care to correct Vice.

To such Remonstrances the Men reply, *That's Admirable;* and the Women usually tell the Good Fathers in a deriding way, *That if their Threats be well grounded, the Mountains of the other World must consist of the Ashes of souls.*

2. English Trader John Lawson Describes Native Sexuality in North Carolina, 1709

As for the *Indian* Women, which now happen in my Way: when young, and at Maturity, they are as fine-shap'd Creatures (take them generally) as any in the Universe. They are of a tawny Complexion; their Eyes very brisk and amorous; their Smiles afford the finest Composure a Face can possess; their Hands are of the finest Make, with small long Fingers, and as soft as their Cheeks; and their whole Bodies

---

John Lawson, *A New Voyage to Carolina,* ed. Hugh Talmage Lefler (1709; Chapel Hill: University of North Carolina Press, 1967), 189–195.

of a smooth Nature. They are not so uncouth or unlikely, as we suppose them; nor are they Strangers or not Proficients in the soft Passion. They are most of them mercenary, except the married Women, who sometimes bestow their Favours also to some or other, in their Husbands Absence. For which they never ask any Reward. As for the Report, that they are never found unconstant, like the *Europeans,* it is wholly false; for were the old World and the new one put into a Pair of Scales (in point of Constancy) it would be a hard Matter to discern which was the heavier. As for the Trading Girls, which are those design'd to get Money by their Natural Parts, these are discernable, by the Cut of their Hair; their Tonsure differing from all others, of that Nation, who are not of their Profession; which Method is intended to prevent Mistakes; for the Savages of *America* are desirous (if possible) to keep their Wives to themselves, as well as those in other Parts of the World. When any Addresses are made to one of these Girls, she immediately acquaints her Parents therewith, and they tell the King of it, (provided he that courts her be a Stranger) his Majesty commonly being the principal Bawd of the Nation he rules over. . . . He likewise advises her what Bargain to make, and if it happens to be an *Indian* Trader that wants a Bed-fellow, and has got Rum to sell, be sure, the King must have a large Dram for a Fee, to confirm the Match. These *Indians,* that are of the elder sort, when any such Question is put to them, will debate the Matter amongst themselves with all the Sobriety and Seriousness imaginable, every one of the Girl's Relations arguing the Advantage or Detriment that may ensue such a Night's Encounter; all which is done with as much Steadiness and Reality, as if it was the greatest Concern in the World, and not so much as one Person shall be seen to smile, so long as the Debate holds, making no Difference betwixt an Agreement of this Nature, and a Bargain of any other. If they comply with the Men's Desire, then a particular Bed is provided for them, either in a Cabin by themselves, or else all the young people turn out, to another Lodging, that they may not spoil Sport; and if the old People are in the same Cabin along with them all Night, they lie as unconcern'd, as if they were so many Logs of Wood. If it be an *Indian* of their own Town or Neighbourhood, that wants a Mistress, he comes to none but the Girl, who receives what she thinks fit to ask him, and so lies all Night with him, without the Consent of her Parents.

The *Indian* Traders are those which travel and abide amongst the *Indians* for a long space of time; sometimes for a Year, two or three. These Men have commonly their *Indian* Wives, whereby they soon learn the *Indian* Tongue, keep a Friendship with the Savages; and, besides the Satisfaction of a She-Bed-Fellow, they find these *Indian* Girls very serviceable to them, on Account of dressing their Victuals, and instructing 'em in the Affairs and Customs of the Country. Moreover, such a Man gets a great Trade with the Savages; for when a Person that lives amongst them, is reserv'd from the Conversation of their Women, 'tis impossible for him ever to accomplish his Designs amongst that People.

But one great Misfortune which oftentimes attends those that converse with these Savage Women, is, that they get Children by them, which are seldom educated any otherwise than in a State of Infidelity; for it is a certain Rule and Custom, amongst all the savages of *America,* that I was ever acquainted withal, to let the Children always fall to the Woman's Lot; for it often happens, that two *Indians* that have liv'd together, as Man and Wife, in which Time they have had several Children; if they part, and another Man possesses her, all the Children go along with the

Mother, and none with the Father. And therefore, on this Score, it ever seems impossible for the Christians to get their Children (which they have by these *Indian* Women) away from them; whereby they might bring them up in the Knowledge of the Christian Principles. Nevertheless, we often find, that *English* Men, and other *Europeans* that have been accustom'd to the Conversation of these savage Women, and their Way of Living, have been so allur'd with that careless sort of Life, as to be constant to their *Indian* Wife, and her Relations, so long as they liv'd, without ever desiring to return again amongst the *English,* although they had very fair Opportunities of Advantages amongst their Countrymen; of which sort I have known several.

As for the *Indian* Marriages, I have read and heard of a great deal of Form and Ceremony used, which I never saw, nor yet could learn in the Time I have been amongst them, any otherwise than I shall here give you an Account of; which is as follows.

When any young *Indian* has a Mind for such a Girl to his Wife, he, or some one for him, goes to the young Woman's Parents, if living; if not, to her nearest Relations; where they make Offers of the Match betwixt the Couple. The Relations reply, they will consider of it, which serves for a sufficient Answer, till there be a second Meeting about the Marriage, which is generally brought into Debate before all the Relations (that are old People) on both Sides; and sometimes the King, with all his great Men, give their Opinions therein. If it be agreed on, and the young Woman approve thereof, (for these Savages never give their Children in Marriage, without their own Consent) the Man pays so much for his Wife; and the handsomer she is, the greater Price she bears. Now, it often happens, that the Man has not so much of their Money ready, as he is to pay for his Wife; but if they know him to be a good Hunter, and that he can raise the Sum agreed for, in some few Moons, or any little time, they agree, she shall go along with him, and betroth'd, but he is not to have any Knowledge of her, till the utmost Payment is discharg'd; all which is punctually observ'd. Thus, they lie together under one Covering for several Months, and the Woman remains the same as she was when she first came to him. I doubt, our *Europeans* would be apt to break this Custom, but the *Indian* Men are not so vigorous and impatient in their Love as we are. Yet the Women are quite contrary, and those *Indian* Girls that have convers'd with the *English* and other *Europeans,* never care for the Conversation of their own Countrymen afterwards.

They never marry so near as a first Cousin; and although there is nothing more coveted amongst them, than to marry a Woman of their own Nation, yet when the Nation consists of a very few People (as now adays it often happens) so that they are all of them related to one another, then they look out for Husbands and Wives amongst Strangers. For if an *Indian* lies with his Sister, or any very near Relation, his Body is burnt, and his Ashes thrown into the River, as unworthy to remain on Earth; yet an *Indian* is allow'd to marry two Sisters, or his Brothers Wife. Although these People are call'd Savages, yet Sodomy is never heard of amongst them, and they are so far from the Practice of that beastly and loathsome Sin, that they have no Name for it in all their Language.

The Marriages of these *Indians* are no farther binding, than the Man and Woman agree together. Either of them has Liberty to leave the other, upon any frivolous Excuse they can make; yet whosoever takes the Woman that was another Man's before, and bought by him, as they all are, must certainly pay to her former

Husband, whatsoever he gave for her. . . . [Y]ou may see Men selling their Wives as Men do Horses in a Fair, a Man being allow'd not only to change as often as he pleases, but likewise to have as many Wives as he is able to maintain. I have often seen, that very old *Indian* Men (that have been Grandees in their own Nation) have had three or four very likely young *Indian* Wives, which I have much wondered at, because to me they seem'd incapacitated to make good Use of one of them.

The young Men will go in the Night from one House to another, to visit the young Women, in which sort of Rambles they will spend the whole Night. In their Addresses they find no Delays, for if she is willing to entertain the Man, she gives him Encouragement and grants him Admittance; otherwise she withdraws her Face from him, and says, I cannot see you, either you or I must leave this Cabin, and sleep somewhere else this Night.

They are never to boast of their Intrigues with the Women. If they do, none of the Girls value them ever after, or admit of their Company in their Beds. This proceeds not on the score of Reputation, for there is no such thing (on that account) known amongst them; and although we may reckon them the greatest Libertines and most extravagant in their Embraces, yet they retain and possess a Modesty that requires those Passions never to be divulged.

The Trading Girls, after they have led that Course of Life, for several Years, in which time they scarce ever have a Child; (for they have an Art to destroy the Conception, and she that brings a Child in this Station, is accounted a Fool, and her Reputation is lessen'd thereby) at last they grow weary of so many, and betake themselves to a married State, or to the Company of one Man; neither does their having been common to so many any wise lessen their Fortunes, but rather augment them.

The Woman is not punish'd for Adultery, but 'tis the Man that makes the injur'd Person Satisfaction, which is the Law of Nations practis'd amongst them all; and he that strives to evade such Satisfaction as the Husband demands, lives daily in Danger of his Life; yet when discharg'd, all Animosity is laid aside, and the Cuckold is very well pleased with his Bargain, whilst the Rival is laugh'd at by the whole Nation, for carrying on his Intrigue with no better Conduct, than to be discover'd and pay so dear for his Pleasure.

The *Indians* say, that the Woman is a weak Creature, and easily drawn away by the Man's Persuasion; for which Reason, they lay no Blame upon her, but the Man (that ought to be Master of his Passion) for persuading her to it.

They are of a very hale Constitution; their Breaths are as sweet as the Air they breathe in, and the Woman seems to be of that tender Composition, as if they were design'd rather for the Bed then Bondage. Yet their Love is never of that Force and Continuance, that any of them ever runs Mad, or makes away with themselves on that score. They never love beyond Retrieving their first Indifferency, and when slighted, are as ready to untie the Knot at one end, as you are at the other.

Yet I knew an *European* Man that had a Child or two by one of these *Indian* Women, and afterwards married a Christian, after which he came to pass away a Night with his *Indian* Mistress; but she made Answer that she then had forgot she ever knew him, and that she never lay with another Woman's Husband, so fell a crying, and took up the Child she had by him, and went out of the Cabin (away from him) in great Disorder.

3. Father Joseph-François Lafitau Praises Native Male Friendships, 1733

The *Athenrosera,* or particular friendships between young people which prevail almost in the same way from one end of America to the other, are one of the most interesting points of their customs because they include one of the most curious comparisons with antiquity, and serve to explain to us the usage, particularly in the Cretan and Spartan Republics.

The legislators of these republics have been slandered by statements made later by some authors that they authorized by their laws what these authors wanted to make us understand by the odious names of *Amator* [lover] and *Amasius* [beloved] [i.e., sodomy]. . . .

The intention of these legislators was . . . to found friendships which had virtue as their principle, which were decent connections, innocent friendships, a meeting of minds, from which even the shadow of crime was lacking, and which were a reciprocal emulation between the one loving and the one loved. . . .

Among the North American Indians, these relationships of friendship carry no suspicion of apparent vice, although there is or may be much real vice. They are very ancient in their origin, very clear in their constant usage, sacred, if I dare say so, in the union which they form, the knots of which are as closely tied as those of blood and nature and can be broken only if one of them, making himself unworthy by cowardly acts which would dishonour his friend, [should] force him to renounce his alliance. Some missionaries have told me that they have seen examples of this. The parents are the first to encourage these friendships and to respect their rights; they [the friends] are chosen in such a way as to be worthy of respect, being founded on mutual merit as they [the Indians] reckon it, on congeniality of manners and qualities fitted to arouse emulation. Thus everyone wants to be the friend of the most highly esteemed men and those who most deserve admiration.

These friendships are purchased by gifts made by the friend to his selected friend; they are kept up by mutual marks of affection; the two become companions in hunting, warfare, and good or bad fortune; they are entitled to food and shelter in each other's lodging. The most affectionate compliment which a friend can make his friend, is to give him this name of friend: finally, these friendships grow old with them and are so well cemented that often there is heroism in them as there is between the Orestes and the Pylades.

Father Garnier told me that he had learned from an Indian that this statement had often been made by the Indians among themselves on the subject of these friendships that, when a captive was burned, it could be regarded as certain that the one named (by the captive) in his death song would soon be taken himself and have the same fate. This father then made this reflection. Even if the omen should be followed by the event, there would be nothing extraordinary in it; for, he said, that captive threatening his torturers as was customary, calls to his help his closest friend

Father Joseph-François Lafitau, *Customs of the American Indians,* ed. and trans. William N. Fenton and Elizabeth C. Moore (1733; Toronto: The Champlain Society, 1974), vol. 1, 361–365.

to avenge him: and the latter, grieving over the loss of his friend of whose fate he soon learns, is not slow, in the hope of getting vengeance, in rushing into the same perils in which he is almost always the victim of the temerity inspired in him by regret for the loss of his friend and his grief at losing him.

4. Father Luis Jayme Attacks Sexual Abuse of Indigenous Women, 1772

With reference to the Indians, I wish to say that great progress would be made if there was anything to eat and the soldiers would set a good example. . . . [L]ittle progress will be made under present conditions. . . . [N]o doubt some of [the soldiers] are good exemplars and deserve to be treated accordingly, but very many of them deserve to be hanged on account of the continuous outrages which they are committing in seizing and raping the women. There is not a single mission where all the gentiles [Indian converts to Christianity] have not been scandalized, and even on the roads, so I have been told. Surely, as the gentiles themselves state, they are committing a thousand evils, particularly those of a sexual nature. The fathers have petitioned Don Pedro concerning these points, but he has paid very little attention to them. He has punished some, but as soon as they promised him that they would work at the presidio, he turned them loose. That is what he did last year, but now he does not even punish them or say anything to them on this point. . . .

At one of these Indian village near this mission of San Diego, which said village is very large, and which is on the road that goes to Monterey, the gentiles therein many times have been on the point of coming here to kill us all, and the reason for this is that some soldiers went there and raped their women, and other soldiers who were carrying the mail to Monterey turned their animals into their fields and they ate up their crops. Three other Indian villages about a league or a league and a half from here have reported the same thing to me several times. For this reason on several occasions when Father Francisco Dumetz or I have gone to see these Indian villages, as soon as they saw us they fled from their villages and fled to the woods or other remote places, and the only ones who remained in the village were some men and some very old women. The Christians here have told me that many of the gentiles of the aforesaid villages leave their huts and the crops which they gather from the lands around their villages, and go to the woods and experience hunger. They do this so that the soldiers will not rape their women as they have already done so many times in the past.

. . . [The converted Indians] all know the natural law, which, so I am informed, they have observed as well or better than many Christians elsewhere. They do not have any idols; they do not go on drinking sprees; they do not marry relatives; and they have but one wife. The married men sleep with their wives only. The bachelors sleep together, and apart from the women and married couples. If a man plays with any woman who is not his wife, he is scolded and punished by his captains. Concerning those from the Californias I have heard it said that they are given to

Father Luis Jayme, *Letter of Luis Jayme, O.F.M.*, ed. and trans. Maynard Geiger (Los Angeles: Dawson's Book Shop, 1970), 38–48. Reprinted by permission of the San Diego Public Library.

sexual vices, but among those here I have not been able to discover a single fault of that nature. Some of the first adults whom we baptized, when we pointed out to them that it was wrong to have sexual intercourse with a woman to whom they were not married, told me that they already knew that, and that among them it was considered to be very bad, and so they did not do so at all. "The soldiers," they told me, "are Christians and, although they know that God will punish them in Hell, do so, having sexual intercourse with our wives. We," they said, "although we did not know that God would punish us for that in Hell, considered it to be very bad, and we did not do it, and even less now that we know that God will punish us if we do so." When I heard this, I burst into tears to see how these gentiles were setting an example for us Christians. Of the many cases which have occurred in this mission, I shall tell of only two, about which it is very necessary that Your Reverence should know, particularly the last one which I shall relate.

First Case

One day about the first of August of the present year of 1772, I went to the Indian village nearest the mission, which is about fifty paces from here, and the Christian Indians said to me: "Father, there is an unmarried woman here who is pregnant." "Well, how can this be?" I said to them. "Have not you told me many times that you do not have sexual intercourse with any woman except your own wife?" "That is true, Father," they said to me. "We do not do so, nor have any of us done so with this woman. On the contrary, according to what the woman says, she was coming from the Rincón village (which is about a league and a half from this mission) when a soldier named Hernandez and a soldier named Bravo and a soldier named Julian Murillo seized her and sinned with her, and, although she was getting away, she is almost blind and could not run very fast, and so it is that she is in this condition without being married." They told me, furthermore, that she was ashamed to be in this condition without being married, and that for this reason she had made many attempts to have an abortion but could not, but that as soon as the creature was born she would kill it. I told her through the interpreter (for, although I understood her some, I used the interpreter so that she could understand better) that she should not do anything so foolish, for God would punish her in Hell, that she should bear the little one and we would give her clothing for it to wear, and we would baptize it, etc. Several times I made this and other exhortations to her so that she would not carry out her evil intentions, but it was to no avail. When the time came for the child to be born, she went to the said Rincón village, where she bore the child and killed it, without my being able to baptize it. The child was killed about the middle of August of this year. The Indians who saw the little boy told me that he was somewhat white and gave every indication of being a son of the soldiers.

Second Case

On the 11th day of September of the present year there went to the Indian village called "El Corral" the soldiers Castelo, Juan María Ruiz, Bravo, and another who, although the Indians did not know his name, they knew his face well, and a sailor named Ignacio Marques. When they arrived at the said Indian village, they asked the Indian women for prickly pear apples, which they graciously gave to them. They then asked them to give them some earthen pots, and when they would not do so, the soldier Castelo went forward to take them by force in front of Marques, the said sailor, and boldly seized one of the women by the hand. The said sailor left the soldiers, giving them to understand that he did not want to cooperate in such iniquity as the soldiers were going to commit, and in fact did commit, as soon as the said sailor left them.

Before the said soldiers sinned with the women, the soldier Castelo and the soldier Bravo threatened a Christian Indian named José Antonio who happened to be at the said Indian village, so that he would say nothing about what he had seen. Soldier Castelo carried a gentile woman into a corral which serves as a part of the enclosure surrounding the said Indian village, and inside the corral the said soldier had sexual intercourse with the woman and sinned with her. When he had raped her, the said soldier came out of the corral, and the soldier Juan María Ruiz entered the same corral and sinned with the said woman. After this they released the woman and went to the Indian village, and the soldier whose name is not known seized another woman violently and carried her into the same corral and sinned with her there. He came out, and the soldier Bravo entered and sinned with her. He came out and the soldier Juan María Ruiz entered and did the same. He came out and the soldier Castelo entered and did the same. They went to the Indian village and the soldier Castelo gave this last woman two tortillas and some red ribbons. The soldier Juan María Ruiz also gave this same woman some ribbons. The two said soldiers also gave the first woman some ribbons. In order that these outrages should not become known, soldiers Castelo and Bravo told José Antonio, the Indian (who is the one already mentioned above, he having been at the Indian village while all this was taking place) that if he told the father they would punish him. The said José Antonio arrived here at the mission and the soldier Castelo gave him two tortillas, warning him not to tell.

On the afternoon of the same day the two women came to tell me about what had happened. They came into the mission weeping, and were seen by many soldiers who were inside. Guessing why they had come, I sent them to the Indian village next to the mission so that the case would not become known to the public. I went to the Indian village after a little while and learned about everything that had happened from the same women with whom the said soldiers had sinned, Diego Ribera serving as my interpreter for greater clarity, he being the one whom I use to teach the Christian Doctrine.

I was informed of this case twice by the said two women, and three times by José Antonio, the said Indian, and they always agreed on everything. This evil was followed by another . . . namely, that this same Indian who had told me about this case was placed in stocks without my being notified, and I took him out in defiance of the corporal of the guard, for I judged, and rightly so, that they were going to punish him so that he would not confess the truth concerning the said case. . . . I beg Your Reverence to do everything possible (as I suppose you will) so that this conquest will not be lost or retarded because of the bad example of these soldiers.

ESSAYS

These essays examine the cross-cultural encounters of Europeans and Native peoples in three different locations. Reflecting on Columbus and Pocahontas as symbols of this encounter, Theda Perdue of the University of North Carolina analyzes English men's observations of Southern indigenous women. European ideas about sex and gender, she argues, legitimated sexual aggression in the colonial context. Antonia I. Castañeda, a historian at St. Mary's University in San Antonio, supports and extends this argument in a case study of sexual violence by Spanish men against Native American women in California. She illuminates the use of rape and sexual abuse of women as a form of terror against an entire population. Jennifer M. Spear of Dickinson College offers a contrasting picture. In New France, sexual unions between European men and Native American women—termed métissage—were common. Spear analyzes the combination of demographic factors, cultural attitudes, and economic considerations that shaped colonial policies toward these relationships and explains why they persisted for so long.

Columbus Meets Pocahontas in the American South

THEDA PERDUE

As icons of the European colonization of the Americas, Columbus and Pocahontas represent opposite sides of the experience—European and Native, invader and defender, man and woman. Biographies and other scholarly writings document their lives and deeds, but these feats pale in comparison to the encounter these two legendary figures symbolize. Columbus embodies European discovery, invasion, and conquest while Pocahontas has become the "mother of us all," a nurturing, beckoning, seductive symbol of New World hospitality and opportunity. The two never actually met in the American South, of course, except metaphorically, but this symbolic encounter involved a sexual dynamic that was inherent to the whole process of European colonization, particularly that of the American South.

John Smith's tale of succor and salvation fixed the Pocahontas image forever in the American mind, and his autobiographical account of peaceful relations with her people, the Powhatans, has exempted Englishmen from the tarring Columbus has received as an international symbol of aggression. The Columbian encounter with Native women seemed, in fact, to be radically different from Smith's. On his initial voyage of discovery, Columbus had relatively little to report about Native women except that they, like men, went "naked as the day they were born." The loss of one of his ships on this voyage forced Columbus to leave about a third of his crew on Hispaniola. When he returned, he found the burned ruins of his settlement and the decomposing corpses of his men. Local Natives related that "soon after the Admiral's departure those men began to quarrel among themselves, each taking as many women and as much gold as he could." They dispersed throughout the island, and local caciques killed them. The men on Columbus's expedition had their revenge: "Incapable of moderation in their acts of injustice, they carried off the women of the islanders under the very eyes of their brothers and their husbands."

Theda Perdue, "Columbus Meets Pocahontas in the American South," *Southern Cultures* 3 (1997): 4–20. Reprinted by permission of *Southern Cultures*.

Columbus personally presented a young woman to one of his men, Michele de Cuneo, who later wrote that when she resisted him with her fingernails, he "thrashed her well, for which she raised such unheard of screams that you would not have believed your ears." In the accounts of the conquistadores, Spaniards seized women as they seized other spoils of war. Such violence contributed to the "black legend" of Spanish inhumanity to Native peoples and stands in stark contrast to early English descriptions of their encounters with Native women.

John Smith, according to his own account, did not face the kind of resistance from Pocahontas and other Native women of the Virginia tidewater that the Spanish had met in the Caribbean. When Smith and a delegation from Jamestown called at the primary town of Powhatan, Pocahontas's father, they discovered that he was away, but the chief's daughter and other women invited the Englishmen to a "mascarado." "Thirtie young women," Smith wrote, "came naked out of the woods, only covered behind and before with a few green leaves, their bodies all painted." They sang and danced with "infernal passions" and then invited Smith to their lodgings. By his account, written with uncharacteristic modesty in the third person, "he was no sooner in the house, but all these Nymphes more tormented him than ever, with crowding, pressing, and hanging about him, most tediously crying, Love you not me? Love you not me?"

The contrast is obvious—the Spanish supposedly raped and pillaged while the English nobly resisted seduction. By focusing merely on the colonizing Europeans, however, we lose sight of the Native women who are central actors in this drama: they are, after all, both the victims of Columbus's barbarity and the seductive sirens luring Smith's party. Despite differences in the ways these women are portrayed in historical sources, their experiences suggest that conquest and colonization had their own sexual dynamic. One of the facts of colonization that rarely surfaces in polite conversation or scholarly writing is sex, yet we know from the written records left by Europeans and from the more obscure cultural traditions of Native people that European men had sexual relations with Native American women. What can the Columbian voyages, the Jamestown colonists, and the experiences of subsequent European immigrants to the American South tell us about the ways in which men and women crossed cultural and racial bounds in their sexual relations? What do these relationships reveal about European views of female sexuality? And how did these views shape European expansion?

One thing seems fairly certain: Native women were never far from the conscious thought of European men, be they Spanish or English. Nudity insured that this was so. Accustomed to enveloping clothes, Europeans marveled at the remarkably scant clothing of the Natives. De Cuneo described the Carib woman whom he raped as "naked according to their custom," and Smith noted that except for a few strategically placed leaves, his hostesses were "naked." De Cuneo and Smith were not alone in commenting on Native women's lack of clothing. The Lord Admiral himself noticed not only that the Caribbean women he encountered wore little but that they had "very pretty bodies." The Jamestown colonists first encountered the prepubescent Pocahontas frolicking naked with the cabin boys. The combination of her youthful enthusiasm as well as her nudity led William Strachey, official chronicler of the colony, to describe Pocahontas as "a well featured, but wanton young girl." Other Europeans also tended to link the absence of clothing to sexuality: Amerigo Vespucci, for whom America was named, noted that "the women . . . go about naked and are very libidinous."

While Native women frequently exposed breasts, particularly in warm weather, they normally kept pudenda covered. When women did bare all, Europeans had another shock in store: Native women in many societies plucked their pubic hair. While some evidence points to female singeing of pubic hair in ancient Greece and even early modern Spain, most Europeans recoiled from hairless female genitalia. Thomas Jefferson, whose interests extended far beyond politics, attempted to explain hair-plucking among Native Americans: "With them it is disgraceful to be hairy in the body. They say it likens them to hogs. They therefore pluck the hair as fast as it appears." Jefferson revealed both the reaction of non-Native men and the artificiality of the practice: "The traders who marry their women, and prevail on them to discontinue this practice say, that nature is the same with them as with whites." However comfortable Euro-American men may have been with visible penises, depilation left female genitalia far more exposed than most could bear. Because women revealed their private parts intentionally, they seemed to be flaunting their sexuality.

Another cultural modification to the female physique also provoked comment. Among many Native peoples, women as well as men wore tattoos. While some Euro-Americans became so enamored of the practice that they adopted it, others regarded tattooing in the same light as make-up applied to make one more physically attractive. The late eighteenth-century Philadelphia physician Benjamin Rush, for example, compared the body markings of Native peoples to cosmetics used by the French, a people whom he described as "strangers to what is called delicacy in the intercourse of the sexes with each other." Unnatural markings on the body, to Europeans, signaled an enhanced sexuality.

As contact between Native peoples and Europeans grew, women gave up tattooing and hair plucking, and they adopted the blouses and long skirts common among non-Native women along the colonial frontier. Other features of Native culture, however, perpetuated the view of Native women as sexually uninhibited. Some Europeans found the humor of Native women to be terribly bawdy. Most women enjoyed teasing and joking, and pranks and jokes with sexual overtones were not necessarily taboo. The teasing Smith endured—"Love you not me? Love you not me?"—provides a good example. One Native woman even managed to shock a Frenchman. Louis-Philippe made a tour of the American West at the end of the eighteenth century, and during his visit to the Cherokees, his guide made sexual advances to several women. "They were so little embarrassed," wrote the future French king, "that one of them who was lying on a bed put her hand on his trousers before my very eyes and said scornfully, *Ah sick.*"

Directness characterized courtship as well as rejection. Smith clearly expressed amazement at the forwardness of the "thirtie young women." In *Notes on the State of Virginia*, Thomas Jefferson compared the "frigidity" of Native men with the assertiveness of women: "A celebrated warrior is oftener courted by the females, than he has occasion to court: and this is a point of honor which the men aim at. . . . Custom and manners reconcile them to modes of acting, which, judged by Europeans would be deemed inconsistent with the rules of female decorum and propriety." When the eptiome of the American Enlightenment attributed Native women with a more active libido than Native men, who could doubt that it was so?

The arrangement and use of domestic space seemed to confirm a lack of modesty on the part of Native women. Native housing afforded little privacy for bathing, changing what little clothes women did wear, or engaging in sexual intercourse. Several generations, as well as visitors, usually slept in the same lodge. The essayist Samuel Stanhope Smith admitted that Indians were unjustly "represented as licentious because they are seen to lie promiscuously in the same wigwam." Nevertheless, few Natives allowed the lack of privacy in their homes to become a barrier to sexual fulfillment. During early eighteenth-century explorations in Carolina, one of John Lawson's companions took a Native "wife" for the night, and the newlyweds consummated their "marriage" in the same room in which other members of the expedition feasted and slept: "Our happy Couple went to Bed together before us all and with as little Blushing, as if they had been Man and Wife for 7 Years."

Most European accounts of Native women in the South commented on their sexual freedom, particularly before they married. In the late eighteenth century, naturalist Bernard Romans observed: "Their women are handsome, well made, only wanting the colour and cleanliness of our ladies, to make them appear lovely in every eye; . . . they are lascivious, and have no idea of chastity in a girl, but in married women, incontinence is severely punished; a savage never forgives that crime." John Lawson suggested that even married women "sometimes bestow their Favours also to some or others in their Husbands Absence." And the trader James Adair maintained that "the Cherokees are an exception to all civilized or savage nations in having no law against adultery; they have been a considerable while under a petti-coat government, and allow their women full liberty to plant their brows with horns as oft as they please, without fear of punishment."

Women in the Southeast sometimes openly solicited sex from Euro-Americans because sex gave women an opportunity to participate in the emerging market economy. Unlike men, who exchanged deerskins, beaver pelts, and buffalo hides with Europeans for manufactured goods, women often had to rely on "the soft passion" to obtain clothing, kettles, knives, hoes, and trinkets. Among some Native peoples a kind of specialization developed according to John Lawson, who claimed that coastal Carolina peoples designated "trading girls." Sometimes prostitution was more widespread. Louis-Philippe insisted that "all Cherokee women are public women in the full meaning of the phrase: dollars never fail to melt their hearts."

Selling sex was one thing; the apparent gift of women by their husbands and fathers was quite another. To Europeans, sex was a kind of commodity, purchased from prostitutes with money and from respectable women with marriage. An honorable man protected the chastity of his wife and daughters as he would other property. Native men in many societies, however, seemed to condone or even encourage sexual relations between Europeans and women presumably "belonging" to them. Even husbands who might object to "secret infidelities" sometimes offered their wives to visitors.

Europeans also viewed the widespread practice of polygyny, or a man taking more than one wife, as adulterous because they recognized only the first as the "real" wife. Many Native people favored sororal polygyny, the marriage of sisters to the same man, and the groom often took sisters as brides at the same time. Since this meant, in European terms, that a man married his sister-in-law, sororal polygamy was incest as well as adultery. Jedidiah Morse, in his *Universal Geography,* wrote: "When a man loves his wife, it is considered his duty to marry her sister, is she has one. Incest and bestiality are common among them." Morse apparently regarded marriage to sisters as serious a violation of European sexual mores as human intercourse with animals; in his mind, both constituted perversion.

Polygynous, adulterous, and incestuous or not, marriage meant little to Indians in the estimation of many Euro-Americans. Lawson, for example, described the ease with which the Native peoples of coastal Carolina altered their marital status: "The marriages of these Indians are no further binding than the man and woman agree together. Either of them has the liberty to leave the other upon any frivolous excuse they can make." The trader Alexander Longe relayed a Cherokee priest's view of his people's lax attitude toward marriage: "They had better be asunder than together if they do not love one another but live for strife and confusion." Europeans would have preferred that they stay together and, despite domestic turmoil, raise their children in an appropriately patriarchal household.

When husband and wife parted, children normally remained with their mothers because Native peoples of the Southeast were matrilineal, that is, they traced kinship solely through women. John Lawson attributed this very odd way of reckoning kin, in his view, to "fear of Impostors; the Savages knowing well, how much Frailty possesses *Indian* women, betwixt the Garters and the Girdle." While paternity might be questioned, maternity could not be. Despite the logic of such a system, Europeans had both intellectual and practical objections. Matrilineality seemed too close to the relationship between a cow and calf or a bitch and puppies: it was, the Iroquois historian Cadwallader Colden asserted, "according to the natural course of all animals." "Civilized" man presumably had moved beyond this "natural course" and had adopted laws, civil and religious, that bound fathers to children and husbands to wives. Europeans who married Native women of matrilineal societies nevertheless had difficulty exercising any control over their children and often abandoned them to their mothers' kin because men had no proprietary interest in their offspring. Thomas Nairne wrote of the Creeks: "A Girles Father has not the least hand or concern in matching her. . . . Sons never enjoy their fathers place and dignity."

Blatant disregard of marital vows and paternal prerogatives was shocking enough, but many Native peoples exhibited little concern for the chastity of their daughters. Jean-Bernard Bossu reported that among Native peoples on the lower Mississippi, "when an unmarried brave passes through a village, he hires a girl for a night or two, as he pleases, and her parents find nothing wrong with this. They are not at all worried about their daughter and explain that her body is hers to do with as she wishes." Furthermore, according to Lawson, "multiplicity of Gallants never [gave] . . . a Stain to a Female's reputation, or the least Hindrance of her Advancement . . . the more *Whorish*, the more *Honourable*."

European men who traveled through the Native Southeast thought that they had stepped through the looking glass into a sexual wonderland. Actually, they had encountered only a fractured reflection of their own assumptions about appropriate sexual behavior. Native women were not as uninhibited as most whites thought. Europeans failed to realize that Native peoples did have rules regulating marriage and sexual intercourse, although the rules were sometimes quite different from their own. In the Southeast, unmarried people could engage freely in sex, but many factors other than marital status regulated and limited sexuality. A warrior preparing for or returning from battle (sometimes much of the summer), a ball player getting ready for a game, a man on the winter hunt (which could last three to four months), a pregnant woman, or a woman during her menstrual period abstained from sex. In other words, Native southerners had to forego sexual intercourse for a far greater percentage of their lives than Europeans.

Furthermore, there were inappropriate venues for sex. Although a Native couple might engage in sex in a room occupied by others, there were places, such as agricultural fields, where amorous encounters were forbidden. Violation of this rule could have serious consequences. According to the trader James Adair, the Cherokees blamed a devastating smallpox epidemic in 1738 on "the adulterous intercourses of their young married people, who the past year, had in a most notorious manner, violated their ancient laws of marriage in every thicket, and broke down and polluted many of their honest neighbours bean-plots, by their heinous crimes, which would cost a great deal of trouble to purify again." For many Native southerners, therefore, a "toss in the hay" would have been a very serious offense.

Native peoples also had rules against incest, but they did not define incest in the same way Euro-Americans did. Intercourse or marriage with a member of a person's own clan, for example, was prohibited, and the penalty could be death. Clan membership, which included all individuals who could trace their ancestry back to a remote, perhaps mythical figure, often ran into the thousands and included many people whom Europeans would not have regarded as relatives. Consequently, the number of forbidden partners was far greater than the number under the European definition of incest. The Cherokees, for example, had seven clans. No one could marry into his or her own clan, nor was the father's clan an acceptable marriage pool. The result was that, for any given Cherokee, almost one third of all Cherokees were off-limits as sexual partners.

Each Native people had particular rules regarding marriage and incest. Many societies permitted men to have more than one wife and to marry sisters. The effect was not necessarily the devaluation of women, as European observers often claimed. Some cultural anthropologists suggest, in fact, that sororal polygamy correlates positively with high female status. In the Southeast where husbands lived with their wives, the marriage of sisters to the same man reduced the number of men in the household and strengthened the control of the women over domestic life. As Morse suggested, sisters often wanted to share a husband just as they shared a house, fields, labor, and children.

Ignorant of Native rules, southern colonials tended to view Native women as wanton woodland nymphs over whose sexuality fathers, brothers, and husbands could exercise little control. Many colonists took full advantage of the situation as they perceived it. Some evidence, however, suggests that southeastern Native women were not as amenable to sexual encounters as Europeans suggested. Louis-Philippe's anecdote reveals a woman, however bold and uninhibited, rejecting a sexual advance. When women did engage in sexual activity, many of them probably succumbed to pressure or force rather than charm.

European culture at this time countenanced considerable violence against women. William Byrd's confidential account of surveying the boundary line between North Carolina and Virginia, for example, describes several episodes of sexual aggression. One young woman, he wrote, "wou'd certainly have been ravish't, if her timely consent had not prevented the violence." This cavalier attitude toward a woman's right to refuse sex characterized much interaction between Native women and Europeans. Race almost certainly exacerbated the situation. The records of the South Carolina Indian trade are replete with Native complaints of sexual abuse at the hands of Europeans. One trader "took a young Indian against her Will for his Wife," another severely beat three women including his pregnant wife whom he killed, and a third provided enough rum to a woman to get her drunk and then "used her ill." Obviously, the women in these incidents were not the ones who were lascivious.

Some Native peoples came to regard sexual misbehavior as the most distinguishing feature of European culture. The Cherokee Booger Dance, in which participants imitated various peoples, portrayed Europeans as sexually aggressive, and the men playing that role chased screaming young women around the dance ground. As it turns out, from the Native perspective, the British colonists of the American South may not have been so terribly different from Columbus's men after all.

The people who do stand in stark contrast are Native men. James Adair, a resident of the Chickasaw Nation and a trader throughout the Southeast, perhaps knew the region's Native cultures better than any other European in the eighteenth century. As the husband of a Chickasaw woman and an occasional member of Chickasaw war parties against the Choctaws, he wrote with authority that "the Indians will not cohabitate with women while they are out at war; they religiously abstain from every kind of intercourse, even with their own wives." While Adair believed, perhaps correctly, that the reason for a period of abstinence was religious, the implications for female captives were clear. "The French Indians," he wrote, "are said not to have deflowered any of our young women they captivated, while at war with us." Even the most bloodthirsty Native warrior, according to Adair, "did not attempt the virtue of his female captives," although he did not hesitate to torture and kill them. Even the Choctaws, whom Adair described as "libidinous," had taken "several female prisoners without offering the least violence to their virtue, till the time of purgation was expired." Adair could not, however, resist the temptation to slander the Choctaws, the Chickasaws' traditional enemy: "Then some of them forced their captives, notwithstanding their pressing entreaties and tears."

Captivity narratives suggest Indian men raped very few, if any, women victims of colonial wars—"a very agreeable disappointment" in one woman's words. Rules prohibiting intercourse immediately before and after going to war may have contributed to the absence of documented sexual violence, but Native views on female sexuality and autonomy may have been equally responsible. Indians apparently did not view sex as property or as one of the spoils of war.

Columbus's men do seem to have equated sex and material plunder. The accounts of the destruction of the Hispaniola settlement link his men's desire for women with a desire for gold. In perhaps a more subtle way, British colonists also considered women to be a form of property and found the Native men's lack of proprietary interest in their wives and daughters incomprehensible. It called into question the Indians' concept of property in general and paved the way for Europeans to challenge Native people's ownership of land. From the second decade of colonization in the South, wealth depended on the cultivation of land, and southerners found the argument that Indians had no notion of absolute ownership particularly compelling.

While Native southerners forcefully maintained their right to inhabit the land of their fathers, they did not, in fact, regard land ownership in quite the same way as the Europeans who challenged their rights to it. They fought for revenge rather than for territory, they held land in common, and they permitted any tribal member to clear and cultivate unused tracts. Land did not represent an investment of capital, and Native southerners did not sell out and move on when other opportunities beckoned. Indeed, the land held such significance for most of them that they suffered severe economic, social, and political disruption rather than part with it. In the 1820s and 1830s, frontiersmen, land speculators, and politicians joined forces to divest Native peoples of their land, and southern state governments and ultimately the federal government took up the aggressors' cause. White southerners made a concerted effort to force their Indian neighbors to surrender their lands and move west of the Mississippi to new territory. What difference did it make, many whites asked, which lands the Indians occupied? With squatters encroaching on them, shysters defrauding them at every turn, and federal and state authorities unwilling to protect them, Native peoples in the South struggled desperately to retain their homelands. They did so for reasons as incomprehensible to Euro-Americans as the sexual behavior of Native women. People who objectified both land and sex had encountered people who did not.

Ultimately, Native southerners lost. Representatives of the large southern tribes—the Cherokees, Chickasaws, Choctaws, Creeks, and Seminoles—signed treaties in which they agreed to move west to what is today eastern Oklahoma. Remnants of some of those tribes as well as other isolated Native communities simply retreated into the shadows and eked out a living on marginal land while the cotton kingdom expanded onto the rich soil that Native peoples had surrendered. In the cotton kingdom, land was saleable rather than sacred, and power not parity characterized sexual relationships.

In recent years we have come to admire Native sensitivity to the natural world and to compare ourselves unfavorably to Indians on environmental issues and attitudes toward the land. Columbus and Pocahontas probably thought about sex at least as often as they did ecology, but we seem incapable of recognizing that their views on sex might have been as different as their ideas about land use. Disney's recent movie, *Pocahontas,* merely perpetuates the notion that romantic love is a universal concept that transcends cultural bounds and has little connection with specific aspects of a culture. The film depicts Pocahontas not as the autonomous person she probably was, but as a subservient young woman submissive to her father, betrothed to the warrior Kocoum, and won by Smith. Pocahontas's love for Smith (and vice versa) resolves conflicts with the Indians, and the English presumably set about the task at hand. "Oh, with all ya got in ya, boys," Governor Ratclife sings, "dig up Virginia, boys." True love, of course, characterized neither the real relationship between Pocahontas and John Smith nor the dealings of Native women and European men. Instead of Disney's John Smith, most Native women really met Columbus. Perhaps in the American South, where Columbus and Pocahontas metaphorically collided so forcefully, we should expand our comparison of Native Americans and Europeans beyond environmental issues and consider the interactions between men and women. Then we might begin to make connections between the materialism and exploitation that have characterized so much of southern history and sexual violence against women.

Sexual Violence in the Spanish Conquest
of California

ANTONIA I. CASTAÑEDA

In the morning, six or seven soldiers would set out together . . . and go to the distant rancherías [villages] even many leagues away. When both men and women at the sight of them would take off running . . . the soldiers, adept as they are at lassoing cows and mules, would lasso Indian women—who then became prey for their un-bridled lust. Several Indian men who tried to defend the women were shot to death.
JUNIPERO SERRA, 1773

In words reminiscent of sixteenth-century chroniclers Bernal Díaz del Castillo and Bartolomé de las Casas, . . . Junipero Serra [the father president of the California missions] described the depredations of the soldiers against Indian women in his reports and letters to Viceroy Antonio María Bucareli and the father guardian of the College of San Fernando, Rafaél Verger. Sexual assaults against native women began shortly after the founding of the presidio and mission at Monterey in June 1770, wrote Serra, and continued throughout the length of California. The founding of each new mission and presidio brought new reports of sexual violence.

The despicable actions of the soldiers, Serra told Bucareli in 1773, were severely retarding the spiritual and material conquest of California. The native people were resisting missionization. Some were becoming warlike and hostile because of the soldiers' repeated outrages against the women. The assaults resulted in Amerindian attacks, which the soldiers countered with unauthorized reprisals, thereby further straining the capacity of the small military force to staff the presidios and guard the missions. Instead of pacification and order, the soldiers provoked greater conflict and thus jeopardized the position of the church in this region.

Serra was particularly alarmed about occurrences at Mission San Gabriel. "Since the district is the most promising of all the missions," he wrote to Father Verger, "this mission gives me the greatest cause for anxiety; the secular arm down there was guilty of the most heinous crimes, killing the men to take their wives." Father Serra related that on October 10, 1771, within a month of its having been founded, a large group of Indians suddenly attacked two soldiers who were on horseback and tried to kill the one who had outraged a woman. The soldiers retaliated. "A few days later," Serra continued, "as he went out to gather the herd of cattle . . . and [it] seems more likely to get himself a woman, a soldier, along with some others, killed the principal Chief of the gentiles; they cut off his head and brought it in triumph back to the mission."

The incident prompted the Amerindians of the coast and the sierra, mortal enemies until that time, to convene a council to make peace with each other and join forces to eliminate the Spaniards. The council planned to attack the mission on October 16 but changed the plan after a new contingent of troops arrived at the

Antonia I. Castañeda, "Sexual Violence in the Politics and Policies of Conquest: Amerindian Women and the Spanish Conquest of Alta California," in Adela de la Torre and Beatriz M. Pesquera, eds., *Building with Our Hands: New Directions in Chicana Studies* (Berkeley: University of California Press, 1993), 15–33. Copyright © 1993 The Regents of the University of California. Reprinted by permission of the University of California Press.

mission. Despite this narrowly averted disaster, the soldiers assigned to Mission San Gabriel continued their outrages.

The soldiers' behavior not only generated violence on the part of the native people as well as resistance to missionization, argued Serra; it also took its toll on the missionaries, some of whom refused to remain at their mission sites. In his 1773 memorial to Bucareli, Serra lamented the loss of one of the missionaries, who could not cope with the soldiers' disorders at San Gabriel. The priest was sick at heart, Serra stated: "He took to his bed, when he saw with his own eyes a soldier actually committing deeds of shame with an Indian who had come to the mission, and even the children who came to the mission were not safe from their baseness."

Conditions at other missions were no better. . . . After spending two years as the sole missionary at [Mission San Luis Obispo], Father Domingo Juncosa asked for and received permission to return to Mexico because he was "shocked at the scandalous conduct of the soldiers" and could not work under such abominable conditions. Even before San Luis Obispo was founded in the early fall of 1772, Tichos women had cause to fear. The most notorious molesters of non-Christian women were among the thirteen soldiers sent on a bear hunt to this area during the previous winter of starvation at Monterey.

The establishment of new missions subjected the women of each new area to sexual assaults. Referring to the founding of the mission at San Juan Capistrano, Serra wrote that "it seems all the sad experiences that we went through at the beginning have come to life again. The soldiers, without any restraint or shame, have behaved like brutes toward the Indian women." From this mission also, the priests reported to Serra that the soldier-guards went at night to the nearby villages to assault the women and that hiding the women did not restrain the brutes, who beat the men to force them to reveal where the women were hidden. Non-Christian Indians in the vicinity of the missions were simply not safe. They were at the mercy of soldiers with horses and guns.

In 1773, a case of rape was reported at San Luis Rey, one at San Diego, and two cases at Monterey the following year. Serra expressed his fears and concern to Governor Felipe de Neve, who was considering establishing a new presidio in the channel of Santa Barbara. Serra told Neve that he took it for granted that the insulting and scandalous conduct of the soldiers "would be the same as we had experienced in other places which were connected with presidios. Perhaps this one would be worse."

Native women and their communities were profoundly affected by the sexual attacks and attendant violence. California Amerindians were peaceful, nonaggressive people who highly valued harmonious relationships. Physical violence and the infliction of bodily harm on one another were virtually unknown. Women did not fear men. Rape rarely, if ever, occurred. If someone stole from another or caused another's death, societal norms required that the offending party make reparations to the individual and/or the family. Appropriate channels to rectify a wrong without resorting to violence existed.

Animosity, when it did surface, was often worked out ritualistically—for example, through verbal battles in the form of war songs, or song fights that lasted eight days, or encounters in which the adversaries threw stones across a river at each other with no intent actually to hit or physically injure the other party. Even among farming groups such as the Colorado River people, who practiced warfare and took women and children captive, female captives were never sexually molested. The Yumas believed that intimate contact with enemy women caused sickness.

Thus, neither the women nor their people were prepared for the onslaught of aggression and violence the soldiers unleashed against them. They were horrified and terrified. One [resident] reported that women of the San Gabriel and other southern missions raped by the soldiers were considered contaminated and obliged to undergo an extensive purification, which included a long course of sweating, the drinking of herbs, and other forms of purging. This practice was consistent with the people's belief that sickness was caused by enemies. "But their disgust and abhorrence," [he states], "never left them till many years after." Moreover, any child born as a result of these rapes, and apparently every child with white blood born among them for a very long time, was strangled and buried. . . .

Serra and his co-religionists had great cause for concern, because the missions were not meeting their principal objective of converting Amerindians into loyal Catholic subjects who would repel invading European forces from these shores. By the end of 1773, in the fifth year of the occupation of Alta California, fewer than five hundred baptisms and only sixty-two marriages had been performed in the five missions then existing. Since the marriages probably represented the total adult converts, that meant that the remaining four hundred converts were children. These dismal statistics fueled arguments for abandoning the California missions. While various reasons may be cited for the failure to attract adult converts, certainly the sexual attacks and the impact of that violence on women and their communities were primary among them. . . .

It is clear that the sexual exploitation of native women and related violence seriously threatened the political and military objectives of the colonial enterprise in California. Repeated attacks against women and summary reprisals against men who dared to interfere undermined the efforts of the priests to attract Amerindians to the missions and to Christianity. They also thwarted whatever attempts the military authorities might make to elicit political or military allegiance from the native peoples.

From the missionaries' point of view, the attacks had more immediate, deleterious consequences for the spiritual conquest of California, because such actions belied significant principles of the Catholic moral theology they were trying to inculcate. As the primary agents of Christianization/Hispanicization, the missionaries argued that they could not teach and Amerindians could not learn and obey the moral strictures against rape, abduction, fornication, adultery, and all forms of sexual impurity while the soldiers persisted in their licentiousness and immorality. Their actions repudiated the very morality the friars were to inculcate.

Early conflict between ecclesiastical and civil-military officials over deployment and discipline of the mission escort soon gave rise to constant bitter disputes centering on the question of authority and jurisdiction over the Indians in California. The conflict over control of the Indians revolved around the issue of their segregation from the non-Indian population. . . . The concern here is to examine [this issue] specifically from the point of view of sex/gender and to define a context for explaining why, despite strenuous efforts by church and state alike, there was little success in arresting the attacks on Indian women.

Serra, for his part, blamed the military commanders and, once appointed, the governor. They were, he said, lax in enforcing military discipline and unconcerned about the moral fiber of their troops.They failed to punish immoral soldiers who assaulted native women, were flagrantly incontinent, or took Amerindian women as concubines. In California, he stated, secular authorities not only condoned the soldiers' assaults on Indian women but interfered with the missionaries' efforts to counter the abuse, and thereby exceeded their authority with respect to Amerindians.

To argue his case against Lieutenant Pedro Fages, the military commander, and to muster political and economic support for the California establishments, Serra made the arduous trip to Mexico City for an audience with Viceroy Bucareli. He left California in September of 1772 and arrived in Mexico the following February. At the viceroy's request, Serra submitted a lengthy work entitled "Report on the General Conditions and Needs of the Missions and Thirty-Two Suggestions for Improving the Government of the Missions." Serra addressed sex/gender issues as part of several grievances against Fages's command. His recommendations for curtailing the sexual violence and general malfeasance of the soldiers were that Fages should be removed and that Spaniards who married Indian women should be rewarded.

Once the viceroy had removed the lieutenant, Serra continued, he should give strict orders to Fages's successor that, upon the request of any missionary, "he should remove the soldier or soldiers who give bad example, especially in the matter of incontinence . . . and send, in their place, another or others who are not known as immoral or scandalous."

Drawing on colonial tradition established much earlier in New Spain, wherein colonial officials encouraged intermarriage with Amerindian noblewomen in order to advance particular political, military, religious, or social interests, Serra suggested that men who married newly Christianized "daughters of the land" be rewarded. . . . Serra asked Bucareli to "allow a bounty for those, be they soldiers or not, who enter into the state of marriage with girls of that faraway country, new Christian converts," [including] . . . two cows and a mule . . . and . . . allotment of a piece of land. Since soldiers were subject to being transferred from one mission or presidio to another, Serra further recommended that he who married a native woman should be allowed to remain permanently attached to his wife's mission.

With this recommendation, . . . Serra hoped to solve several related problems. He sought to curb the sexual attacks on Indian women as well as to induce soldiers to remain and become permanent settlers in Alta California. Theoretically, soldiers would thereby remain on the frontier, and formal and permanent unions with Indian women would allay the natives' mistrust and help to forge a bond between them and the soldiers. These marriages would thus help to ease Indian-military tensions while also cementing Catholic family life in the region. . . .

The document that resulted from the official review of Serra's memorial, the *Reglamento Provisional*—generally known as the *Echeveste Regulations*—was the first regulatory code drawn up for California. The *Echeveste Regulations* acted favorably on twenty-one of Serra's thirty-two original recommendations, including the removal of Fages as military commander.

Implementation of the new regulations, however, did not stop the abuse of women or the immorality of the soldiers. Serra continued to blame the civil-military authorities. . . . [I]n the summary of Franciscan complaints against [the newly appointed governor, Felipe de Neve], which Francisco Panagua, guardian of the College of San Fernando, sent Viceroy Mayorga in 1781, Father Panagua wrote that "another consequence . . . of the aversion which the said Governor [Neve] has for the religious, is that the subordinates . . . live very libidinously in unrestrained and scandalous incontinence as they use at will Indian women of every class and strata." Serra . . . charged that Neve allowed fornication among the soldiers, "because, so I have heard him say, . . . it is winked at in Rome and tolerated in Madrid."

Serra's charges against Fages, Rivera, and Neve were not well founded. As head of the California establishments, each was fully cognizant that the soldiers' excesses not only undermined military discipline, and thus their own command, but also seriously jeopardized the survival of the missions and the presidios. Fundamentally, the assaults against women were unwarranted, unprovoked, hostile acts that established conditions of war on this frontier. Although the native peoples by and large did not practice warfare, they were neither docile nor passive in the face of repeated assaults. The people of the South were especially aggressive. The country between San Diego and San Gabriel remained under Indian control for a long time. It was in this region that the Indians marshaled their strongest forces and retaliated against the Spaniards. Some of the engagements, such as the one at San Gabriel in 1771, were minor skirmishes. Others were full-fledged attacks. In 1775 at Mission San Diego, for example, a force of eight hundred razed the mission, killed one priest and two artisans, and seriously wounded two soldiers. Women participated and sometimes even planned and/or led the attacks. In October 1785, Amerindians from eight *rancherías* united under the leadership of one woman and three men and launched an attack on Mission San Gabriel for the purpose of killing all the Spaniards. Toypurina, the twenty-four-year-old medicine woman of the Japchivit *ranchería,* used her considerable influence as a medicine woman to persuade six of the eight villages to join the rebellion. The attack was thwarted. Toypurina was captured and punished along with the other three leaders.

Throughout their terms, Fages, Rivera, and Neve were keenly aware that Amerindians greatly outnumbered Spain's military force in the fledgling settlement and that, ultimately, the soldiers could not have staved off a prolonged Indian attack. Neve's greatest fear, expressed in his request to Bucareli for more commissioned officers, was that "if an affair of this kind [disorders caused by soldiers] ever results in a defeat of our troops, it will be irreparable if they [the Indians] come to know their power. We must prevent this with vigor."

Therefore, during their respective administrations, the military authorities enforced Spain's legal codes, as well as imperial policy regarding segregation of Amerindians from non-Indians as a protective measure for the former. They prosecuted soldiers for major and minor crimes, and they issued their own edicts to curb the soldiers' abuse of Amerindians in general and women in particular. Their authority [to convict and sentence], however, was circumscribed by Spain's highly centralized form of government. . . .

Ever concerned that Amerindians would discover the real weakness of the Spanish position in California, Neve sought to prevent the sexual attacks, and thereby to defuse the military and political conflicts they gave rise to, by forbidding all troops, including sergeants and corporals, from entering Indian villages. Only soldiers escorting the priests on sick calls were exempt from this order, and then the soldier was not to leave the missionary's side. Escort guards were strictly admonished against misconduct and were severely punished if they disobeyed. In the same vein, he prohibited soldiers of the mission guard from spending the night away from the mission—even if the priests demanded it. . . .

Governor Fages was equally emphatic when he issued the following order in 1785: "Observing that the officers and men of these presidios are comporting and behaving themselves in the mission with a vicious license which is very prejudicial because of the scandalous disorders which they incite among the gentile and Christian women, I command you, in order to prevent the continuation of such abuses, that you circulate a prohibitory edict imposing severe penalties upon those who commit them."

A decade later, Viceroy Branciforte followed up Neve's earlier order with his own decree prohibiting troops from remaining overnight away from the presidios, because among other reasons this practice was "prejudicial to good discipline and Christian morals." Governor Diego de Borica, who succeeded Fages in 1794, issued a similar order the following year. These edicts had little effect.

Soldiers and civilian settlers alike disregarded the civil laws against rape as well as military orders against contact with Amerindian women outside of narrowly proscribed channels. The records verify that sexual attacks continued in areas adjacent to missions, presidios, and pueblos throughout the colonial period. Amerindian women were never free from the threat of rapacious assaults. The missionaries continuously reported that soldiers "go by night to nearby villages for the purpose of raping Indian women." . . . [M]any more cases must surely have gone unreported.

Why, despite strenuous efforts by officials of both church and state, did the sexual attacks persist unabated? Why, despite the obviously serious political and military conflicts that assaults ignited, did they continue? In view of extensive legislation, royal decrees, and moral prohibitions against sexual and other violence, what, in the experience of the men who came here, permitted them to objectify and dehumanize Indian women to the degree that chasing and lassoing them from mounted horses and then raping them reveals?

Until recently, scholars attributed sexual violence and other concurrent social disorders in early California to the race and culture of the mixed-blood soldier-settler population recruited or banished to this frontier. . . . Institutional studies generally concurred with Serra's view that the soldiers were recruited from the scum of the society. Serra had repeatedly beseeched Bucareli to send "sturdy, industrious Spanish families" and asked him to advise the governor of the Californias "not to use exile to these missions as punishment for the soldier whom he may detest as insolent or perverse."

In the last two decades, the conditions that shaped institutional development on this frontier have been reexamined [and] studies of the social history of the people recruited to Alta California have been undertaken. As a result, the earlier interpretations have been rejected. Scholars now conclude that the slow development of colonial institutions in California was attributable to limited resources, lack of uniform military codes, and other structural problems—and not to the racial or social-class origins of the soldier-settler population.

Instead, the mixed-blood recruits—who themselves derived from other frontier settlements—were admirably able to survive the harsh privations and onerous conditions. In so doing, they established lasting foundations of Spanish civilization in California and the Southwest. Although the *cuera* (leather-jacket) soldiers were indeed unruly and undisciplined, their behavior reflected a particular informality and a "peculiar attitude of both officers and men." According to revisionist studies, the isolation and distance from the central government, a shared life of hardship and risk, and the fact that blood and marriage ties existed among officers and common soldiers all contributed to this attitude of informality and independence. . . . [T]he racially mixed settlers responded to the often brutal conditions on the far northern and Pacific frontiers by creating a distinct frontier culture, characterized by self-reliance, individualism, regionalism, village orientation, resistance to outside control, innovativeness, family cohesiveness, and the preservation of Roman Catholicism as a unifying force. . . .

To . . . understand the soldier-settler violence toward native women, we must examine the stratified, patriarchal colonial society that conditioned relationships between the sexes and races in New Spain; the contemporary ideologies of sex/gender and race; and the relations and structures of conquest imposed on this frontier. While rape and other acts of sexual brutality did not represent official policy on this or any other Spanish frontier, these acts were nevertheless firmly fixed in the history and politics of expansion, war, and conquest. In the history of Western civilization writ large, rape is an act of domination, an act of power. As such, it is a violent political act committed through sexual aggression against women.

"The practice of raping the women of a conquered group," writes historian Gerda Lerner, "has remained a feature of war and conquest from the second millennium to the present." Under conditions of war or conquest, rape is a form of national terrorism, subjugation, and humiliation, wherein the sexual violation of women represents both the physical domination of women and the symbolic castration of the men of the conquered group. These concepts and symbolic meanings of rape, . . . are rooted in patriarchal Western society—in the ideology that devalues women in relation to men while it privatizes and reifies women as the symbolic capital (property) of men. In this ideology, rape has historically been defined as a crime against property and thus against "territory." Therefore, in the context of war and conquest, rape has been considered a legitimate form of aggression against the opposing army—a legitimate expression of superiority that carries with it no civil penalty. In nonmilitary situations, punishment for rape and other crimes of sexual violence against women in Western civilization has, until very recently, generally been determined by the social condition or status of the women violated and by the status of the violator.

In eighteenth-century California, the status of Amerindian women—as members of non-Christian, indigenous groups under military conquest on Spain's northernmost outpost of empire—made them twice subject to assault with impunity: they were the spoils of conquest, and they were Indian. In the mentality of the age, these two conditions firmly established the inferiority of the Amerindian woman and became the basis for devaluing her person beyond the devaluation based on sex that accrued to all women irrespective of their sociopolitical (race, class) status. . . .

From their earliest contact with Amerindian peoples, Europeans established categories of opposition, or otherness, within which they defined themselves as superior and Amerindians as inferior. These categories were derived from the Aristotelian theory that some beings are inferior by nature, and therefore should be dominated by their superiors for their own welfare, and from the medieval Spanish concept of "purity of blood," which was based on religion and which informed the sense of national unity forged during the reconquest. These ideas—which were fundamentally political concepts that separated human beings into opposing, hierarchical subject-object categories—prevailed during the era of first contact with Amerindians and the early conquests of the Americas.

By the late eighteenth century, a different political concept—racial origin—defined place and social value in the stratified social order of colonial New Spain. Race was inextricably linked to social origin and had long been a symbol for significant cleavages in society; it was one primary basis for valuation—and devaluation—of human beings. . . .

Two aspects of the devaluation of Amerindian women are especially noteworthy. First and foremost, it is a political devaluation. That is, it is rooted in and driven by political considerations and acts: by war, conquest, and the imposition of alien sociopolitical and economic structures of one group over another. Second, the devaluation rationalized by conquest cuts across sex. At this level, women and men of the conquered group are equally devalued and objectified by the conquering group. Amerindian women and men were both regarded as inferior social beings, whose inferiority justified the original conquest and continued to make them justifiably exploitable and expendable in the eyes of the conqueror. . . .

Although the ideological symbols of sociopolitical devaluation changed over time—from religion to socioracial origins to social class—the changing symbols intersected with a sex/gender ideology that has remained remarkably constant from the fifteenth to the twentieth century. As the term implies, the sex/gender ideology defines two categories of opposition—sex and gender—within which women are characterized as superior or inferior in relation to others.

With respect to sex stratification, women are placed in opposition and in an inferior position to men, on the assumption that in the divine order of nature the male sex of the species is superior to the female. In this conception, the ascribed inferiority of females to males is biologically constructed.

The opposition centering on gender revolves around sexual morality and sexual conduct. This opposition creates a level of superior-inferior or good-bad stratification based on social and political value-centered concepts of women's sexuality. This dichotomization provides a very specific, socially constructed, "sexual morality" category for valuing or devaluing women.

. . . [T]his ideology makes woman a pivotal element in the property structure and institutionalizes her importance to the society in the provisions of partible and bilateral inheritance. It also places woman's value, also termed her "honor," in her sexual accessibility—in her virginity while single and, once wed, in the fidelity of her sexual services to the husband to ensure a legitimate heir.

Within this construct, women are placed in opposition to one another at two extremes of a social and moral spectrum defined by sexuality and accessibility. The good woman embodies all the sexual virtues or attributes essential to the maintenance of the patriarchal social structure: sexual purity, virginity, chastity, and fidelity. Historically, the norms of sexual morality and sexual conduct that patriarchal society established for women of the ruling class have been the norms against which all other women have been judged. . . .

Since the linchpins of these ideological constructs are property, legitimacy, and inheritance, a woman excluded from this property/inheritance structure for sociopolitical reasons (religion, conquest, slavery, race, class), or for reasons based on sexual immorality (any form of sexual misconduct), is consequently excluded from the corresponding concepts and structures of social legitimacy. A woman so excluded cannot produce legitimate heirs because she is not a legitimate social or sexual being.

The woman who is defined out of social legitimacy because of the abrogation of her primary value to patriarchal society, that of producing heirs, is therefore without value, without honor. She becomes the other, the bad woman, the embodiment of a corrupted, inferior, unusable sex: immoral, without virtue, loose. She is common property, sexually available to any man that comes along.

A woman . . . thus devalued may not lay claim to the rights and protections the society affords to the woman who does have sociopolitical and sexual value. In colonial New Spain, as in most Western societies until the very recent period, the woman so demeaned, so objectified, could be raped, beaten, worked like a beast of burden, or otherwise abused with impunity.

The soldiers, priests, and settlers who effected the conquest and colonization of Alta California in the last third of the eighteenth century perceived and acted toward Amerindians in a manner consistent with the ideology and history of conquest—regarding them as inferior, devalued, disposable beings against whom violence was not only permissible but often necessary. For, despite the Laws of the Indies, the contradictions in the ideology and corresponding historical relations of conquest were great from the very beginning. These contradictions were generally exacerbated, rather than resolved, across time, space, and expansion to new frontiers.

From the very beginning, the papal bulls and scholarly (ideological) debates that affirmed the essential humanity of Amerindians and initiated the legislation to effect their conversion and protection sanctioned violence and exploitation under certain conditions. Loopholes in the royal statutes that were technically intended to protect Amerindians and guarantee their rights, but more specifically protected the crown's interest in Indian land and labor, had permitted virulent exploitation of Indians since the laws were first passed.

More contemporary military and civil laws, such as those enacted by Neve, Fages, and Borica, carried severe penalties for illegal contact with or maltreatment of Indians; but these laws were especially contradictory because they were intended to curb certain kinds of violence by soldiers who were trained to kill Indians and who were sent to California to effect the temporal (military) conquest of this region. Thus, violence [including sexual violence] against Amerindians was permissible when it advanced the particular interests of the Spanish Conquest, but punishable when it did not. . . .

Finally, perhaps the greatest contradictions were those of the greatest champion of Amerindian rights—the Catholic church. On the one hand, Catholic clergy sought to remove Amerindians from contact with Spaniards, in order to protect them from the exploitation and violence of conquistadores, soldiers, and colonists; on the other hand, Jesuits, Franciscans, and other religious orders relied heavily on corporal punishment in their programs to Christianize and Hispanicize native people. While proclaiming the humanity of Amerindians, missionaries on the frontier daily acted upon a fundamental belief in the inferiority of the Indian. Their actions belied their words.

Accordingly, in his lengthy memorial of June 19, 1801, refuting the charges of excessive cruelty to Amerindians leveled against the Franciscans by one of their own, Father President Fermín Francisco de Lasuén disputed the use of extreme cruelty in the missions of the New California. Force was used only when absolutely necessary, stated Lasuén; and it was at times necessary because the native peoples of California were "untamed savages . . . people of vicious and ferocious habits who know no law but force, no superior but their own free will, and no reason but their own caprice." Of the use of force against neophyte women, Lasuén wrote that women in the mission were flogged, placed in the stocks, or shackled only because they deserved it. But, he quickly added, their right to privacy was always respected—they were flogged inside the women's dormitory, called the *monjero* (nunnery). Flogging the women in private, he further argued, was part of the civilizing process because it "instilled into them the modesty, delicacy, and virtue belonging to their sex."

A key element in the missionaries' program of conversion to Christianity included the restructuring of relations between the sexes to reflect gender stratification and the corollary values and structures of the patriarchal family: subservience of women to men, monogamy, marriage without divorce, and a severely repressive code of sexual norms.

In view of the fact that ideologies, structures, and institutions of conquest imposed here were rooted in two and a half centuries of colonial rule, the sexual and other violence toward Amerindian women in California can best be understood as ideologically justified violence institutionalized in the structures and relations of conquest initiated in the fifteenth century. In California as elsewhere, sexual violence functioned as an institutionalized mechanism for ensuring subordination and compliance. It was one instrument of sociopolitical terrorism and control—first of women and then of the group under conquest.

Interracial Unions in French Louisiana

JENNIFER M. SPEAR

There are here . . . young men and soldiers who are in a position to undertake farms. They need wives. I know only this one way to hold them.
—JEAN-BAPTISTE MARTIN D'ARTAGUIETTE, 1710

When the French colonization of Louisiana began in the early eighteenth century, *commissaire ordonnatuer* d'Artaguiette and other Louisiana administrators were faced with a problem they believed could be solved only by increasing the immigration of single Frenchwomen into the colony. From 1699 through the 1720s, administrators and missionaries were constantly concerned with the "concubinage among the backwoodsmen and soldiers" with Indian women. These secular and religious

Jennifer M. Spear, "'They Need Wives': Métissage and the Regulation of Sexuality in French Louisiana, 1699–1730," in Martha Hodes, ed., *Sex, Love, Race: Crossing Boundaries in North American History* (New York: New York University Press, 1999), 35–59. Reprinted by permission of New York University Press and the author.

officials believed that relationships between Frenchmen and Indian women were "retard[ing] the growth of this colony" by discouraging male Louisiana colonists from settling down and establishing themselves as farmers. . . . Officials believed that the presence of more Frenchwomen would allow the backwoodsmen, *engagés,* or indentured servants, and discharged soldiers to find wives among the European population and, in turn, that the resulting marriages to European women would encourage the establishment of a stable and self-sufficient colony. In this essay, I examine the ways in which Louisiana administrators and missionaries constructed the presence of sexual relations between Frenchmen and Indian women as a hindrance in their attempts to create a European colony, and how they came to believe that Frenchwomen could become the colony's saviors. Their reactions to métissage, or interracial unions, and their reasons for turning to Frenchwomen were greatly influenced by how they constructed cultural difference and by their desire to manage sexuality: of Europeans, both male and female, and of Indians. . . .

France's interest in Louisiana originated in New France and flowed down the Mississippi River to the Gulf of Mexico; in many ways, its early development echoed that of New France. . . . [I]n 1699 the Canadian Pierre Le Moyne, sieur d'Iberville, accompanied by his brother, Jean Baptiste Le Moyne, sieur de Bienville, established the first permanent French encampment near present-day Biloxi.

. . . [M]any of the earliest Euro-Louisianians came by way of New France, and they were overwhelmingly male. Because imperialist and militarist intentions predominated in the early years, the French population of Louisiana was scattered, and most of the first colonists were military personnel. . . . After the military personnel, the [next] largest group of Euro-Louisianians consisted of trappers, hunters, and *coureurs de bois* [unlicensed fur traders]. This predominance of men, and the fact that many were from New France, had a profound impact on the formation of relationships with local Indian women.

. . . The Canadian immigrants brought with them cultural attitudes and a history of interactions with Indians that differed from those of their French *confrères,* or counterparts. Coming from the frontier society of New France, these Canadians were used to a certain degree of personal freedom. . . . [Governor] Bienville's successor, Antoine de Lamothe Cadillac, . . . described them as "a heap of the dregs from Canada, jailbirds without subordination for religion and for government." . . .

This perception of the Canadians' lawlessness and insubordination stemmed partially from their intimate associations with Indians and their apparent acceptance of an "Indian way of life." . . . [T]he hunters, trappers, and *coureurs de bois* . . . had quickly learned to adapt to Indian customs and norms in order to facilitate trade . . . [and] often . . . [integrated] themselves into Indian trade and kinship networks through marriage to Indian women. . . . Bienville complained in 1706, "several marriages of Frenchmen with Indian women [had been] performed by the missionaries who are among the Indians." . . .

In addition to these individual alliances designed to facilitate trade, there were official practices that broke down the cultural barriers between European men and Louisiana Indians and encouraged personal, and perhaps intimate, contact between the Frenchmen and Indian women. The first was the custom of sending young French boys, usually orphans, to live in Indian villages to learn their languages in order to later serve as diplomatic go-betweens or interpreters. Iberville and Bienville also intended these boys to become "cultural spies," as Bienville noted that a boy he left with the Chickasaw "can write and informs me often about what is happening in this village." Yet, as historians have noted of New France, it is very likely that this practice led, "in many cases, [to the formation of] a taste for the life they never would lose."

The custom of sending soldiers and other colonists to live in Indian villages during times of famine also broke down cultural barriers. Although France was supposed to be sending regular provisions to its colony, shipments often never arrived or were delayed, and the foods spoiled. . . . [I]n 1706, . . . Bienville, "seeing that the food supplies were fast diminishing and that no vessel was on the way to bring some, gave permission to several persons of the garrison to go hunting or to go live as best they could among the savage nations friendly to the French." Until Louisiana achieved self-sufficiency, its European residents were dependent on local Indians, especially for food supplies, and administrators occasionally had to disperse the colonists among Indian villages. . . .

André Pénicaut, . . . who stayed with the Colapissas and Nassitoches in the winter of 1706, . . . recalled in a narrative published in 1723 [that when] he and fellow colonists arrived at the village, "they embraced us, the men as well as the women and girls, all [were] delighted to see us come to stay with them." Pénicaut lodged with the chief of the Nassitoches and wrote that he

> was not sorry . . . for in his house I received every possible favor. He had two daughters that were the most beautiful of all the savage girls in the district. The older one was twenty; she was called Oulchogonime, which in their language means the good daughter. The second was only eighteen, but was much taller than her older sister. She was named Ouilchil, which means the pretty spinner.

By February 1707, Bienville sent out word for all the Frenchmen to return to Mobile, causing Pénicaut and his colleagues to "bec[o]me quite melancholy." Upon returning to Mobile, however, they were pleased "to behold the provisions that had come for us and to find wine in the lot, which we had not had among the Colapissas. The wine consoled us for the loss of the favors of their girls." While never explicitly stating that he or his fellow Frenchmen engaged in sexual relationships with Colapissas or Nassitoches women, Pénicaut did refer to a kiss between his host's older daughter and Picard, a fellow Frenchmen, claiming, "I was not so sorry about this as I would have been if it had been the younger daughter kissing him." Whether or not sexual relations took place, these occasional stays in Indian villages fostered a familiarity between Indians and Frenchmen that officials would rather have done without.

In *The History of Louisiana,* Antoine Simon Le Page du Pratz, who lived in Louisiana from 1718 to 1734, indicated that at least some Frenchmen were spending more time interacting with Indian women than they were with Indian men. In describing the Natchez Indians, he wrote,

> Tho' the women speak the same language with the men, yet, in their manner of pronunciation, they often soften and smooth the words, whereas the speech of men is more grave and serious. The French, by chiefly frequenting the women, contracted their manner of speaking, which was ridiculed as an effeminacy by the women, as well as the men, among the natives.

Le Page du Pratz's comment . . . suggests the presence of a gendered frontier along which Indians and Europeans interacted. . . .

While European men like Pénicaut and Le Page du Pratz have left evidence of their interactions with Indian women, no Indian women left records of their reasons for engaging in relationships with European men. Some Indian women may have initiated relationships with French traders because it gave them access to European goods that they had grown to rely on; as conduits of these goods, they may have gained status in their own communities. In addition, Indian fathers may have desired military and trade alliances, as seen in Jesuit Father le Petit's comment that the Illinois were "inviolably attached to the French, by alliances which many of that Nation had contracted with them, in espousing their daughters." Pointing to another possible motivation, Le Page du Pratz claimed that a Natchez chief's wife begged him to marry her daughter "that I might have it in my power to civilize their nation by abolishing their inhuman customs, and introducing those of the French." While it is possible that this exchange took place, it is most likely that Le Page du Pratz interpreted the Natchez woman's reasons, which may have concerned economic or political alliance building, through his own ethnocentric lenses, placing himself in the role of the "civilizing" European. Another possible reading is that the Natchez, like Iberville and Bienville, wanted to plant "cultural spies" among the French.

These practices . . . as well as the marriages between Indian women and European traders took place in Indian villages. Other interactions between Indian women and European men took place within the French establishments and demonstrate how sites of contact played a role in determining the nature of these relationships. Interactions that took place within Indian villages were more likely to be consensual, while those occurring in French villages were more likely to be exploitative. As early as 1710, there was a thriving black market in Indian slave women, supplied by Indians in the interior and by raids on nearby villages undertaken by Canadian and Frenchmen themselves. Le Page du Pratz purchased a Chitimacha woman "in order to have a person who could dress our victuals." This unnamed woman remained with him for many years, even refusing her father's offer to buy her back. . . . [A]ccording to the censuses of 1721, there were 51 Indian slaves in the New Orleans area and 139 in the Mobile-Biloxi area. Although these censuses do not list the gender of the Indian slaves, later censuses document that female Indian slaves outnumbered male ones by almost two to one.

While Le Page du Pratz and others claimed to be seeking domestic help when they bought Indian slaves, [Governor] Cadillac, among others, was not convinced that this was the real reason European men kept female slaves. In 1713 he noted that "[t]he Canadians and the soldiers who are not married have female Indian slaves and insist that they cannot dispense with having them to do their washing and to do their cooking or to make their sagamity and to keep their cabins." However, Cadillac argued, if these slaves were only serving as domestic help, "it ought not to prevent the soldiers from going to confessional, or the Canadians either." Cadillac believed that European men were buying Indian slave women to serve as concubines rather than for domestic help.

Father Henry de la Vente, the curate of Mobile, agreed with Cadillac that female Indian slavery was thinly disguised concubinage. Complaining about the religious and moral turpitude he observed among Euro-Louisianans, he wrote: "They prefer to maintain scandalous concubinages with young Indian women, driven by their proclivity for the extremes of licentiousness. They have bought them under the pretext of keeping them as servants, but actually to seduce them, as they in fact have done." Sister Marie-Madeleine Hachard, an Ursuline nun, echoed la Vente's concern when she wrote that "not only debauchery, but dishonesty and all the other vices reign here more than elsewhere."

Although in this instance Cadillac, the secular governor, and la Vente, a religious curate, agreed, generally secular and religious opinions on the two forms of métissage differed. Religious officials were concerned with converting Indian souls and maintaining religiosity among the Euro-Louisianians. They believed that marriage, a relationship sanctified by European church and state, could serve as a "civilizing" vehicle, leading to the cultural colonization of Indian women and their children. Concubinage, by contrast, would encourage licentiousness among both Indians and Euro-Louisianians, resulting in the Indianization of the latter. Secular officials, on the other hand, feared that promoting or even allowing Indian-European marriages legitimated an alternative and potentially destabilizing way of life. These differences are most apparent in the decade-long conflict between la Vente and secular officials, particularly Bienville and d'Artaguiette's successor as *commissaire ordonnateur,* Jean-Baptiste du Bois Duclos, over which form of métissage was worse—marriage or concubinage—and what actions needed to be taken to limit its effects. The debate began when la Vente sought official sanction from Louisiana administrators and from the superiors of the foreign missions for the marriages he and his priests had performed between European men and Indian women.

La Vente believed that allowing Indian-European marriages would discourage French and Canadian men from "maintain[ing] scandalous concubinages." . . . In his proposal to legitimate Indian-European relationships, la Vente was building on past policies of both missionaries and secular officials in New France. Since 1648, missionaries had been struggling to control the relationships between French fur traders and Indian women and thought that legitimating them through marriage would do so. Jean-Baptiste Colbert, French Minister of the Navy in the 1660s, "urged very strongly that the native Indian population be Christianized, civilized, and constrained to settle and intermarry with the French," instituting a policy of Frenchification. . . . Yet . . . these attempts at Frenchification failed as Canadian men tended to adopt Indian ways and the Indians were not attracted by European "civilization."

[Governor] Bienville probably had these past failures in mind when he opposed la Vente's proposal, claiming that la Vente was responsible for "authorizing [the Frenchmen who are scattered among the Indians] to live there as libertines under the pretext that they have wives among them." Although he had occasionally sent soldiers and colonists to live temporarily among the Indians, Bienville believed that for the successful colonization of Louisiana, Frenchmen needed to reside in French settlements, under French authority, and not with the Indians on a permanent or even semipermanent basis. . . . While no French or Louisiana officials prohibited these relationships outright, in 1735 the Superior Council did order that all métissage marriages be approved by the state, indicating that secular officials were concerned with regulating, rather than prohibiting, such relationships.

Perhaps anticipating Bienville's opposition to legitimating French-Indian marriages, la Vente also requested that officials "issue an ordinance to forbid the French of Mobile from taking Indian women as slaves and especially from living with them under the same roof in concubinage." [Governor] Cadillac concurred, arguing that all unmarried military men, "from the governor to the lowest officers," should be permitted only male slaves. . . .

Bienville, however, . . . claimed that [this] would be difficult to implement, as "everybody represents to me the indispensable need that they have of taking care of their households and backyards." Even though he thought la Vente was deliberately trying to "annoy the officers and colonists," Bienville did . . . "oblig[e] all those who are concerned to send [the female slaves] to sleep in the houses in which there are Frenchwomen," a move that, he claimed, "does not fail to be a very great inconvenience for [the masters]."

While secular administrators may not have encouraged or desired these relationships, they preferred to turn a blind eye to illicit and presumably transitory ones rather than legitimate them through marriage. Their fear was that marriage to Indians would Indianize the French colonists and prevent the establishment of a stable colony. Unlike the missionaries, who stressed the power of European social institutions such as marriage to convert and "civilize" Indians, secular administrators believed that cultural differences overrode the supposedly civilizing influences of marriage. Duclos pointed to a few examples of Indian-French marriages that had survived, though

> not because [the wives] have become Frenchified, if one may use that term, but it is because those who have married them have themselves become almost Indian, residing among them and living in their manner, so that these Indian women have changed nothing or at least very little in their manner of living.

Louisiana officials feared "losing" male Euro-Louisianians to an Indian way of life partly because their constructions of Indian sexuality and marriage practices conflicted with their notions of how to create a stable European society.

Many male European commentators in early Louisiana perceived Indian women as more sexual or more promiscuous than European women (or at least the ideal European woman). One of the first things many commented on was the relative nudity among Indians. In describing the first time he met the Bayogoulas, Iberville wrote:

> The women wear only a sash of bark, most of which are red and white. . . . They are sufficiently concealed by this garment, the strands in continuous motion. Many girls six to seven years of age do not wear sashes; they conceal their nakedness with a small bundle of moss, held by a string which runs between the thighs and is fastened to a waistband.

Pénicaut commented that Pascagoulas women wore only "a single hank of moss which passed between their legs and covered their nakedness, the rest of their bodies being quite nude." For Europeans, nakedness was an indication of an unrestrained sexuality.

Polygamy was also seen by the French as representative of immorality. Bernard Diron d'Artaguiette, commandant at Mobile . . . , claimed that "polygamy is in practice here [by the Natchez] and among all the Indian nations which I have seen." Chiefs and other elite men contracted marriages with several women in order to build economic and political alliances, and as an indication of status and power. For Diron d'Artaguiette, however, polygamy and an unrestrained Indian sexuality were linked because he believed that the former led to women's ability to leave their husbands "without the least complaint being made by those whom they leave." Duclos also pointed to women's apparent sexual freedom in his opposition to la Vente's proposal[:]

> [W]e shall find very few Indian women who will be willing to marry Frenchmen. Accustomed to a certain sort of dissolute life that they lead in their villages and to leave the husbands with whom they are not pleased in order to take others they will never be able to accustom themselves and even less to remain with them the rest of their lives. . . . Furthermore it happens very often that they leave their French husbands and go and remarry Indians in other villages.

. . . This ability to change spouses "when it seems good to them" resulted, according to Father le Petit, in an "indifference to the conjugal union." In the minds of Louisiana administrators, the instability of Indian marriages would carry over to Indian-French marriages and undermine their struggle to establish a secure colony.

The perceived ease of divorce or separation . . . indicated a female sexuality far more independent than [the French commentators] were used to. Diron d'Artaguiette noted that young girls were taught that they were "the mistresses of their own bodies (to use their own expression)." Taken as a whole, European commentators saw Indian women as "lustful and devoid of restraint," "naturally inclined towards love," and willing to prostitute themselves to "the Frenchmen, to whom they refuse none of their favors, in return for a few glass beads or other trifles." But it was not just Indian women's sexuality that was blamed for encouraging métissage. D'Artaguiette also pointed to the "stimulating" climate and to the backwoodsmen and soldiers who were "young men for the most part Canadians, that is to say very vigorous."

Some administrators complained that French and Canadian men would select local Indian women over Frenchwomen if they had the choice. Cadillac wrote that many colonists were "addicted to vice principally with Indian women whom they prefer to Frenchwomen." . . . The naval officer Tivas de Gourville described the Canadians as "hunters and backwoodsmen who are of a strong and vigorous age and temperament . . . who like the sex, and not finding any who can hold them, as wanderers among the Indian nations and satisfy their passions with the daughters of these Indians." . . .

Given these constructions of Indian women's and Canadian men's sexuality, administrators and missionaries feared the results of métissage on a number of levels, stemming not only from the desire to regulate Indians but also from the need to regulate the Euro-Louisianians. As [historian] Ann Stoler has argued in regard to French Indochina and the Dutch East Indies, "it was through the policing of sex that subordinate European military and civil servants were kept in line and that racial boundaries were thus maintained." The administrators' greatest concern was how these relationships would affect the establishment of Louisiana as an economically viable colony. La Chaise complained that "None of those voyageurs clear any group or make any settlements." Relationships, let alone sanctioned marriages, with Indian women were not seen by administrators as conducive to creating stable families. D'Artaguiette argued that marriages to Indian women would "not cause . . . any great change at all in the Indians," but would encourage Frenchmen to lead "with these wives a life as nomadic as before." . . .

Administrators were less concerned with the morality of the colonists, although they did complain about the Canadian men's licentiousness, and preferred that Euro-Louisianians engage in immoral but fleeting relationships with Indian women rather than have those relationships sanctified and made permanent. The missionaries, on the other hand, were greatly concerned with the moral state of the colony, its colonists, and its indigenous inhabitants. . . . While both religious and secular officials wanted to see the successful colonization of Louisiana, they disagreed over the method to achieve this goal. For the administrators, the presence of Indians offered the French settlers an alternative way of life that needed to be discouraged. The missionaries, on the other hand, were more concerned with breaking down Indian culture and assimilating individual Indians into French "civilization." Regardless of experiences in New France, they still believed the Frenchification of Indian women would follow from marriages with Frenchmen. At the same time, they were opposed to illicit relationships of any kind.

For Louisiana *habitants*, the key issue regarding these marriages was the question of succession, illustrating the centrality of property in European conceptions of marriage. Under French law, an Indian widow was entitled to receive half of her French husband's estates, and if there were no children the property acquired during the marriage went to her Indian heirs, rather than to her husband's French heirs. *Habitants* complained that many of these "Indian heirs frequently ran away with what was left by the deceased," and that it was impossible to force them to make good on debts held against the estates. . . . In 1728 the Superior Council decreed that a Frenchman should be appointed as tutor, if there were children, or, if there were none, as curate, who would control the property left by Frenchmen to their Indian wives and children. With or without children, the widow would receive a pension of one-third of the estate. This decree included a provision "that this pension should cease in case she returned to dwell among her tribe."

Although these concerns were articulated in terms of property rights, questions of French identity, citizenship, and nationality permeated the legal discourse. Would the children of French-Indian marriages be Indian? Would they be French? Or would they be something new, a people in between? Duclos opposed la Vente's proposal, arguing, "experience shows every day that the children that come from such marriages are of an extremely dark complexion," causing the adulteration of "the whiteness and purity of the blood in the children." If these were the only children born in Louisiana, "it would become a colony of halfbreeds who are naturally idlers, libertines and even more rascals as those of Peru, Mexico and the other Spanish colonies give evidence." While the Superior of Foreign Missions to whom la Vente wrote had no objections to Indian-French marriages, "there was still a fear of mingling by these marriages good blood with bad and of producing in the colony only children of a hard and idle character." It was not only Euro-Louisianians who worried about the results of Indian-French marriages or cultural intermingling more generally. One Natchez elder also expressed anxiety regarding [what the French translated as] purity of blood, blaming Frenchmen for "debauch[ing] the young women, and taint[ing] the blood of the nation," . . . [and] making [the] women "vain and idle." Stung Serpent, another Natchez, concurred: "our women were more laborious and less vain than they are now."

These concerns over "purity of blood" and "halfbreeds" illuminate the racial boundaries that the French in Louisiana were constructing. When the Bayougoulas offered women to Iberville and his party in 1700, Iberville "made them understand that their skin—red and tanned—should not come close to that of the French, which was white." Color here was an indicator of social and sexual distance. In his original proposal, la Vente himself distinguished between the southern Indians and the northern ones, who were "whiter, more laborious, cleverer, neater in the household work and more docile than those of the south": in other words, more akin to the construction of European women. Pénicaut also drew implicit comparisons between white and Indian womanhood. Describing Tourimas and Capas women, he wrote that "they are quite pretty and white-complexioned."

In a long comparison of the Nassitoches and Colapissas, Pénicaut wrote:

> The Nassitoches are handsomer and have better figures than the Colapissas, because the Colapissas' bodies, men's and women's, are all tattooed. They prick almost their entire bodies with needles and rub the pricks with willow ash crushed quite fine, which causes no inflammation of the punctures. The arms and faces of Colapissas women and girls are tattooed in this way, which disfigures them hideously; but the Nassitoches, men as well as women and girls, make no use of such punctures, which they loathe. That is why they are so much better looking; *besides, they are naturally whiter.*

Here Pénicaut conflated race, savagery, civilization, and beauty, inscribing them onto the body. While the last line seems almost an afterthought, "whiteness" lies at the center of Pénicaut's aesthetic. For the French colonizing Louisiana, a discourse of color, embodying racial and cultural differences, was present from the start: a discourse shaped by previous French experiences in New France and by knowledge of Spanish and English colonization elsewhere in the New World.

Constructions of unrestrained sexuality of both Indian women and some European men, together with the racialized fears of "mixing blood," led secular officials to oppose any proposals that would legitimate marriages between Indian women and European men, thereby in some ways legitimating a non-European way of life. The Navy Council at Louvre agreed, declaring that "Marriages of this sort must be prevented as much as possible and girls will be sent from here when it will be possible to do so." Some of the blame for these relationships was laid at the feet of the "vigorous" backwoodsmen, Canadians, and soldiers, but administrators, clerics, and other commentators also believed that these men could be reformed and redeemed through marriage to Frenchwomen. As d'Artaguiette wrote to Pontchartrain, the young men and soldiers "need wives. I know only this one way to hold them."

When the complaints about métissage were reported to Pontchartrain in 1712, he noted that "We ought to send women." Over and over, Louisiana administrators wrote to France begging for more Frenchwomen, stressing that only marriage to Frenchwomen would encourage the young settlers, many of them discharged soldiers or backwoodsmen, to establish farms. . . . [S]everal administrators, including d'Artaguiette, argued that "of all the remedies [to check the course of concubinage] the most sure is to send women there." . . . François de Mandeville . . . suggested that "if about forty girls who would provide for themselves were sent there, they would first get married and being married they would work to support their families in mutual rivalry." While Bienville and la Vente disagreed over the appropriateness of marriages between Indian women and Frenchmen, both believed that the immigration of European women was the best solution. In 1710 la Vente returned to France and, participating in the recruitment effort, relayed the concerns of d'Artaguiette and others about "the necessity that exists for having girls to draw in [to the settlements] the backwoodsmen."

France had previous experiences in recruiting women for the colonies. Between 1662 and 1673, authorities sent more than seven hundred women to New France in order to "satisfy the colony's need for marriageable women." These women, known as the *filles du roi,* or the king's girls, since their dowries were provided by the Crown, were usually orphans and often illiterate. They were mostly recruited from the Hôpital Général du Paris, which served as a house of detention and correction for prostitutes, vagrants, kept women, and other criminals but was also an orphanage. More than 80 percent married within six months of arrival. . . .

At first, Louisiana officials requested any woman and every woman. De Gourville suggested recruiting women from the Paris asylums, who would not be missed. To persuade these women to emigrate, he recommended giving them free passage and eighteen to twenty months of subsistence. Other Louisiana administrators wanted "hard-working people and girls" who would be able to perform the labor necessary in a young colony: cultivating the land, reproducing, and teaching the Indian men and women. D'Artaguiette wrote that the best immigrants would be "families of farmers, selecting those in which there are many girls who would be married to Canadians." . . .

After some experience, Louisiana administrators became more selective about what sorts of European women they wanted sent. . . . The ideal female immigrants, in the minds of Louisiana officials, were farmers' daughters who were used to hard work and would not be distracted by vanity.

French officials did not ignore these requests. In 1704 Pontchartrain wrote to Bienville notifying him that the *Pélican* was on its way to Louisiana, carrying "twenty girls to be married to the Canadians and others who have begun to make themselves homes on the Mobile in order that this colony may be firmly established." This was the first shipment of *épouseuses,* or women specifically sent "to marry and civilize the rough woodsmen and populate the wilderness." The . . . *Baron de la Fosse* in 1713 [brought] Cadillac, his wife and children, and several "Breton girls, who had come of their own accord." The *Loire,* which left France in 1720, carried dressmakers, bakers, cooks, and laundresses. Immigration picked up between 1718 and 1721 with the arrival of 7,020 Europeans, including 1,215 women. Shipments of *épouseuses* ended in 1728 with the arrival of the *filles à cassette,* or "casket girls," named after the casket of dress articles they were given for their new lives in Louisiana.

While Louisiana officials had high expectations for these women, not all who arrived as *épouseuses* in Louisiana were, in the words of one Louisiana historian, "the best women for founding a colony." Scholars have estimated that between one-fifth and one-half were prostitutes. Anecdotal evidence indicates that many, especially those who arrived in the 1720s, had been recruited from the Hôpital Général du Paris. . . . Because it was still a house of detention and correction, Louisiana settlers were concerned that the recruits were all "fallen women." . . . Chassin, an officer in the Illinois country, complained that the women being sent were unsuitable for officers to marry.

Several are becoming impatient but we let them grumble. The Company has already sent four or five hundred girls but officers and those who hold any rank cannot make up their minds to marry such girls who in addition to the bad reputations that they bring from France give reason to fear that some also bring remnants of infirmities of which they have been imperfectly healed. . . .

Officials were not unaware of these concerns. When Minister of the Navy Colbert instituted subsidized immigration for women into New France, he looked for "marriageable girls whose backgrounds had been investigated to ensure that they were morally healthy as well as physically fit." Pontchartrain, echoing his predecessor, claimed that the *Pélican* "girls have been brought up in virtue and piety" and had been recruited from "places that cannot be suspected of any dissoluteness," so that "none at all may be sent except those of recognized and irreproachable virtue." He ordered Bienville to "be careful to establish them as best you can and to marry them off to men capable of supporting them with some sort of comfort." Pénicaut noted that the *Pélican* women "were quite well behaved, and so they had no trouble finding husbands."

[The] women who arrived aboard the *Baron* in 1713 were not so well received, as they landed under a cloud of rumor and scandal. The *épouseuses* aboard the *Baron* were under the chaperonage of Cadillac and his wife. Cadillac accused the ship's crew of misbehaving toward these women, particularly condemning Sieur de Richebourg as "a man who indulges in all sorts of debaucheries. . . . seduc[ing] my wife's chambermaid." Some of the Canadians on board the same vessel, "being witnesses of what happened in regard to them, spoke ill of them as soon as they landed." As a result, only two of the twelve women had married by October. It was not only rumors that hindered these women's marriages, however. Duclos commented that they were "extremely ugly," while Cadillac noted, "these girls are very poor having neither linen nor clothes nor beauty." . . .

Cadillac recommended that "it would be well to marry off several of these girls to soldiers who are courting them and who could support them, for fear that they may be debauched since they are quite destitute." Again, a year later, Cadillac issued a request for women "suitable for marriage to officers and refined and educated colonists."

Not all the Hôpital recruits would have been prostitutes or other criminals. When the *Maréchal de Villars* arrived in 1719, it brought twenty "girls from the poorhouse of La Rochelle." These women were fourteen to twenty-seven years old; the ages at which they had been left at the poorhouse ranged from birth to fourteen. Pénicaut similarly described the girls he saw arrive in 1721 as fourteen to fifteen years old and having been "brought up in this house from infancy," indicating that these girls were probably the orphaned or abandoned children of the women detained at the Hôpital. . . .

Many of these women did not come voluntarily to Louisiana. In 1719 ninety-five women arrived aboard the *Mutine*, "sent by the king," while thirty-eight "exiled women" arrived aboard the *Deux Frères* and *Duc de Noailles*. Working against voluntary emigration to Louisiana was the fact that the colony suffered from an unsavory reputation among the common people of France. Conditions in Louisiana were those of a frontier society that had not yet become self-sufficient. Death rates were high for incoming immigrants, and settlers still relied on shipments of provisions

from France for wine, clothing, and food staples. When they first arrived in Louisiana, the women, according to Dumont de Montigny, "were lodged in the same house, with a sentinel at the door. Leave was given to see them by day and make a selection, but as soon as it was dark, entrance to the house was forbidden to all persons." The unpleasantness of being on display as bachelors paraded past was compounded by those such as Pénicaut who referred to the *épouseuses* as "merchandise that was soon distributed, so great was the dearth of it in the country."

It is not clear how many women found husbands and how many settlers were deterred by rumors of impurity or the "unattractiveness" of the women. Dumont de Montigny reported that "these girls were not long in being provided for and married. . . . In fact, had there arrived at the time as many girls as there were soldiers and workmen on the island, not one would have remained without a husband." There was at least one woman, however, who apparently refused to marry. In 1706, two years after the arrival of the *Pélican,* Bienville complained that "There is one of the twenty girls who were sent to Mobile who is quite unwilling to marry." He wrote to Pontchartrain requesting permission to "oblige . . . her to do so like the others since there are several good suitors who are sighing for her." Louis XIV granted governor-elect de Muy permission to "oblige her to do so" under the threat of being returned to France. The king did allow de Muy to determine for himself whether she could be "useful to the colony while living as she does either for the instruction of the daughters of the inhabitants in the principles of religion or to teach them to work." If de Muy determined that this unnamed woman would be useful, he could postpone her forced return to France. Just as French male immigrants to New France had found freedom from Old World customs and mores, so too did French women who emigrated to Louisiana.

Some of these imported women did establish themselves in the colony and occasionally became matriarchs among the "first families." While some . . . were promised support by the Company of the Indies until they got married, others supported themselves in a variety of ways, including prostitution. Cadillac complained of one woman who was "selling herself to all comers, the Indians just like the whites." Unfortunately for the Louisiana administrators who espoused the civilizing effects that Frenchwomen would have on Louisiana, the colony seems to have had the opposite effect on some Frenchwomen. Périer and Salmon acknowledged that conditions in the colony did not help in preventing single women, especially orphan girls, from resorting to vice.

La Chaise complained in 1725 that "there are many other women . . . who have no husbands and who are ruining the colony"; he recommended that all the immigrants who had been forced to Louisiana, men and women, be returned to France. A few months later, the Council of Louisiana argued for "the necessity of purging the colony of . . . a number of women of bad life who are entirely lost." Other women were destined to end up where they began. In 1727 Governor Périer and *commissaire ordonnateur* la Chaise noted, "There are many women and girls of bad life here," and recommended the building of "a house of correction here in order to put in it the women and girls of bad lives who cause a public scandal." Périer asked the Ursuline nuns to "take care of the girls and women of evil life." . . . While administrators had previously believed that Frenchwomen would secure the establishment of families and farms in Louisiana, by the late 1720s, they found themselves faced with women who, in the words of la Chaise, "are useless and who do nothing but cause disorder."

Even with the increased population of Frenchwomen, administrators and clerics were unable to eradicate métissage between Indian women and Euro-Louisianian men as both concubinage and marriages continued to occur. Father Raphäel complained in 1726 that while "the number of those who maintain young Indian women . . . to satisfy their intemperance is considerably diminished, there still remain enough to scandalize the church and to require an effective remedy." . . . In 1745 [a mixed] marriage appeared in the Superior Council records in the will of Charles Hegron. Hegron bequeathed half his estate to "François, an Indian woman, his legitimate wife." The remainder of his estate was to be "divided between his two children, the issue of his legitimate marriage." Hegron's concern with stressing the legitimacy of his marriage, and therefore of his children, probably stemmed from a fear that his fellow Euro-Louisianians would not accept the legitimacy of his bequests to his Indian wife and children. Indeed, the Superior Council did appoint a tutor for his widow, determining that she was incompetent to manage the estate herself. Relationships between Indian women and Euro-Louisianian men continued throughout the eighteenth century, although the debates over their existence subsided from public view. With the decrease in Louisiana's Indian population, the increase in the African Louisianian population, and the entrenchment of slavery, Euro-Louisianians shifted their concerns about métissage onto the licit and illicit relationships between white men and black women, ignoring those few Indian–Euro-Louisianian relationships that persevered.

◖ F U R T H E R   R E A D I N G

Karen Anderson, *Chain Her by One Foot: The Subjugation of Native Women in Seventeenth-Century New France* (1991).
James Axtell, ed., *The Indian Peoples of Eastern America: A Documentary History of the Sexes* (1981).
Evelyn Blackwood, "Sexuality and Gender in Certain Native American Tribes: The Case of Cross-Gender Females," *Signs* 10 (1984): 27–42.
James F. Brooks, "'This Evil Extends Especially . . . to the Feminine Sex': Negotiating Captivity in the New Mexico Borderlands," *Feminist Studies* (Summer 1996): 279–309.
Charles Callender and Lee M. Kochems, "The North American Berdache," *Current Anthropology* 24 (1983): 443–470.
Carol Devens, *Countering Colonization: Native American Women and Great Lakes Missions, 1630–1900* (1992).
John Mack Faragher, "The Custom of the Country: Cross-Cultural Marriage in the Far Western Fur Trade," in Lillian Schlissel et al., eds., *Western Women: Their Land, Their Lives* (1988), 199–215.
Rayna Green, "The Pocahontas Perplex: The Image of Indian Women in American Culture," *Massachusetts Review* 16 (1975): 698–714.
Ramón A. Gutiérrez, *When Jesus Came, the Corn Mothers Went Away: Marriage, Sexuality, and Power in New Mexico, 1500–1846* (1991).
Martha Hodes, ed., *Sex, Love, Race: Crossing Boundaries in North America* (1999).
Albert L. Hurtado, *Intimate Frontiers: Sex, Gender and Culture in Old California* (1999).

Richard Lee, "Politics, Sexual and Non-sexual, in an Egalitarian Society," in Eleanor
    Leacock and Richard Lee, eds., *Politics and History in Band Societies* (1982), 23–36.

Beatrice Medicine, "Warrior Women: Sex Role Alternatives for Plains Indian Women," in
    Patricia Albers and Beatrice Medicine, *The Hidden Half: Studies of Plains Indian
    Women* (1983), 267–280.

June Namias, *White Captives: Gender and Ethnicity on the American Frontier* (1993).

Jacqueline Peterson, "Women Dreaming: The Religiopsychology of Indian White Marriages
    and the Rise of Metis Culture," in Lillian Schlissel et al., eds., *Western Women: Their
    Land, Their Lives* (1988), 47–76.

Will Roscoe, *The Zuni Man-Woman* (1991).

Nancy Shoemaker, ed., *Negotiators of Change: Historical Perspectives on Native American
    Women* (1994).

Richard C. Trexler, *Sex and Conquest: Gendered Violence, Political Order, and the European
    Conquest of the Americas* (1995).

Sylvia Van Kirk, "The Role of Native Women in the Fur Trade Society of Western Canada,"
    in Susan Armitage and Elizabeth Jameson, eds., *The Women's West* (1987), 53–62.

Harriet Whitehead, "The Bow and the Burden Strap: A New Look at Institutionalized
    Homosexuality in Native North America," in Sherry B. Orner and Harriet Whitehead,
    eds., *Sexual Meanings* (1981).

Walter L. Williams, *The Spirit and the Flesh: Sexual Diversity in American Indian Culture*
    (1986).

CHAPTER
3

Regulating Sexuality in

the Anglo-American Colonies

Historians' knowledge of sexuality in British North America depends greatly on legal and judicial records that document laws passed, trials conducted, and punishments meted out. These records not only reveal the varieties of sexual crimes and illicit sexual behavior, they allow us to examine the norms that defined legitimate sexual relations. Laws about sexuality covered a wide range of acts and pairings believed to disturb the social order of the settler colonies. Ideas about sexuality were in flux in the early modern Atlantic world and varied from colony to colony. Differences in religious orientation, labor systems, demographic composition, and political authority all played a role in the ways that sexuality was understood and regulated.

In Puritan New England, trials for fornication, adultery, sodomy, and bestiality defined, as well as enforced, proper sexual conduct. Perceiving sexual sins as divine judgments and fearful that their godly community would be undermined, Puritans undertook the vigilant surveillance of nonmarital sexual behavior. Colonial societies were organized around patriarchal households, with property-owning men exercising authority over their wives and children and policing the labor and persons of servants and slaves. Laws about sexual conduct upheld patriarchal authority. In such colonies as Virginia, in which involuntary servitude developed early and extensively, sexual regulations helped also to define the terms of racial slavery: white men might rape black women with impunity; the children of enslaved women were slaves, regardless of their paternity; all black men were denied social status as fathers; free white women who bore children of color were condemned to servitude for their sexual violation of racial boundaries. Examining these laws closely reveals how they maintained the familial order, regulated labor, and formed and preserved racial and class hierarchies.

Colonial trial records reveal how civil and religious authorities understood sexuality and projected their power. In the hands of skillful historians, these trials also reveal other sources of influence and authority in settler communities. Midwives and groups of neighbor women claimed a role in judging and regulating the sexual behavior of other women. Even laborers and servants might convey their views about elite men who committed sodomy. This evidence, however fragmentary and partial, suggests that popular ideas about sexuality were not always the same as the official views expressed by ministers and colonial governors. How did they differ?

70

DOCUMENTS

The legal codes of Massachusetts and Virginia reveal both the social categories to which persons were assigned and the sexual transgressions that most often occurred between people in different positions. Document 1 excerpts Massachusetts's capital laws, which defined certain sexual acts that so deeply violated moral codes that they were deemed punishable by death. The Virginia laws, as excerpted in Document 2, policed sexual relations in ways that maintained hierarchies of rank and race: servants, slaves, and masters; African, English, and Indian. What are the reasons for the different emphases in these laws?

Despite these efforts to regulate sexuality, erotic desires were not always contained, or even explainable. In Document 3, Governor William Bradford sought to understand the disturbing outbreak of sodomy and buggery in the Plymouth colony in 1642, which challenged his belief that the Puritans had established a godly society. What does his analysis suggest about the larger anxieties and fears preoccupying the Puritans? Testimony taken before Virginia governor John Pott in 1629 (Document 4) turned on the identity of Thomas or Thomasine Hall, who replied to those who inquired that he was "both man and woman." Those who associated with Hall believed that this transvestite must be one or the other. Who was Hall? What were others' views toward Hall? And what does this case tell us about gender and sexual identity in the past?

1. Massachusetts Colony's Laws on Sexual Offenses, 1641–1660

. . . If any man or woeman shall lye with any beaste or bruite creature by Carnall Copulation, They shall surely be put to death. And the beast shall be slaine and buried and not eaten.

If any man lyeth with mankinde as he lyeth with a woeman, both of them have committed abhomination, they both shall surely be put to death.

If any person committeth Adultery with a married or espoused wife, the Adulterer and Adulteresse shall surely by put to death. [1641] . . .

If any man LYETH WITH MAN-KINDE as he lieth with a woman both of them have committed abomination, they both shall surely be put to death, unles the one partie were forced, or be under fourteen years of age in which case he shall be severely punished. *Levit. 20.13.* [1649] . . .

If any man shall RAVISH any maid, or single woman, committing carnal copulation with her by force, against her own will; that is above the age of ten years, he shall be punished either with death, or with some other greivous punishment, according to circumstances, as the Judges, or General Court shall determine. [1649] . . .

"The Body of Liberties" (1641) and "Capital Laws" (1660), in William H. Whitmore, ed., *The Colonial Laws of Massachusetts* (Boston: City Council of Boston, 1889), 55, 128, 129, 153.

Fornication.

It is Ordered by this Court and Authority thereof, That if any man commit *Fornication,* with any single woman, they shall be punished, either by enjoyning marriage, or fine, or corporal punishment, or all or any of these, as the Judges of the Court that hath Cognizance of the cause shall appoint. [1642]

2. Virginia Regulates Sex Among Servants, Slaves, and Masters, 1642–1769

WHEREAS many great abuses & much detriment have been found to arise both against the law of God and likewise to the service of manye masters of families in the collony occasioned through secret marriages of servants, their masters and mistresses being not any ways made privy thereto, as also by committing of fornication, for preventing the like abuses hereafter, *Be it enacted and confirmed by this Grand Assembly* that what man servant soever hath since January 1640 or hereafter shall secretly marry with any mayd or woman servant without the consent of her master or mistres if she be a widow, he or they so offending shall in the first place serve out his or their tyme or tymes with his or their masters or mistresses, and after shall serve his or their master or mistress one compleat year more for such offence committed, And the mayd or woman servant so marrying without consent as aforesaid shall for such her offence double the tyme of service with her master and mistress, And a ffreeman so offending shall give satisfaction to the master or mistress by doubling the value of the service and pay a ffine of five hundred pounds of tobacco to the parish where such offence shall be comitted, And it is also further enacted and confirmed by the authority of this Grand Assembly that if any man servant shall comit the act of fornication with any mayd or woman servant, he shall for his offence, besides the punishment by the law appointed in like cases, give satisfaction for the losse of her service, by one whole year's service, when he shall be free from his master according to his indentures, And if it so fall out that a freeman offend, as formerly he shall be compelled to make satisfaction to the master or mistris of the said woman servant by his service for one compleat year, or otherwise give forthwith such valuable consideration as the commissioners in their discretion shall think fitt. [1642–1643] . . .

Concerning secret Marriages.

WHEREAS many greate abuses and much detriment hath been found to arise both against the lawe of God and likewise to the service of many masters of ffamilies in this collonie, occasioned through secret marriages of servants, their masters and mistresses not any waies made privie thereunto, As also by comitting of ffornication; for the prevention of the like abuses hereafter, *Bee it enacted,* and confirmed

William Waller Hening, ed., *The Statutes at Large; Being a Collection of all the Laws of Virginia, 1619–1792* (1809–1823; Charlottesville: Jamestown Foundation/University Press of Virginia, 1969), vol. 1: 252–253, 438–439; vol. 2: 167, 168, 170; vol. 3: 86–87, 447–448, 452–454; vol. 8: 358.

by this Grand Assembly that what servant soever hath since January, 1656, or here-after shall secretly marrie with any maid or woman servant without the consent of her master or mistresse, (if she be a widowe) hee or they soe offending shall in the first place serve out his or their times with his or their master or mistresse, and after shall serve his or their said master or mistresse, one complete yeare more for such offence comited, And the maid or woman servant so marrying without consent as aforesaid shall for such her offence to her master or mistresse serve one year after her freedom by indenture, And a freeman so offending shall give satisfaction to the master or mistresse by doubling the valew of the service.

And it is also further enacted and confirmed by the authoritie of this Grand Assembly that if any mans' servant shall hereafter comit the act of ffornication with any maid . . . [he shall] . . . give satisfaction for the loss of her service to her said master or mistresse by his service of one compleat yeare, or pay fifteen hundred pounds of tobacco and give securitie to save harmeless the parish and her said master or mistresse, and defraye all charge of keeping the child, And a freeman so offending shall for his offence pay fifteen hundred pounds of tobacco or one year's service to the master or mistresse of the woman or maid servant of whom hee shall gett a bastard, As also give securitie to save the parish and her said master and mistresse harmelesse & defray all charge about keeping the child, And the woman servant so offending to suffer according to lawe, Also be it enacted that every per-son comitting ffornication shall pay five hundred pounds of tobacco to the [u]se of the parish where the said act is comitted or be whipt. [1657–1658] . . .

Women servants gott with child by their masters after their time expired to be sold by the Churchwardens for two yeares for the good of the parish.

WHEREAS by act of Assembly every woman servant haveing a bastard is to serve two yeares, and late experiente shew that some dissolute masters have gotten their maides with child, and yet claime the benefitt of their service, and on the contrary if a woman gott with child by her master should be freed from that service it might probably induce such loose persons to lay all their bastards to their masters; *it is therefore thought fitt and accordingly enacted, and be it enacted henceforward* that each woman servant gott with child by her master shall after her time by indenture or custome is expired be by the churchwardens of the parish where she lived when she was brought to bed of such bastard, sold for two yeares, and the tobacco to be imployed by the vestry for the use of the parish. [1662] . . .

Men servants getting any bastard child to make satis-faction to the parish after their service ended.

WHEREAS by the present law of this country the punishment of a reputed father of a bastard child is the keeping the child and saving the parish harmlesse, and if it should happen the reputed father to be a servant who can noe way accomplish the penalty of that act, *Be it enacted by the authority aforesaid* that where any bastard child is gotten by a servant the parish shall take care to keepe the child during the time of the reputed fathers service by indenture or custome, and that after he is free the said reputed father shall make satisfaction to the parish. [1662] . . .

*Negro womens children to serve according to the condi-
tion of the mother.*

WHEREAS some doubts have arrisen whether children got by any Englishman upon a negro woman should be slave or ffree, *Be it therefore enacted and declared by this present grand assembly,* that all children borne in this country shalbe held bond or free only according to the condition of the mother, *And* that if any christian shall commit ffornication with a negro man or woman, hee or shee soe offending shall pay double the ffines imposed by the former act. [1662] . . .

An Act for suppressing outlying Slaves.

. . . And for the prevention of that abominable mixture and spurious issue which hereafter may encrease in this dominion, as well by negroes, mulattoes, and Indians intermarrying with English, or other white women, as by their unlawfull accompanying with one another, *Be it enacted by the authoritie aforesaid, and it is hereby enacted,* that for the time to come, whatsoever English or other white man or woman being free shall intermarry with a negroe, mulatto, or Indian man or woman bond or free shall within three months after such marriage be banished and removed from this dominion forever, and that the justices of each respective countie within this dominion make it their perticular care, that this act be put in effectuall execution. *And be it further enacted by the authoritie aforesaid, and it is hereby enacted,* That if any English woman being free shall have a bastard child by any negro or mulatto, she pay the sume of fifteen pounds sterling, within one moneth after such bastard child shall be born, to the Church wardens of the parish where she shall be delivered of such child, and in default of such payment she shall be taken into the possession of the said Church wardens and disposed of for five yeares, and the said fine of fifteen pounds, or whatever the woman shall be disposed of for, shall be paid, one third part to their majesties for and towards the support of the government and the contingent charges thereof, and one other third part to the use of the parish where the offence is committed, and the other third part to the informer, and that such bastard child be bound out as a servant by the said Church wardens untill he or she shall attaine the age of thirty yeares, and in case such English woman that shall have such bastard child be a servant, she shall be sold by the said church wardens, (after her time is expired that she ought by law to serve her master) for five yeares, and the money she shall be sold for divided as is before appointed, and the child to serve as aforesaid. [1691] . . .

An act concerning Servants and Slaves.

I. *Be it enacted, by the governor, council, and burgesses, of this present general assembly, and it is hereby enacted, by the authority of the same,* That all servants brought into this country without indenture, if the said servants be christians, and of christian parentage, and above nineteen years of age, shall serve but five years; and if under nineteen years of age, 'till they shall become twenty-four years of age, and no longer. . . .

IV. *And also be it enacted, by the authority aforesaid, and it is hereby enacted,* That all servants imported and brought into this country, by sea or land, who were not christians in their native country, (except Turks and Moors in amity with her majesty, and others that can make due proof of their being free in England, or any other christian country, before they were shipped, in order to transportation hither) shall be accounted and be slaves, and as such be here bought and sold notwithstanding a conversion to christianity afterwards. . . .

XVIII.   And if any women servant shall be delivered of a bastard child within the time of her service aforesaid, *Be it enacted, by the authority aforesaid, and it is hereby enacted,* That in recompence of the loss and trouble occasioned her master or mistress thereby, she shall for every such offence, serve her said master or owner one whole year after her time by indenture, custom, and former order of court, shall be expired; or pay her said master or owner, one thousand pounds of tobacco; and the reputed father, if free, shall give security to the church-wardens of the parish where that child shall be, to maintain the child, and keep the parish indemnified; or be compelled thereto by order of the county court, upon the said church-wardens complaint: But if a servant, he shall make satisfaction to the parish, for keeping the said child, after his time by indenture, custom, or order of court, to his then present master or owner, shall be expired; or be compelled thereto, by order of the county court, upon complaint of the church-wardens of the said parish, for the time being. And if any woman servant shall be got with child by her master, neither the said master, nor his executors[,] administrators, nor assigns, shall have any claim of service against her, for or by reason of such child; but she shall, when her time due to her said master, by indenture, custom or order of court, shall be expired, be sold by the church-wardens, for the time being, of the parish wherein such child shall be born, for one year, or pay one thousand pounds of tobacco; and the said one thousand pounds of tobacco, or whatever she shall be sold for, shall be emploied, by the vestry, to the use of the said parish. And if any woman servant shall have a bastard child by a negro, or mulatto, over and above the years service due to her master or owner, she shall immediately, upon the expiration of her time to her then present master or owner, pay down to the church-wardens of the parish wherein such child shall be born, for the use of the said parish, fifteen pounds current money of Virginia, or be by them sold for five years, to the use aforesaid: And if a free christian white woman shall have such bastard child, by a negro, or mulatto, for every such offence, she shall, within one month after her delivery of such bastard child, pay to the church-wardens for the time being, of the parish wherein such child shall be born, for the use of the said parish fifteen pounds current money of Virginia, or be by them sold for five years to the use aforesaid: And in both the said cases, the church-wardens shall bind the said child to be a servant, until it shall be of thirty one years of age.

XIX.   And for a further prevention of that abominable mixture and spurious issue, which hereafter may increase in this her majesty's colony and dominion, as well by English, and other white men and women intermarrying with negros or mulattos, as by their unlawful coition with them, *Be it enacted, by the authority aforesaid, and it is hereby enacted,* That whatsoever English, or other white man or woman, being free, shall intermarry with a negro or mulatto man or woman, bond or free, shall, by judgment of the county court, be committed to prison, and there remain, during the space of six months, without bail or mainprize; and shall forfeit and pay ten pounds current money of Virginia, to the use of the parish, as aforesaid. [1705] . . .

An Act to amend the Act, intituled an
Act to amend the Act for the better
government of Servants and Slaves.

I.   WHEREAS by an act of the General Assembly made in the twenty-second year of his late majesty George the second, intituled An Act directing the trial of slaves committing capital crimes, and for the more effectual punishing conspiracies and insurrections of them, and for the better government of negroes, mulattoes, and Indians, bond or free, the county courts within this dominion are impowered to punish outlying slaves who cannot be reclaimed, by dismembering such slaves; which punishment is often disproportioned to the offence, and contrary to the principles of humanity: *Be it therefore enacted, by the Governor, Council, and Burgesses, of this present General Assembly, and it is hereby enacted by the authority of the same,* That it shall not be lawful for any county court to order and direct castration of any slave, except such slave shall be convicted of an attempt to ravish a white woman, in which case they may inflict such punishment; any thing in the said recited act, to the contrary, notwithstanding. [1769] . . .

3. William Bradford Witnesses "Wickedness Breaking Forth" in Puritan Plymouth, 1642

Marvelous it may be to see and consider how some kind of wickedness did grow and break forth here, in a land where the same was so much witnessed against and so narrowly looked unto, and severely punished when it was known, as in no place more, or so much, that I have known or heard of; insomuch that they have been somewhat censured even by moderate and good men for their severity in punishments. And yet all this could not suppress the breaking out of sundry notorious sins (as this year, besides other, gives us too many sad precedents and instances), especially drunkenness and uncleanness. Not only incontinency between persons unmarried, for which many both men and women have been punished sharply enough, but some married persons also. But that which is worse, even sodomy and buggery (things fearful to name) have broke forth in this land oftener than once.

I say it may justly be marveled at and cause us to fear and tremble at the consideration of our corrupt natures, which are so hardly bridled, subdued and mortified; nay, cannot by any other means but the powerful work and grace of God's Spirit. But (besides this) one reason may be that the Devil may carry a greater spite against the churches of Christ and the gospel here, by how much the more they endeavour to preserve holiness and purity amongst them and strictly punisheth the contrary when its ariseth either in church or commonwealth; that he might cast a blemish and stain upon them in the eyes of [the] world, who use to be rash in judgment. I would rather think thus, than that Satan hath more power in these heathen lands, as some have thought, than in more Christian nations, especially over God's servants in them.

2. Another reason may be, that it may be in this case as it is with waters when their streams are stopped or dammed up. When they get passage they flow with more

---

William Bradford, "Wickedness Breaks Forth" and "A Horrible Case of Bestiality" (1642), in *Of Plymouth Plantation, 1620–1647*, ed. Samuel Eliot Morison (New York: Knopf, 1952), 316–317, 320–322.

violence and make more noise and disturbance than when they are suffered to run quietly in their own channels; so wickedness being here more stopped by strict laws, and the same more nearly looked unto so as it cannot run in a common road of liberty as it would and is inclined, it searches everywhere and at last breaks out where it gets vent.

3. A third reason may be, here (as I am verily persuaded) is not more evils in this kind, nor nothing near so many by proportion as in other places, but they are here more discovered and seen and made public by due search, inquisition and due punishment; for the churches look narrowly to their members, and the magistrates over all, more strictly than in other places. Besides, here the people are but few in comparison of other places which are full and populous and lie hid, as it were, in a wood or thicket and many horrible evils by that means are never seen nor known; whereas here they are, as it were, brought into the light and set in the plain field, or rather on a hill, made conspicuous to the view of all. . . .

. . . There was a youth whose name was Thomas Granger. He was servant to an honest man of Duxbury, being about 16 or 17 years of age. (His father and mother lived at the same time at Scituate.) He was this year detected of buggery, and indicted for the same, with a mare, a cow, two goats, five sheep, two calves and a turkey. Horrible it is to mention, but the truth of the history requires it. He was first discovered by one that accidentally saw his lewd practice towards the mare. (I forbear particulars.) Being upon it examined and committed, in the end he not only confessed the fact with that beast at that time, but sundry times before and at several times with all the rest of the forenamed in his indictment. And this his free confession was not only in private to the magistrates (though at first he strived to deny it) but to sundry, both ministers and others; and afterwards, upon his indictment, to the whole Court and jury; and confirmed it at his execution. And whereas some of the sheep could not so well be known by his description of them, others with them were brought before him and he declared which were they and which were not. And accordingly he was cast by the jury and condemned, and after executed about the 8th of September, 1642. A very sad spectacle it was. For first the mare and then the cow and the rest of the lesser cattle were killed before his face, according to the law, Leviticus xx.15; and then he himself was executed. The cattle were all cast into a great and large pit that was digged of purpose for them, and no use made of any part of them.

Upon the examination of this person and also of a former that had made some sodomitical attempts upon another, it being demanded of them how they came first to the knowledge and practice of such wickedness, the one confessed he had long used it in old England; and this youth last spoken of said he was taught it by another that had heard of such things from some in England when he was there, and they kept cattle together. By which it appears how one wicked person may infect many, and what care all ought to have what servants they bring into their families.

But it may be demanded how came it to pass that so many wicked persons and profane people should so quickly come over into this land and mix themselves amongst them? Seeing it was religious men that began the work and they came for religion's sake? I confess this may be marveled at, at least in time to come, when the reasons thereof should not be known; and the more because here was so many hardships and wants met withal. I shall therefore endeavour to give some answer hereunto.

1. And first, according to that in the gospel, it is ever to be remembered that where the Lord begins to sow good seed, there the envious man will endeavour to sow tares.

2. Men being to come over into a wilderness, in which much labour and service was to be done about building and planting, etc. such as wanted help in that respect, when they could not have such as they would, were glad to take such as they could; and so, many untoward servants, sundry of them proved, that were thus brought over, both men and womenkind who, when their times were expired, became families of themselves, which gave increase hereunto.

3. Another and a main reason hereof was that men, finding so many godly disposed persons willing to come into these parts, some began to make a trade of it, to transport passengers and their goods, and hired ships for that end. And then, to make their freight and advance their profit, cared not who the persons were, so they had money to pay them. And by this means the country became pestered with many unworthy persons who, being come over, crept into one place or other.

4. Again, the Lord's blessing usually following His people as well in outward as spiritual things (though afflictions be mixed withal) do make many to adhere to the People of God, as many followed Christ for the loaves' sake (John vi.26) and a "mixed multitude" came into the wilderness with the People of God out of Egypt of old (Exodus xii.38). So also there were sent by their friends, some under hope that they would be made better; others that they might be eased of such burthens, and they kept from shame at home, that would necessarily follow their dissolute courses. And thus, by one means or other, in 20 years' time it is a question whether the greater part be not grown the worser?

4. Thomas or Thomasine? A Case of Transvestism in Virginia, 1629

Examinations taken before *John Pott* Esq[r] governo[r] the 25th day of *March A[nno]* [1629]

ffrancis England of the age of twenty yeares or thereabouts sworne and examined saith That *Thomas Hall* (being examined by Cap: *Basse* wether hee were man or woeman (as himselfe did confesse to this [witness]) toulde this [witness] that hee answered Cap[t]: *Basse* that hee was both man and woeman[.] And this [witness] further sayth that the said *Hall* being at *Atkins arbor* one *Nicholas* . . . asked him why hee went in weomans aparell the said *Hall* answered in the hearing of this dep[onent,] *I goe in weomans aparell to gett a bitt for my Catt*[.] And hee further sayth that there was a Rumo[r] and Report that the said *Hall* did ly wth a maid of M[r] *Richard Bennetts* called *great Besse*[.] And hee likewise sayth that hee this [witness] and one *Roger Rodes* being at the upper plantation after it had beene rumored that the said *Hall* was a man and that hee was put in mans apparell the said *Hall* being then there with them, the said *Rodes* tould *Hall thou hast beene reported to be a woman and now thou art proved to bee a man, I will see what thou carriest*[.]

H. R. McIlwaine, ed., *Minutes of the Council and General Court of Colonial Virginia, 1622–1632* (Richmond, Va.: The Colonial Press/Everett Waddey Co., 1924), 194–195.

Whereuppon the said *Rodes* laid hands uppon the said *Hall,* and this [witness] did soe likewise, and they threw the said *Hall* on his backe, and then this [witness] felt the said *Hall* and pulled out his members whereby it appeared that hee was a Perfect man, and more hee cannot depose.

John Atkins of the age of 29 yeares or thereabouts sworne and examined deposeth and sayth that Mr Stacy having reported that *Hall* now a servante unto this [witness] was as hee thought a man and woeman, not long after, the said *Hall* (being then servante to Rob^{te} *Eyros* and *John Tyos*) and being at *Nicholas Eyros* his howse[,] *Alice Longe Dorothye Rodes* and *Barbara Hall* being at that tyme in the said howse, upon the said Report did search the said *Hall* and found (as they then said) that hee was a man but the said *Tyos* swore the said *Hall* was a woeman (as the said *Dorothy Rodes* did often affirme unto this depo[nent]). Whereuppon Cap: *Basse* examined the said *Hall* in the presence of this dep[onent] whether hee were man or woeman, the said *Hall* replyed hee was both only hee had not the use of the mans p[ar]te [penis] . . . was a peece of fleshe growing at the . . . belly as bigg as the topp of his little finger [an] inch longe[.] [W]hereuppon Capt: *Basse* Commanded [him] to bee put in woemans apparell, but the aforesaid searchers were not fully resolved, but stood in doubte of what they had formerly affirmed, and being (about the twelveth of *february*) at this [witness']s house the said *Hall* dwelling wth him, and finding the said *Hall* asleep did againe search him and then allsoe found the said *Hall* to bee a man and at that presently called this [witness] to see the proof thereof, but the said *Hall* seeming to starre as if shee had beene awake[,] this [witness] lefte him and at that instant Could see nothing[.] But the *Sunday* following, those serchers being againe assembled and the wife of *Allen Kinaston* and the wife of *Ambrose Griffen* being in Company wth them were again desirous to search the said *Hall,* and having searched him in the [presence] of this Deponent did then likewise finde him to bee a man[.] Whereuppon this [witness] asked him if that were all hee had to wch hee answered[,] *I have a peece of an hole* and thereuppon this dep[onent] commanded him to lye on his backe and shew the same[.] And the said woemen searching him againe did againe finde him to bee a man[.] Whereuppon the s[aid witness] did Comaunde him to bee put into mans apparell[.] And the day following went to Captaine *Basse,* and tould him that the said *Hall* was founde to bee a man and desired that hee might be punished for his abuse[.] And this dep[onent] further sayth that the said *Hall* (as this dep[onent] hath heard) did question the said *Alice Long* for reporting that hee had layen wth a mayd of Mr *Richard Bennetts,* to wch shee answered, *I reported it not,* but *Penny* [?] *Tyos* his man reported soe much[.] And this is all this [witness] can say.

Thomas Hall examined saith that hee being born at or neere *Newcastle uppon Tyne* was as hee hath been often tould Christned by the name of *Thomasine* and soe was called and went Clothed in woemans apparell there untill the age of twelve years at wch age the said [Hall's] mother sent him to his Aunte in *London* and there hee lyved ten [?] yeares untill *Cales* Ac[ti]on [i.e., a military engagement], at wch tyme a brother of his being pressed for that service. . . . [Hall] Cut of his heire and Changed his apparell into the fashion of man and went over as a souldier in the *Isle of Ree* being in the habit of a man, from whence when he was retorned hee came to *Plymouth,* and there hee changed himselfe into woemans apparell and made bone lace and did other worke wth his needle, and shortly after Shipping being ready for a voyage into this Country hee Changed againe his apparell into the habit of a man and soe came over into this Country.

It was thereuppon at this Co^{rt} ordered that it shall bee published in the planta-tion where the said *Hall* lyveth that hee is a man and a woeman, and all the Inhabi-tants there may take notice thereof and that hee shall goe Clothed in mans apparell, only his head to bee attired in a Coyfe and Croscloth wth an Apron before him[.] And that hee shall finde sueties for his good behavio^r from Quarter Co^{rt} to Quarter Co^{rt} untill the Co^{rt} shall dischardge him and Capt *Nathaniell Basse* is ordered to see this order executed accordingly.

◧ E S S A Y S

These scholars imaginatively probe court records and other sources to gain insight into a history that would otherwise be difficult to explore. Kathleen Brown, of the University of Pennsylvania, places the case of Thomas or Thomasine Hall in context. She illumi-nates the concerns of Hall's neighbors and colonial authorities, elite and popular beliefs about sexual and gender identity, and the disarray in colonial society that not only per-mitted but even decreed Hall's transvestism. Although common people insisted on binary sexual categories of male and female, they acknowledged in practice that gender identity could be more ambiguous, both masculine and feminine. Consider how Brown reaches these conclusions. Are there other interpretations of Thomas or Thomasine Hall? Like Brown, Richard Godbeer, of the University of California at Riverside, contrasts elite and popular discourse in a study of sodomy in the New England colonies. Ministers and magistrates regarded sodomy as an unnatural, immoral, and disorderly act. Ordinary people, however, recognized that some men had a predilection for sodomy, and they were reluctant to prosecute their neighbors for this behavior, especially if they were of high social standing. Godbeer challenges the prevailing theory that before the modern period people understood the erotic dimension of life in terms of carnal *acts* rather than sexual *identities*. This dichotomy, he argues, is too absolute: sodomitical desire might have been acknowledged by those who enacted and encountered it.

"Changed . . . into the Fashion of Man": The Politics of Sexual Difference in a Seventeenth-Century Anglo-American Settlement

KATHLEEN BROWN

In 1629, the gender identity of servant Thomas Hall stirred controversy among the residents of Warrosquyoacke, Virginia, a small English settlement located across the James River from what the English optimistically called "James Cittie." A recent migrant, Hall soon became the subject of rumors concerning his sexual identity and behavior. A servant man's report that Hall "had layen with a mayd of Mr. Richard Bennetts" may initially have sparked the inquiry that led to questions about Hall's sex. Although fornication was not an unusual offense in the colony—the skewed sex ratio of nearly three men to every one woman and the absence of effective means for

" 'Changed . . . into the fashion of man': The Politics of Sexual Difference in a Seventeenth-Century Anglo-American Settlement" by Kathleen Brown from *Journal of the History of Sexuality* 6 (1995): 171–193. Copyright © 1995 by the University of Texas Press. All rights reserved.

restraining servants' sexual activities produced a bastardy rate significantly higher than that in England—Hall's response to the charge and the subsequent behavior of his neighbors were quite out of the ordinary. When allegations of sexual misconduct and ambiguous sexual identity reached the ears of several married women, Hall's case spiraled into a unique community-wide investigation that eventually crossed the river to the colony's General Court at Jamestown.

Court testimony revealed that while in England, Hall had worn women's clothing and performed traditionally female tasks such as needlework and lace making. Once in Virginia, Hall also occasionally donned female garb, a practice that confused neighbors, masters, and plantation captains about his social and sexual identity. When asked by Captain Nathaniel Bass, Warrosquyoacke's most prominent resident, "whether he were man or woeman," Hall replied that he was both. Confounded by the discrepancy between Hall's purported male identity and his appearance, another man inquired why he wore women's clothes. Hall answered, "I goe in weomans aparell to gett a bitt for my Catt." As rumors continued to circulate, Hall's current master John Atkins remained unsure of his new servant's sex. But the certainty that Hall had perpetrated a great wrong against the residents of Warrosquyoacke with his unusual sartorial style led Atkins to approach Captain Bass, "desir[ing] that hee [Hall] might be punished for his abuse."

Unable to resolve the issue, Warrosquyoacke locals sent Hall's case to the General Court at Jamestown, where details of the community investigation and Hall's personal history were recorded by the clerk. Two witnesses testified to the community's multiple efforts to gather physical evidence. Hall, meanwhile, provided justices with a narrative history of his gender identity. Together, this testimony constitutes the main documentary trail left by the person known variously as Thomas or Thomasine Hall. Other colonial records reveal only a few additional details about this unusual servant and the unprecedented investigation of Hall's body, sexual history, and identity.

Despite the paucity of evidence, Hall's case presents a nonetheless richly detailed glimpse of an early modern community's responses to gender transgression, exposing to view a multiplicity of popular beliefs about sexual difference and the variety of uses to which they could be put by groups of people with different stakes in the social order. In contrast to most of the known European cases of gender transgression in the early modern period, the brief transcript of the Hall case contains a vivid description of the efforts of ordinary people (whom I define here as individuals who did not participate directly in formal legal, medical, or scientific theorizing about sexual difference) to determine a sexually ambiguous person's identity. Faced with an individual who did not conform to conventional gender categories, the residents of Warrosquyoacke gathered empirical evidence about Hall's physical body. The subsequent need to report their findings to a superior court compelled people who normally did not articulate their views on sexual difference to define the essence of maleness and femaleness. . . .

Hall's case also offers a unique chance to compare popular concepts of sexual difference, about which little is known, with elite medical and scientific discourses, about which much has been written in recent years. Several scholars have argued that until the early nineteenth century, medico-scientific theories of sexual difference were not based on a model of anatomical incommensurability. Rather, many early modern medical theorists and scientists worked within a predominantly

Galenic framework. . . . Women were not a separate sex, according to this model of difference, but an imperfect version of men. Lacking the vital heat to develop external genitalia, women's deformed organs remained tucked inside. Many early modern writers noted, however, that strenuous physical activity or mannish behavior could cause a woman's hidden testicles and penis to emerge suddenly, an occurrence contemporaries explained as evidence of Nature's unerring tendency toward a state of greater perfection. . . .

Scientific discourses that emphasized anatomical parallels and mutability ultimately left the lion's share of the work of producing gender distinctions to legal and religious institutions, local custom, and daily performance. Borrowing liberally from religious and medical texts that assumed women's inferiority, legal interpreters enshrined gender differences in the laws governing marriage, property, and accountability for crime. Christian theologians similarly reaffirmed gender differences in their divergent assessments of men's and women's capacity for reason and their condemnations of boundary violations as sinful and defiling. In daily life, meanwhile, family and neighbors naturalized gender boundaries by insisting on the continuity of identity established and affirmed through clothing, names, work, and the public approbation accorded to heterosexual relationships. Law, religion, and custom thus stabilized gender although they did so without access to a stable biological concept of sexual difference.

When challenges to early modern categories of manhood and womanhood arose in Christian Europe, as in the case of hermaphroditism or transvestism, the burden of explicating gender differences fell primarily to the legal apparatus in consultation with academically trained doctors and scientific investigators. . . . [T]he courts, which were mainly concerned to preserve clear gender boundaries rather than explore anomalies, had the power to coerce individuals to alter their gender performances. Rather than insisting that the hermaphrodite had a "true" core sex that could be determined anatomically, early modern legal authorities urged the individual to adopt either a male or female identity. Echoing religious and philosophic treatises that categorized hermaphrodites as monsters, legal discourse reaffirmed gender boundaries by refusing to admit sexual ambiguity legally.

Transvestism, which typically took the form of women dressing as men during the sixteenth and seventeenth centuries, represented a different sort of challenge. While the hermaphrodite embodied the slippery dualism of all sexual identities under the Galenic one-sex model, the transvestite undermined society's ability to use clothing to stabilize distinct sexual identities. . . . Early modern theologians denounced transvestism as a violation of prohibitions spelled out in Deut. 22:5: "the woman shall not wear that which pertaineth unto a man, neither shall a man put on a woman's garment, for all that do so are abominable unto the Lord thy God." Legal institutions similarly attempted to police gender boundaries by punishing cross-dressing harshly. . . .

Complicating the effort to retrieve popular discourses of sexual difference is the fact that accounts of Hall's body and past, like most accounts of early modern gender transgression, were presented in a legal setting where they were subject to the needs of the court. Despite this legal context, the testimony in the Hall case still permits a comparison between community examinations of an ambiguous individual and the subsequent legal process. Energetic and heterogenous community investigations of Hall's identity reflected different philosophies and tactics from those used by Virginia's General Court. While justices inquired politely into Hall's past, seeking historical answers to the question of his identity, most of his neighbors responded to his fluctuating persona with aggressive curiosity about what lay hidden in his breeches. The settler population also had great difficulty reaching consensus; no single popular discourse of sexual difference informed their inquiries, nor did they agree about the meaning of their findings. . . .

Perhaps the most compelling feature of Hall's case is Hall him/herself. Hall's life disrupted the attempts of justices and neighbors alike to treat gender as a set of natural categories. For Hall, the "performance" of gender identity appeared to be as malleable as a change of clothes and at least partially motivated by opportunities for employment. The burgeoning commerce, migration, and national rivalries of the early modern Atlantic world, moreover, had in many ways helped to produce Hall's complex personality. When asked to explain his/her gender identity, Hall produced a narrative in which the visible signs of gender were not passive manifestations of a naturalized, internal identity, but communiqués actively authored and manipulated for public consumption. While Hall seemed utterly at ease with gender as a choice of self-presentation distinct from the issues of identity—a posture I will examine more closely—his metamorphoses provoked both his community and the colonial arm of the state to discover and affix a permanent identity. . . . Hall received a comparatively mild punishment, raising additional questions about the significance of this case.

Let us turn now to the colony of Virginia and to Warrosquyoacke, the settlement where neighbors and plantation commanders found Hall's fluctuating identity so perplexing.

By 1629, Virginia had enjoyed several years of peace and prosperity but was nevertheless considered an undesirable and dangerous place by many English men and women. Two decades of warfare with local Indians culminated in an Indian attack upon the English population in 1622, a bloody event that tarnished the colony's early image as a paradise for settlers. Reports of rampant disease, maltreated servants, and backbreaking labor, moreover, filtered back to England, discouraged female migrants, and exacerbated the skewed sex ratio and climate of lawlessness that prevailed among the colony's predominantly young, male, and unmarried settlers. The difficulty of attracting dedicated ministers and supporting churches in a region where the sparse European population was scattered over miles of riverine settlements rather than clustered in towns further contributed to the colony's reputation for godlessness and immorality. In addition, by 1629, the colonial economy was firmly committed to the production of tobacco, a New World tropical commodity that had become fashionable to royal and aristocratic circles throughout Europe. Despite the efforts of local officials to encourage economic diversification, most of the colony's landowners devoted themselves to tobacco and to procuring the labor necessary to its production. English laborers, especially men, were the preference of most planters, although by 1629 a newcomer to Virginia might have seen English women or African laborers, male and female, hoeing rows of tobacco.

A fledgling plantation in a colony where everything was relatively new, Warrosquyoacke had been an English settlement for less than seven years when Thomas Hall arrived. Founded on the site of an Indian village, the settlement consisted of two plantations devoted to the production of tobacco: "Bennett's Welcome" . . . [and] "Basse's Choice." . . .

Compared to the English cities and towns the Virginia colonists had left behind, Warrosquyoacke was a tiny community filled with newcomers. It is doubtful that the settlement ever exceeded two hundred people during the 1620s. . . . Of the sixteen individuals named in the Hall testimony, seven can be positively identified as residents of the colony in 1625. . . . [O]nly three appear to have lived in Warrosquyoacke before 1627 [w]hen Hall moved [there]. . . .

Only two of those named in the court testimony could boast a lengthy tenure in Warrosquyoacke: [Captain Nathaniel] Bass, the plantation commander [and proprietor], and Alice Long, who had married and borne at least one child in Virginia since her arrival in the colony in 1620. At thirty-nine and twenty-seven, respectively, both individuals were seasoned veterans of the south-side plantations, embodying whatever traditions had endured the traumatic and disrupted history of English settlement. In 1629, while Bass enjoyed a position of political authority [representing the plantation in the House of Burgesses], Long claimed informal influence among the several dozen women in the settlement. Although the records do not reveal how she spent her days, it is likely that as a married woman and mother of nearly ten years' residency, she had witnessed betrothals, delivered babies, nursed the sick, and buried many dead. Bass may have been the settlement's official representative, but Long undoubtedly knew the intimate details of the lives of many of its residents.

A few other individuals who became involved in the Hall case had been in the colony, if not in Warrosquyoacke itself, for several years before Hall's arrival. John Atkins, Hall's new master at the time of the inquest at Jamestown, arrived in the colony in 1623. Roger Rodes, who appears to have been living in Jamestown in 1625, was married to Dorothy Rodes, one of the matrons who assisted Alice Long in her investigation of Hall's body. John Tyos, described in the court testimony as a former master of Hall's, also had a history in the colony long enough to have included association with at least two men named Thomas Hall.

The last individual to have a major role in Warrosquyoacke's attempts to determine Hall's identity was John Pott, the governor of the colony who presided over the colony's General Court. A medical doctor who had lived in the colony since 1620, Pott did not reside in Warrosquyoacke, but on one of several tracts of land he had acquired on the north side of the James River. By the time of Hall's case, Pott had overcome several setbacks to achieve a position of political and economic prominence in the colony. In 1629, with much of the earlier controversy behind him, Pott moved up from being a council member to assume the role of acting governor of the colony.

The community investigations of Hall's body that took place in Warrosquyoacke in early 1629 occurred not at the behest of Governor Pott, however, but as a consequence of local concerns for social order. Lacking many of the traditional institutions of English village life, the small English community depended instead on highly personal forms of authority. Despite the high mortality in Warrosquyoacke, the steady influx of immigrants, and the dispersed pattern of settlement, its size and situation may have rendered social relations even more intimate than those in the smallest English villages. The anonymity made possible by immigration and settlement among strangers was thus offset by sparse population. This was not an intimacy built on families tightly interwoven for several generations, however, or long-standing geographical rootedness—conditions that did not prevail even in many English villages—but on a very limited universe of face-to-face interactions.

As Warrosquyoacke residents mobilized personal networks to address Hall's transgression, at least three converging lines of authority emerged. The first—embodied by Bass and Bennett—derived its strength from the official mandates of the governor, the General Court, and the Crown. The second, which included John Tyos and John Atkins, represented the community of masters and their interests in maintaining existing labor arrangements with servants. The third, a source of authority largely internal to the community, was constituted by women such as Alice Long and Dorothy Rodes.

Boasting nearly as much influence as its male counterparts, female authority in Warrosquyoacke accrued from the important role granted midwives and matrons by English law. In cases in which the condition of a woman's body could influence the verdict or sentence, English courts constituted an investigatory jury of women to conduct an examination. After searching the subject's body for evidence of recent sexual activity, pregnancy, or childbirth (or, in case of suspected witchcraft, suspicious marks), the matrons reported their findings to the court. . . . With minor deviations, the tradition of summoning the matrons' jury appears to have continued in Virginia. . . .

The authority of the Warrosquyoacke matrons might also have derived from the heightened significance of their legal and historical functions in Virginia. In a small community that lacked rival institutions of historical memory, Long and Rodes . . . were repositories of information about community relationships, personal histories, and identities. These activities did not naturally constitute female authority. Rather, women's authority derived from . . . their claims to interpret female bodies—a practice that required constituting the subjects of their inquiry (women) as well as their own authority to make sense of these bodies. Female authority to interpret female bodies depended in part, however, on the apparent naturalness of sexual categories. Without the existence of two sexes, women's claims to special knowledge would have been unfounded and their unique roles in courtroom and community unnecessary. Women such as Long and Rodes thus had an important stake in protecting gender boundaries and enforcing the rules governing sexual behavior. Their authority resided in categories of sexual difference that Hall's changes of clothes threatened to undermine.

This then was Warrosquyoacke in 1629, a community less than ten years old overseen by men and women with a maximum of six or seven years of colonial life under their belts, where intimate forms of authority diverged along gendered lines.

The first to lay hands on Hall for the purposes of gathering information was a group of women whose interest had been piqued by a "report" that Hall was both a man and a woman. Groups of women usually searched only other women at the request of a local court; their authority to glean information from bodies rarely crossed gender lines and they did not usually initiate a search without the backing of local officials. With Hall's then-master, John Tyos, claiming his servant was female, however, the women decided that it was appropriate to intervene. Searching Hall's person for evidence of his sexual identity, Alice Long, Dorothy Rodes, and a third woman, Barbara Hall, concluded that "hee was a man." Despite this new evidence, Master Tyos continued to swear to Hall's female identity, provoking John Atkins, who was contemplating the purchase of Hall, to take the problem to plantation commander Captain Bass.

Confronted with the array of conflicting evidence—the rumors of Hall's hermaphroditism and alleged fornication, Hall's master's claim that his servant was a woman, and the married women's findings that he was male—Bass asked Hall point-blank "whether hee were man or woeman." Hall answered that he was both, explaining that although he had what appeared to be a very small penis ("a peece of flesh growing at the . . . belly as bigg as the topp of his little finger [an] inch long"), "hee had not the use of the man's p[ar]te." Hearing this confession, Bass ordered Hall to put on women's clothes. Although difficult to prove in court, male impotence was considered sufficient grounds for the annulment of marriages; it became for Bass, in this instance, a sufficient condition for determining female gender identity. An individual who lacked male sexual functions and sometimes dressed like a woman, Bass may have reasoned, could safely be classified as a woman.

Bass's decision did not sit well with the group of married women who claimed to have seen evidence of Hall's manhood. But with Hall parading about Warrosquyoacke in the mandated female attire, they also began to "doubte of what they had formerly affirmed." Trooping over to Hall's residence at the home of his new master, John Atkins, the group searched the female-clad Hall while he slept, confirming their original judgment that he was a man. In an unusual breech of etiquette, moreover, they insisted that Master Atkins view the proof for himself. Atkins tiptoed to Hall's bed but lost his nerve when "shee" stirred in her sleep. So convincing a woman was Hall that Atkins abandoned the idea of undressing the sleeping servant. In subsequent descriptions of this incident before the General Court, Atkins found it impossible to describe Hall with other than female pronouns.

Tenacious in their quest to reveal the "truth" to Atkins and to two other women who had joined their ranks—and perhaps still harboring doubts themselves—the married women planned a third search of Hall's person. When Atkins finally saw the evidence of Hall's manhood he was unimpressed and asked Hall "if that were all hee had." Perhaps Atkins, like Hall himself, doubted the significance of the small "peece of flesh" protruding from Hall's belly and wondered whether there might be other anatomical clues. Describing his identity for the first time as the presence of female anatomy rather than as a lack or deformity of maleness, Hall told Atkins that he had "a peece of an hole." Atkins immediately insisted that Hall lie down and "shew" these female credentials. After searching together in vain for Hall's vagina, Atkins and the married women concluded that Hall could not be a hermaphrodite. Although Hall's penis may have been tiny and in poor working order, it became for Atkins and the matrons, in the absence of other "evidence" of femaleness, the dominant criterion for Hall's social identity. In sharp contrast to the language Hall used to describe his own freewheeling sense of chosen identities, Atkins ordered Hall to "bee put into" male apparel and urged Captain Bass to punish him for his "abuse."

As soon as Captain Bass reversed his decision about Hall's gender identity and proclaimed him to be a man, Hall became fair game for the men of Warrosquyoacke. Hearing a "rumor and report" of Hall's tryst with Mr. Richard Bennett's maid Great Besse, Francis England and Roger Rodes took advantage of a chance meeting with Hall to conduct their own impromptu investigation. Rodes declared, "Hall thou hast beene reported to be a woman and now thou art p[ro]ved to bee a man, I will see what thou carriest." Assisted by England, Rodes threw Hall onto his back. England later told the General Court that when he "felt the said Hall and pulled out his members," he found him to be "a perfect man."

The declarations of evidence and the conclusions drawn from that evidence bring us as close as I believe we will ever be to ordinary seventeenth-century English people's articulated beliefs in the essence of sexual difference and their deployment of those beliefs to serve their own political and social interests. Three groups of people—the married women, Hall's former and present masters, and the plantation commander—participated actively in these searches of Hall's person. In the absence of a county court and church, these groups represented the community's interests in determining Hall's gender. Significantly, each group also had a personal stake in defending the boundaries of maleness and femaleness. Married women, who normally interpreted women's bodies for legal authorities, intervened because Hall's crossing of gender lines challenged fundamental gender differences on which their authority was based. Hall's masters' interest in determining the sex of their servant suggested the significance of gender to the allocation of labor, an especially important issue in this new settlement so single-mindedly devoted to producing tobacco. Hall's gender identity may have influenced Master John Atkins in the work he assigned him, the sexual intimacies he did or did not attempt, and the company he allowed his servant to keep. Male servants would likely be pressed into participating in the militia at some point during their service. Male and female servants also received different freedom dues and were expected to assume different social and economic roles at the end of their terms. Charged with keeping order in the community, plantation commanders sought a permanent identity for Hall that would mollify the displeased masters and matrons of the community, restore Hall to his proper place in that community, and, above all, establish the commander's ability to resolve community conflicts successfully.

Roger Rodes and Francis England, whose interests in Hall's identity were slightly more attenuated but who nonetheless asserted their right to intervene, constituted a fourth group. Lacking any formal authority to search bodies except in the case of grand jury inquests into murder, Rodes and England could not claim the customary role or territorial interest of the matrons, the immediate interests of masters, or the political authority of the plantation commander. . . . Yet the two men still intruded themselves into the process, perhaps seeing the unprecedented nature of the case as an opportunity for expanding the scope of their own authority in the community, for satisfying their curiosity, or for punishing Hall informally for his masquerade.

The matrons of Warrosquyoacke, the community's plantation commander, and Hall's masters were initially at odds over the issue of his gender, issuing conflicting conclusions and repeating their processes of gathering evidence as they struggled to move toward a consensus. After the matrons' initial examination of Hall and their conclusion that he was a man, Captain Bass undermined them, reasoning from Hall's confession of impotence, rather than from the women's testimony, that Hall was a woman. The married women did not let this breech of their traditional legal role go unchallenged. To do so would have been to suffer a severe loss of credibility and influence. It seems that they may also have harbored doubts about the nature of the evidence they had uncovered, for they quickly instigated a second search. When this examination confirmed their initial pronouncement, they enlisted a man from the group of masters with an interest in Hall's case, thereby creating a coalition of women and men to confront Captain Bass. Despite their influence in Warrosquy-oacke, women's word alone was not sufficient to lead Bass to change his mind. In league with Atkins, however, the married women's information persuaded Bass to contradict his own command and order Hall to don male clothes.

In addition to their difficulties with rival male authorities in their community, however, the married women faced the challenge of interpreting Hall's unusual body. As they did not describe their findings in detail—or those descriptions did not reach the records of the General Court—we can only speculate about their analysis of the evidence. The presence of a penis, however small and ineffective, seems to have weighed heavily in their conclusion that Hall was a man. But their articulated doubts and subsequent search for a vagina suggests the difficulty of fitting Hall's body into familiar categories. . . . Unlike the bodies of men, a woman's body was believed to bear the marks of her sexual and reproductive history. Married women in most early modern European societies wielded influence in courtrooms in part because they had constructed a folk science of extracting sexual histories from female bodies by "read-ing" these marks. Virginity, recent sexual intercourse, rape, childbirth, sex with the devil—all carried corresponding physical signs in the science of midwifery and were probably equally significant, if not as systematically delineated, for matrons called on by their communities to translate this evidence into legal testimony. Hall's penis may not then have been the only reason the women defined him as male. The absence of a readable set of female genitalia—not to be confused with the absence of that genitalia altogether—may also have led the women to pronounce Hall a man in con-tradiction to Hall's own declarations and the opinions of two men, including his cur-rent master. Implicitly, the women reaffirmed that femaleness consisted not simply of conformity to a particular genital anatomy, but of a quality of plastic impression-ability such that sexual and reproductive histories could be gleaned from the body. By both of these criteria, Hall's body proved ineligible for womanhood.

Curiously, the matrons of Warrosquyoacke chose not to involve Great Besse, the servant rumored to have had a tryst with Hall, in their deliberations. In the absence of any additional information about Hall's alleged lover, we can only com-ment on the possible and probable reasons for her silence in the court record. Besse could possibly have been one of the tiny number of Africans who lived in the colony after 1619 and, as a consequence, may not have spoken much English; the chances are, however, that she would have been described in the testimony as a "negor" rather than as a "servant maid." It is less likely that Besse was an Indian, as few Indians were held as servants or slaves in the colony until the middle of the century. A less intriguing but more plausible scenario is that Besse was an English-woman whose link to Hall was so quickly proven to be unfounded that there was no need to pursue her testimony.

Able to reach only a shaky consensus on the question of Hall's gender identity and unsure of how to punish his transgression, Warrosquyoacke locals sent Hall's case to the General Court at Jamestown. Under the leadership of the recently in-stalled governor, John Pott, the General Court declined to initiate their own search of Hall's body. . . . Nor did the Court invite the married women to report their find-ings directly. They listened instead to Francis England's and John Atkins's accounts of Hall's gender mutability and then "examined" Hall juridically, eliciting a narra-tive of gender identity.

Hall explained that he had been christened Thomasine in England and dressed accordingly in women's clothes. When "she" reached the age of twelve, an age at which many girls would have taken up residence with neighbors or relatives to learn housewifery, Thomasine was sent by her mother to London to live with an aunt. During her ten-year residence in the city, Thomasine could have witnessed the crossover of male and female aristocratic fashions that so disturbed James I. London's female street culture might also have had a profound impact on the young Thomasine, offering lessons in market savvy, sexuality, and marriage to all who listened to the ribald balladry of an itinerant performer or picked up a discarded broadside.

If at this point in Hall's narrative justices harbored hopes that an established pattern of female identity, deeply rooted in Hall's childhood, would put an end to the confusion, they were to be sadly disappointed. Hall continued, informing the justices that when his brother was pressed into military service, Thomasine "Cut of[f] his heire and Changed his apparell into the fashion of man" to become a soldier in the English force that intervened on behalf of French Huguenots at the Isle of Rhe. Twenty-four years old when he made this transformation, Hall was indeed lucky to survive his first year as a man. The military adventure proved to be a debacle, with nearly half of the eight thousand English troops killed or left behind in France. Upon returning to England, Hall "changed himself into woeman's apparell," resuming both female identity and needlework. Residing in the port of Plymouth, which was by the mid-1620s a point of embarkation for many colonial voyages, Hall remained a woman until the opportunity arose to sail for Virginia. He "changed againe his apparell into the habit of a man and soe came over into this Country" sometime late in 1627.

Both the evidence gathered by the community and Hall's own historical narrative of identity figured in the General Court's sentence of Hall. Compelling Hall to don men's breeches, the court acknowledged the weight of the physical manifestations of sex that were of such importance to the diligent matrons of Warrosquyoacke. Governor Pott may have encouraged this anatomical interpretation of gender identity, having previously served the colony as a doctor. But the court did not find the physical evidence or the sentence of an imposed (and permanent) male identity sufficient. Their order that the male-clad Hall should mark his head and lap with female accessories—"a Coyfe and Croscloth with an Apron before him"—attested to their power to punish by inscribing dissonant gender symbols on an offender, in this case, by demeaning a man with the visible signs of womanhood. Such a sentence mimicked Hall's crime of diminishing the integrity of his male identity with female garb. The sentence may also have been the justice's admission that self-confessed impotence, cross-dressing, and a history of female identity compromised an individual's claims to the political and legal privileges of manhood.

The court's decision that Hall should wear male attire topped by the apron and headdress of a woman seems at one level to affirm Hall's claim to a dual nature by creating a separate category for him. Yet Hall himself never expressed his hermaphroditism in this fashion, choosing instead to perform his identity serially as either male or female. The judges' mandate of a permanent hybrid identity for Hall was thus both a punishment and an unprecedented juridical response to gender ambiguity. Denying Hall the right to choose a single identity—a marked departure from the usual European treatment of hermaphrodites—the judges asserted the importance of permanence for social constructs of gender even as they failed to define

its essence. They may have believed they had found a creative solution to the problem of defending the boundaries of both maleness and femaleness from Hall's transgressive behavior. That they chose to shame him rather than inflict brutal corporeal
punishment suggests that the court recognized Hall's value to his masters and to the
colony as a laborer.

The court never addressed the matter of Hall's culpability for fornication. Nor
did it address the consequences of the court-ordered hermaphroditic identity for
Hall's future sexual activity. Rather, it concerned itself with "publish[ing]" the fact
that Hall was "a man and a woeman" in Warrosquyoacke so that "all the Inhabitants
there may take notice thereof." In doing this the court may have sought to prevent
unwitting men from committing sodomy with the ambiguous Hall. Perhaps, too,
the justices were trying to warn unsuspecting women not to allow him too much intimacy. They did take the precaution of requiring Hall to find sureties for his good
behavior until the local court of Warrosquyoacke discharged him. Good behavior
in this case seems to have meant both constancy of performed identity and compliance with the court-ordered signature of hermaphroditism, the mixture of male
and female garb.

. . . The court's decision to have Hall wear the clothing of both man and woman
did not solve many of the dilemmas that had initially compelled Warrosquyoacke
residents to approach their plantation commander. Master Atkins, for instance, was
probably no closer to determining Hall's work assignment or freedom dues than he
had been at the beginning of the investigation. Sadly, we will never know just how
Hall's community addressed the problems raised by the court's sentence.

Despite the differences between the General Court's focus on establishing
identity from a narrative of performance and the Warrosquyoacke matrons' insistent search for readable physical evidence, the two groups may have shared a belief
in the essential historicity of female identity. . . .When Hall's body proved resistant
to being read [for the impressions of sexual histories], the married women may
have been inclined to see the "peece of flesh" as a penis and to categorize "him" as
a man. For the General Court, conversely, Hall's historical narrative of sexual identity. . . made it difficult for the court to assign him a legal identity. . . . Although
courts across the early modern world recognized maturation to manhood as an inherently teleological feature of male identity, adult manhood brought a stabilizing
conclusion, vulnerable only to age and death. Hall's changes of gender as an adult
may thus have precluded him from the privileges of manhood, provoking the court
to tag him with clothing that symbolized the mutable quality of female bodies.

Although it is easy to appreciate the unique features of the Hall case, it is no
less important to identify the broad contours of early modern Atlantic history that
are implicated in Hall's narrative of identity. . . .

Hall anchored his account of shifting identities in the major historical events
of the early seventeenth century. In his narrative, English military mobilization
provoked the initial transformation "into the fashion of a man." Military defeat and
a return to England led to a reaffirmation of female social identity and domestic
work. England's colonial aspirations in the New World created an opportunity for
migration that Hall rather significantly decided to seize as a man.

Hall's mutability was also emblematic of the ambiguous and tentative identities
of English peoples recently settled in the New World. Many conditions contributed

to the instability of English identities in Virginia, but among the most significant
challenges were the encounter with a Native American gender division of labor that
differed significantly from that of the English, the demands of the colonial economy
for a more flexible division of labor than that which existed in England, the difficulty of translating English symbols and institutions of political authority into a
colonial idiom, and the existence of powerful women in a society committed to, but
only partially able to replicate, English-style patriarchal institutions. Hall's self-
fashioned gender identity presented a baffling challenge to these already shaky
articulations of English identity and political authority. Reports of Hall's hermaphroditism led to public refutations of the conclusions of matrons, masters, and plantation commanders. Hall's ability to tangle the lines of authority, forcing residents of
Warrosquyoacke to improvise, was perhaps most evident in the unprecedented coed
search for female genitalia. The attempts of community leaders and justices to define and "fix" Hall's identity reveals the complex ways in which the ideal of clear
gender distinctions was an integral part of their vision of an orderly, stable society.

In addition, Hall's narrative of identity appears to conform to the patterns of
other gender transgression narratives of the same period. In the story of Elena de
Cespedes, a sixteenth-century Spanish individual of indeterminate sex, the transformation from femaleness to maleness is similarly described as including the adoption of male dress and military service, leading ultimately to a series of inspections
at the hands of neighbors, local magistrates, and the Inquisition. Catalina de Erauso,
an early seventeenth-century Spanish nun, metamorphosed her gender by changing
her name and her habit and fleeing to the New World, where she served in the Spanish army. Upon returning to Spain in 1624, she received a pension and papal permission to continue dressing like a man. Several Dutch women, including Maritgen
Jens and Maria van Antwerpen, changed their identities to leave low-paying employment in needlework and domestic service for more promising careers in silk
thread production and the military. Perhaps most significant to this analysis is the
tale of Mary Frith, which circulated in printed form in London during the years of
Hall's residence there and may have influenced Hall's presentation of personal history as a series of choices about gender performance. Known colloquially as Moll
Cutpurse, Frith experimented with serial identities before deciding to invent a costume that reflected her self-definition as neither man nor woman. Although there is
no evidence of Hall's literacy, the popularity of Frith's tale makes it probable that
even an illiterate London resident might have heard about her.

Several themes in these other stories resonate particularly well with those of
Hall's own narrative: economic exigencies brought about by limited opportunities
for female employment; the cutting of hair, an act replete with classical, biblical,
and sexual meaning; the donning of male clothes for the first time; the establishment of male identity performatively through military service; and the preference
for embarking on colonial adventures as a man. Like the other gender transgressors, Hall described his identity as the performance of tasks and roles. . . .

. . . The similarities in their stories suggest that, by the early seventeenth century, the Atlantic world may already have had its own sexual culture in which the
narratives of gender identity and those of mercantilism and colonization had become mutually implicated in the practice of exploration, conquest, migration, and
commodification.

What distinguishes Hall from the other subjects of these tales is the identity revealed by investigation. In almost every other case of nonaristocratic gender transgression in the early modern period, the ambiguous or "passing" individual is revealed to be a hermaphrodite or a female transvestite. The end of Hall's story takes an unexpected turn, however, with the matrons' conclusion that Hall was really a man. Before 1800, cases of male transvestism outside of aristocratic circles and the theater were extremely rare, and especially unusual in the context of Europe's Atlantic colonies.

. . . In a world in which dressing as a man brought women expanded economic and political opportunities, Hall found it difficult to suppress his female identity. Although he offered a pragmatic and environmental explanation for his cross-dressing . . . which implied the occasional economic advantages of being a woman, very few of his contemporaries, male or female, would have agreed with him. Despite the attendant risks and disadvantages of being female in the seventeenth century, Hall found it personally useful, necessary, or comfortable to dress occasionally as a woman.

Set against other transgression narratives of the period, Hall's stands apart both for the conclusions of his examiners that he was male and for the inability of seventeenth-century medical or economic theories to explain his transformation. Neither moving to a state of greater perfection nor adopting a more expansive social role, Hall left his contemporaries—and, indeed, leaves us—baffled. We might hypothesize that early colonial Virginia, a settlement in which English women were scarce, may have afforded enough opportunities for upward mobility to tempt an individual like Hall to try to take advantage of them. He had, after all, renounced his male identity when such opportunities presented themselves in England. Yet such a theory raises as many questions as it answers. If early seventeenth-century Virginia was so favorable a place for women, why did more women not flock to the colony or more men attempt to pass as female? A more plausible explanation may lie with Hall himself. Perhaps "his" female identity was so deeply embedded as a consequence of a childhood and adolescence of female training and identification that he could not shed it. . . .

We can only speculate about what, if anything, the different conclusions about Hall's sex may have had in common. . . . As the perplexity of Hall's neighbors and the sentence meted out by the General Court suggest, ordinary people's concepts of sexual difference could not be easily reconciled with the behavior of an individual who periodically "changed himself . . . into the fashion of man."

Sodomy in Colonial New England

RICHARD GODBEER

Nicholas Sension settled in Windsor, Connecticut, around 1640, married in 1645, and became a prosperous member of his community during the ensuing years. Sension's marriage was childless, but his life appears to have been otherwise unexceptional save in one regard: in 1677, he appeared before the colony's General Court,

Richard Godbeer, " 'The Cry of Sodom': Discourse, Intercourse, and Desire in Colonial New England," *William and Mary Quarterly*, 3rd Series, 52 (April 1995): 259–286. Reprinted by permission of the Omohundro Institute of Early American History and Culture, *William and Mary Quarterly*.

charged with sodomy. The frank and detailed testimony presented to the court by neighbors and acquaintances left no room for doubt that Sension had made sexual advances to many men in his community over a period of three decades. These advances, deponents claimed, had often taken the form of attempted assault:

> I was in the mill house . . . and Nicholas Sension was with me, and he took me and threw me on the chest, and took hold of my privy parts. [c. 1648]

> I went out upon the bank to dry myself [after swimming], and the said Sension came to me with his yard or member erected in his hands, and desired me to lie on my belly, and strove with me, but I went away from him. [c. 1658]

On other occasions Sension had offered to pay for sex: "He told me," claimed Peter Buoll, "if I would let him have one bloo [blow] at my breech he would give me a charge of powder."

Town elders had investigated Sension's behavior and reprimanded him informally on two occasions, first in the late 1640s and again in the late 1660s. Both investigations were prompted by complaints from relatives of young men who had been approached by Sension. Yet no formal action was taken against him until 1677. Fortunately for the defendant, although several men came forward at the trial to describe his unsuccessful overtures, only one claimed that Sension had actually "committed the sin of sodomy." Because this was a capital crime that required two witnesses for a conviction, Sension could be found guilty only of attempted sodomy. And although convicted of the lesser charge, he was not even whipped or fined, though his entire estate was placed in bond for his good behavior. Sension died twelve years later. No information survives to indicate whether he changed his ways as a result of the prosecution.

Nicholas Sension's experience raises questions about attitudes toward sex in early New England and the effects of illicit sexual behavior on social relations in local communities. This [essay] explores sodomy as a sexual category and as a social issue in colonial New England. In seeking to understand sodomy and its place in the sexual culture of the northern colonies, I make two assumptions that underlie recent theoretical and historical scholarship. First, sex as a physical act must be distinguished from sexuality, the conceptual apparatus that men and women use to give meaning and value to sexual attraction and its enactment. People never simply have sex; at some level of consciousness, they interpret their behavior in terms of their own and their culture's attitudes toward sex. Sexual acts are thus always "scripted." Second, the meanings ascribed to sex vary from one culture to another, from one place to another, and from one time to another. Although members of different societies may experience similar physical impulses and engage in similar acts, they understand them differently. Sexual categories have no universal signification; they are cultural products, emerging from and contingent on their specific context. Thus, if we are to understand past people's experience of sex, we need to jettison our own notions of sexuality in favor of the categories that they used. Indeed, we cannot assume that sexuality or even desire functions as an independent causal agent in all versions of human subjectivity. Sex acquires meaning in many cultures only as a function of political, economic, social, and religious ideologies.

Theological and legal formulations in early New England, which together constituted the region's official discourse, had no place for desire or sexual orientation as distinct realms of motivation. Puritan thinkers condemned sexual "uncleanness" in general and sodomy in particular as sacrilegious, disorderly acts that resulted from innate depravity, the expression of which did not have to be specifically sexual. The word "lust" denoted any "fleshly" impulse that distracted men and women from "spiritual" endeavors; illicit sex, drunkenness, and personal ambition were equally lustful in Puritan eyes. Official statements on sodomy were sometimes inconsistent in their details, but two fundamentals united them: neither ministers nor magistrates thought of sodomitical acts as being driven by sexual orientation, and they were unequivocally hostile toward those who committed sodomy.

While some ordinary people (by which I mean those who were not invested with clerical, legislative, or judicial authority) doubtless perceived and judged sodomy along lines similar to those advocated by their leaders, others ascribed to it somewhat different meanings and values. The attitudes of colonists toward sodomitical behavior as it occurred in their communities are much more elusive than the legal and theological viewpoints promulgated through sermons, laws, and judicial decisions. Even more obscure are the ways in which people who were attracted to persons of the same sex viewed their own physical impulses. Legal depositions do survive that embody such responses, however, albeit in fragmentary and often oblique form. Whereas ministers perceived sodomy as one of many acts, sexual and nonsexual, that expressed human depravity, some lay persons apparently recognized a specific inclination toward sodomitical behavior in certain individuals. The extant sources reveal a few occasions on which New Englanders, sensing that official discourse was of limited use in making intelligible their actual experiences and observations, created what seemed to them more appropriate categories and frameworks of meaning. This informal and inchoate discourse did not go so far as to invoke a "homosexual" identity as such, but it does seem to have posited an ongoing erotic predilection that transcended the acts themselves. Villagers and townspeople were, moreover, seldom willing to invoke official sanctions against sodomy, despite theological and legal denunciation. Whatever their leaders' expectations, they viewed and treated sodomy on their own terms.

The purpose of this [essay] is to show that attitudes toward sodomy in colonial New England were more varied than has been assumed, in two ways. First, while religious and legal statements match scholarly impressions of premodern sexual discourse as focused on *acts* rather than *identity,* popular perceptions of sodomy sometimes appear closer to the latter, though we should take care not to invest them with a twentieth-century sensibility. Second, not all New Englanders shared the virulent horror of sodomitical acts expressed in official discourse. Some appear to have found other, nonsexual aspects of a person's behavior more significant in determining his or her social worth. What emerges most clearly from the surviving evidence is that, as in so many aspects of their lives, New Englanders were pragmatic in their responses to sodomy, focusing on practical issues rather than moral absolutes.

Responsibility for "put[ting sex] into discourse" in early New England rested with the clergy. It was they who provided the official lens through which colonists were supposed to view sexual impulses. Ministers did not perceive sex as inherently dangerous or evil. Rejecting with scorn the "popish" advocacy of a single and celibate life, Puritans on both sides of the Atlantic taught that God had ordained sexual relations between husband and wife not only to procreate but also to express marital affection. "Conjugal love," wrote Samuel Willard, should be demonstrated through "conjugal union, by which [husband and wife] become one flesh." This oneness was "the nearest relative conjunction in the world . . . follow[ing] from a preference that these have each of other in their hearts, above all the world." Clerics condemned sexual relations in any context other than marriage. All variants of nonmarital sex, they argued, desecrated the bodies and endangered the souls of the perpetrators. "Uncleanness," warned Samuel Danforth, "pollutes the body, and turns the temple of the holy ghost into a hog-sty, and a dog's kennel."

Clerical condemnation of sex outside marriage was not indiscriminate. When New England ministers addressed their congregations on the subject of sexual uncleanness, they were careful to distinguish between different kinds and degrees of offense. Speaking in 1673, Danforth argued that "abominable uncleanness" could be "expressed by and comprehended under these two terms, *fornication,* and *going after strange flesh.*" Danforth explained that *"fornication"* was to be "taken in a large sense" to include four offenses: "whoredom" ("the vitiating of a single woman"), adultery, incest, and "self-pollution." The second category, *"going after strange flesh,"* incorporated sodomy ("filthiness committed by parties of the same sex") and bestiality ("when any prostitute themselves to a beast"). Willard, discussing the Seventh Commandment in a 1704 sermon, used different terminology to make a similar distinction. He told his congregation that "unlawful and prohibited mixtures" could be "ranked under two heads": "natural" and "unnatural." Sodomy and bestiality, he claimed, were "unnatural" because of "the species and sexes" involved, whereas "fornication" (sex "between persons who are single"), adultery, polygamy, and incest were "(in some sense) more natural" because they came "within the compass of the species and sexes."

Danforth and Willard classified sexual acts in terms of those involved and their relationships to each other: their marital status, sex, and species. They and other commentators made a clear distinction between illicit sex performed by a man and woman and that between either two persons of the same sex or a human being and an animal. Clerics believed that women as well as men might engage in sodomitical acts. John Cotton referred to the "unnatural filthiness . . . of man with man, or woman with woman," Thomas Shepard to "secret whoredom, self-pollution, speculative wantonness, men with men, women with women," Charles Chauncy to "unnatural lusts of men with men, or woman with woman," and Samuel Whiting to "unnatural uncleanness . . . when men with men commit filthiness, and women with women." Those who pursued "strange flesh" disrupted the natural order and crossed scripturally ordained boundaries between sexes and species. Such behavior was thus more clearly sinful and disorderly than was uncleanness between a man and a woman. Sodomy, argued John Rayner, was "more against the light of nature" than other sexual offenses between human beings and therefore "needed the more to be restrained and suppressed." Clerical denunciations of sodomy were harsh and unequivocal. New England, wrote Chauncy, was "defiled by such sins." These were, declared Cotton Mather, "vile . . . unutterable abominations and confusions." They should be punished "with death, without mercy."

Although ministers defined sodomy as involving two persons of the same sex, the notion of sexual orientation had no place in their discourse; nor did they evoke desire as an independent agency that gave rise to sexual acts. They explained sodomy just as they did all other sins, sexual and nonsexual: it was driven by the innate corruption of fallen humanity and embodied disobedience to God's will. . . . Because sodomitical uncleanness was founded in universal corruption, the temptation to commit sodomy afflicted everyone. Even those who remained innocent of particular sinful acts were guilty in their hearts if not in deed. Shepard reminded his congregation that they were all guilty of "heart whoredom, heart sodomy, heart blasphemy, heart drunkenness, heart buggery, heart oppression, [and] heart idolatry." . . .

. . . Throughout the seventeenth century, ministers were quite unequivocal in their definition of sodomy [as] . . . sex between men or between women. Ministers did not discuss the possibility that anal sex between a man and a woman or nonprocreative sex in general might constitute sodomy. They focused on the violation of boundaries between the sexes, not rectal penetration or sodomy's nonreproductive character. The word had for them a distinct meaning, even though the phenomenon to which it referred should, they insisted, be understood in tandem with, not in isolation from, other sins.

New England laws against sodomy generally followed clerical example in defining the crime as an act that involved "parties of the same sex." The legal codes, however, focused much more specifically on male sex than did clerical pronouncements. The Plymouth, Massachusetts, Connecticut, and New Hampshire laws quoted verbatim Leviticus 20:13: "If any man lyeth with mankind, as he lyeth with a woman, both of them have committed abomination; they both shall surely be put to death." Rhode Island adopted the language of Romans I:26–27, defining sodomy as "a vile affection, whereby men given up thereto leave the natural use of woman and burn in their lusts one toward another, and so men with men work that which is unseemly." . . .

New Haven's sodomy law [passed in 1655] differed . . . from the codes adopted elsewhere in New England. Much more detailed and including a broad range of sexual acts, its definition of sodomy incorporated sex between men and between women, anal penetration by men of women and children, male or female ("carnal knowledge of another vessel than God in nature hath appointed to become one flesh, whether it be by abusing the contrary part of a grown woman, or child of either sex"), and vaginal penetration of a girl prior to puberty ("carnal knowledge of . . . [the] unripe vessel of a girl"). Each of these acts was to be treated as a capital crime. The law added that masturbation "in the sight of others . . . corrupting or tempting others to do the like, which tends to the sin of sodomy, if it be not one kind of it," could also justify death, "as the court of magistrates shall determine." The sexual acts encompassed by the New Haven law had two common characteristics, as the law itself explained. Each was nonprocreative, "tending to the destruction of the race of mankind," and each was "unnatural . . . called in scripture the going after strange flesh, or other flesh than God alloweth." Unlike clerical formulations and the laws enacted elsewhere in New England, the New Haven code viewed sodomy as a range of acts that frustrated reproduction, not simply as uncleanness between members of the same sex. The Assistants interpreted biblical references to strange flesh and unnatural sex as referring to the misuse of genital organs, not the gender of the persons to whom they were attached. Seen from this perspective, sodomy became a catchall term for any nonreproductive and therefore unnatural act committed by human beings. The act need not even involve a penis, since the law also encompassed sex between women.

Why New Haven rejected a simple restatement of biblical injunction in favor of a lengthy, unusually explicit, and broadly conceived formulation is a mystery. If this sodomy law had been the first to appear in New England, it might be tempting to argue for a narrowing definition of the crime as years passed. Yet other northern colonies had already adopted laws that specified sex between men as their purview. New Haven's code was thus anomalous, not part of a trend. The General Court may have hoped that a far-reaching definition of the crime would facilitate legal process in dealing with sex offenders, reacting against the restrictive format used elsewhere. If so, no other colony followed New Haven's example. The New Haven law remained in effect for only 10 years since the colony united with Connecticut in 1665 and thereafter came under Connecticut's legal code.

On only two known occasions did women appear before New England courts on charges of "unclean" behavior with each other. In 1642, Elizabeth Johnson was whipped and fined by an Essex County quarterly court for "unseemly practices betwixt her and another maid." Sara Norman and Mary Hammon, both of Yarmouth, Plymouth Colony, were presented in 1649 for "leude behaviour each with other upon a bed." In neither case does the brief court record suggest that the magistrates categorized the offense as sodomitical or, indeed, that they categorized it at all save as "lewd" and "unseemly." The use of these vague adjectives may reflect judicial uncertainty about the classification of sexual intimacy between women as well, perhaps, as a reluctance to describe the acts in question.

Except for New Haven's, New England sodomy laws referred only to sex between men. . . .

. . . [O]n neither side of the Atlantic[, however,] did sodomy laws specify the point at which physical intimacy became a capital offense. There was no consensus among English legal experts as to whether penetration was necessary for conviction. . . .

[In colonial New England, definitions] of the crime and of the criteria for conviction doubtless varied from one magistrate to another and from one case to another, so that generalizations are problematic. But one broad feature does seem fairly clear: courts rarely accepted either intent or physical intimacy short of penetration as grounds for execution. They took care to distinguish between sodomy, attempted sodomy, and other acts tending to sodomy. Ejaculation without penetration did not constitute sodomy in their view of the crime, although it was indicative of intent and could substantiate a lesser charge of sodomitical filthiness. This interpretation of the laws reflected the rigorous standards of proof that the New England judicial system sought to enforce in all capital cases. It was also consistent with the treatment of sex in official discourse, whether legal or theological, as a specific physical act rather than as a form of desire. Magistrates and ministers referred to "sodomy" and "sodomitical" activity but not to "sodomites" or to any specifically homoerotic impulse.

Securing evidence that would justify a conviction for sodomy was no easy matter. Most courts had only circumstantial evidence on which to base their deliberations: deponents may have seen the accused in compromising circumstances, but they rarely claimed to have witnessed penetration itself. The two-witness rule made conviction even less likely, and so in most cases the court could find only that relations to some degree sodomitical had taken place. Edward Michell of Plymouth Colony, for example, was whipped in 1642 for "his lude & sodomiticall practices tending to sodomye with Edward Preston." A year earlier, William Kersley, also of Plymouth Colony, had been presented for "uncleane carriages towards men that he hath lyen withall." The indictment made no mention of sodomy itself, presumably because the court did not anticipate finding any concrete proof. Kersley's case does not appear to have proceeded further, suggesting that the testimony available against him was too flimsy to substantiate even a crime of lesser degree.

Given these problems, it is not surprising that only two individuals, William Plaine and John Knight, are known to have been executed for sodomy in colonial New England. In neither of their cases was the route to conviction straightforward. Plaine appeared before the Assistants at New Haven in 1646, accused of having "committed sodomy with two persons in England" and of having "corrupted a great part of the youth of Guilford [New Haven Colony] by masturbations, which he had committed, and provoked others to the like above a hundred times." Despite this impressive record, the governor refused to condemn Plaine until he had sought the advice of magistrates and ministers in Massachusetts. Only when his consultants declared that Plaine "ought to die" did the court sentence him accordingly. In 1655, the New Haven General Court found John Knight guilty only of "a sodomitical attempt" on a teenaged boy, but the Assistants eventually decided that Knight's clear intention to commit sodomy, in conjunction with other "defiling ways" and his having been found guilty by a previous court of sexually abusing a neighbor's child, justified the death sentence.

Magistrates and ministers viewed sodomy as a sacrilegious and disorderly act but not as an expression of desire or sexual identity. Yet some men did have an ongoing sexual interest in members of the same sex that was recognized as such by their neighbors, even though the persistent and specific impulse that they identified was not acknowledged in official discourse. Surviving court depositions show that popular perceptions of sodomy were by no means always consistent with official teachings. Whereas ministers sought to understand sodomy as it related to other sins such as sloth and disobedience, townspeople and villagers saw it as a distinct phenomenon. And whereas magistrates focused on the act of penetration, deponents in sodomy prosecutions seem to have found intent equally significant. New Englanders were, furthermore, remarkably slow to act against offenders. The evidence suggests that there was no consensus within local communities as to how (or whether) to respond to sodomy.

New Englanders were sometimes well informed about sodomitical behavior in their midst and the attempts of those who were so inclined to establish local networks. John Allexander of Plymouth Colony, tried in 1637 for "lude behaviour and uncleane carriage" with Thomas Roberts, was found by the court "to have beene formerly notoriously guilty that way." He had apparently sought "to allure others thereunto." [Allexander's notoriety presumably originated with men who did not welcome his overtures and who sought to warn others against him, but Roberts may not have been the only man to accede.] Five years later, in 1642, when Edward Michell and Edward Preston appeared before the same colony's court for "lude practises tending to sodomye," Preston was also accused of "pressing" a third man, John Keene, to join them. Keene had refused and reported the incident. The court ordered him "to stand by" while Michell and Preston were whipped. Although Keene had "resisted the temptation, & used meanes to discover it," the judges suspected that "in some thing he was faulty," presumably in having given Preston reason to think that he might be amenable. . . .

The depositions presented at Nicholas Sension's trial in 1677 documented one Connecticut man's prolonged quest for sexual partners among his fellow townsmen. Sension had approached a number of men repeatedly, but the young fellow on whom he fixed his attentions most assiduously was Nathaniel Pond, a servant in the Sension household. Pond had complained to his brother Isaac about his master's "grossly lascivious carriages toward him, who did often in an unseemly manner make attempts tending to sodomy." Several witnesses claimed to have seen Sension attempt sodomy with Pond, mostly in the sleeping quarters at Sension's house, where the master seems to have prowled at night, a sexual predator among his servants. Sension's interest in Pond does not appear to have been purely physical. In conversation with neighbor Joshua Holcombe, he spoke of the "fond affections which he had toward" Nathaniel. Pond's feelings about the relationship were clearly ambivalent. On the one hand, he resented his master's attempts to sodomize him and complained about them to his brother. On the other, when Sension responded to a local investigation of his behavior by offering to release Pond from his indenture, the young man refused, claiming that "he was loathe [sic] to leave him who had the trouble of his education in his minority." Nathaniel, who referred to his master as "Uncle Sension," may well have felt a loyalty and affection toward the man that Sension misinterpreted as an invitation to physical intimacy.

Nathaniel Pond was not the only male servant with whom Sension tried to have sex. Most of the men he approached were, like Pond, in their teens or early twenties. Sension appears to have been interested in penetrating men whose age and status placed them in a position subordinate to himself; his sexual impulses were articulated in the context of power relations. . . . For most sodomy prosecutions in early New England there survives only a brief record of the charge and outcome; in some cases, we do not even know the names of those involved, let alone their age or status relative to each other. But the social context that emerges from the unusually informative transcripts for Sension's trial does at least suggest that for men attracted to members of the same sex in New England as elsewhere in early modern English culture, intercourse, hierarchy, and power were closely intertwined.

Although his interest in sodomizing men was bound up with the expression of social power, Sension characterized his many sexual overtures as a distinct realm of activity. When neighbor William Phelps berated Sension for attempting to seduce various young men, Sension admitted that he had "long" practiced "this trade." It is not clear from Phelps's deposition whether he or Sension introduced the word "trade" into their conversation; indeed, Phelps may have used it retroactively. The application of the term to Sension's "sodomitical actings," by whomever, is significant because "trade" implied a specific calling or way of life. Use of that term to describe Sension's behavior indicates a sense of its significance, distinctiveness, and permanence in his life. "Trade" as a signifier went well beyond the act-oriented view of sodomy propounded by official discourse. It fitted Sension's own experience much better than did authorized categories. Phelps's deposition, then, provides a rare glimpse of ordinary people creating their own sexual taxonomy, their own discourse.

Yet even if Sension originated or participated in that creative process, doing so did not enable him to discard religious values that condemned the acts in which he wanted to engage. Testimony at his trial revealed that he had been tormented by his attraction to men. John Enno deposed that one night he saw Sension slip into bed with one of his servants, masturbate against him, and then go into the adjoining room, where Enno "heard Sension pray God to turn him from this sin he had so long lived in." . . .

Sension was concerned about his fate in this world as well as the next and real-ized the legal dangers that faced him. He described his affection for Pond as "fool-ish," and Enno, who had witnessed several incriminating incidents, told the court that Sension had begged him "to say nothing of these things." Far from being brazen about his attempts at sex with the young men who slept in his house, he was clearly scared and did his best to dissimulate when caught in the act. Samuel Wilson testi-fied that one night in 1671 he "lay back to back" with Nathaniel Pond when Sension came to the bed and started to fondle Pond's "breech," whereupon Wilson "turned about." Sension immediately pulled his hand "out of the bed and said he had come for some tobacco." But neither private warnings from local court members and the fear of more formal proceedings against him, nor repeated rejection, nor spiritual misgivings could deflect Sension from his "trade."

Sension's predilections were apparently well known. Whether or not he found willing partners in and around Windsor, Sension had a reputation for being sexually aggressive that made at least some of his neighbors and acquaintances nervous of him. When Thomas Barber, another man's servant, found he was expected to sleep with Sension "in a trundel bed" during a stay in Hartford, he was "unwilling and afraid" to do so "because of some reports he had heard formerly concerning him." Barber overcame his apprehension, partly because he was reluctant to make "dis-turbance in a strange house" and partly because members of the General Court "lay in the chamber" and so "he hoped no hurt would come of it." But not long after Barber got into bed, Sension "strove to turn [Barber's] back parts upwards and attempted with his yard to enter his body." Barber now found himself "in a great strait," on the one hand "fearing to disturb the courtiers in the other bed" and on the other "fearing he should be wronged." The anxious servant "turned his elbow back to Sension's belly with several blows which caused him to desist for that time." Barber "slept in fear all night, and in [the] morning told his master . . . that he would lie no more with Goodman Sension."

Sension's persistence, despite his notoriety and the danger in which that placed him, may have been encouraged by the live-and-let-live attitude adopted by the elders of Windsor. After investigating his sexual aggression toward Pond, town elders insisted only that Sension shorten the young man's indenture by one year and pay him forty shillings "for his abuse." The primary concern seems to have been to compensate Pond, not to punish Sension. It is striking that community leaders allowed Pond to stay in the Sension household and, in general, that Sension was able to pursue his "trade" for over three decades before being brought to trial. There were those in and near Windsor who had long condemned Sension's interest in men and feared that others might be seduced into similar behavior. It was, William Phelps claimed, the "hazard" of Sension "infecting the rising generation" that drove him to initiate the first inquiry into Sension's "actings." Barber was not the only young man who was displeased by his attentions. When Sension got into bed with Daniel Saxton and tried to mount him, Saxton "thrust him off" and declared, "You'll never leave this devilish sin till you are hanged." Saxton left his master before his apprenticeship was completed and told several acquaintances that he did so because of Sension's attempt to have sex with him. Yet the community as a whole seems to have been remarkably tolerant of Sension's behavior.

Issues of power may have figured in Sension's impunity as well as in his choice of partners. The status accorded him as one of the wealthiest householders in town probably shielded him to some degree, and indeed, at the trial's conclusion, the security offered by his estate enabled him to escape corporal punishment. Reluctance to tear the fabric of community life by taking formal action against an established citizen and employer may also have counterbalanced disapproval of his sexual proclivities. Sension's popularity among his neighbors and acquaintances may have helped protect him. The court depositions are remarkable for their lack of hostility to the accused, save in regard to his sexual behavior. Sension's evident attraction to men did not undermine the general esteem in which he was held. Thomas Barber, whom Sension had tried to sodomize in Hartford, declared that he was "much beholden" to the accused for "entertainment in his house" and "therefore [was] much troubled that he should be any instrument to testify against him in the least measure." Similar feelings on the part of other Windsor citizens may have long delayed legal proceedings against him.

Why then the community's change of heart in the late 1670s? The key event seems to have been the death of Nathaniel Pond in 1675, after which Sension's approaches to other young men became more frequent. This would have provided his enemies with ammunition to secure the support, however grudging, of formerly loyal neighbors such as Barber. There is no evidence from the preceding decades to suggest that any of Sension's neighbors actually condoned his behavior, but neither does it appear that many people in Windsor, apart from the targets of Sension's lust, cared sufficiently about his sexual tastes to advocate a strong community response. Legal prosecution became possible only when the social disruption brought about by Sension's advances seemed to outweigh his worth as a citizen.

There are remarkable parallels between the Sension case and a superficially quite different situation that developed in another Connecticut community in the mid-eighteenth century. Stephen Gorton, minister at the Baptist church in New London, was suspended from his position in 1756 for "unchaste behaviour with his fellow men when in bed with them." Like Sension, Gorton was a married man who had apparently exhibited his attraction to men "in many instances through a number of years." In 1726, he had appeared before the New London county court for "hav[ing] lasciviously behaved himself towards sundry men, endeavouring to commit sodomy with them." The charge had been dismissed for lack of evidence, but in 1757 the General Meeting of Baptist Churches judged that his "offensive and unchaste behaviour, frequently repeated for a long space of time," indicated "an inward disposition . . . towards the actual commission of a sin of so black and dark a dye." The meeting did not explain what it meant by "inward disposition" but went on to recommend that Gorton absent himself from the Lord's Supper for "several months at least" to "give thereby the most effectual evidence" of his "true humiliation" and reformation. The assumption that Gorton could overcome his proclivities suggests that the meeting viewed his "crime" in terms consistent with earlier religious formulations, as an expression of inner corruption that afflicted everyone but that sinners could defeat with Christ's support. Yet although the phrase was not being used to denote a permanent or specifically sexual orientation, it did depict Gorton's depravity as expressing itself in a particular and consistent form. The plain facts of Gorton's sexual history prompted the meeting to recognize attraction to men as an ongoing facet of his life. The official judgment against him was a diplomatic and subtle response to the situation: it used language in ways that did not actually breach the parameters of authorized discourse but pushed standard categories to their very limits in accommodating local impressions of Gorton's behavior.

Like Sension, Gorton managed to survive more or less unscathed, despite his sexual reputation. Gorton's notorious interest in men caused such discomfort that "many" members left the church "on that account." According to his opponents in 1756, the church had "been broken thereby." Yet once Gorton acknowledged and confessed his sins, the remaining members voted by a two-thirds majority to restore him to the pastorate. Almost three quarters (71.4 percent) of the voting women favored Gorton's restoration, whereas only half (52.2 percent) of the men did so. This suggests that Gorton's reputation and behavior made his male parishioners particularly nervous, possibly because they felt threatened by his sexual tastes.

How can we explain the congregation's apparent inaction during the three decades between 1726 and 1756 and then its willingness to reinstate him? Gorton's clerical office is unlikely to have afforded him much protection, considering the frequency with which New Englanders challenged unsatisfactory ministers. It seems more plausible that elders had berated Gorton informally and were hoping that he would mend his ways without their having to initiate formal proceedings. Throughout the colonial period, New England communities preferred to handle problematic behavior through informal channels; they resorted to ecclesiastical discipline or the legal system only when private exhortation failed. Although most of the surviving information about sodomitical activity comes from court records, townspeople and villagers did not see such behavior primarily as a legal problem.

The likelihood that members who disapproved of Gorton's inclinations were interested primarily in reclaiming rather than punishing or dismissing him is strengthened by the church's treatment of Gorton even after it was driven to formal proceedings against him. Gorton was not the only man accused of "unchaste behaviour" with others of the same sex to benefit from faith in the possibility of spiritual renewal. Ebenezer Knight, a member of the First Church at Marblehead, Massachusetts, suspended from communion in 1732 for his "long series of uncleanness with mankind," was restored to full membership after spending six years in Boston and convincing the membership that he had seen the error of his ways. Why the church finally took action against Knight is unclear, but his expressions of repentance and the assuaging effect of an extended absence brought about his reacceptance into the church community.

There is another possible explanation for the New London congregation's behavior. While some of the church members disapproved of Gorton's behavior and so either sought his spiritual reclamation or lobbied for his removal, others may have been less perturbed by his activities, as long as they did not become a public embarrassment. Most of the correspondence relating to the dispute between pastor and congregation addressed not Gorton's exploits, but the fact that "rumour, offense, and reproach" arising from them had now reached "distant parts and different churches." Indeed, the most striking aspect of local hostility toward Gorton is that church members seem to have been more concerned with rumors having "spread abroad in the world" than with Gorton's actual behavior. Gorton's flock resorted to disciplinary proceedings against him only when the spread of scandal made action imperative. The church members who left the congregation may well have done so rather than stay to fight for his dismissal because they realized that their brethren were either inclined to mercy or did not see Gorton's "unchaste" acts as a serious issue in its own right. If so, their hunch was borne out by the events of 1756.

The impunity with which men such as Gorton pursued their sexual inclinations suggests an attitude on the part of their neighbors that was far removed from the spirit of official pronouncements on the subject. We should not downplay too much the effectiveness of such pronouncements: they may well have deterred individuals from experimenting with sodomy and doubtless incited condemnation of those who committed it. Others may have neglected to act against sodomitical behavior because they were slow to recognize or label it as such. . . . Sexual advances made by a master toward a male servant could be understood in terms of the power dynamic between the two individuals; there was no compelling need to treat the sexual act as distinct from the broader relationship or to label it explicitly as sodomy. Those unable or unwilling to do so may well have been disturbed by what they saw but were unable to respond because the behavior was undefined.

New Englanders who did identify and condemn sodomy often may have been deterred by the rigorous demands of the legal system from taking formal action against offenders. Just as colonists waited to prosecute suspect witches until they had accumulated enough evidence to mount a credible prosecution, so when dealing with men like Sension hostile neighbors and acquaintances may have delayed for similar reasons. Informal measures by local magistrates or church elders constituted an attractive alternative to the expensive and often intractable legal system. Moreover, addressing the situation through nonjuridical channels was less direful than invoking capital law and so would have appealed to those who wanted to proceed against offenders but did not want to endanger the lives of those involved. If the local standing of the offender was also an element, as in the Sension case, an informal investigation would provide a more discreet way of addressing the situation. And finally, just as a cunning person's social value as a healer might offset suspicions of "*maleficium*" and protect her for many years from prosecution as a witch, so the positive attributes of men such as Sension might counterbalance disapproval of their sexual propensities. Risking the loss of a good neighbor and the disruption of social and economic relations in the local community might well have struck the practical minded as too high a price to pay for the expunging of the unclean.

We cannot assume that a majority of New Englanders took their leaders' strictures against sodomy all that seriously. . . . Some incidents relating to sodomy may never have reached court or church records because local communities handled such matters informally; others may have gone unreported because too few people were upset for prosecution to be worthwhile. In the Sension and Gorton cases, formal action was taken only when illicit behavior became socially disruptive or threatened to damage the community's reputation. It seems plausible that lay responses to sodomy ranged from outright condemnation to a live-and-let-live attitude that did not go so far as to condone such behavior but that did enable peaceful cohabitation, especially if the individual concerned was an otherwise valued member of the local community. The weight of opinion does not appear to have rested with those actively hostile toward sodomy.

During the years between Nicholas Sension's trial and the proceedings against Stephen Gorton, the metropolis of London provided the setting for a transformation in the relationship among sodomy, social identity, and gender. By the early eighteenth century there had emerged in London a distinct and visible sodomitical subculture. Men who were attracted to their own sex could meet others with similar tastes in recognized gathering places such as particular taverns, parks, and public latrines. . . . They became "mollies," in contemporary parlance. In "molly houses" scattered across London it was customary to adopt effeminate behavior; some mollies cross-dressed. One visitor to a molly house in the Old Bailey observed "men calling one another 'my dear' and hugging, kissing, and tickling each other as if they were a mixture of wanton males and females, and assuming effeminate voices and airs." Many were dressed as women, "completely rigged in gowns, petticoats, headcloths, fine laced shoes, furbelowed scarves, and masks."

Unlike the word "sodomy," which had been used to describe specific acts, "molly" denoted a more broadly conceived identity that included not only sexual attraction to other men but also clearly delineated patterns of self-presentation, even of personality. . . . In focusing on persons instead of acts and in its application to a particular group instead of fallen humanity in general, the molly represented a major shift in the classification of sexual attraction between men away from "sodomy" and toward what thinkers in the late nineteenth century would term "homosexuality." . . . Surviving evidence from [the North American colonies] gives no signs of a subculture such as London offered. Nor did attacks on cross-dressing in the colonies imply that the wearing of female clothes was related to sodomitical behavior; effeminacy and sodomy were separate categories in early America.

Recent scholarship . . . shows that modern notions of sexual identity began to develop [in other major European cities] long before they became crystallized in the taxonomy that now dominates sexual discourse. The New England evidence suggests that making a clear-cut distinction between premodern conceptions of sodomy as an *act* and the modern construction of a homosexual *identity* is problematic not only for eighteenth-century urban culture but also for early modern popular attitudes in the provinces and colonies. To argue that New Englanders identified a distinct sodomitical sexuality would be to stretch the evidence far beyond the bounds of credibility. But exposure to the recurrent impulses of men like Nicholas Sension does seem to have led neighbors and acquaintances to treat sodomy as a condition rather than as an act; it became in their minds a habitual course of action that characterized some men throughout their lives. . . .

The boundaries between official and popular attitudes should not be overdrawn. In the judgment against Gorton, we see an ecclesiastical body adapting authorized categories so as to incorporate social observation, mediating between doctrinal formulations and reports of actual behavior. Some people doubtless used official categories to interpret what they saw going on around them. Yet the surviving evidence suggests that other men and women identified in certain individuals an ongoing predilection for members of the same sex. The latter response, which falls somewhere between the paradigms focused on act and identity, was quite different from the authorized view of sodomy. That difference was more than a function of rhetoric or occasion: it evinced distinct interpretive responses to sex, one determined by a theological system, the other more empirical.

The long-term survival of apparently incorrigible offenders suggests that many New Englanders either did not condemn sodomy as readily as their leaders or else took the view that acting against such behavior was less important than maintaining the social integrity and reputation of their communities. People who felt compelled to do something may often have preferred private exhortation to public confrontation, partly because of the difficulties inherent in legal prosecution and partly because informal channels were more discreet. But others seem to have felt no compulsion to do anything, in some cases perhaps because they did not identify the behavior as specifically sodomitical and in others because they did not particularly care. Difficult though it was to secure a conviction for sodomy in a New England court, the greater challenge for those who favored legal action was persuading their neighbors to join them in pressing charges, even against "notorious" individuals like John Allexander. Thus the citizens of Windsor allowed Nicholas Sension to avoid prosecution for over thirty years and to live as a respected member of his community, despite his "sodomitical actings." And thus the Baptist congregation in eighteenth-century New London would delay for several decades before acting against even a pastor who was known for his sodomitical "disposition."

FURTHER READINGS

Kathleen M. Brown, *Good Wives, Nasty Wenches, and Anxious Patriarchs: Gender, Race, and Power in Colonial Virginia* (1996).

Catherine Clinton and Michele Gillespie, eds., *The Devil's Lane: Sex and Race in the Early South* (1997).

Nancy F. Cott, "Divorce and the Changing Status of Women in Eighteenth-Century Massachusetts," in Michael Gordon, ed., *The American Family in Social-Historical Perspective* (1978), 115–139.

Cornelia Hughes Dayton, "Taking the Trade: Abortion and Gender Relations in an Eighteenth-Century New England Village," *William and Mary Quarterly* 48 (January 1991): 19–49.

Kai T. Erickson, *Wayward Puritans: A Study in the Sociology of Deviance* (1968).

Thomas A. Foster, "Deficient Husbands: Manhood, Sexual Incapacity, and Male Marital Sexuality in Seventeenth-Century New England," *William and Mary Quarterly* 56 (1999): 723–744.

A. Leon Higginbotham and Barbara Kopytoff, "Racial Purity and Interracial Sex in the Law of Colonial and Antebellum Virginia," *Georgetown Law Journal* 77 (August 1989): 1967–2029.

Carol Karlsen, *Devil in the Shape of a Woman* (1987).

Barbara S. Lindemann, "'To Ravish and Carnally Know': Rape in Eighteenth Century Massachusetts," *Signs* 10 (1984): 63–68.

Kenneth A. Lockridge, *On the Sources of Patriarchal Rage* (1992).

Edmund S. Morgan, "The Puritans and Sex," *New England Quarterly* (December 1942): 591–607.

Robert F. Oaks, "'Things Fearful to Name': Sodomy and Buggery in Seventeenth-Century New England," *Journal of Social History* 12 (1978): 268–281.

Ann Marie Plane, *Colonial Intimacies: Indian Marriage in Early New England* (2000).

Elizabeth Reis, *Damned Women: Sinners and Witches in Puritan New England* (1997).

Daniel Scott Smith and Michael Hindus, "Premarital Pregnancy in America, 1640-1971," *Journal of Interdisciplinary History* 5 (1975): 537–570.

Merril D. Smith, *Breaking the Bonds: Marital Discord in Pennsylvania, 1730–1830* (1991).

Merril D. Smith, ed., *Sex and Sexuality in Early America* (1998).

Colin L. Talley, "Gender and Male Same-Sex Erotic Behavior in British North America in the Seventeenth Century," *Journal of the History of Sexuality* 6 (1996): 385–408.

Roger Thompson, *Sex in Middlesex: Popular Mores in a Massachusetts County, 1649–1699* (1986).

Paula Treckel, "Breastfeeding and Maternal Sexuality in Colonial America," *Journal of Interdisciplinary History* 20 (1989): 25–51.

Laurel Thatcher Ulrich, *Good Wives* (1980).

Kathleen Verduin, "'Our Cursed Natures': Sexuality and the Puritan Conscience," *New England Quarterly* 56 (1983): 220–237.

Helena M. Wall, *Fierce Communion: Family and Community in Early America* (1990).

Michael Warner, "New English Sodom," *American Literature* 64 (March 1992): 19–47.

Gender Conflict and
Sex Reform in the
Early Nineteenth Century

The beginning of the nineteenth century was a time marked by "sexual disarray" and visible gender tension. Premarital pregnancy rates rose rapidly in the years after the Revolutionary War, so that by 1800, one woman in three was pregnant at marriage. The average age at marriage and the proportion of women who never married also rose. Parental authority over courtship declined, and young women seemed increasingly vulnerable sexually. Stories of women victimized by male seducers, their sexual aggression unchecked by law or moral censure, circulated widely in fiction and news accounts.

The erosion of customary parental and communal controls over sexual relations occurred as the "market revolution" transformed American society in the early nineteenth century. Social relationships became increasingly defined through commercial transactions rather than kinship and neighborhood, a development that simultaneously created greater opportunities for personal autonomy and greater risks of sexual danger. Individuals' choices were often limited by their civil status or economic position. Women had few property rights, and their wages were about half that paid to men. Earning a meager living as domestic servants, seamstresses, and factory hands, urban working-class women struggled to negotiate the terms of their sexual transactions with men. Prostitution thrived, and sexual violence was common.

Even as the market revolution destabilized older traditions of sexual regulation, new ideals of gender and sexuality arose in the early decades of the nineteenth century. Books of advice for young people on courtship and marriage multiplied. Many health reformers articulated new concerns about "excessive" sexual practices and uncontrollable urges, focusing especially on nymphomania among women and masturbation among men. Reformers offered an amazing number of proposals to remodel sexual relations. Some suggested limited sexual intercourse between couples or male withdrawal before ejaculation, as a form of self-control and family limitation. Radical experiments proliferated, from the Shakers' lifelong celibacy to the utopian Oneida Association's sharing of sexual partners and property. Despite the vast differences in these proposals, they were directed to the same goal: making sexual impulses subject to rational decision making and restraint. Why did this new emphasis on individual will and sexual self-control develop?

Influenced by evangelical Protestantism, the emergent middle class found the new ideals of spiritual self-improvement and sexual self-control especially appealing. They became central to middle-class identity, although in different ways for men and women. While advice books endorsed self-restraint for men to achieve middle-class success and respectability, they also claimed that virtuous women were naturally chaste and morally superior. Some middle-class women embraced this ideology and used it to assert new political claims. In the 1830s and 1840s, they established societies for moral reform that condemned male sexual predators and demanded laws against seduction. How did these new sexual ideals change the relative power of women and men? Was an ideology of female purity empowering for women—and if so, for which women? What did these new ideals of sexuality and gender mean for working-class women and men?

D O C U M E N T S

In the late eighteenth century, gender and class inequalities marked sexual relations in troubling ways, as Document 1 reveals. This 1793 report of the trial of Henry Bedlow, a wealthy "rake" accused of raping a young, working-class woman in New York, reveals the legal protection and social acceptance of male sexual aggression, as well as the misogynist belief that women were weak and untrustworthy. These attitudes were challenged in the 1830s by a widespread movement for "moral reform," spearheaded by Northern white women who fought the sexual double standard, male sexual privilege, and prostitution. In 1838, the Boston Female Moral Reform Society published a call to Christian women to reject licentious men from respectable society; this call, Document 2, not only asserted a new gender ideology of women's sexual purity and moral superiority, but claimed women's right to agitate for social change.

Principles of self-restraint and discipline infused the new sexual ideals in the early nineteenth century and were circulated by advice books for both men and women. Document 3 is an excerpt from health reformer William Alcott's *The Young Woman's Book of Health,* which defined nymphomania and recommended bathing, sleeping, and dietary rules to prevent it. Another health reformer, Sylvester Graham (best known for inventing the graham cracker), advised men in Document 4 that chastity in marriage was as important as sexual fidelity. Married men should indulge their sexual impulses once a month, practice withdrawal before ejaculation as a form of birth control, and avoid masturbation. An emphasis on self-control increasingly shaped the sexual practices of Americans, although it coexisted with other beliefs. In his private journal for 1852–1853, a portion of which is reprinted in Document 5, Navy drummer and sailor Philip C. Van Buskirk described the all-male society aboard a Navy ship, where sodomy, masturbation, and intergenerational sex were generally accepted; Van Buskirk revealed his struggles against these tendencies and his drive for sexual self-control.

1. A Trial for Rape in New York, 1793

On Tuesday, the 8th of October, 1793, at the court of Oyer and Terminer, and Gaol delivery for the County of New York, came on the trial of *Henry Bedlow,* for committing a rape on the body of *Lanah Sawyer,* spinster, a young girl of about 17 years of age. . . .

LANAH SAWYER, who, being sworn, testified, That . . . on a Sunday evening, the latter end of August, she was going through Broadway, and received several insults from some Frenchmen, whose language she could not understand; and that the Prisoner came up, rescued her, and then attended her home to her father's house in Gold Street. . . .That he told her his name was lawyer Smith. On the Sunday following, she met him again—he accosted her—they entered into conversation. . . . He conveyed her home, and departed. In the morning, a Mr. Hone, who lived opposite to her, observed what a smart Beau she had got. She told him it was a lawyer Smith; but Mr. Hone said it was not, for it was *Harry Bedlow,* a very great rake; she said it could not be, as he had said his name was lawyer Smith. On the Wednesday evening following, being the 4th of September, she was sitting on her father's stoop, and the Prisoner came up to her, asked her to take a walk, and told her that Miss Steddiford (whom she had before mentioned to him to be a young lady of her acquaintance) would, with another gentleman, accompany them. That she went with the prisoner to the house of Mr. Steddiford, but found his daughter out; that Bedlow suggested they had gone to the battery. She accordingly went with him towards that place, down Broadway. They stop'd at Corre's, and took some ice cream, and afterwards proceeded to the Battery, round which they walked twice. During this time she heard the clock strike and counted twelve; this alarmed her, she mentioned her fears to the Prisoner, but he quieted them by telling her it was only ten. They then returned, and going into Broadway, met three watchmen, who upon being asked by Bedlow, told them it was one o'clock. They then went on to John–Street, where she was going to turn down, but the Prisoner would not let her. He kept his arm around her, and brought her on to Ann-Street, which he wanted her to turn down, but she would not, as she knew there were vacant lots there—had heard the street was filled with bad people, and thought it improper for a young girl to go down there. He kept tight hold of her;—she screamed, and he stopt her mouth. She then, for the first time, began to suspect his intentions. He then dragged her along to opposite the Brick–Meeting–house, with one arm round her, the other having both her hands; he then knocked with his stick at the door of Mrs. Cary: Mrs. Cary opened the window; he desired admittance; she refused, saying that her doors were locked—that her husband was out of town, and she could not open them. The Prosecutrix, during this, escaped from the Prisoner, and ran near to the corner of Nassau–Street; Bedlow dragged her back again; she again escaped, and fled quite to the corner; he forcibly made her return; she again ran away, almost exhausted, and not knowing what she did, ran upwards; the Prisoner followed her, told her she should not go back again, and keeping tight hold of her, bro't her to

Report of the Trial of Henry Bedlow, for Committing a Rape on Lanah Sawyer (New York: n.p., 1793), 3–6, 9–10, 20, 22, 62.

Ann–Street, she resisting; he carried her down there, took her through a vacant lot, keeping fast hold of her arms, and going backwards himself, drew her through a passage, pushed open a gate, led her thro' a garden, where they were obstructed by bushes—then came to a back door, at which he knocked and demanded admittance; the door was opened by Mrs. Cary, who said, "there is a room;" the Prisoner dragged her into it; she screamed; he called for a candle, which was afterwards put in at the door by Mrs. Cary, and the door was then shut. Bedlow then pulled off his coat and waistcoat, during which, the Prosecutrix screamed and endeavored to escape, that he then seized her, stopped her mouth, and laughed loud to prevent her screams from being heard; he then threw off her hat, tore the pins out of her gown, and placing her before him, drew it off her shoulders; he asked her consent three or four times, which she refused, calling him a brute, a dog, and a villain; he next asked her consent to put out the candle, which she likewise refused, and he put it out without; afterwards he tore the strings of her petticoats, and kicked them off with his feet; upon this he threw her down on the bed, and pulled off his own cloaths, during which, she tried to effect an escape, but was prevented by him. He then threw himself upon her, laid his left arm across her throat, so that she was almost choaked, and did not suppose she could live many minutes, and *had his ends of her.* These words were explained by leading questions (the answers to which thro' delicacy we omit; but they amounted to proof of the fact)[.] She did not feel his right arm at all, nor knew what he did with it; afterwards he turned his back and went to sleep; she then arose to look for the door, but came across the window, tried to open it, but could not; she next found the door, felt a latch but could not open it; felt all over for bolts and found one; Bedlow hearing her, got up and forced her to bed again, but did not offer any new violence. . . . [A]fter some time he arose, opened the shutter, and she discovered it to be broad day; he dressed himself, told her to do the same, and to make haste, as he supposed Mrs. Cary wished them to be gone; that he went away; she staid, dressed herself, and coming out into the passage, was met by Mrs. Cary, who said, "deary, you may go out at the back or the front door, as I have looked out and there is nobody in the street"; the prosecutrix replied she would go out at the front door, and did not care if the first man she met was her father, or some relation or acquaintance. . . .

Mr. THOMPSON.

Gentlemen of the Jury,

IT is now my duty, as the youngest counsel for the Prisoner, to open the nature of his defence. . . .

[F]irst, as the nature of the crime of which he is accused, and the serious consequences involved in the event of this trial, are too well known to you, in opening the cause, I shall pass them over in silence, on mentioning that it is an accusation easy to be made, hard to be proved, but harder, much harder to be defended by the party accused, though perfectly innocent. As it is an offense of so dark a nature, so easily charged by the woman, and the negative so difficult to be proved, putting the life of a citizen in the hands of a woman, to be disposed of almost at her will and pleasure; you therefore will find it necessary in the first place to determine with the strictest scrutiny into the character and conduct of her upon whose evidence he must stand or fall. Her character, her conduct, to entitle her to be that evidence who shall take away the life of a citizen, ought not only to be perfectly chaste, but through the whole scene should not leave the slightest suspicion of impropriety; she ought indeed to be a person who would have avoided the house in which she pretends the fact was committed, as she would have avoided her own ruin. The first ground of our defence she has furnished from the relation of the facts themselves. . . . [K]ind Providence, who sometimes protects the innocent, has furnished us with that evidence which cannot leave the least suspicion upon your minds of his guilt, but will indeed disclose a scene of fraud and falshood; clearly shew that the measure of her iniquity is full; and that she yielded herself up a willing sacrifice on the altar of prostitution.

I now proceed to state the substance of the prisoner's evidence, which in many instances will correspond with that offered on the part of the people; and indeed the first evidence we shall offer, will begin at the time the Prosecutrix and the Prisoner came to the house of Mrs. Cary, which was nearly between 10 and 11 in the evening of Wednesday night; that the Prisoner with Miss Sawyer, while at Mrs. Cary's front door, were in a very agreeable conversable mood, and that there were no noise or tokens of violence appearing to be offered by the Prisoner to Miss Sawyer; that after continuing some time they walked off arm in arm; that they had been gone above an hour or longer, when Mrs. Cary and the family were alarmed by the barking of dogs in the back yard; that at this time the Prisoner and Miss Sawyer came into the lane from Ann–Street to the gate that leads into Mrs. Cary's garden; that this gate was fastened by a heavy latch with a nail over it, which was inserted for greater security; that the Prisoner left Miss Sawyer on the out side of the gate, while he climbed over the fence and unbolted the gate, and let Miss Sawyer through into the garden. . . . Mrs. Cary came to the door, and enquired who was there; whereupon the Prisoner replied a friend; on hearing the Prisoner's voice, she knew him, opened the door, and introduced him into the room, and presently handed a candle to them; that while Mrs. Cary was at the door, there was no noise or signs of violence. . . .

An eminent writer of the English law . . . defines Rape to consist "in the carnal knowledge of a woman, forcibly and against her will." Has the Prosecutrix proved any force? Has she proved a violation against her will? . . . Mr. Bedlow may have been highly culpable, and yet not guilty of a Rape. He may have seduced this girl; yet he did not force her. Overcome by his assiduities, his attentions, his address, his persuasions, she may have fallen a victim to seduction, but she has not experienced the monstrous brutality of a rape. The Prisoner is known to be a gallant man, fond of women, one who will not refuse the favors of the Fair, and one perhaps, who will go considerable lengths in soliciting their consent to his wishes; but he is not known to be a wretch, so lost to every sense of honor and decency, as to be capable of satisfying his lustful appetite by a recourse to the brutality of force. Besides, his character as a man of gallantry, is by no means a circumstance against him, it is strongly in his favor; accustomed to the company of women; a genteel figure; an insinuating address; would probably open sufficient avenues to the gratification of his pleasures, and prevent the necessity of force from ever occurring to his mind. His character, gentlemen, is almost a demonstrative proof, that seduction, and not rape, was the crime committed. . . .

What is [Lanah Sawyer's] reputation? A cloud of witnesses have sworn that she is a modest, discreet, prudent girl. It is true, before this discovery, she might have been so esteemed. She may have had the art to carry a fair outside, while all was foul within. She may have appeared modest, discreet and prudent to her neighbour-hood, while she was the very reverse, when not under their observation. Possibly before this affair, there were no means of judging of her discretion and prudence. Never before in the way of temptation, she had been innocent for the want of oppor-tunity. But gentlemen, facts speak for themselves; the testimony of a whole neigh-borhood in her behalf, is not so strong and convincing, as what she herself has disclosed. Determine her character from her own evidence. . . .

After a Trial, which lasted 15 hours, the Jury retired, and in the space of 15 minutes, returned, finding a verdict of—NOT GUILTY.

2. Boston Female Moral Reformers Condemn "Licentious Men," 1838

JUST TREATMENT OF LICENTIOUS MEN.
ADDRESSED TO CHRISTIAN MOTHERS, WIVES, SISTERS, AND
DAUGHTERS.

DEAR SISTERS:—As members with us of the body of the Lord Jesus Christ, we take the liberty of addressing you on a subject near our hearts, and of the deepest interest to our sex. We ask your serious attention, while we press upon your con-sciences the inquiry, "Is it right to admit to the society of virtuous females, those unprincipled and licentious men, whose conduct is fraught with so much evil to those who stand in the relation to us of sisters?" True, God designed that man should be our protector, the guardian of our peace, our happiness, and our honor; but how often has he proved himself a traitor to his trust, and the worst enemy of our sex? The deepest degradation to which many of our sex have been reduced, the deepest injuries they have suffered, have been in consequence of his perfidy. He has betrayed, and robbed, and forsaken his victim, and left her to endure alone the untold horrors of a life embittered by self-reproach, conscious ignominy, and ex-clusion from every virtuous circle. Is there a woman among us, whose heart has not been pained at the fall and fate of some one sister of her sex? Do you say the guilty deserve to suffer and must expect it? Granted. But why not let a part of this suffer-ing fall on the destroyer? Why is he caressed and shielded from scorn by the coun-tenance of the virtuous, and encouraged to commit other acts of perfidy and sin, while his victim, for one offence, is trampled upon, despised and banished from all virtuous society[.] The victim thus crushed, yields herself to despair, and becomes a practical illustration of the proverb that, "A bad woman is the worst of all God's creatures." Surely, if she is worse, after her fall, than man equally fallen, is there not reason to infer that in her nature there is something more chaste, more pure and

"Just Treatment of Licentious Men. Addressed to Christian Mothers, Wives, Sisters and Daughters,"
Friend of Virtue, January 1838, 2–4.

refined, and exalted than in his? Is it then not worth while to do something to prevent her from becoming a prey to the perfidy and baseness of unprincipled man, and a disgrace to her sex? Do you ask, what can woman do, and reply as have some others, "We must leave this work for the men?" Can we expect the wolf, ravenous for his prey, to throw up a barrier to protect the defenceless sheep? As well might we expect this, as to expect that men as a body will take measures to redress the wrongs of woman.

. . . [A] Moral Reform is the first of causes to our sex. It involves principles, which if faithfully and perseveringly applied, will preserve the rights and elevate the standing of our sex in society. As times have been, the libertine has found as ready a passport to the society of the virtuous, as any one, and he has as easily obtained a good wife, as the more virtuous man. But a new era has commenced. Woman has erected a standard, and laid down the principle, that man shall not trample her rights, and on the honor of her sex with impunity. She has undertaken to banish licentious men from all virtuous society. And mothers, wives, sisters, and daughters will you lend your influence to this cause? Prompt action in the form of association will accomplish this work. Females in this manner must combine their strength and exert their influence. Will you not join one of these bands of the pious? The cause has need of your interest, your prayers, and your funds. Come then to our help, and let us pray and labor together.

3. Health Reformer William Alcott Discusses Nymphomania, 1855

Uterine Madness, or Nymphomania

This disease, most happily, is rare. I have not seen half a dozen cases of it in twenty-five years. Indeed, I am not without hope that it is less frequent than formerly. And yet, as long as a single case of so dreadful a disease can be found, the young should be apprised of its existence and character. . . .

The best account I have seen of the causes of this disease is as follows. The writer, having made the usual division into predisposing and exciting causes, thus goes on:

> In the former should be included all circumstances capable of producing an exaltation of excitement in the brain and nervous system, such as the reading of lascivious and impassioned works, viewing voluptuous paintings, romantic conversations, associating with corrupt companions, frequent visits to balls or theatres, disappointed love, the too assiduous cultivation of the fine arts, the influence of imitation on beholding it in others, the abuse of aphrodisiac remedies, or of spirituous liquors, or of aromatics and perfumes, which excite too much the brain and general sensibility.
>
> The causes which act directly upon the genital organs (the exciting causes), and which may afterwards act sympathetically upon the brain, are masturbation, the abuse of coition, pruritus of the vulva, inflammation of the nymphae, clitoris, neck of the uterus and ovaries; to which we may add the irritation of ascarides in the rectum; and,

William A. Alcott, *The Young Woman's Book of Health* (New York: Miller, Orton, and Mulligan, 1855), 215–219.

finally, the use of drastic purgatives, and the internal or extensive external employment of cantharides.

One thing should be mentioned, in passing, concerning its resemblance to *pruritus*—mentioned above, as one of its causes. They are sometimes mistaken for each other. But they need not be. Nymphomania is accompanied by venereal desire; but in pruritus, though there is a most intolerable itching, there is seldom any sexual impulse or desire; indeed, it is usually the very reverse of all this.

Warm baths have been recommended in this disease; but, as it seems to me, without due consideration. I do not believe that any sensible practitioner would be willing to risk them. The cold bath—I mean the use of cold water on the whole surface of the body—is far preferable.

Indeed, the whole treatment, both external and internal, should be cooling. None but cooling drinks are at all admissible, and none but the most bland food. Farinaceous food—bread of various kinds, arrowroot, sage, tapioca, rice, and potatoes—with mild sub-acid fruits, and milk, is the best. Animal food, especially salted animal food, and old salted butter, should be avoided as carefully as if they were rank poison.

Opposed as I am to the use of medicine in most female diseases, my views of its application in nymphomania will be easily guessed. I regard it as not only useless in this disease, but positively and greatly hurtful. I never knew the least benefit derived from it.

There is one surgical operation which has occasionally been resorted to; but in a book for young women, it is entirely unnecessary to describe it. What they need is, to know the causes, that they may know how to prevent it. For here, if nowhere else in the wide world, prevention is better than cure—immensely better.

The Scriptures speak of a period in the early history of our world when the thoughts of mankind were only evil, and that continually. The thoughts and imagination of every female afflicted with this species of madness are in the same predicament.

It often happens, moreover, that these unhallowed thoughts and feelings are fed and nurtured by reading doubtful romances, if not even those books which are printed with a special design to excite lascivious feelings. This suggests an important item in the treatment of these persons. It consists in watching over and endeavoring to control and direct about their mental food, no less than their physical.

If the mind cannot be rightly directed in any other way, it may be advisable to travel, but not without a judicious companion, as a protector. But even in this there will be some danger of too great excitement. The country is preferable to the city, to travel in; and a private carriage better than the tumult and whirl of railroads and steamboats.

My views of feather beds are already fully known; but if there be a case in which, more than any other, they are inadmissible, it is that of nymphomania. The coarsest, most porous, and coolest beds are to be secured; and if a companion is admissible at all, a judicious selection should be made. Better sleep entirely alone than with those whose imprudence will tend to perpetuate the disease.

Nor should there be the least indulgence in late hours in the morning. The patient should leave the bed the instant she wakes. One evil connected with comfortables and feather beds is, that, by their unnatural warmth and stimulus, they tempt to late hours in the morning.

Artificial heat in sleeping-rooms for young women who are afflicted with this disease is also to be shunned with the greatest care and solicitude. They are of doubtful utility to any body; but here there is no apology for them.

The frequent recommendation to marry, as a means of removing the tendency to this disease, must not be received and acted upon without a good deal of qualification. It may be useful; but it is also true that it may be utterly inadmissible. On this point, consult the proper authorities.

4. Sylvester Graham Lectures Young Men on Self-Restraint, 1839

Young men, in the pursuit of illicit commerce with the other sex, generally contemplate the act, for a considerable time before its performance,—their imagination is wrought up, and presents lewd and exciting images,—the genital organs become stimulated, and throw their peculiar influence over the whole system; and this, to the full extent of its power, acts on the mental and moral faculties, and is thence again reflected with redoubled energy upon the genital and other organs. The sight, or touch of the female body, and especially the bosom, &c., greatly increases the excitement, and thus the ardor and power of the passion are augmented continually, and more in proportion to the difficulties in the way, until indulgence takes place, when the excitement is intense and overwhelming, and the convulsive paroxysms proportionably violent and hazardous to life. . . . But, between the husband and wife, where there is a proper degree of chastity, all these causes either entirely lose, or are exceedingly diminished in their effect. They become accustomed to each other's body, and their parts no longer excite an impure imagination, and their sexual intercourse is the result of the more natural and instinctive excitements of the organs themselves;—and when the dietetic and other habits are such as they should be, this intercourse is very seldom.

Moreover, a promiscuous commerce between the sexes would be terribly pernicious to the female and to the offspring, as well as to the male. Debility, abortion, barrenness, and painful diseases of various forms, would be the inevitable result in the female; and that peculiarly loathsome, virulent and ruinous disease which is generated and perpetuated by such commerce, and which has already been so dreadful a scourge to millions of the human family, would prevail on every hand, and become a common calamity of society. . . .

. . . [A]s a general rule, it may be said to the healthy and robust, it were better for you not to exceed, in the frequency of your indulgences, the number of months in the year; and you cannot habitually exceed the number of weeks in the year, without in some degree impairing your constitutional powers, shortening your lives, and increasing your liability to disease and suffering; if indeed you do not thereby actually induce disease of the worst and most painful kind; and at the same

Sylvester Graham, *A Lecture to Young Men on Chastity* (Boston: George W. Light, 1839), 72–74, 83–89.

time transmit to your offspring an impaired constitution, with strong and unhappy predispositions. . . .

. . . Remember, my young friends, the end of your [body's] organization! Recollect that the *final cause* of your organs of reproduction—the propagation of your species—requires but seldom the exercise of their function!—and remember that the higher capabilities of man qualify him for more exalted and exalting pleasures than lie within the precincts of sensual enjoyment!—and remember, also, that by all we go beyond the real wants of nature, in the indulgence of our appetites, we debase our intellectual and moral powers, increase the carnal influences over our mental and moral faculties, and circumscribe our field of rational acquisition and enabling pleasures.

Who, then, would yield to sensuality, and forego the higher dignity of his nature, and be contended to spend his life and all his energies in the low satisfactions of a brute! when earth and heaven are full of motives for noble and exalting enterprise?—and when time and eternity are the fields which lie before him, for achievements of virtue, and happiness, and immortality, and unperishing glory?

There is a common error of opinion among young men, which is, perhaps, not wholly confined to the young,—that health requires an emission of semen at stated periods, and that frequent nocturnal emissions in sleep are not incompatible with health. Nay, indeed, "many entertain the notion that to give loose to venereal indulgence, increases the energy and activity of the mind, sharpens the wit, gives brilliancy and power to the imagination, and beautiful and sublime flights to fancy!"—All this is wrong,—entirely, dangerously wrong! Health does not absolutely require that there should ever be an emission of semen from puberty to death, though the individual live an hundred years:—and the frequency of involuntary, nocturnal emissions, is an indubitable proof, that the parts at least, are suffering under a debility, and morbid irritability, utterly incompatible with the general welfare of the system: and the mental faculties are always debilitated and impaired by such indulgences.

If an unmarried man finds himself troubled with concupiscence, let him be more abstemious, and less stimulating and heating in his diet, and take more active exercise in the open air, and use the cold bath under proper circumstances; and there will be no necessity for an emission of his semen:—especially if, with proper chastity of mind, he avoids lewd images and conceptions. And if a married man finds himself inclined to an excess of sexual indulgence, let him adopt the same regimen, and he will soon find that he has no reason to complain of what he calls his natural propensity. All men can be chaste in body and in mind, if they truly desire it, and if they use the right means to be so. But it is a perfect mockery, to talk about our inherent and ungovernable passions, while we take every measure to deprave our instinctive propensities, and to excite our passions, and render them ungovernable and irresistible.

By far the worst form of venereal indulgence, is self-pollution; or, what is called "Onanism." . . .

. . . [I]t is wholly unnatural; and, in every respect, does violence to nature. The mental action, and the power of the imagination on the genital organs, forcing a vital stimulation of the parts, which is reflected over the whole nervous system, are exceedingly intense and injurious; and consequently the reciprocal influences between the brain and the genital organs become extremely powerful, and irresistible, and destructive. The general, prolonged, and rigid tension of the muscular and nervous tissues, is excessively severe and violent. In short, the consentaneous effort, and concentrated energy of all the powers of the human system, to this single forced effect, cause the most ruinous irritation, and violence, and exhaustion, and debility to the system.

5. Navy Drummer Philip C. Van Buskirk's Private Journal, 1852–1853

SEPTEMBER 1852.

Friday, 17. . . .

An Old Reprobate on the wrong side of *fifty seven,* came to me yesterday at breakfast time with a present of fruit which I accepted as a kind of just due for services I had often rendered him, and I thought they were offered as such. At dinner time I was waited upon with another present, which I also accepted; and at suppertime was again urged to partake of the old fellow's liberality, but declined. Beginning to think of what might be the *motive* of the old Main-mast man's sudden *liberality,* I soon perceived myself to be in that condition which is attached to all boys upon first entering the service—*the being the object of a S———te's desires.* Thinking of this fact mortified me a little; I considered the man's age—my own age—and the fact that my past conduct had been studied & so regulated by decency as to leave no ground for disesteem, and this consideration led me to doubt whether the old fellow really did harbour such horrible thoughts & attach them to the *idea drummer.*

   After tattoo I betook myself to rest, occupying a space of the Gun Deck immediately a-port of the Main mast & between the pumps and Main Hatch—my usual place of resort, in the day for reading or sewing, & at night for sleeping. My pallet consists of the *Marine's* great-coat-bag and a watch coat, with my fatigue jacket for pillow. As before said, I laid down yesterday after tattoo, and very soon fell asleep. In the night I was awakened—some one tugged at my arm—I thought of the old main mast man, & guessed correctly that it was he, but betrayed no symptoms of having been awaked.

   He tugged again & edged upon my pallet—Another tug and another edging, and he stretched out his unoccupied hand and rested it on my head. Considering the game as played long enough, I coughed and made other symptoms of awaking, freed my hand, altered my position, and very gently kicked the fellow away. As he did not leave the place at the instance of my kicking, I set up, and roughly—contemptuously—told him to 'clear out'.

Drummer Philip C. Van Buskirk's Private Journal and Remark Book entries: September 17, September 22, October 22–23, 1852; August 19, October 19, 1853. Manuscripts and University Archives, University of Washington, Seattle, Wash.

Wensday [*sic*], 22. . . .

Suspicious Conduct. Since the 17th of this month, I have every night shared my *pallet* with . . . Joe . . . , and this conduct is food for scandal. A Quartermaster, quick to criminate, attacked me the other day with—'*Well! You lays alongside o'boys now o'nights, do you*', upon which ensued the following dialogue: Æ. 'Of lates I rate a chicken—to be sure!—what next? Q. 'Why aint you ashamed of yourself to have a boy alongside of you all night'. Æ. 'Not exactly, considering who the boy is, and that nothing bad results from our sleeping together—Q. Who the boy is! why that boy would —— a jackass'—Æ. 'I do'nt care if he would —— a jackass—I know that he do'nt —— me. Every night passed with me by the boy is a night spent in inno-cence—when he sleeps with me, he is out of harm's way; if he did'nt sleep with me, he'd certainly sleep with somebody else, &, in that case, bad consequences might in-deed result. Q. Oh, Hell! now do you mean to say that you sleeps alongside o' boys o'nights and do'nt do nothing? Æ. Well now you may as well drop the subject—I see you are a little more interested than you ought to be—you are jealous.' &c.

Joe does'nt any longer sleep with me; he deserted me yesterday to take up his *residence* with a Main-topman. I have now lost patience with the youngster, and must of necessity express less friendship in manner towards him, that he may feel the odium which guilt is calculated to excite.

OCTOBER, 1852.

Friday, 22. . . .

*Sin * * *. I would most willingly spare myself this remark. Towards the close of last night, I awoke from a sleep and found myself on the point of involuntary pollution; consciousness returned just before the moment of consummation, which took place without any opposition of my will, though I believe it come into play.*

Saturday, 23. . . .

I'D THINK NATURE had cursed me at my birth—that I am damned—that I am rapidly going down the stream of perdition—destined to misery here and Hell here-after; but no; to think so would be to meet Hell half way. Between me and the grave are yet years, and there is yet hope. I was led on last night by a series of evil thoughts to the perpetration of that damning crime—the bane of my soul. Oh! I am a miserable dog—I am Hell's own—a favorite child—unless the devils themselves abhor my conduct.

Angels abhor me; and so would men, if they only knew me. I abhor myself— would fly my own polluting presence.

AUGUST 1853.

Friday, 19. . . .

Conversation, last night, with an old sailor on the subject of manual pol[l]ution.
Æ. Well, White, what's your opinion of those men who have to do with boys? If you were King, would'nt you kill every one of 'em?

WHITE. Yes; Every feller that lives ashore and does *that*, I'd shoot him—yaas, by —, I'd shoot him.

Æ. And if you had a navy, would'nt you kill every man in it found guilty of *that?*

WH. No;—what can a feller do? —three years at sea—and hardly any chance to have a woman. I tell you, drummer, a feller *must do so*. Biles and pimples and corruption will come out all over his body if he do'nt.

Æ. White, you have given me your opinion candidly and openly. I'll be equally as candid with you: *If I were King, I would kill every man at sea or ashore found guilty of this dreadful practice, and I would never have mercy*—See here, have you ever read any books on this subject?

W. No.

Æ. Well you are most damnably mistaken about this practice "being *healthy!*" I'll lend you a little book to-morrow that tells all about it.

W. Thankee—I'll read it.

OCTOBER, 1853.

Wensday, 19. . . .

PÆDERASTY—SODOMY. To prevent confusion of meaning which might in future ensue upon a wrong use of the terms *paederasty* and *sodomy* in these Notes, I will now as clearly as possible define the meaning I have thought belonging to them. I first met with *"paederasty"* in Gibbon's Rome. . . . I understand the word to mean *the practice of sodomy between two males where the* hand *of each is used to pollute the other,* or *where one performs with the* hand *this horrid office for another.* On board of ships, paederasty (called "shaking") is not looked upon as a form of sodomy, but considered innocent and undeserving of reproach. I extend the signification of *Sodomy* to embrace every horrid unnatural use of the organs of generation: and as such, embracing *Paederasty,* where one must act for another, *Onanism,* where one acts for himself, and lastly *the laying down of a male to act as a* woman *to another male,* which form alone sailors call "sodomy".

⬛ E S S A Y S

These two historians of women consider the social and sexual changes of the early nineteenth century from the increasingly divergent perspectives of middle-class and working-class women. Christine Stansell of Princeton University explores both cross-class relationships and the culture of working-class youth in New York City. Her analysis of the case of Henry Bedlow, a "gentleman" charged with raping seamstress Lanah Sawyer, reveals the class and gendered assumptions that governed many sexual interactions. Power relations among working-class men and women were more open to negotiation, Stansell argues, and in some ways represented an improvement for working-class women. Nancy F. Cott of Yale University examines the sexual ideology of an emerging middle class, and explores the origins of the Victorian idea that women were by nature less carnal and lustful than men. Middle-class women embraced "passionlessness"—a desexualized definition of womanhood—because it downplayed their vulnerability to men; defined them in moral, intellectual, and spiritual terms; and gave them some power over sexual and reproductive choices. Compare the responses of middle-class and working-class women to male assumptions about sexuality. How did the notion that women were passionless relate to the sexual double standard and women's vulnerability to rape, seduction, and abandonment? What was working-class women's relationship to the ideology of passionlessness?

Male License and Working-Class Women's Sexuality

CHRISTINE STANSELL

[T]he republican beliefs of the Revolution, broadly disseminated among New York laboring men, amplified and strengthened assumptions of female subservience and male authority that were already widely current in eighteenth-century Anglo-American society. Elite women in the decades after the war had held onto some ideological and cultural resources that protected and even improved their perceived position. Laboring women, however, had barely examined the possibilities the Revolution held out for their sex; moreover, their class position made them more vulnerable to sexual antagonisms which grew worse in the next twenty years.

It was not that patriarchal views of women were anything new, or that there was a direct causal relation between republican politics and contemptuous attitudes toward women. Rather, the ideological climate of the post-Revolutionary decades seems to have reinvigorated, rather than undercut, an already established, popularly based misogyny. Women had never rated high in the canons of eighteenth-century thought. Seventeenth-century dissenting Protestantism had done something to elevate female status by breaking with a centuries-old European tradition that viewed women as daughters of Eve, mankind's ill fortune, prey to vanity, folly and concupiscence. Yet the old suspicions of women cropped up on all levels of seventeenth-century American religious society, from ministers' sermons to judgments against village shrews to witchcraft accusations. In the eighteenth century, . . . Eve's vices lingered on, to be translated into the quintessentially feminine follies that advice and etiquette books admonished women to curb and men to beware of. Although the ideas in these writings were not necessarily those of their readers (not to speak of all those who did not read books), they nonetheless reveal what literate men and women thought in all possibility they could expect of themselves and each other.

From this perspective, the belief in women's potential for deviousness is striking. Women's dependent status supposedly fostered in them all the vices and stratagems of the weak: They were foolish, easily corrupted by flattery, immodest and frivolous, artful and vain. And *because* they were so prone to these vices, they were rightfully and properly dependent on men for direction and moral authority. Thus Lord Chesterfield, whose letters (collected and published as an advice manual) were popular on both sides of the Atlantic, made one of his typically low assessments of the female character: "They have but two passions, vanity and love," he remarked. Chesterfield was a confirmed misogynist, and his ideas define the outer

Christine Stansell, *City of Women: Sex and Class in New York, 1780–1860* (New York: Knopf, 1986), 20–30, 83, 86–92, 95–96, 98–99. From *City of Women* by Christine Stansell, copyright © 1982, 1986 by Christine Stansell. Used by permission of Alfred A. Knopf, a division of Random House, Inc.

limits of articulated antagonisms toward women, but he was by no means alone. More liberal-minded writers implicitly sided with him, if not in the tactics he advocated, then at least with his low estimation of female character. Throughout the century, a variety of reform-minded Anglo-American writers, from Mary Wollstonecraft to Benjamin Franklin, held up an alternative ideal of female piety, modesty and prudence; although they proposed that the sources of women's defects lay not in their nature but in their upbringing, they, too, implied that the female character was morally deficient.

Even in a society that talked about liberty as much as did post-Revolutionary America, such weak and willful people could not be left to their own devices. To exercise virtue and ensure the capacity to maintain the republic, a citizen had to be *independent:* that is, he had to be at liberty to act according to his own reasoned judgments about what served the public good. . . . No one who depended on another could fully exercise republican virtue, and thus no dependent—woman, servant, child or slave—possessed the moral status necessary for citizenship. Thus the ideological legacy of the Revolution shaped men's—including laboring men's—sense of their place in the gender system as well as in the entirety of American society. The political importance of the male-headed household was confirmed; republican patriarchalism was synonymous with citizenship; independence demanded the subordination of morally suspect dependents. . . . Women, then, were rightfully subjected within their households to the authority of those male heads who could properly watch out for their interest and protect the liberties of all.

The implications of republican ideology for women were not all negative. Popular republicanism, with its stress on the reasonable abilities of all human beings, provided women themselves some ways to attack the belief in the innate folly of their character. During the Revolution and the early national period, women, especially the wives and daughters of patriot leaders, raised tentative questions about women's rights (recall Abigail Adams's admonition to her husband at the beginning of the Revolution to "remember the ladies"). They also improved the social estimation of their sex by creating a republican imagery of motherhood. If virtue was necessary to citizenship, they proclaimed, then women could play a part in the new republic as mothers who educated their sons in republican values. Gone were the follies of the lady; reason and prudence, not vanity and frivolity, would characterize the republican mother. For privileged women, this perspective on woman's social role was to foster, in turn, the nineteenth-century cult of domesticity. . . .

There were, then, competing republican images, one group invented and promoted primarily by women, the other inherited from the past and articulated chiefly by men. On balance, it was the latter that prevailed, especially (we will see) in regard to laboring women. As in any revolution, only a self-conscious women's movement could have made real for women the emancipatory potential of the patriots' ideas of liberty. Not only did the American Revolution do little to improve the female condition; in many ways it strengthened negative opinions of women. Indeed, by the 1790s, the campaign for recognition of women's full dignity had *lost* ground, especially in New York, where British influence remained strong among the elite. There, republican motherhood (whatever its appeal to high-minded patriots) ran against the grain of a culture that took its cues from Regency London. "The sink of British manners and politics," Benjamin Rush acerbically termed fashionable

New York. However ardently New York women may have worked to enhance the dignity of their sex, their efforts occurred in a city where self-styled libertines swaggered about the streets, the blood sports beloved by Regency rakes persisted as popular pastimes and the double standard of sexual behavior remained a source of unabashed masculine pride.

If anything, male license for sexual aggressiveness increased in the two decades after the Revolution, especially toward women in public. . . .

These antagonisms toward women were never fully elaborated into explicit ideas that men considered and debated. Mostly, assumptions about women were expressed within a structure of feeling rather than a body of explicit ideas. What shaped the gender relations of ordinary people were unconscious or half-conscious beliefs, intuitions, reactions—the culturally conditioned sense of what was obvious and proper, a matter of common sense. Republican ideas of government, authority and power supported already familiar justifications of sexual hierarchies. To understand the roots and implications of these darker perceptions of women, we must piece together fragments.

A series of events in 1793 provides an especially valuable source of information about how men could act out and explain to themselves their hostilities toward women, and how those hostilities connected with popular politics. Harry Bedlow, a gentleman, was charged with raping seventeen-year-old Lanah Sawyer, a seamstress and daughter of a seaman. Sawyer had met Bedlow one evening when she was out walking; he introduced himself as "Lawyer Smith" and asked to see her again. When the pair walked out together, Bedlow at first treated his companion to chaste and genteel entertainments, ice cream and a tour around the Battery. On the way back, however, well after midnight, he demanded payment for his favors and either forced the girl (according to her) or invited her (according to him) into a bawdy house, where they spent the night and had sexual "connection."

Bedlow's defense in the ensuing trial constitutes a digest of misogynist thought girded by class contempt. Rather than defending Bedlow's intentions or actions, his phalanx of distinguished attorneys shrewdly shifted the focus of the trial from the duplicity of the seducer to the weak-mindedness of the seduced. The girl, they argued, should have been better attuned to the etiquette of debauchery. When a poor girl meets a rich man on the street, what else should she assume but that he intends to make use of her sexually? "Considering the difference of their situations, to what motive could she attribute his assiduities? Could she imagine that a man of his situation would pay her any attention . . . unless with a view of promoting illicit commerce? Was it probable that Lawyer Smith had any honorable designs in his connection with a sewing girl?" This was not rape but seduction by an accomplished practitioner of the art, the counsel proudly affirmed.

This argument drew on very old beliefs about men's rights to women's bodies. But the identification of heterosexual relations with treachery and cold-blooded exploitation was particularly characteristic of eighteenth-century Anglo-American culture. In the lawyers' argument that Bedlow's intentions were perfectly clear— what else could a gentleman want with a poor girl?—courting appears as a barely concealed contest of duplicity between men and women. The prescriptive literature of the times viewed frank sexual hostility as a fact of polite society. "The greater part of either sex study to prey upon one another," avowed the fashionable London preacher Dr. Fordyce, author of a popular advice manual published in an American edition in 1787; thank goodness, he added parenthetically, men had the edge. "The world," he lamented, "in too many instances, is a theatre of war between women and men. Every stratagem is tried, and every advantage taken, on the side of both." Courtship was a war of wits, each sex jockeying to turn the other to its own exploitative uses. Marriage was a prolonged siege of female guile against male authority: *Female Policy Detected: or the Arts of a Designing Woman Laid Open* ran the title of one popular satire. In this context, writers exhorted men to use dissimulation as a weapon. Reasonable men, Lord Chesterfield wrote, only trifled with women and always kept in mind that "they" could turn vicious: "It is necessary to manage, please, and flatter them, and never to discover the least marks of contempt, which is what they never forgive"—all the more difficult, since contempt was just what Chesterfield assumed would be uppermost in men's minds. Although Chesterfield's views of women were especially derisive, the popular reception of the *Letters* shows the extent to which polite society tolerated extreme sexual antagonisms and saw sexual aggression—even brutal aggression—as one way for gentlemen to get on in the world.

While men's power in the struggle derived from their superior authority, reason and intelligence (their "strength and daring," as Fordyce put it), women's flowed from "passion." If chastity was the cardinal virtue of womanhood, passion was its chief vice. Passion was women's legendary carnality, the curse of Eve, capacious receptacle for all the foolishness, wantonness and greed of the sex. It knew no limits of age. Any female could be a passionate creature, as the defendants in trials for child rape sometimes contended. The attorney for a weaver charged with raping a thirteen-year-old girl in 1800, for example, based the argument for the defense on the claim that carnality comprised the essence of even a female child's character: "The passions may be as warm in a girl of her age as in one of more advanced years." As for the traduced Lanah Sawyer, it was her "desire of gratifying her passions," the defense attorneys argued, which led her to entertain the man's acquaintance in the first place. Passion was not simply lasciviousness, but sexual greed fused with other kinds of acquisitiveness in a peculiarly female mode of exploitation. By these lights Sawyer was not the victim she appeared; only trickery, "art," preserved the appearance of innocence—a "fair outside, while all was foul within."

After fifteen minutes of deliberation in the Bedlow/Sawyer rape trial, the jury returned a verdict of not guilty. The acquittal touched off a riot, in which a crowd of six hundred (men, it seems) converged on the bawdy house where the accused, Bedlow, had taken the girl. The mob ransacked it, and proceeded on to several other brothels and the houses of Bedlow's attorneys before mounted militia turned them back.

Against the backdrop of the bloody events in France in 1793, political passions—pro- and antirevolutionary—ran high in the new republic. In the Bedlow affair, popular dissatisfaction with the privileged crystallized into an image of aristocratic sexual license. Sympathy for the girl herself does not seem to have been particularly important in the affair. Her own father vowed "if his daughter was wrong he would turn her out of doors" and loyalty not to the girl but to the father, a man "well known amongst the seafaring People," seems to have motivated the "Boys, Apprentices, Negroes and Sailors" who made up the crowd. The spectacle of gentlemanly license protected by a court was what touched off a wave of "popular indignation," turning a drama of female sexual vulnerability into a conflict between men.

Into this fray entered "Justitia," probably a woman of some learning, certainly a highly literate one (her real identity remains hidden). Angered by Bedlow's acquittal, Justitia wrote a letter to the newspaper denouncing Bedlow as "a *wretch* . . . whose character is too vile to be portrayed" and took the occasion to air some of her own sexual grievances. The attack on the bawdy houses had been, no doubt, "a matter of great grief for many of our *male* citizens," she observed with unladylike sarcasm, "considering what comfortable hours they have passed in these peaceful abodes far from the complaints of a neglected wife." She went on to suggest—archly—that the bawdy houses might be policed far more effectively if it weren't for the fact that the magistrates themselves patronized them.

Justitia's intrepid foray into print set off a flurry of abuse. No respectable woman could even know of such things, her respondents maintained sardonically. They dropped hints about her identity and to top if off belittled the "weakness of her misunderstanding and the indelicacy of her pen." The exchange quickly shifted ground from the political matter of the bawdy houses to the question of Justitia's own honor. In the end she was reduced to recruiting a gentleman who, she informed her adversaries in her final letter, would call on the writer who had most directly sullied her name through his imputations. These were not women's matters, Justitia had learned, even if rape and prostitution directly concerned them. Men guarded the public discourse of sexuality.

In the Bedlow case and the Justitia exchange, the implicit sexual connotations of the weak-mindedness of women became explicit. Popular views of female folly converged with the notion of passion. Both were defects that warped women's ability to act reasonably. Dominated by emotional imperatives, women could not comport themselves with the fairness and independence required of the citizen. In the trial, Bedlow's attorneys, drawing on such assumptions, had suggested that unleashing women in a court of law in itself threatened the civil process. The life of a citizen (rape was a capital crime until 1796) was in jeopardy because of a woman's testimony, and such testimony was inherently suspect. "Putting the life of a citizen in the hands of a woman to be disposed of almost at her will and pleasure," the defense grimly characterized the proceedings, and went on to denounce the legitimacy of all female testimony in the trial as fundamentally compromised by the supposedly loose sexual proclivities of the women in question. The female neighbors had testified that Lanah Sawyer was a girl of good character, unlikely to go to bed willingly with Bedlow. In response, the prosecution argued that the neighbor women's testimony was worthless, since by virtue of their sex and their humble position, they knew nothing of good character themselves: "Their being of the same condition of life with the Prosecutrix gives us a right to doubt what they mean." The sexual practices of such women—"accustomed . . . to allowing male friends liberties"—partook of the same vices which deformed Sawyer's character.

The intersection of class and gender, then, signified a sexual wantonness that weakened women's credibility. More broadly, assumptions about female passion discredited women's authority over their own persons. Men could with some justification make women, especially laboring women, their sexual prey, since a foul nature exempted the latter from the customary protections of virtuous womanhood.

Justitia had stepped out of place, thereby abnegating those protections, by venturing into the public discourse of sexual politics. Other women did so simply by walking unescorted on the streets. Harassing women in public was a favorite entertainment of the "bloods," rakes whose chief pastime was lounging about the streets. . . . A phalanx of young men hung about the streets, ready to jeer and jolt a victim. "If she essays to proceed by the wall, they instantly veer that way, and defeat her intention. In this manner she is often obliged to pass and repass several times in front of the line, each one making his impertinent remarks on her as she tried to get forward—'An Angel, by H———s!' 'Dam'd fine girl, by g———d!' 'Where do you lodge, my dear?'" "Language the most obscene, and actions the most gross" accompanied the hooting and catcalling. Laboring women, more likely than ladies to be out on the streets alone, must have been frequent targets. Certainly the effect of the insults (which included "the drawing up of the upper, or pouting out of the nether lip, accompanied with a sort of hissing") was to stigmatize women as rightful prey on the streets. . . .

. . . Contempt for women was not the attitude exclusively of wealthy gentlemen. Indeed, it was probably a bond that men shared across class lines in a "plebeian" culture where sporting gentlemen might consort with workingmen at bawdy houses and cockfighting rings and in political affrays. Images of women as bawds and tricksters were a staple in the conversations of laboring people, and the lusty moll of sailors' ballads and journeymen's jokes was close kin to the greedy whore of the gentlemen's lore. The figure of the affable wench, an integral part of the bawdy popular culture of the early eighteenth century, was still alive in the first two decades of the nineteenth. Sometimes amiable, sometimes scheming, she was one way or the other out to get her way with men. For "The Orange Woman," a Dublin girl in a sailors' broadside, this meant simply satisfying her carnal appetites. "I always fancy pretty Men,/Wherever I can find 'em," the "hearty buxom Girl" declares unabashedly.

> I'll never marry, no indeed,
>   For Marriage causes trouble;
> And after all the priest has said,
>   'Tis merely hubble bubble.
> The rakes will still be counted rakes,
>   Not hymen's chains can bind 'em. . . .

"And so," she happily concludes

> Preventing all mistakes
> I'll kiss where'er I find 'em.

The Orange Woman was a sailor's dream come true, the proverbial whore with a heart of gold who took pleasure in men and asked for little in return. . . .

Real women, of course, demanded a return on their favors, and other renditions of the bawd from before the Revolution also indicate laboring men's view that sexuality was a female weapon, the instrument by which women duped men and then took them for all they were worth. "A father said to his son, what is your wife quick already?" ran a joke from an almanac aimed at a readership of skilled workers. "Yes, said he, a pox on her, she is too quick, for we have been married but a month, and she is ready to lie in." The source of humor in such jokes was a shared view of women as inseparable from the babies they bore and of both babies and women as parasites on men's lives. "A man complained to his wife she brought him nothing. You lie like a rogue, says she, for I bring you boys and girls without your help." . . .

. . . The double standard, by these lights, was a legitimate male weapon in sexual warfare rather than a regrettable consequence of male lust—the construction the Victorians would later give it. So was sexual antagonism and even, sometimes, sexual violence. True, there were powerful ideological traditions, including republicanism, that celebrated the family as an entity of heterosexual harmony and mutuality. This cooperative image, however, stood in tension with another view of the family as a place for disciplining women, a means of cloistering them and protecting society at large from their depredations.

It was not these assumptions alone, of course, that consigned women to the family and men to the public world. Centuries of tradition dictated that women be responsible for household labor and that they be excluded from many kinds of public life. But the assumptions about women's nature did legitimate this familiar division, constraining women from walking the streets, engaging in a trade or seeking amusement for themselves. Meanwhile, the structures of household life that supported beliefs in masculine authority and female moral weakness eroded under economic and social pressures. The consequent rearrangements in women's work, part and parcel of the experience of proletarian life, were in many cases to aggravate sexual hostilities. The working-class city of the nineteenth century, however, would also create openings for more amiable negotiations between the sexes. . . .

. . . [S]ingle women helped to create a youth culture of sexual and commercial pleasures, purchased with wages and time freed up from domestic obligations and family discipline. . . .

. . . Sexuality was often the ticket of admission—the key to social pleasure, the coin of heterosexual exchange.

Antebellum working-class youth culture encompassed the bawdy houses and some of the traditional rowdy pastimes of what was still a rough maritime town, but as early as 1820 it also occupied new corners of the city. Holiday excursions to the country, for example, were special treats in which women included themselves. . . .

"Walking out" was another way young men and women met. Walking out was a prelude to courting, a means of flirting and pairing off. Young girls fell into walking out as they hung about the streets in groups in the course of doing their daily chores. Walking out was a patterned promenade on the avenues and in public places like City Hall Park; there, on Broadway and the Bowery, the crowds and the jumble of people and classes shielded the young from the scrutiny of their neighborhoods. If walking out gave young women greater independence from adult supervision, however, the custom also provided, as in Lanah Sawyer's case, the latitude for some disastrous mistakes. As single women ventured outside the restrictions of their neighborhoods, they left behind the protections that kin and neighbors provided in enforcing men's sexual propriety. Although flirtations on the avenues were freer, they were also more dangerous, especially in a city where seduction, even debauchery, remained sources of male self-esteem into the antebellum years. . . .

. . . Being on one's own was, in general, a very risky business. The trials suffered by Caroline, whom Ezra Stiles Ely met in 1811 in his ministry to the Almshouse, show how seriously a girl could injure herself in cutting herself loose from her family. Caroline had been engaged to a young man in her hometown in Vermont; with her mother's blessing, the pair went off to visit his parents in another town, where the suitor promised they would marry. They eloped instead to New York, where he took a room for them in a waterfront boardinghouse. Shortly thereafter he abandoned Caroline, leaving her penniless and infected with gonorrhea. Without friends or kin in the city, she went to the Almshouse for treatment, where her country looks and repentant ways brought her to the minister's attention. But despite her professions of repentance to Reverend Ely, Caroline had seen enough of New York in her short stay to perceive that "keeping company" with men could be a way of supporting herself alone in the city. So when she left the Almshouse cured, she made her way back "on the town," to the same boardinghouse where she had lived with her young man, to support herself through prostitution.

Caroline's story shows both the pleasures and the dangers involved when a girl set off on her own. Courtship was one part of a system of barter between the sexes, in which a woman traded sexual favors for a man's promise to marry. Premarital intercourse then became a token of betrothal. This was, however, a problematic exchange for the woman, since she delivered on her part of the bargain—and risked pregnancy—before the man came through with his. In the settled European and rural communities in which this practice was rooted, a young woman could count on family, neighbors and (in Ireland) local magistrates to hold the man to his vows should she become pregnant while courting. Even in the more volatile circumstances of cities, neighbors and kin did what they could to supervise courtships. One of Lanah Sawyer's neighbors, for instance, had warned her that the "smart beau" who walked her home one night was not "lawyer smith" at all but "Harry Bedlow, a very great rake. . . ." The already developed *genteel* code of female chastity had little bearing here. It was not "walking out" for which the neighbor admonished Lanah Sawyer, but the reputation of the one with whom she walked. Other young couples consummated their courtships practically under the eyes and with the tacit knowledge of the girls' families. In 1800, for instance, a respectable Quaker family watched calmly while a cousin, Alma Sands, disappeared into various bedrooms with the boarder Levi Weeks. The warmth of the courtship was occasion for remarks, but not the form the courtship was taking; the family assumed that the sexual activity was in itself proof (in general) of the pair's commitment and (in particular) of Levi Weeks's seriousness. "I always thought Levi a man of honor," attested the aunt, "And that he did not intend to promise further than he could perform."

When people moved around, however, from city to city, from the Old World to the New, and from country to city (as in Caroline's case), these methods of ensuring male responsibility weakened. A young woman on her own in New York could enjoy the pleasures of promenading the avenues in fine dresses purchased with her own wages, but those "frolics" . . . could also leave her bereft, stranded, and pregnant. Even single girls like Lanah Sawyer and Alma Sands, surrounded by people with an eye to their well-being, could run into trouble with men in the mobile and anonymous circumstances of the city. The neighbor's warnings failed to dissuade Lanah Sawyer from a disastrous liaison; Alma Sands was murdered the night she was to marry Levi Weeks and suspicions that Weeks had tried to evade his obligations by killing the girl led to his indictment for the crime. The slow breakdown of betrothal practices was perhaps one reason that the Sawyer rape case became a *cause célèbre*. Like the trial of Harry Bedlow, the Sands murder also became a magnet for popular fantasies and fears. Hundreds of people came to view the girl's body; rumors swirled about the murderer's identity and the details of the killing; peddlers hawked handbills which conjured up "ghouls and goblins . . . dancing devils . . . accounts of witchcraft . . . strange and wonderful prophecies." These were early and especially lurid acts in a narrative of seduction and betrayal that had probably already touched many urban families, and that in ensuing decades was to become a staple of nineteenth-century popular melodrama.

Early in the century, then, single women claimed their part in a youthful milieu where they could conduct—to a greater or lesser degree—their own pleasures and affairs. But sexual territory was also dangerous ground where the same mobility that gave women some degree of freedom—the continual movement of people in and around each others' lives—also rendered them more vulnerable to male entrapment and abandonment.

The mentality of early national life also enhanced that vulnerability. As long as rakes like Harry Bedlow remained exemplars of fashion, and as long as laboring men looked on women as antagonists to be outfoxed and outmaneuvered, severe sorts of exploitativeness toward young women—especially young women of spirit—would seem legitimate and unremarkable. And as long as the heterosexual marketplace of leisure remained closely connected to the older, male-dominated milieu of the bawdy houses, different conceptions of relations between men and women had little chance to emerge. The development of new possibilities awaited a more distinct working-class culture, where men's consciousness of how much they held in common with other wage earners—in other words, a working-class consciousness—would lead them to look more kindly on their female peers. This was a culture where the self-conscious community of class experience would to some degree encompass women, and where the slumming gentleman would prove an unwelcome guest. . . .

That milieu began to materialize in the 1830s on the Bowery, the broad avenue running up and down the east side of the island. . . . In the two decades before the Civil War, it became a byword for working-class culture. . . . Evenings on the Bowery were the special province of young people. At the end of the working day and on Saturday night, the dance halls, oyster houses and the famed Bowery Theater, built in 1827, came alive with workingwomen, journeymen and laborers looking for marital prospects, sexual encounters and general good times. In many ways, this culture resembled that of the bawdy houses. Men set the tone, and abusiveness toward women, if no longer explicitly celebrated in jokes and songs, still entered into the proceedings. Still, Bowery culture involved changes in the relations of single, young men and women; it marginalized older forms of misogyny and celebrated instead the possibilities of gregariousness between the sexes. While the reality often fell short, the ideal still represented an opening in gender relations. . . .

Through the 1830s, the peculiar features of Bowery life—vociferous crowds at the theaters, riotous volunteer fire companies and truculent street gangs—became sufficiently well known to cohere into a cultural identity recognizable to outsiders; in the early 1840s, the Bowery produced its first metropolitan "type," the Bowery Boy. Valorous, generous and unabashedly rough-hewn in manners and speech, the Boy descended from the Bowery "fire laddie" of the famed workingmen's volunteer fire companies in the 1830s; unlike the latter, however, the Bowery Boy aspired to fashion and style. . . .

. . . One of the accoutrements of the Boy's persona was "his girl hanging on his arm" . . . a young workingwoman: a factory girl, shopgirl, milliner, dressmaker, book folder, map colorer, flower maker, or seamstress. Wage work and the loosening of domestic obligations that wages purchased made her presence possible. George Foster, the would-be Dickens of the New York scene, noted how such young women emerged in a crowd at the end of the workday, streaming toward the east side: "all forming a continuous procession which . . . loses itself gradually in the innumerable side-streets leading thence into the unknown regions of Proletaireism in the East End." Many of them ended up on the Bowery, sashaying up and down the avenue with crowds of girlfriends or on the arms of their young men. For women, the allure seems to have been exclusively heterosexual. Although the beginnings of a gay male subculture were just visible—Whitman, for one, was part of it—the social conditions for a lesbian milieu seem to have been absent in what was still a heavily masculine culture. Still, the young women of the Bowery, decked out in fancy clothes, beckoned to every newly arrived country girl, a collective symbol of certain pleasures of city life. . . .

. . . The Bowery was not egalitarian in its gender relations, but Bowery style did repudiate some kinds of antagonisms toward women, primarily those that were bound up with blatant class exploitation. While voyeuristic "aristos" had found some welcome at turn-of-the-century bawdy houses, gentlemen looking for liaisons with working girls ran into frank hostility on the Bowery. "The b'hoys are little inclined to disguise the open contempt and hatred he inspires," Foster reported of the gentleman intruder. "Should he become at all demonstrative in his attention to any of the ladies," he was likely to come to blows with her protectors. Abram Dayton, who himself had once been a gentleman looking for a good time on the avenue, remembered how risky flirtations could be. "The Broadway exquisite who ventured 'within the pale' was compelled to be very guarded in his advances towards any fair one . . . any approach to familiarity either by word or look was certain to be visited by instant punishment." Women joined in. "The g'hals themselves despise him," Foster noted of the "aristo." If a fight developed, Dayton recalled, the women rallied to the Boys' side, cheering them on as in a faction fight in Ireland or a street fight in New York.

The Boys' antagonism to the prowling outsider was a way by which they defined exclusive rights to "their" women. The workingmen's own sense of the widening distance between rich and poor, Broadway and the Bowery, employer and employee, colored their perceptions of working-class women. The rise of the Bowery was inseparable from the growth of working-class consciousness between 1830 and 1860. In this context, the rough version of republican ideology that the Bowery Boys inherited—the celebration of the virtues of manual labor and physical prowess, the virile patriotism, the truculence toward outside authority—promoted a change in republican views of women. Like their eighteenth-century predecessors, Bowery men saw public life—in their case, working-class life—as a place where men were the main show and women the supporting cast. But in contrast to earlier attitudes, theirs was a paternalist stance that stressed the protective rather than antagonistic elements of their involvement with women. The visibility of the Bowery Gals must have contributed to this shift. As independent wage earners, women themselves cast off some symbolic associations with dependency.

The Boys' defense of their female guests was certainly not egalitarian or comradely, but neither was it overtly misogynist. For all the limitations of working-class paternalism, . . . this paternalism still granted working-class women a greater ability to lay claim to some respect. On one level, the Boys, in delineating their turf, laid claims to territory in women. But on another, they challenged the unabashed sexual predation of the gentleman. In doing so, they acknowledged some obligations to their female companions, albeit in a fundamentally patronizing way.

The expansive heterosexuality of the Bowery, however, also competed with the rougher side of its working-class republicanism: the bellicosity, the masculinism (women on the sidelines), the localism and the insular loyalties. In the 1830s, the Boweryites' pugnacious defense of their rights against interfering outsiders erupted not only in melees with rival fire companies and gangs but in antiblack, antiabolitionist riots and the first stirrings of anti-immigrant nativism. . . . A culture so concerned with vaunting its male insiders—the true American boys—at the expense of everyone else (the Irish, the English, the blacks, the wealthy and genteel) must often have cast women as parasitic outsiders.

Thus while working-class consciousness undermined some features of eighteenth-century misogyny, still others persisted. Sexual hostilities may have gone underground, but they did not disappear, either from the Bowery or from the wider working-class world around it. The abuse of women, especially sexual abuse, remained a male prerogative; for some, it became a form of recreation. Group rapes, virtually unknown in the court records of the early nineteenth century, appear occasionally in court proceedings after 1830. "Getting our hide" was one perpetrator's term for a gang rape. The assailants were the same sorts of young workingmen who frequented the Bowery; their victims might have been, in other circumstances, their companions at the dance halls or oyster shops. . . .

. . . In a city where women were taking new territory for themselves, the intentions of both parties in a heterosexual encounter could be murky. . . .

Insofar as sex retained its associations to exchange and money, women's presence in a *commercial* culture of leisure, based on the purchase of pleasures, could in itself imply sexual willingness. . . . Caroline Wood, who charged a suitor with rape in 1858, seemed to have drifted—perhaps knowingly, perhaps unwittingly—into widening circles of erotic commitment. She had met the young man at a "place of amusement" and agreed to a rendezvous late one afternoon. As the pleasures he provided expanded from ice cream to an omnibus ride up Broadway to a boat trip to Newark to an excursion to the Jersey countryside, so did his sense of his sexual rights. By the time they left Newark he had raped her, and by the time they returned to New York he was introducing her as his wife. . . . Of her relation to her assailant, she protested to the court, "I never went with him to any place of public amusement. He never made me presents of the value of anything."

. . . Young men had long taken the sexual favors they believed women owed them; if necessary, they did so by force. The difference in a commercial milieu lay in what men viewed as a courtship. In household and neighborhood settings, women built up a sense of sexual obligation over a period of time and in a series of encounters. But when they met their partners in the hurly-burly of the dance halls and pleasure gardens, they could find themselves sexually accountable for just one night's round of beers and oysters.

Thus among the men of New York's working-class youth culture, older kinds of sexual exploitation and misogynistic abuse survived, albeit in new forms. While class-conscious notions of respect and protectiveness toward workingwomen could mitigate their harshest behavior, men continued to prey upon women outside the dance halls. Forced sex in courting became, if anything, more omnipresent as courting itself became more attenuated. Women alone on the streets continued to be targets for seduction and rape. The Boweryites may have despised gentlemen rakes, but the working class itself had plenty of seducers and rapists within its own ranks.

Still, while the Bowery marginalized rather than eradicated male predation, it also encouraged greater reciprocity, sexual and social, between young men and women. As was the case elsewhere in New York life, men took more than they gave. But a commercial culture that depended on the exchange of money for amusement and pleasure at least had this effect: Its practices of heterosexual exchange implied a more contingent notion of men's rights over women. Commercial culture promoted the assumption that women owed sexual favors in return for men's generosity. From women's perspective, this was hardly egalitarian, but it was an improvement on the view that women were legitimate targets for sexual coercion simply by virtue of their sex.

Passionlessness: An Interpretation of Victorian Sexual Ideology, 1790–1850

NANCY F. COTT

In 1903 Havelock Ellis announced that the notion of women's sexual "anaesthesia," as he called it, was a nineteenth-century creation. He had researched literary and medical sources from ancient Greece to early modern Europe and discovered, to his own amazement, that women had generally been thought to desire and enjoy sexual relations more than men. Ellis and his contemporaries initially sought the source of the idea that women lacked sexual passion in the generations immediately preceding their own. The late nineteenth century was an era of contention over female sexuality, physiology, health, dress, and exercise, and one in which medical opinion had become an authoritative sector of public opinion. Since investigators have found rich documentation on these controversies, particularly in medical sources, they have been little induced to look beyond them. Until quite recently, historians tended not only to follow Ellis's chronological bias but, like him, to associate the idea that women lacked sexual passion with social repression and dysfunction. Now that attitude has been challenged by the possibility that nineteenth-century sexual ideology held some definite advantages for women, and by the claim that ideology reflected or influenced behavior far less than had been thought.

Nancy F. Cott, "Passionlessness: An Interpretation of Victorian Sexual Ideology, 1790–1850," *Signs* 4 (Winter 1978): 219–236. Copyright © 1978 by The University of Chicago Press. Reprinted by permission of The University of Chicago Press.

A full appraisal of the idea that women lacked sexual passion requires an investigation of its origins. My purpose is to offer a hypothesis, if not a proven case, regarding the initiation and reception of that central tenet of Victorian sexual ideology which I call "passionlessness." I use the term to convey the view that women lacked sexual aggressiveness, that their sexual appetites contributed a very minor part (if any at all) to their motivations, that lustfulness was simply uncharacteristic. The concept of passionlessness represented a cluster of ideas about the comparative weight of woman's carnal nature and her moral nature; it indicated more about drives and temperament than about actions and is to be understood more metaphorically than literally.

Obviously, a single conception of women's sexuality never wholly prevails. Western civilization up to the eighteenth century, as Ellis discovered, accentuated women's concupiscence: a fifteenth-century witch-hunters' guide warned, for instance, that "carnal lust . . . in women is insatiable." But the Christian belief system that called unsanctified earthly women the devil's agents allowed, on the other hand, that women who embodied God's grace were more spiritual, hence less susceptible to carnal passion, than men. Nineteenth-century views of female sexuality were also double edged: notions of women's inherent licentiousness persisted, to be wielded against women manifesting any form of deviance under the reign of passionlessness. Acknowledging that notions of women's sexuality are never monolithic, I would nonetheless emphasize that there was a traditionally dominant Anglo-American definition of women as *especially* sexual which was reversed and transformed between the seventeenth and the nineteenth centuries into the view that women (although still primarily identified by their female gender) were *less* carnal and lustful than men.

The following pages focus on early appearances of the idea of female passionlessness, discuss its social context, and analyze if and why it was acceptable, especially to women. The documents in this test case are limited to New England; to apply the interpretive paradigm to literate, Protestant, middle-class women elsewhere would require further testing. I have looked to women's public and private writings in order to put the women involved in the forefront and prevent viewing them as passive recipients of changing ideas. My other sources are largely didactic and popular works, especially religious ones, which influenced women. Most of what is known about sexual ideology before the twentieth century comes from "prescriptive" sources—those manuals, essays, and books that tried to establish norms of behavior. Although religious views, expressed in sermons and tracts, were the most direct and commanding "prescriptions" from the seventeenth through the early nineteenth centuries, they have not been so finely combed for evidence of sexual norms as has been medical advice, a comparable source of "prescriptions" for the later nineteenth century. Religious opinion is particularly relevant to this inquiry because of the churches' hold on the female population. Women became a majority in the Protestant churches of America in the mid-seventeenth century and continued to increase their numerical predominance until, by the mid-nineteenth century, "Christian" values and virtues and "female" values and virtues were almost identical. In my view, the ideology of passionlessness was tied to the rise of evangelical religion between the 1790s and the 1830s. Physicians' adoption of passionlessness was a second wave, so to speak, beginning at mid-century. By the time that physicians took up the question of passionlessness and attempted to reduce the concept to "scientific" and somatic quantities the idea had been diffused through the spiritual realm and had already engendered its own opposition.

Early American prescriptive and legal documents suggest that the New England colonists expected women's sexual appetites to be comparable with men's, if not greater. Calvinists assumed that men and women in their "fallen" state were equally licentious, that sexual drives were natural and God-given in both sexes, and had their proper outlet in marriage. If anything, the daughters of Eve were considered more prone to excess of passion because their rational control was seen as weaker. And yet it was objectionable for women to exercise the sexual initiative; regardless of women's sexual drives, the religious and social context required female subordination. Puritan theology weakened but did not destroy the double standard of sexual morality. In colonial law, for example, fornication was punished equally in either sex, but adultery was defined by the participation of a married woman. A married man did not commit adultery but fornication—unless he took up with another man's wife. In Massachusetts until the Revolutionary period, a wife's adultery was always cause for her husband to divorce her, but wives had little success in freeing themselves from unfaithful husbands. Men also won suits to recover "damages" from their wives' lovers. As Keith Thomas has put it, such suits reflected the underlying tenet of the double standard: "the view that men have property in women and that the value of this property is immeasurably diminished if the woman at any time has sexual relations with anyone other than her husband." There was vast potential for sexual exploitation in a society in which women's sexual nature was considered primary and their social autonomy was slight. The physical and biological consequences of sexual adventure also burdened women more heavily than men in an era lacking effective means to prevent conception or infection.

In the second century of colonial settlement one finds many more numerous prescriptions for the role of women. The reasons for this increase are diverse: new class concern for standards of distinction and taste, the spread of literacy, the growth of printing and journalism, and "enlightened" interest in reformulating social systems and personal relations in "natural," "rational," rather than scriptural, terms. Britain led in discussions of female character and place, setting sex-role conventions for the literate audience. Since British social ideals became more influential in the mid-eighteenth century with the decline in Puritanism, the diffusion of Protestant energies, and the growth of an affluent urban class in the colonies, British "prescriptions" must be taken into consideration. At least three phases of British opinion contributed to the development of the idea of passionlessness. In the beginning of the century when spokesmen for the new professional and commercial middle class began explicitly to oppose aristocratic pretension, vanity, and libertinism, reforming writers . . . portrayed sexual promiscuity as one of those aristocratic excesses that threatened middle-class virtue and domestic security. Their kind of propriety led to an ideal of sexual self-control, verbal prudery, and opposition to the double standard of sexual morality (for the sake of purity for men rather than justice for women). Due to their influence, in part, "the eighteenth century witnessed a redefinition of virtue in primarily sexual terms." . . . By elevating sexual control highest among human virtues the middle-class moralists made female chastity the archetype for human morality.

Out of the upper class came a different prescriptive genre, the etiquette manual. The ones most available to middle-class women in America, such as . . . John Gregory's *A Father['s] Legacy to His Daughters,* consistently held that woman was made for man's pleasure and service; woman was strong only insofar as she could use her own weakness to manipulate the opposite sex (within the bounds of social propriety). These authors advised a great deal of restraint and affection (not to mention deception) in women's behavior. At the same time, modesty and demureness took center stage among the female virtues enshrined. According to [historian] Keith Thomas, the idea of passionlessness emerged in this context as an extension of the ideal of chastity needed to protect men's property rights in women; it was a reification in "nature" of the double standard. Yet it must be objected that in the nineteenth century women who believed in passionlessness usually rejected the double standard of sexual morality. Modesty was the quintessential female virtue in works such as Gregory's, but, amid the manipulative and affected tactics advised, it connoted only demure behavior—a good act—not, necessarily, passionlessness. Indeed, the underlying theme that women had to appeal to men turned modesty into a sexual ploy, emphasizing women's sex objectification. John Gregory did hint that sexual desire was weaker in women, with their "superior delicacy," than in men. He was sure that nature had assigned to wives rather than husbands the "reserve" which would prevent "satiety and disgust" in marital relations. But not until a third phase at the close of the century did emphasis move implacably from modesty to passionlessness, under the Evangelical aegis.

The British Evangelicals were conservative reformers horrified at the French Revolution and its "godlessness"; they worked to regenerate Protestantism in order to secure social and political order. Like earlier middle-class moralists, the Evangelicals opposed aristocratic blasphemies and profligacy, cherished family life, and advocated chastity and prudence in both sexes. Because they observed women's greater piety, and hoped that women would influence men and the next generation, they focused much of their proselytizing zeal on women. In contrast to earlier eighteenth-century didacts, they harped on the theme that women were made for God's purposes, not man's. Thomas Gisborne, for example, clearly considered women moral beings responsible for themselves and to society. His call for self-conscious moral integrity on women's part directly opposed Gregory's insinuations about the shaping of women's behavior to men's tastes; he objected that such behavior was "not discretion, but art. It is dissimulation, it is deliberate imposition." . . .

. . . Evangelicals linked moral agency to female character with a supporting link to passionlessness. Their insistence on sincerity or "simplicity," accompanying their emphasis on women's moral potential, caused them to imply that women were virtuous by nature. Continuing to stress the female virtue of modesty, Evangelicals could not (in contrast to Gregory) allow that modesty was a behavior assumed to suit society's conventions and men's preferences. If women were to act modest and sexually passive, and also act without affectation, then, logically, they must be passionless. Gisborne said women had "quicker feelings of native delicacy, and a stronger sense of shame" than men. The anonymous author of *Female Tuition* claimed the female sex was "naturally attached to purity."

Hannah More's work perfected the transformation of woman's image from sexual to moral being. Her *Strictures on the Modern System of Female Education* called for the rescue of religion and morality and located her constituency among her own sex. She detailed further than any predecessor the power that women could command, first making clear that this was power derived from their moral and spiritual endowment, not from their winning or endearing (sexual) ways. "It is humbling to reflect," More began her *Strictures,* "that in those countries in which fondness for the mere persons of women is carried to the highest excess, *they are slaves;* and that their moral and intellectual degradation increases in direct proportion to the adoration which is paid to mere external charms." More offered a resounding alternative to the idea that women were made for men's pleasure—but at the price of a new level of self-control. Since she believed that human nature was corrupt, her educational program consisted of repression as much as enhancement. Her outlook revealed to women a source of power (in moral influence) and an independence of men (through reliance on God) in a female world view that inspired and compelled women throughout the nineteenth century. In her refusal to see women as childish and affectedly weak beings, designed only "to gratify the appetite of man, or to be the upper servant," she agreed with her contemporary, Mary Wollstonecraft. Despite the spectrum of difference between More and Wollstonecraft in politics and personal behavior, they both abhorred "libertine notions of beauty" and "weak elegancy of mind" in women, wished to emphasize women's moral and intellectual powers rather than their "mere animal" capacities, and expected reformed women to reform the world. Their two critiques rose from shared indignation that women were degraded by their sexual characterization.

The new focus on moral rather than sexual determinants of female character in didactic works at the end of the eighteenth century required a reversal in Protestant views of women. In Puritan ideology, earthly women were the inheritors of Eve's legacy of moral danger. By the mid-eighteenth century, however, New England ministers had discarded similes to Eve, probably in deference to their predominantly female congregations, and portrayed women as more sensitive to the call of religion than men. Nineteenth-century Protestantism relied on women for its prime exemplars and symbols. Between 1790 and 1820 particularly, as an evangelical united front spread across the United States and Britain, the clergy intensified their emphasis on women as crucial advocates of religion. Evangelical Protestants constantly reiterated the theme that Christianity had raised women from slaves in status to moral and intellectual beings. The tacit condition for that elevation was the suppression of female sexuality. Christian women were "exalted above human nature, raised to that of angels"; proper understanding of the gospel enabled women to dismiss the earthly pride or sensuality that subjected them to men's whims. The clergy thus renewed and generalized the idea that women under God's grace were more pure than men, and they expected not merely the souls but the bodies of women to corroborate that claim.

The pastors had a double purpose in training their eyes on the moral rather than the sexual aspect of woman's being. It enabled them to welcome women as worthy allies and agents of Protestantism, which seemed more and more essential as men's religious commitment dissipated. Second, a world view in which woman's sexual nature was shadowed behind her moral and spiritual endowment eclipsed her primitive and original power over men, the power of her sexuality. The evangelical view, by concentrating on women's spiritual nature, simultaneously elevated women as moral and intellectual beings and disarmed them of their sexual power. Passionlessness was on the other side of the coin which paid, so to speak, for women's admission to moral equality.

The correlation between passionlessness and a distinctly improved view of women's character and social purpose begins to suggest the appeal of the concept to women. By replacing sexual with moral motives and determinants, the ideology of passionlessness favored women's power and self-respect. It reversed the tradition of Christian mistrust based on women's sexual treacherousness. It elevated women above the weakness of animal nature, stressing instead that they were "formed for exalted purity, felicity, and glory." It postulated that woman's influence was not ensnaring but disinterested. It routed women out of the cul-de-sac of education for attractiveness, thus allowing more intellectual breadth. To women who wanted means of self-preservation and self-control, this view of female nature may well have appealed, as Hannah More's views appealed. It remains to be seen in what social circumstances such views came to the fore.

There was extraordinary turbulence in sexual patterns and definitions in the late eighteenth century. The traditional system under which parents exercised authority over their children's marriage choices was breaking down. This change might seem to imply greater freedom for youth of both sexes in choosing their spouses. Since men conventionally exercised the sexual/marital initiative, however, the demise of parental control probably meant a relative decline in the leverage available to marriageable women, who no longer had their parents operating openly on their behalf and could not assume that role themselves. Eliza Southgate, an articulate and well-to-do eighteen-year-old of Maine, remarked in 1800 that women sensed their "inequality of privilege" most grievously "in the liberty of choosing a partner in marriage; true, we have the liberty of refusing those we don't like, but not of selecting those we do." Owing primarily to the changing sex ratio, the average age at which women first married rose from a low of about twenty years in the early colonies to about twenty-three by the Revolutionary period, while men's age at first marriage fell slightly. The proportion of women who never married rose appreciably in the same period, and the remarriage rate of widows dropped. One might interpret these statistics favorably to mean that "those who wed may have taken longer to consider the implications of such actions and the alternatives," or even that it was now "possible for unmarried men and women to find a satisfying role." But since marriage was the principal means women had of supporting themselves, one could argue that the number of desperate and exploitable women multiplied. While marriage was the likeliest source for economic security for a woman, marital subjection remained the living symbol of women's general subjection to men. In Abigail Adams's famous request to her husband John in 1776 to "remember the ladies," her central complaint was not women's political disenfranchisement but husbands' legal exercise of "unlimited power" over their wives. Turning Revolutionary rhetoric to marital relations, Abigail reminded John that "all men would be tyrants if they could," and urged that a new law code "put it out of the power of the vicious and lawless to use us with cruelty and indignity with impunity." Her objections evoke the double spectres, of sharper victimization or greater equity, borne before women's eyes during these Revolutionary years. Did women's marital status trouble her because it had become, of late, more abject, or because some hints of improvement in women's marital power precipitated her demand for further change?

During the same decades, the prebridal pregnancy rate rose dramatically. At peak years between 1760 and 1800, one-third to one-half of all recorded legitimate first births were the result of premarital sexual intercourse in several New England towns where the same measure was one-tenth or one-twentieth in the seventeenth century. Again, numerous and contradictory interpretations can be drawn from these figures. The increase in prebridal pregnancy could be ascribed to a general increase in premarital sexual activity, which in itself could possibly represent greater individual and sexual freedom for both sexes, or just as possibly indicate greater vulnerability and exploitation of women. Or, premarital sexual activity could have remained constant but have led more frequently to marriage and legitimation. The continued reign of a double standard of sexual morality made it unlikely that sexual "freedom" came without cost to women. A content analysis of nine New England magazines between 1777 and 1794 has shown that characters in both fiction and nonfiction regularly advocated punishment or ostracism for the male partner in illicit sex and sympathy for the female as the victim of force or misguided ignorance. In actual portrayals of illicit sexual encounters, however, the males involved escaped scot-free and the women almost always suffered punishment or ostracism. On this injustice the young wife of a lawyer in Haverhill, Massachusetts, reflected in 1802: "Man boasts superior strength of mind, I would have him prove it, by avoiding or conquering temptation; but man disgraces his godlike reason, and yields to a thousand follies, to give them no harsher name—and passes through the world in high repute, such conduct would blast the reputation of poor weak woman. . . . 'tis an unrighteous custom, which gives such license to our lords of the creation." She was not alone in protesting men's combination of sexual license with their claim to righteous social power. On the eve of her marriage, Sarah Connell of Concord, New Hampshire, lamented a local instance of seduction and betrayal, empathizing with the many unprotected girls who had "fallen victim to the baseness of those who call themselves lords of the Creation."

The sexual exploitation possible in contemporary disruption of marital and sexual patterns was probably more obvious to women because of heightened expectations on their part. The clergy, adopting a more positive image of women in their sermons, no longer presented marriage as a hierarchical relationship but stressed that women were complementary, and piously influential, marriage partners. The rhetoric of the American Revolution glorified women's role further by connecting it with the success of the national experiment. In an abrupt reversal in 1773, Massachusetts women were victorious if they petitioned their governor and council for divorce on account of their husbands' adulteries; and women's overall success in obtaining divorce was almost equal to men's in the decade after 1776. If not the most isolated farmers' wives, then literate women, living in populated areas sharing in the commerce of goods and ideas, were particularly likely to anticipate better treatment.

A vision of sexual equity arising from awareness of sexual injustice brought feminist writers into the open during the same years. Judith Sargent Murray of

Gloucester, Massachusetts, began criticizing female education in the 1770s, anticipating the themes of More and Wollstonecraft. Under the pseudonym "Constantia"
she argued that men's presumed superiority in rationality was due to their superior
education and continued advantages, not to any inherent preeminence. She demanded that women have opportunity to cultivate other means than sexual attraction. Pointing out that the typical upbringing of girls trivialized their minds and
made them rely on physical beauty, she urged women to develop aspirations, a
"reverence of self," moral and intellectual integrity, and the capacity for self-
fulfillment. Constantia put her hopes in the female academies springing up. Another pseudonymous feminist, an "aged matron" of Connecticut who published
The Female Advocate in 1801, wished to disabuse the world of the idea that woman
was inferior to man or made for men's uses. God and Nature, she claimed, had
given the two sexes "equality of talents, of genius, of morals, as well as intellectual
worth," and only male arrogance had invaded that equality. Men had deprived
women of education and experience while they themselves "engross[ed] all the
emoluments, offices, honors and merits, of church and state." In her eyes the sexual
double standard epitomized male usurpation of power, because it allowed a man to
flaunt the arts of seduction without losing public esteem while it condemned a
woman forever if she once succumbed to a deceiver. *The Female Advocate*'s images
of women's powerlessness and vulnerability contrasted with its portrayal of men's
aggrandizement of power and seductive wiles. Yet its author was optimistic that
"well informed mind[s]" would be "the mean of enabling us [women] to possess
some command over ourselves."

Polite ladies' magazines, which first appeared in the 1780s with the growth of
a literate female audience, unintentionally paraded the contemporary controversy
over sexual definitions. They celebrated female intellectual accomplishments and
aimed not to cater to homemakers' tastes but to "improve and amuse" ladies'
minds. In this "polite" entertainment, the subjects of fornication, prostitution, adultery, seduction, and betrayal were legion. By and large, the stories and essays in
these magazines broadcast the view that women's modus operandi was sexual, and
consisted in manipulating men. But they also gave the impression that women met
victimization and downfall more often than they gained influence and happiness
through the solicitation of men's passions. The sexual definition of women could
undermine their control of encounters with men. . . . A serious "Scheme for Increasing the Power of the Ladies" called on women to end the double standard by
refusing to tolerate fashionable "rakes"; like Hannah More, the writer emphasized
that it was up to women to reverse their complaisance with and degradation under
the existing code. Sarah Connell concluded her account of her acquaintance's
seduction with similar sentiment: "Did every virtuous female show her detestation
of the libertine by wholly renouncing his society, there would be a much smaller
number of them."

Only a handful of New England women at this time questioned the political inequi-
ties of their situation, but sexual and marital subjection—unequal sexual prerogatives—seem to have rankled a much larger population. As *The Female Advocate*
pointed out, women had to conform to male tastes and wait to be chosen but resist
seduction or suffer ostracism for capitulating; men, meanwhile, were free to take

the first step, practice flattery, and escape the consequences of illicit sexual relations. In sexual encounters women had more than an even chance to lose, whether
by censure under the double standard, unwanted pregnancy and health problems, or
ill-fated marriage. In this perspective, women might hail passionlessness as a way to
assert control in the sexual arena—even if that "control" consisted in denial. Some
scholars have claimed that women adhered to the ideology of passionlessness to
bolster their position in a disadvantageous marriage market, that is, to play "hard to
get" with conviction. More essentially, passionlessness served women's larger interest by downplaying altogether their sexual characterization, which was the cause
of their exclusion from significant "human" (i.e., male) pursuits. The positive contribution of passionlessness was to replace that sexual/carnal characterization of
women with a spiritual/moral one, allowing women to develop their human faculties and their self-esteem. The belief that women lacked carnal motivation was the
cornerstone of the argument for women's moral superiority, used to enhance
women's status and widen their opportunities in the nineteenth century. Furthermore, acceptance of the idea of passionlessness created sexual solidarity among
women; it allowed women to consider their love relationships with one another
of higher character than heterosexual relationships because they excluded (male)
carnal passion. "I do not believe that men can ever feel so pure an enthusiasm for
women as we can feel for one another," Catherine Sedgwick recorded in her diary
of 1834 upon meeting Fanny Kemble, "—ours is nearest to the love of angels." . . .
That sense of the angelic or spiritual aspect of female love ennobled the experience
of sisterhood which was central to the lives of nineteenth-century women and to the
early woman's rights movement. Women considered passionlessness an important
shared trait which distinguished them favorably from men.

    It must not be assumed that women who internalized the concept of passion-
lessness necessarily shunned marriage. The pervasive ideology of romantic love,
and also the evangelical conflation of the qualities of earthly and spiritual love,
bridged the gap and refuted the ostensible contradiction between passionlessness
and marriage. On a practical level, belief in female passionlessness could aid a
woman to limit sexual intercourse within marriage and thus limit family size. . . .
The conviction and the demand that it was woman's right to control reproduction,
advocated by health reformers in the 1850s and promulgated in the movement for
"voluntary motherhood" in subsequent decades, depended on the ideology of female passionlessness. [Historian] Linda Gordon has shown the feminist basis of
the argument for voluntary motherhood in the claim that women had the right to
refuse their husbands' sexual demands, despite the legal and customary requirements of submission to marital "duty."

    The degree to which a woman might incorporate the idea of passionlessness is
revealed in an 1845 letter of Harriet Beecher Stowe to her husband. Responding to
his revelations about "licentiousness" on the part of certain clergymen, she wrote:
"What terrible temptations lie in the way of your sex—till now I never realized it—
for tho I did love you with an almost insane love before I married you I never knew
yet or felt the pulsation which showed me that I could be tempted in that way—
there never was a moment when I felt anything by which you could have drawn me
astray—for I loved you as I now love God. . . . " Angelina Grimké's passionless attitude was a feminist affirmation of woman's dignity in revulsion from male sexual

domination. To the man who would become her husband she revealed her judgment "that men in general, the vast majority, believe most seriously that women were made to gratify their animal appetites, *expressly* to minister to their pleasure—yea Christian men too." She continued: "My soul abhors such a base letting down of the high dignity of my nature as a woman. How I have feared the possibility of ever being married to one who regarded *this* as the *end*—the great design of marriage. In truth I may say that I never was reconciled to the compound [relat]ions of marriage until I read Combe on the Constitution of man this winter."

Yet a belief so at odds with the traditional appreciation of female sexuality, and one which seems to mid-twentieth-century sensibilities so patently counterproductive, so symbolic of the repression and subordination of women, cannot be interpreted simply. Historians' frequent assumption that men devised the ideology of female passionlessness to serve their own interests—"to help gentlemen cope with the problem of controlling their own sexuality"—is partial (in both senses of the word) but not illogical. An ideal of male continence, of virtuous and willed repression of existing carnal desires (as distinct from passionlessness, which implied absence of carnal motivation), figures in nineteenth-century directions for men's respectability and achievement in the bustling new world of industrial capitalism. In one aspect, female passionlessness was a keystone in men's construction of their own self-control. But Howard Gadlin has underlined the paradox of the ideology, as well as reason for its diffusion and rootedness, in his remark that "the nineteenth-century double standard was the vehicle for a desexualization desired by both men and women for opposing purposes. Men wanted to desexualize relationships to maintain their domination; women wanted to desexualize relationships to limit male domination."

Both women's participation in the creation of Victorian sexual standards and the place of passionlessness in the vanguard of feminist thought deserve more recognition. The serviceability of passionlessness to women in gaining social and familial power should be acknowledged as a primary reason that the ideology was quickly and widely accepted. Yet feminists were the first to question and oppose the ideology once it was entrenched. When prudery became confused with passionlessness, it undermined women physically and psychologically by restricting their knowledge of their own sexual functioning. From the first, women health reformers and moral reformers rejected this injurious implication while fostering the positive meanings of passionlessness. Feminist opposition arose when the medical establishment adopted passionlessness and moved the grounds for judging the concept from the spiritual to the somatic. When female passionlessness came to be insisted upon literally, more than one woman reacted as Rebecca Harding Davis did: "In these rough and tumble days, we'd better give [women] their places as flesh and blood, with exactly the same wants and passions as men." Mary Gove Nichols claimed: "A healthy and loving woman is impelled to material union as surely, often as strongly, as man. . . . The apathy of the sexual instinct is caused by the enslaved and unhealthy condition in which she lives." Several woman's rights activists of the later part of the century, including Isabella Beecher Hooker, Alice Stockham, and Elizabeth Cady Stanton, discussed among themselves their belief in the existence and legitimacy of female sexual drives, even while the movement of which they were part banked on women's superior morality and maternal instinct as chief supports. Consistent with the general conflicts and contradictions in sexual ideology after 1860, feminists perceived oppression in prudery while clinging to the promises that passionlessness held out.

The ideology of passionlessness, conceived as self-preservation and social advancement for women, created its own contradictions: on the one hand, by exaggerating sexual propriety so far as to immobilize women and, on the other, by allowing claims of women's moral influence to obfuscate the need for other sources of power. The assertion of moral integrity within passionlessness had allowed women to retrieve their identity from a trough of sexual vulnerability and dependence. The concept could not assure women full autonomy—but what transformation in sexual ideology alone could have done so?

FURTHER READING

Ben Barker-Benfield, *The Horrors of the Half-Known Life: Male Attitudes toward Women and Sexuality in Nineteenth-Century America* (1976).

———, "The Spermatic Economy: A Nineteenth-Century View of Sexuality," *Feminist Studies* 1 (1972): 45–74.

Janet Farrell Brodie, *Contraception and Abortion in Nineteenth-Century America* (1994).

Patricia Cline Cohen, *The Murder of Helen Jewett: The Life and Death of a Prostitute in Nineteenth-Century New York* (1998).

Julie Dunfey, "'Living the Principle' of Plural Marriage: Mormon Women, Utopia, and Female Sexuality in the Nineteenth Century," *Feminist Studies* 10 (Spring 1983): 7–25.

Lawrence Foster, *Religion and Sexuality: Three American Communal Experiments of the Nineteenth Century* (1981).

———, *Women, Family, and Utopia: Communal Experiments of the Shakers, the Oneida Community, and the Mormons* (1991).

Carol Groneman, *Nymphomania: A History* (2000).

John S. Haller, Jr., and Robin M. Haller, *The Physician and Sexuality in Victorian America* (1974).

Susan Lee Johnson, "Bulls, Bears, and Dancing Boys: Race, Gender, and Leisure in the California Gold Rush," *Radical History Review* (1994): 4–37.

Louis J. Kern, *An Ordered Love: Sex Roles and Sexuality in Victorian Utopias* (1981).

Jan Lewis, "The Republican Wife: Virtue and Seduction in the Early Republic," *William and Mary Quarterly* 4 (1987): 689–721.

———, "'Sally has been Sick': Pregnancy and Family Limitation among Virginia Gentry Women, 1780–1830," *Journal of Social History* 22 (Fall 1988): 5–19.

Kevin J. Mumford, "'Lost Manhood' Found: Male Sexual Impotence and Victorian Culture in the United States," *Journal of the History of Sexuality* 3 (1992): 33–57.

Stephen Nissenbaum, *Sex, Diet, and Debility in Jacksonian America: Sylvester Graham and Health Reform* (1980).

Ellen K. Rothman, "Sex and Self-Control: Middle-Class Courtship in America, 1790–1840," *Journal of Social History* 15 (1982): 409–425.

E. Anthony Rotundo, *American Manhood* (1993).

Cynthia Eagle Russett, *Sexual Science: The Victorian Construction of Womanhood* (1989).

Carroll Smith-Rosenberg, *Disorderly Conduct: Visions of Gender in Victorian America* (1984).

Amy Gilman Srebnick, *The Mysterious Death of Mary Rogers: Sex and Culture in Nineteenth-Century New York* (1995).

Sexuality, Race, and Violence in Slavery and Freedom

The painful experience of sexuality and violence in slavery casts a long shadow on American racial relations to the present day. Views of racial difference have long been rooted in powerful and persistent sexual stereotypes—the "pure" white woman, the black male rapist. Racial slavery was a sexual institution as well as an economic and political one. White masters owned the bodies of enslaved black women and could beat and rape them with impunity, force them into sexual relations with other slaves, and sell their children for profit. Even the most upstanding white men believed it their entitlement to have sex in the slave quarters; their wives, dependent on slaves in the household, had little power to stop their husbands' adulterous affairs. How did African Americans cope with this system of racial and sexual oppression? Historians have begun to document the injuries of rape and sexual abuse as a form of "soul murder" caused by extreme physical and psychological damage. Black men, helpless to protect their wives and daughters, were also victims. Other scholars emphasize that black women and men did everything possible to resist white efforts to define and control their sexuality. They asserted their humanity and dignity against all odds by celebrating marriage, forming extended families, socializing children, and building a sense of community.

Sexual violence continued after Emancipation, not only against black women but also against black men. Black men were increasingly portrayed as inherently licentious and uncontrollable. Lynching—the murder and sometimes castration of black men by white mobs—was justified by the accusation that they had raped or insulted white women. This charge inverted the actual dynamics of sexual violence. As civil rights activist Ida B. Wells-Barnett documented, lynching was used most often against black men who had asserted their freedom from white domination, often as business or political leaders. Others had been involved in consensual sexual relationships with white women. In the crusade to restore white supremacy in the post-Reconstruction South, lynching was a systematic form of terror; despite the activism of Wells and others, it was never made a federal crime.

The influence of slavery on sexuality and marriage within African-American culture has been controversial ever since Emancipation. Some commentators, both black and white, have stressed the disruption of parental and marital bonds by sale and sexual violence. According to that view, fragile marriages, single mothers, and absent fathers are the legacy of slavery. Other commentators have stressed the resilience of kinship ties and the stability of black extended families, despite the exploitation of slavery and continuing racial discrimination. From that perspective, poverty rather than culture is at the root of contemporary problems in black communities. Much more than historical interpretation is involved in these debates: sexual conduct is not only a private matter, especially for socially subordinate groups, but a matter of politics and public policy.

D O C U M E N T S

Escaped slaves described sexual violence against black women as an evil inherent in slavery. In Document 1, Lewis Clarke, speaking to a sympathetic abolitionist audience in 1842, explained how these assaults violated his sense of manhood. Interviewed in 1863 by the American Freedmen's Inquiry Commission (Document 2), J. W. Lindsay—born to a free woman but kidnapped as a child—described sexual coercion and the treatment of mixed-race children. Esther Hill Hawks, a white physician who went South to teach ex-slaves during the Civil War, recorded the rape and torture of a woman "Susan Black" in her 1865 diary (Document 3). Harriet Jacobs's celebrated autobiography, *Incidents in the Life of a Slave Girl,* published in 1861 (Document 4), offered one of the frankest discussions of the sexual dimension of racial slavery published by abolitionists. Written to appeal primarily to white women, Jacobs's narrative struggles simultaneously to validate the strict code of sexual conduct shared by many white and black women and to recognize the limitations that slavery placed on women's moral autonomy.

After Emancipation, the right to marry was held by the former slaves to be a key tenet of freedom, as letters to the Freedmen's Bureau attest (Document 5). Violent opposition to black autonomy—whether economic, political, or sexual—arose in the decades after the Civil War. In Document 6, William H. Stallings testified to a Congressional committee in 1871 about the Ku Klux Klan's lynching of a mixed-race couple and the use of ritualized sexual violence to control blacks and whites. Most whites in the South and North justified lynching because they believed that black men habitually raped white women. Documenting the true reasons for lynching, activist Ida B. Wells-Barnett smashed that myth in her brilliant pamphlet *Southern Horrors* (Document 7).

1. Fugitive Slave Lewis Clarke Explains Why "A Slave Can't Be a Man," 1842

"I can't tell these respectable people as much as I would like to; but jest think for a minute how you would like to have *your* sisters, and *your* wives, and *your* daughters, completely, teetotally, and altogether, in the power of a master.—You can picture to yourselves a little, how you would feel; but oh, if I could *tell* you! A slave woman an't allowed to respect herself, if she would. I had a pretty sister; she was whiter than I am, for she took more after her father. When she was sixteen years

Lewis Clarke, "Leaves from a Slave's Journal of Life," *National Anti-Slavery Standard,* October 20 and 27, 1842, reprinted in *Slave Testimony,* ed. John W. Blassingame (Baton Rouge: Louisiana State University Press, 1977), 156–158.

old, her master sent for her. When he sent for her again, she cried, and didn't want to go. She told mother her troubles, and she tried to encourage her to be decent, and hold up her head above such things, if she could. Her master was so mad, to think she complained to her mother, that he sold her right off to Louisiana; and we heard afterward that she died there of hard usage.

"There was a widower in Kentucky, who took one of his women slaves into the house. She told her master one day that seven of the young girls had poked fun at her for the way she was living. This raised his *ambition.* 'I'll teach 'em to make fun!' said he. So he sent the woman away, and ordered the young girls to come to him, one by one." (An ill-mannered and gross laughter, among the boys of the audience, here seemed to embarrass him.) "Perhaps I had better not try to tell this story," he continued, "for I cannot tell it as it was; though surely it is more shameful to have such things *done,* than it is to *tell* of 'em. He got mad with the girls, because they complained to their mothers; but he didn't like to punish 'em for that, for fear it would make a talk. So he ordered 'em to go out into the field to do work that was too hard for 'em. Six of 'em said they couldn't do it; but the mother of the seventh, guessing what it was for, told her to go, and do the best she could. The other six was every one of 'em tied up naked, and flogged, for disobeying orders. Now, who would like to be a slave, even if there was nothing bad about it but such treatment of his sisters and daughters? But there's a worse thing yet about slavery; the worst thing in the whole lot; though it's all bad, from the butt end to the *pint.* I mean the *patter-rollers* (patrols). I suppose you know that they have patter-rollers to go round o' nights, to see that the slaves are all in, and not planning any mischief? Now, these are jest about the worst fellows that can be found; as bad as any you could pick up on the wharves. The reason is, you see, that no decent man will undertake the business . . . [and] they have to put all power into their hands to do with the niggers jest as they like. If a slave don't open his door to them at any time of night they break it down. They . . . act just as they please with his wives and daughters. If a husband dares to say a word, or even look as if he wasn't quite satisfied, they tie him up and give him thirty-nine lashes. If there's any likely young girls in a slave's hut, they're mighty apt to have business there; especially if they think any colored young man takes a fancy to any of 'em. Maybe he'll get a pass from his master, and go to see the young girl for a few hours. The patter-rollers break in and find him there. They'll abuse the girl as bad as they can, a purpose to provoke him. If he looks cross, they give him a flogging, tear up his pass, turn him out of doors, and then take him up and whip him for being out without a pass. If the slave says they tore it up, they swear he lies: and nine times out of ten the master won't come out agin 'em; for they say it won't *do* to let the niggers suppose they may complain of the patter-rollers; they must be taught that it's their business to obey 'em in everything; and the patter-roller knows that very well. Oh, how often I've seen the poor girls sob and cry, when there's been such goings on! Maybe you think, because they're slaves, they an't got no feeling and no shame? A woman's being a slave, don't stop her having genteel ideas; that is, according to their way, and as far as they can. They know they must submit to their masters; besides, their masters, maybe, dress 'em up, and make 'em little presents, and give 'em more privileges, while the whim lasts; but that an't like having a parcel of low, dirty, swearing, drunk patter-rollers let loose among 'em, like so many hogs. This breaks down their spirits dreadfully, and makes 'em wish they was dead.

"Now who among you would like to have your wives, and daughters, and sisters, in such a situation? This is what every slave in all these States is exposed to. . . .

. . . No; this is the cruelty of the thing—A SLAVE CAN'T BE A MAN. He *must* be made a brute; but he an't a brute, neither, if he had a chance to act himself out. Many a one of 'em is right smart, I tell you. But a horse *can't* speak, and slave *darn't;* and that's the best way I can tell the story."

2. J. W. Lindsay Describes Sexual and Family Relations Under Slavery, 1863

You, who come from the States, have often heard slavery described, but it has never been painted so bad as it is. Say, for instance, you were married, (I will put it in that form), and you had a lot of slave women around you. You bring up a tier of children by your wife, and another tier of children by your slave women. By & by your children grow up, and those you had by your wife have children by those you had by your slave women, and then you take those same children and sell them.

There are very few mulattoes that come from pure white women, though I have known some cases of that kind; they mostly come from white men. There are men who will buy a sprightly, good looking girl, that they think will suit their fancy, and make use of them in that way. I knew a man by the name of Ben Kidd—a desperate mean man to his slaves—who had three or four slave women, and some of them he had children by. He kept a stallion in his barn, and he made one of his women tend upon that stallion and used to meet her at that barn. She had a husband, too; but that made no difference; he used her whenever he saw fit. He generally carried a white oak cane, one end very heavy, and if the women did not submit, he would make nothing of knocking them right down. He had a boy by one of his colored women, and he would take hold of his hair, and lift him up as high as your head, and let him fall down, and almost knock the breath out of him. He was the worst man I ever saw. I don't think the poor white women of the south are any better than the women of the north, but there is a restriction on the blacks. It is given out that they will be hanged if they trouble a white woman. There are cases where white women fall in love with their servants. There was a 'Squire Green, who had a slave and he & his mistress knocked up a young one between them. There was a great talk made about it, & the child was sent off South. A colored child wouldn't be treated any better, if from a white woman, than one from a black woman by a white father. There are some few slaveholders who thinks a good deal of their children by their slaves, & some have sent their children north. Some of them have been to Oberlin. There are some slaveholders who have got pretty refined feelings about them, though they are great men to go into these depredations. Sometimes they get really attached to their mistresses. Sometimes white mistresses will surmise that there is an intimacy between a slave woman & the master, and perhaps she will make a great fuss & have her whipped, & perhaps there will be no peace until she is sold. I have seen

J. W. Lindsay, interviews by Benjamin Drew and Samuel Gridley Howe, 1863, American Freedmen's Inquiry Commission, Record Group 94, National Archives, reprinted in *Slave Testimony,* ed. John W. Blassingame (Baton Rouge: Louisiana State University Press, 1977), 400–401.

slaveholders with little bits of children on a horse, whom they were taking from home to sell—children not more than three or four years old. They want a little money, & take a baby off & get one or two hundred dollars for him.

3. Dr. Esther Hill Hawks Recounts the Rape of "Susan Black," 1865

I have in school a woman of this name whose history has greatly interested me. She is about thirty six years of age, quite black, but with good features, bright and intelligent. She was born of pure African parents and has always lived in one family, to whom she is still greatly attached. The first notice taken of her, which she remembers, by her old master, was when she was about twelve yrs old. One day he called her to go into the shed with him—saying jocosely that he was afraid, but his eldest daughter hearing it said to Susan "You keep away from Pa don't go in there", however, he called again soon, and she went after him. When there, he caught hold of her, held her and in spite of her frightened resistance—with his handkerchief stuffed in her mouth, committed *rape* on such a child. She was sick for three weeks after. On her recovery he used her as he liked. When about thirteen she gave birth to a son. She wasn't going to nurse it or care for it and [it] was placed in the hands of her sister to bring up. This is the only child which she has ever had which greatly enraged her master and he whipped her several times, saying that she destroyed her children and he liked the breed to well "to allow it to run out."

He had daughters older than she and when one of them married, Susan was a part of the marriage parties. Susan lived quite happily with her young mistress, married a fellow-slave, had a "real wedding" in church as she expressed it, and until the breaking out of the rebellion had no serious troubles. Her husbands master was quite indulgent to him, and gave him many privilleges, so one night when out fishing with two others, the temptation to go out to see the yankees was too great to be overcome—and he went; Susan, meanwhile was living up in the country. Her Master, now Maj. Henry Rivers [C.S.A.], on learning that her husband had gone, undertook to console her by offering her joint stock, in his affections with his wife. Tried entreaties, money, which she threw in his face, and lastly whippings and threats. Susan would'nt tell her mistress of her persecutions fearing to make her unhappy so poor Susan bore in silence his abuses, till one day, after exhausting all his powers to make her yield to his desires, he had her stripped naked, tied up and then with his own hands beat her 'till the feaver of passion had subsided. Susan said he would take particular pains to beat her over the pubis; until she was terribly swolen and the blood run down her legs and stood in pools on the floor. She showed me her body and limbs and they are now covered with frightful great white scars. As soon as she was sufficiently recovered she resolved to endeaver to make her escape and if possible join her husband somewhere. She succeeded in reaching this City and was secreted in a small room, by her father, great search was made for her—but she remained in security—twice dressed in boys clothes, she attempted to cross the water to Morris Is. but was frightened back. This was about two months

Gerald Schwartz, ed., *A Woman Doctor's Civil War: Esther Hill Hawks's Diary* (Columbia: University of South Carolina Press, 1992), 154–155.

before the fall of Ft. Wagna [Wagner]—and from that time 'till the occupation of this place by our troops, she was confined to one small room, only daring to venture out in the evening. When our soldiers marched into the city Susan was wild with delight—which she hardly knew how to express. As the troops marched through the street, coming opposite to her she pulled of [off] her shawl and spread it down for them to walk on. The officers gallantly stepped aside and raised their hats in recognition of her delicate compliment—Susan's husband came over to Port Royal and enlisted in the 1*st.* S.C. Regt, was a good soldier, got disabled was discharged and came back here with the "Yankee soldiers" to find his wife, which he was not long in doing and they are now living here as quietly and happily as though they had only lived prosy ordinary lives like other people.

4. Harriet Jacobs Relates Incidents in the Life of a Slave Girl, 1861

I now entered on my fifteenth year—a sad epoch in the life of a slave girl. My master [Dr. Flint] began to whisper foul words in my ear. Young as I was, I could not remain ignorant of their import. I tried to treat them with indifference or contempt. The master's age, my extreme youth, and the fear that his conduct would be reported to my grandmother, made him bear this treatment for many months. He was a crafty man, and resorted to many means to accomplish his purposes. Sometimes he had stormy, terrific ways, that made his victims tremble; sometimes he assumed a gentleness that he thought must surely subdue. Of the two, I preferred his stormy moods, although they left me trembling. He tried his utmost to corrupt the pure principles my grandmother had instilled. He peopled my young mind with unclean images, such as only a vile monster could think of. I turned from him with disgust and hatred. But he was my master. I was compelled to live under the same roof with him—where I saw a man forty years my senior daily violating the most sacred commandments of nature. He told me I was his property; that I must be subject to his will in all things. My soul revolted against the mean tyranny. But where could I turn for protection? No matter whether the slave girl be as black as ebony or as fair as her mistress. In either case, there is no shadow of law to protect her from insult, from violence, or even from death; all these are inflicted by fiends who bear the shape of men. The mistress, who ought to protect the helpless victim, has no other feelings towards her but those of jealousy and rage. The degradation, the wrongs, the vices, that grow out of slavery, are more than I can describe. They are greater than you would willingly believe. Surely, if you credited one half the truths that are told you concerning the helpless millions suffering in this cruel bondage, you at the north would not help to tighten the yoke. You surely would refuse to do for the master, on your own soil, the mean and cruel work which trained bloodhounds and the lowest class of whites do for him at the south. . . .

I longed for some one to confide in. I would have given the world to have laid my head on my grandmother's faithful bosom, and told her all my troubles. But Dr. Flint swore he would kill me, if I was not as silent as the grave. Then, although my

Harriet A. Jacobs, *Incidents in the Life of a Slave Girl, Written by Herself* (1861), ed. Jean Fagan Yellin (Cambridge: Harvard University Press, 1987), 27–29, 31–33, 37–39, 53–56.

grandmother was all in all to me, I feared her as well as loved her. I had been accustomed to look up to her with a respect bordering upon awe. I was very young, and felt shamefaced about telling her such impure things, especially as I knew her to be very strict on such subjects. Moreover, she was a woman of a high spirit. She was usually very quiet in her demeanor; but if her indignation was once roused, it was not very easily quelled. I had been told that she once chased a white gentleman with a loaded pistol, because he insulted one of her daughters. I dreaded the consequences of a violent outbreak; and both pride and fear kept me silent. But though I did not confide in my grandmother, and even evaded her vigilant watchfulness and inquiry, her presence in the neighborhood was some protection to me. Though she had been a slave, Dr. Flint was afraid of her. He dreaded her scorching rebukes. Moreover, she was known and patronized by many people; and he did not wish to have his villainy made public. It was lucky for me that I did not live on a distant plantation, but in a town not so large that the inhabitants were ignorant of each other's affairs. Bad as are the laws and customs in a slaveholding community, the doctor, as a professional man, deemed it prudent to keep up some outward show of decency. . . .

The Jealous Mistress

Mrs. Flint possessed the key to her husband's character before I was born. She might have used this knowledge to counsel and to screen the young and the innocent among her slaves; but for them she had no sympathy. They were the objects of her constant suspicion and malevolence. She watched her husband with unceasing vigilance; but he was well practised in means to evade it. . . .

After repeated quarrels between the doctor and his wife, he announced his intention to take his youngest daughter, then four years old, to sleep in his apartment. It was necessary that a servant should sleep in the same room, to be on hand if the child stirred. I was selected for that office, and informed for what purpose that arrangement had been made. . . . The first night the doctor had the little child in his room alone. The next morning, I was ordered to take my station as nurse the following night. A kind Providence interposed in my favor. During the day Mrs. Flint heard of this new arrangement, and a storm followed. I rejoiced to hear it rage.

After a while my mistress sent for me to come to her room. Her first question was, "Did you know you were to sleep in the doctor's room?"

"Yes, ma'am."

"Who told you?"

"My master."

"Will you answer truly all the questions I ask?"

"Yes, ma'am."

"Tell me, then, as you hope to be forgiven, are you innocent of what I have accused you?"

"I am."

She handed me a Bible, and said, "Lay your hand on your heart, kiss this holy book, and swear before God that you tell me the truth."

I took the oath she required, and I did it with a clear conscience.

"You have taken God's holy word to testify your innocence," said she. "If you have deceived me, beware! Now take this stool, sit down, look me directly in the face, and tell me all that has passed between your master and you."

I did as she ordered. As I went on with my account her color changed frequently, she wept, and sometimes groaned. She spoke in tones so sad, that I was touched by her grief. The tears came to my eyes; but I was soon convinced that her emotions arose from anger and wounded pride. She felt that her marriage vows were desecrated, her dignity insulted; but she had no compassion for the poor victim of her husband's perfidy. She pitied herself as a martyr; but she was incapable of feeling for the condition of shame and misery in which her unfortunate, helpless slave was placed. . . .

The Lover

Why does the slave ever love? Why allow the tendrils of the heart to twine around objects which may at any moment be wrenched away by the hand of violence? . . .

There was in the neighborhood a young colored carpenter; a free born man. We had been well acquainted in childhood, and frequently met together afterwards. We became mutually attached, and he proposed to marry me. I loved him with all the ardor of a young girl's first love. But when I reflected that I was a slave, and that the laws gave no sanction to the marriage of such, my heart sank within me. My lover wanted to buy me; but I knew that Dr. Flint was too wilful and arbitrary a man to consent to that arrangement. From him, I was sure of experiencing all sorts of opposition, and I had nothing to hope from my mistress. She would have been delighted to have got rid of me, but not in that way. It would have relieved her mind of a burden if she could have seen me sold to some distant state, but if I was married near home I should be just as much in her husband's power as I had previously been,—for the husband of a slave has no power to protect her. Moreover, my mistress, like many others, seemed to think that slaves had no right to any family ties of their own, that they were created merely to wait upon the family of the mistress. I once heard her abuse a young slave girl, who told her that a colored man wanted to make her his wife. "I will have you peeled and pickled, my lady," said she, "if I ever hear you mention that subject again. Do you suppose that I will have you tending *my* children with the children of that nigger?" The girl to whom she said this had a mulatto child, of course not acknowledged by its father. The poor black man who loved her would have been proud to acknowledge his helpless offspring.

Many and anxious were the thoughts I revolved in my mind. I was at a loss what to do. Above all things, I was desirous to spare my lover the insults that had cut so deeply into my soul. I talked with my grandmother about it, and partly told her my fears. I did not dare to tell her the worst. She had long suspected all was not right, and I confirmed her suspicions. I knew a storm would rise that would prove the overthrow of all my hopes.

This love-dream had been my support through many trials; and I could not bear to run the risk of having it suddenly dissipated. There was a lady in the neighborhood, a particular friend of Dr. Flint's, who often visited the house. I had a great respect for her, and she had always manifested a friendly interest in me. . . . The lady listened with kindly sympathy, and promised to do her utmost to promote my wishes. She had an interview with the doctor, and I believe she pleaded my cause earnestly; but it was all to no purpose.

How I dreaded my master now! Every minute I expected to be summoned to his presence; but the day passed, and I heard nothing from him. The next morning, a message was brought to me: "Master wants you in his study." I found the door ajar, and I stood a moment gazing at the hateful man who claimed a right to rule me, body and soul. I entered, and tried to appear calm. I did not want him to know my heart was bleeding. He looked fixedly at me, with an expression which seemed to say, "I have half a mind to kill you on the spot." At last he broke the silence, and that was a relief to both of us.

"So you want to be married, do you?" said he, "and to a free nigger."

"Yes, sir."

"Well, I'll soon convince you whether I am your master, or the nigger fellow you honor so highly. If you *must* have a husband, you may take up with one of my slaves."

What a situation I should be in, as the wife of one of *his* slaves, even if my heart had been interested!

I replied, "Don't you suppose, sir, that a slave can have some preference about marrying? Do you suppose that all men are alike to her?"

"Do you love this nigger?" said he, abruptly.

"Yes, sir."

"How dare you tell me so!" he exclaimed, in great wrath. After a slight pause, he added, "I supposed you thought more of yourself; that you felt above the insults of such puppies."

I replied, "If he is a puppy I am a puppy, for we are both of the negro race. It is right and honorable for us to love each other. The man you call a puppy never insulted me, sir; and he would not love me if he did not believe me to be a virtuous woman."

He sprang upon me like a tiger, and gave me a stunning blow. It was the first time he had ever struck me; and fear did not enable me to control my anger. When I had recovered a little from the effects, I exclaimed, "You have struck me for answering you honestly. How I despise you!" . . .

A Perilous Passage in the Slave Girl's Life

After my lover went away, Dr. Flint contrived a new plan. He seemed to have an idea that my fear of my mistress was his greatest obstacle. In the blandest tones, he told me that he was going to build a small house for me, in a secluded place, four miles away from the town. I shuddered; but I was constrained to listen, while he talked of his intention to give me a home of my own, and to make a lady of me. Hitherto, I had escaped my dreaded fate, by being in the midst of people. . . .

And now, reader, I come to a period in my unhappy life, which I would gladly forget if I could. The remembrance fills me with sorrow and shame. It pains me to tell you of it; but I have promised to tell you the truth, and I will do it honestly, let it cost me what it may. I will not try to screen myself behind the plea of compulsion from a master; for it was not so. Neither can I plead ignorance or thoughtlessness. For years, my master had done his utmost to pollute my mind with foul images, and to destroy the pure principles inculcated by my grandmother, and the good mistress of my childhood. The influences of slavery had had the same effect on me that they had on other young girls; they had made me prematurely knowing, concerning the evil ways of the world. I knew what I did, and I did it with deliberate calculation.

But, O, ye happy women, whose purity has been sheltered from childhood, who have been free to choose the objects of your affection, whose homes are protected by law, do not judge the poor desolate slave girl too severely! If slavery had been abolished, I, also, could have married the man of my choice; I could have had a home shielded by the laws; and I should have been spared the painful task of confessing what I am now about to relate; but all my prospects had been blighted by slavery. I wanted to keep myself pure; and, under the most adverse circumstances, I tried hard to preserve my self-respect; but I was struggling alone in the powerful grasp of the demon Slavery; and the monster proved too strong for me. I felt as if I was forsaken by God and man; as if all my efforts must be frustrated; and I became reckless in my despair.

I have told you that Dr. Flint's persecutions and his wife's jealousy had given rise to some gossip in the neighborhood. Among others, it chanced that a white unmarried gentleman had obtained some knowledge of the circumstances in which I was placed. He knew my grandmother, and often spoke to me in the street. He became interested for me, and asked questions about my master, which I answered in part. He expressed a great deal of sympathy, and a wish to aid me. He constantly sought opportunities to see me, and wrote to me frequently. I was a poor slave girl, only fifteen years old.

So much attention from a superior person was, of course, flattering; for human nature is the same in all. I also felt grateful for his sympathy, and encouraged by his kind words. It seemed to me a great thing to have such a friend. By degrees, a more tender feeling crept into my heart. He was an educated and eloquent gentleman; too eloquent, alas, for the poor slave girl who trusted in him. Of course I saw whither all this was tending. I knew the impassable gulf between us; but to be an object of interest to a man who is not married, and who is not her master, is agreeable to the pride and feelings of a slave, if her miserable situation has left her any pride or sentiment. It seems less degrading to give one's self, than to submit to compulsion. There is something akin to freedom in having a lover who has no control over you, except that which he gains by kindness and attachment. A master may treat you as rudely as he pleases, and you dare not speak; moreover, the wrong does not seem so great with an unmarried man, as with one who has a wife to be made unhappy. There may be sophistry in all this; but the condition of a slave confuses all principles of morality, and, in fact, renders the practice of them impossible.

When I found that my master had actually begun to build the lonely cottage, other feelings mixed with those I have described. Revenge, and calculations of interest, were added to flattered vanity and sincere gratitude for kindness. I knew nothing would enrage Dr. Flint so much as to know that I favored another; and it was something to triumph over my tyrant even in that small way. I thought he would revenge himself by selling me, and I was sure my friend, Mr. Sands, would buy me. He was a man of more generosity and feeling than my master, and I thought my freedom could be easily obtained from him. The crisis of my fate now came so near that I was desperate. I shuddered to think of being the mother of children that should be owned by my old tyrant. I knew that as soon as a new fancy took him, his victims were sold far off to get rid of them; especially if they had children. I had seen several women sold, with his babies at the breast. He never allowed his offspring by slaves to remain long in sight of himself and his wife. Of a man who was not my master I could ask to have my children well supported; and in this case, I felt confident I should obtain the boon. I also felt quite sure that they would be made free. With all these thoughts revolving in my mind, and seeing no other way of escaping the doom I so much dreaded, I made a headlong plunge. Pity me, and pardon me, O virtuous reader! You never knew what it is to be a slave; to be entirely unprotected by law or custom; to have the laws reduce you to the condition of a chattel, entirely subject to the will of another. You never exhausted your ingenuity in avoiding the snares, and eluding the power of a hatred tyrant; you never shuddered at the sound of his footsteps, and trembled within hearing of his voice. I know I did wrong. No one can feel it more sensibly than I do. The painful and humiliating memory will haunt me to my dying day. Still, in looking back, calmly, on the events of my life, I feel that the slave woman ought not to be judged by the same standard as others.

The months passed on. I had many unhappy hours. I secretly mourned over the sorrow I was bringing on my grandmother, who had so tried to shield me from harm. I knew that I was the greatest comfort of her old age, and that it was a source of pride to her that I had not degraded myself, like most of the slaves. I wanted to confess to her that I was no longer worthy of her love; but I could not utter the dreaded words.

As for Dr. Flint, I had a feeling of satisfaction and triumph in the thought of telling *him*. From time to time he told me of his intended arrangements, and I was silent. At last, he came and told me the cottage was completed, and ordered me to go to it. I told him I would never enter it. He said, "I have heard enough of such talk as that. You shall go, if you are carried by force; and you shall remain there."

I replied, "I will never go there. In a few months I shall be a mother."

He stood and looked at me in dumb amazement, and left the house without a word. I thought I should be happy in my triumph over him. But now that the truth was out, and my relatives would hear of it, I felt wretched. Humble as were their circumstances, they had pride in my good character. Now, how could I look them in the face? My self-respect was gone! I had resolved that I would be virtuous, though I was a slave. I had said, "Let the storm beat! I will brave it till I die." And now, how humiliated I felt!

5. Chaplain A. B. Randall Writes About the Freedpeople's Ideal of Marriage, 1865

Little Rock Ark Feb 28th 1865

[To Brig. Gen. L. Thomas]

Weddings, just now, are very popular, and abundant among the Colored People. They have just learned, of the Special Order No' 15. of Gen Thomas by which, they may not only be lawfully married, but have their Marriage Certificates, *Recorded;* in a *book furnished by the Government.* This is most desirable; and the order, was very opportune; as these people were constantly loosing their certificates. Those who were captured from the "Chepewa"; at Ivy's Ford, on the 17th of January, by

A. B. Randall to Brig. Gen. L. Thomas, February 28, 1865, in Ira Berlin and Leslie Rowland, eds., *Families and Freedom* (New York: New Press, 1997), 163–164.

Col Brooks, had their Marriage Certificates, taken from them; and destroyed; and then were roundly cursed, for having such papers in their posession. I have married, during the month, at this Post; Twenty five couples; mostly, those, who have families; & have been living together for years. I try to dissuade single men, who are soldiers, from marrying, till their time of enlistment is out: as that course seems to me, to be most judicious.

The Colored People here, generally consider, this war not only; their *exodus,* from bondage; but the road, to Responsibility; Competency; and an honorable Citizenship— God grant that their hopes and expectations may be fully realized. Most Respectfully

[Chaplain] A. B. Randall

6. William H. Stallings Testifies About Ku Klux Klan Lynchings, 1871

ATLANTA, GEORGIA, November 6, 1871.

WILLIAM H. STALLINGS sworn and examined.

By the CHAIRMAN:

Question. State your age, where you were born, where you now live, and what is your present occupation.

Answer. I am thirty-eight years old; I was born in the city of Augusta, in this State, and now live there; I am a carpenter by trade—a mechanic.

Question. We have had a great deal of testimony, it is proper to say, before us with respect to certain disguised bands of men going about at night and committing various acts of lawlessness. State whether there are any such in your community, and what you know about them there, of your own knowledge or upon reliable information?

Answer. I have never heard of any in the county of Richmond to my recollection. I think that in 1868 or 1869—I paid very little attention to it at the time—at a station called Dearing, on the Georgia road, between here and Augusta, about one or two hundred yards this side of the station, is what is called the water-pump or tank. One night while we were stopping at that station getting wood and water, two men came through the car I was in; they looked to me as if they had their coats turned wrong side outwards, with red flannel linings, and their faces blacked or smutted; they ran through the car and went out. About a couple of minutes afterwards, about two miles this side of Barnett, I saw on the side of the railroad embankment a row of men, twenty-five or thirty, maybe forty, I could not count them as the train was going by, they were all dressed in white; they raised their hands, and I heard them make a noise, but I could not hear what they said; that was all I ever saw of them. There was so much of it going on through the country at the time that I did not pay much attention to it.

Report of the Joint Select Committee to Inquire into the Affairs of the Late Insurrectionary States, House Report, 42nd Cong., 2nd Sess., no. 22 (1872): Georgia—Sub-Committee, 1119–1120.

Question. Were they understood to be going about over the country at that time?

Answer. Yes, sir; there was a great deal of it.

Question. Have you seen any traces of their acts?

Answer. As I stated before, there has been so little action taken about it throughout this State, a great many said here that the United States Government was going to give no protection to us—that is, the republican party; that I gave very little attention to anything after the spring of 1869 or the fall of 1868. But I think it was in the latter part of 1869, or the early part of 1870, that I saw two men who said they were taken out of jail in Jefferson County and had their ears taken off. I talked with one while the other stood off some eight or ten feet from me; I could see that his ear was all bound up. . . .

Question. Have you had any reliable information of any other cases than that?

Answer. Yes, sir; I have heard Doctor M. E. Swinney, of Augusta, relate a case of a colored man and a white woman in Jackson County.

Question. What was that case as he related it to you?

Answer. Well, they were accused of cohabiting together. He said that the colored man was taken out into the woods, a hole dug in the ground and a block buried in it, and his *penis* taken out, and a nail driven through it into the block; that a large butcher or cheese knife, as they call it, very sharp, was laid down by him, and lightwood piled around him and set on fire; the knife was put there so that he could cut if off and get away, or stay there and burn up. Doctor Swinney said that he cut it off and jumped out. Doctor Swinney did not tell me that he saw this himself, but he said he knew the parties concerned in it. I have heard him say often that he knew all the parties who did it. After the colored man did this, they took the woman, laid her down on the ground, then cut a slit on each side of her orifice, put a large padlock in it, locked it up, and threw away the key, and then turned her loose. She went so for two or three days, and then sent for Doctor Swinney to cut it out. I do not know whether he said he cut it out or got there just as the other physician had done it; but he saw the place.

Question. Did he prescribe for the woman?

Answer. I do not know; I do not recollect whether he said he did or not.

Question. He stated that he knew the parties who were concerned in it?

Answer. Yes, sir; he stated that he knew the parties. And there was another case I have heard him speak of, of the Creech family, father and son, and a negro woman in the same county. I have sat down and listened to him state all this at several different times.

Question. What was the case of the Creech family?

Answer. I do not recollect what they were accused of; but they had a grocery and sold liquor; that was one thing, for he said he had often stopped there and taken a drink himself, as he was going to his place from the railroad station. He spoke of several letters that were written to Creech ordering him to leave there. Creech advised with him what to do, and he advised him to leave just as quickly as possible, or they would kill him. A few days after that the body of the young man was found in the creek about two hundred yards from the house, and his father and the body of the colored woman were found in a mill-pond. I do not recollect how far off they said the mill-pond was from there; it was right in the neighborhood.

Question. You do not recollect what they had against Creech?

Answer. One thing, I think, was about selling liquor.

7. Ida B. Wells-Barnett Exposes the Myth
of the Black Rapist, 1892

Wednesday evening May 24th, 1892, the city of Memphis was filled with excitement. Editorials in the daily papers of that date caused a meeting to be held in the Cotton Exchange Building; a committee was sent for the editors of the "Free Speech" an Afro-American journal published in that city, and the only reason the open threats of lynching that were made were not carried out was because they could not be found. The cause of all this commotion was the following editorial published in the "Free Speech" May 21st, 1892, the Saturday previous.

"Eight negroes lynched since last issue of the 'Free Speech' one at Little Rock, Ark., last Saturday morning where the citizens broke (?) into the penitentiary and got their man; three near Anniston, Ala., one near New Orleans; and three at Clarksville, Ga., the last three for killing a white man, and five on the same old racket—the new alarm about raping white women. The same programme of hanging, then shooting bullets into the lifeless bodies was carried out to the letter.

Nobody in this section of the country believes the old thread bare lie that Negro men rape white women. If Southern white men are not careful, they will over-reach themselves and public sentiment will have a reaction; a conclusion will then be reached which will be very damaging to the moral reputation of their women." . . .

. . . [T]he leading citizens met in the Cotton Exchange Building the same evening, and threats of lynching were freely indulged, not by the lawless element upon which the deviltry of the South is usually saddled—but by the leading business men, in their leading business centre. Mr. Fleming, the business manager and owning a half interest [in] the Free Speech, had to leave town to escape the mob, and was afterwards ordered not to return; letters and telegrams sent me in New York where I was spending my vacation advised me that bodily harm awaited my return. Creditors took possession of the office and sold the outfit, and the "Free Speech" was as if it had never been.

The editorial in question was prompted by the many inhuman and fiendish lynchings of Afro-Americans which have recently taken place and was meant as a warning. Eight lynched in one week and five of them charged with rape! The thinking public will not easily believe freedom and education more brutalizing than slavery, and the world knows that the crime of rape was unknown during four years of civil war, when the white women of the South were at the mercy of the race which is all at once charged with being a bestial one.

Since my business has been destroyed and I am an exile from home because of that editorial, the issue has been forced, and as the writer of it I feel that the race and the public generally should have a statement of the facts as they exist. They will serve at the same time as a defense for the Afro-American Sampsons who suffer themselves to be betrayed by white Delilahs.

The whites of Montgomery, Ala., knew J. C. Duke sounded the keynote of the situation—which they would gladly hide from the world, when he said in his paper,

Ida B. Wells-Barnett, *Southern Horrors. Lynch Law in All Its Phases* (New York: New York Age, 1892), reprinted in *Southern Horrors and Other Writings: The Anti-Lynching Campaign of Ida B. Wells, 1892–1900,* ed. Jacqueline Jones Royster (Boston: Bedford/St. Martin's, 1997), 51–54, 58–62.

"The Herald," five years ago: "Why is it that white women attract negro men now more than in former days? There was a time when such a thing was unheard of. There is a secret to this thing, and we greatly suspect it is the growing appreciation of white Juliets for colored Romeos." Mr. Duke, like the "Free Speech" proprietors, was forced to leave the city for reflecting on the "honah" of white women and his paper suppressed; but the truth remains that Afro-American men do not always rape (?) white women without their consent.

Mr. Duke, before leaving Montgomery, signed a card disclaiming any intention of slandering Southern white women. The editor of the "Free Speech" has no disclaimer to enter, but asserts instead that there are many white women in the South who would marry colored men if such an act would not place them at once beyond the pale of society and within the clutches of the law. The miscegenation laws of the South only operate against the legitimate union of the races; they leave the white man free to seduce all the colored girls he can, but it is death to the colored man who yields to the force and advances of a similar attraction in white women. White men lynch the offending Afro-American, not because he is a despoiler of virtue, but because he succumbs to the smiles of white women. . . .

There is hardly a town in the South which has not an instance of the kind which is well-known, and hence the assertion is reiterated that "nobody in the South believes the old thread bare lie that negro men rape white women." Hence there is a growing demand among Afro-Americans that the guilt or innocence of parties accused of rape be fully established. They know the men of the section of the country who refuse this are not so desirous of punishing rapists as they pretend. The utterances of the leading white men show that with them it is not the crime but the *class*. Bishop Fitzgerald has become apologist for lynchers of the rapists of *white* women only. Governor Tillman, of South Carolina, in the month of June, standing under the tree in Barnwell, S.C., on which eight Afro-Americans were hung last year, declared that he would lead a mob to ["]lynch a *negro* who raped a *white* woman[.]" So say the pulpits, officials and newspapers of the South. But when the victim is a colored woman it is different. . . .

In Nashville, Tenn., there is a white man, Pat Hanifan, who outraged a little Afro-American girl, and, from the physical injuries received, she has been ruined for life. He was jailed for six months, discharged, and is now a detective in that city. In the same city, last May, a white man outraged an Afro-American girl in a drug store. He was arrested, and released on bail at the trial. It was rumored that five hundred Afro-Americans had organized to lynch him. Two hundred and fifty white citizens armed themselves with Winchesters and guarded him. A cannon was placed in front of his home, and the Buchanan Rifles (State Militia) ordered to the scene for his protection. The Afro-American mob did not materialize. Only two weeks before Eph. Grizzard, who had only been *charged* with rape upon a white woman, had been taken from jail, with Governor Buchanan and the police and militia standing by, dragged through the streets in broad daylight, knives plunged into him at every step, and with every fiendish cruelty a frenzied mob could devise, he was at last swung out on the bridge with hands cut to pieces as he tried to climb up the stanchions. A naked, bloody example of the blood-thirstiness of the nineteenth century civilization of the Athens of the South! No cannon or military was called out in his defense. He dared to visit a white woman.

At the very moment these civilized whites were announcing their determination "to protect their wives and daughters," by murdering Grizzard, a white man was in the same jail for raping eight-year-old Maggie Reese, an Afro-American girl. He was not harmed. The "honor" of grown women who were glad enough to be supported by the Grizzard boys and Ed Coy, as long as the liaison was not known, needed protection; they were white. The outrage upon helpless childhood needed no avenging in this case; she was black. . . .

The appeal of Southern whites to Northern sympathy and sanction, the adroit, insiduous plea made by Bishop Fitzgerald for suspension of judgment because those "who condemn lynching express no sympathy for the *white* woman in the case," falls to the ground in the light of the foregoing.

From this exposition of the race issue in lynch law, the whole matter is explained by the well-known opposition growing out of slavery to the progress of the race. This is crystalized in the oft-repeated slogan: "This is a white man's country and the white man must rule." The South resented giving the Afro-American his freedom, the ballot box and the Civil Rights Law. The raids of the Ku-Klux and White Liners to subvert reconstruction government, the Hamburg and Ellerton, S.C., the Copiah County Miss., and the Lafayette Parish, La., massacres were excused as the natural resentment of intelligence against government by ignorance.

Honest white men practically conceded the necessity of intelligence murdering ignorance to correct the mistake of the general government, and the race was left to the tender mercies of the solid South. Thoughtful Afro-Americans with the strong arm of the government withdrawn and with the hope to stop such wholesale massacres urged the race to sacrifice its political rights for sake of peace. They honestly believed the race should fit itself for government, and when that should be done, the objection to race participation in politics would be removed.

But the sacrifice did not remove the trouble, nor move the South to justice. One by one the Southern States have legally (?) disfranchised the Afro-American, and since the repeal of the Civil Rights Bill nearly every Southern State has passed separate car laws with a penalty against their infringement. The race regardless of advancement is penned into filthy, stifling partitions cut off from smoking cars. All this while, although the political cause has been removed, the butcheries of black men at Barnwell, S.C., Carrolton, Miss., Waycross, Ga., and Memphis, Tenn., have gone on; also the flaying alive of a man in Kentucky, the burning of one in Arkansas, the hanging of a fifteen year old girl in Louisiana, a woman in Jackson, Tenn., and one in Hollendale, Miss., until the dark and bloody record of the South shows 728 Afro-Americans lynched during the past 8 years. Not 50 of these were for political causes; the rest were for all manner of accusations from that of rape of white women, to the case of the boy Will Lewis who was hanged at Tullahoma, Tenn., last year for being drunk and "sassy" to white folks.

These statistics compiled by the Chicago "Tribune" were given the first of this year (1892). Since then, not less than one hundred and fifty have been known to have met violent death at the hands of cruel bloodthirsty mobs during the past nine months.

To palliate this record (which grows worse as the Afro-American becomes intelligent) and excuse some of the most heinous crimes that ever stained the history of a country, the South is shielding itself behind the plausible screen of defending the honor of its women. This, too, in the face of the fact that only *one-third* of the 728 victims to mobs have been *charged* with rape, to say nothing of those of that one-third who were innocent of the charge. A white correspondent of the Baltimore Sun declares that the Afro-American who was lynched in Chestertown, Md., in May for assault on a white girl was innocent; that the deed was done by a white man who had since disappeared. The girl herself maintained that her assailant was a white man. When that poor Afro-American was murdered, the whites excused their refusal of a trial on the ground that they wished to spare the white girl the mortification of having to testify in court.

This cry has had its effect. It has closed the heart, stifled the conscience, warped the judgment and hushed the voice of press and pulpit on the subject of lynch law throughout this "land of liberty." Men who stand high in the esteem of the public for christian character, for moral and physical courage, for devotion to the principles of equal and exact justice to all, and for great sagacity, stand as cowards who fear to open their mouths before this great outrage. They do not see that by their tacit encouragement, their silent acquiescence, the black shadow of lawlessness in the form of lynch law is spreading its wings over the whole country.

Men who, like Governor Tillman, start the ball of lynch law rolling for a certain crime, are powerless to stop it when drunken or criminal white toughs feel like hanging an Afro-American on any pretext.

Even to the better class of Afro-Americans the crime of rape is so revolting they have too often taken the white man's word and given lynch law neither the investigation nor condemnation it deserved.

They forget that a concession of the right to lynch a man for a certain crime, not only concedes the right to lynch any person for any crime, but (so frequently is the cry of rape now raised) it is in a fair way to stamp us a race of rapists and desperadoes. They have gone on hoping and believing that general education and financial strength would solve the difficulty, and are devoting their energies to the accumulation of both.

The mob spirit has grown with the increasing intelligence of the Afro-American. It has left the out-of-the-way places where ignorance prevails, has thrown off the mask and with this new cry stalks in broad daylight in large cities, the centres of civilization, and is encouraged by the "leading citizens" and the press.

▮ E S S A Y S

Historical accounts of African-American life under slavery have tended to emphasize either the exploitation of slaves by white planters or the relative autonomy of slave culture "from sundown to sunup." In distinctive ways, these two essays move beyond this dichotomy by focusing on slaves' sexuality and their relationships both with masters and with other slaves. Historian Brenda E. Stevenson of UCLA argues that slaves' intimate lives were subject to their masters' control, but emphasizes that slaves formed enduring, flexible kinship bonds that supported their resistance to domination. At the same time, she opens to view the relationships between black women and men, including marriage and, in a controversial finding, polygyny. She explores both sides of black men's effort to carry out ideals of manliness: many sought marriage and tried to protect their families, but others exploited women sexually. Historian and biographer Nell Irvin Painter of

Princeton University insists that we must look more closely at the patterns of psychological abuse and damage brought about by the habitual rape, sexual harassment, and battering of enslaved women—what she powerfully terms "soul murder." She urges historians to probe beneath the surfaces of historical evidence, and employs feminist and psychological theory to suggest the immediate and long-term costs to black people of slavery's sexual abuse, child neglect, violence, and anger.

Slave Marriage and Family Relations

BRENDA E. STEVENSON

African American romance and marriage within the context of the institution of slavery could be the most challenging and devastating of slave experiences. From the initiation of a romance, black men and women had to confront and compromise with their masters about control of their intimate lives, aware that their owner typically had the final say about if and when they could marry, and even who. Even after a slave's marriage, his or her master still commonly decided when slave husbands and wives could see each other, if and when they could live or work together, the fate of their children, and sometimes even the number of children they had.

Slaves nonetheless had their own way of doing things, refusing to concede too much, sometimes refusing to concede at all. If the slave master's interference in the slave's personal life was interminable, so too was the slave's resistance to this kind of intervention. Like their owners, slave attitudes and decisions about courtship and marriage were shaped by gender convention and community concerns, but not necessarily the same conventions or concerns. The matrifocality of many slave families, for example, meant that the realities of slave manhood and womanhood differed substantially within the context of family life from those whose familial experiences were nuclear and patriarchal. Likewise, extended families and slave communities were important, not just because they monitored slave behavior and maintained slave values, thereby protecting the integrity of the community. Members of slave communities also actually played substantial physical, material, and emotional roles in the lives of slaves. To a large extent, they were the slave's family. The presence of meaningful kinship ties embodied in the extended family or community, therefore, allowed slaves to take on a variety of marital arrangements and familial structures. One's master might have had the final authority, but there also were other slaves and slave institutions that exerted influence, perhaps more influence than masters realized. Within the broad contours of slave life that masters insisted on designing, slaves found spaces of their own, choosing what lines to and not to cross as they constructed their own domestic terrain.

It was a terrain structured by diverse, yet nonetheless respected rules and standards. Those who wanted to marry, for example, had to consult their parents or other black authority figures first. The man usually initiated the process, asking for permission from the would-be bride, her kin, and their owners. "First you picks out de gal you wants, den ax her to marry up with you," Levi Pollard explained. "[D]en go to Mars en ax him ifen you ken have her. If Mars like dat couple den he says yes." Pollard's recollection suggests that male slaves and owners controlled much of this process, but mothers and elderly women also held power in certain slave quarters, particularly in relation to younger slave women. They could control vital aspects of a woman's courtship and marriage, sometimes even to the exclusion of owners or slave men.

The predominance of matrifocality and the large percentages of slave women in smaller holdings, therefore, had significant impact on slaves' domestic lives, giving slave women great influence in their families and communities. It was an influence not recognized in the larger society's hierarchy, but nonetheless functional in the slave's world view. Elderly slave women who had lived in the quarters for years, particularly where adult females were in the majority, were accorded great respect. Their long lives and the wisdom assumed derived from it, their years of service to their families, and their knowledge of their community's history were the basis for their authority. Likewise, mothers who raised their children without paternal input commanded their children's obedience and deference.

Female power in slave families and communities was not power that they took lightly or used sparingly. Ex-slave Philip Coleman, for example, admitted that "there was a likely girl" that he "took a great fancy to" and wanted to marry. According to Coleman, his owner approved of the match and the young woman did too, but the girl's mother "put up so strong [an] objection that the wedding . . . was called off." Caroline Johnson Harris explained of her courtship and marriage that "Ant Sue," and not her master, had to give permission to the slave couples in her quarters before they could marry. As an elder and a holy woman, "Ant Sue" especially compelled communal respect. Harris recalled that when she and her prospective husband approached the powerful woman for her blessing, "She tell us to think 'bout it hard fo' two days, 'cause marryin' was sacred in de eyes of Jesus." Having followed her directions carefully, Caroline and Mose (the would-be-fiancé) returned to "Ant Sue" and told her that, after much consideration, they still wanted to marry. The elderly woman then assembled the other members of the slave community and asked them to "pray fo' de union dat God was gonna make. Pray we stay together an' have lots of chillun an' none of 'em git sol' way from de parents." A broomstick ceremony followed her prayer, but not before "Ant Sue" queried the couple again about the certainty of their decision.

"Ant Sue's" and the discriminating mother's control carried considerable weight in their slave communities. Masters who were unaware of or disinterested in slaves' distribution of social power within their world claimed that their authority as owner took priority. If the couple had the same master, there usually was no problem in gaining his or her permission, although sometimes an owner would question each about their feelings before giving consent. If the couple had different owners, both masters had to give their permission and usually the husband and wife continued to live separately after their marriage. "My father was owned by John Butler and my [mother] was owned by Tommy Humphries," Loudoun [Virginia] slave George Jackson explained. "When my father wanted to cum he had to get a permit from his massa. He would only cum home on Saturday. He worked on the next plantation joinin' us." A few owners bought a favorite slave's spouse. William Gray of "Locust Hill" just outside of Leesburg, for example, purchased

Emily, the wife of his male slave George, after their first child was born in 1839. The couple had five more children during the next eight years. Gray later sold the slave family to a local farmer in 1853, "all at their own request" for $3200.

Emily and George, as most slaves, probably had a brief, "informal" wedding. Despite its brevity and seeming informality, however, slave weddings and the commitments they symbolized were extremely important events for black families and communities. William Grose, for example, was appalled when a new master insisted that he marry again simply because he had been sold far away from his first wife. He was equally distressed when the owner presented him with a new wife without any "ceremony." Slave marriage rituals varied considerably. "Jumping the broom" was popular among some. Georgianna Gibbs remembered that when the slaves on her farm married they had to "jump over a broom three times" before they actually were considered married. . . .

Those slaves who did not "jump the broom" solemnized their marriages in other ways. Slave masters sometimes participated, reading a few words from the Bible or giving their own extemporaneous text. Tom Epps recalled that he had heard of "jumping the broomstick," but "us never did nothin' like dat in our place." Instead, the slaves participated in a ceremony whereby the "Marsa would hol' a light, read a lil' bit an' den tell 'em dey was married."

On very rare occasions, local ministers actually officiated. Ex-slave Fannie Berry remembered with delight her wedding to a free black man named John Taylor. Because she was a favorite of her owners, she was able to have the ceremony in her mistress's front parlor, a minister perform the service, and many slaves and local free blacks attend. A festive reception followed with "ev'ything to eat you could call for." Berry's husband worked on the railroad, and she saw him only occasionally until after general emancipation. Her abroad marriage was typical even if her lavish nuptials were not.

Fannie's owner let her marry the man she chose. Yet inevitably some masters refused to respect the choices that their slaves made about their private lives. Despite family or community support, those slaves who defied their masters paid a high price. Still slaves willingly, and sometimes willfully, chose to marry in spite of their owner's wishes. Martha and David Bennett, for example, married without her master's permission. David belonged to Captain James Taylor and Martha was a slave of George Carter. Taylor seemed not to resent the union, but evidence suggests that Carter felt otherwise—Martha reported that Carter had had her stripped naked and "flogged" "after her marriage." . . .

. . . Martha's marriage begs a number of important questions not only about the reasons why slaves married who they married, but also about the kinds of marriage and family styles they deemed acceptable.

Slaves so frequently married persons belonging to other masters that Martha's behavior does not seem odd. . . . [M]any slaves had abroad marriages and matrifocal households.

. . . Complex rules of exogamy, notions of slave manhood and womanhood, and a desire to extend one's social world beyond one's residential community were significant considerations. So too was the slave's psychological need to establish some "emotional distance" between oneself and one's loved ones, to say nothing of the slave's cultural heritage. All these factors contributed to what "choices" slaves made about their domestic lives within the context of the rigid constraints that masters imposed.

The slaves' great concern about marriage to a close blood relation, for example, could have influenced greatly the numbers of abroad marriages that existed even among quarters . . . where there were many men and women from which to choose a spouse. In generations-old quarters . . . , long years of intermarriage and procreation created intricate and complex kinship ties, ties that may have been discernible only to slave community members. While older quarters housed particularly stable communities because of extended family networks, they also contained closely connected kin (first cousins, for example) whom slaves would consider ineligible as marriage partners. . . . [M]any masters seemed to have realized that their slaves were upholding stringent rules of exclusion. Georgia Gibb's recollection that her master "never sell none of his slaves, but he'd always buy more . . . dat keeps de slaves from marrying in dere famblies" suggests her owner's knowledge of operative rules of exogamy.

Martha Bennett, therefore, may have looked for a husband outside of Carter's slaveholding because his quarters presented her with a preponderance of male kin. There also may have been other reasons why she agreed to marry abroad. Growing up in communities filled with matrifocal slave families, it is not surprising that slave women like Martha were socialized to function in such. Slave women may have foreseen other benefits as well. Having abroad husbands and matrifocal households, for example, allowed them a kind of management of their children and day-to-day domestic life that live-in husbands may not have. . . . [M]atrifocality had the potential to define . . . slave womanhood in ways that were quite distinct from free womanhood. Likewise, abroad marriages could give women greater domestic power, ideally affording them the moral sanctity of marriage, but also lessening some of their responsibilities—physical and emotional—to their husbands.

Slave men like David Bennett would have had other motives for choosing an abroad wife, some linked to African American conventions of manhood and leisure. Nineteenth-century black men, as white, often viewed travel and "adventure" as a "natural" desire and activity of a "man." [Abroad marriage meant an extended social world for slave men. "Slaves always wanted to marry a gal on 'nother plantation cause dey could git a pass to go visit 'em on Saddy nights," ex-slave Tom Epps recalled. These descriptions and others not only suggest the delight slave men gained from "travel" to their wives' homes and the opportunity those excursions afforded them to broaden their community. It also allowed slave husbands a "break" from their daily physical and psychological routines.] . . . The slave husband's sense that his "manhood" in part hinged on his ability to protect his wife and children inspired some to marry abroad—at least he did not have to witness his family's daily abuse. When local slave Dan Lockhart's wife was sold to a man who lived eight miles away from him, he believed it was "too far" and he managed to get his owner to sell him to someone who lived closer. He stayed with his new master for more than three years before he decided to run away to avoid seeing his wife and children being whipped. He explained that he "could not stand this abuse of them, so I made up my mind to leave." . . .

Love and romance were as important reasons as any that slaves insisted on choosing their spouses even if it meant a long-distance marriage. The story of Loudoun slave William Grose and his free black wife is instructive. Grose's owner never approved of his abroad marriage to the free woman, for he feared that she would find some means to help William escape. Eventually he decided that the best way to protect his investment was to sell William to a long-distance trader. Sent to New Orleans, he was sold again, this time as a domestic to a creole widower. Grose's new owner, who seemed to have several slave wives himself, insisted that William marry another woman. "He sent for a woman, who came in, and said he to me, 'That is your wife,'" William explained. "I was scared half to death, for I had one wife whom I liked, and didn't want another. . . . There was no ceremony about it—he said Cynthia is your wife."

It is not certain from Grose's autobiographical account whether or not he and Cynthia ever lived as husband and wife, but he continued to care deeply for the Loudoun free black woman he had married. Remarkably, the two managed to remain in contact. A year later, Grose's Virginia wife arrived in New Orleans and managed to get a position as a domestic in the same family in which he worked (an American family he had been hired out to serve), and the two secretly carried on their marriage. Grose's master eventually found out about their relationship and she was forced to leave New Orleans. But this was not the end of their story. "After my wife was gone," William confessed, "I felt very uneasy. At length, I picked up spunk, and said I would start." William finally managed to escape to Canada where he, his Loudoun wife, and their children finally were reunited.

The history of William Grose, his free black wife, and their struggle to remain married in spite of his owners' opposition is an incredible and rare one. Yet the kind of determination they demonstrated was more common than one might imagine. Unfortunately, few were able to triumph, but many made admirable attempts. . . .

The kinds of decisions about their intimate lives that slaves made, even given the many restrictions which encumbered them, were very important to their sense of individuality, control, and self-esteem. For those slaves like the Groses . . . and even the Bennetts, therefore, it obviously was just as important, if not more so, to marry the person whom they "chose," even when they knew they would have to live apart, as to marry someone simply to please their master or because they could expect to share a home with that person on a daily basis.

"Marsa used to sometimes pick our wives fo' us," Charles Grandy complained. "Wasn't no use tryin' to pick one," he added resentfully, "cause Marsa wasn't gonna pay but so much for her. All he wanted was a young healthy one who looked like she could have children, whether she was purty or ugly as sin." Most slaves knew that their owners preferred that they marry within their own holding. To do so allowed masters to claim as property all children born to these cohabitative couples, usually considerably more in number than those born of abroad marriages. Slaveholders also believed that couples who resided together reduced security problems, eliminating the need to give passes for conjugal visits and providing masters with the potent threat of selling or hurting slave family members in order to insure obedience.

The large numbers of abroad marriages, the substantial incidence of serial marriages, even the rare examples of polygamy, therefore, can be linked both to the slave's lack of control over his or her domestic life and to his or her resilient assertion of control. . . . One of the most compelling examples of slave choice and its impact on slave marital structures and relations is that offered by ex-slave Israel

Massie. Massie insisted that slave men and women not only "understood" polygynous marital relations, but some sought them out. His insistence helps to further establish the premise that slaves adopted a variety of marriage and family styles and that they were comfortable with that variety. According to Massie, slaves sometimes made a conscious choice to create certain marital arrangements and family structures which were not monogamous and nuclear.

"Naw, slaves didn't have wives like dey do now," he began his explanation. "Ef I liked ya, I jes go an' tell marster I wanted ya an' he give his consent." "Ef I see another gal over dar on another plantation, I'd go an' say to de gal's marster, 'I want Jinny fer a wife.' . . . Hit may be still another gal I want an' I'll go an' git her. Allright now, dars three wives an' slaves had as many wives as dey wanted." Massie insisted that the multiple wives of one slave man "didn't think hard of each other" but "got 'long fine together." He illustrated antebellum slave polygyny with an example from his own farm. "When Tom died," he continued, "dar wuz Ginny, Sarah, Nancy, an' Patience." According to Massie, all of Tom's wives came to his funeral and publicly mourned for him. "Do ya kno' . . . dem women never fou't, fuss, an' quarrel over dem men folks? Dey seemed to understood each other."

Polygyny, or something akin to it in which a slave man had longstanding, contiguous intimate relationships with more than one woman, probably was a much more popular alternative among slaves than heretofore has been realized. The unavailability of marriageable slave men in smaller holdings and the scarce number of men in those slave communities hit particularly hard by the domestic slave trade provided the physical conditions for polygamy, particularly when coupled with pressures (internal and external) on women to "breed." Moreover, at least scarce knowledge of ancestral domestic arrangements (in Islamic or many traditional African religious groups) and a continual tradition of matrifocality among slaves provided cultural sanction for polygamy. Still few actual accounts of slave polygyny remain. This probably is because polygynous marriages could not be legalized after general emancipation. Given the general predilection of local churches, northern missionaries, teachers, and the Freedmen's Bureau to establish monogamy among freed slaves, polygynous or polygamous relationships after emancipation may have been largely ignored, or given some kind of culturally bound, misleading label such as "promiscuous couplings," "immoral" behavior, or adultery that have hidden from view the practice of polygamy among freed slaves.

Federal, state, and private agencies coerced freedmen and women to change this aspect of their lives, or at least to camouflage it from public scrutiny. Massie again is instructive, alluding to the reasons why polygyny ended with emancipation: "Now, out of all dem wives, when Lee surrendered, ya choose from dem one 'oman an' go an' git a license an' marry her. Some turned all dey wives loose an' got a new wife from some t'other place." Massie, and probably many other ex-slaves, was aware that it was illegal for "free" people to have more than one spouse. Former slaves, hoping to legitimize their domestic world through acquisition of the marriage "license," had to publicly abandon polygyny. Regardless of the reason for this postbellum change, however, it is clear that Massie, and the slaves he referred to, acted as if monogamy, even serial monogamy, was not the only marriage alternative or ideal they had as slaves. . . .

. . . Slave females, who were more likely than males to remain in their families of birth through adolescence, received most of their gendered socialization from their mothers, other female kin, or community women. Usually by the time slave girls reached their teens, these women already had prepared them to take on the most important commitments of their adult lives—motherhood and marriage. Slave women taught their girls that as adults it would be their responsibility to cook, clean, bear, and rear children for their families, all this despite the labor demands of masters. They were supposed to take pride in their "womanly" skills and service they rendered their families. . . .

A woman's role as head of a matrifocal family mandated that she make some of her family's most vital decisions and suffer the consequences if her master or her abroad husband disagreed. It meant that she had to act protectively and aggressively for the sake of her dependents, often in open conflict with her owner. Slave mothers, for example, routinely rebelled against the poor material support owners provided, especially the amount and quality of their food. Few hesitated to steal, lie, and cheat in order to guarantee their physical survival or that of their children. . . .

Slave women across age, cultural, and occupational lines were forthright in their appreciation of self-reliant, determined black females who had the wherewithal to protect themselves and theirs, confrontationally if need be. Of course, most women were not able to act in any openly confrontational manner for fear of severe retaliation. But it is clear that slave women held great pride and esteem for those who did so. These were the women whom other slave females spoke most often about in "heroic" terms, attributing to them what seem like (and may have been) fantastical deeds and attitudes. Thus, while white southern society believed that this kind of female conduct was unfeminine, if not outright masculine, slave women utilized aggressive, independent behavior to protect their most fundamental claims to womanhood; that is, their female sexuality and physicality, and their roles as mothers and wives.

True stories about slave female rape and physical abuse, for example, abound in the records produced by slaves. Most slave women found no way to fight back (and win). Those women who found some manner to resist emerged in the lore and mythology of slave women as both heroic and ideal. Slave mothers, in fact, often told stories of these women to their daughters as part of their socialization. Virginia Hayes Shepherd, for one, spoke in glowing terms of three heroic slave women she had known personally or through her mother's stories—one successfully avoided the sexual pursuit of her owner, while the other two refused to be treated in the fields like men, that is, to be worked beyond their physical endurance as childbearing women.

Seventy years after her emancipation, Minnie Folkes still felt the pain of witnessing her mother being whipped by her overseer. Yet her explanation of the older woman's suffering (that she had refused "to be wife to dis man") and her description of how her mother had taught her to protect herself from sexual abuse ("muma had sed 'Don't let nobody bother yo principle; 'cause dat wuz all yo' had'") are tinged with pride and respect. The elder Folkes was determined to have control of the physical attributes of her womanhood even if it meant routinely withstanding brutal beatings. Her resistance was a powerful lesson to Minnie.

Fannie Berry told many accounts of female slave resistance to sexual abuse, including her own. But she was most proud of Sukie Abbott's daring rebuff of both her owner's sexual overtures and the slave trader's physical violation. Both Berry and Abbott rightfully linked the two as equally dehumanizing.

Sukie was the Abbott house slave who, according to Berry, had been the target of her master's unwarranted sexual advances. One day while Sukie was in the kitchen making soap, Mr. Abbott tried to force her to have sex with him. He pulled down her dress and tried to push her onto the floor. Then, according to Berry, "dat black gal got mad. She took an' punch ole Marsa an' made him break loose an' den she gave him a shove an' push his hindparts down in de hot pot o' soap. . . . He got up holdin' his hindparts an' ran from de kitchen, not darin' to yell, 'cause he didn't want Miss Sarah Ann [his wife] to know 'bout it." A few days later, Abbott took Sukie to the slave market to sell. The defiant women again faced sexual abuse and physical invasion as potential buyers stared, poked, and pinched her. According to Fannie, Sukie got mad again. "She pult her dress up an' tole those ole nigger traders to look an' see if dey could fin' any teef down dere. . . . Marsa never did bother slave gals no mo," Berry concluded with relish.

Many witnesses at the slave market that day no doubt thought Sukie vulgar and promiscuous, a perfect picture of black "womanhood." Fannie Berry concluded something altogether different. In Berry's estimation, Sukie had exacted a high price from the men who tried to abuse her. It was true that the slave woman had lost her community when Mr. Abbott sold her in retaliation for her resistance; but she still managed to deny her owner his supposed right to claim her "female principle." She also demanded that her new buyer see her for what she was, a woman, not an animal, by insisting that he acknowledge her female sexual organs. Perhaps most important, Sukie's response to Mr. Abbott's attempted rape deterred him from violently pursuing other slave women on his plantation. . . . Fannie Berry's rendition of the Sukie Abbott biography, whether true or embellished, is an important example of the kinds of stories of female heroism and humanity that slave women told and retold as a kind of inspirational socialization and legitimizing process.

Thus the story had to be told within a certain context to give the desired effect. Neither Fannie nor Sukie probably would have approved of a woman baring her sexual organs publicly if the circumstances had been different. Slave women usually frowned on blatant female sexual exhibition or promiscuity. This is not to say that they were ashamed of their sexuality. Nor were they shy about the promise of sexual pleasure and human procreation that they as women embodied. There were rules, however, which guided their sexual expression, rules which many of them respected and tried to incorporate in their social lives.

Sex in the female slave world, for example, was part of the culture of adults. As girls grew older, it was acceptable for them to become more aware of the significance and value of their sexual power, to realize that women, through their sexuality, provided great service to their families and communities. A woman's body in the world of slaves was an important, complex symbol. Her body, therefore, was a sign, in the face of heart-wrenching tragedy and oppression, of human pleasure, immortality and future security. Many expected that much about a young woman should suggest the sensuality and immortality that she (as a sexual, procreative being) held. A single women's dress, hair, walk, dance, and language could and sometimes were supposed to be sexually suggestive. Yet girls and adolescents still were not supposed to yield to the temptation of sexual intercourse out of a sheer desire for sexual pleasure. That right and responsibility was reserved for married women, those who were soon to be married, or those who wanted to bear children.

The diverse cultures of slaves produced varying guidelines about a woman's sexual behavior and responsibility. Some mothers, for example, went to great lengths to shield their daughters from sex until after they were married. Others acted differently, expecting young women to marry after they became pregnant or gave birth to their first child. Usually, however, sex was communally sanctioned only for those women who were ready to marry, to have children, or both. Matrifocality was such a widespread phenomenon among slaves that many slave elders did not always demand marriage before intercourse or even before the birth of a first child. Extended families and operative slave communities were good support networks for single mothers and children. A woman with a child, regardless of her marital state, however, had to be willing to take that responsibility seriously. If her family and community came to her aid, the community expected that she, and later the child, would give back in kind.

Of course the conditions of life for slave females often made any social rules difficult to maintain. Moreover, rules of sexual expression differed for slave men and women. To complicate the matter even further, black men often were not the only ones that slave women had to respond to and negotiate sexual contact. When assumptions of male sexual prerogative and female submission shared by both black and white men influenced their relationships with slave women, men of either race might have used whatever advantage they had to seduce or even to exploit and sometimes abuse these women. . . .

. . . Slave wives, even abroad wives, were expected to submit to their husband's will, particularly those who had regular contact. A woman's submission to her man went hand in hand with her service to her family and community. . . .

And while many slave couples did not live together on a daily basis and many abroad wives believed they had to take on an aggressive, protective, somewhat independent stance with regard to family matters, many slave husbands still wanted to be their families' protectors and supporters. Thomas Harper, for example, was a local blacksmith who decided to escape to Canada because he "thought that it was hard to see . . . [his family] in want and abused when he was not at liberty to aid or protect them." . . . Numerous Loudoun black men . . . managed to secure the freedom of their wives and/or children in order to insure that they could protect them. . . .

A wife's submission and service to her husband, therefore, was supposed to be rewarded by his efforts to aid and protect her and her children. Sex complicated this brokered balance because it virtually was impossible for some slave women to submit to their husband's desire for sexual exclusivity. Loudoun slave masters who believed that they held sexual rights to their female slave property continued to be an enormous problem for couples. Some masters actually reserved the most attractive slave women for themselves, regardless of the woman's marital status or even their age. Loudoun planter George Carter, for example, was known to purchase female adolescents for his sexual pleasure. Writing to the wealthy bachelor in 1805, William Forbes was explicit about Carter's preferences: "Girls are more frequently for sale than boys—would you object to a very likely one—*a virgin*—of about 14 or 15." Several years later, Carter's sister Sophia sternly criticized her brother's infamous behavior. Writing in response to her accusations, Carter admitted his history but added by way of an explanation: "My habits like most men are vicious & corrupt," "a Sin" that he was "only answerable for" to his God.

Indeed, George Carter's declaration that he was only one of many was well founded. Loudoun county census takers in 1860 described 27 percent of resident slaves and 51 percent of local free blacks as mulatto. Miscegenation was frequent, but not spoken about openly. Slaves, threatened with whippings and sale, typically had the most to lose from exposing slave/master sexual liaisons. Once the threat of public exposure surfaced, slaveholding families did not hesitate to blame and punish the slave women. Liz McCoy painted a not unusual scenario: "Aunt Charlotte . . . was sold to Georgia away from her baby when de Chile won't no more 3 months. . . . [She] had a white baby by her young master. Dats why dey sold her south." A slaveholder reacted typically to an incident of miscegenation within his family that had become public knowledge. "She had offended in my family," he explained of his son's concubine, "and I can only restore confidence by sending her out of hearing [to Georgia]."

Miscegenation is a sterile, emotionless term that often shrouds acts of sexual submission characterized by violence and degradation. The women and their biracial children clearly were the true victims in these situations; but slave men also could face grave consequences. Many often found themselves in the precarious, if not dangerous, position of competing with slaveholding men for the same slave women. Slave beaus and husbands could suffer brutal physical and emotional consequences if a slaveholding man wanted his woman. Undoubtedly when white men raped black women they did so not only to subject these females to a violent and dehumanizing experience, but also to emasculate husbands and male kin. The various reactions of male slaves, therefore, were equally responses to their own sense of powerlessness as they were a recognition of the physical and psychological pain that these females experienced. "Marsters an' overseers use to make slaves dat wuz wid deir husbands git up, [and] do as they say," one ex-slave man noted. "Send husbands out on de farm, milkin' cows or cuttin' wood. Den he gits in bed wid slave himself. Some women would fight an' tussel. Others would be [h]umble—feared of dat beatin'. What we saw, couldn't do nothing 'bout it. My blood is b[o]ilin' now [at the] thoughts of dem times. Ef dey told dey husbands he wuz powerless."

When slave husbands did intervene, they suffered awful retaliatory actions—sometimes permanent separation from their families, severe beatings, or murder. Many probably felt as did Charles Grandy, who concluded of the fatal shooting of a male slave who tried to protect his wife from the advances of their overseer: "Nigger ain't got no chance." Some slave husbands targeted the female victims of rape rather than the powerful white males who attacked them. Regardless of whomever they struck out at, however, their responses usually had little effect on the abusive white men involved.

But not all sexual relations between slave women and white men were physically coerced, just as not all sex between slave women and men was voluntary. Masters and slave men had many ways to gain control of and manipulate black women's sexuality. Some slave women responded to material incentives like food, clothing, and better housing that white men offered in exchange for sexual favors. Certainly they were much more able than slave suitors to "romance" slave women with gifts and promises of a better life. Others promised, and sometimes granted, emancipation. The unavailability of marriageable slave men, particularly for those women who lived in small holdings, also could have been something of a coercive factor. It is not inconceivable that some of these women established sexual/marital relations with available white men, just as these kinds of demographic conditions may have enjoined some to commit to polygynous relations with whatever black men were available.

One also cannot discount the impact on biracial sexual relations of a combination of factors endemic to life in a racialist constructed society, including internalized racism and a desire to identify with and be accepted by the "superior" race. Under these circumstances, some slave women may have agreed to become concubines to, or may have even desired, white men. Racially mixed slave women who were socialized to be more culturally akin to whites than blacks could be particularly vulnerable to the sexual overtures of white men. Ary, for example, was a quadroon slave woman raised, as the favored domestic, in the home of her father's brother. By the time she reached young womanhood, she had become the concubine of her young master, her paternal first cousin. Convinced that she was her father's favorite child, Ary often boasted of her elite white parentage and her young master's love for her. Remembering her lover's pronouncement that she was to have nothing to do with "colored men" because they "weren't good enough" for her, Ary was determined not to associate too closely with any blacks.

Despite Ary's belief that white men were superior to black, men of both races lived by a double and privileged sexual standard. Tales of male sexual prowess were applauded in the slave community, while female promiscuity was frowned on. Masters followed the same sexual code in their white communities and, therefore, understood only too well the importance of sexual conquest to the male ego. Some undoubtedly used the masculine esteem derived from sexual triumph to help convince slave men to act as "breeders." West Turner was born in about 1842 and remembered well the tales of breeding men: "Joe was 'bout seven feet tall an' was de breedinges' nigger in Virginia," he began one story. "'Member once ole Marsa hired him out to a white man what lived down in Suffolk. Dey come an' got him on a Friday. Dey brung him back Monday mo'nin'. Dey say de next year dere was sebenteen little black babies bo'n at dat place in Suffolk, all on de same day." . . .

Slave men traditionally applauded their sexual potency, celebrating it in song, dance, jokes, and heroic tales. Unlike slave women, men did not have to restrict their sexual activity to marital or procreative duties. A man could derive great status from having sexual relations with as many women as possible, or as many times as possible with one woman, without marriage or children being at issue. Even elderly men like Cornelius Garner still spoke proudly of their youthful sexual verve and refused to accept that the possibility of infertility diminished their record of sexual performance or their status as men. Speaking of his three wives, Garner boasted: "Pretty good ole man to wear out two wives, but de third one, ha, ha may wear me out." When asked if he had any children, Garner was quick to answer that he had never had any children, but that that was not his fault: "I did what God tole me. 'Wuk and multiply,' ha ha. I wuked but 'twon't no multiplying after de wuk."

The emphasis that slave men placed on their sexual prowess had profound impact on slave courtship and marriage, particularly when they treated their women as sexual objects to pursue and dominate, often without a hint of marriage or long-standing commitment. The impact of slavery on the relationships that slave males had with their families, especially the women in their families, may have helped to exaggerate female sexual objectification. . . . [The] constant experience and fear of separation, along with the need to be able to adjust, physically and emotionally, to it, may have inhibited some slave men from allowing themselves to construct complex relationships with the women with whom they came in contact, resulting instead in their sexual objectification.

A song that ex-slave Levi Pollard sang proudly when interviewed summarizes some aspects of slave sexual relations. From the first stanza on, it is a celebration of slave male eroticism, sexual casualness, and female slave objectification.

> Black gal sweet,
> Some like goodies dat de white folks eat;
> Don't you take'n tell her name,
> En den if sompin' happen you won't ketch de blame.
>
> Yaller gal fine,
> She may be yo'ne [yours] but she oughter be mine,
> Lemme git by
> En see what she mean by de cut er dat eye.
> Better shet dat door,
> Fo'de white folks'll believe we er t[e]arin' up de flo'.
>
> When a feller comes a-knockin',
> Dey holler Oh, sho,
> Hop light ladies,
> Oh, Miss Loo. . . .
>
> . . . De boys ain't a gwine,
> When you cry boo hoo,
> Hop light, ladies,
> Oh, Miss Loo. . . .

Pollard's song not only is about sexual relations in the quarters, but specifies the kind of sexual control that slave and white men joked about or perhaps hoped to have over slave women. . . . [I]t documents, in the words of slave men themselves, many of the popularized perspectives they held about sex and the female slave. It is replete with allusions to vital issues of slave sexuality, including: competition for slave women across and within racial lines ("Some like goodies dat de white folks eat;" "She may be yo'ne but she oughter be mine"); questions of paternity and sexual responsibility ("Don't you take'n tell her name,/ En den if sompin' happen you won't ketch de blame"); the voyeuristic essence of slaveholders' interest in slaves' private lives ("Better shet dat door/ Fo' de white folks'll believe we er t'arin' up de flo'"); female promiscuity ("When a feller comes a-knockin',/Dey holler Oh, sho"); and the ways in which slave women used their sexual attractiveness and femininity to manipulate slave men ("De boys ain't a gwine, /When you cry boo hoo/ Hop light, ladies").

Particularly interesting, in relation to the continuing discussion of matrifocality, is the text's suggestion that some slave men avoided taking responsibility for children born of casual sexual liaisons ("Don't you take'n tell her name,/ En den if sompin' happen you won't ketch de blame"). If this is true, then the impact on the lives of those slave women involved, their children and their communities could have been significant. Did single and married slave men in fact contribute significantly to the numbers of matrifocal slave families by refusing to acknowledge their children by women to whom they were not publicly tied? This song suggests that a woman's family or community might hold a man accountable if his identity could be documented.

The contours of slave society, however, diminished the opportunity for a woman, or her family, to authenticate such paternity claims. Since most slaveholders were much more likely to give their slave men, rather than their women, passes to travel from one farm to the next, it was not difficult for these men to avoid sexual accountability. . . .

Slave girls and women recently separated from the "protection" and advice of their kin as pawns in the domestic slave trade must have been especially vulnerable to the sexual and romantic advances of local dandies. For those females whose families and communities demanded that they remain sexually inactive until after marriage, or at least marry once they became pregnant, the decision of a slave man not to admit paternity could mean a lowering of a woman's esteem within her kin network.

Casual sex in the quarters, therefore, rarely had casual consequences. When casual sex translated into adultery, stakes were very high. Slave men were jealous not only of the sexual attention that white men paid their wives, but also of the flirtations and seductions of other black men. Slave women were equally intolerant. . . .

. . . Overall, . . . slaveholders usually did not promote slave marriages, families, or related values unless they believed it would benefit themselves in one way or another. For the slave master the slave family had two important roles: it gave an owner the opportunity to manipulate for the owner's benefit a slave's concern for his or her family; and it was the center of slave procreation.

Some masters undoubtedly promoted long-term slave marriages if the couple proved to be amply fertile. Betsy and Henry Jackson, for example, had fifteen children. Although they lived on neighboring farms in Loudoun, Mrs. Jackson's owner seemed to have had no objection to Henry's conjugal visits every Saturday and Sunday. Loudoun planter William H. Gray bought his slave woman Emily in 1839 along with her small child Lizzie. At that time Emily, who was married to Gray's slave George, was pregnant with another child. By 1853, Emily and George had increased Gray's slave property by another four children. Although there is no evidence to suggest that the Jacksons' owner or William H. Gray pressured their slaves to have children, there are testimonies from other slaves as well as documentation within planters' papers which indicate that slave breeding was a concern of many slaveholders. "The masters were very careful about a good breedin' woman. If she had five or six children she was rarely sold," one ex-slave explained, as did several others. Likewise, owners and traders did not hesitate to advertise young female slaves as "good breeding wenches" and buyers interested in purchasing female adolescents and adults routinely inquired of their general health and specifically their ability to bear children.

Sometimes slave owners promised female slaves material rewards such as larger food allowances, better clothing, or more spacious cabins if they would consent to have many children. Some undoubtedly accepted these incentives, while others resented their masters' attempts to control their bodies. A slave woman's sexuality and her reproductive organs were key to her identity as a woman and she claimed a right to have power over that identity. "Muma had sed 'Don't let nobody bother yo' principle'; 'cause dat was all yo' had," Minnie Folkes explained of her reticence to have sexual relations even after she married. Some female slaves in fact may have taken the matter of reproduction into their own hands, secretly using contraceptive methods in order to maintain control over their procreation. One slave woman, for example, indicated that she was able to regulate her childbearing when she explained that she used to have a child every Christmas, "but when I had six, I put a stop to it, and only had one every other year."

Masters often suspected slave females of using contraceptives and inducing miscarriages, but rarely were able to prove it. Eliza Little, for example, spoke of her owner's attempts to discover information about "a slave girl who had put her child aside." He beat several of the slaves and inquired of the incident, but was unable to get the details of this carefully guarded secret of the female slave community. A few slave mothers went so far as to commit infanticide. The Loudoun *Democratic Mirror* reported on November 11, 1858, for example, that the court had found a slave woman named Marietta guilty of infanticide and ordered her deportation to the lower South.

Sometimes what slaveholders might have construed as a slave woman's resistance to bearing children, however, was a result of temporary or permanent female infertility. Given their overall poor physical condition due to heavy work loads, regular harsh treatment, nutritionally deficient diets, and limited access to proper medical attention, it is not difficult to understand why many black women were unable to reproduce as quickly as some of their owners might have wanted. . . .

. . . A "typical" slave woman might begin to have occasional sexual relations during her mid- to late teens. She usually conceived her first child when she was almost nineteen; her second when she was almost twenty-one. If by then she had settled into a marital relationship that allowed her to have conjugal sexual relations at least once a week, she might have four other children who would be born alive; and perhaps four to five miscarriages or still births before she reached menopause. . . .

. . . The development of a strong sense of identity and community ethos was one of the most important ways slaves coped with and resisted the stress on their domestic relations. Slave kin, for example, hoped to teach their children not only how to survive as individuals, but also the importance of the slave community and their responsibility to help others. They emphasized the value of demonstrating respect for other slaves and, in complete opposition to the lessons of owners, instructed their youngsters in a code of morality that paid homage to blacks rather than to whites. They preached against lying to and stealing from one another, the importance of keeping slave secrets, protecting fugitive slaves, and sharing work loads. Teachers working among contraband slaves in Virginia noted the affection that slaves held for one another and the many polite courtesies they extended among themselves. . . .

But slaves, like other Loudouners, were not always successful in their attempts to withstand long-term pressures on their domestic or social relations. As individuals with the same range of emotions and capable of the same moral triumphs and failures as free persons, many acted inappropriately toward their loved ones. Adultery was not the only internal problem which occasionally plagued Loudoun slave marriages and rocked slave families or communities. The slave quarters often was a place of smoldering emotions and anger. Disagreements and frustrations could erupt into violence, while verbal and physical abuse were sometimes responses to complicated issues of discord within slave marriages and families. Spousal abuse was not uncommon[.] . . . Child abuse and neglect also were well-documented phenomena.

. . . The continual demands of the domestic slave trade, coupled with the other devastating conditions slave owners imposed, sometimes effectively eroded slave communities and family networks that had been functional for generations. Those who witnessed and were part of this destruction could not escape its physical or emotional impact. . . .

Despite all this, the Loudoun slave family survived and served many of its constituents well. It did not necessarily exist or function in the ways of other southerners. Slaves drew on rich African, European, and American cultural heritages, but also were forced by oppressive socioeconomic and political conditions and diverse domestic climates to construct domestic ideals and functional families that were different from the "norm." Given the difference that their status and cultures made in all other aspects of their lives, certainly it is not surprising that enslaved blacks in the American South also defined family life differently.

Soul Murder and Slavery

NELL IRVIN PAINTER

The Sojourner Truth whom we know [is] . . . an eloquent black feminist abolitionist. But this figure did not come ready-made; Truth's was the kind of past that had to be transcended. A poor, despised slave and freedwoman, Truth defeated tremendous personal odds to remake herself into an embodiment of power. . . .

Sojourner Truth . . . had not always been self-confident. Born a slave in Ulster County, New York, at the end of the eighteenth century, she was Isabella Van Wagener (or Van Wagner) in the mid-1830s, when she spent three years in a commune headed by a tyrant. The leader of Truth's community was a man who had been born Robert Matthews and who had changed his name to the "Prophet Matthias." Within what he called his "kingdom," Matthias made all the rules and broke them at will; he flew into hour-long rages and ranted at his followers whenever the spirit

Nell Irvin Painter, "Soul Murder and Slavery: Toward a Fully Loaded Cost Accounting," in Linda K. Kerber, Alice Kessler-Harris, and Kathryn Kish Sklar, eds., *U.S. History as Women's History: New Feminist Essays* (Chapel Hill: University of North Carolina Press, 1995), 125–146. Copyright © 1995 by the University of North Carolina Press. Used by permission of the publisher and author.

moved him. He made them call him "Father" and appropriated the best of everything for himself, from houses and furniture and carpets and silver to the richest white woman in the community, even though she was married to someone else. As is so often the case in movements built around a charismatic leader who sets himself above worldly laws and common decency, the Matthias kingdom came to ruin over unorthodox conjugal arrangements and allegations of murder. Isabella Van Wagener was his devoted follower until he left her. She did not leave him.

Why are people (even people like Sojourner Truth) continually attracted to communities headed by autocrats who abuse their followers verbally, physically, and sexually? One answer is to be found in the psychological scars that disfigure so many adherents. Leaders who emerge from emotionally trying backgrounds wield power aggressively, and they hold a singular appeal to people who were abused, especially sexually, as children. Such was the case with Sojourner Truth, who was a slave for the first thirty years of her life and who dictated and published in 1850 her recollections of bondage in the Hudson Valley of New York. The *Narrative of Sojourner Truth* has taught me a great deal about how crucial slavery was to the formation of identity, whether the subject was a northerner or a southerner. As a historian of the American South, I might have been tempted before writing about Sojourner Truth to equate slave society with southern society and to speak only of southerners in the relation between slavery and psychology. This, after all, has been the habit in American historiography since the mid-nineteenth century, a habit that I have now broken in my own work. Having evaded the regional snare, I write a good deal nonetheless about the South, for the historical scholarship on slavery is mainly southern. Even so, this regional tilt should not obscure the prevalence of the institution: In the seventeenth and eighteenth centuries, slavery was a national phenomenon, and its effects were by no means limited to the South.

We all know on a certain, almost intuitive level that violence is inseparable from slavery, but historians rarely trace the descent of that conjunction. In this essay I accept that unhappy task. My aim is to examine the implications of soul murder . . . and use them to question the lacunae in historians' descriptions of American society during the era of slavery. My hope is that a more complete accounting—what bookkeepers would term a "fully loaded cost accounting"—of the costs of slavery, most notably the tragic overhead costs that were reckoned in the currency of physical abuse and family violence, will yield a fuller comprehension of our national experience. With the broad geography of American slavery in mind, I take as my theme "Soul Murder and Slavery," which does not stop at the borders of the South.

This work is interdisciplinary, drawing on the history of American slavery, feminist scholarship on women, the family, and the workplace, and on the thought of sociologists and psychologists regarding children. My questions have their roots in second-wave feminism of the 1960s. . . . By focusing attention on women's lives, feminist scholarship has made women visible rather than taken for granted and queried the means by which societies forge gender out of the physical apparatus of sex. While some feminist thinkers have analyzed women's writing and gender, recently other intellectuals and activists have turned a spotlight on a protected, potent social institution: the family. Even though families, as the site of identity formation, shape the elaboration of politics, and even though public policy profoundly influences families, family dynamics have generally been treated as private and separate from the public realm and have not traditionally figured prominently in the writing of history.

Historiographical blindness toward families still persists, even though the source material is abundant. Turning new eyes on evidence that has been at hand forever, feminist historians are able to hear subaltern voices and recognize phenomena that had not previously been investigated seriously. What were long termed "discipline" and "seduction" of the young and powerless, who were described as feckless and oversexed, we can now call by their own names: child abuse, sexual abuse, sexual harassment, rape, battering. Psychologists aggregate the effects of these all-too-familiar practices in the phrase *soul murder,* which may be summed up as depression, lowered self-esteem, and anger. . . .

Sexual abuse, emotional deprivation, and physical and mental torture can lead to soul murder, and soul-murdered children's identity is compromised; they cannot register what it is that they want and what it is that they feel. . . . [T]hey often identify with the person who has abused them, and they may express anger toward themselves and others. Abused persons are more at risk for the development of an array of psychological problems that include depression, anxiety, self-mutilation, suicide attempts, sexual problems, and drug and alcohol abuse. Victims of soul murder do not inevitably turn into abusers—there is no direct or predictable line of cause and effect—but people who have been abused or deprived as children grow up at risk psychologically.

We surely cannot translate twentieth-century psychology directly into the mentalities of eighteenth- and nineteenth-century societies, because many aspects of life that we regard as psychological were, in earlier times, connected to religion. Spirituality then, as now, varied considerably from person to person and from group to group; with the passage of time, religious sensibilities were subject to fundamental alterations. American religion generally changed in the aftermath of the Great Awakening of the early eighteenth century and the Second Great Awakening of the early nineteenth century. The various evangelicals, especially Methodists and Baptists, deeply influenced what we would call the psychology of Americans, as well as the terms in which they envisioned and communicated with their gods.

Despite differences of mentality wrought by greater or lesser religiosity, psychology—when used carefully, perhaps gingerly—provides a valuable means of understanding people and families who cannot be brought to the analyst's couch. Ideally historians could enter a kind of "Star Trek" realm of virtual reality in which we could hold intelligent conversations with the dead, then remand them to the various hells, purgatories, and heavens and return to our computers. Lacking this facility, we can only read twentieth-century practitioners and enter the archives with our eyes wide open.

Even without the benefit of an esoteric knowledge of psychology, we readily acknowledge the existence of certain conventions associated with slavery: the use of physical violence to make slaves obedient and submissive, the unquestioned right of owners to use the people they owned in whatever ways they wished. But we may need to be reminded that these habits also translate into a set of ideals that were associated with white women in middle- and upper-class families and into another set of ideals identified with evangelical religion. Submission and obedience, the core values of slavery, were also the key words of patriarchy and piety.

Because the standard of slavery calibrated values in other core institutions, slavery deserves recognition as one of the fundamental influences on American family mores and, by extension, on American society as a whole. Religion, democracy, the frontier, patriarchy, and mobility are all recognized as having played their part in the making of American families and American history. Slavery also counted, and not merely for Americans who experienced it as captive, unpaid laborers.

No matter how much American convention exempts whites from paying any costs for the enslavement of blacks, the implications of slavery did not stop at the color line; rather, slavery's theory and praxis permeated the whole of slave-holding society. Without seeking to establish one-to-one relationships or direct lines of causality, I will pose questions and suggest answers that may foster more comprehensive and feminist thinking about American history. Ironically, perhaps, names that have only recently been coined help reinterpret the past. . . .

American habits of thought . . . have rendered the experience of slaves utterly invisible in the literature of child abuse. No one at all disputes the fact that these children and women endured hurts that they did not forget, yet these victims do not currently figure in the consideration of the effects of child abuse and sexual harassment. . . .

For most scholars of child abuse and sexual abuse, slavery possesses neither a literal meaning nor consequences; it serves only as a potent, negative metaphor. As a historian familiar with the institution that existed throughout most of American territory into the early nineteenth century, I *do* want to think literally: I want to investigate the consequences of child abuse and sexual abuse on an entire society in which the beating and raping of enslaved people was neither secret nor metaphorical.

The first step is to think about slaves as people with all the psychological characteristics of human beings, with childhoods and adult identities formed during youthful interaction with others. As ordinary as is the assumption that white people evolve psychologically from childhood to adulthood, to speak of black people in psychological terms can be problematical, for this history has a history. Much of scholars' and readers' reluctance to deal with black people's psychology goes back to the 1960s debate over Stanley Elkins's *Slavery: A Problem in American Institutional and Intellectual Life,* which provoked extensive criticism and revision.

Acknowledging the "spiritual agony" inherent in American slavery, Elkins compared slavery in the American South with Nazi concentration camps, in which, he thought, an all-encompassing system of repression infantilized people who had been psychologically healthy. Elkins wrote that on southern plantations and in Nazi concentration camps, inmates *"internalized"* their masters' attitudes. Drawing a flawed analogy between concentration camps, which existed for a few years, and slavery, which persisted over many generations and was psychologically more porous, Elkins argued that the closed system of slavery produced psychologically crippled adults who were docile, irresponsible, loyal, lazy, humble, and deceitful, in short, who were Sambos. With regard to both slavery and concentration camps, Elkins's methodology was more psychological than archival, and he also overlooked resistance in both contexts. In the American South, Elkins ignored the significance of slave families and communities and the long tradition of resistance and revolt. . . .

The scholarship that appeared in the 1970s and 1980s provided a more complete view of slaves and slave families than Elkins had presented in the broken-up character of Sambo. Yet since the thunder and lightning of the Elkins controversy— even after the appearance of extensive revisionist writing—scholars and lay people have avoided, sometimes positively resisted, the whole calculation of slavery's psychological costs. The Sambo problem was solved through the pretense that black people do not have psyches.

The prevailing wisdom says that strong black people functioned as members of a group, "the black community," as though black people shared a collective psyche whose only perception was racial, as if race obviated the need to discuss black people's subjective development. Within this black community, the institution of "the black family" appeared preternaturally immune to the brutality inherent in slavery. Black patriarchy with a human face appears in much of this post-Elkins writing, particularly in the case of the well-intentioned work of Herbert Gutman, which refuted a 1965 report by Daniel Patrick Moynihan that blamed poverty and criminality on black families. In family groups or as individuals, slaves emerged from historians' pages in the pose of lofty transcendence over racist adversity. Any analysis hinting that black people suffered psychological trauma as a result of the vicious physical and emotional practices that slavery entailed seemed tantamount to recapitulating Elkins and admitting the defeat of the race at the hands of bigots.

Rejecting that reasoning is imperative, because denying slaves psychological personhood improverishes the study of everyone in slave-holding society. . . .

Slave owners, slaves, jurists, abolitionists, and historians all have recognized personal violence as a component of the regulation of owned labor; as Charles Pettigrew, a slaveholder, wrote to his son: "It is a pity that . . . Slavery and Tyranny must go together and that there is no such thing as having an obedient and useful Slave, without the painful exercise of undue and tyrannical authority." Tyrannical authority there was in abundance, and slave children's parents, even when they were present, could not save their babies. It was as though a slave mother's children were not her own, a former slave recalled: "Many a day my old mamma has stood by an' watched massa beat her chillun 'till dey bled an' she couldn' open her mouf." From an entirely different vantage point, southern judiciaries acknowledged that owners needed and should lawfully exercise total power over their slaves. The central legal tenet of slavery was summed up by a southern judge: "The power of the master must be absolute, to render the submission of the slave perfect." . . .

On the personal level, the evidence of this kind of discipline is heartbreaking, whether between master and slave, slave parent and child, or across the generations. When he was a child, fugitive slave narrator William Wells Brown witnessed the harrowing scene of his mother being flogged for going late into the fields. Years later Brown recalled that "the cold chills ran over me, and I wept aloud." Sojourner Truth, who was beaten as a slave in New York's Hudson Valley in the early nineteenth century, beat her own children—to make them obedient and to stop their hungry cries when her work prevented her from feeding them. . . .

Masters beat slave children to make them into good slaves. Slave parents beat children to make them regard obedience as an automatic component of their personal makeup that was necessary for survival in a cruel world, a world in which they were to be first and always submissive. In other words, slave parents beat slave children to make them into good slaves. Their motives differed radically, but the aims of masters and parents coincided.

Parents and owners taught slave children to quash their anger when they were beaten, for anger was a forbidden emotion for slaves to display before owners. A Virginia owner summed up the prevailing wisdom among his peers in these phrases: "They Must obey at all times, and under all circumstances, cheerfully and with alacrity." Suppression of this kind of anger is one of the characteristics of what psychologist Alice Miller terms the "poisonous pedagogy" of child abuse, and it has certain fairly predictable effects on its victims: feelings of degradation and humiliation, impaired identity formation, suppression of vitality and creativity, deadening of feeling of self, anger, hatred, and self-hatred on the individual level and violence on the social level.

Slave children, particularly those whose mothers worked in the fields, were also very likely to suffer physical and emotional neglect, because their mothers were rarely allowed much time off the job to spend with their children. . . .

The slave trade, which disrupted an estimated one-third of all slave families in the antebellum South, also took a devastating emotional toll, as antislavery writing and iconography illustrated. As a young child in New York State, Sojourner Truth lived with her own parents, but they were chronically depressed as a result of having sacrificed their children to the market, one after the other. Such forfeiture would have been tantamount to having one's child die, and Truth's grieving parents lost ten children to this callous trade.

In slave societies, neglect was routine, abuse was rampant, and anger was to be suppressed. The question regarding the neglect and physical abuse of slave children is not whether they took place—everyone agreed that they did—but rather, what they meant to the children and adults who experienced them. Did the whipping that was so central a part of child rearing and the enforcement of discipline among slaves affect them and their families as child abuse traumatizes twentieth-century victims?

There is evidence that the child abuse of slavery imposed enormous costs. The relationship between abuse and repercussion is not simple or predetermined, but the damage is frequent enough to be recognizable. For countless women and children, these injuries were magnified by the intimate nature of the abuse.

Like child beating in slavery, the sexual torment of slave women and children has been evident for more than a century. Some of this mistreatment occurred in situations that we now recognize as sexual harassment on the job, and some occurred within households—which were work sites for hundreds of thousands of slave women—and with overtones of incest. One well-known figure exemplifies both patterns.

While many ex-slave narratives mention master-slave sexuality, the most extended commentary on the sexual harassment of slave women comes from Harriet Jacobs, who was a slave in Edenton, North Carolina. Writing under the pseudonym Linda Brent, Jacobs published a narrative in 1861, entitled *Incidents in the Life of a Slave Girl.* Jacobs's character, Linda, becomes the literal embodiment of the slave as sexual quarry in the testimony of slaves. We know from the work of critic Jean Yellin that *Incidents in the Life of a Slave Girl* is autobiography, and that Jacobs's master harassed her sexually from the time she was thirteen. Her narrative is a story of pursuit, evasion, and, ultimately, escape, although in order to evade her owner Jacobs had to spend seven years closed up in her grandmother's tiny attic crawl space, unable to stand up straight, sweltering in the summer, cold in the winter. As portrayed in *Incidents in the Life of a Slave Girl,* much of Jacobs's life in North Carolina revolved around avoiding her master's advances.

Jacobs says that without her master's having succeeded in raping her, he inflicted injuries that young female slaves frequently suffered and that we would consider psychological. As she became nubile, she says, her master began to whisper "foul words in my ear," which robbed her of her innocence and purity, a phenomenon that psychologists call inappropriate sexualization, which encourages a child to interpret her own value primarily in sexual terms. Describing the effect of her master's "foul words" and the angry and jealous outbreaks from her mistress, Jacobs says she became, like any slave girl in her position, "prematurely knowing in evil things," including life in a household cum work site that was suffused with predation, infidelity, and rage.

Jacobs commits an entire, highly charged chapter of *Incidents in the Life of a Slave Girl* to "The Jealous Mistress." The angry figure of the jealous mistress, frequently ridiculed, never seriously investigated, is so common in the literature of slavery as to have become a southern trope. Perhaps because I have my own jealous mistress, so to speak, I am certain that the figure deserves a longer, much longer look. My jealous mistress is Gertrude Thomas, of Augusta, Georgia, who kept a journal from the time she was fourteen years old in 1848 until 1889, when she was fifty-five. . . .

Although she was a jealous mistress, Gertrude Thomas becomes more easily understandable as the victim of adultery. According to the ostensible mores of her community, she stood near the pinnacle of society (as a woman, she was denied space at the very top). She was a plantation mistress in a society dominated by the minuscule proportion of white families that qualified as planters by owning twenty or more slaves; she was an educated woman at a time when only elite men could take higher education for granted; and she was white in a profoundly racist culture. Yet neither Gertrude Thomas's economic or educational advantages nor her social status protected her from what she saw as sexual competition from inferior women. She knew, as Mary Chesnut and her friends knew, that they were supposed to pretend not to see "what is as plain before their eyes as the sunlight." The deception did not ease the discomfort, for Thomas knew and wrote that white men saw women—whether slave or free, wealthy or impoverished, cultured or untutored, black or white—as interchangeable. She and other plantation mistresses failed to elevate themselves sufficiently as women to avoid the pain of sharing their husbands with their slaves.

Preoccupied by the issue of competition between women, Thomas realized and recorded with tortuous indirection a central fact of her emotional life: that female slaves and female slaveholders were in the same sexual marketplace and that in this competition, free women circulated at a discount due to the ready availability of women who could be forced to obey. The existence in the same market for sex of women who were literally property lowered the value of Gertrude Thomas and her mother as sexual partners. The concept of women as property has long been evident to feminists as a powerful means of keeping women subjected.

The traffic in women, a phrase coined by the early twentieth-century American anarchist, Emma Goldman, is shorthand for cultural practices that anthropologists . . . and psychoanalysts . . . have seen as basic to human nature but that feminists have identified with patriarchy and considered devastating to women. . . . [T]he notion of such a traffic is useful both literally and metaphorically with regard to American society during its nearly three centuries of slavery. Over the course of those ten or more generations, rich white women saw themselves in competition for the attention of husbands whose black partners were ideal women: Slave women had to come when summoned and were conceded no will of their own. Gertrude Thomas knew moments of despair over her husband's infidelities, but if she contemplated suicide, she censored the thought. Testimony from Kentucky captures marital strife more vividly.

Andrew Jackson, an ex-slave narrator, had belonged to a fiery preacher he called a "right down blower." Though the owner's preaching moved his congregation to tears, at home he and his wife quarreled bitterly over his attraction to their enslaved cook, Hannah. Jackson recalled hearing the wife accuse the preacher of having gone into the kitchen to see Hannah, which the preacher denied. "I know you have, you brute," Jackson quotes the wife crying, "I have a great mind to cut my own throat!" To this, Jackson says, the preacher replied, "I really wish you would." The wife understood his meaning: "Yes I presume you do, so that you could run to the kitchen, as much as you please, to see Hannah." Andrew Jackson concluded that slaveholders "had such bad hearts toward one another" because they treated their slaves so brutally.

At the same time that jealous mistresses were angry over their husbands' adulterous conduct, slave women like Harriet Jacobs who were the husbands' prey realized fully that mistresses saw themselves (not the slaves) as the victims in these triangles. Slave women resented what they envisioned as their mistresses narcissistic self-pity, and they returned their mistresses' anger in kind. Jacobs's outrage at her mistress is part of a larger phenomenon. . . . Slave women's anger has etched yet more deeply the unsympathetic portrait of women who held slaves. Today we can see that more was at stake than contention over the ultimate title of victim.

What slaves could seldom acknowledge and historians did not see is that attachment often lay at the core of slave women's resentment. With slave families constantly subject to disruption, mistresses often functioned as mothers—good or bad—to their young female slaves. In this sense, the bitterness that Linda Brent felt as the prey of her master emerged against her mistress, just as victims of incest often hate their mothers for not saving them from the sexual advances of fathers and stepfathers. Psychiatrist Judith Herman says that many sexually abused children feel deeply betrayed because their mothers or mother figures are not able to protect them. Victims who do not display anger at their abusers may displace their rage on to nonabusing but impotent parental figures: mothers. The psychological dynamics of the heterogeneous households of slavery explicate attitudes and behaviors that cannot be explained if we deny to slaves the personhood that we grant to our own contemporaries.

It has been difficult for historians to view interracial households as families and slaves as workers and as people, but such understanding places the sexual abuse of slave women and children (including boys) within categories that are now familiar and that we now term sexual harassment. One of the founders of the field, Catharine A. MacKinnon, noted in the 1970s that poorer women seem more likely to suffer physical harassment than middle-class and career women, whose abuse is more often verbal. This should alert us to the triple vulnerability of slave women; they were among the poorest of working women and members of a race considered inherently inferior, and, if they were domestic servants like Harriet Jacobs, they spent long hours in the company of the men who had power over them.

Psychologists say that children and young women who are sexually abused, like children who are beaten, tend to blame themselves for their victimization and consequently have very poor self-esteem. They may also see their sexuality as their only means of binding other people to them as friends or allies. Recent scholarship outlines a series of long-term psychological repercussions of sexual abuse and incest: depression, difficulty sleeping, feelings of isolation, poor self-esteem, difficulty relating to other people, contempt for all women including oneself, revictimization, and impaired sexuality that may manifest itself in behaviors that can appear as frigidity or promiscuity. It is doubtful that slaves possessed an immunity that victims lack today.

While it is tempting to see all slaves as strong people who were able to transcend the savagery to which they were subjected from very early ages, ex-slave narratives also bear witness to much psychological hurt. What today's psychologists call anger, depression, and problems of self-esteem come through ex-slave narratives and attest to slaves' difficulty in securing unqualified trust. Theologian Benjamin Mays discerned the theme of personal isolation that pervaded black slave religion and that is movingly emblemized in spiritual songs. Their titles are embedded in American memory: "Sometimes I Feel Like a Motherless Child," "Nobody Knows the Trouble I've Seen," "I'm a Long Way from Home." We are used to hearing such sentiments as poignant artistry, but they are also testimonies of desolation. Slaves' situation within a system built on violence, disfranchisement, and white supremacy was analogous to that of twentieth-century victims of abuse, and some slaves, like people today, responded with self-hatred, anger, and identification with the aggressor. As understandable as such responses would have been, they are not all there is to the story.

Were this analysis to stop here, it might seem to invite a rerun of the controversy over Stanley Elkins's *Slavery,* for I might seem to be saying, like Elkins, that slavery inflicted psychic wounds so severe that slaves were massively disabled psychologically. This is *not* a recapitulation of Stanley Elkins, because my arguments exceed Elkins's in two important ways: I insist, first, that slaves had two crucial means of support that helped them resist being damaged permanently by the assaults of their owners and their fellows; and second, that owners also inflicted the psychic damage of slavery upon themselves, their white families, and, ultimately, on their whole society.

Since the 1959 publication of Elkins's *Slavery,* historians such as John Hope Franklin and Earl E. Thorpe have presented evidence of the ways in which slaves seized the initiative and found "elbow-room" within a system that was meant to dehumanize them. Once historians began to seek it, confirmation of slaves' resistance and survival appeared in abundance. The testimony comes from slaves and from owners, and it affirms that most slave women and men were able to survive slavery in a human and humane manner, particularly if they lived where they were surrounded by other blacks who were actual or fictive kin. Historians have concentrated their attention on the half or so of slaves in the antebellum South who lived on plantations with twenty or more bondspeople, and those were the people more likely to belong to a community of slaves. They did not, however, represent the totality of Americans who were enslaved. So far, unfortunately, the other half of southern slaves and virtually all northern slaves, who were surrounded by mostly white people, have received little scrutiny. Slaves living in isolation would hardly have benefited from the psychological support that a slave community could provide.

Historians like Deborah White and John Blassingame show that plantation slaves' psychic health depended largely on two essential emotional counterweights to owners' physical and psychological assaults: the slaves' own families and a system of evangelical religious beliefs that repudiated the masters' religious and social ideology of white supremacy and black inferiority. Blassingame sees slave families as a source of psychic protection from slavery's onslaught and considers families "an important survival mechanism." . . . [Deborah White] shows how slave women working together created their own internal rank ordering. Although their owners and other whites might dishonor and mistreat them, slave women forged "their own independent definition of womanhood" through their own web of women's relationships, which functioned as an antidote to slavery's degradation.

. . . Ex-slave narratives from the nineteenth and twentieth centuries make it clear that slaves could reject their masters' assumptions that slaves were constitutionally inferior as a people and that they deserved to be enslaved.

Slave religion also buttressed a countervailing belief system by promising that equity would ultimately prevail in God's world. During and after slavery, religion was an important means through which powerless people preserved their identity, as in the case of Sojourner Truth. . . . [B]lack people forged their own evangelical religion, which could be apocalyptic and reassuring . . . [A] belief in the impending apocalypse, a perennial theme in American evangelicalism, served the particular needs of the black poor by promising that there would soon come a time when God would judge all people, that he would punish the wicked, who were the slaveholders, and reward the good, who were the slaves. . . .

Psychologists have noted that in situations where the individual is totally powerless, faith in a greater power than the self becomes a potent means of survival. Slaves with a firm religious belief were able to benefit from this nonmaterial source of support, which we recognize today in the methodology of twelve-step programs for overcoming addiction that begin by putting one's fate in the hands of a greater power than the self.

In their appeal to countervailing ideologies, supportive communities, and spirituality, slaves were, in a sense, behaving like good feminists seeking means of lessening the power of oppression and sexual abuse in their lives. Having been identified and set apart as a despised race, slaves found it easier to create alternative ideologies than the white people—including women—who owned them and who told them what to do. There is no denying that white ladies were able to oppress slaves, but even so, the ladies lacked access to much of their society's other kinds of power. Of all the people living in slave-holding societies who might have benefited from an alternative system of values, rich white women were least likely to forge one. . . .

Owning as well as owned families paid a high psychological and physical cost for the child and sexual abuse that was so integral with slavery. First, despite what black and white scholars assume about the rigidity of the color bar, attachment and loss often transcended the barriers of race and class and flowed in both directions. The abuse of slaves pained and damaged nonslaves, particularly children, and forced those witnessing slave abuse to identify with the victim or the perpetrator.

Second, the values and practices of slavery, in particular the use of violence to secure obedience and deference, prevailed within white families as well. The ideals of slavery—obedience and submission—were concurrently and not accidentally the prototype of white womanhood and of evangelical piety, which intensified the prestige and reinforced the attraction of these ideals. Nineteenth-century evangelical religion meant various things to its many believers, and it could compel them toward startlingly different ideological conclusions, as exemplified in the North in the Jacksonian era. After the abolition of slavery in the North, evangelicalism fostered a profusion of convictions, including abolitionism and feminism; in the region still committed to slavery, however, evangelicalism produced no reforming offshoots that were allowed to flourish. Instead, unquestioning evangelical piety was more valued, and piety was another word for submission and obedience, terms that also figured prominently in the language of the family. . . .

Slavery accentuated the hierarchical rather than the egalitarian and democratic strains in American culture, thereby shaping relations within and without families and politics. Patriarchal families, slavery, and evangelical religion further reinforced one another's emphasis on submission and obedience in civil society, particularly concerning people in subaltern positions.

. . . Proslavery apologists often insisted that the maintenance of slavery depended on the preservation of patriarchy within white families, arguing that white women, especially rich women, must remain in their places and be submissive to their fathers and husbands so that slaves would not conceive notions of equality. Similar motives prohibited white men from acknowledging publicly that white women commonly labored in southern fields at tasks that the culture reserved rhetorically for women who were enslaved. The reasoning of proslavery apologia ran from women's honor to gender roles to black men–white women sex, skipping over the reality of white men's sexual use and abuse of black women in a manner that twentieth-century readers find remarkable: for its silences, its intertextuality, and its unabashed patriarchy. Of course, there is nothing at all contradictory between family feeling and hierarchy, between attachment and the conviction that some people absolutely must obey others.

Hierarchy by no means precludes attachment. Just as young slaves attached to the adults closest to them, white as well as black, so the white children and adults in slave-owning households became psychologically entangled with the slaves they came to know well. When Sojourner Truth's son, Peter, was beaten by his owner in Alabama, his mistress (who was Sojourner's mistress's cousin) salved his wounds and cried over his injuries. That story concluded with Peter's mistress's murder by the very same man, her husband, who had previously abused Peter. Like Peter's murdered mistress, other slave owners, especially women, grieved at the sight of slaves who had been beaten. . . .

As slave-owning children grew into adults, their identification with victims or victimizers often accorded to gender. . . . [M]istresses could be cruel tormentors of their slaves. But in comparison with masters, white women were more likely to take the side of the slaves, while white men nearly unanimously identified with the aggressor as a requisite of manhood. Becoming such a man did not happen automatically or painlessly. . . .

Fathers ordinarily did the work of inculcating manhood, which included snuffing out white children's identification with slaves. In 1839 a Virginian named John M. Nelson described his shift from painful childhood sympathy to manly callousness. As a child, he would try to stop the beating of slave children and, he said, "mingle my cries with theirs, and feel almost willing to take a part of the punishment." After his father severely rebuked him several times for this kind of compassion, he "became so blunted that I could not only witness their stripes with composure, but *myself* inflict them, and that without remorse." . . .

So far in this discussion, only slaves have figured as the victims of physical and psychological abuse. But the ideals of slavery affected families quite apart from the toll they exacted from the bodies and psyches of blacks. Thanks to the abundance of historical scholarship that concentrates on antebellum southern society, it is possible to reach some generalizations regarding whites. But even in the slave South, historians have been much less aware of the abuse of white women than of the oppression of black slaves. . . .

Petitions for divorce and church records show that wife beating was a common motive for the attempted dissolution of marriages and the expulsion of men and women from church membership. Doubtless this was true in nonslave-holding regions as well. . . . [L]egislators and church leaders routinely urged women to remain in abusive unions and to bear abuse in a spirit of submission. In the hard-drinking antebellum South, which was well known for rampant violence against slaves and between white men, white women had little recourse when their husbands beat them, for, in general, the southern states were slow to grant women the legal right to divorce or to custody of their children in cases of separation. Until the 1830s, southern states lacked divorce laws, and state legislatures heard divorce petitions on a case-by-case basis. The result was a small number of divorces granted inconsistently and according to the social and economic status of the petitioner in her community.

The disposal of the small number of cases of incest that came before judges also illuminates the reasoning of the men who exercised power in the slave South. As in instances of wife beating, so in cases of incest, judges preferred to investigate the flaws of the female petitioner, who, even despite extreme youth, usually came to be seen as consenting. Not surprisingly, incest seldom became public, but when it entered the criminal justice system, the girls in question were likely as not seen as accomplices in their own ravishment.

In the interests of preserving patriarchy, victims of incest, like victims of wife abuse, were abandoned by law and sacrificed to the ideal of submission. . . . [S]outhern lawmakers and judges who were anxious to regulate racialized sexuality were loathe to punish white men for sexual violence against white or black women and children.

Incest and wife beating do not usually appear in general studies of the antebellum South, where the received wisdom . . . is that planter families came to be child-centered and companionate. Such a vision fails even to allow for the level of familial abuse that psychologists see as usual in twentieth-century households, where, according to the American Medical Association, one-quarter of married women will be abused by a current or former partner at some point during their lives. Were planter families more straightforwardly loving than we? I think not.

Aristocrats were skilled at keeping and preserving appearances, as I know from experience with Gertrude Thomas. Only by reading her 1,380-page journal repeatedly was I able to discover her secrecy and self-deception. In this case, the secret I discovered was adultery, for both her father and her husband had outside wives and children. Her journal never reveals her other family secret, her husband's drunkenness, which was only preserved orally in family lore.

Then and now, family violence and child sexual abuse are usually concealed, and the people with the most privacy, the wealthy, are better at preserving their secrets than poor people, who live their lives in full view of the rest of the world. Scholars have connived with wealthy families to hide child sexual abuse among people of privilege, which one psychologist concludes is "most conspicuous for its presumed absence." This is an old, old story. . . .

Some historians are ready to examine their sources more critically. Recent books by Richard Bushman and critic Jay Fliegelman alert us that by the late eighteenth and early nineteenth centuries, wealthy Americans had come to prize gentility so highly that they spent enormous amounts of time and energy creating pleasing appearances. . . . [T]he letters, speeches, and journals that historians have used as the means of uncovering reality and gauging consciousness ought more properly to be considered self-conscious performances intended to create beautiful tableaux. People with sufficient time, space, and money modeled themselves on characters in novels and acted out what they saw as appropriate parts. What was actually taking place at home was another story entirely, which was not necessarily preserved for our easy investigation. If historians are to understand the less attractive and deeply buried aspects of slave society, the scales will have to fall from their eyes. They will have to see beyond the beauty of performance and probe slavery's family romance more skeptically.

Once we transcend complete reliance on the written record, deception clues are not hard to see: The eloquent violence, alcoholism, and invalidism of eighteenth- and nineteenth-century America (and especially of the nineteenth-century South) could not be concealed, and they point to the existence of compelling family secrets. . . .

Historians need to . . . look beneath the gorgeous surface that cultured slave owners presented to the world, and pursue the hidden truths of slavery, including soul murder and patriarchy. The task is essential, for our mental health as a society depends on the ability to see our interrelatedness across lines of class and race, in the past, as in the present.

FURTHER READING

Peter W. Bardaglio, *Reconstructing the Household: Families, Sex, and the Law in the Nineteenth-Century South* (1996).

Gail Bederman, "'Civilization,' the Decline of Middle-Class Manliness, and Ida B. Wells's Antilynching Campaign," *Radical History Review* 52 (1992): 5–30.

Mary Frances Berry, "Judging Morality: Sexual Behavior and Legal Consequences in the Late Nineteenth-Century South," *Journal of American History* 78 (1991): 835–856.

Carol Bleser, ed., *In Joy and in Sorrow: Women, Family, and Marriage in the Victorian South, 1830–1900* (1991).

Victoria E. Bynum, *Unruly Women: The Politics of Social and Sexual Control in the Old South* (1992).

Catherine Clinton, "Bloody Terrain: Freedwomen, Sexuality, and Violence during Reconstruction," *Georgia Historical Quarterly* 76 (1992): 313–332.

────── and Michele Gillespie, eds., *The Devil's Lane: Sex and Race in the Early South* (1997).

Angela Davis, "Reflections on the Black Woman's Role in the Community of Slaves," *Black Scholar* 3 (December 1971): 2–15.

Laura F. Edwards, *Gendered Strife & Confusion: The Political Culture of Reconstruction* (1997).

Annette Gordon-Reed, *Thomas Jefferson and Sally Hemings: An American Controversy* (1997).

Herbert G. Gutman, *The Black Family in Slavery and Freedom, 1750–1925* (1976).

Jacquelyn Dowd Hall, "The Mind That Burns in Each Body: Women, Rape, and Racial Violence," in Ann Snitow et al., eds., *Powers of Desire* (1983), 328–349.

Saidiya V. Hartman, *Scenes of Subjection: Terror, Slavery, and Self-Making in Nineteenth-Century America* (1997).

Darlene Clark Hine, "Rape and the Inner Lives of Black Women in the Middle West: Preliminary Thoughts on the Culture of Dissemblance," in Ellen Carol DuBois and Vicki L. Ruiz, *Unequal Sisters* (1990), 292–297.

Martha Hodes, ed., *Sex, Love, Race: Crossing Boundaries in North America* (1999).

────── , *White Women, Black Men: Illicit Sex in the Nineteenth Century South* (1997).

Thelma Jennings, "'Us Colored Women Had to Go Through a Plenty': Sexual Exploitation of African-American Slave Women," *Journal of Women's History* 1 (1990): 45–74.

Linda O. McMurry, *To Keep the Waters Troubled: The Life of Ida B. Wells* (1999).

Anthony S. Parent, Jr., and Susan Brown Wallace, "Childhood and Sexual Identity under Slavery," *Journal of the History of Sexuality* 3 (1993): 363–401.

Peggy Pascoe, "Miscegenation Law, Court Cases, and Ideologies of 'Race' in Twentieth Century America," *Journal of American History* 83 (1996): 44–69.

Robyn Wiegman, "The Anatomy of Lynching," *Journal of the History of Sexuality* 3 (1993): 445–467.

Love and Intimacy in Nineteenth-Century America

Victorians have long been stereotyped as prudish and repressed, but historians in recent years have discovered a nineteenth-century world of passion, romance, and love. What was the character of Americans' intimate relationships, sexual desire, and physicality? Some argue that the ideology of "separate spheres" and "passion-lessness" distanced men and women. Social etiquette proscribed public intimacy, and many believed women's bodies were for reproductive purposes only. In their private writings, however, many women and men adhered to notions of romantic love, and sometimes recorded passionate desires for their lovers and spouses.

Even more striking is the evidence of intense emotional bonds among women throughout the nineteenth century. Young middle-class women developed crushes or "smashes" on other women at school and in church; intimate friendships often lasted a lifetime. Some working-class and frontier women passed as men not only for economic gain—to work in male occupations—but to marry and live with the women they loved. Intimate female friendships were considered different in nature from women's attachments to men. Notions of sisterhood likened them to kinship, not romance, and thus they were generally seen as compatible with marriage. The romantic language women used in their letters and diaries needs to be examined closely. Was this a conventional style of expression in the nineteenth century? In what ways do these writings suggest sexual desire and physical intimacy? Nineteenth-century Americans assumed that women's affections were "pure"— that is, asexual. Would women's close friendships have been as readily accepted if they were regarded as sexual?

Men also sought out male companionship, shared beds, and wrote long, emotional letters to each other. Because men were regarded as sexual beings beyond the reproductive domain, the sexual potential of their relationships was more generally acknowledged. Still, in a period before "the homosexual" had emerged as a distinct identity, the lines between platonic love and sexual desire were blurred. Walt Whitman, for instance, denied that his poetry celebrated physical sex between men but could not conceal its homoeroticism.

During the late nineteenth century, medical scientists superseded evangelical ministers as experts on sexuality, and sexual desire became a more explicit part of commercial culture. Knowledge of female sexual passion and of sexual variation

*began to surface—with varied consequences. Romantic attachments between
women or between men now were scrutinized as "abnormal" desires and labelled
sexual inversion; homosexuals were condemned as insane or deviant. Yet people
with same–sex desires could begin to find indirect validation in the new sexology
that described, however negatively, the contours of an emerging sexual identity.*

DOCUMENTS

Public writings and private papers document a rich world of romance, passion, and
friendship in the nineteenth century. Writing under the pseudonym Mary Forrest in her
1861 book *Women of the South* (Document 1), Julia Deane Freeman distinguished between male-female relationships and "Woman-Friendship." Walt Whitman's "Calamus"
poems (Document 2), published in the 1860 edition of *Leaves of Grass,* "celebrate[d]
the need of comrades"; he wrote obliquely yet powerfully of his love of men. Private
letters offer other pictures. Writing to her "dear soldier boy" during the Civil War
(Document 3), a woman discussed the pleasures of sexual intercourse, the struggle for
self-control, and the suffering of an unintended pregnancy that ended with a dead fetus
(whether by abortion, miscarriage, or stillbirth is not clear). In Document 4, a Smith
College student described her crush on another student, drawing upon the language of
heterosexual courtship to describe her feelings. Was this an adolescent crush, a lesbian
relationship, or something that cannot be defined in modern categories?

In the late nineteenth century, doctors and sexologists began to label female
friendships as sexual perversions and to promote a medical discourse on homosexual
identity. A notorious murder case in 1891 revealed these new ideas. In Document 5,
Dr. T. Griswold Comstock described Alice Mitchell—who killed her female lover after
they were prevented from marrying—as a case of hereditary sexual perversion, which
he regarded as a form of mental disease.

1. Julia Deane Freeman Praises
"Woman-Friendship," 1861

All the world gives ready credence to the possibility of friendship between man and
man—some people are even inclined to believe that the immutable attachment of
Orestes and Pylades, of Æneas and Achates, may be repeated among men in these
inconstant modern times;—but the devotion of woman to one of her own sex, the
sincerity with which she clasps the hand or presses the lip of woman, the genuine-
ness of her self-sacrifices daily made for a beloved sister, are subjects of a vast
amount of skepticism. Philosophic writers, poets, wits, have openly declared their
disbelief in the existence of the strange phenomena of woman-friendships. . . .

On the other hand, . . . [w]e have [Shakespeare's] illustration of woman-
friendship, in its consummate beauty, portrayed in the passionate, protecting love
of Beatrice for Hero in "Much Ado About Nothing," and in "As You Like It," a still
stronger picture in the self-renouncing, absolute devotion for Rosalind of the gentle
Celia, who startles her wrathful father with the declaration:

Mary Forrest [Julia Deane Freeman], "Woman-Friendship," in *Women of the South Distinguished in Literature* (New York: Derby & Jackson, 1861), 99–102.

> ———If she be a traitor,
> Why, so am I; we still have slept together,
> Rose at an instant, learn'd, play'd, eat together,
> And wheresoe'er we went, like Juno's swans
> Still we went coupled and inseparable!

When the implacable Duke banishes Rosalind, Celia replies:

> Pronounce that sentence then on me, my liege,
> I cannot live out of her company.

Shakspeare against the world! for who knew the world one half so well!

Not only are we impressed by the conviction that his glowing portraitures of woman-friendship are life-drawn; not only have we perfect faith in the possibility of a thoroughly unselfish, all-absorbing attachment between two women, but we entertain the belief that there are certain female minds so constituted that a tender friendship with one of the same sex is positively *indispensable to happiness*. Such natures experience an irresistible impulse to confide in one who, enlightened by her own yearnings and failings, can understand feminine wants and frailties—who can look upon feminine insufficiencies, not from a strong, manly, but a weak, womanly point of view.

A woman may be the most irreproachable of wives to the best of husbands, and yet feel a void in her affections, a chamber in her large heart unfilled—a something needful lacking, if there by no Celia into whose ear she can pour the history of her joys and sorrows—to whom she can turn for advice, and lenient judgment, and comprehending sympathy.

There are trivial domestic difficulties, petty annoyances, perplexing positions with which no woman of tact will trouble and bewilder her husband by relating to him. If he is a man of decided intellect, he will not attach any importance to these small crosses, will not even understand these minor miseries, and the wife is thrown back upon her own resources, vexed and disheartened by her failing attempt to enlist his aid or sympathy. If he is a man of limited mental powers, he will be more annoyed than she, and will only increase her vexations without disentangling a single thread of the fine web of dilemmas, into which she is snared. But to a sympathetic female companion, a woman may enter into all the details of these insignificant trials, and, clasping a friend's hand, she may search for and discover the clue that can guide her out of her domestic labyrinth.

The higher love—the love for man—neither absorbs nor forbids the lower, the friendship for woman. They are distinct, emotional capacities which may be coexistent in one heart. They are evidences of rich, spiritual organization. If they dwell together in pristine purity, one affection strengthens rather than weakens the other.

Who can deny that two women, through a mysterious affinity, may become, and recognize each other as sisters in heart? Who can doubt that there is a bond of sisterhood between their spirits, as real and as strong as the tie of blood between sisters? And if this be true, must not that internal kinship outlive even the dissevering stroke of death, and proclaim them *true sisters* in the great hereafter? But in this lower sphere, what name can we give to their attachment but that of "woman-friendship?"

2. Walt Whitman's Poetic Embrace of Comrades and Lovers, 1860

In paths untrodden,
In the growth by margins of pond-waters,
Escaped from the life that exhibits itself,
From all the standards hitherto published—from
    the pleasures, profits, conformities,
Which too long I was offering to feed my Soul;
Clear to me now, standards not yet published—
    clear to me that my Soul,
That the Soul of the man I speak for, feeds, rejoices
    only in comrades;
Here, by myself, away from the clank of the world,
Tallying and talked to here by tongues aromatic,
No longer abashed—for in this secluded spot I can
    respond as I would not dare elsewhere,
Strong upon me the life that does not exhibit itself,
    yet contains all the rest,
Resolved to sing no songs to-day but those of manly
    attachment,
Projecting them along that substantial life,
Bequeathing, hence, types of athletic love,
Afternoon, this delicious Ninth Month, in my
    forty-first year,
I proceed, for all who are, or have been, young
    men,
To tell the secret of my nights and days,
To celebrate the need of comrades.

Whoever you are holding me now in hand,
Without one thing all will be useless,
I give you fair warning, before you attempt me
    further,
I am not what you supposed, but far different.
Who is he that would become my follower?
Who would sign himself a candidate for my
    affections? Are you he?

The way is suspicious—the result slow, uncertain,
    may-be destructive;
You would have to give up all else—I alone would
    expect to be your God, sole and exclusive,

Walt Whitman, "Calamus," *Leaves of Grass* (Boston: Thayer & Eldridge, 1860), 341–342, 344–346, 357–358, 371, 377.

A long while, amid the noises coming and going
  —of drinking and oath and smutty jest,
There we two, content, happy in being together,
  speaking little, perhaps not a word.

Here my last words, and the most baffling,
Here the frailest leaves of me, and yet my
  strongest-lasting,
Here I shade down and hide my thoughts—I do not
  expose them,
And yet they expose me more than all my other
  poems.

3. A Woman Writes Her Lover During the Civil War, 1865

Watkins March 7th [1865]

My Dear Soldier Boy;

Well, my love I have at last received that letter you sent by Jaynes, and I will answer it[.] I sent you one the same day he left or I would have written before, and now I want you to *observe* that I have taken a sheet that is closely ruled and am going to put just as many words on a line as I can. You spoke about my letters turning so cold and not as they *used* too. Well, John to tell you the *truth,* I felt so sad, I had no heart to write any other way or to write much, after I found out about things I could not do anything. I felt sick most of the time and did not feel able to write. oh! I can tell you John no human being knows what I have suffered for over two months nor no one shall never know. I am happy to say, I am free from the burden[.]

I feel happy now, and will write you just as I feel now, not as I have felt. You could if you had known all about it have not helped the matter. But we were not "*sure*" that time. We must have got overpowered and I do not wonder at it much for at times it went ever so nice. and it was *wonderous pleasant* to keep at it, was it not? You ask if I would not like to warm your bed? Yes I indeed I would, but we must stop *here,* just where we are now until we are married. I cannot run the risk again. While *you* are in the *Army,* without we were married no money could tempt me although I love it just as well and if I were with you it would make me fight myself all the *while,* but it must be so. Ma took the *little* [?] and made his home in a bed of *ashes* there to be eaten up. I might have done as you told *me* b[u]ryied it but I was a little to[o] sick for that then. Oh! think not I *love* you less no indeed. I love *you* more and more each day of my *life*[.] oh! I feel so often that if I could fly, how often would I go to you[,] how often I feel almost wild when I get to thinking of you. Oh! could any one *love* more dearly and truly! could any one long more to be with another than I do to be with you *forever. Pray* think not that I am *changed* or anything of that sort.

Letter to "My Dear Soldier Boy," March 7, 1865, in John Tuttle and Arvilla Raplee Andrews Papers, 1843–1902, Collection #3790, box 1. Rare and Manuscript Collections, Kroch Library, Cornell University, Ithaca, N.Y.

it is not so. You know I have been told enough time and again to change me if there was any such a thing and I had felt inclined to have believed it *half*, but I have always thought you *honest* in *every respect*. therefore I took no thought about it.

Oh what a lovely day how is it with you are you having pleasant weather now? I was up to Reading to church last Sabbath. went in a load we thought it would be the last sleigh ride we would get this season as it was thawing very fast and we found it bare ground part of the way and it was[.] Oh! John there is to be a show here this week of smaller folks than Tom *Thumb* and [?]. I wish you were here to see them. You say you have not heard from Tubbs in a long while why is it? does he not answer your letters, or what is the matter. Em asked me a few days ago if I knew where he was now. John I would like to have sent you a lot of dried beef &c. by Jaynes, but I dare not for fear he would not have wanted to have taken it. I dare not ask him. He seemed so sober that day he called I felt real sorry for him. is he a nice fellow? he said he felt perhaps it would be the last time he would get home. but I hope all may be happily disapointed and may return safely to those who feel so anxious for them and who loves them so dearly and truly.

Oh! What would we do if they should not oh! how could we spare them[?] I think it all over sometimes and try to prepare myself for the worst that might come. and oh! you do not know how it does affect me[.] I feel almost wild and I have to drive those sad very sad thoughts from my mind. I have dreamed a number of times that you were dead and I always feel so gloomy all the next day. I cannot get it out of my mind. I had a very pleasant dream a few nights ago. I thought you had come home to stay and that we were in a cosy little home of our own and oh! how pleasant it was. I was so happy. everything was so nice. I got so happy that it woke me up and I could not get to sleep again thinking about it. They will not have to draft in *Dix* but I guess they will in Reading. Homer says he shall go if he is drafted any how, he talks strange about it sometimes I think. I guess he does not mean it all. he wants to see how bad his folks wants him to stay. he told me you had sent him some sharp letters about going or not going. Well I do hope and pray this cruel war will soon close and in the right way and no more will be asked *for.* and those we love may soon very soon come home to us. Yes John I do pray daily for *you* and hope that my prayers may be answered. You must pray also. Do you? I hope so.

Please write soon and often as you can. I will do the same. Yours always[.]

4. A Smith College Student Discusses Her "Crush," 1881

Northampton, Mass. Sept. 17
1881

My dear faithful Cora—

This Sabbath evening finds me alone in my little room, taking up my pen to speak a few words to you—you who abide ever so near, so dear, so true. Do you know what another wonder in my wonderful life has been wrought? If you could only see this beautiful home, everywhere so neat, dainty, refined—almost luxurious.

Eleanor Rose Larrison to "My dear faithful Cora," September 17, 1881, typescript, in Smith College Archives, Smith College, Northampton, Mass.

If you could only see this kind pleasant gentleman and lady, Mrs. and Mr. Welton, who call me "Eleanor" and treat me as a daughter. And isn't it wonderful that I am to live with them in a relation as much as possible like that of a daughter?— that they would trust me so much beforehand as to take me into their home and hearts, looking forward to my being a cheerful companion, as [a] real member of the family? How did it come about, you will wonder? I was at Fort Ann, waiting to hear from letters which I had sent out in various directions, to determine my [?]. . . . I had tried to get a place to work for my board and take a few studies. I had no idea of being able [?] Mon. The letter came from Mrs. Jones which, true friend that she is, had been working to find some place for me here. How she ever found me such a nice nest, I cannot think: it all came about in so [?] a way that I love to think that it was almost immediately from God's own hand. I now hope to be able to take all but senior work, but I hold myself subject to the convenience of the faculty. I have a pretty little room—a soft tint of blue about it. The house is not pretentious on the outside but very comfortable inside. It is right opposite Mrs. Payne's. I can run in there when I get lonesome. I must confess I have been so today, but I would not give it much vent. It came from seeing Helen. Isn't it strange how the sight of one dear familiar face when we are in a new strange place into which we are not yet fitted will stir up the deeps? I went over to her room in the Dewey House and we walked to the Edwards Church together, and after church she walked part way home with me. She is enjoying keenly the new life in the college houses—so social, nice and refined. I fear me—I am half jealous. I am so far away from her now—for I have a walk of half a mile or more to college.

But still I am a happy grateful girl tonight—so glad to be here at all, and then to be so luxuriously situated and to have the prospect of finishing my course—isn't it glor[i]ous? Am I not blessed? As Miss Hersey said this morning (she walked with Helen and me as far as our church)—"Doesn't Providence take good care of you, though!" But I do feel the responsibility it has upon me to be noble and self-sacrificing—to love for others—to love with a patient much-suffering love like Christ's. Pray for me—that I may find strength for all that the year will demand of me as I do for you, my dear. Now goodnight. . . .

Sunday, Sept. 25. Cora, what a comfort you are to me! To me, our friendship defies time and space, bodily weakness and suffering on your part, and a busy life making its never-ending demands on me. I fly to the thought of your faithful love as a refuge when cares oppress, and it contributes to make up the happiness of my bright hours. There is such a sense of rest in the thought of this friendship of ours. I have no jealous pangs. I know you love me; your loving sympathy surrounds me like the atmosphere. And I know I love you. I do not have to anxiously question myself about it.

I am led to think of this by the unrest which Helen causes me so often. I know but too well how much I love her. She is dearer to me than any one here in Northampton which is saying much; for how many lovely characters, many friends who have done great things for me, many people whom I love and [?] all but a very few elsewhere. I did not seek or choose that it should be so. It came from God—and in His own exuding excellent way—a way which seems to the world blinded soul like chance. I came very gradually to love her so well. I had known her long, in a certain way. I could not help myself, so I know that it was sent to me.

But I cannot feel sure of her. I know it is her nature, always to keep the best in reserve; but I have not such an overweening estimate of my powers of pleasing as to believe that I hold my place with her unless she gives me some evidence of the fact—now and then. Sometimes she is coaxed out of her ice wall, and the change is sweetness itself. She is so very lovely when she is gracious! It nurses in me such an ecstasy of joy that I half wonder at myself. She is so very different from me that I find in her something of the same sort of charm that some women find in men. She is "manly, as a woman may be womanly"—[?] strong. I never would choose to make advances to her, but am unspeakably happy when she smooths my cheek with her hand, or lays it on my head, looking down at me with the dewy light in her dark grey eyes, and calls me by some one of her many names for me—perhaps "Marchioness" (which she has dubbed me since we read Old Curiosity Shop) or "Little Mother." She has a way of putting a great deal into a commonplace act or word sometimes.—but unfortunately I am twenty-five, and she twenty-one next Sunday. I am a senior and she a sophomore, and she said once, "I am so proud—I am afraid of letting anybody know how much I care for them, for fear that they do not love me so much." Perhaps this is why I cannot seem to get very near her since we came to N———. But I cannot be sure, you see. I have not known her long enough, I have not tested and tried her love. There is some thing feverish in this up and down existence—these alternations between doubt and distress, and ecstatic happiness. As much better is a long tried friendship where both parties have arrived at the love which if not yet perfect, is yet near enough it to cast out fear, as the settled steadfast love of its hearts on their golden wedding day is better than the jealous pangs, the doubts and fears, of the lover in the days of early courtship.

I must tell you a bit about one Sunday night at Fort Ann—the last we spent in Helen's home—two weeks ago tonight. We had gone up to our room and Helen had gone to bed. I sat by the table and as I did not feel sleepy yet, and she said she wasn't, I proposed what I knew would give her pleasure—to read some bits from Cora's letters. She assented eagerly; once in our home at Mrs. Turner's I had read her a little and she said she wished she could hear them every Sunday night just before going to bed. So I read quite a while. The[n] we talked a little bit about you, and then she sprang up and said she must read me some of May's dear letter. . . . So I lay on the bed and she sat up and read to me and indeed they were dear letters. I have such a tender heart for that sensitive, suffering high-souled, orphan girl. Instead of begrudging her Helen's love I sometimes wonder if she has as much of it as she deserves. She says so often "You have other friends; I have nobody but you" (No other girl friend) She is as far removed from anything in the sentimental line as you can possibly imagine, and so the way in which she clings to Helen and her expressions of her love, even though she is continually trying to hold them back, touch me more than I can tell you. I sympathize with her intensity. Helen is not intense in the way we are. I sometimes grow skeptical and wonder if she does really care very deeply for either of us. And yet if not why should she rouse so much love in us? And she says "It makes me angry to have May say, 'You don't, you can't love and do'", she says she cannot express her deepest feelings. She must always let somebody else express them for her. All her life she says she has suffered from being thought cold.

Well, I wonder if you are bored? Please don't be. I want you to like Helen, because I do, and she likes you. Do please let me talk about her yet a little more, for she has cost me all the tears I have shed since I came back to Northampton, and I will have at least the little comfort of praising her to another I love. Did I ever try to describe her to you? Now [I] will first try a bit, and then if you should ever see a worthy picture of her you can see how far my description varies from the impression you get. (But most of her pictures do not represent her at all) She has a face which one would notice in a crowd—a large strong face which I would once have characterized by the adjective *plain,* and now would say was almost handsome—say rather noble: that fits best—a large face almost entirely colorless surrounded by very dark brown hair which lies in little natural loose rings next to her face—eyebrows and eyelashes very dark which give her eyes the effect of being black but they are dark grey—those most expressive eyes, which deepen and soften and kindle. (Miss Roberts, a stylish young lady who used to sit by Helen last spring at Mrs. Clark's table, said that she had "beautiful eyes—dangerous eyes—only she didn't know how to use them—she did not know that she could do what she likes with those eyes[."]) Her nose is regular but quite massive, and her lips are firm but full and very pale. Her chin and mouth give the character to her face as they do not retreat in the least and have a powerful look. She has a large strong chin. The face all together is as I said a noticeable one. I like it particularly in profile. The strength is brought out there best. Of all adjectives, noble describes her best. She has such a scor[n] of little low meannesses of character and conduct.

There, I am through talking about her: but as she has made such a large share in this week's history it was but fair she should take up much space in my journal letter. . . .

Sunday, Oct. 2.—Dear, I will add a few words and send this letter on, for I want to bridge over the silence. . . .

I wish you were here where you might enjoy the flowers in our garden. I carried a lovely birthday bouquet to Helen today—heliotrope, tuberoses, English violets, carnation pinks, rose geranium leaves. . . .

Well, Cora, if I could only see you tonight—only look in and see how you look once more. Shall I never never have that picture of you? You know I have nothing by that poor photo taken before you were ill. How are you? Do send me a word at least. When, O when shall I see you again?

Your own loving
Nelly

5. Alice Mitchell as a "Case of Sexual Perversion," 1892

The facts about Alice Mitchell will long be treasured in medical works on insanity, and mental and moral perversion. The medical scholar will study the case in all its lights and shades, while the public will only recall that she suddenly, in a terrible manner, with a razor, cut the throat of her dearest companion and friend, Freda Ward, a young lady of an excellent family. The natural impulse of every one was

T. Griswold Comstock, "Alice Mitchell of Memphis: A Case of Sexual Perversion or 'Urning,'" *New York Medical Times* 20 (September 1892): 170–173.

that summary justice should be dealt to avenge such an unprovoked crime. A few among the people of Memphis were so horrified that they even suggested violence. Fortunately the law took its course.

As a matter of medical jurisprudence, it is of great interest and importance that such a case should be inquired into and thoroughly analyzed by the medical profession, and I may add by the most careful and reliable medical experts. The very first impression is, that there must be something radically abnormal in the mental and physical development of such a murderess—and so it was.

The facts were that there was an unnatural affection existing between Alice Mitchell and Freda Ward. Alice Mitchell seems to have been the ardent one. The love they had for each other, to the public, seems something hard to conceive or explain, but to experts in insanity it is nothing unusual. Alice exhibited in her passion for Freda Ward all the impulses of the male sex for a female. She was to have been dressed as a man and take the bridegroom's part in the marriage ceremony. She had already even arranged with a clergyman to perform the services, but Miss Ward's friends interfered and they were separated. This disturbed Alice. When riding out with a friend, she meets Miss Ward. She suddenly stops and alights from the carriage, and overtaking Miss Ward deliberately cuts her throat with a razor which she carried for the purpose. She jumps into her buggy and drives rapidly home. She was arrested. She confessed the dreadful deed. She said she murdered her best friend because she loved her. For six months while in prison she did not exhibit any remorse or regret, but showed great devotion for the photograph of Miss Ward. And during the trial, and while the verdict was being rendered, her conduct was scarcely altered. The most reasonable conclusion of the jury, and those who have made a study of the alienated mental condition of those who commit such homicides, is, that the motive must have come of mental delusion. By scientific experts it is recognized as insanity of a peculiar kind. Alice having been indicted for murder, her attorneys looked at once into the antecedents of the family for mental aberrations. They learned that the mother of Alice in her first confinement, which occurred in St. Louis, had child-bed fever and puerperal insanity, and was confined in an asylum, and that before the birth of Alice she was deranged, and this aberration continued until sometime after labor. I attended the mother of Alice in her first confinement in St. Louis more than thirty years ago. She became insane just after delivery and her mania was of the acute form with fever. I attended her for a month and then advised that she be sent to an asylum. She was sent to the State Asylum at Fulton, where she remained for some time—I think six months. Within a few days after her return home from the asylum, she was first informed of the death of her child, and then her mind became again unbalanced. This demented condition, however, continued only a few days, but she did not recover from the shock. She remained melancholy for a long time, suffering from hallucinations, and was infatuated with the most groundless prejudices and fears. I had occasion to see her for some three years until the family removed from St. Louis to Memphis, and I could always remark a peculiar expression about her eyes which would bring to mind her former furious delirium. I mention this matter since it is a most important factor in the case of Alice, and must not be overlooked. The fact of a real engagement of marriage with one of her own sex indicated at once that she was what is known in forensic medicine as a *sexual pervert*. On the 19th of July, 1891, a judicial enquiry was instituted before Judge Du Bose, of the criminal court of Memphis, to examine into the sanity or rather the insanity of Alice Mitchell. A commission was issued and sent from Memphis to St. Louis to take my evidence regarding the particulars of the first confinement of the mother when puerperal mania followed. Also a hypothetical case was cited describing the life of the mother, her antecedents, her family history, and mentioning the fact that others members of her family had been of unsound mind. It also described the particulars and all the peculiarities of the life of Alice, from the date of her birth up to the time of the murder of Miss Ward. . . . My affidavit stated that from the antecedents of the mother, Alice was a sexual pervert and affected with emotional monomania, without doubt hereditary, and that her condition was one of *paranoia,* resulting in homicidal mania, and consequently her condition might be regarded as intrinsic insanity. That Alice is a sexual pervert and a *paranoiac* is quite probable, and the jury unanimously decided that she was insane. . . .

Here I may say something of sexual perverts. It is a revolting subject for the laity, for they have no toleration for anything of that kind. It is strictly a scientific matter of professional interest and of great importance to the medical expert. Until recently, little has been said upon this subject in text-books of insanity. It is mentioned in the recent works of Spitzka and Shaw, but for a full elucidation we must examine the work of Krafft-Ebing, Professor of Nervous Diseases in the University of Vienna.

He describes the *"vita sexualis"* of perverts, such as Alice Mitchell, under the classification *"Urnings."* This term, used frequently by German writers upon forensic medicine, refers to those who in a sexual sense are only stimulated when consorting with their own sex. It applies to those who indulge in unnatural sexual practices. But it especially includes sensuality and sexual desire of one female for another, and a disgust for a male. The same may be said of males—mutatis mutandis. Krafft-Ebing describes the "Lesbian Love"—(tribadism), saphismus, cunnilingus, fellators, pædicatio mulierum, sadismus, masochismus and fetischismus. Sadismus is a fierce, wild sensuality and lust, together with cruelty before, during and after coitus. Masochismus is another form of perverted lust during the act of constupration or coitus, accompanied with cruelty and special acts to terrorize and injure the female. Fetischismus or erotic fetischism refers to the "urning" or pervert, who superstitiously adores and worships some article of clothing or some organ of the person loved; or the odor of the person loved excites the orgasm, while the desire of natural coitus is disregarded. In some cases of these unnatural perverts, under the head of "Sadismus" or "Masochismus," the subject, before he can accomplish the sexual act, must, in order to induce priapism, practice cruelty to the woman or upon some animal; *e.g.,* he will bring along a live chicken, a duck, a rabbit or a dog and decapitate it in her presence. And then only can he be excited to complete the sexual act. In these cases coitus is only performed when accompanied by acts of horrid cruelty, or murder after its completion. The awful murders of "Jack the Ripper," in Clerkenwell, London, can be accounted for only on this theory.

Subjects like Alice Mitchell, who come under the classification of "Urnings," are all given to cruelties to the lower animals. This seems to have been the case with her, as proved by the evidence at the trial. These facts are all unpleasant matters to deal with, but they were germane in dealing with this young woman, and they are verified by numerous cases quoted in the authoritative work of Krafft-Ebing, extending through 432 pages. It is a sad truth that the existence of sexual perverts is of frequent occurrence, especially among the upper class of society. . . . Sexual perverts readily recognize each other, although they may have never met before, and there exists a mysterious bond of psychological sympathy between them. Instances have been authenticated to me where such perverts when meeting another of the same sex, have at once recognized each other, and mutually become acquainted and have left in company with each other to practice together their unnatural vices. I am informed by an expert in nervous diseases, that in New York, upon the elevated railroad, these perverts travel and frequently meet others of the same sex, and leave the cars in order to be in each other's private company. . . .

The sexual function and passion are not to be trifled with. For it is nothing less than the keystone of society, and plays a great rôle in forensic medicine. . . . The practices of sexual perverts I have alluded to, but they can not be described—they are fit to be studied only by competent medical men. These individuals are naturally objects of disgust to the laity, but in a professional man they excite the deepest sympathy. We have known many cases, sad to say, among the ministers of the Gospel—in high places—who were perverts, and one case not long since in the medical profession. Some of the most unnatural crimes that are chronicled in the newspapers result from mental aberrations that affect the sexual system. And again, the practice of a neurotic vice will intensify delusions and insanity in a sexual pervert.

Among such persons, Krafft-Ebing mentions manustupration, pædicatio mulierum, saphism, libidinous constupration with intense violence and the killing of their victims, sadismus and masochismus—which are frequently practiced. Among sexual perverts, jealousy is always a prominent passion, and Alice Mitchell's separation from Freda Ward seems to have excited the most intense jealousy, and the fire of this passion at the time burning in her breast was a motive for her to commit the homicide. The sexual relations of the human race are indeed mysterious, and when practiced in any unnatural manner, Nature will certainly avenge herself upon the offender. Mental disturbance and insanity will often follow.

The case of Alice Mitchell will be instanced for a long period hence as *un cas célebre,* and we feel that the verdict of the jury declaring that she was insane was just and proper. The relation of insanity to perverted sexuality is one of the most delicate matters that the physician has to treat, and it can be readily appreciated that in such cases the advice of experts and specialists in medical jurisprudence should be sought. Our mental organization and its workings are something that we can not entirely fathom, but the safety of society requires us to guard with constant care all persons who are in any way mentally irresponsible.

If the mind is deranged, self-control is lost and the acts of the person alienated may not only endanger his own life, but may be a constant menace to society. Physically, Alice Mitchell was a woman, but psychically her cerebral functions were those of a male, and still her preferences, like other Urnings—were for her own sex. All this came from an abnormal neuro-psychical development, and, as we believe, was inherited. The insanity of her mother was undoubtedly its prime cause, and that the mother was deranged before the birth, and the mania continued after the delivery, is a legitimate reason for placing the daughter in the category of one not responsible for the dreadful murder which she committed. It was then indeed a case of sexual perversion from hereditary taint, and was probably intensified by unnatural practices—primitive degenerative insanity; though of these we can only conjecture, as there was nothing of the kind elicited by the evidence. Insanity in such cases is more liable to be transmitted from mother to offspring of the same sex than to any male issue.

This case of Alice Mitchell, not only to the family of the pervert, and to the afflicted family whose daughter was so ruthlessly murdered, and to society in general, is indeed sad, and must cast its dark shadows far and wide. To the medical profession it suggests more thorough and exact study of mental disease.

▶ E S S A Y S

Carroll Smith-Rosenberg's path-breaking 1975 article on romantic friendships among women has become a classic in the history of sexuality. In it, she describes an intimate "female world" that was accepted even by women's husbands. Rejecting a dichotomy between emotional and physical intimacy, Smith-Rosenberg of the University of Michigan asks us to imagine a past in which female same-sex relationships were not stigmatized as "deviant" because they were not understood as "sexual." Her sources are primarily the letters of white, middle-class women in the North.

In response to this provocative essay, many other historians have probed women's private writings and analyzed intimate relationships. Sociologist Karen V. Hansen of Brandeis University uncovers a romantic friendship between two African-American women that was not only emotional and loving but explicitly erotic and physical; their love came under criticism when it threatened to interfere with heterosexual relationships. Hansen points toward the sexual nature of erotic friendships, not only among these two black women but perhaps among other women as well. Historian Karen Lystra of the California State University at Fullerton questions Smith-Rosenberg's assumptions about the emotional distance between women and men, and argues that sexualized courtship and conjugal affection characterized the world of Victorians.

The Female World of Love and Ritual

CARROLL SMITH-ROSENBERG

The female friendship of the nineteenth century, the long-lived, intimate, loving friendship between two women, is an excellent example of the type of historical phenomena which most historians know something about, which few have thought much about, and which virtually no one has written about. It is one aspect of the female experience which consciously or unconsciously we have chosen to ignore. Yet an abundance of manuscript evidence suggests that eighteenth- and nineteenth-century women routinely formed emotional ties with other women. Such deeply felt, same-sex friendships were casually accepted in American society. Indeed, from at least the late eighteenth through the mid-nineteenth century, a female world of varied and yet highly structured relationships appears to have been an essential aspect of American society. These relationships ranged from the supportive love of

Carroll Smith-Rosenberg, "The Female World of Love and Ritual: Relations between Women in Nineteenth-Century America," *Signs* 1 (1975): 1–29. Copyright © 1975 by The University of Chicago Press. Reprinted by permission of The University of Chicago Press.

sisters, through the enthusiasms of adolescent girls, to sensual avowals of love by mature women. It was a world in which men made but a shadowy appearance.

Defining and analyzing same-sex relationships involves the historian in deeply problematical questions of method and interpretation. This is especially true since historians, influenced by Freud's libidinal theory, have discussed these relationships almost exclusively within the context of individual psychosexual developments or, to be more explicit, psychopathology. Seeing same-sex relationships in terms of a dichotomy between normal and abnormal, they have sought the origins of such apparent deviance in childhood or adolescent trauma and detected the symptoms of "latent" homosexuality in the lives of both those who later became "overtly" homosexual and those who did not. Yet theories concerning the nature and origins of same-sex relationships are frequently contradictory or based on questionable or arbitrary data. In recent years such hypotheses have been subjected to criticism both from within and without the psychological professions. . . .

I would like to suggest an alternative approach to female friendships—one which would view them within a cultural and social setting rather than from an exclusively individual psychosexual perspective. Only by thus altering our approach will we be in the position to evaluate the appropriateness of particular dynamic interpretations. Intimate friendships between men and men and women and women existed in a larger world of social relations and social values. To interpret such friendships more fully they must be related to the structure of the American family and to the nature of sex-role divisions and of male-female relations both within the family and in society generally. The female friendship must not be seen in isolation; it must be analyzed as one aspect of women's overall relations with one another. The ties between mothers and daughters, sisters, female cousins and friends, at all stages of the female life cycle constitute the most suggestive framework for the historian to begin an analysis of intimacy and affection between women. Such an analysis would not only emphasize general cultural patterns rather than the internal dynamics of a particular family or childhood; it would shift the focus of the study from a concern with deviance to that of defining configurations of legitimate behavioral norms and options.

This analysis will be based upon the correspondence and diaries of women and men in thirty-five families between the 1760s and the 1880s. These families, though limited in number, represented a broad range of the American middle class, from hard-pressed pioneer families and orphaned girls to daughters of the intellectual and social elite. It includes families from most geographic regions, rural and urban, and a spectrum of Protestant denominations ranging from Mormon to orthodox Quaker. Although scarcely a comprehensive sample of America's increasingly heterogeneous population, it does, I believe, reflect accurately the literate middle class to which the historian working with letters and diaries is necessarily bound. It has involved an analysis of many thousands of letters written to women friends, kin, husbands, brothers, and children at every period of life from adolescence to old age. . . . It is my contention that an analysis of women's private letters and diaries which were never intended to be published permits the historian to explore a very private world of emotional realities central both to women's lives and to the middle-class family in nineteenth-century America.

The question of female friendships is peculiarly elusive; we know so little or perhaps have forgotten so much. An intriguing and almost alien form of human relationship, they flourished in a different social structure and amidst different sexual norms. Before attempting to reconstruct their social setting, therefore, it might be best first to describe two not atypical friendships. These two friendships, intense, loving, and openly avowed, began during the women's adolescence and, despite subsequent marriages and geographic separation, continued throughout their lives. For nearly half a century these women played a central emotional role in each other's lives, writing time and again of their love and of the pain of separation. Paradoxically to twentieth-century minds, their love appears to have been both sensual and platonic.

Sarah Butler Wister first met Jeannie Field Musgrove while vacationing with her family at Stockbridge, Massachusetts, in the summer of 1849. Jeannie was then sixteen, Sarah fourteen. During two subsequent years spent together in boarding school, they formed a deep and intimate friendship. Sarah began to keep a bouquet of flowers before Jeannie's portrait and wrote complaining of the intensity and anguish of her affection. Both young women assumed nom de plumes, Jeannie a female name, Sarah a male one; they would use these secret names into old age. They frequently commented on the nature of their affection: "If the day should come," Sarah wrote Jeannie in the spring of 1861, "when you failed me either through your fault or my own, I would forswear all human friendship, thenceforth." A few months later Jeannie commented: "Gratitude is a word I should never use toward you. It is perhaps a misfortune of such intimacy and love that it makes one regard all kindness as a matter of course, as one has always found it, as natural as the embrace in meeting."

Sarah's marriage altered neither the frequency of their correspondence nor their desire to be together. In 1864, when twenty-nine, married, and a mother, Sarah wrote to Jeannie: "I shall be entirely alone [this coming week]. I can give you no idea how desperately I shall want you. . . ." After one such visit Jeannie, then a spinster in New York, echoed Sarah's longing: "Dear darling Sarah! How I love you & how happy I have been! You are the joy of my life. . . . I cannot tell you how much happiness you gave me, nor how constantly it is all in my thoughts. . . . My darling how I long for the time when I shall see you. . . ." After another visit Jeannie wrote: "I want you to tell me in your next letter, to assure me, that I am your dearest. . . . I do not doubt you, & I am not jealous but I long to hear you say it once more & it seems already a long time since your voice fell on my ear. So just fill a quarter page with caresses & expressions of endearment. Your silly Angelina." Jeannie ended one letter: "Goodbye my dearest, dearest lover—ever your own Angelina." And another, "I will go to bed . . . [though] I could write all night—A thousand kisses—I love you with my whole soul—your Angelina."

When Jeannie finally married in 1870 at the age of thirty-seven, Sarah underwent a period of extreme anxiety. Two days before Jeannie's marriage Sarah, then in London, wrote desperately: "Dearest darling—How incessantly have I thought of you these eight days—all today—the entire uncertainty, the distance, the long silence—are all new features in my separation from you, grevious to be borne. . . . Oh Jeannie. I have thought & thought & yearned over you these two days. Are you married I wonder? My dearest love to you wherever and *who*ever you are." Like many other women in this collection of thirty-five families, marriage brought Sarah and Jeannie physical separation; it did not cause emotional distance. Although at first they may have wondered how marriage would affect their relationship, their affection remained unabated throughout their lives, underscored by their loneliness and their desire to be together.

During the same years that Jeannie and Sarah wrote of their love and need for each other, two slightly younger women began a similar odyssey of love, dependence and—ultimately—physical, though not emotional, separation. Molly and Helena met in 1868 while both attended the Cooper Institute School of Design for Women in New York City. For several years these young women studied and explored the city together, visited each other's families, and formed part of a social network of other artistic young women. Gradually, over the years, their initial friendship deepened into a close intimate bond which continued throughout their lives. The tone in the letters which Molly wrote to Helena changed over these years from "My dear Helena," and signed "your attached friend," to "My dearest Helena," "My Dearest," My Beloved," and signed "Thine always" or "thine Molly." . . .

The intensity and even physical nature of Molly's love was echoed in many of the letters she wrote during the next few years, as, for instance in this short thank-you note for a small present: "Imagine yourself kissed a dozen times my darling. Perhaps it is well for you that we are far apart. You might find my thanks so expressed rather overpowering. I have that delightful feeling that it doesn't matter much what I say or how I say it, since we shall meet so soon and forget in that moment that we were ever separated. . . . I shall see you soon and be content."

At the end of the fifth year, however, several crises occurred. The relationship, at least in its intense form, ended, though Molly and Helena continued an intimate and complex relationship for the next half-century. The exact nature of these crises is not completely clear, but it seems to have involved Molly's decision not to live with Helena, as they had originally planned, but to remain at home because of parental insistence. Molly was now in her late twenties. Helena responded with anger and Molly became frantic at the thought that Helena would break off their relationship. Though she wrote distraught letters and made despairing attempts to see Helena, the relationship never regained its former ardor—possibly because Molly had a male suitor. Within six months Helena had decided to marry a man who was, coincidentally, Molly's friend and publisher. Two years later Molly herself finally married. The letters toward the end of this period discuss the transition both women made to having male lovers—Molly spending much time reassuring Helena, who seemed depressed about the end of their relationship and with her forthcoming marriage.

It is clearly difficult from a distance of 100 years and from a post-Freudian cultural perspective to decipher the complexities of Molly and Helena's relationship. Certainly Molly and Helena were lovers—emotionally if not physically. The emotional intensity and pathos of their love become apparent in several letters Molly wrote Helena during their crisis: "I wanted so to put my arms round my girl of all the girls in the world and tell her . . . I love her as wives do love their husbands, as *friends* who have taken each other for life—and believe in her as I believe in my God. . . . If I didn't love you do you suppose I'd care about anything or have ridiculous notions and panics and behave like an old fool who ought to know better. I'm going to hang on to your skirts. . . . You can't get away from [my] love." Or as she wrote after Helena's decision to marry: "You know dear Helena, I really was in love with you. It was a passion such as I had never known until I saw you. I don't think it was the noblest way to love you." The theme of intense female love was one Molly again expressed in a letter she wrote to the man Helena was to marry: "Do you know sir, that until you came along I believe that she loved me almost as girls love their lovers. *I know I loved her so.* Don't you wonder that I can stand the sight of you." This was in a letter congratulating them on their forthcoming marriage.

The essential question is not whether these women had genital contact and can therefore be defined as heterosexual or homosexual. The twentieth-century tendency to view human love and sexuality within a dichotomized universe of deviance and normality, genitality and platonic love, is alien to the emotions and attitudes of the nineteenth century and fundamentally distorts the nature of these women's emotional interaction. These letters are significant because they force us to place such female love in a particular historical context. There is every indication that these four women, their husbands and families—all eminently respectable and socially conservative—considered such love both socially acceptable and fully compatible with heterosexual marriage. Emotionally and cognitively, their heterosocial and their homosocial worlds were complementary.

One could argue, on the other hand, that these letters were but an example of the romantic rhetoric with which the nineteenth century surrounded the concept of friendship. Yet they possess an emotional intensity and a sensual and physical explicitness that is difficult to dismiss. . . . A survey of the correspondence and diaries of eighteenth- and nineteenth-century women indicates that Molly, Jeannie, and Sarah represented one very real behavioral and emotional option socially available to nineteenth-century women.

This is not to argue that individual needs, personalities, and family dynamics did not have a significant role in determining the nature of particular relationships. But the scholar must ask if it is historically possible and, if possible, important, to study the intensely individual aspects of psychosexual dynamics. Is it not the historian's first task to explore the social structure and the world view which made intense and sometimes sensual female love both a possible and an acceptable emotional option? From such a social perspective a new and quite different series of questions suggests itself. What emotional function did such female love serve? What was its place within the hetero- and homosocial worlds which women jointly inhabited? Did a spectrum of love-object choices exist in the nineteenth century across which some individuals, at least, were capable of moving? Without attempting to answer these questions it will be difficult to understand either nineteenth-century sexuality or the nineteenth-century family.

Several factors in American society between the mid-eighteenth and the mid-nineteenth centuries may well have permitted women to form a variety of close emotional relationships with other women. American society was characterized in large part by rigid gender-role differentiation within the family and within society as a whole, leading to the emotional segregation of women and men. The roles of daughter and mother shaded imperceptibly and ineluctably into each other, while the biological realities of frequent pregnancies, childbirth, nursing, and menopause bound women together in physical and emotional intimacy. It was within just such a social framework, I would argue, that a specifically female world did indeed develop, a world built around a generic and unself-conscious pattern of single-sex or homosocial networks. These supportive networks were institutionalized in social conventions or rituals which accompanied virtually every important event in a woman's life, from birth to death. Such female relationships were frequently supported and paralleled by severe social restrictions on intimacy between young men and women. Within such a world of emotional richness and complexity devotion to and love of other women became a plausible and socially accepted form of human interaction.

An abundance of printed and manuscript sources exists to support such a hypothesis. Etiquette books, advice books on child rearing, religious sermons, guides to young men and young women, medical texts, and school curricula all suggest that late eighteenth- and most nineteenth-century Americans assumed the existence of a world composed of distinctly male and female spheres, spheres determined by the immutable laws of God and nature. The unpublished letters and diaries of Americans during this same period concur, detailing the existence of sexually segregated worlds inhabited by human beings with different values, expectations, and personalities. Contacts between men and women frequently partook of a formality and stiffness quite alien to twentieth-century America and which today we tend to define as "Victorian." Women, however, did not form an isolated and oppressed subcategory in male society. Their letters and diaries indicate that women's sphere had an essential integrity and dignity that grew out of women's shared experiences and mutual affection and that, despite the profound changes which affected American social structure and institutions between the 1760s and the 1870s, retained a constancy and predictability. The ways in which women thought of and interacted with each other remained unchanged. Continuity, not discontinuity, characterized this female world. Molly Hallock's and Jeannie Fields's words, emotions, and experiences have direct parallels in the 1760s and the 1790s. There are indications in contemporary sociological and psychological literature that female closeness and support networks have continued into the twentieth century—not only among ethnic and working-class groups but even among the middle class.

Most eighteenth- and nineteenth-century women lived within a world bounded by home, church, and the institution of visiting—that endless trooping of women to each others' homes for social purposes. It was a world inhabited by children and by other women. Women helped each other with domestic chores and in times of sickness, sorrow, or trouble. Entire days, even weeks, might be spent almost exclusively with other women. Urban and town women could devote virtually every day to visits, teas, or shopping trips with other women. Rural women developed a pattern of more extended visits that lasted weeks and sometimes months, at times even dislodging husbands from their beds and bedrooms so that dear friends might spend every hour of every day together. When husbands traveled, wives routinely moved in with other women, invited women friends to teas and suppers, sat together sharing and comparing the letters they had received from other close women friends.

Secrets were exchanged and cherished, and the husband's return at times viewed with some ambivalence. . . .

Friends did not form isolated dyads but were normally part of highly integrated networks. Knowing each other, perhaps related to each other, they played a central role in holding communities and kin systems together. Especially when families became geographically mobile women's long visits to each other and their frequent letters filled with discussions of marriages and births, illness and deaths, descriptions of growing children, and reminiscences of times and people past provided an important sense of continuity in a rapidly changing society. Central to this female world was an inner core of kin. The ties between sisters, first cousins, aunts, and nieces provided the underlying structure upon which groups of friends and their networks of female relatives clustered. Although most of the women within this sample would appear to be living within isolated nuclear families, the emotional ties between nonresidential kin were deep and binding and provided one of the fundamental existential realities of women's lives. . . .

Women frequently spent their days within the social confines of such extended families. Sisters-in-law visited each other and, in some families, seemed to spend more time with each other than with their husbands. First cousins cared for each other's babies—for weeks or even months in times of sickness or childbirth. Sisters helped each other with housework, shopped and sewed for each other. Geographic separation was borne with difficulty. A sister's absence for even a week or two could cause loneliness and depression and would be bridged by frequent letters. Sibling rivalry was hardly unknown, but with separation or illness the theme of deep affection and dependency reemerged.

Sisterly bonds continued across a lifetime. In her old age a rural Quaker matron, Martha Jefferis, wrote to her daughter Anne concerning her own half-sister, Phoebe: "In sister Phoebe I have a real friend—she studies my comfort and waits on me like a child. . . . She is exceedingly kind and this to all other homes (set aside yours) I would prefer—it is next to being with a daughter." Phoebe's own letters confirmed Martha's evaluation of her feelings. "Thou knowest my dear sister," Phoebe wrote, "there is no one . . . that exactly feels [for] thee as I do, for I think without boasting I can truly say that my desire is for thee."

Such women, whether friends or relatives, assumed an emotional centrality in each others' lives. In their diaries and letters they wrote of the joy and contentment they felt in each others' company, their sense of isolation and despair when apart. The regularity of their correspondence underlines the sincerity of their words. Women named their daughters after one another and sought to integrate dear friends into their lives after marriage. As one young bride wrote to an old friend shortly after her marriage: "I want to see you and talk with you and feel that we are united by the same bonds of sympathy and congeniality as ever." After years of friendship one aging woman wrote of another: "Time cannot destroy the fascination of her manner . . . her voice is music to the ear. . . ." Women made elaborate presents for each other, ranging from the Quakers' frugal pies and breads to painted velvet bags and phantom bouquets. When a friend died, their grief was deeply felt. Martha Jefferis was unable to write to her daughter for three weeks because of the sorrow she felt at the death of a dear friend. . . .

These female friendships served a number of emotional functions. Within this secure and empathetic world women could share sorrows, anxieties, and joys, confident that other women had experienced similar emotions. One mid-nineteenth-century rural matron in a letter to her daughter discussed this particular aspect of women's friendships: "To have such a friend as thyself to look to and sympathize with her—and enter into all her little needs and in whose bosom she could with freedom pour forth her joys and sorrows—such a friend would very much relieve the tedium of many a wearisome hour. . . ." These were frequently troubles that apparently no man could understand. When Anne Jefferis Sheppard was first married, she and her older sister Edith (who then lived with Anne) wrote in detail to their mother of the severe depression and anxiety which they experienced. Moses Sheppard, Anne's husband, added cheerful postscripts to the sisters' letters—which he had clearly not read—remarking on Anne's and Edith's contentment. Theirs was an emotional world to which he had little access.

This was, as well, a female world in which hostility and criticism of other women were discouraged, and thus a milieu in which women could develop a sense of inner security and self-esteem. As one young woman wrote to her mother's long-time friend: "I cannot sufficiently thank you for the kind unvaried affection & indulgence you have ever shown and expressed both by words and actions for me. . . . Happy would it be did all the world view me as you do, through the medium of kindness and forbearance." They valued each other. Women, who had little status or power in the larger world of male concerns, possessed status and power in the lives and worlds of other women.

An intimate mother-daughter relationship lay at the heart of this female world. The diaries and letters of both mothers and daughters attest to their closeness and mutual emotional dependency. Daughters routinely discussed their mother's health and activities with their own friends, expressed anxiety in cases of their mother's ill health and concern for her cares. Expressions of hostility which we would today consider routine on the part of both mothers and daughters seem to have been uncommon indeed. On the contrary, this sample of families indicates that the normal relationship between mother and daughter was one of sympathy and understanding. . . . Something of this sympathy and love between mothers and daughters is evident in a letter Sarah Alden Ripley, at age sixty-nine, wrote her youngest and recently married daughter: "You do not know how much I miss you, not only when I struggle in and out of my mortal envelop and pump my nightly potation and no longer pour into your sympathizing ear my senile gossip, but all the day I muse away, since the sound of your voice no longer rouses me to sympathy with your joys or sorrows. . . . You cannot know how much I miss your affectionate demonstrations." A dozen aging mothers in this sample of over thirty families echoed her sentiments. . . .

Daughters were born into a female world. Their mother's life expectations and sympathetic network of friends and relations were among the first realities in the life of the developing child. As long as the mother's domestic role remained relatively stable and few viable alternatives competed with it, daughters tended to accept their mother's world and to turn automatically to other women for support and intimacy. It was within this closed and intimate female world that the young girl grew toward womanhood. . . .

At some point in adolescence, the young girl began to move outside the matrix of her mother's support group to develop a network of her own. Among the middle class, at least, this transition toward what was at the same time both a limited autonomy and a repetition of her mother's life seemed to have most frequently coincided with a girl's going to school. Indeed education appears to have played a crucial role in the lives of most of the families in this study. Attending school for a few months, for a year, or longer, was common even among daughters of relatively poor families, while middle-class girls routinely spent at least a year in boarding school. These school years ordinarily marked a girl's first separation from home. They served to wean the daughter from her home, to train her in the essential social graces, and, ultimately, to help introduce her into the marriage market. It was not infrequently a trying emotional experience for both mother and daughter.

In this process of leaving one home and adjusting to another, the mother's friends and relatives played a key transitional role. Such older women routinely accepted the role of foster mother; they supervised the young girl's deportment, monitored her health and introduced her to their own network of female friends and kin. Not infrequently women, friends from their own school years, arranged to send their daughters to the same school so that the girls might form bonds paralleling those their mothers had made. . . .

Even more important to this process of maturation than their mother's friends were the female friends young women made at school. Young girls helped each other overcome homesickness and endure the crises of adolescence. They gossiped about beaux, incorporated each other into their own kinship systems, and attended and gave teas and balls together. Older girls in boarding school "adopted" younger ones, who called them "Mother." Dear friends might indeed continue this pattern of adoption and mothering throughout their lives; one woman might routinely assume the nurturing role of pseudomother, the other the dependency role of daughter. . . . Helena played such a role for Molly, as did Sarah for Jeannie. Elizabeth Bordley Gibson bought almost all Eleanor Parke Custis Lewis's necessities—from shoes and corset covers to bedding and harp strings—and sent them from Philadelphia to Virginia, a procedure that sometimes took months. Eleanor frequently asked Elizabeth to take back her purchases, have them redone, and argue with shopkeepers about prices. These were favors automatically asked and complied with. Anne Jefferis Sheppard made the analogy very explicitly in a letter to her own mother written shortly after Anne's marriage, when she was feeling depressed about their separation: "Mary Paulen is truly kind, almost acts the part of a mother and trys to aid and *comfort me,* and also to *lighten my new cares.*"

A comparison of the references to men and women in these young women's letters is striking. Boys were obviously indispensable to the elaborate courtship ritual girls engaged in. In these teenage letters and diaries, however, boys appear distant and warded off—an effect produced both by the girls' sense of bonding and by a highly developed and deprecatory whimsy. Girls joked among themselves about the conceit, poor looks or affectations of suitors. Rarely, especially in the eighteenth and early nineteenth centuries, were favorable remarks exchanged. Indeed, while hostility and criticism of other women were so rare as to seem almost tabooed, young women permitted themselves to express a great deal of hostility toward peer-group men. When unacceptable suitors appeared, girls might even band together to harass them. When one such unfortunate came to court Sophie DuPont she hid in her room, first sending her sister Eleuthera to entertain him and then dispatching a number of urgent notes to her neighboring sister-in-law, cousins, and a visiting friend who all came to Sophie's support. A wild female romp ensued, ending only when Sophie banged into a door, lacerated her nose, and retired, with her female cohorts, to bed. Her brother and the presumably disconcerted suitor were left alone. These were not the antics of teenagers but of women in their early and mid-twenties.

Even if young men were acceptable suitors, girls referred to them formally and obliquely: "The last week I received the unexpected intelligence of the arrival of a friend in Boston," Sarah Ripley wrote in her diary of the young man to whom she had been engaged for years and whom she would shortly marry. Harriet Manigault assiduously kept a lively and gossipy diary during the three years preceding her marriage, yet did not once comment upon her own engagement nor indeed make any personal references to her fiancé—who was never identified as such but always referred to as Mr. Wilcox. The point is not that these young women were hostile to young men. Far from it; they sought marriage and domesticity. Yet in these letters and diaries men appear as an other or out group, segregated into different schools, supported by their own male network of friends and kin, socialized to different behavior, and coached to a proper formality in courtship behavior. As a consequence, relations between young women and men frequently lacked the spontaneity and emotional intimacy that characterized the young girls' ties to each other.

Indeed, in sharp contrast to their distant relations with boys, young women's relations with each other were close, often frolicsome, and surprisingly long lasting and devoted. They wrote secret missives to each other, spent long solitary days with each other, curled up together in bed at night to whisper fantasies and secrets. In 1862 one young woman in her early twenties described one such scene to an absent friend: "I have sat up to midnight listening to the confidences of Constance Kinney, whose heart was opened by that most charming of all situations, a seat on a bedside late at night, when all the household are asleep & only oneself & one's confidante survive in wakefulness. So she has told me all her loves and tried to get some confidences in return but being five or six years older than she, I know better. . . ." Elizabeth Bordley and Nelly Parke Custis, teenagers in Philadelphia in the 1790s, routinely secreted themselves until late each night in Nelly's attic, where they each wrote a novel about the other. Quite a few young women kept diaries, and it was a sign of special friendship to show their diaries to each other. . . . Girls routinely slept together, kissed and hugged each other. Indeed, while waltzing with young men scandalized the otherwise flighty and highly fashionable Harriet Manigault, she considered waltzing with other young women not only acceptable but pleasant.

Marriage followed adolescence. With increasing frequency in the nineteenth century, marriage involved a girl's traumatic removal from her mother and her mother's network. It involved, as well, adjustment to a husband, who, because he was male came to marriage with both a different world view and vastly different experiences. Not surprisingly, marriage was an event surrounded with supportive, almost ritualistic, practices. . . . Young women routinely spent the months preceding their marriage almost exclusively with other women—at neighborhood sewing bees and quilting parties or in a round of visits to geographically distant friends and relatives. Ostensibly they went to receive assistance in the practical preparations for

their new home—sewing and quilting a trousseau and linen—but of equal importance, they appear to have gained emotional support and reassurance. . . .

Sisters, cousins, and friends frequently accompanied newlyweds on their wedding night and wedding trip, which often involved additional family visiting. Such
extensive visits presumably served to wean the daughter from her family of origin.
As such they often contained a note of ambivalence. Nelly Custis, for example, reported homesickness and loneliness on her wedding trip. "I left my Beloved and
revered Grandmamma with sincere regret," she wrote Elizabeth Bordley. "It was
sometime before I could feel reconciled to traveling without her." Perhaps they also
functioned to reassure the young woman herself, and her friends and kin, that though
marriage might alter it would not destroy old bonds of intimacy and familiarity.

Married life, too, was structured about a host of female rituals. Childbirth,
especially the birth of the first child, became virtually a *rite de passage,* with a
lengthy seclusion of the woman before and after delivery, severe restrictions on her
activities, and finally a dramatic reemergence. This seclusion was supervised by
mothers, sisters, and loving friends. Nursing and weaning involved the advice and
assistance of female friends and relatives. So did miscarriage. Death, like birth, was
structured around elaborate unisexed rituals. . . . Virtually every collection of letters and diaries in my sample contained evidence of women turning to each other
for comfort when facing the frequent and unavoidable deaths of the eighteenth and
nineteenth centuries. While mourning for her father's death, Sophie DuPont received elaborate letters and visits of condolence—all from women. No man wrote
or visited Sophie to offer sympathy at her father's death. Among rural Pennsylvania Quakers, death and mourning rituals assumed an even more extreme same-
sex form, with men or women largely barred from the deathbeds of the other sex.
Women relatives and friends slept with the dying woman, nursed her, and prepared
her body for burial.

Eighteenth- and nineteenth-century women thus lived in emotional proximity
to each other. Friendships and intimacies followed the biological ebb and flow of
women's lives. Marriage and pregnancy, childbirth and weaning, sickness and death
involved physical and psychic trauma which comfort and sympathy made easier to
bear. Intense bonds of love and intimacy bound together those women who, offering
each other aid and sympathy, shared such stressful moments.

These bonds were often physical as well as emotional. An undeniably romantic
and even sensual note frequently marked female relationships. This theme, significant throughout the stages of a woman's life, surfaced first during adolescence. As
one teenager from a struggling pioneer family in the Ohio Valley wrote in her diary
in 1808: "I laid with my dear R[ebecca] and a glorious good talk we had until about
4[A.M.]—O how hard I do *love* her. . . ." Only a few years later Bostonian Eunice
Callender carved her initials and Sarah Ripley's into a favorite tree, along with a
pledge of eternal love, and then waited breathlessly for Sarah to discover and respond to her declaration of affection. The response appears to have been affirmative.
A half-century later urbane and sophisticated Katherine Wharton commented upon
meeting an old school chum: "She was a great pet of mine at school & I thought as I
watched her light figure how often I had held her in my arms—how dear she had
once been to me." Katie maintained a long intimate friendship with another girl.
When a young man began to court this friend seriously, Katie commented in her

diary that she had never realized "how deeply I loved Eng and how fully." She wrote over and over again in that entry: "Indeed I love her!" and only with great reluctance left the city that summer since it meant also leaving Eng with Eng's new suitor.

Peggy Emlen, a Quaker adolescent in Philadelphia in the 1760s, expressed similar feelings about her first cousin, Sally Logan. The girls sent love poems to each other (not unlike the ones Elizabeth Bordley wrote to Nellie Custis a generation later), took long solitary walks together, and even haunted the empty house of the other when one was out of town. Indeed Sally's absences from Philadelphia caused Peggy acute unhappiness. So strong were Peggy's feelings that her brothers began to tease her about her affection for Sally and threatened to steal Sally's letters, much to both girls' alarm. In one letter that Peggy wrote the absent Sally she elaborately described the depth and nature of her feelings: "I have not words to express my impatience to see My Dear Cousin, what would I not give just now for an hours sweet conversation with her, it seems as if I had a thousand things to say to thee, yet when I see thee, everything will be forgot thro' joy. . . . I have a very great friendship for several Girls yet it dont give me so much uneasiness at being absent from them as from thee. . . . [Let us] go and spend a day down at our place together and there unmolested enjoy each others company." . . .

Tender letters between adolescent women, confessions of loneliness and emotional dependency, were not peculiar to Sarah Alden, Peggy Emlen, or Katie Wharton. They are found throughout the letters of the thirty-five families studied. They have, of course, their parallel today in the musings of many female adolescents. Yet these eighteenth- and nineteenth-century friendships lasted with undiminished, indeed often increased, intensity throughout the women's lives. . . . Eunice Callender remained enamored of her cousin Sarah Ripley for years and rejected as impossible the suggestion by another woman that their love might some day fade away. Sophie DuPont and her childhood friend, Clementina Smith, exchanged letters filled with love and dependency for forty years while another dear friend, Mary Black Couper, wrote of dreaming that she, Sophie, and her husband were all united in one marriage. . . . Eliza Schlatter, another of Sophie's intimate friends, wrote to her at a time of crisis: "I wish I could be with you present in the body as well as the mind & heart—I would turn your *good husband out of bed*—and snuggle into you and we would have a long talk like old times in Pine St.—I want to tell you so many things that are not *writable.* . . ."

Such mutual dependency and deep affection is a central existential reality coloring the world of supportive networks and rituals. In the case of Katie, Sophie, or Eunice—as with Molly, Jeannie, and Sarah—their need for closeness and support merged with more intense demands for a love which was at the same time both emotional and sensual. Perhaps the most explicit statement concerning women's lifelong friendships appeared in the letter abolitionist and reformer Mary Grew wrote about the same time, referring to her own love for her dear friend and lifelong companion, Margaret Burleigh. Grew wrote, in response to a letter of condolence from another woman on Burleigh's death: "Your words respecting my beloved friend touch me deeply. Evidently . . . you comprehend and appreciate, as few persons do . . . the nature of the relation which existed, which exists, between her and myself. Her only surviving niece . . . also does. To me it seems to have been a closer union than that of most marriages. We know there have been other such between two men and also between two women. And why should there not be. Love is spiritual, only passion is sexual."

How then can we ultimately interpret these long-lived intimate female relationships and integrate them into our understanding of Victorian sexuality? Their ambivalent and romantic rhetoric presents us with an ultimate puzzle: the relationship along the spectrum of human emotions between love, sensuality, and sexuality.

One is tempted, as I have remarked, to compare Molly, Peggy, or Sophie's relationships with the friendships adolescent girls in the twentieth century routinely form—close friendships of great emotional intensity. Helena Deutsch and Clara Thompson have both described these friendships as emotionally necessary to a girl's psychosexual development. But, they warn, such friendships might shade into adolescent and postadolescent homosexuality.

It is possible to speculate that in the twentieth century a number of cultural taboos evolved to cut short the homosocial ties of girlhood and to impel the emerging women of thirteen or fourteen toward heterosexual relationships. In contrast, nineteenth-century American society did not taboo close female relationships but rather recognized them as a socially viable form of human contact—and, as such, acceptable throughout a woman's life. Indeed it was not these homosocial ties that were inhibited but rather heterosexual leanings. While closeness, freedom of emotional expression, and uninhibited physical contact characterized women's relationships with each other, the opposite was frequently true of male-female relationships. One could thus argue that within such a world of female support, intimacy, and ritual it was only to be expected that adult women would turn trustingly and lovingly to each other. It was a behavior they had observed and learned since childhood. A different type of emotional landscape existed in the nineteenth century, one in which Molly and Helena's love became a natural development.

Of perhaps equal significance are the implications we can garner from this framework for the understanding of heterosexual marriages in the nineteenth century. If men and women grew up as they did in relatively homogeneous and segregated sexual groups, then marriage represented a major problem in adjustment. From this perspective we could interpret much of the emotional stiffness and distance that we associate with Victorian marriage as a structural consequence of contemporary sex-role differentiation and gender-role socialization. With marriage both women and men had to adjust to life with a person who was, in essence, a member of an alien group.

I have thus far substituted a cultural or psychosocial for a psychosexual interpretation of women's emotional bonding. But there are psychosexual implications in this model which I think it only fair to make more explicit. . . .

. . . [W]e are well aware that cultural values can affect choices in the gender of a person's sexual partner. We, for instance, do not necessarily consider homosexual-object choice among men in prison, on shipboard or in boarding schools a necessary indication of pathology. I would urge that we expand this relativistic model and hypothesize that a number of cultures might well tolerate or even encourage diversity in sexual and nonsexual relations. Based on my research into this nineteenth-century world of female intimacy, I would further suggest that rather than seeing a gulf between the normal and the abnormal we view sexual and emotional impulses as part of a continuum or spectrum of affect gradations strongly affected by cultural norms and arrangements, a continuum influenced in part by observed and thus learned behavior. At one end of the continuum lies committed heterosexuality, at the other uncompromising homosexuality; between, a wide latitude of emotions and sexual feelings. Certain cultures and environments permit individuals a great deal of freedom in moving across this spectrum. I would like to suggest that the nineteenth century was such a cultural environment. That is, the supposedly repressive and destructive Victorian sexual ethos may have been more flexible and responsive to the needs of particular individuals than that of the mid-twentieth century.

An Erotic Friendship Between Two African-American Women

KAREN V. HANSEN

Addie Brown, a free-born African-American domestic worker, wrote letters before, during, and immediately after the Civil War to her "only dear and loving friend," Rebecca Primus, an African-American school teacher. In May, 1861, in characteristically vivid prose, Addie wrote to Rebecca: "Your most affec[tionate] letter to me was like a peices of meat to hungere wolfe." Addie and Rebecca's letters tell the story of a passionate relationship that endured nine years of intermittent separation, the ebb and flow of their romantic love, and male suitors attempting to woo each of them. Theirs was not a secretive liaison. It was highly visible and deeply enmeshed in the domestic networks of Hartford's African-American community.

Because Rebecca preserved a cache of letters, the resonant voices of these two remarkable yet ordinary women fill a silence about free-born African-American women of the nineteenth century. Addie and Rebecca spoke their minds and hearts to each other, not intending their words to be published. They worked hard and loved fiercely. Through their friendship they provided a safe space, as Patricia Hill Collins labels it, to voice confidently their point of view and reaffirm their self-conceptions.

The correspondence between Rebecca and Addie fills a gap in the literature about African-American women in the nineteenth century. This flourishing scholarship has creatively drawn from the limited available evidence to explore women's activism in the abolitionist movement, the church, the club movement, the struggle for Black men's suffrage, anti-lynching campaigns, and everyday acts of rebellion. However, primarily because of the dearth of primary sources written by ordinary women, historical analysis has focused largely on organizations and on women in positions of leadership. As a result, intimate friendships between women have remained a relatively unexplored area. The historical and literary writing about Black women in the nineteenth century places Addie and Rebecca in an over-arching context, but their letters alone forge new ground in documenting friendships and everyday life in the North. Moreover, like the Black women abolitionists studied by Shirley Yee, Addie and Rebecca were "not passive victims of oppression, but active

---

Karen V. Hansen, "'No Kisses Is Like Youres': An Erotic Friendship between Two African-American Women during the Mid-Nineteenth Century," *Gender and History* 7 (August 1995): 153–182. Reprinted by permission of Blackwell Publishers.

participants in efforts to help their families and communities and to secure racial equality." As agents of their own livelihoods, they created networks of support and exchange, sought and found employment, indulged in a passionate friendship with each other, and battled racism in the urban North.

Approximately 120 of Addie Brown's letters to Rebecca Primus and fifty of Rebecca's letters to her family, written between 1859 and 1869, have been preserved. Addie's almost illegible handwriting, poor grammar, and cryptic references make her letters difficult to decipher. At the same time, there is a magic to her letters, a rhythm to her speech, a forthrightness about her feelings, and a drama to her emotional turmoil that immediately captivates the reader. Because Rebecca's direct replies to Addie are missing, it is necessary to infer Rebecca's reactions and perspective. Rebecca's responses can be gauged and partially reconstructed from the conversational way that Addie writes. In a typical letter, Addie laments their separation, reports local gossip, and searches for affirmation of mutual love. She then turns to the questions posed in Rebecca's last letter. Rebecca's letters to her family paint a fuller portrait of her. Her correspondence illustrates her eloquence and grace, and reveals her dedication to her vocation and to the improvement of conditions for African Americans. Evidence of Addie's importance to Rebecca lies in the fact that it was Rebecca who preserved Addie's letters for sixty-two years.

The letters of Rebecca Primus and Addie Brown also prompt us to reinterpret the sexuality of women's friendships. . . . [S]tudies of white middle-class women . . . have found that close bonds between women in the nineteenth century often became passionate and sometimes erotic. My research on friendship between working-class white women finds a similar romantic attachment amongst women who otherwise rejected middle-class notions of womanhood. This literature on romantic friendship has sparked a scholarly debate about the degree to which women's affection for one another simply expressed the romantic discourse dominant in the nineteenth century, reflected a unique women's culture, or revealed a lesbian sexual practice. It has also generated controversy regarding the degree to which society unproblematically accepted the intense emotional relationships between women. Collectively these studies challenge contemporary readers to reconsider sexual categories such as homosexuality and heterosexuality, and to appreciate the fluidity of boundaries in nineteenth-century sexuality. Addie Brown and Rebecca Primus push us further to reanalyze the literature on romantic friendship. . . .

At first glance, Addie and Rebecca seem an unlikely pair, and precisely how they met remains a mystery. Rebecca was born in 1836 to a family who had resided in Connecticut for several generations. Her father, Holdridge Primus, worked as a clerk in a grocery store for forty-seven years and her mother, Mehitable Primus, was self-employed as a dress-maker, a highly skilled position. The Primuses owned their home at 20 Wadsworth Street in Hartford. In 1850, the household claimed $1,200 worth of real estate, far exceeding the average wealth of free Blacks in the North.

Mehitable Primus, along with other Christian worshipers, rejected the segregation of local white churches and founded the Talcott Street Congregational Church in 1833. Within the Black community, the church reigned supreme as a central place for gathering, educating and organizing. The Talcott Street Church was also known as the "First Colored Church" and the "Fifth Congregational." The other

Black church in Hartford was the Methodist Episcopal–Zion's Church, founded in 1836. Both churches sponsored fairs, festivals, concerts and political forums throughout the 1860s. . . . For over sixty years, Mehitable Primus actively participated in the congregation and in its numerous secular events.

Rebecca, the eldest of four children, obtained a high school education and became a highly respected teacher. Her Christianity, her "missionary spirit," and her determination to improve the conditions of freed slaves motivated her to venture southward after the Civil War. . . . In this act alone, she was daring. She described herself as liking speed—"fast driving and quick movements in any body or any thing." At the same time, she was sensible and proud of her capacities as a wage earner. From her family and community she inspired respect, admiration, and awe. Addie described her as "a fastidious young lady." Conferring respectability in the Black community often reflected a class consciousness and defied white society's opinions to the contrary.

Rebecca's conception of respectable womanhood did not prompt her to shrink from confrontation or political commitment. Through the sponsorship of Hartford's newly established Freedmen's Aid Society, she went South in the fall of 1865 to establish a school for ex-slaves. In Royal Oak, Maryland, Rebecca taught seventy-five day and evening students of various ages. Rebecca's letters reveal her enduring commitment to improving the condition of African Americans as she raised money from her Hartford community to construct a school house in Maryland, and worked relentlessly to persuade local citizens as well. In 1867, she wrote: "Their invariable plea is we're all poor, just out of bondage, and times are hard with us &c. My reply is, very true, nevertheless, we must have a school house." Rebecca worked in Maryland for four years, and the local community named the school the Primus Institute in her honor.

Rebecca wrote home from Maryland about verbal harassment, physical abuse, and threats to the lives of teachers from the North who acted as moral crusaders in a racially stratified and deeply hostile political and social environment. With great dignity, Rebecca bravely set a high standard of treatment: "These white people want all the respect shown them by the col^d people. I give what I rec. & no more."

Maltreatment by whites was not unique to the South, however. The North maintained segregationist laws and customs as well, and even within radical abolitionist circles, African Americans had to fight for equal treatment. Connecticut, Rebecca's home state, had abolished slavery by 1800, but permitted out-of-state slaveholders unlimited transit with their slaves until 1837. . . . For Rebecca and the free Black community, neither equal access to public facilities nor the right to personal dignity came without a struggle.

Addie Brown, an orphan five years Rebecca's junior, was eighteen when her correspondence to Rebecca begins. She remains invisible in nineteenth-century government documents. Addie lamented the fact that she had to make her way in the world without the support of family ties. Rebecca's relative abundance of kin and education contrasted sharply with Addie's dearth. Nonetheless, Addie's buoyant and charismatic personality finds a voice in her vivid but functional writing style, an unmistakable divergence from Rebecca's more circumspect, polished eloquence. She combined passion, earnestness, and sensuality, all the while sustaining a commentary on the moral appropriateness of people's behavior, and avidly reading novels. A tall woman with great force of personality, Addie characterized herself as "singular," an adjective she used to describe women whom she found contentious. Addie judged others quickly and harshly for moral transgressions or for disagreeing with her.

Black women found few jobs open to them outside of laundry and domestic service, and Addie Brown was no exception. Hartford's prosperity in the 1860s did not guarantee economic security to free Blacks, for they were excluded from factory jobs and most of the skilled trades. Addie made a living alternately as a seamstress (a low-skilled and poorly paid position), a domestic servant, a worker in a dye factory, an assistant cook, and shortly before she died at the age of twenty-nine, a teamster (a driver of a team of horses). She recognized the limits of her narrow horizons: "You say don't allow myself to indulge in glumy forebodings for the future. How can I help it? I can't get any work. I have no money, and I stand to live out to service long at the time. That all I can aspire in this place." Like most domestic servants in the nineteenth-century United States, Addie changed jobs and shifted households repeatedly. In fact, she moved at least eight times between 1859 and 1868. She strove to maintain her status as a seamstress and to avoid the even more punishing work that many of her peers were forced to take: "I went to see Mrs. Manings. She looks just the same, up to eyes in washing. I hope I will never have to take in washing for my livelyhood." Addie regarded laundry, a grueling chore largely relegated to poor African-American women, as an employment of last resort.

Despite her dire economic situation, Addie was unafraid of employers who overstepped their bounds. Speaking of the small-minded, autocratic supervisor at a white household where she worked, Addie wrote: "I don't like her. You know how I am with any one I don't like." Addie felt even more intolerant of racism and segregation at white churches. In 1867, while working at Miss Porter's School in Farmington, Connecticut, she attended church only once. After regularly attending the Talcott Street Church in Hartford, she had no patience for white segregationists who maintained separate seating for African Americans, and so refused to attend church while in Farmington.

Addie worried about her right to love Rebecca because Rebecca was older, more educated, and obviously of a higher status within the Black community. She explored the disparities in her and Rebecca's status by discussing a novel she had recently read, which in her mind exemplified the dilemmas within her relationship with Rebecca. *Women's Friendships,* published in 1850 by Grace Aguilar, tells a tale of friendship between the aristocratic Lady Ida and the naive, middle-class Florence Leslie. Aguilar conveys the honor of a passionate attachment between white women and illustrates the power of true friendship to change their lives. The disparity in class status between Lady Ida and Florence precipitates a crisis when Lady Ida marries into the upper echelons of English society at the same time that a series of misfortunes leave Florence penniless, fatherless, and doubtful about the respectability of her parentage. Addie found the book captivating in part because in her estimation, the protagonists' relationship mirrored her own with Rebecca. In an enthusiastic letter, Addie confided that Florence loved Lady Ida as "I do you." Yet the book's message must have been disturbing. "Friendship demands equality of station, true affections devoid of selfishness," Addie wrote to Rebecca. Identifying with Florence, Addie speculated about the fate of mixed-class relationships: "I fear this warm attachment must end in disappointment, fully as I can sympathize in its present happiness." . . .

Rather than simply a romantic outpouring of sentiment, the passion between Addie and Rebecca that suffuses the letters expressed a self-consciously sexual relationship. Although they left no evidence of genital contact, their friendship included passion, kisses and what I call "bosom sex," and competed with their heterosexual relationships. My interpretation of the sensuality of their relationship takes on greater meaning in the context of what is known about women's friendships in the nineteenth century. Since the historical scholarship is largely based on the experiences of white middle-class women, there are obvious limitations. Regardless, the literature frames the physical intimacy between women as part of a sexual continuum, with fluid boundaries between heterosexuality and homosexuality. Writing at great distances, white women, working-class and middle-class, both single and married, professed their great love for each other. These liaisons included physical expressions such as kissing, hugging, and sharing a bed, but were not considered improper or sexual, either by the women themselves or by their communities. They were presumed not to involve genital contact and frequently occurred in the context of heterosexual marriage.

No comparable body of evidence exists for Black women in the nineteenth century. Historians and literary critics have turned to African-American fiction to try to construct what might have happened in relationships between women and in everyday life. The significance of Addie and Rebecca's correspondence is thus twofold. One, it is the only collection of writings by Black women who were not related, not abolitionists, and not famous that documents an intimate relationship. Two, it differs from the white women's correspondence in many ways, most importantly, in that it documents an explicitly erotic—as distinct from romantic—friendship.

Embedded in an extensive network of social and economic relationships, Addie and Rebecca embraced friendship and sisterhood, yet surpassed both. They pronounced the language of friendship inadequate to their situation: "I need never name the tie which exist between us. Friendships, this term is not applicable to you. And you even say that you are not worthy of it. Call it any thing else." Although Addie protested when Rebecca deemed herself unworthy of the high office of friend, she nevertheless celebrated the honorable nature of friendship. Four years later she declared, "You have been more to me then a <u>friend</u> or <u>sister</u>." Both Rebecca and Addie realized that the language of friendship, even when fused with the language of kinship, proved inadequate for capturing the complexity of their relationship. Their struggle with language is endemic both to the study of friendship and to friendship itself.

Intense amorous feeling permeates the correspondence between Addie and Rebecca in the early 1860s. Predating the late nineteenth-century novels by African-American women, but thematically anticipating them, Addie's letters use the language of romance and love. While imagining a rendezvous of their souls, Addie fantasized, "Methink my <u>Dearest Sister</u> I am near the, breathing the same air with your arm gently drawn around me, my head reclining on your noble breast in perfect confidence and love." These declarations of love follow patterns observed within U.S. society as a whole. In her study of nineteenth-century romantic love, Karen Lystra points out that private life provided an arena of "personal unmasking and freedom from etiquette" where lovers freely disclosed their innermost feelings. . . . In the tradition of great undying love in the nineteenth century, Addie suffered through their separations:

> Darling I will try and express my feelings when I see you better. O it's useless for I can't. Rebecca, when I bid you good by it's seem to me that my very heart broke. I have felt wretched ever since. Sometime I feel that I could not live one hour to another. My Darling Friend I shall never be happy again unless I am near you eather here on earth or in heaven. Since you have left me I want nothing. O Rebecca, why can't I be with you? Will I never have that pleasure? Don't tell me no, for I must.

Letter-writing consoled her little: "Do not be surprise to hear from me again. I am heart sick to see you once more." Rebecca tried to console Addie: "you say absence streng[th]ens friendship and our love will not grow cold. Mine will never. I will always love you and you only."

One key exchange that shaped my interpretation of Addie and Rebecca's relation-ship occurred in the autumn of 1867. In her letter, Addie revealed a sexual practice that for me threw startling new light on their then eight-year-old friendship. She wrote reassuring Rebecca that she did not suffer from loneliness at Miss Porter's School where she worked as an assistant cook: "The girls are very friendly towards me. I am eather in they room or they in mine, every night out ten and sometime past. One of them wants to sleep with me. Perhaps I will give my consent some of these nights. I am not very fond of whit[ie] I can assure you." Although nineteenth-century custom encouraged sharing a bed, the sexual innuendo did not escape Rebecca's notice. When she wrote back inquiring about Addie's new bed partner, Addie replied quickly:

> If you think that is my bosom that captivated the girl that made her want to sleep with me, she got sadly disappointed injoying it, for I had my back towards all night and my night dress was butten up so she could not get to my bosom. I shall try to keep your f[avored] one always for you. Should in my excitement forget, you will partdon me I know.

In this most explicit passage, Addie reveals a sexual practice whose particulars she assumed Rebecca would understand. Sleeping with a woman involved providing access to her breasts. By preventing this fondling, Addie disappointed her bed part-ner. Addie articulated what some historians of women have long suspected, that the passion expressed by nineteenth-century women was not solely cerebral. However, in the absence of comparable explicitness in the letters of white women, scholars have had to imagine the details. Without this interchange, Addie's correspondence more closely parallels the letters of white middle-class women. With the inter-change complete with sexual innuendo, it provides graphic evidence of the erotic dimension of the relationship.

For two reasons, we can surmise that "bosom sex" was part of Addie's rela-tionship with Rebecca as well. First, Rebecca reacted jealously. She worried that Addie might forsake their exclusive relationship when she learned of other women's sexual interest in Addie. Addie recognized that in the heat of a passionate moment she might abandon reason and fail to observe Rebecca's sacred privileges.

Two weeks later, Addie responded somewhat defensively to Rebecca's deeper probe of the incident:

> I thought I told you about the girl sleeping with me whether I injoyed it or not. I can't say that I injoyed it very much. I don't care about her sleeping with me again. I don't know what kind of an excitement I refer to now. I pesume I know at the time. I can't recalled.

Thereafter Addie changed the subject and it did not resurface in the subsequent letters.

Second, we can assume that "bosom sex" was part of Addie and Rebecca's relationship because the exchange revealed that Addie and Rebecca shared assumptions about what could happen between sleeping partners. Had Rebecca lacked knowledge about Addie's night-time practices, she would not have responded jealously. She knew Addie "injoyed" her sexuality, and was perhaps prone to getting carried away in a moment of passion. Addie flaunted her power over Rebecca, evidenced in her arrogant retort: "Should in my excitement forget, you will partdon me I know." Indisputably, Addie and Rebecca had a romantic friendship, one common to nineteenth-century womanhood. However, they also indulged in an erotic sensuality.

In her letters, Addie expressed her longing for Rebecca by evoking the image of Rebecca's bosom. Writing from Hartford in the autumn of 1860, Addie addressed a note to her "cherish friend":

> O my Dear Dear Rebecca when you press me to your dear bosom O how happy I was. Last night I gave any thing if I could only layed my poor aching head on your bosom. O Dear how soon will it be I can be able to do so? . . . It is very gloomy here. If I was only near you now. I rather have my head on your lap then pencil the few lines to you . . . Addie
>
> P.S. except a sweet kiss. I will imprint on here so look good.

The imagery of breasts evokes notions of comfort, nurturing and maternity as well as female sexuality. In an 1861 letter, Addie wrote:

> How I have wanted to see you. If I only could have rested my head on your bosom for a moments give vent to my feeling. I have been sad. I am so ful some time that I could take a knife and cut my heart out, perhaps then I feel better. If I could be with you daily, I know that I would be happy. Well, that can't be.

"Bosom talk" appears everywhere in the correspondence.

In her other letters, Addie often spoke of exchanging caresses, kisses, and hugs, and of sharing a bed. In one 1859 letter, Addie prefers the memory of Rebecca's kisses to those offered by Mr. Games, the Black man who headed the household where she worked as a domestic servant: "How I did miss you last night. I did not have anyone to hug me up and to kiss. Rebecca, don't you think I am very foolish? I don't want anyone to kiss me now. I turn Mr. Games away this morning. No kisses is like youres." Sensuality figured centrally in Addie's satisfaction with Rebecca. "I wish I was going to be [embraced in] you loving arms to night. How happy I would be. Well, I guess the time will soon arrises when I will have that most exquisite pleasure so doing."

Addie repeatedly compared her feelings toward Rebecca to those between women and men.

You are the first girl that I ever <u>love</u> so and you are the <u>last</u> one. Dear Rebeca, do not say anything against me <u>loving</u> you so, for I mean just what I say. O Rebbeca, it seem I can see you now, casting those loving eyes at me. If you was a man, what would things come to? They would after come to something very quick. What do you think the matter? Don't laugh at me. I not exactly crazy yet.

The echoes of a marital vow appear in an 1860 letter: "Yours for ever, untill death parts us." In 1865 Addie delighted in the fantasy of a marriage to Rebecca: "What a pleasure it would be to me to address you <u>My Husband</u>." Addie found the prospect of loving someone else—male or female—with the same intensity virtually unfathomable. All evidence indicates that Rebecca reciprocated Addie's love with the same fervent passion:

> Rebecca, my Darling, you can't imagine what pleasure I take in perusing those notes. Its send such a thrilling sensation through me, particular were you say, "I do indeed love you with my whole heart." My Dear you say I am entirely ignorant of the depth of your love. Not quite my persuous Darling. I am little wise of it. I can't help being so to see how much you do for me daily.

Anxiety and conflict accompanied infatuation in Rebecca and Addie's romantic friendship, as they did for other friends and lovers in the nineteenth century. Romantic "love brought anxiety in its wake," along with numerous other emotions such as sympathy, longing, joy, pain, jealousy and sadness. Both Addie and Rebecca felt the plague of insecurity at different points in their relationship. In 1862, at the height of their proclamations of love, they agonized over their tumultuous emotional journey. That September, Addie implied that they had just reconciled after reaching the brink of estrangement. Addie had perceived an alteration in Rebecca's attachment to her: "Dearest Sister, I hope you feeling will never again change towards me. To think I was on edge of loseing your <u>purest</u> love. O how my heart leap for joy when I think I have regain it, as strong as it was before, perhaps stronger." Three days later she wrote: "I feel sad to night for I don't think you have got over the feeling you had towards me when you bid me good night. It seem cold and would not even kiss me. That something you have never done yet." Rebecca, in turn, felt vulnerable to Addie's moods and uncertain about how to interpret them. Addie replied:

> Sweat Sister, I have peruse your note again. It make the six time. I cannot perceive why you thought thus I was indifferent towards you that A.M. My Darling, I did not feel so, although I felt sad that morning. I awoke before you. I imprint several kisses upon your lips and gave you a fond imbrace. While I was in that position a shade of sadness stole over me and it has not been remove yet.

Addie eventually smoothed over the hurt feelings by going through the ritual of reassuring her beloved.

The tenor of their bond shifted perceptibly over the nine years of Addie's correspondence. Their relationship changed as Rebecca and Addie grew older and were intermittently separated. Their passion erupted in 1860, and flourished and peaked in 1862 through outpourings of the heart and conflicted misunderstandings about commitment. Beginning in 1863 the correspondence virtually evaporates for two-and-a-half years, presumably because they were both living in Hartford. When their correspondence resumes in the fall of 1865, after Rebecca went South to teach, the letters tone down and reflect a deeper, more mature relationship. While their love did not abate, their infatuation did. Addie continued to refer to Rebecca as her beloved and cherished sister. At the same time, she began addressing her letters to her "adopted sister," indicating a decline in emotional intensity, although rooted more stably in kinship. When Addie talked about Mr. Joseph Tines, her new suitor, she made it clear that she did love him, but not *passionately*. Passion was the hallmark of her love for Rebecca. . . .

The level of explicit eroticism and passion in the letters declined, but did not disappear. In January, 1866, Addie wrote: "Dearest friend & only Sister, I will never doubt your <u>love</u> for me again. You say you put my picture under your pillow. I wish I had the pleasure laying along side of you." Addie's references to Rebecca's bosom consistently alluded to their emotional intimacy and shared confidence but referred less often to their sensual love. In May, 1866, Addie wrote, "My Dear & Adopted Sister, I truly wish that I could exchange pen and paper for a seat by your side and my head reclining on your soft bosom and having a pleasure chit chat with thee." Bosoms became more exclusively a symbol of safety, intimacy, and unconditional love. A more dramatic shift in tone occurred after the summer of 1866. Addie's letters got shorter in 1867 and became much more matter of fact, with little if any emotional embellishment. Nonetheless, the jealous exchange over Addie's sleeping partner took place in the winter of 1867. Throughout the nine years of Addie's correspondence, despite these transformations in the relationship, Rebecca figured as the centerpiece to Addie's emotional well-being.

The intense romantic friendship between Addie Brown and Rebecca Primus was recognized, facilitated, and sanctioned by their kin and friends within the African-American community, but not without some ambivalence. . . . Shortly after Rebecca went South for the first time [in January 1866], Addie visited the Primus household and found that the family had recently received a letter from Rebecca, which Bell Primus, Rebecca's sister, offered to show her. A neighbor, Mr. James, came in when she handed over the letter and provocatively inquired if it was a "gentleman letter." Fully aware the letter was from Rebecca, he may have thought the letter was written to Addie. Regardless, he intentionally implied that the letter was romantic, one properly written by a gentleman to a lady. His question suggested that the relationship between Addie and Rebecca was one most appropriate between a man and a woman, not two women. Mrs. Primus came to Addie's defense, Addie reported in her letter to Rebecca:

> She said I thought as much of you if you was a gentleman. She also said if either one of us was a gent we would marry. I was quite surprise at the remark. Mr. James & I had quite a little arguement. He says when I find some one to <u>love</u> I will throw you over the shoulder. I told him, "never."

Addie inserted a line above the text: "I have unshaken confidence in your love. I do sincerely believe." Mr. James's insinuation that the right man would prompt the two women to abandon their love for each other offended Addie. Mrs. Primus's understanding of the commitment Addie and Rebecca made to one another and her willingness to defend the association caught Addie off guard, although it pleased her greatly.

. . . Addie indignantly responded to Mr. James's implication that she showered her love on Rebecca only because no men were interested in her. In fact, she did have male suitors; Joseph Tines, a worker on a steam ship, was courting her. Regardless, subsequent correspondence reveals that having a beau did not prevent her from ardently loving Rebecca and pledging a commitment first and foremost to her.

This episode reveals the acceptance and support the Primus kin gave to Addie and Rebecca, but also suggests that, at least in the eyes of Mr. James, Rebecca and Addie's relationship crossed previously observed but unspoken boundaries. Their community and kin recognized their mutual attachment as unusually powerful, yet they actively facilitated and fortified the relationship. What permitted, indeed encouraged, the relationship to flourish?

African Americans in the Northeast lived mainly in the major cities; nevertheless they were a small group. In Hartford, the state capital, African Americans composed 2.4 per cent of the population in 1860. On the day she first traveled to Baltimore, Maryland, Rebecca Primus commented, "I guess I have already seen almost as many colored people as there are in the whole of Hartford." . . .

Like many African-American communities in the North, Hartford had flourishing systems of exchange; people shared food, loaned money, traded goods and services, ran errands, and conducted business with one another. Addie and Rebecca fully participated in these networks. Their communities overlapped, although they were not identical. In the web of the Primus family network, Mehitable Primus cared for Addie through several illnesses and regularly found her employment; Rebecca loaned "a large portion" of one of her pay checks to her boarding housekeepers, Mr. and Mrs. Thomas; and Rebecca and Addie borrowed money from each other. Virtually every letter sent between them carried greetings and wishes for good health sent by neighbors and friends. The conveyances reveal that the members of the domestic networks were aware of Addie and Rebecca's constant communication and their commitment to each other. In turn, Addie and Rebecca both gossiped about people's health, their whereabouts, premarital pregnancies, and foiled courtships. Rebecca and Addie's immersion in these webs of relations signifies that the Black community in Hartford accepted them as full-fledged members.

In the African-American tradition, Addie and Rebecca claimed each other as sisters, expecting unconditional and enduring support. From slave ships to Southern plantations to free communities in the North, Americans of African heritage have created "fictive kin" to supplement biological ties and to establish systems of socioeconomic exchange. Rebecca invited Addie to address her as sister in the spring of 1862. Addie responded:

> My dearest here is [nise] question. You ask a favor and that is this, too <u>call</u> you my <u>sister</u>. And then you ask me if it will be agreeable. O My Darling, Darling, you know it would. It has been my wish for sometime I dare not [voice]. My Dear I cannot find words to express my feeling to you.

Fully embracing Rebecca as her sister/partner, Addie signed several letters, "Addie Brown Primus."

In the process of accepting Rebecca as kin, Addie also adopted the Primus kin network. After a visit in 1859, Addie wrote, "I was treated so rich by all the family . . . you Dear Ma, there is no one like her if you was to [search] all over United States."

Mehitable Primus advised Addie, found her employment, and shared Rebecca's letters with her. Her daughters, Rebecca's sisters Henrietta and Bell, similarly drew Addie into their orbit. Although Addie did not address Mehitable Primus in kin terms, she regarded her as a pillar of her domestic network. . . .

Rebecca's kin embraced Addie in all of her "singularity" and sensuality. Deeply involved in kin dynamics, Addie helped to mediate Rebecca's relations with her family. In the fall of 1862, Addie strongly urged Rebecca not to leave home. The person most likely to suffer would have been Rebecca's mother, whom Addie wanted to protect. (However, because of her own interest in Rebecca's proximity, this intervention cannot be seen as completely selfless.) Later, after Rebecca had moved to Maryland, Addie told her of Henrietta Primus's conflicted feelings about her. In the wake of Rebecca's successes, Henrietta felt undereducated and insufficiently accomplished, and turned to Addie for comfort. . . .

Addie created conflict in her relationships with men in the Primus network. . . . Addie's relationship with Rebecca's only brother, Nelson Primus, a prominent portrait painter based in Boston, prompted conflict with Rebecca. In 1862, Addie pleaded with Rebecca not to be angry at her for flirting with Nelson:

> I shall not be as friendly with your brother as I have been. I know you don't like it and I also understand another member of the family don't like it. You know I like your family very much and sometime like to be in there society very much. But for the future I will treat him as I would any other young man acquaintance.

Thereafter Nelson only rarely appears in Addie's letters. As with Nelson, Addie's flirtatiousness with Thomas Sands, Rebecca's cousin, eventually led to what Addie characterized as misperceptions about the nature of the relationship and her intentions. In 1867, Bell Sands, Thomas's wife, began circulating rumors insinuating that Thomas and Addie were romantically involved. Henrietta warned Addie that her engagement with Joseph Tines would be threatened if her fiancé learned about the letters that they exchanged. Interestingly, the suggestion of romantic interest in two of the men in the Primus family network—Nelson Primus and cousin Thomas Sands—proved troublesome, whereas with a woman it did not. That said, Thomas Sands was married, which put his flirtation in a different category. (Addie denied improper involvement.) However, Addie's intense attachment to Rebecca did not provoke the same reservations. Perhaps the family viewed her relations with Rebecca as transitional, a stage during young adulthood that would not interfere with eventual heterosexual marriage. While her relationships with women were sometimes contentious, they were always more important. Addie terminated her relations with men in the network in order to sustain those with the women. . . .

Although they appeared to harbor no misgivings about the passion the women felt for each other, Addie and Rebecca's kin tried to assist them in negotiating their relationships with men. While supporting the friendship, they warned that it should not interfere with male-female courtship. In their admonitions to Addie about her open proclamations of devotion to Rebecca, they acknowledged the depth and strength of her feelings. For instance, Rebecca's Aunt Emily cautioned Addie that she would be wise not to tell her Hartford beau, Joseph Tines, that she loved Rebecca better than anyone. Addie wrote to Rebecca:

> How I have miss you. I have lost all; no more pleasure for me now. Aunt Emily ask me last eve if I was going to carry that [sober] face until you return. She also said if Mr. T[ines] was to see me, think that I care more for you then I did for him. I told, I did love you more then I ever would him. She said I better not tell him so. It would be the truth and most else.

Addie's avowed preference for Rebecca, like her argument with Mr. James, reveals that the community knew about the primacy of these two women's attachment to each other. At the same time, their ties were not regarded as exclusive, but rather as compatible with social obligations and heterosexual partnership, as long as they finessed the situation skillfully.

Consistent with this attitude, for both Addie and Rebecca, involvement with each other did not preclude relationships with men. Addie admitted to her attraction to men. However, her devotion to Rebecca created obstacles for those men drawn to her. Addie's admirers quickly learned that they had to vie with her love for Rebecca. Despite Aunt Emily's advice, Addie measured all other affections against this standard of unconditional and ardent love. In Addie's eyes, no one else could even approach this pinnacle of devotion. Addie relayed the news of a proposal from a sailor, Mr. Lee, in 1862: "He said it will not be long before he will return and make me his wife. He said that he has met with gr[at] many ladies since he is be gone but none compare with his sweat Addie. He says his love is stronger than ever." A reassuring line quickly followed: "Dear Rebecca, I never shall love any person as I do you." While relaying her news, she simultaneously confided and tried to provoke jealousy in her beloved. . . .

After Addie moved to Hartford from New York City in 1862, Mr. Lee receded in importance, but Addie's attempts to foster competition continued. However, as Addie and Rebecca's relationship changed, so too did the way Addie talked about her suitor. In 1865, she made sure that Rebecca met Mr. Joseph Tines, a man whose employment on a steam ship, the *Granite State,* brought him regularly up the Connecticut River through Hartford. When Rebecca left for Maryland, Mr. Tines "says I must not worry to much, best of friends must part. How can I help it, for all is gone? No one feel as I do about you and nev[er] will." However, Rebecca remained Addie's primary love object: "I had the pleasure of seeing Mr. Tines twice last week . . . I shall miss him very much. If you was here I should not care very much. He seems to be rather doubtful of my <u>love</u> for him. I do love him but not passionately and never will." . . .

Addie approached marriage in the practical way she approached her work rather than the romantic way she thought about friendship. Assessing her situation as a single woman without kin, engaged in a low-wage occupation, she pragmatically weighed the economic and social advantages of potential marriage against the dangerous prospect of a bad relationship or difficult childbirth. Marriage seemed a risky venture that promised little and guaranteed less: "I guess no ones know what triall that married people has to goes through, not only triall but how they have to suffer." . . . Still, Addie concluded: "Dear Rebecca, if I should ever see a good chance I will take it, for I'm tired roving around this unfriendly world." At the age of twenty, Addie wearied of the struggle to make her own way in the world and saw marriage as a solution—a way to forge a partnership and to establish a secure home base.

A life with Rebecca seemed remote and unlikely. Female-headed households were more common in Black communities than in white communities, especially in urban areas. Because of a higher mortality rate for Black men and more job opportunities for women, many cities, such as Boston and Providence in the North and Charleston and Washington, D.C., in the South, had more women than men. This meant that "the decision not to marry was unconventional," according to [historian] James Oliver Horton, "but it offered one means of reconciling the conflicting responsibilities placed on black women." Thus, "unmarried women were not common, but neither were they unique." The Black community's reaction to two romantically involved women setting up a household together is a subject virtually untouched in historiography. In 1861 Addie wrote from New York City:

> I want to ask you one question. That is, will you not look at my marrying in a different light then you do? Look at this my Darling, I'm here with Mother, perhaps see you about three time in a year. I'm sometimes happy, more time unhappy. I will get my money regular for two or three week and then iregular. What would you rather see me do, have one that truly <u>love</u> me that would give me a happy home, and or give him up and remain in this home, or part of me? Rebecca, if I could live with you or even be with you some parts of the day, I would never marry.

This response to Rebecca indicates that Rebecca opposed Addie's thoughts of marriage, but also resisted her suggestion to live together. Both women realized that marriage posed a threat to their relationship. Five years later, after Addie agreed to marry Mr. Tines, she had second thoughts. She postponed the wedding several times. Even when a firm date was arranged, she felt ambivalent. "I very serious thoughts and make me feel unhappy at times. I often wonder if every [ones] feels as I do." As if fulfilling a prophecy, Addie's correspondence to Rebecca abruptly halts near the time of her wedding. She moved to Philadelphia to live with the Tines family, and died of tuberculosis two years later at the age of twenty-nine.

Although we do not have a comparable account of Rebecca's courtship, we have a few facts with which to work. Rebecca taught in Royal Oak, Maryland, until June of 1869 when the Hartford Freedmen's Aid Society dissolved and called its teachers home. Upon returning, she accepted a position as the Assistant Superintendent of the Sabbath School at the Talcott Street Congregational Church. In 1872, Charles H. Thomas, Rebecca's former landlord in Maryland and a recent widower, moved north to Hartford, presumably to pursue Rebecca, and lived temporarily with the Primus family. An ex-slave who had purchased his own freedom, he was an established horse trainer and sawmill engineer when Rebecca met him in 1865, and was deeply involved in Maryland's Reconstruction politics. He actively helped to facilitate the building of Rebecca's schoolhouse and served on the school committee. . . .

. . . After he and Rebecca married in 1872, they settled near Rebecca's parents, but Rebecca's life was not easy. Charles suffered a severe head injury in an accident in the late 1880s, and was mentally incompetent and destitute for the last several years of his life. After he died in 1891, Rebecca returned home to live with her mother on Wadsworth Street. There she resided until her mother died in 1899. At that point Rebecca moved to a boarding house, where she lived until 1932 when she met her death at the age of 95.

Eventually, both Addie and Rebecca married men. Addie felt attracted to men as well as women, she enjoyed their attentions, and liked to boast of her allure to both sexes. While she remained ambivalent about her relationships with men, she recognized the economic advantages of heterosexual marriage, however marginal. At the same time, because Black men had few occupational opportunities, received low wages, and faced periodic unemployment, married women regularly had to work. Marriage did not promise a life free of labor or from the threat of destitution. Yet African-American working women who did not marry suffered economic hardships throughout their lives. In the mid-nineteenth-century United States, women engaged in wage labor had to struggle to eke out an independent livelihood. Although some women lived with female kin because they did not marry or because their husbands died or deserted them, most women did not have the option of choosing a female partnership over heterosexual marriage. Addie knew that ultimately she would have to find a husband, for economic reasons at the very least.

Addie and Rebecca forged a fierce, enduring bond with each other despite their difference in age, family security, education, class status, and personality. They respected and valued themselves and each other in a culture that denigrated Black women. Their mutuality helped to stave off the crippling effects of racial and gender oppression. The surviving correspondence began in 1859, revealing an intense infatuation fraught with insecurities. The nature of their relationship shifted over time, and while their passion may have waxed and waned, their commitment to one another did not. Addie identified Rebecca as a sister; she was her family, her best friend, her beloved, one who offered unconditional love, attention, affection, help, advice and comfort. Rebecca, in turn, relied on Addie for help with her personal affairs, adoration, passionate love, and sensuality.

The domestic networks of the African-American community in Hartford strengthened the two young women's connection by embracing them as individuals and as a couple, by intertwining their work and social lives, and by accepting their offerings to the community. They understood Addie and Rebecca's relationship as analogous to a heterosexual partnership, an honorable commitment based on mutual attachment. As long as this commitment did not completely usurp relationships with men, the community did accept Addie and Rebecca falling in love, prioritizing their friendship, and becoming sisters. However, the community and culture did not endorse their consideration of a life-long partnership that excluded men.

When I initially began reading the Primus Family collection, I was struck with the similarities between Rebecca and Addie's relationship and the romantic friendships among white working-class and middle-class women of the same period. The correspondence jubilantly celebrated the relationship and drew from the flowery language of romantic love so prevalent in the nineteenth century. With erotic overtones, it referred to physical moments of intimacy. Like the white women's relationships, this relationship flourished in the context of a predominantly heterosexual society. Addie and Rebecca enjoyed the widespread acceptance of female friendship in nineteenth-century America, and adapted the conventional language of romantic love to express their attachment. Although Addie and Rebecca circulated primarily in the Black community, they also participated in and were influenced by the dominant white culture. By her profound identification with a white British aristocrat, Addie made it clear that her own imagination did not observe strict color or class lines. . . .

[Nevertheless] Addie and Rebecca's relationship poses important contrasts to the existing literature on white women. Unlike the white middle-class women's friendships, Addie and Rebecca's relationship was not cultivated and nurtured in a separate women's world. It was part and parcel of the Black community and domestic networks that included women and men. Moreover, as Black women, Addie and Rebecca were subject to racial harassment and to employment and wage discrimination. Their opportunities were few and resources scarce. Although legally free, as Black women they did not have access to even the limited citizenship of white women. They began writing when four million Blacks were enslaved. A civil war divided the nation over, among other things, the status of Black Americans. In the face of wrenching debates that disputed the humanity of African Americans and a ravaging war over whether they could be owned as private property, Addie and Rebecca lived with great dignity, bravely commanding respect from the furthest reaches of their communities. . . .

We can interpret the practice of "bosom sex" in many ways; I suggest three. One alternative is that Addie and Rebecca were not romantic friends, but rather lesbian lovers for whom "bosom sex" was part of their sexuality. In agreement with others studying nineteenth-century sexuality, I find it inappropriate to label the relationship as lesbian. The term was not part of mid-nineteenth-century parlance and not part of the culture's consciousness. I am persuaded by John D'Emilio's argument that "lesbian" signifies an identity unique to twentieth-century industrial capitalism. A second possibility is that only Addie, Rebecca, and their coterie of lover/friends practiced "bosom sex," making it a feature of one small sub-culture. A third interpretation is that many or most romantic friends engaged in "bosom sex." Although scholarship has not yet unearthed explicit evidence, it is possible that women's silence about it reflects either its taken-for-granted nature or the customary sexual silence of the time. The casual references to bosoms throughout the letters of romantic friends could be further evidence of its commonality. The practice may have been viewed as natural, pleasurable, and an appropriate means of expressing affection for or attraction to another woman.

While other interpretations are possible, I think it is virtually certain that Addie, her white friend from Miss Porter's School, and Rebecca were not the only practitioners of "bosom sex." The case of Addie and Rebecca challenges the assumption in the literature on white women's romantic friendships that such relationships were socially acceptable because of their marked difference from heterosexual relationships. While Addie and Rebecca's family and friends did not endorse a same-gender partnership that excluded marriage, they accepted these women's partnership as similar to a heterosexual one. Perhaps white women's friendships were not accepted merely because they were presumed to be platonic. Understanding sexual relationships between women in the nineteenth century will always be a challenge, because of the centrality of texts as historical evidence, their unspoken assumptions, and their multiplicity of meanings. Assessing the pervasiveness of "bosom sex" necessitates re-examining the extant evidence with new eyes and continuing to search for more documents by both Black and white women.

Sexuality in Victorian Courtship and Marriage

KAREN LYSTRA

"Lie still and think of the Empire" is the wedding-night advice Queen Victoria was supposed to have given her daughter, thus representing the quintessential in Victorian repression and prudery. Among American Victorians, passionlessness in female sexuality has been characterized as the dominant ideology. It was an ideology propounded in ministerial and medical advice as well as in some feminist tracts, but it was not the ideal that guided men or women in the conduct of their private lives. Queen Victoria's daughters across the Atlantic did not take her advice to heart, if they heard it at all.

Middle-class American women gave no private indication that they believed in an ideal of female passionlessness. This does not mean that there was no sexual dysfunction among them, or that they had perfect sex lives by their standards or ours. But married women did not treat their sexual feelings as abnormalities. Many indicated that they accepted themselves as sexual beings. Individual personality factors influenced the way women expressed their physical desires, but it is clear that they did not consider themselves freaks, deviants, or even strange for having sexual needs or expressing sexual interest to men in *private.*

Married men showed no shock, horror, or even mild displeasure at their wives' physical interest. In fact, they seemed pleased by these private expressions of desire for them. There were surely passionless marriages, but passionlessness was not a dominant ideal within middle- to upper-middle-class American marriages. Moreover, romantically attached married men cared about their spouses' sexual responses. This did not mean that either husband or wife looked for identical sexual satisfaction. But under the spell of romantic love an ethic of mutuality seemed to operate in the Victorian bedroom. Nineteenth-century married men and women sometimes expressed a genuine interest in pleasing each other in physical as well as non-physical ways.

Although before marriage, Victorian sexuality was more ambiguous and potentially stressful, this should not be attributed to the belief in female passionlessness. Ironically, nineteenth-century couples might have found courtship less stressful if passionlessness had been a dominant Victorian courtship ideal. In fact, both men and women saw sexual desire as the natural physical accompaniment and distillation of romantic love. Some indeterminate level of sexual expression and satisfaction was acceptable in Victorian courtships when individuals were in love and the expectation of marriage was strong. Intercourse, however, was a physical boundary not to be crossed until after marriage. This was the crux of the courtship ambiguity. Sexual expression was approved as a symbol of love and typically accompanied nineteenth-century middle-class courtship. During a period in which love was intensively cultivated in a structure of privacy and minimal parental supervision, intercourse was supposedly postponed while some ambiguous level of erotic

expression symbolizing love was condoned. For some couples, this created few noticeable problems, but for others the tensions were tangible.

Nonetheless, married or unmarried, American Victorians recognized and
expressed sexual desire, interest, and passion. Even humor surrounded sexual exchanges between nineteenth-century Victorian couples. There were earthy sexual
comments by both sexes. Some women and men enjoyed the bawdiness of sexual
experience unvarnished by sentimental rhetoric. Moreover, Victorians seemed to
derive considerable pleasure from speaking of sex in private. Even the more reticent managed to convey that erotic activity was central to their view of male-
female relationships. But if sex could be respectably "raunchy" in Victorian
relationships, it could also be luxuriantly romantic. The mutual identification of
two people "in love" was often symbolized by sexuality itself. Under the right circumstances, sex might be viewed as a romantically inspired religious experience, a
sacrament of love. The latter was perhaps the most culturally significant meaning
attached to Victorian sexuality.

The fusion of love and sex, or rather the investment of sexuality with the
meanings of romantic love, may seem unremarkable. Yet the nineteenth-century
view of sex as the ultimate expression of love had remarkable cultural consequences. Imbued with romantic love, sex was seen as an act of self-disclosure, not
so much in the sense of revealing one's body as one's essential identity. Sex was
identified with the inner life and was perceived as part of the privileged revelation
of an "authentic" self. Properly sanctioned by love, sexual expressions were read
as symbolic communications of one's real and truest self, part of the hidden
essence of the individual. This was the most salient meaning of sex to American
Victorians. Thus any sexual behavior that was not the honest expression of an individual's "truest" self was deeply offensive to Victorian culture.

Historians have concluded, on the basis of public exhortations, that nineteenth-
century women downplayed their lower-status sexual/carnal side and emphasized
their higher-status spiritual/moral capacities. The implication is that the sexual was
at odds with the moral or spiritual in nineteenth-century culture, especially with
respect to women. This is a major stumbling block to understanding Victorian sexuality. Actually Victorians joined the sexual and the spiritual or moral in the concept
of true love. Romantic ideology bridged the gap between purity and sex for Victorian women as well as men. For example, one nineteenth-century adviser defined
true love as "Love in its truest, purest, highest form is that of strong, unselfish affection blended with desire—an honorable desire implanted by nature in the breast of
men and women and which is only to be condemned when it is perverted and seeks
gratification in forbidden ways." Sex could be sacred and sexuality might be spiritual, if affection were blended with desire.

In private discussions couples equated their love of one another with their sexual desire and pleasure. Desire was often cast as the sign and seal of romantic love.
The son of a Presbyterian minister pined for his wife during the separation necessi-
tated by his preparation for their move from Illinois to California: "When I lie
down at night my mind is filled with thoughts of you, not *bad* thoughts but I do so
long to have you beside me again and I find nothing to fill the vacant place in my
arms and my heart. Nothing which I can closely fold up to my heart and feel blest
in possessing. My dear wife you must come to me soon. I must have you with me."

An unmarried woman, Betsey Meyers, also employed the common physical metaphors of love: "Oh if you knew how mutch I love you, you would have no occasion to fear that I would ever break my promises, for if you are as constant to me as I am to you, those vowes which we have made, will never be broken untill Death seperates us for ever, for my mind is constantly on you, you are my though[t]s by day and my dreams by night, some times I fancy in my dreams that you are by my side, and your arm around my waist and my hand in yours, and that you again lead me back to our old haunts of love and pleasures but when I awake I find it but a dream and the dear delusion flyes from me, and I again sink back upon my bed and bedew the pillow with my tears. Oh that I had the wings of a dove that I might fly to your bosom and enjoy your embraces, but as I have not I must content myself as well as I can untill you come which I hope will be vary soon." This unmarried woman's yearnings for love were inextricably bound in memories of physical expression and pleasure.

Celebrating eleven years of marriage, Lincoln Clark so intertwined sexuality with love, bodily pleasure with the metaphors of the heart, that love and sex were inseparable: "What would all this world be if we could not pour out the heart to those who care for us, and who have given us evidence that they care for us by smiles in health and angelic devotion in sickness. I want to put my arms around your waist—and kiss you and pat your black hair and say how sweet! It would do me just as much good as it did ten years and a half ago—and I have the vanity to believe that the pleasure would not all be on one side, and this idea enhances it to me: you say you can not 'say' you love: well I will say it, and you may express it as you please—the thing itself is the *sunshine* of earth." Though the diction was uncommonly fine, the use of sex and physical desire as symbols of romantic love was not unusual. In private expression, romantic love and sex were intertwined in the everyday system of cultural meaning.

Although sexuality was romanticized, it could at the same time be funny and sensate. Alice Baldwin, a respectable army wife, was far from sentimental about her sexual feelings. Separated from her husband during his military campaigns against the Indians, she wrote after two years of marriage, "Oh how rejoiced I will be to see your dear face once more to feel myself clasped in your sheltering arms. Those dear strong arms have always loved and comforted me. . . ." A traditional woman in Victorian terms, Alice Baldwin conceived of her own role as a strictly subordinate one in relationship to men. Alice was no feminist, which makes it all the more fascinating when in 1870 she reported to her husband on a flashing she received in a train station: "There was a man showed his 'conflumux' to me at one station where we stopped in Illinois while I was looking out of the window. I thought he might have saved himself the trouble because I had seen one before. . . ." Her matter-of-fact reporting and earthy nonchalance were not what might be expected of a nineteenth-century lady if one read only certain medical and religious tracts on the female nature.

In later letters, she blatantly taunted her husband after learning that he had wavered between marrying her or another woman, Nellie Smith. "Aunt Mary," Alice wrote, "said you asked her advice about it you didnt know whether to marry her or me. Mr. Frank D. Baldwin, if I had known you was in such a quandry I would have settled the matter at once by giving you the mittens. I felt real queer and strange when I heard you had half a mind to marry another girl. I thought I held *undivided* you[r] love. Well its too late now. Nellie Smith dont know what she escaped. She would have been killed at one nab: of your old long Tom!!!" Alice unabashedly referred to "old long Tom," a nineteenth-century slang term for a penis.

Alice Baldwin's feigned irritation at her husband was expressed in a humorous if vulgar attack on the recently revealed rival for her husband's love. The nature of the attack, however, turned the ideology of the Victorian lady around, for instead of deriding her rival as sexually loose and lacking in purity, she ridiculed her competitor's sexual inadequacy. In doing so, she conveyed a wholesome confidence in her husband's sexual appetite and her own physical response. Allie Baldwin was frustrated by many aspects of her sex role, but not her role in the marriage bed. For example, she responded to a sexual tease by her husband with another of her own. "I got your letter last night . . . ," she wrote; "so you have been casting sly glances at Mrs. Sowters Bubbies [slang for breasts]. You ought to be ashamed. I intend to show mine to somebody before long." Alice Baldwin's thinking about sex roles was fairly mundane. Her audacity with regard to sex was *not* tied to any overt inclination toward social change and cultural innovation. . . .

Emily Lovell was a housewife who observed many of the traditional nineteenth-century sex-role distinctions. She worried over her children, fussed over her husband's clothes, and conceived of her role as a behind-the-scenes one. Yet as far as her sexuality was concerned, she expressed her passion openly and enthusiastically. She closed a Civil War letter by saying: "Now beloved—one of my heart—embrace me—and love me as I do desire—kiss me over and over again—while I say beloved one good bye—."

"Dearest," she wrote two days later, "I have come to the end of my paper and have left no room for a nice long and loving embrace—would that it were such—so darling come and let me put my arms around thee and beg you to write so often as you can—one more look of affection—one more kiss—and a few tears—I'll go—your own poor loving wife." She longed not just to be the object of his embraces and kisses but to be his passionate active lover: "I write you darling one a little messenger yesterday but on the arrival this morning of another song of Love, from thee, I could not help saying a few words . . . would that I could *kiss you all over*—and then *eat you up.* . . ." Whether Emily meant her last phrase as a euphemism for oral sex or simply as general slang for physical enjoyment, she was not after all reporting on an actual event. What is significant is the intent she expressed—the open avowal of her sexual desires and the unselfconscious way she characterized herself as a sexual aggressor. Her husband Mansfield was equally enthusiastic: "Kiss me dear sweetheart, a thousand warm and loving kisses, take me to your beautiful arms and let me for a while enjoy a heaven upon earth." He encouraged Emily to play the active sexual role and reveled in the prospect of *her* sexual aggression. This exchange took place after thirteen years of marriage.

While women could be enthusiastic, and occasionally forceful, in expressing their physical desire, masculine sexual imagery tended to be more aggressive than female sexual imagery. One man, courting a young woman in 1838, teased her about their physical relationship by asking if she would give him "one kiss" for the gift he was bringing her. He joked that even her mother would approve, then continued: "I have written so much about kissing, don't be afraid I shall devour you for then I should have no one to kiss." Albert Janin gave no such assurances to his lover: "May I confess that I am always wondering whether I shall find opportunities for folding you in my arms and covering you with kisses, as in the happy past." Janin warned his fiancée that she should strengthen her ribs because he intended to "fold you in my arms à la boa constricter."

John Marquis also expressed sexual longing and affection in a more aggressive masculine style. During his first year of marriage, while his wife was on a short visit away from home, John pined: "The nights are long and sad I do not sleep well without you . . . expect to be smothered to death when I see you." Anticipating a long-awaited reunion with his fiancée, James Hague also reflected an active masculine physical style: "Well, I hope I shall have my arms around the old girl herself before many weeks and if I don't behave with great impropriety then it will be for better reasons that I can now foresee. I'll just squeeze her and hug her, and kiss her forehead and eyes—yes I'll kiss them again and again, and when I have looked at them to my heart's content I'll kiss them again, and her cheeks and lips and throat, and I'll take liberties with her back hair and pull out her hair pins, and tousle and tumble her up generally until she boxes my old ears and goes up stairs to set herself straight. Won't that be nice, old Loveliness? glorified, exalted, ecstatic, radiant; and don't I wish I was there now. . . ."

It would be a mistake, however, to draw the contrast between the expressive styles of Victorian men and women too starkly. Individual differences, combined with the difficulties of untangling the subtle signals of sexual desire, suggest caution. There was no subtlety, moreover, in the next invitation by Alice Baldwin, "How are you this hot day? I am most roasted and my chemise sticks to me and the sweat runs down my legs and I suppose I smell very sweet, dont you wish you could be around just now." Alice was aware of her body and obviously enjoyed her erotic self. She savored her sexual appetite in this aggressively teasing invitation to her husband.

Sexual enthusiasm was expressed in the private correspondence of both married and unmarried nineteenth-century couples. With regard to sex, however, courtship exchanges differed from marital exchanges in at least one important respect. During courtship, correspondence offers glimpses of both physical and psychological tensions created by the traditional interdiction against premarital intercourse. Nevertheless, there seemed to be little ambiguity in middle- to upper-middle-class Victorian courtship over petting, caressing, kissing, and other non-genital forms of sexual interaction. In fact, the acceptable range of sexual conduct before marriage was wide. . . .

The physical aspects of nineteenth-century courtship induced tensions as well as satisfactions. The romantic view of sexuality had the potential to create confusion over the meaning of purity in courtship. Though the taboo against intercourse before marriage remained powerful, the belief that love might sanctify sex could sometimes blur the legitimate boundaries of erotic behavior before marriage. But this potential tension might also remain dormant in Victorian courtship. Women such as Eliza Trescot had no doubts determining or trouble maintaining her sense of legitimate sexual expression during courtship. She clearly felt that some avenues of physical expression were closed to her before marriage. But she promised Eldred [Simkins] that, once married, she would demonstrate her love: "Never mind, one of these days when I have a right to be 'that sweet name' I will lose my reserve and let my words as well as actions, show how very dear you are to me." She accepted the physical side of her love, but approved of its fullest expression only within the marriage vows. Nevertheless, outside matrimonial boundaries, she was willing to hold and be held by him, to touch and be touched. . . .

Mary Smith, more reserved about her sexual feelings than Eliza Trescot, had probably conducted a less physical courtship. She was less certain of the permissible range of sexual expression before marriage. Mary and her fiancé Samuel were also separated throughout most of their courtship. Apparently worried about her physical desires as the wedding day approached, Mary confessed: "though I would fain be all loveliness yet while I feel so much of evil rioting in my bosom how *can* I conceal it?" Mary appeared anxious to reveal her physical feelings to Samuel, a Baptist minister, but she was worried about the reception she might receive from him. She remarked that she preferred physical converse to letters, adding suggestively, "I might and probably should appear *still more* naughty yet I would rather even prefer that—for then I could disguise nothing—now much is repressed." Mary was a religious woman who lived in a world of high moral seriousness, yet she did not see herself as passionless. Her passion might be "naughty," and even "evil" before marriage, but she recognized it in herself and did not disown it. Respecting the "evil rioting" in her bosom, she asked Samuel: "how *can* I conceal it? I know not how, even if I could." She clearly wanted him to recognize her physical desires; perhaps she was even seeking reassurance that her sexual feelings were acceptable to him. Her statements reflect, however euphemistically, the strength of her sexual feelings and her need to express them in spite of her sense of moral restraint.

Samuel responded to her revelations with a characteristic didactic piety, telling her that he believed their recognition of the warfare between spirit and flesh was encouraging because it proved they were trying to live more spiritual and godly lives. Yet he urged her to be careful "because I tremble lest the cup of pleasure should be dashed from our lips before it is tasted." It seems unlikely that Samuel was referring simply to platonic love. Samuel hinted more than once at his physical interest in their relationship. He compared his relationship with God to his relationship with her: "The present has been truly an autumnal day. The fall of the leaf approaches. Well, we will fear neither change nor decay, if the encircling of the everlasting arms may only be our refuge. I long, my dear, for your presence with me. I need earthly soothers, as well as a friend in heaven." Obviously, Samuel hoped to be encircled by less everlasting arms.

As their wedding day approached, Samuel revealed: "I am looking forward, my dear, with anxious longing to the day of our union. The thought that it is so near unsettles my thoughts and almost wholly unfits me for the performance of any duty whatever." His unsettled thoughts rested upon the imminent "consummation" of their marital vows: "I cherish the hope that all will be joyously and happily, yea, and to our eternal joy and happiness, consummated."

Mary also anticipated the consummation of their wedding vows, using qualifiers that added parental overtones to her sexual meaning: "and might we not anticipate blessed results from the sweet union we are now so ardently longing to be consummated?" Many couples gave evidence of courtships full of sexual exploration and playful physicality. Mary and Samuel appear to have been satisfied with, or forced by separation to settle for, less physical intimacy than the nineteenth-century courtship ethos allowed.

But indications from Mary, less than two years later, were that her relationship to Samuel had been successful in all respects, including the physical. She teased him confidently: "You seem always prospered truly—even when you made choice of a *wife*. Well you have one that adores you, if you have nothing more—and if you have a score of wives, who would all give you as many sons apiece, you would not after all I think find among them all any more affection or much more enjoyment. What think you my beloved?" Mary had traveled to her family home to await the arrival of their second child, whom she described as a "love-token." Writing during this hiatus, she expressed a casual enthusiasm toward the sexual dimension of their life together: "I wish I could see you for one second—how delightful to have one sweet kiss—well we shall have a good number packed away and ready, when we meet."

Marriage was a significant sexual threshold for courting couples and inter-course was supposed to wait until they crossed over to the "other side." Some couples found this sexual boundary definite and relatively untroubling, while others were deeply vexed. Though it is virtually impossible to quantify such a subjective division, evidence suggests that the symbolic equation of sex and romantic love left Victorian courting couples vulnerable to tensions on the physical side of courtship. In middle- to upper-middle-class courtship romantic love was cultivated during a commonly unchaperoned period of premarital relations. Yet until marriage, physical consummation, justified by "the heart," was forbidden. Ironically, those most deeply devoted to the feelings of romantic love were expected to forgo what their own culture defined as concomitant physical expression. . . .

The unprecedented and unmatched decline in the native-born white birth rate in the nineteenth century combined with the evidence that passionlessness was not a dominant ideal much less a practice in middle-class romantic relationships suggests that sex was separated from procreation in the Victorian marriage. The idea . . . that abstinence was *the* Victorian choice of birth control is false. A number of birth control techniques were available to nineteenth-century couples who saw sex as something important in their lives outside of the desire to have children. While couples may have practiced intermittent abstinence in the form of the rhythm method or safe period in a woman's cycle, or abstinence may have resulted from physical disabilities or emotional estrangement, the predominant attitude of married couples in this study toward sex (within a continuum of course) was a positive and highly valued expression of love. . . .

In the nineteenth century the conception of female sexuality as vested in the woman herself gained credibility. Historians essentially agree that there was an increasing tilt (not a complete revolution) in the view of female sexuality away from something a woman's father owned, and then her husband, toward something that only she "possessed," but the trend has been to associate female control of sexuality with the Victorian woman's right to say "no" to her husband in the bedroom. Historians have argued that the emphasis on female control of sexuality often de-pended upon a rationale of negative trust: woman's sexual desire was thought to be "naturally" weaker than a man's. Therefore, husbands should wait upon their wives' physical needs. Denominated as "voluntary motherhood" by nineteenth-century feminists, women's right to say no in the bedroom was championed by the woman's movement as well as a host of public-spirited moral guardians. What has been less noticed, however, is that female sexuality was also conceived more positively within the meaning of romantic love. The recognition of women's right to sexual self-possession included the equally important right to say "yes." That is, Victorian women controlled their sexuality, not just on the basis of an image of themselves as sexless or passionless but on the grounds of their individuality. . . .

. . . In other words, when sex became romanticized, it became part of the act of self-expression over which each individual was sovereign. Romantic ideology gave women a rationale for treating sexual expression as part of themselves and as compatible with their spiritual, moral capacities. In fact, both men and women identified sex as a component of the romantic ideal of free and open communication and saw physical expression as part of the gift of self, indisputably owned by the woman, and not immoral (except for coition before marriage) if motivated by love. The romantic ideology of self-expression completely overshadowed the ideology of passionlessness in private life.

Sex was progressively separated from procreation through cultural values as well as birth control techniques. Historians have agreed upon the availability of douches, diaphragms, condoms, and the knowledge of the rhythm method and coitus interruptus in nineteenth-century America. This meant that a couple could, if motivated, rely upon something other than female passionlessness to restrict the size of their families. This is not to say that evidence of women who conceived of themselves as passionless cannot be found, nor is it meant to imply that women did not fear pregnancy. . . . Nonetheless, Victorian sexual relationships could be intensely erotic with no necessary sense of female sexuality as unnatural or impure when separated from reproduction.

Furthermore, men could cooperate in the family limitation process. While urging his wife to come to Washington, where he was serving a term in Congress, Lincoln Clark exclaimed, "How much I want to see you. *Cautious!* How are your *lady conditions?*—safe or dangerous—tell me. . . ." Lincoln was inquiring about her period and appears worried about the effectiveness of their birth control practices: "I feared you had some such trouble as you mention—I think it must be the result of exposure and cold at Springfield—that it can be the existence of a 'condition' I do not believe—there has been in my opinion no *adequate cause;* neither do I believe it to be the result of age—you had best lose no time in consulting Dr. Collins—you might pay severely for delay or false modesty." Apparently Julia had not menstruated since they last slept together, and she was afraid of another pregnancy. Though Lincoln's use of "*adequate cause*" (which he underlined) remains ambiguous, other exchanges indicate he was probably defending some form of birth control he or they had used during their last sexual encounter.

For example, after a visit home, Lincoln returned to Washington and wrote: "How is your special lady health? No harm I hope." Five months later he inquired: "Hope your health is good—How is that? Are you in any danger?—Will you not be a good, healthy, fat merry old Lady after a while? Come as soon as you can." Though the Clarks were not always confident of the success of their birth control efforts, he was committed to family limitation. . . .

Not all nineteenth-century couples practiced family planning, however. Mary and Elkanah Walker seem to have left the size and spacing of their family to

"God's will." Mary commented in her diary: "I find my children occupy so much of my time that if their maker should see fit to withhold from me any more till they require less of my time and attentions I think I shall at least be reconciled to such an allotment." By contrast, a friend of Augusta Hallock wrote about her first baby, "Twas not a mistake Gusta, but because we wanted one, dont let anyone see this letter because as you say I am going to write just as I would talk, I have got a man that is pretty well posted about such affairs. . . ." This young mother wanted her friend to know that her pregnancy was *not* an accident. This is a striking disclaimer because it is based upon a normative assumption, at least between these two friends, of family limitation in marriage.

FURTHER READING

Katy Coyle and Nadiene Van Dyke, "Sex, Smashing and Storyville in Turn-of-the-Century New Orleans," in John Howard, ed., *Carrying On in the Lesbian and Gay South* (1997), 54–72.

Rebecca McDowell Craver, *The Impact of Intimacy: Mexican-Anglo Intermarriage in New Mexico: 1821–1846* (1982).

Marylynne Diggs, "Romantic Friends or a 'Different Race of Creatures'? The Representation of Lesbian Pathology in Nineteenth-Century America," *Feminist Studies* 21 (1995): 317–340.

Martin Duberman, "'Writhing Bedfellows' in Antebellum South Carolina: Historical Interpretation and the Politics of Evidence," in Martin Duberman et al., eds., *Hidden from History* (1989), 153–168.

Lisa Duggan, "The Trials of Alice Mitchell: Sensationalism, Sexology, and the Lesbian Subject in Turn-of-the-Century America," *Signs* 18 (1993): 791–811.

Lillian Faderman, *Surpassing the Love of Men* (1981).

John Donald Gustav-Wrathall, *Take the Young Stranger by the Hand: Same-Sex Relations and the YMCA* (1998).

Lisa J. Lindquist, "Images of Alice: Gender, Deviancy, and a Love Murder in Memphis," *Journal of the History of Sexuality* 6 (1995): 30–61.

Robert K. Martin, "Knights-Errant and Gothic Seducers: The Representation of Male Friendship in Mid-Nineteenth-Century America," in Martin Duberman et al., eds., *Hidden from History* (1989).

D. Michael Quinn, "Male-Male Intimacy among Nineteenth-Century Mormons: A Case Study," *Dialogue: A Journal of Mormon Thought* 28 (1995): 105–128.

Ellen Rothman, *Hands and Hearts: A History of Courtship in America* (1984).

E. Anthony Rotundo, "Romantic Friendship: Male Intimacy and Middle-Class Youth in the Northern United States, 1800–1900," *Journal of Social History* 23 (1989): 1–25.

Leila Rupp, *A Desired Past: A Short History of Same-Sex Love in America* (1999).

Nancy Sahli, "Smashing: Women's Relationships before the Fall," *Chrysalis* 6 (1979): 17–27.

San Francisco Lesbian and Gay History Project, "'She Even Chewed Tobacco': A Pictorial Narrative of Passing Women in America," in Martin Duberman et al., eds., *Hidden from History* (1989), 183–194.

Steven Seidman, "The Power of Desire and the Danger of Pleasure: Victorian Sexuality Reconsidered," *Journal of Social History* 23 (Fall 1990): 47–67.

Carroll Smith-Rosenberg, *Disorderly Conduct: Visions of Gender in Victorian America* (1985).

Siobhan Somerville, "Scientific Racism and the Emergence of the Homosexual Body," *Journal of the History of Sexuality* 5 (1994): 243–266.

Martha Vicinus, "'They Wonder to Which Sex I Belong': The Historical Roots of the Modern Lesbian Identity," *Feminist Studies* 18 (1992); 467–497.

Free Love, Free Speech, and Sex Censorship

Public controversy about sexuality during the late nineteenth century centered on sexually explicit language and obscenity. Many issues were debated: To what extent should sexual language be used in public? Is frank discussion of sexuality beneficial or harmful, and to whom? What role, if any, should the government play in regulating sexual speech?

The participants on both sides of this debate were middle-class reformers who hoped to elevate sexuality and to eliminate the double standard and prostitution. Some considered sexual speech morally corrupting and sought to suppress it by making obscenity a criminal offense. Leading the campaign was Anthony Comstock, who founded the New York Society for the Suppression of Vice in 1872. This organization seized sexually explicit books and pamphlets, photographs, and newspapers advertising condoms and abortifacient drugs; Comstock's attack extended to children's literature and Walt Whitman's Leaves of Grass. *Anti-vice crusaders' lobbying led Congress in 1873 to pass the Postal Act, often called the Comstock Act, which prohibited Americans from sending obscene material through the U.S. mail. Comstock was appointed Postal Inspector and enforced the law vigorously.*

Advertisements for photographs of naked women and men engaged in sexual acts, pornographic literature, and sexual devices appeared frequently in print. Patent medicine manufacturers and physicians wooed customers with promises of quick, confidential cures for unwanted pregnancies, sexually transmitted diseases, and impotence. Published in newspapers and even family-oriented magazines, such ads reveal widely held conceptions of male and female sexuality and common sexual concerns. Their continued appearance attests to the reading public's demand for sexual information.

Comstock interpreted the obscenity law broadly, prosecuting not only publishers of pornography but also sex education advocates. Opposing sexual prudery were women and men who believed open discussion of sexual matters was essential to personal and social health. Ranging from birth control supporters to sex radicals who called themselves "Free Lovers," they attacked the hypocrisy of Victorian society. Open and broad discussion of the body, sexuality, personal relationships, and social institutions, they believed, would lead to moral improvement.

In the 1870s, a widely discussed sex scandal intensified this debate. Victoria Woodhull and her sister, Tennessee Claflin, published rumors that Henry Ward

Beecher, a prominent Protestant minister (and brother of author Harriet Beecher Stowe), had had an adulterous affair with parishioner Elizabeth Tilton, whose husband Theodore was a leading Republican. The "Beecher-Tilton scandal" became the focus of national media attention. Even those who believed the charges against Beecher attacked Woodhull for publishing them. This experience led Victoria Woodhull and other sex radicals to defend free speech and criticize sexual hypocrisy even more openly than before.

Whose interests were served by the censorship of sexual speech? What do the beliefs of the law's proponents and opponents tell us about ways of conceiving of sexuality in the late nineteenth century?

D O C U M E N T S

These advertisements for sexual images and literature appeared from the 1860s through the 1890s in the *National Police Gazette* (Document 1), which published sensational stories of crime and titillating tales of sexual adventure for male readers. Often written in euphemistic language, these ads addressed widely felt sexual anxieties. Although abortion was illegal, drugs to induce miscarriage were also advertised. In Document 2, Dr. Ely Van De Warker, writing in 1873, described the methods of sale and advised doctors on how to detect women's use of these preparations. Such advertising fueled Anthony Comstock's anti-vice campaign. In *Traps for the Young* (Document 3), he explained its rationale: sexually explicit literature and images arouse lust, which then leads inexorably to immoral sexual acts, crime, and social decay. In his view, the protection of youth justified state intervention limiting free speech.

Radical sex reformers challenged Comstock's perspective during the 1870s. Victoria C. Woodhull, in a speech to "fifteen thousand people" in 1873 (Document 4), compared popular fears of sex reform to scarecrows—straw men set up to silence public discussion. She exposed sexual hypocrisy, criticized marriage laws, and espoused free love, or the voluntary union of women and men. Free-love advocate Ezra H. Heywood was prosecuted for publishing *Cupid's Yoke;* the passages selected in Document 5 include those marked by the censor and prosecutor as "obscene and indecent." The Heywoods' sexual radicalism, like that of Victoria C. Woodhull, was rooted in the philosophical ideal of individual autonomy and an anarchistic faith in the capacity of men and women to exercise self-control without external constraint.

1. *National Police Gazette* Advertisements for Sexual Literature and Devices, 1867, 1886, 1893

SAMARITAN'S GIFT!
The most Certain Remedy ever Used!!
"YES, A POSITIVE CURE"
FOR GONORRHOEA, GLEET, STRICTURES, &c. . . .
ONLY TEN PILLS TO BE TAKEN TO EFFECT A CURE.
They are entirely vegetable, having no smell, nor any permanent taste . . .
Cures in from two to four days, and recent cases in "twenty-four hours."

National Police Gazette, April 13, 1867, 4; October 9, 1886, 14–15; September 2, 1893, 15.

No exposure, no trouble, no change, whatever.

Let those who have despaired of being cured, or who have been gorged with sickening and disgusting drugs, at once use the Samaritan's Gift. . . .

For Syphilis or Venereal Diseases, the Samaritan's Root and Herb Juices is the most potent, certain and effectual remedy ever prescribed. It reaches and eradicates every particle of the venereal poison. Will remove every vestigate of impurities from the system, as well as all the bad effects of mercury. . . .

Important to Females.
DR. CHEESEMAN'S PILLS.

The combination of ingredients in these Pills is the result of a long and extensive practice. They are mild in their operation, and cannot do harm to the most delicate; certain in correcting all irregularities, Painful Menstruations, removing all obstructions, whether from cold or otherwise. . . .

DR. CHEESEMAN'S PILLS.

Have been a Standard Remedy for over thirty years, and are the most effectual one ever known for all the complaints peculiar to Females. To all classes they are invaluable, inducing, with certainty, periodical regularity. They are known to thousands, who have used them at different periods throughout the country, having the sanction of some of the most eminent physicians in America. . . .

[April 13, 1867, p. 4]

FRENCH!

Adventures of a French doctor with his female patients—a rare book—166 pages of fancy reading, choice tid bits and 10 male and female illustrations. By mail, well sealed, 50 cents: 3 books same nature, all different, for $1. Mail or express. . . .

SPORTING MEN

HUSH! You Can Get Them. Gents only.

Full pack, 53 Genuine Transparent Cards. "Hold to Light;" secreted views; male and female; old-timers. Mailed secure. 50¢. per pack: 2 packs, 90¢.

The Magic Revealer, watch charm, ivory, opera glass, magnifies 1,000 times, racy scenes from nature, sample 25¢., 3 different 50¢.; 1 doz. $1.40; stamps taken.

20 Spicy Photos from nature; pretty French girls rich and rare, in interesting positions, only 25¢.

Cabinets [photographs]! Old-timers (in act), highly colored, 3 best, 25¢.

RUBBER ARTICLE for **Gents,** 25¢. each; 3 for 50¢.

All of the above goods **complete,** for a **$1** bill.

[October 9, 1886, pp. 14–15]

SEXUAL POWER

Positively and Permanently Restored in 2 to 10 days, effects in 2 hours; almost immediate relief. No nauseating drugs, minerals, pills or poisons, but the delicious MEXICAN CONFECTION, composed of fruits, herbs and plants. The most POWERFUL tonic known. Restores the Vigor, Snap and Health of youth. Sealed Book free, giving full particulars. . . .

SELF-ABUSE

Cured.   Parts Enlarged.   FREE Remedy.

A victim of youthful errors causing Emisions, Small Parts, Lost Manhood, Varicocele, Nervous Debility, etc., will send (sealed) FREE to all fellow-sufferers a simple means of certain self-cure which he discovered after trying in vain all known remedies. . . .

[September 2, 1893, p. 15]

2. Dr. Ely Van De Warker Discusses the Sale of Abortifacient Drugs, 1873

The sale of these dangerous preparations [abortifacients] is enormous, so far as I am able to form a conclusion. The sale is increasing. Every facility is afforded for the ready sale of these drugs. The daily press accepts the advertisements of the proprietors of these articles, and such are the profits arising from the sales that they are able to purchase the most prominent and expensive places in the papers for the pernicious notices. It is not uncommon to find their notices published in the advertising department of what are regarded as first-class magazines. And, to the shame of the religious community be it written, it is very common to find these advertisements occupying prominent places in so-called religious journals. Every school-girl knows the meaning and intent of these advertisements. Nor is this the worst: almost every woman believes in the power of advertised pills or drops to accomplish the end for which they are recommended. These wares are unblushingly exposed for sale on the shelves of drug-stores, and are as boldly asked for.

Here is a trade which, without stretching a single existing law, may be called illegal and illicit, carried on in open daylight, in the full knowledge of this newspaper-reading public. It is almost impossible to say that women make a misapplication of the wording of these advertisements. An able and intelligent editor once said to me that they carefully excluded all advertisements which seemed to be of a criminal nature. As the term "female irregularity" is invariably interpreted, it means that a woman is irregular when her courses fail to appear, no matter what the cause of the interruption; and thus all "irregularities" being removed, as advertised by these nostrums, these advertisements never fail of being as direct a bid for the attention of the pregnant woman, as those advertisements are which embody a caution for the lady in a "delicate situation" not to use them. . . .

. . . It is an axiom among business-men, that advertising is the life of business, and surely advertising is the life of this trade. Take away from the makers of these demoralizing compounds their facilities for reaching the public notice, and their wares will not be on the shelves of the retail druggist. This prostitution of the great lever of public education and progress is a sacrilege which demands immediate atonement. Upon the shoulders of the law-makers rest many sins of the law-breakers. If, through want of wholesome laws, or defects in existing statutes, an article which has a malignant influence upon the morals of the community is openly sold, it is sure to find criminal purchasers. In view of the extent of this trade, I am

Ely Van de Warker, "The Criminal Use of Proprietary or Advertised Nostrums," *New York Medical Journal* 17 (1873): 23–28, 33–34.

forced to believe that in relation to this crime there exists a moral obliquity in all ranks of native-born society. . . .

The chief source of danger lies not in the abortion, but in the use of drugs, which are of themselves fatal poisons. Savin, tansy, and rue, are examples of drugs which, even when taken with care, are liable to jeopardize the woman's life, without disturbing the contents of the womb. These drugs may also be named as potent abortifacients when their use is persevered in with small doses. . . .

I know many married women who have gone years without the birth of mature children, who resort habitually to some one of the many advertised nostrums with as much confidence of "coming around" as if they repaired to the shop of the professional abortionist. I could detail several cases of this kind, if absolute proof of the dangerous nature of these compounds were necessary. I think but few medical men would be inclined to deny any power, as abortifacients, to these mixtures. It must be borne in mind that, when these compounds are used with criminal intent, they are resorted to in a desperate emergency, and with a reckless disregard for personal safety. Under these circumstances, any thoroughly purgative drug might prove an efficient abortifacient; persistence in the use and excess in the dose being the conditions necessary. . . .

In the morbid anxiety for relief from their unpleasant burden, many women take enormous doses of these mixtures. One case came to my knowledge, in which a young woman took repeatedly doses of fifteen pills of the kind called "Sir James Clark's," in her desperate anxiety. The only result was hypercatharsis and extreme prostration, and months after her health was not restored. In this case no pregnancy existed. It is in this tendency to overdose, rather than underdose, that the chief power of these mixtures, as fœticidal agents, lies. . . . One specimen of an extensively-advertised mixture of what is known as "periodical drops" was given me by a married lady who had taken two teaspoonfuls, and was obliged to desist because of its irritating effects upon the stomach. . . . Another preparation, also well known, and of which there are extensive sales, is composed mainly of oils dissolved in alcohol, and in which a futile attempt is made to mask the odor and color of oil of tansy by wintergreen and coloring-matter. While these two are the most dangerous of the many mixtures I have seen, there are others which are simply inert. . . . How many more of the scores of these nostrums, which have been advertised and sold for the purpose of correcting "female irregularities," are pure humbugs, in their composition, it is impossible to say. The term "humbug" here must be used in an extenuating sense; for the fact that these inert mixtures are sold to those with a criminal intent, and are purposely made innocuous, is, strange to say, an evidence of honesty not yet wholly destroyed. If the question is asked to what extent the use of these advertised preparations is actually dangerous to life, I must say that, so far as my observation goes, all of them examined by me, with the exception of the two already mentioned, are free from any direct poisonous action upon the human system. But, their effects upon the health are most disastrous. Hæmorrhoids, nervous prostration, debility, a persistent gastric and intestinal irritation, and irritation of the bladder, are results which I believe uniformly follow their criminal use. . . .

The law passed in 1868, to check the sale of obscene publications and prints, relates also to obscene advertisements of patent medicines; but would not prevent the publication of advertisements of nostrums calculated to correct "female irregularities," as these advertisements are carefully worded, and could in no sense be called obscene. Yet a trade is permitted in a class of nostrums the very advertisement of which, no matter how carefully and delicately worded, must have a very injurious effect upon the minds of both sexes. One of the most dangerous of these moral effects is the result of the open manner in which the sale of these nostrums is carried on, and the character of the magazines and newspapers which publish the advertisements. To suppress the advertisement, either in newspapers, or by circulars or handbills, of any drug or mixture which is claimed to act as an emmenagogue, or to correct menstrual irregularity, of whatever name or nature, must be as legitimate a matter for corrective legislation as the liquor-traffic, or any other evil, the suppression of which is deemed for the good of society.

In offering, therefore, for the consideration of the Medico-Legal Society, an amendment to the law of 1868, I do so with great diffidence as to the legal part of the remedy, but not with lessened faith that the enactment of such an amendment, and its rigid enforcement, would be a lasting measure for the correction of public morality.

3. Anthony Comstock Condemns Obscene Literature, 1883

Each birth begins a history. The pages are filled out, one by one, by the records of daily life. The mind is the source of action. Thoughts are the aliment upon which it feeds. We assimilate what we read. The pages of printed matter become our companions. Memory unites them indissolubly, so that, unlike an enemy, we cannot get away from them. They are constant attendants to quicken thought and influence action.

Good reading refines, elevates, ennobles, and stimulates the ambition to lofty purposes. It points upward. Evil reading debases, degrades, perverts, and turns away from lofty aims to follow examples of corruption and criminality.

This book is designed to awaken thought upon the subject of *Evil Reading,* and to expose to the minds of parents, teachers, guardians, and pastors, some of the mighty forces for evil that are to-day exerting a controlling influence over the young. There is a shameful recklessness in many homes as to what the children read.

The community is cursed by pernicious literature. Ignorance as to its debasing character in numerous instances, and an indifference that is disgraceful in others, tolerate and sanction this evil.

Parents send their beloved children to school, and text-books are placed in their hands, while lesson after lesson and precept after precept are drilled into them. But through criminal indifference to other reading for the children than their text-books, the grand possibilities locked up in the future of every child, if kept pure, and all the appetites and passions controlled, are often circumscribed and defeated at its threshold of life. This book is a plea for the moral purity of children. It is an appeal for greater watchfulness on the part of those whose duty it is to think, act, and speak for that very large portion in the community who have neither intellect nor judgment to decide what is wisest and best for themselves. It brings to parents the question of their responsibility for the future welfare of their offspring.

Anthony Comstock, *Traps for the Young* (New York: Funk & Wagnalls, 1883), reprint ed. Robert Bremner (Cambridge: Harvard University Press, 1967), 5–6, 132.

If a contagious disease be imported to these shores in some ship, at once the vessel and her passengers are quarantined. The port is promptly closed to the disease. The agent that brings it is estopped from entering the harbor until the contagion has been removed. It is the author's purpose to send a message in advance to parents, so that they may avert from their homes a worse evil than yellow fever or small-pox. Read the facts, and let them speak words of warning.

The author, during an experience of nearly eleven years, has seen the effects of the[se] evils. . . . If strong language is used, it is because no other can do the subject justice.

This work represents facts as they are found to exist. If it shall be the means of arousing parents as to what their children read, of checking evil reading among the young, or of awakening a public sentiment against the prevailing wickedness of the day, the writer will be content. . . .

Because men will deny, scoff, and curse is no reason why these truths should not be laid before the minds of thinking men and women. . . .

Our youth are in danger; mentally and morally they are cursed by a literature that is a disgrace to the nineteenth century. The spirit of evil environs them.

Let no man be henceforth indifferent. Read, reflect, act. . . .

This moral vulture [obscene literature] steals upon our youth in the home, school, and college, silently striking its terrible talons into their vitals, and forcibly bearing them away on hideous wings to shame and death. Like a cancer, it fastens itself upon the imagination, and sends down into the future life thousands of roots, poisoning the nature, enervating the system, destroying self-respect, fettering the will-power, defiling the mind, corrupting the thoughts, leading to secret practices of most foul and revolting character, until the victim tires of life, and existence is scarcely endurable. It sears the conscience, hardens the heart, and damns the soul. It leads to lust and lust breeds unhallowed living, and sinks man, made in the image of God, below the level of the beasts. There is no force at work in the community more insidious, more constant in its demands, or more powerful and far-reaching than lust. *It is the constant companion of all other crimes.* It is honeycombing society. Like a frightful monster, it stands peering over the sleeping child, to catch its first thoughts on awakening. This is especially true where the eye of youth has been defiled with the scenes of lasciviousness in the weekly criminal papers, or by their offsprings, obscene books and pictures. The peace of the family is wrecked, homes desolated, and society degraded, while it curses more and more each generation born into the world. . . .

4. Victoria C. Woodhull Denounces "The Scare-Crows of Sexual Slavery," 1873

My Brothers and Sisters.—I am going to tell you some plain truths to-night. I know I shall not please all your ears. I value the good opinion of you all, but I value the truth more, and if to gain the former I must withhold one iota of the latter I shall fail in securing it. Your good opinion I crave, for I feel that you are my friends—friends to

Victoria C. Woodhull, "The Scare-Crows of Sexual Slavery," *Woodhull and Claflin's Weekly,* September 27, 1873, 3–7, 14.

the great human race, and he or she who is this, though they hate me with a deadly hatred, is my friend; but public opinion I stamp in the mud. . . . I will speak the truth, I will be heard; but you may kill me afterward if you will. I have but one sentiment in my soul, and that is to do what in me lies to lift up the down-trodden and enslaved of earth, and to inaugurate equality and happiness in the world. I have no kindred, less than the human race, who demand or can have service of me. My life is dedicated to this work, and I come to you to speak such words as will make your souls sink in horror and your curses to rest upon yourselves, that you have so long quietly permitted these things to go on unrebuked. I would, if it were possible, wring from you the declaration that you would know no rest again until these wrongs be righted. It must come to this. The world is to be made free and beautiful, and happy because so, and methinks I can see in the not distant future, a time when misery and heartaches and poverty and all unhappiness shall be banished the earth, and the entire human family, both in earth and spirit life, fully and harmoniously united, singing the glad songs of the redeemed. But before this can be, other and terrible things must be. . . .

If a stranger visit the farming districts of the New England States in the month of June, he will observe in many newly-planted corn-fields the most hideous-looking objects, fashioned after the human form. . . .

But now observe upon what the efficiency of these men of straw depends. There they stand motionless, with not so much as the power to raise a hand for harm or good; but the crows, having just sense enough to see in them the resemblance to their great enemy—man—carefully avoid coming within their domain; and thus through ignorance is the young corn saved.

But scare-crows are found in other than corn fields, and for other purposes than to save young corn. . . .

[It is] the social field, whose scare-crows it is our special province at this time to consider. I know them all to be "men of straw" merely, that the lightest puff, the slightest breath of truth will topple over and expose to the world, if it will but look on them as they fall. . . .

. . . The enemy invade the fields where we have sown the seeds of social reform, which are just beginning to make its withered and whitened surface look green again, and on our ground erect these scare-crows to prevent the crows, the ignorant among people, from coming to partake of the feast of gladness that is here spread. . . .

But what is all this about? Well, it is a part of the contest between despotism and freedom. . . .

Freedom, in general terms, means simply this: that each and every individual has the right in his or her own proper person to make such use of any or all his powers and capacities as he or she may elect to do. Anything less than this is not freedom— it is restriction, and restriction exercised by any person or aggregate of persons over another person is despotism, but the rule of social order must be either freedom or despotism: it cannot be a mixture of both. . . .

. . . "[B]ut you know society must protect itself, must regulate things in some way, or else what would become of us all?"

Now, this is just the point, Mr. Objector. It is simply none of your business what other people do; nor any of the business of society what any of its members do, unless they interfere with somebody else without his or her consent. . . . If freedom be a right possessed by all individuals, it cannot matter what use may be made of it. It must be adopted as the basic principle, and be assured that the results will take care of themselves. Having adopted freedom as opposed to despotism, all its logical deductions are also adopted. It is impossible that anything founded on truth should result in error. If the foundation be right the structure built upon it will not fall from any basic defects.

"But," replies the objector, "I cannot understand about this business. If there be no law to compel people to live together, everything will be in confusion, the family will be broken up; and this is the safeguard of society, morality and everything else that is good and pure. Everything will go to the bad directly if it be not maintained by all the safeguards that can be thrown around it. No! no! It will never do to break up the family."

And thus [another] scare-crow is elevated to be in turn demolished. To begin, we deny in toto everything you have said. The very safeguards that you have thrown around the family to make it pure and holy have made instead, a community of little hot hells, in which the two principals torment each other until one or the other gives up the contest, and by which the seeds of devilism are sown in all the children who may unfortunately for themselves and society, result. These safeguards to virtue and morality have made almost every wife a prostitute and every husband a sexual monster, and compel them both against their better natures, to continually go from bad to worse.

Compel people to live together, would you? Of all the monstrous propositions, this is the most monstrous. As a theory, it is absurd enough; but as a practice it is simply revolting infernalism. Even the condition of prostitutes, of which there is so much pretended commiseration, is to be preferred to this! They have the right to refuse to cohabit when they choose; but the poor wife is denied even this. She must submit or take a thrashing, perhaps! . . .

. . . [I]n the new social order of society, women will be individually independent of men for support. From the beginning it will be known that they are not to be educated as sexual slaves for man, merely. In place of this, it will be well understood that no man owes them anything, and that all their intercourse will be governed by a maxim of equivalents in love. It may be necessary to inform men, but it is not to inform women, that in such conditions there will be no undesired pregnancy; whereas, now, four-fifths of the children who are born are unwelcomed.

Next, when a woman becomes pregnant, it will be held immediately that she is laboring for society in the fact that she is to replenish its natural decrease. She will become the especial care of society and, while she is performing this sacred duty, be paid the highest wages received by any class, and be treated accordingly during the entire period of gestation and lactation, when the fruit of her labor will of right belong to society and she return to her common industrial pursuits. . . .

We have not yet disposed of all the scare-crows, and the next one that is erected to frighten the people, of freedom, is license—a most terrible spectre indeed, one from which the multitude falls back in dismay, almost convinced that it is impossible to discover freedom where this monster stands guard over the way. This monster assumes, if all restriction to liberty be removed, that license is thereby granted to everybody to do all sorts of bad things, and that a great many people will immediately proceed to do all these bad things.

First of all, every woman, except those of our household, will incontinently go to the bad, indulging in the most outrageous extremes of all sorts of debauchery;

while the men, everybody excepting "ourselves" of course, will also incontinently proceed to commit rape upon every woman who is so unfortunate as to fall in their way. Age of either extreme will fail to command respect when men are free, and terror and horror will reign triumphant. So much for the assumptions.

But hold, dear sir. Are you not making yourself just a little r[i]diculous? Did you not say that all the women would immediately rush into the arms of every man they should meet, let it be in the street, in the car or wherever else; that even negroes would not escape the mad debauch of white women? Now observe. If this be so, upon whom are these outrages, by men, to be committed? Do you not see if every woman is of her own accord to rush to debauchery, that it will be entirely unnecessary for men to resort to any sort of force whatever, or even to resort to persuasion. A splendid commentary on woman, indeed. . . .

. . . All the laws that can be made regarding sex, and be in harmony with the general theory, maintained in everything else, are such as would punish sexual intercourse obtained by force—in other words, rape; and this is the end of the whole question. . . .

License in love where consent is made a necessary qualification, by the guarantee of freedom to women to refuse, if they will, is simply an absurdity. . . .

. . . Marriage licenses sexuality, while nothing else does; and the horrors that are practiced under this license, are simply demoniacal; almost too horrible to be even thought of without shuddering, how much more so to relate! There is nothing else but marriage that licenses a man to debauch a woman against her will. There is no sexual license except in marriage.

But those who would save this institution by force, having attempted to defend it, and thereby having invited us to the contest, we must not hesitate to drag from their hiding-places the terrific skeletons that marriage has left in almost every household; and it must be expected that it will be done mercilessly. . . . I have declared relentless warfare against it. . . .

Going a little backward to the early days of abolitionism, it is found that the same system of warfare that is now proposed was waged by the heroes of that freedom. They not only attacked slavery upon the question of abstract right, but they also attacked it in the concrete, in its practices. Individual instances of cruelty, as well as the general tendency of the system, were pointed out and depicted with all the terrible effect of truth. Individual offenders were compelled into the light and held up to public detestation, and were made a by-word to the fullest possible extent. . . .

Now through just such experiences have the holders of sexual slaves got to be compelled. All the horrors of this slavery will have to be dragged to the light, and whenever individual offenders can be caught they must be exposed. All this may be seemingly hard; nevertheless it is the only method by which the atrocities to which the system has given birth, can be unearthed, and its own foundation shattered. Many are the tales of horror and brutal violence that have been related of negro slavery, where the lash of the driver was depicted until their hearers almost felt its stings in their own flesh, and almost the red streams flowing down their own backs, and these appealed to the souls of men and women until they were ready to do whatever was needed to destroy a monster that could cause such suffering to a single human being. But I am fully convinced that all the suffering of all the negro slaves combined, is as nothing in comparison to that which women, as a whole, suffer. . . .

It is an unpleasant thing to say that women, in many senses, are as much slaves as were the negroes, but if it be true, ought it not to be said? I say, a thousand times, yes! And when the slavery to which they are subjected is compared to that which the negro endured, the demand for its consideration increases again, still a thousand times more.

Perhaps it may be denied that women are slaves, sexually, sold and delivered to man. But I tell you, as a class, that they are, and the conclusion cannot be escaped. Let me convince all doubters of this. Stand before me, all ye married women, and tell me how many of you would remain mistresses of your husbands' homes if you should refuse to cohabit sexually with them? Answer ye this, and then tell me that ye are free, if ye can! I tell ye that you are the sexual slaves of your husbands, bound by as terrible bonds to serve them sexually as ever a negro was bound to serve his owner, physically; and if you don't quite believe it, go home and endeavor to assert your freedom, and see to what it will lead! You may not be made to feel the inevitable lash that followed rebellion on the part of the negro, but even this is not certain; yet lashes of some sort will surely be dealt. Refuse to yield to the sexual demands of your legal master, and ten to one he will turn you into the street, or in lieu of this, perhaps, give you personal violence, even to compelling you to submit by force. . . .

. . . I know what it is to be both [a labor slave and a sexual slave]. I have traveled the icy pavements of New York in mid-winter, seeking employment, with nothing on my feet except an old pair of india-rubber shoes, and a common calico dress only to cover my body, while the man who called me wife and who made me his sexual slave, spent his money upon other women. I am not speaking whereof I know not. My case may be thought an extreme one, but I know of thousands even worse. Then tell me I shall not have the right to denounce this damned system! Tell me I shall be sent to Sing Sing if I dare expose these things! Open your Sing Sings a thousand times, but none of their terrors shall stop a single word. I will tell the world, so long as I have a tongue and the strength to move it, of all the infernal misery hidden behind this horrible thing called marriage. . . .

Would to Heaven I could thunder these facts forth until women should be moved by a comprehension of the low degradation to which they have fallen, to open rebellion; until they should rise *en masse* and declare themselves free, resisting all sexual subjection, and utterly refusing to yield their bodies up to man, until they shall grant them perfect freedom. . . .

Go preach this doctrine, then, ye who have the strength and the moral courage: No more sexual intercourse for men who do not fully consent that all women shall be free, and who do not besides this, also join the standard of the rebellion. It matters not if you be wife or not, raise your voice for your suffering sex, let the consequences to yourself be what they may. They say I have come to break up the family; I say amen to that with all my heart. I hope I may break up every family in the world that exists by virtue of sexual slavery, and I feel that the smiles of angels, the smiles of those who have gone on before, who suffered here what I have suffered and what thousands are suffering, will give me strength to brave all opposition, and to stand even upon the scaffold, if need be, that my sisters all over the world may be emancipated, may rise from slavery to the full dignity of womanhood.

5. Ezra Heywood Advocates Sexual Self-Government, 1878

Love, in its dual manifestations, implies agreement, he who loves and she who re-
ciprocates his feeling therein binding themselves, neither to hurt the other, nor
evade any moral or pecuniary obligation which the incarnate fruits of their passion
may present. When a man says of a substantial girl, "She suits me"—that is, she
would be to him a serviceable mate,—he does not often as seriously ask if he is
likely to suit her; still less, if this proposed union may not become an ugly domestic
knot which the best interests of both will require to be untied. Whether the number
outside of marriage, who would like to get in, be greater or less than the number inside who want to get out, this mingled sense of esteem, benevolence, and passional
attraction, called love, is so generally diffused that most people know life to be in-
complete until the calls of affection are met in a healthful, happy and prosperous
association of persons of opposite sex. That this blending of personalities may not
be compulsive, hurtful, or irrevocable; but, rather, the result of mutual discretion—
a free compact, dissolvable at will—there is needed, not only a purpose in lovers to
hold their bodies subject to reason; but also radical change of the opinions, laws,
customs, and institutions which now repress and deprave natural expressions of
love. Since "falling in love" is not always ascension, growth, (as it should be), but
often degradation; as persons who meet in convulsive embraces may separate in
deadly feuds,—sexual love here carrying invigorating peace, there desolating
havoc, into domestic life,—intelligent students of sociology will not think the marriage institution a finality, but, rather, a device to be amended, or abolished, as enlightened moral sense may require. . . .

    . . . The popular idea of sexual purity, (freedom from fornication or adultery,
abstinence from sexual intercourse before marriage, and fidelity to its exclusive
vows afterwards), rests on intrusive laws, made and sustained by men, either ignorant of what *is* essentially virtuous, or whose better judgment bows to Custom
that stifles the cries of affection and ignores the reeking licentiousness of marriage beds. Is coition pure only when sanctioned by priest or magistrate? Are
scandal-begetting clergymen and bribe-taking statesmen the sources of virtue?
The lascivious instincts prevalent among men, the destructive courses imposed on
women, and the frightful inroads of secret vice on the vitality of youth of both
sexes, all show the sexual nature to be, comparatively, in a savage state, and that
even public teachers have not begun to reason originally on questions of love,
virtue, continence and reproduction.

    While love denotes movement in one person towards another, and tends to over-
leap unnatural barriers, its proposals are, nevertheless, subject to rejection; created
and nourished by the object of attraction, it is self-limiting. Free love, then, gener-
ates, but never annuls moral obligations. If selfish, love is invasive; but, the person
assailed, has a natural right of resistance; and, if a woman or girl, her effort in self-
defence will be reinforced by disinterested strength around her. . . . She is "safe"
among men, not through laws which deny liberty, but by prevailing knowledge of

Ezra Heywood, *Cupid's Yokes* (Princeton, Mass.: Cooperative Publishing Co., 1878), 3, 5–6, 10–12.

the fact that Nature vests in herself the right to control and dispose of her own person. If lovers err, it is due, not to liberty, but to ignorance, and the demoralizing effect of the marriage system. If free to go wrong, disciplined by ideas, they will work out their own salvation in the school of experience. The free love "delusion" consists in the belief that persons recognized in law as capable of making a sexual contract are, when wiser by experience, morally able to dissolve that contract; and that love is not so depraved as to be incapable of redemption and self-government.

An original impulse of Nature, love has laws of its own; but, coerced by custom, its natural intent and scope are not generally understood. We were all trained in the school of repression, and taught that, to love otherwise than by established rules, is sinful. To get out of one's body to think, to destroy all his old opinions, is almost necessary, to enable him to approach and investigate a new subject impartially. The grave tendencies of the love question, its deep-seated hold on human destiny, its momentous relations to government, religion, life, and property, make any revolution in its doctrines, or institutes, difficult and alarming, if not perilous. But, since nothing is fixed but natural right, the most radical method of treatment is the most truly conservative. Evils like libertinism and prostitution, which have baffled the wisest human endeavor, will yield only to increasing intelligence, and the irresistible forces of Conscience. I beg my readers, therefore, to bring to this subject honest intent to know truth and obey it. That the grand impulse of love is capable of greater good than has yet come of it, is certain; that this noblest element of human being does not logically lead to the marital and social ills around us, is equally evident. The way out of domestic infelicity, then, must lie through larger knowledge of the nature of love and of the rights and duties involved in its evolution. . . .

Though man may "propose," and woman "accept," a notion inhabits the average male head that the irresistibly attractive force of woman's nature makes *her* responsible for any mutual wrong-doing. Thinking woman at the bottom of all mischief, when a male culprit is brought into court, the French ask "Who is she?" In saying that Mrs. Elizabeth R. Tilton "thrust her love on him unsought," the Rev. Henry Ward Beecher thereby indicates how much there is in him of the "old Adam," who said to the "Lord God," interviewing him after he had indulged in the "forbidden fruit," "The woman whom thou gavest to be with me, she gave me of the tree, and I did eat." The insanity plea put forward in courts of law by aggrieved "husbands" who . . . murder men that are attracted to their "wives," also affirms, in a round-about way, the supposed inability of a man to control himself when under the spell of woman's enchantment. Contrary to the old law which regarded the husband and wife as one, and the husband that one, when the twain sin, *she* is held responsible, and he is excused on the ground that he was over-persuaded, and too weak to withstand her wishes. From the Garden of Eden to [Henry Ward Beecher's] Plymouth Church, skulking has been the pet method of man to escape from the consequences of sexual indiscretion. Beecher's confessions and "letters of contrition," with his later denials, sadly illustrate the pathetic penitence, the sniveling cowardice, and brazen-faced falsity with which "great men" endeavor to appease, cajole, and defy equivocal public opinion. The harsh judgments pronounced on women, which abound in the literature of all ages, are equalled only by the evidences of ludicrous puerility which men display when confronted with their sexual "deeds done in the body." The tragic anarchy which now distracts social life originates first in the legal denial of the right of people to manage their own sexual affairs; and secondly in the supposed exemption from moral responsibility of either man or woman in love.

The facts of married and single life, one would suppose, are sufficiently startling to convince all serious-minded people of the imperative need of investigation, especially of the duty of young men and women to give religiously serious attention to the momentous issues of sexual science. But, on the threshold of good intent, they are met by established ignorance forbidding them to inquire. It is even thought dangerous to discuss the subject at all. In our families, schools, sermons, lectures, and newspapers, its candid consideration is so studiously suppressed that children and adults know nothing of it, except what they learn from their own diseased lives and imaginations, and in the filthy by-ways of society. Many noble girls and boys, whom a little knowledge from their natural guardians, *parents, and teachers,* would have saved, are now, physically and morally, utter wrecks. Where saving truth should have been planted, error has found an unoccupied field, which it has busily sown, and gathers therefrom a prolific harvest. The alarming increase of obscene prints and pictures caused both Houses of the U. S. Congress, March 1, 1873, to pass a bill, (or, rather an amendment of the Post Office Act of June, 1872), which was immediately signed by the President, said to be "For the suppression of Obscene Literature," and from which I make the following extract:

§148.—That no obscene, lewd, or lascivious book, pamphlet, picture, paper, print, or other publication of an indecent character, nor any article or thing designed or intended for the prevention of conception or procuring of abortion, nor any article or thing intended or adapted for any indecent or immoral use or nature, nor any written or printed card, circular, book, pamphlet, advertisement, or notice of any kind giving information, directly, or indirectly, where, or how, or of whom, or by what means either of the things before mentioned may be obtained or made, nor any letter upon the envelope of which, or postal card upon which indecent or scurrilous epithets may be written or printed, shall be carried in the mail; and any person who shall knowingly deposit, or cause to be deposited, for mailing or delivery, any of the hereinbefore-mentioned articles or things, or any notice, or paper containing any advertisement relating to the aforesaid articles or things, and any person who, in pursuance of any plan or scheme for disposing of any of the hereinbefore-mentioned articles or things, shall take or cause to be taken, from the mail any such letter or package, shall be deemed guilty of a misdemeanor, and, on conviction thereof, shall, for every offense, BE FINED NOT LESS THAN ONE HUNDRED DOLLARS NOR MORE THAN FIVE THOUSAND DOLLARS, OR IMPRISONED AT HARD LABOR NOT LESS THAN ONE YEAR NOR MORE THAN TEN YEARS, OR BOTH, IN THE DISCRETION OF THE JUDGE.

I Credit Congress and President Grant with good intentions in framing this "law;" for, ignorant of the cause of the evils they proposed to correct, they were probably unaware of the unwarrantable stretch of despotism embodied in their measure, and of the use which would be made of it. . . . Appointed special supervisor of the U. S. Mails (by what authority I am unable to learn); and, by religio-sectarian intolerance, constituted censor of the opinions of the people in their most important channel of inter-communication, [Anthony Comstock] is chiefly known through his efforts to suppress newspapers and imprison editors disposed to discuss the social question. In November, 1872, he procured the arrest and imprisonment of Victoria C. Woodhull and her editorial associates for publishing a preliminary

ventilation of the "Brooklyn Scandal," which afterwards filled American newspapers. . . . John A. Lant, editor and publisher of the N. Y. Toledo Sun . . . says:—
"Judge Benedict to-day sentenced me to imprisonment in Albany Penitentiary one
year and six months.["] . . . Mr. Lant's crime is sending through the mails his newspaper, containing criticisms of the "scandal" and of the Rev. Henry Ward Beecher!
Mr. Comstock's relation to Mr. Lant, as heretofore to Mrs. Woodhull . . . is that of a
religious monomaniac, whom the mistaken will of Congress and the lascivious
fanaticism of the Young Men's Christian Association have empowered to use the
Federal Courts to suppress free inquiry. The better sense of the American people
moves to repeal the National Gag-Law which he now administers, and every interest of public and private morality demands thorough discussion of the issue which
sectarian pride and intolerance now endeavor to postpone.

E S S A Y S

What are the effects of sexual speech on children, morality, and public order? Should
speech be regulated? These questions lay at the heart of the debate over censorship
in the late nineteenth century. Jesse F. Battan, of the California State University at
Fullerton, closely examines the writings of such radical sex reformers as Ezra and
Angela Heywood, who fought Anthony Comstock's efforts to limit and purify sexual
language. They believed that the open discussion of sexuality—using direct, explicit
language to expose Victorian hypocrisy and prudery—would lead to a transformation
in the sexual and social relations of women and men. Battan shows how sex radicals
forced Americans to consider the power of words, a confrontation that often resulted
in their arrest and vilification. Shirley J. Burton, of the National Archives and Records
Administration (Southeast region), looks at the actual impact of censorship by examining prosecutions in Chicago under the Comstock Law, which prohibited the mailing of
obscene material. Although a number of prosecutions involved pornography, sex education literature, and contraceptive information—which Comstock had labeled harmful
to public morality—in fact most of the prosecutions targeted private correspondence
between individuals. As Burton observes, the very ambiguity in the definition of
"obscenity" allowed the state to enlarge its power to intervene in sexual matters.

"The Word Made Flesh": Language, Authority, and
Sexual Desire in Late Nineteenth-Century America

JESSE F. BATTAN

In a letter written to Ezra Heywood, editor of an obscure monthly newspaper called
The Word, a reader described an experience she had had with her daughter. "The
other day," she wrote in 1881, "my little girl, who is in her twelfth year, came to me
and said, 'Mama, what does "fuck" mean?'" The girl's mother quickly asked her
where she had heard such a word. "Why, today at school, Willie ———— said to

me, 'Mamie, won't you fuck me?'" her daughter breezily replied. Rather than express shock or condemn her child's youthful inquiry, the woman responded by telling her "exactly what it meant." In doing so she described the act in "plain English words of four letters" and used her own body, as well as "a well-executed photograph of the male organ in [a] state of erection," to demonstrate the physiological issues involved in sexual intercourse.

On the face of it, the writing and publication of this letter is startling. In an age that has been characterized by its prudery, reticence, and censorship, such sentiments and such language seem quite out of place. This reaction, however, is primarily the result of a gap in our understanding of the diversity of the sexual culture of nineteenth-century America. Although recent scholarship has done much to supplant the traditional view of the monolithic power of the repressive sexual morality that emerged by the 1830s, we still know much more about Victorian efforts to shape sexual ideology and behavior than we do about those who opposed them. Little is known, for example, of the activities of nineteenth-century sexual radicals— the self-described "Free Lovers"—who rejected the ideas advocated in Victorian "primers for prudery." Studies that have been done on these reformers have concentrated primarily on the legal struggles that accompanied their efforts to disseminate birth control information or to defend First Amendment freedoms. These studies, however, have not paid sufficient attention to the battles over words—the politics of language—that were central to the conflicts that occurred between competing sexual ideologies. The goal of this essay is to examine these struggles to define the nature of public language from the perspective of those who attempted to expand the limits of sexual discourse as well as from the point of view of those who sought to constrict it.

Throughout the nineteenth century, heated debates occurred over the meaning of words and their proper usage. These linguistic controversies took a variety of forms and reflected large-scale changes in the structure of American life. Urbanization, industrialization, social and geographic mobility, and the emergence of a democratic culture all worked to undermine stable patterns of deference by multiplying the ways in which all forms of knowledge were communicated. The number of voices making themselves heard, as well as the linguistic styles they used, was expanding. Preexisting boundaries, based on gender and class distinctions, that had served to limit access to the public domain of expression and expertise were being destroyed. As a result, the question of who could speak and write and the context in which this would occur became politically divisive issues. These battles over language were an outgrowth of the struggles between competing groups who strongly believed that words could shape the new social world that was emerging.

Waging war against the growing use of vernacular forms of speech, for example, linguistic conservatives argued that diction, syntax, and word choice reflected the essential character of men and women and determined the nature of society itself. The sensuality aroused by the use of slang undermined the internalized hierarchy of reason over desire. Further, colloquialisms and informal language created a false intimacy that destroyed the "natural" hierarchy between the refined and the vulgar, which was the basis of a stable social order. These linguistic purists—whose numbers included journalists, clergymen, and educators—insisted that the proper use of words would promote reticence and reserve, rather than garrulity and familiarity, and would recreate a social world in which proper deference would reign over an unchecked egalitarianism.

Nowhere was the struggle between linguistic purity and vulgarity more evident than in the conflict over words used to describe sexuality. Although the contending voices in this dialogue supported diametrically opposed ideas on the nature of sexuality and the role it should play in the creation of their vision of the ideal society, all were convinced of its power and sought to monitor and guide it. Linking consciousness to conduct, the participants in this struggle believed that the erotic imagination and the behavior it inspired could be controlled if the words used to describe sexuality were carefully chosen. They all believed, in short, that language could be used to regulate the expression of sexual desires.

Efforts to use language to control erotic images and impulses escalated throughout the nineteenth century. In fact, they played a central role in the development of Victorian sexual ideology. Motivated by their distrust of sensual desires, Victorian moralists worked to inculcate a sense of shame in response to erotic stirrings and promoted chastity in thought and speech as well as in conduct. Convinced that individual health and social stability required the strict regulation of sexual desires, they correspondingly attempted to circumscribe the social geography of sexual discussions by sharply distinguishing between language that was appropriate for public and for private life. Their attempts to eradicate linguistic and artistic forms of "obscenity" that began with local, extralegal actions of vice societies in the 1830s and culminated in the enactment of the Postal Act of 1873 (known as the Comstock Act) grew out of this desire to restrict sexuality to the private arena.

By severely limiting what could be said, where it could be said, and who could say it, Victorian moralists attempted to suppress any discussion of sexuality that had not been carefully neutered. Those empowered to discuss this topic—clergymen, physicians, and moral reformers—engaged in conversations filled with biblical images of sin and redemption, medical metaphors of sickness and health, and obtuse euphemistic references that carefully filtered out any hint of sensuality. Fearful of the stark imagery connoted by vulgar language, they condemned words that incited forms of sexual behavior threatening to the institutions and relationships they had created to control erotic desires. Rather than reflect a conspiracy of silence that sought to eliminate all discussions of sexual issues, the goal of Victorian prudery was to use language to properly socialize desire.

Within the expanding terrain of public language in the nineteenth century, however, there were also many attempts to create alternative ways of writing about sexuality. The most radical attempts were made by the Free Lovers. The Free Lovers first appeared in the 1850s, when the term "free love" became more than a derisive epithet used to describe any form of sexual behavior that deviated from prescribed norms. It instead denoted a system of ideas that challenged Victorian sexual ideology. During this time the term "Free Lover" was also capitalized and used as a descriptive noun to indicate membership in a loosely knit but highly self-conscious group of politically and socially active men and women. Drawing on the ideas of utopian reformers of the early nineteenth century, the Free Lovers sought to regenerate society by reconstructing the relationships that regulated the expression of human emotions.

One of the most important ways in which the Free Lovers sought to achieve their goals centered on their use of "obscene" language. Their use of such language to promote their radical ideas, they claimed, was not motivated by a desire to titillate their audience. Rather, it reflected their fundamental desire to eradicate a sexual culture they saw as corrupt and corrupting. Much more was at stake here than simply free speech: the Free Lovers' war against Victorian prudery was an attempt to fundamentally transform American society through the revitalization of language.

Like their orthodox counterparts, the Free Lovers believed that what was said in public influenced what was performed in private. In contrast to conservative moralists, however, they argued that the unwillingness to candidly discuss every aspect of human physiology led not to purity and health but to vulgarity and disease. By exercising their right to investigate the "sexual question" and to communicate their findings, they tried to create an alternative sexual discourse. Sexual health could be achieved, they maintained, only after "the prudishness, the false modesty that shrinks from open and fearless discussion of everything pertaining to the sexual nature of men and women" had been overcome. Not denial but confrontation, not euphemisms but direct expression, not "suppression or prohibition, but education and enlightenment" would destroy unhealthy behavior and return the sexual appetites of men and women to their "natural" condition. In their reform ideology, the purification of the physical body as well as the body politic depended on the open examination of human sexuality.

In order to use language to transform consciousness and behavior, the editors of Free Love newspapers published materials that challenged the fundamental tenets of Victorian sexual ideology. Among the most influential were Moses Harman, editor of *Lucifer, the Light-Bearer,* and Ezra Hervey Heywood, editor of *The Word.* These newspapers provided a forum in which they and their audience could describe their sexual experiences without fear of censorship. For example, they published articles that rejected the image of childhood as a state of sexual innocence and argued for an education that would expose children to the "facts" of human sexuality rather than the "soothing-syrup of legalized duplicity and fashionable deceit!" Defending their right to disseminate birth control information, these editors also printed advertisements and articles that described a variety of contraceptive practices, and they initiated a series of debates on the benefits and problems created by their use.

Heywood and Harman also paraded before the eyes of their readers striking examples of "aberrant" sexual behavior. Their newspapers were filled with vivid accounts of wives driven to illness or early graves by the unbridled lusts of their husbands. Sadie Magoon of Los Angeles, for example, related a typical case of one woman who had married what most considered to be "a good man." His constant sexual demands, however, soon destroyed her health. "The sparkle left her eye, and the bloom her cheeks. She grew thin and had a peculiar gait, and at last could no longer walk at all, and was confined to her bed and in time became partially paralyzed." But the horror continued. Even while bedridden and placed under a nurse's care, when her day nurse left she was at the total mercy of her husband, a "human brute," who continued to gratify his desires. "Through his constant nightly abuses she was, to quote from her nurse and my informant," wrote Magoon, "'raw as beef steak.'" The plight of this woman, as well as the experiences of countless others who were similarly treated, were publicized as examples of "the hidden mysteries of the marriage institution." Since the "secrets of the inner temple of home" were guarded more closely than "those of the cloister," the Free Lovers insisted that the conspiracy of silence had to be broken for the liberation of the enslaved to begin.

In addition to these stories of "women who slowly perished" as a result of the "sexual excesses forced on them" by their husbands, the editors of Free Love newspapers also published accounts of other forms of sexual "perversion." In a letter that found its way into the columns of *Lucifer* in 1890, for example, Dr. Richard V. O'Neill, a New York physician, described his treatment of a woman whose mouth and throat were filled with "venereal ulcers" as a result of her husband "putting his private organ into his wife's mouth," as well as his contact with a man who sought a cure for his "*insatiable* appetite for *human semen* [emphasis in original]." The patient, who claimed to have inherited this disease from his father, complained that he had traveled far and wide in order "to find men to allow him to 'suck them off' as he says." Further, the patient confessed that he had often engaged in oral sex with members of his family, men as well as women, who would "*suck* each other's *private parts* in the presence of each other."

In the hands of the Free Lovers, deviant behavior was neither celebrated nor condemned. Rather, they believed that only by publicly acknowledging these acts of perversion in clear language could they be understood and eliminated. As Harman argued, the "cancers that are eating the life out of our social system can never be cured by the covering up or plastering over process. The evil must be laid bare in all its native hideousness. The healing influences of nature's air and sunshine must be allowed to do their work if ever the patient is to be cured." Straining against the conspiracy of silence that confined the discussion of these "hidden crimes" to "private circles," these sexual muckrakers publicized them in order to create a groundswell of public outrage and inspire political action that would effectively meliorate the conditions they described. . . .

By far the most radical nineteenth-century critique of linguistic prudery was carried on by Angela Fiducia Tilton Heywood and her husband and comrade, Ezra Heywood. Together, they achieved considerable notoriety in the 1870s and 1880s by using words that offended almost everyone, including some Free Lovers. While the Free Lovers regarded themselves as supporters of "the most unpopular of all unpopular reforms," the Heywoods' ideas on the power of words to effect changes in consciousness and behavior placed them at the cutting edge of even this most radical of movements. Stephen Pearl Andrews, an ardent critic of many aspects of Victorian society, observed in 1883 that the "boldness of speech" in which they expressed their views on marriage and sexuality "frightened and repelled the conservatives on the one hand, and even more their own associates in the reformatory world, who were not ready to be committed to so much." In the important struggle for the freedom to speak openly about the "sex question," Andrews concluded, they were "the extreme case; if they can be endured, anybody can."

As the publisher of unorthodox notions and obscene language, it was Ezra Heywood who faced the wrath of the censors and the judicial system empowered to impose their will. It was Angela Heywood, however, who provided the most outspoken defense of their "habit of saying naughty words, and shocking the whole world by saying them." Such words, she argued, effectively exposed the gap between private behavior and public language. The use of "naughty words," however, would do more than illuminate the hypocrisy of the old moral order. The language of sexual candor also held the power to transform social relationships. For Angela Heywood, words were symbols of vibrant truths, the expression of which would destroy the artificial inhibitions that sustained all forms of inequality. By enabling men and women to communicate their emotions in a more direct way, words could liberate them from destructive forms of consciousness and behavior.

Angela Heywood's desire to openly discuss every aspect of human sexuality developed at an early age. "As a girl," she recalled in 1889, "I used to say, in myself, 'When I grow up I shall deal with men's penises, write books about them; I mean to and I will do it.'" An odd goal for a nineteenth-century woman, yet it was one that she realized nonetheless. Her ambitions were in part inspired by her intellectual heritage. Born in Deerfield, New Hampshire, she traced her lineage on her mother's side to John Locke. From her mother, Lucy M. Tilton, Angela inherited her distaste for the prudery of "'learned' men and 'refined' women" as well as the corresponding view that sexuality was worthy of "respect and study." Raised on a farm and alerted to the natural processes of animal reproduction, she early learned to regard human sexuality with reverence. "From babyhood," she wrote in 1884, "I was taught to have sacred regard for the human body-form and all its belongings, to call penis 'penis' and womb 'womb'; it never occurred to me that it could be considered indelicate or 'vulgar' to speak, orally or writtenly, of sex organs by their proper names."

Moreover, as a young woman she was drawn to the ideas of a circle of abolitionists and transcendentalists whom she regarded as her "immediate teachers," which included William Lloyd Garrison, Wendell Phillips, Thomas Wentworth Higginson, Bronson Alcott, Theodore Parker, Ralph Waldo Emerson, and Walt Whitman. As a result of her contact with what Stephen Pearl Andrews described as "the old antislavery ranks," when she began to explore the sex question she "carried their *Abolitionist* boldness of speech into that subject." While the antislavery radicals may have inspired her willingness to speak out, the essential element of Angela Heywood's critique of linguistic prudery—the belief in the redemptive power of words themselves—was most influenced by what [literary critic] F. O. Matthiessen has described as the "transcendental conception of language."

By the mid-nineteenth century, writers such as Emerson, Parker, Alcott, and Whitman had developed a sharp critique of the linguistic shifts that accompanied the development of Victorianism as a cultural system. Modern civilization, with its emphasis on "respectability," conformity, and materialism, had alienated man from his natural environment. Reflecting this fall from grace, the essential link between words and the physical and spiritual realities they represented had been destroyed. As Emerson argued in 1836, the "corruption of man is followed by the corruption of language." . . .

For these transcendentalists, the solution to both forms of corruption lay in the redemptive power of language. By reconnecting words to things, language would be revitalized. It could then provide men and women with a clear, coherent, and ultimately harmonizing vision of their physical desires, the natural world, and the spiritual truths they symbolized. Influenced by German idealism and English romanticism, the transcendentalists looked to the language of the "folk"—in this case, the earthiness of Elizabethan Saxon English—as the source for authentic forms of communication. The rehabilitation of language and society, they argued, would only occur when the words and phrases spoken in fields and streets replaced the language found in dictionaries and literature. . . .

In addition to democratizing the sources of language, the transcendentalists expanded the perimeters of what it could describe. All experiences, ranging from cooking and cleaning to courting and loving, were worthy of discussion. Moreover, as Emerson argued, such discussions should include words—even "obscene" words—normally "excluded from polite conversation." Carrying this idea further, Whitman insisted that the reconnection of words to things would only occur after the "forbidden voices . . . of sexes and lusts" had been freed from the censor's grip. Once men and women had learned to "publicly accept, and publicly name, with specific words" every aspect of human sexuality without resorting to the euphemisms of genteel society, that which had formerly been "indecent" would be "clarified and transfigur'd." . . .

Along with ideas imbued by her mother or learned from radical thinkers, Angela Heywood's desire to challenge the linguistic purity created by what she referred to as "the compound of silks, insinuation, laces, and mincing called society" was also driven by her own experiences as a working woman. Taught the value of work at an early age, Angela engaged in a variety of occupations, ranging from domestic servant, seamstress, farmhand, and innkeeper to librarian, writer, and platform speaker. As one who maintained a lifelong sympathy for the plight of working women, Angela always resented the fact that "shop-girls, mill-girls, and house-girls [are] regarded below par in social life simply because they work and have not means accumulated from others' earnings." Moreover, as Stephen Pearl Andrews observed in 1883, her contempt for "the superciliousness and pretension of superiority by the rich and 'cultured'" was influenced by the ways in which working girls were verbally and physically treated by the men and women of the professional and leisured classes. In a short biographical sketch, Andrews perceptively noted that Angela Heywood and "others of her order were constantly approached and tempted or insulted by men of the so-called superior classes." From such contacts she early learned that the "private language and lives" of these men were "utterly corrupt," but in public their words and deeds "were delicate and refined to the last degree." Angela Heywood's firsthand experience with the "organized hypocrisy" of genteel society, combined with her "natural and inherited revolt against a pretended sanctity, propriety and culture on the part of the polished hypocrites," led to her firm "determination that folks shall hear openly talked about what in secret they dwell on as the staple of their lives; that the hypocrisy shall be exposed; that the inflated pretense of virtue which does not exist shall be punctured and collapsed."

As a self-described "word painter," Angela attempted to use words to reveal the brutality and unhappiness bred by Victorian sexual ideology. Her goal was to communicate the inner truths obscured by genteel language and reintroduce men and women to what she referred to as a transcendent "throbbing" or vitalistic "rhythmic Reality." By enunciating "words of fire and power," connections could be drawn between the symbol and the truth it represented, dissipating the foggy mists spun by Victorian prudery. In pursuit of what she called "Fleshed Realism," she sought to make the word flesh, a transforming force that would draw its power for change from the essential truths it reflected. The radical alteration of the sexual lives of men and women—the rehabilitation of desire—would result from the revitalization of the language used to describe sexuality.

Angela Heywood's efforts to revise what she termed "sex-nomenclature" extended even to the very names of the sexual organs and their functions. This became a cause célèbre when she began advocating the use of the "Anglo-Saxon" designation for "two well known objects and their associative use"—namely, "c[ock], c[unt] and f[uck]." Her use of the infamous "three words" created quite a stir, not only among genteel moralists, but within the Free Love movement itself. Notoriety, however, was not her goal. Her defense of the use of these words grew out of her earlier attempts in the 1870s to include the word "penis" in her lectures. Angela's insistence that this word be used in public discourse was inspired by her belief that a new language would equalize the relationship between men and women. Since women did not possess "formulas of expression concerning the male generative organ," she insisted, "woman's generative organ has, for ages, been a foot-ball in men's talk." Because of this gap in women's vocabulary, "no companionable exchange in dialect" had been possible. The dialogue between men and women thus had always been lopsided, in favor of men.

Seeking to realign the balance of power, Angela Heywood argued that in *The Word,* as well as in nature, "Penis goes with Womb," and she warned that their "'cultured' readers" would have to get over their distaste for it. "If man says 'womb' without rising heat or dishonest purpose," she argued, "why should not woman say 'penis' without blushing squirm or sheepish looks." "Penis and Womb," she announced, "have arrived in Literature" and should become permanent fixtures in any discussion of the intimate lives of men and women.

Eventually, however, Angela grew dissatisfied with the Latinate designations of the sexual organs. For her, the term "penis" no longer adequately described the male organ's power and vigor. "What mother can look in the face of her welcome child and not religiously respect the rigid, erect, ready-for-service, persistent male-organ that sired it?" she mused in 1887. "Penis is a smooth, musical, almost feminine word," she argued, and should be replaced by the word "cock" as the symbolic designation of the male organ. "Built projective, carrying the seed of Life, ordained to propose what woman may accept, man is instinctively true to nature in coining the word cock to define creative power," she insisted. Preferring Saxon words, she maintained that they "exactly define sex-organs and their mutual use." Why should people be afraid of such words, she wondered. "In literature we have cocks as weathervanes, cocks as faucets, cocks as fowls, cocked hats, cocked rifles and cocks as leading gentlemen members of clubs." This word would have more power, and be truer to its function, if it were used to describe the male reproductive organ. Even though "Latin names and devious phrases prevail in literary and scientific discourse," she urged Americans to incorporate "plain English" designations of the "sexual organs and their use" into their everyday speech and writing. Only then, she insisted, would "predatory penis-commerce" cease to exist.

For Angela Heywood, it was "not the pen only, but the penis" that was "mightier than the sword." Or rather, it was the penis guided by the pen and what it represented—conscious thought, discussion and choice—that would lead to the regeneration of public and private life. As long as sexual desire is not *spoken out about, in the mental, social, and literary world, so long will disaster mar sex-experience."*

While in the past the improper use of man's sexuality had transformed it into a powerful force of destruction, by discussing its nature and the consequences of its expression men could learn to control their desires and redeem themselves by treating women with respect. "An *irresponsible* penis manufactures 'prostitutes,' 'harlots,' 'whores,' 'strumpets,'" she stated, but "a conscientious penis *glorifies* woman."

Stressing the importance of "intelligent, natural, honest, plain-speaking," Angela emphasized her belief that communication should precede physical contact. When men and women speak honestly to one another, the "light beam of thought" creates cooperation through understanding. "Such graceful terms as hearing, seeing, smelling, tasting, fucking, throbbing, kissing, and kin words, are telephone expressions," Angela argued, "lighthouses of intercourse centrally immutable to the situation." While feelings can be communicated through touch, a more intimate form of contact would be established if men and women demonstrated a "spontaneous, expressive candor." Once they "think" about each other as well as "feel" one another, once they place "man's penis under scrutiny of day-light Thinking as well as in test of physical, mid-night Feeling," the unhealthy images fostered by the prudery of orthodox morality would be erased and the dark side of sexuality would disappear.

Through her creation of a new "human grammar," Angela sought to realize "Sex-Unity," or the harmonious relation between the sexes. Such a "natural mode" of expression would free women from forms of communication that reinforced their powerlessness. . . . By controlling language and "keeping the mysteries of Sex, the secrets of coition, the momentous potencies of Love and Parentage deep *hidden* in dark places" beyond their reach, men maintained their control over women. Autonomy for women would be achieved only after a revolution in the ways in which affectional relationships are discussed, envisioned, and experienced. And the agent of revolution, Angela asserted, will be "the force of woman's tongue" calling men's "penises, over-loaded with white, child-making blood . . . to order." In the past, she concluded, women had been "ears and men mouths; now *we* must speak also."

By eliminating the artificial boundaries that separated public life from private life and exposing the hypocrisy of social elites, Angela sought to inaugurate a revolution in class as well as in gender relationships. The liberation of women from their bondage to men was part of a larger struggle to free both women and men from a system of economic and political domination. Striking out at the oppression bred by the centralized control of knowledge, Angela argued that those in power were fearful of the circulation of ideas. The "church-state grip" on sexual knowledge, she wrote, keeps "women and labor" in a condition of "subjected destitution." The power of elites, she contended, was maintained by their "usurpation of the means of education, legalized censorship of the press, of behavior and morals." As a result, "propertyless workers" were rendered the "helpless slaves of privileged robbers." Economic and political equality would only be realized after the power that orthodox moralists gained by "falsifying words" had been destroyed.

Just as women, properly armed with an expressive sexual vocabulary, were to be responsible for their own liberation in private life, the economically downtrodden and politically powerless were to be revolutionary agents for change in public life. . . . The raw language used by the "girls and boys of the street," who described their bodies without the affectation of restraint, would redeem society. True civilization, she concluded, "comes *up* from the masses, not down from the classes."

For Angela Heywood, the reconstruction of gender and class relationships awaited the revitalization of the language of sexual discourse. "When fit words please the ear as physical-human beauty pleases the eye, when sentences are quick with warm, throbbing life; when LANGUAGE, in original power and charming surprise, is the perennial miracle Spontaneity allows it to be; when souls know bodies, and mind informs matter well-enough to help us meet and work in the realm of ethical possibility," the millennium will be at hand. A "new literature," she argued, would create "new social harmonies, a new heaven and a new earth." Reconnecting words to things, obscene language would inaugurate the social and emotional transformations that Victorian moralists were struggling to forestall. As a result of her linguistic innovations, class and gender hierarchies would be destroyed, and equality and intimacy would replace inequality and formality in *public* as well as in *private* relationships.

From the perspective of both the Free Lovers and those who tried to censor their efforts, the restriction or expansion of sexual discourse held the key to the structure and character of the social order itself. While both groups celebrated a common vision of an ideal world in which health and virtue flourished, each was convinced that the ideas and patterns of behavior advocated by their opposing faction led only to disease and immorality.

Anthony Comstock, for example, who spent his professional career putting gamblers, pornographers, and quack doctors behind bars, claimed that he knew of "nothing more offensive to decency, or more revolting to good morals" than the publications of Free Lovers such as Angela and Ezra Heywood. He found them to be "foul of speech, shameless in their lives, and corrupting in their influence," and he warned of certain "ruin and death" awaiting those entranced by their doctrines. Their goal, he argued, was to destroy the moral "restraints" that ensured premarital chastity and marital fidelity. In pursuit of this end, they held "public meetings where foul-mouthed women" lectured to audiences who were reduced to an "enervated, lazy, shiftless, corrupt breed of human beings, devoid of common decency, not fit companions, in many cases, to run with swine."

In their struggles "to protect the morals of the community" and prevent "the libertine and rake from poisoning the minds" of the young, moralists such as Anthony Comstock underscored the power of words to unleash or restrain "the baser passions." This is clearly demonstrated in Comstock's description of a young man confronting a piece of "obscene literature." . . . In the conservative Victorian imagination, mental purity was maintained only by avoiding words and images that elicited sensual thoughts. "Good reading refines, elevates, ennobles, and stimulates the ambition to lofty purposes," Comstock concluded, while "evil reading debases, degrades, perverts, and turns away from lofty aims to follow examples of corruption and criminality."

In contrast, the Free Lovers envisioned themselves as sexual scientists pursuing knowledge that would liberate men and women from the corrupting influences of orthodox morality. Moses Harman clearly expressed this in his response to a reader's request for aid in obtaining "obscene books and pictures." "Lasciviousness and salacity are signs of abnormality or perversion, due primarily to ignorance," he wrote, "and the pure minded will make use of these symptoms as the physician does the symptoms of disease, and guided by these symptoms try to assist the sufferer to health or sanity."

For the Free Lovers, mental purity was gained through education. They explained away the heightened prudishness displayed by censors like Comstock as a manifestation of the guilt they felt toward their own overheated sexual imaginations. "If Anthony Comstock will seriously and carefully examine into his own emotional condition," wrote one of Angela Heywood's supporters in 1890, "he will find himself troubled, and seriously so, with perverted and depraved emotions, which he should immediately try to correct, by a scientific course of hygiene." As Angela herself argued, the "pretense that English words, which so exactly define sex-organs and their mutual use, are indelicate, is a part of that *mental* disease which, insisting that ignorance guarantees social purity, enacts 'obscenity statutes' to *hinder increase of physiological knowledge!*" Rather than an effort to maintain moral purity, the Free Lovers viewed the activities of these censors as a conspiracy on the part of church, state, and genteel society to perpetuate economic and emotional slavery.

While they shared a common goal—mental purity—orthodox moralists and sexual radicals were thus divided by their differing views on how to realize it. In contrast to genteel efforts to avoid discussing unsavory topics, the Free Lovers fought to expand the dimensions of public discourse to include the exploration of private issues. This difference cost the Free Lovers dearly. The "war of words," wrote David W. Hull after the arrest of his brother Moses Hull in 1876, often led to "actual battles" fought by men and women who were willing to "come forward and face the danger."

In rural areas and in small towns, for example, linguistic prudery was enforced primarily by community leaders who controlled access to knowledge, as well as through more informal controls, such as gossip, social ostracism, and the ever present "scarecrow" of respectability, Mrs. Grundy. In these village environments, the Free Lovers also faced mobs of local citizens, who torched their homes and printing offices and confiscated and burned their publications. Further, it was not uncommon for those on the lecture circuit to be attacked by armed toughs who threatened, and frequently delivered, violence against their persons as well as their property.

In urban centers, where knowledge was more easily disseminated and a consensus on moral issues was more difficult to maintain, efforts to censor language relied on more formal controls. With the passage of the Postal Act, which empowered Comstock and his agents to examine letters, newspapers, journals, and books sent through the mails for "obscene" content, the federal government joined ranks with the growing number of local reform societies after the Civil War who used the police and courts to prosecute sexual radicals. Ezra Heywood, for example (whose experience was far from unique), was arrested and convicted in 1890 for publishing the letter quoted at the beginning of this essay. At the age of sixty-one, he was sentenced to two years in prison.

Even though, as Walt Whitman observed in 1882, the linguistic prudery of "good folks" found in "good print everywhere" seemed to "lingeringly pervade all modern literature, conversation and manners," it is important to remember that it did not go unchallenged. It is equally important to note that this challenge provoked an intense reaction. Throughout the last three decades of the nineteenth century, the Free Lovers were confronted by a wide range of enemies. "Mobs from the streets, local and national 'government,' 'religious' intolerance, lascivious superstition, the Pharisees of 'morality' and the Pharisees of 'culture' have all in turn wrestled with the Free Love Idea," Ezra Heywood defiantly proclaimed, "and all have been thrown by it."

While Ezra Heywood's views on the Free Lovers' ability to circumvent the forces that sought to silence them were overly optimistic, the hardships they endured as a consequence of their battles with censorship were essential to shaping sexual discourse in the nineteenth century. Unlike pornographers and abortionists, whose acts were clothed in secrecy until exposed by Comstock and his agents, the Free Lovers courted prosecution in order to uncover the duplicity of genteel society. "Called to public discourse on sex-issues" in response to the efforts of orthodox moralists "to suppress [the] investigation of [sexual] questions by invasive 'statutes,'" as Angela Heywood observed in an article tellingly entitled "Penis Literature," they met the forces of censorship head on and openly challenged their power to place controls on sexual discourse. In consequence, the Free Lovers faced the full wrath of their censors and continually tested the limits of their authority. As one of their contemporaries argued, by publishing "words morally certain to provoke arrest," the Free Lovers expanded the margins of free speech and provided a buffer that "marked the limits of safety" in which more moderate critics of Victorian society and culture could operate.

Moreover, by bringing to light the "wail of suffering" and the "cries of distress" of those ill served by Victorian sexual ideology, the Free Lovers showed many people that their discomfort was not unique and emboldened them to speak out against Victorian ideas and institutions. By revealing the private experiences hidden by public discourse, they were able to criticize Victorian moralists for not living up to the very values they espoused. . . .

. . . The Free Lovers exposed the connection between the language used by the "'upper' ten" and the "'lower' million" in order to eliminate the destructive consequences of the hypocrisy bred by the separation of public and private life and by the rift between words and things. To accomplish this, they liberated sexual discourse from the mincing words of prudes and from the sniggering vulgarity of back-street conversations and promoted a vocabulary that allowed men and women to regain control over their erotic and emotional lives. . . .

While their willingness to shock "public sensibilities" by exploring issues previously "tabooed or held to be improper for public discussion" was the source of their strength as reformers, it was also responsible for the unsavory reputation the Free Lovers gained at the hands of conservative moralists. Held up as symbols of depravity, they were relegated to the margins of social discourse, both in their own day and in the decades that followed. Zacariah Chafee, Jr., for example, while researching an entry on Ezra Heywood for the *Dictionary of American Biography*, noted in 1929 that because Heywood had "strayed so far from the paths of orthodoxy," no other biographical dictionary had been "willing to soil its pages with any mention of him." More than sixty years later, the radical ideas and activities of Free Lovers such as Moses Harman and Angela and Ezra Heywood still remain largely unexplored. Nonetheless, in order to understand the battles that shaped the sexual culture of nineteenth-century America, it is necessary to restore their efforts to re-define the limits of public language to the historical record.

Seeking to understand the relationship between language, authority, and desire, the Free Lovers used words to bring subconscious ideas into the arena of conscious thought and rational control, celebrated their power to regenerate the individual and transform society, and explored the relationship between language and the con-struction of the gendered self, the social self, and, in ways that intertwined the two, the sexual self. Only by viewing these activities within the framework of the broader nineteenth-century concern with the power of words to shape conscious-ness and behavior—as well as with the powers that words represent and serve—can we fully understand the reasons why the Free Lovers risked so much to expand the discourse of desire.

The Criminally Obscene Women of Chicago

SHIRLEY J. BURTON

Perhaps the most famous woman ever denounced as obscene in Chicago was Fahreda Mahzar, who assumed the stage name "Little Egypt" when she performed at the 1893 World's Columbian Exposition. Dressed in a gauze shirt, vest, and skirts reaching nearly to her ankles, Mahzar moved her feet and legs only slightly as she danced, swaying her arms and torso in an undulating motion which critics condemned as indecent, but Little Egypt's performance was one of the most pop-ular attractions of the fair, which also boasted a spectacular electrical lighting dis-play, a scholarly symposium introducing Frederick Jackson Turner's frontier thesis, and a new mechanical amusement called the Ferris wheel. Little Egypt's pro-moters described her performance at "A Street in Cairo" as the *danse du ventre,* but Anthony Comstock, the nation's foremost censor, called it the "hootchie cootchie" and demanded it be shut down.

When a newspaper reported that Bertha Palmer, queen of Chicago society and president of the fair's Board of Lady Managers, had taken a group of friends to Little Egypt's performance, Palmer indignantly denied the accusation and added her voice to that of George Davis, one of the fair's most influential committeemen, who demanded that the show be closed. In the flurry of controversy that followed, Ida Craddock, a Chicago shorthand expert, sex counselor, and Social Purist, sent Palmer a four-page defense of the dance, describing it as "a religious memorial in-culcat[ing] purity and self-control." Bertha Palmer remained publicly unpersuaded, but Little Egypt stayed in business, probably because the show was simply too pop-ular for the fair directors to close.

While Little Egypt avoided the censorship of the law, Ida Craddock did not. Continuing her defense of the performance, Craddock wrote an article called "The Danse du Ventre," which was published in the *Chicago Clinic,* a medically oriented

Shirley J. Burton, "Obscene, Lewd, and Lascivious: Ida Craddock and the Criminally Obscene Women of Chicago, 1873–1913," *Michigan Historical Review* 19 (1993): 1–16. Copyright © 1993 by Central Michigan University. Reprinted by permission of the editor.

journal, which Anthony Comstock, as the Post Office's "special agent" charged with enforcing the federal obscenity statute, declared unmailable. It was Craddock's first brush with the federal censor, but it would not be her last. It is Ida Craddock, rather than Little Egypt, who better typifies the women prosecuted between 1873 and 1913 under the federal obscenity law in the U.S. District Court for the Northern District of Illinois—the "criminally obscene" women of Chicago. Their prosecutions, documented in legal records, help to illuminate the complex dynamic in which criminal law functions as social control, and to elucidate the ideological regroupings and changing social standards that energize that dynamic. In doing so, they enrich the historical perspective of an earlier generation's attempts to deal with censorship, reproductive rights, and the legislation of morality.

Few criminally obscene women of Chicago ran afoul of the law by providing titillating amusements such as Little Egypt's. Rather, many intentionally risked the censure of the law by pressing a social agenda that conflicted with prevailing standards of sexual propriety, public discourse, and accepted female behavior; others found themselves in unexpected legal difficulties while attending to private matters.

The 1873 federal obscenity law, the Comstock Law, was rooted in the sexual reform impulses of an emerging middle class. Reformers hoped to eliminate prostitution and venereal disease, confine sexuality within the private sphere, and attain a single sexual standard of marital chastity for both women and men. They were influenced more than a little by the Victorian masturbation phobia that viewed the body as a closed energy system depleted by the "expenditure" of sexual fluids, but reformers did not agree how change would be best achieved. Vice crusaders like Anthony Comstock argued for government suppression of sexually explicit materials, which they believed threatened self control and contributed to moral decay: masturbation, extra-marital sex, and prostitution. Those like Ida Craddock, however, maintained that sex could be better regulated through education, open public dialogue, and the free exchange of information. The 1873 obscenity statute represented a significant victory for the advocates of government censorship of public sexual expression, and was an important step in the transfer of social control from the family and church to civil law.

Although Anthony Comstock's lobby for the federal obscenity statute is often described as a "one-man" campaign, he was well-funded by a group of wealthy businessmen and supported by several influential congressmen. In 1873 his views were representative of much of middle-class America. Comstock's success also benefited from the prevailing public opinion of political morality, which was at a low ebb in the wake of the Credit Mobilier scandal, in which the Union Pacific Railroad bribed politicians to avoid an investigation into fradulent contracts subsidized by government funds. Many congressmen were pleased to lend their support to legislation which purported to elevate moral standards.

The bill that passed without debate on 3 March 1873 was significantly stronger than any previous federal or state anti-obscenity legislation. It prohibited, in the language of the statute, sending "obscene, lewd, and lascivious" materials through the mail, [including] "any article or thing intended for the prevention of conception or procuring of abortion" and advertisements for those articles or things. Anthony Comstock benefited from this ambigu[ous language] when he was appointed Special Agent to enforce the statute, and he became the most powerful censor in the country. Comstock's personal definition of obscenity would be virtually the law of the land until his death 42 years later.

Anthony Comstock had been outraged by the French postcards that circulated among the troops during the Civil War, and by the sexually explicit items he found abundantly available in New York City afterwards. These were the "traps for the young" about which he wrote a book—the lures and snares to entice youths, especially young boys, into masturbation, promiscuous sex, and their physical, intellectual, and moral decay. As for contraceptives and abortifacients, like many Social Purists Comstock thought them the stuff of the brothel, "abominations" that promoted debilitating sexual over-indulgence while evading pregnancy—the time-honored deterrent and betrayer of illicit sex.

Ida Craddock, however, based her defense of the *danse du ventre* upon a different agenda of moral reform. Like Anthony Comstock, she advocated marital fidelity and limited sexual relations; and like him she condemned prostitution, masturbation, oral sex, contraception, and abortion. Like other Social Purists, she aimed toward a single sexual standard for women and men. Even if Comstock could have tolerated Craddock's arguments for the propriety of the sexual impulse, he could not permit her to argue it publicly. In the privately-printed pamphlets provided to her clients, Ida Craddock insisted that women and men each had sexual impulses needing resolution. She advocated both nudity and active female participation in sexual relations. Disagreeing that sex should be restricted to procreation, Craddock assured her readers that moderate sexual activity "never debilitates," but "freshens and renews." But she also advised limiting the frequency of sexual relations through self-control. It was perhaps this dual commitment to female sensuality and self-control that brought her to the defense of Little Egypt, who seemed to personify the sensual, but unseduced woman.

Craddock repeatedly argued for open public dialogue. "I need make no plea for the propriety of my subject," she wrote. "What concerns us all is eminently fit for discussion by all, and too much light cannot be thrown upon it." She presented her views explicitly in pamphlets such as "Letter to a Prospective Bride," "Advice to a Bridegroom," "The Wedding Night," and "Right Marital Living." Her pamphlets emphasized the necessity of gentleness, patience, and mutuality in sexual intercourse. Social Purists had long decried the sexual brutalization of women which their supposed Victorian "passionlessness" and "submissiveness" seemed to invite. Although the grisly stories of innocent brides going mad on their wedding nights and of married women suffering permanent physical disability from the sexual demands of their brutish husbands were undoubtedly exaggerated, there is little doubt that ignorance did abound.

Ida Craddock provided sexual counseling in a small office on Dearborn Street in Chicago. Those too modest to come to her personally could take advantage of her mail course titled "Regeneration and Rejuvenation of Men and Women Through the Right Use of the Sexual Function." For ten dollars the subscriber received two booklets and a sheet of diagnostic questions. Craddock responded in two separate letters of instruction; additional letters cost five dollars and extra copies of the pamphlets were available by mail for fifty cents each. Her use of the mail put Craddock on another collision course with Anthony Comstock, one with repercussions far greater than the dispute over Little Egypt's performance. Their confrontation came in 1899, when the *Chicago Clinic* published "Right Marital Living." Although the article drew little public reaction, it attracted Comstock's attention and he decided that Craddock should be stopped.

Ida Craddock was indicted in the federal court at Chicago on 27 October 1899, under Postal Law 3893, the federal Comstock Law. She stayed out of jail only because criminal lawyer and free speech advocate Clarence Darrow posted her $500 bond. Her indictment quoted only excerpts from the offending pamphlet because it was, in the language of the court, too "obscene, lewd, and lascivious" to be entered into the official record. Craddock initially pleaded not guilty. After the prosecution subpoenaed Anthony Comstock and Henry Blackwell, widower of conservative feminist Lucy Stone, as witnesses, Craddock, sensing her cause lost, changed her plea to guilty in return for a suspended sentence. For the next week she was so depressed that she considered suicide.

Craddock's pamphlet fell within the first of the four major categories of materials prosecuted under the federal obscenity law: "obscene" printed materials, contraceptives and abortifacients, "obscene" private correspondence, and threatening or defamatory letters. Approximately one in five of the defendants indicted in the Chicago court were, like Ida Craddock, charged with mailing "obscene" books or pictures—Anthony Comstock's "traps for the young." These banned materials included a wide variety of sexually explicit books—erotic classics like Boccaccio's *Decameron;* contemporary, "realistic" literature by Zola and Balzac; and suggestive, forgotten titles such as "Confessions of a Typewriter Girl" and "Irish Mollie, The Queen of the Demi-Monde." They also included Charles Knowlton's influential *Fruits of Philosophy,* and Dr. Alice B. Stockham's pamphlet titled "The Wedding Night."

A specialist in obstetrics and gynecology, Stockham was best known for her popular home medical book on painless childbirth, *Tokology.* However, neither her medical credentials nor her conservative views protected Stockham's writings from prosecution. . . . Her theory of "karezza" advocated strictly limiting the frequency of sexual relations, and advised both women and men to avoid orgasm. Although her publications supported a standard of sexual conduct of which even Anthony Comstock could hardly disapprove, he did object to her means of promoting it, and in 1905 the Chicago court found Stockham guilty of violating the federal obscenity statute.

The suppression of contraceptives and abortifacients, a primary concern of Anthony Comstock and the consensus he represented, accounted for only one in four of the Chicago prosecutions. Women accused of mailing birth control materials or information were, like their male counterparts, often associated with the medical and health professions. One out of six persons indicted for this offense, and four of the five women defendants who can be identified by occupation, were physicians like Ida Lincoln, who offered to provide an abortifacient by mail in response to an 1898 decoy letter. Bertha Hasenclever, wife of a physician, offered a "regulator" that she promised "will cure you without fail within ten days." Jennie Thomas provided her goods or services at the public baths she operated on State Street.

However, most of the obscenity prosecutions in the Chicago court were not directed at the commerce in either sexually explicit publications or in contraceptives and abortifacients. Instead, they targeted private correspondence—"obscene" letters or postcards sent through the mail. While mail inspectors could not lawfully examine first class mail without the permission of the recipient, the extant records suggest this legal nicety was often observed in the breach. Most "obscene" letters and cards were personal communications, sometimes between feuding neighbors or quarreling family members, even correspondence between husband and wife. About twenty per cent of the Chicago prosecutions were for correspondence categorized as threatening or defamatory, which lent itself to abuse in personal and political disputes. Jessie Crone, for example, was fined $25 for writing the following lines: "Mrs. Marks. If you do not return my cup at once I shall have you put behind bars." In 1913, Illinois Governor E. F. Dunne received a letter demanding the removal of a state official. "As a Mother and a Christian," the letter began, "allow me to protest against the retention of Rufus Potts as Insurance Commissioner . . . not only has his business been to boast of *fixing legislators* to vote for Brewery Measures . . . Governor, will it be necessary to remind you of his HORRIBLE CRIME with the LITTLE SPRINGFIELD GIRL? Her SPIRIT cries aloud from the GRAVE. . . . [signed] A Suffragette." This "obscene" woman turned out to be a man, Percy B. Sullivan, who was indicted for mailing the letter, a charge which the court later dismissed. Sometimes prosecuted correspondence was intended to report the misconduct of a spouse. Mary Adair was convicted of writing the following to a Mrs. Griffin:

> It pains me to inform you again of your husband's unfaithfulness to you his wife. He makes an excuse into McCormick saloon for a drink she makes right out of H[?]oops Tea Store to him. . . . I'd advise you to come at once to 3513 Halsted Street . . . and let her know that you [are] his wife.

For this bit of tattling, a jury convicted Adair of mail obscenity, and fined her ten dollars.

Other letters declared "obscene" appear to be solicitations from prostitutes. James M. Searles, who apparently was planning a trip from the Oklahoma Territory to Chicago, received invitations from three different Chicago women during July and August of 1901. "I can manage to be with you all the time you are here," one promised. Vina Fields's offense was mailing change-of-address announcements to her customers when she relocated her brothel. One side of the cards announced the new location of "Vina Fields House of Pleasure," and the other bore "four . . . verses of lewd doggerel so obscene, lewd, and indecent" to be unfit to enter into the court record. Fields's house of prostitution in Chicago's infamous "Levee" district employed only African-American women. It had an exclusively white clientele, and was one of the most famous brothels in the city. . . .

Fields managed to postpone her court date by providing a physician's certification that she was recovering from typhoid fever and unable to leave her room. But she eventually faced a jury, which agreed that the notices were obscene and found her guilty.

An overview of the prosecutions of the Chicago court from 1873 through 1913 permits several generalizations. First, an obscenity prosecution was a serious matter likely to end in a criminal penalty. Although the conviction rate of the Chicago court fails to substantiate Anthony Comstock's claim of 90%, percentages do vary from 41% for mailing threatening or defamatory letters to 74% for "obscene" books or pictures. Fines were often substantial, and prison sentences a possibility.

Second, mail obscenity was a middle-class crime. Analyzed by occupation, the largest group of defendants, sixty individuals (25%) derived their livelihood from sales and service occupations. Admittedly, unlicensed medical practitioners, "backroom abortionists," and true smut dealers are difficult to identify. However, more names of professional than "working" class persons appear in the criminal dockets. The prosecutors, moreover, were middle class. In Chicago, obscenity regulation served less as a means of an empowered middle class exerting social control over a lower one, than of a reform-minded middle class controlling itself.

Third, the Chicago evidence supports the argument that the federal obscenity law played a significant role in late-nineteenth century efforts to keep sex tied to reproduction. The law not only suppressed contraceptives and abortifacients, it also targeted sexual dialogue such as "free love" tracts. Reformers like Ida Craddock did not explicitly threaten the tie between sexuality and reproduction, although their insistence upon the legitimacy of erotic pleasure validated an emerging concept of sensual pleasure as an autonomous force in respectable sexual relationships. Conservative Alice Stockham embraced the restrictive ideal up to and past its logical limit, but was prosecuted when she disseminated her views publicly. Mary Adair's letter may have been simply a well-intended attempt to bring Mrs. Griffin's husband back into the conjugal fold, but she breached the law (and a male-dictated code of female conduct) by bringing marital infidelity into public discourse.

A more focused analysis of the Chicago prosecutions illuminates the roles played by women in this dynamic of criminal law and social control. The prosecution of women increased steadily between 1873 and 1913 (rising from 3% of the total defendants during the first decade of the study to 12% during the last). Once charged, women pleaded guilty at about the same rate as men (41% to 49%), and were convicted at about the same rate (67% to 64%). After being indicted and tried in a somewhat egalitarian manner, however, women benefited from the traditional paternalism of the court when it meted out punishment. Their fines were typically only a quarter of those assessed to men ($30 compared to $124). Alice Stockham and Vina Fields were notable exceptions, perhaps for no better reason than their "unfeminine" ability to pay. The court's paternalism extended to sentencing; convicted males sometimes faced prison terms but only one female ever did.

One of the most notable differences between female and male defendants is the offenses for which they were prosecuted. Women most often were charged with violating the private aspects of the law (mailing private correspondence) and men with breaching its public aspects (illegally offering goods for sale). Prosecutions of items for sale predominated during the first decade that the law was in force, then receded as the percentage of private offenses—that is, "obscene," "threatening," or "defamatory" personal communications—rose along with the number of female defendants. Women accused of violating the public aspects of the law were usually charged with offering contraceptives, abortifacients, or sex manuals by mail. All of the defendants indicted for mailing blatantly titillating nude pictures or literature were male.

These court records provide a unique lens through which to view the recurring struggle between regulation and choice, and a useful elucidation of the nineteenth-century struggle over reproductive rights. The 1873 postal prohibition of contraceptives (use was never illegal) and abortifacients (which were illegal only if used after "quickening") was at odds with, but did not deter, the unremitting trend toward lower birth rates that demographers have tracked. Many women quietly chose a course of personal conduct at odds with social mores and the public policy established by law, but, by the end of the century, the social consensus had shifted perceptibly, enforcement lagged, and the law was gradually being redefined to better represent prevailing standards.

The criminally obscene women of Chicago were a part of that changing dynamic. The persistent challenges of activists like Ida Craddock and Alice Stockham kept the law in the public dialogue and malleable for change when the consensus allowed. Vina Fields and Bertha Hasenclever tested the extent to which deviation from social standards would be tolerated. . . . Victorian "horror of the flesh" was more a romantic ideal than reflective of the way real people lived their lives. Both prostitution and abortion were necessary safety valves for a sexually repressed middle class, and Vina Fields's place within the racist patriarchal model is clear. Left for years to operate her illegal business in Chicago's vice district, Fields faced the censure of the law only when she violated her patrons' privacy with personal correspondence. To conclude that Little Egypt escaped the censure of the law because her provocative performance affirmed, rather than threatened, the patriarchal model may be an over-simplification, but her role as a seductive, rather than a sensual woman is a nuance that may have eluded Ida Craddock.

Soon after her legal difficulties in Chicago, Craddock made a portentous decision and moved to New York, Anthony Comstock's bastion, where she would soon deliberately defy the most powerful censor in the country. With a reformer's zeal, she believed that she had been "divinely led here to New York to face this wicked and depraved man Comstock in open court and to strike the blow which shall start the overthrow of Comstockism." It was Craddock's end rather than Comstock's, however, which was at hand. On 5 March 1902, she was arrested under New York's "little Comstock law" and sentenced by the Special Sessions Court to three months in the City Prison Workhouse on Blackwell's Island. Craddock "took her sentence in stoic silence," a newspaper reported, "and looked neither to right nor left as she was led across the bridge to the Tombs."

After completing her sentence, Craddock was released and immediately re-arrested under the federal Comstock Law. She secured a continuance to work on her legal defense and to write an exposé of conditions on Blackwell's Island. When her case came before the New York Circuit Court, a jury found her guilty once again. On the morning she was to be sentenced, Craddock drank lamp oil and slashed her wrist. In a long note to her mother she wrote, "I maintain my right to die as I have lived, a free woman, not cowed into silence by any other human being."

For a time, Ida Craddock became a martyr around whom free speech advocates rallied. Physician Juliet H. Severance expressed their shock and outrage in a public letter. "Ida Craddock," she wrote, "was a pure-minded, intelligent woman, working with a clean conscience for the good, as she believed, of humanity. . . . She has been hounded to the death by these blood-hounds of the law." Emphasizing the difficulty of the unfranchised woman facing the American legal system she added, "I am glad I am not a man, and have had no hand or voice in enacting the many unjust laws that are a disgrace to the age in which we live."

In addition to the tragedy of Ida Craddock, the data examined in this study document the slow start of prosecution under the Comstock Law in the Chicago court. Only one indictment was returned in the first year, another in the second, none in the third, and two during the fourth. Only thirty-two persons were prosecuted (about four percent of the total number of criminal cases) during the Comstock Law's first decade. By the second decade, however, prosecutions had increased to about ten percent, where they remained for the duration of the study.

Law is a tool of power groups, and criminal prosecutions have been described both as a form of social control and as expression of moral aversion. In popular discourse, "obscenity" expresses repugnance and condemnation. Like "insanity," a legal term lacking definition in medicine or psychiatry but nevertheless used to justify legal action, the designation "obscenity" also allows a legal remedy for ambiguously defined crimes. One of the continuing criticisms of the Comstock Law—its ambiguous definition of obscenity—was one of its major strengths in terms of social control. Critics complained that the only way to test the legality of a thing was in court, and contended that as long as obscenity was determined on a case-by-case basis potential transgressors could only know they were committing a violation after the fact. This very amorphousness, however, insured that the authority of the statute would remain at the disposal of the court and the power base it represented.

Nor was the court restricted by the original intent of the statute. As the power and authority of the courts increased, so did the latitude of interpretation given to the judiciary. The framers of the Comstock Law placed postal restrictions on specific things such as "obscene" books and pictures, contraceptives and abortifacients, and "obscene" or threatening and defamatory letters and cards. It soon became apparent that to be censured as "obscene" by the court, these did not require the presence of specific words or pictures—Cleland's *Fanny Hill* provides ample evidence that euphemisms were sufficient. In application, the law sought to prohibit specific behavior, not just the representations specified in the statute, and to enforce the values of the power groups which empowered, staffed, and supported the judicial system.

FURTHER READING

Jesse F. Battan, "The 'Rights' of Husbands and the 'Duties' of Wives: Power and Desire in the American Bedroom, 1850–1910," *Journal of Family History* 24 (1999): 165–186.

Nicola Beisel, *Imperiled Innocents: Anthony Comstock and Family Reproduction in Victorian America* (1997).

Martin Henry Blatt, *Free Love and Anarchism: The Biography of Ezra Heywood* (1989).

Paul S. Boyer, *Purity in Print: The Vice-Society Movement and Book Censorship in America* (1968).

Janet Farrell Brodie, *Contraception and Abortion in Nineteenth-Century America* (1994).

John M. Craig, "'The Sex Side of Life': The Obscenity Case of Mary Ware Dennett," *Frontiers* 15 (1995): 145–166.

Carl Degler, "What Ought to Be and What Was: Women's Sexuality in the Nineteenth Century," *American Historical Review* 79 (1974): 1467–1490.

Edward de Grazia, *Girls Lean Back Everywhere: The Law of Obscenity and the Assault on Genius* (1992).

Ellen Carol DuBois and Linda Gordon, "Seeking Ecstasy on the Battlefield: Danger and Pleasure in Nineteenth Century Feminist Sexual Thought," *Feminist Studies* 9 (1983): 7–25.

Richard Wightman Fox, *Trials of Intimacy: Love and Loss in the Beecher-Tilton Scandal* (1999).

Barbara Goldsmith, *Other Powers: The Age of Suffrage, Spiritualism, and the Scandalous Victoria Woodhull* (1998).

Rochelle Gurstein, *The Repeal of Reticence* (1996).

John Paull Harper, "Be Fruitful and Multiply: Origins of Legal Restrictions on Planned Parenthood in Nineteenth-Century America," in Carol Berkin and Mary Beth Norton, eds., *Women of America: A History* (1979), 245–269.

Helen Lefkowitz Horowitz, "Victoria Woodhull, Anthony Comstock, and Conflict over Sex in the United States in the 1870's," *Journal of American History* 87 (2000): 403–434.

Louis J. Kern, "Stamping Out the 'Brutality of the *He*': Sexual Ideology and the Masculine Ideal in the Literature of Victorian Sexual Radicals," *ATQ* [*The American Transcendental Quarterly*] 5 (1991): 225–239.

Clelia Duel Mosher, *The Mosher Survey: Sexual Attitudes of 45 Victorian Women*, ed. James Mahood and Kristine Wenburg (1980).

David J. Pivar, *Purity Crusade: Sexual Morality and Social Control, 1868–1900* (1973).

Elizabeth Pleck, "Feminist Responses to 'Crimes Against Women,' 1868–1896," *Signs* 8 (1983): 451–470.

Hal D. Sears, *The Sex Radicals: Free Love in High Victorian America* (1977).

Steven Seidman, "Sexual Attitudes of Victorian and Post-Victorian Women: Another Look at the Mosher Survey," *Journal of American Studies* 23 (1989): 68–72.

Altina L. Waller, *Reverend Beecher and Mrs. Tilton: Sex and Class in Victorian America* (1982).

C H A P T E R
8

Prostitution and Working-Class Sexuality in the Early Twentieth Century

In the early twentieth century, prostitution and working-class sexuality became the subject of intense public scrutiny, anxiety, and fascination. Crusading journalists investigated forced prostitution and offered sensational stories of "white slavery" to the public. Reformers cracked down on brothels and established houses of refuge to rehabilitate the "fallen sisterhood," while the government investigated the importation of immigrant women into the American sex trade. Although targeting prostitution, reformers saw it as symptomatic of a broader sexualization of American culture—an emergent pattern of dating, dancing, music, and talk that was lax, promiscuous, and reinforced by commercial interests.

Many working-class women at this time, both immigrant and American-born, entered prostitution to make ends meet, seeing it as more lucrative than the factory jobs and domestic work of most employed women. Some immigrants, however, were kidnapped or sold, imported into the United States, and forced into the "white slave traffic." Despite this name, it was Chinese women who were most exploited by the organized prostitution trade, as a result of specific U.S. immigration and labor policies, as well as Chinese immigrants' family and sexual patterns. Chinese men were recruited to work as migrant laborers and typically emigrated without wives or families; moreover, interracial marriages were barred by law. These conditions fostered a profitable business in the virtual enslavement of Chinese prostitutes. This example suggests that we must consider familial, economic, and political contexts in order to assess women's sexual agency and victimization.

Millions of immigrants brought their own standards of sexual decorum and behavior from Eastern and Southern Europe, Asia, and Latin America to the United States. Such traditional customs as arranged marriages and chaperonage often proved difficult to sustain in the nation's bustling urban centers. Indeed, the new sexual style reformers feared was, to a large extent, pioneered by the working-class, American-born sons and daughters of immigrants. Against the strictures of parents, some sought out sexual encounters, intimacy, and personal autonomy in the darkness of movie theaters, the abandon of dance halls, and the shadows of tenements. For working-class women, however, these pleasures had to be weighed against the sexual dangers they faced, including harassment, rape, venereal disease, and unwanted pregnancy, as well as the harm to their reputations. Moreover, working-class women's economic and family situations placed severe constraints on their lives. Earnings were so low that they often exchanged sexual favors for meals, clothes, and recreation. In this context, how did working women distinguish between vice and virtue, respectability and prostitution? To what extent were they free to make choices about their sexuality? And what were the consequences of those choices?

D O C U M E N T S

Public concern in the early twentieth century focused on respectable women lured into white slavery against their will. In an excerpt from the U.S. Immigration Commission's investigation of international sex trafficking (Document 1), a federal agent explained the recruitment of immigrant women into prostitution: Who were they, and why did they enter this trade? In Document 2, Chinese immigrant Wong Ah So told how she became a prostitute, before she was rescued by reformer Donaldina Cameron's mission in San Francisco. Her story of sexual slavery contrasts with the views expressed by Cantonese men in Chinatown. In rhymes that sometimes adopted women's voices (Document 3), they wrote of wives left behind in China, prostitutes walking American streets, and their own confusion witnessing American-born women's freer sexual conduct. In Document 4, Eduardo Migliaccio, a popular actor of the Italian immigrant stage known as "Farfariello," also told of the pleasures and confusions of an immigrant courting in the New World. Migliaccio wrote his song "'*O Cafone c' 'a Sciammeri a*" in standard Italian, Italian dialects, and "Italglish," a fusion of English and Italian (try reading it aloud). The title translates as "the peasant with the lightweight overcoat," suggesting the immigrant who is able to purchase goods in America unaffordable in Italy and is now putting on airs; *sciammeria* is also a *double entendre,* meaning a "quickie." The dances of working-class youth signified sexual danger to many reformers and parents. One group, the Committee on Amusements and Vacation Resources of Working Girls issued an explicit warning (Document 5) about "tough dancing" in New York's commercial halls. In Document 6, a Czech newspaper in Chicago, *Denni Hlasatel,* defended the morality of the community's dance halls and its young women. Finally, in Document 7, anarchist and feminist Emma Goldman put the "traffic in women" in a broader perspective in a famous 1911 article; in it, she attacked middle-class hypocrisy and moralism as she explained how social conditions led to prostitution.

1. A Government Agent Explains the White Slave Traffic, 1911

To the motive of business profit is due beyond question the impulse which creates and upholds this traffic. The procurers who seduce or otherwise entice the women to leave their foreign homes, the importers who assist them in evading the law or who

---

U.S. Immigration Commission, *Reports: Importation and Harboring of Women for Immoral Purposes,* Senate Document No. 753, 61st Cong., 3rd Session (Washington: Government Printing Office, 1911), 65–69.

bring them into the United States for sale, the pimps and keepers of disorderly houses who exploit them body and soul, have only profit in view. The work is strictly foreign commerce for profit.

Although very many of the girls are brought here innocent, betrayed into a slavery rigid in its strictness and barbarous in its nature, the prize offered to the victim is only that of higher wages and better economic conditions. The much greater number of women who have already been living an immoral life abroad and who come to the United States willingly to continue open-eyed the practices of their former life, come to secure higher wages, often profits ten times as great as those they have received in Europe. Even though they are subject to their pimps and have little or no opportunity to save for themselves, there is yet the opportunity for higher gains, a higher economic standard of living, an opportunity for travel, and the interest of a new environment, and perhaps at times a hope of a real betterment of conditions. But the persons chiefly responsible for the development of the traffic are not the women themselves, but the keepers of houses, the pimps, and the procurers, who live by their exploitation. . . .

This recruiting is carried on both here and abroad. The procurers, with cunning knowledge of human nature, play upon the weaknesses of vanity and pride, upon the laudable thrift and desire to secure a better livelihood, upon the praiseworthy trust and loyalty which innocent girls have for those to whom they have given their affection, even upon their sentiments of religion, to get their victims into their toils; and then in the pursuit of their purposes, with a cruelty at times fiendish in its calculating coldness and brutality, they exploit their attractions to the uttermost. If the woman is young and affectionate, as often happens, the procurer makes her acquaintance, treats her kindly, offers to assist her in securing a better livelihood. Her confidence and affection won, she is within his power, and is calculatingly led into a life of shame. If the procurer is a woman, the innocent girl is usually promised pleasant work for large pay.

In this connection, also, it is obviously impossible to give statistics showing whether the greater number are recruited abroad, or whether they are induced or compelled to enter the business after their arrival in the United States. In either case the methods of recruiting do not differ materially. Though in all probability many are innocent, the majority of women and girls who are induced to enter this country for immoral purposes have already entered the life at home and come to this country as they would go elsewhere, influenced primarily by business considerations. According to reports made by Marcus Braun, a special agent of the Bureau of Immigration and Naturalization, who investigated in Europe the exportation of women to America for immoral purposes, there is a practical certainty of greatly increased earnings. So far as the more degraded women in eastern and southeastern Europe—Poland, Roumania, and elsewhere—are concerned, the earnings would probably be from five to ten times as much. On the other hand, the opportunities of their securing any material share of their earnings for their own uses is no greater, possibly not so great.

With this class of women the women procurers are probably almost as successful as the men. They call the attention of the girls to the attractiveness of a voyage abroad, to the new and interesting experiences to be met with in a new country, and especially to the greatly increased earnings and the consequent opportunities to gratify their desire for luxury and display.

To the innocent girls the woman procurer offers only the inducement of work, and usually work of a menial nature, though at higher pay than that to which the girl has been accustomed at home. In one case known to the Commission a girl left her home in Europe with the consent of her parents to act as maid to the woman procurer; and there are doubtless numerous instances in which women, sometimes those of a better class, such as nurses, are offered good positions at high pay.

The investigation leads the Commission to the belief, however, that more of the recruiting of innocent young girls in Europe is done by men procurers than by women; and possibly even with women of the professional class they may be somewhat more successful, as while they can promise just as much in the way of pleasure and pay as can the woman procurer, they also probably lead the women to believe that they can assure them better protection and a greater security in the evasion of the law.

Correspondence captured in raids instituted by agents of the Commission shows some of these methods of recruiting. These letters are extremely valuable "human documents" relating to persons of the class in question. The men seem to feel affection for their families; they talk tenderly with reference to the fortunes or misfortunes of their mothers or relatives; they send polite greetings to one another and to their friends. At the same time they discuss the characteristics of the women in question with the same coolness with which they would name the good points of a horse or a blooded dog which they had for sale. Extracts from some of the captured letters follow:

> An absolutely new number—tall, handsome of figure and body, 20 years and 6 months old. She wants to earn money.
> The brother of Antoine and Pierre, nicknamed "dealers in live stock." I do not want to ask any favors of them; they are great rascals.
> A woman the like of whom you can never find; young, beautiful, most . . . and who fully decided to leave. You can well understand I gave them a song and dance. . . . Without praising her highly, she is as beautiful as it is possible to find in this world, and I hope she will serve your purpose well. . . . I will send you her photograph. Her beautiful teeth alone are worth a million.

Far more pitiful, however, are the cases of the innocent girls. A French girl seized in a raid of a disorderly house in Chicago stated to the United States authorities that she was approached when she was but 14 years of age; that her procurer promised her employment in America as a lady's maid or a companion, at wages far beyond any that she could ever hope to get in France; that she came with him to the United States, and upon her arrival in Chicago was sold into a house of ill fame.

The testimony of a girl of only 17 taken in a typical case in Seattle in 1909 shows some of the methods used in recruiting their victims by those engaged in the traffic. Flattery, promises of work, love-making, promise of marriage to a wealthy person, seduction without marriage, kind treatment for a month or two, travel with the procurer as wife, continual deception; then an explanation to the girl of the life awaiting her, which in her innocence she could not understand, experience in a house of ill fame in Montreal, Canada, personal brutality, even physical violence, being allowed not one cent of the hard-earned money; then transportation to Vancouver, to Prince Rupert, to Alaska, and to Seattle, in every city being forced to earn money in a shameful life, with total earnings of more than $2,000, none of which she was able to retain; finally release by arrest and readiness to be deported if only the story of her shame can be kept from father and mother, sisters and brothers. This is but one of many such cases.

Edwin W. Sims, United States district attorney in Chicago, makes the following statement, the evidence for which is on file in his office:

> The hirelings of this traffic are stationed at certain points of entry in Canada where large numbers of immigrants are landed to do what is known in their parlance as "cutting-out work." In other words, these watchers for human prey scan the immigrants as they come down the gang plank of a vessel which has just arrived and "spot" the girls who are unaccompanied by fathers, mothers, brothers, or relatives to protect them. The girl who has been spotted as a desirable and unprotected victim is properly approached by a man who speaks her language and is immediately offered employment at good wages, with all expenses to the destination to be paid by the man. Most frequently laundry work is the bait held out, sometimes housework or employment in a candy shop or factory.
>
> The object of the negotiations is to "cut out" the girl from any of her associates and to get her to go with him. Then the only thing is to accomplish her ruin by the shortest route. If she can not be cajoled or enticed by the promises of an easy time, plenty of money, fine clothes, and the usual stock of allurements—or a fake marriage—then harsher methods are resorted to. In some instances the hunters really marry their victims.
>
> As to the sterner methods, it is, of course, impossible to speak explicitly beyond the statement that intoxication and drugging are often resorted to as a means to reduce the victim to a state of helplessness, and sheer physical violence is a common thing.

Those who recruit women for immoral purposes watch all places where young women are likely to be found under circumstances which will give them a ready means of acquaintance and intimacy, such as employment agencies, immigrant homes, moving-picture shows, dance halls, sometimes waiting rooms in large department stores, railroad stations, manicuring and hairdressing establishments. The men watching such places are usually suave in manner, well dressed, and prosperous looking. They become acquainted as intimately as possible with the young aliens, then use every conceivable method of betraying them.

Many of the girls now engaged in prostitution have told agents of the Commission of the desire of procurers and disorderly-house keepers to obtain innocent young girls. They consider them particularly desirable because they have no pimp to demand a share of their earnings or to remove them from the disorderly house at will, and they will last longer, and therefore be more profitable. The proprietor of such a house will even pay a large price for such a girl. Among the papers taken from the Dufaur house, Chicago, in June, 1908, was a letter from a man in London asking Dufaur to send $200 for the passage of himself and a woman from London to Chicago, and a receipt showing that the money had been received from Dufaur. Another letter was from a woman in Brussels addressed to Mr. and Mrs. Dufaur asking if they had a place for the writer's 18-year-old sister who wished to come to America. Still other evidence showed that Dufaur had paid $1,000 for an exceptionally attractive girl.

To secure entries into the country contrary to law, these immoral women or the deluded innocent victims of the procurers are usually brought in as wives or relatives of men accompanying them; as maids or relatives of women accompanying them; as women entering alone, booked to friends or relatives or to a home, and representing themselves as looking for work; as wives coming to men supposed to be their husbands, or, in the case of Japanese, their proxy husbands. Many imported women are brought by way of New York. Of late, many come through Canada. On the Pacific coast, San Francisco and Seattle are the chief ports of entry.

. . . [S]ome Japanese women doubtless come to this country to meet their proxy husbands when their purposes are entirely legal and proper; but it can be readily seen how liable the custom is to abuse, and in the opinion of the immigrant inspectors a large majority of the women coming in this way are intended for purposes of prostitution. If, however, the marriage ceremony is duly performed, the officials feel that nothing more can be done. It is practically impossible to prove the intention before the fact. . . .

Chinese women can enter this country under the law only when appearing as wives or daughters of the Chinese men who are of the admitted classes, such as merchants, students, travelers, government officials. Doubtless in many instances women are brought in as wives of members of these exempt classes and are then sold to keepers of houses. Under the conditions ruling in the Chinese quarters of our cities, such women become really slaves; doubtless in many cases they have been slaves at home. Unless they are redeemed through purchase by some man who is ready to marry them their position is practically that of permanent slavery, although theoretically they are allowed in certain instances to earn the money for the purchase of their liberty. Under the methods of exploitation followed in Chinese houses, as well as those kept by others, such self-purchase is, however, almost, if not quite, impossible.

A plan followed frequently in importing Japanese women for immoral purposes is to marry them upon their arrival to Japanese men whose status as native Americans has been established. In some instances Americans pretend to marry Japanese girls in Japan and bring them into America as their wives. Doubtless these cases are rare.

2. Wong Ah So Describes Her Experiences as a Prostitute in the Early 1920s

I was born in Canton Province, my father was sometimes a sailor and sometimes he worked on the docks, for we were very poor.

I was 19 when this man came to my mother and said that in America there was a great deal of gold. Even if I just peeled potatoes there, he told my mother I would

Social Science Institute, Fisk University, *Orientals and Their Cultural Adjustment: Interviews, Life Histories and Social Adjustment Experiences of Chinese and Japanese . . . in the United States,* Social Science Source Documents, no. 4 (Nashville: Fisk University, 1946), 31–33. Reprinted by permission of Fisk University.

earn seven or eight dollars a day, and if I was willing to do any work at all I would earn lots of money. He was a laundryman, but said he earned plenty of money. He was very nice to me, and my mother liked him, so my mother was glad to have me go with him as his wife.

I thought that I was his wife, and was very grateful that he was taking me to such a grand, free country, where everyone was rich and happy.

When we first landed in San Francisco we lived in a hotel in Chinatown, a nice place, but one day, after I had been there for about two weeks, a woman came to see me. She was young, very pretty, and all dressed in silk. She told me that I was not really Hucy Yow's wife, but that she had asked him to buy her a slave, that I belonged to her, and must go with her, but she would treat me well, and I could buy back my freedom, if I was willing to please, and be agreeable, and she would let me off in two years, instead of four if I did not make a fuss. She said that so I would be quieter about it. I did not believe her, I thought that she was lying to me. So when Hucy [Y]ow come I asked him why that woman had come and what she meant by all that lying. But he said that it was true; that he was not my husband, he did not care about me, and that this was something that happened all the time. Everybody did this, he said, and why be so shocked that I was to be a prostitute instead of a married woman. I asked him, "What is a prostitute? Am I not your wife?" And he said, "Couldn't I just say that you were my wife? That does not make it so. Everybody does this sort of thing. The woman gave me money just to bring you over."

I was in that life for seven months, and then I was released. I don't know just how it came about, but I know it was through a friend of my father's that I met at a banquet.

It was a party given by the Tong men, where slave girls are invited, who sit and eat and drink with the men. Suddenly I saw a friend of my father's come in, a man who had seen me less than a year ago. Although I was all dressed up so grand he recognized me, and the first chance he had, he came and asked me, "Are you not so and so's daughter?"

Of course, under the circumstances, I refused to admit that I knew my own parents, for fear that I would disgrace them, but he insisted, and finally he took me aside and forced me to admit it, and asked, "How is it that you have come to this?" He explained that if I would tell him all he would find some way to get me out of that. So I told him all.

The reason why I did not tell him at first was because I wanted to shield my mother. I felt that my father was absolutely innocent, because one day I heard him tell my mother that if any evil should befall me in America he would hold her responsible, and I felt that now the evil was done and there was no need for her to suffer for it.

About ten days after the party and the interview with this man I was rescued and taken to the mission. I don't know just how it happened because it was all very sudden. I just know that it happened. I am learning English and to weave, and I am going to send money to my mother when I can, I can't help but cry, but it is going to be better. I will do what Miss Cameron [head of the Presbyterian Mission Home] says.

3. Cantonese Rhymes from San Francisco's Chinatown, 1911–1915

Husband is in North America.
He leaves me so easily for some gain!
This makes me lonely, as I guard the scented
    bedroom by my lonesome self,
Giving up the gaiety of life at the age of
    twenty-two!
It's so frustrating.
This cold bedding keeps me from sleep.
I light the lamp, and again write him a letter
    from home,
Dear love, I ask, have you decided when to
    return?

Hitching up with a nice young man—
This whore sure has good vision.
Suddenly she quits her profession and her prayers
    are answered;
Rids herself of the infamous label and becomes his
    second wife.
It's a big deal for her:
She wanders the streets no more.
Now she retires to learn the manners of a family
    woman;
She's spared from being flesh and skin for hire.

The beautiful lass, an American-born,
A barbaric little princess.
She follows the Western example and lives the
    American way;
She doesn't accept her parents' strict discipline.
Harboring high ideals,
She chooses her own mate.
Falling in love with one who shares her likes,
She agrees to have sex with him before picking out
    the wedding day.

Native-borns call each other brother and sister.
They live in the American way.

Marlon K. Hom, *Songs of Gold Mountain: Cantonese Rhymes from San Francisco Chinatown* (Berkeley: University of California Press, 1987), 129, 226, 230, 320. Reprinted by permission of the Regents of the University of California and the University of California Press.

Holding hands, they say they're off to a picture
  show.
Actually, they're going to a hotel!
Enjoying their longings and desires,
So what if people gossip;
The two of them entwined in deep passion;
She may become pregnant, but that's nothing strange!

4. "Farfariello" Sings About Courting and Marriage in America, 1910

Me piace questa terra americana,	I like this American soil,
Perche' qua siamo tutte quante equale	Because here we're all equal
E il presidente m' hadda da' la mano,	And the president has to give his hand,
A me come la da' al frato carnale.	To me like he gives it to his blood brother.
Mo che saccio ll' America,	Now that I know America,
Nun tengo cchiu' crianza,	I don't have anymore respect [for others],
Ammarcio col principio,	I am guided by the principle,
Nisciuno e' mmeglio 'e me	That no one is better than me
Si tu si nnato principe,	Whether you're born a prince,
O tu si scenziato.	Or if you're an intellectual.
Io tengo la sciammeria	I have a lightweight overcoat
E songo 'o stesso 'e n' ato	And I'm the same as any other
Dezze bicos Franci'	That's because Frankie
Mi laiche dis contri'	Me like this country[.]
A lu paese mio pe fa ll'ammore,	To court in my village,
Te 'a mettere il cortiello nella sacca	You have to put a knife in your pocket
O lu pate o lu frate per ll'annore,	Either the father or the brother for honor,
La ponta de lu naso te ll'ammacca	Will dent the tip of your nose
Ma qua ll'ammore **e'olrraite,**	But here lovemaking is alright,
Overamente e'bello,	Actually it's beautiful,
Il padre penza e' dollare,	The father thinks of dollars,
Il frate penza 'e **ghelle**	The brother thinks of girls
Percio la strada e' libera,	That's why the road is clear,
Aperta so' li porte.	The doors are open.
La chiamme: **Come daune.**	You call her: Come down.

Eduardo Migliaccio ("Farfariello"), *'O Cafone c' 'a Sciammeri a"* (1910), Eduardo Migliaccio Collection, box 2, Immigration History Research Center, University of Minnesota, St. Paul, Minn. Translated by Nancy Carnevale and Maria Galetta. Reprinted by permission of the Immigration History Research Center and Nancy Carnevale and Maria Galetta.

T' a pigli e te la puorte.
   Dezze bicose Franci',
   Mi laiche dis contri'.

Si tu te nzure dalli parte noste,
Passe lu guai e nun nce fai cchiu'
   niente,
Quell'e' e quelle'e' cumpa', care te
   costa,
*O fosse **olrraite** o fosse malamente*
Ma qua dentro all'America,
Si nun te pare bbona,
Scasse lu matremmonio
E te la vai a cagna'
*Dice: **misto no laiche.***
Fai na carta mbollata,
E quello lesto il sinneco,
Te ne prepara n'ata
   Dezze bicose Franci'
   Mi laiche dis contri'.

You get her and you take her away.
   That's because Frankie,
   Me like this country.

If you get married around our parts,
You've got troubles and you can't do
   anything,
That's what she is *compare*, she'll
   cost you dear,
If she's alright or if she's bad
But here in America,
If she doesn't seem good to you,
Break the marriage
And go exchange her
Say: Mister, no like.
Make a notarized document,
And the mayor will quickly,
Prepare you another [wife]
   That's because Frankie
   Me like this country.

5. Reformers Condemn "Tough Dancing," c. 1910

The attention of the Committee on Amusements and Vacation Resources of Working Girls of New York City, has been directed to the wide-spread diffusion of certain forms of dancing, and its contribution to delinquency. After investigation, our committee has reported that conditions in this regard challenge the immediate consideration of all who are interested in the welfare of young men and young women.

We need your co-operation in our efforts to suppress "tough" dancing which, according to our investigators, is being practiced to an alarming extent. We feel that once the public conscience is aroused to the gravity of the situation, means will be adopted whereby all dancing of this character will be prohibited.

We have ascertained that these dances, commonly designated as the "slow rag," "lovers' two-step," "bunny hug," "turkey trot" and "walk back" are, in reality, modified varieties and conventional adaptations of a dance which had its origin in houses of prostitution, whence it spread first to the dives and tenderloin dance halls and thence to a large number of the dance halls of the city.

This dance has spread so that it is now danced at all but the most select dances, although of course, in its more or less modified forms, but it does not, in the progress of modification, lose one whit of its disreputable identity and demoralizing influence.

Committee on Amusements and Vacation Resources of Working Girls broadside (c. 1910), Lillian Wald Collection, box 28, folder "Parks and Playgrounds—Correspondence," Rare Book and Manuscript Library, Columbia University, New York.

It is not sufficient here, in referring to this dance, to merely designate it as improper, or immodest, or "tough," nor is it enough to indicate it by the names by which it is known since the uninformed would fail to identify it from round dancing. It is distinctly not round dancing, or dancing in which the participants stand too close.

In order that the character and influence of this dance may be known, and that those in charge of young people may detect it in its various forms, it might be well to define it specifically. What particularly distinguishes this dance is the motion of the pelvic portion of the body, bearing in mind its origin. It is this feature of the dance that renders it dangerous to the morals of those who have learned it.

It should be explained that the milder forms of this dance, such as the moderated "lovers' two-step," the "bunny hug," the combined two-step and walk back, and the subdued "turkey trot," in which this characteristic side to side swaying of the pelvis is subdued, is the same immoral dance. Once learned, the participants can, at will, instantly decrease or increase the obscenity of the movements, lowering the hands from the shoulders to the hips and dancing closer and closer until the bodies touch.

In fact so common is this procedure, that it may be said to be almost characteristic of the dance. Hence the absurdity of the argument made by some that "as long as they dance it in its moderated variety it won't hurt them any." It is this milder form of the dance that is being taught to the unsuspecting. The positions and movements of the dance, no matter how slight they may be, are pernicious.

This form of dance, particularly in conjunction with liquor drinking, has become the principal means through which girls are now being led astray, seduced or procured in the dance halls which have, within the last few years, sprung up in every city throughout the country. These are not opinions, but statements of facts, which may be readily corroborated.

We urge the importance of recognizing the distinction between legitimate dancing and this hideous perversion which, generally speaking, is not dancing at all, but a series of indecent antics, to the accompaniment of music. It would be unfair to condemn the art of dancing because of the intrusion of this objectionable variety.

We should state that this dance in its several varieties began to spread only within the last five or six years. Has any dancing of this description come to your notice? Will you not reply to this letter, assuring us of your interest and co-operation in the elimination of this most pernicious influence in our civil life?

6. An Immigrant Newspaper Defends Czech Dance Halls, 1917

The *Chicago American*, which is published and owned by Mr. [William Randolph] Hearst, of unsavory repute, has been printing a series of articles headed, "Our Little Daughters," as an initiation of a crusade against certain halls in which dancing and other entertainment are offered to the patrons. These halls are . . . branded as places

---

"In the Interest of Our Halls," *Denni Hlasatel.* March 23, 1917, in Works Project Administration, *Chicago Foreign Language Press Survey.* Chicago Public Library, Chicago, Ill.

where the body and mind of young girls are exposed to moral corruption, where drunkenness is in order, and which lead directly to the police courts. The avowed purpose of the articles is a hint for the authorities to close these halls and disrupt any kind of pleasure that may be derived from them. There are some good points in the movement, if only those propagating it would clear up the issue beginning at the right place, and use discrimination.

Because good judgment is not found in the articles, we object to them; their survey does not extend only to places where an orgy is indulged in every evening— these articles invade our immigrant dance halls; they attack our places of decent recreation. The venom of the reports is especially directed against two of our halls; one article turned against the hall of the Sokol Chicago, the other against the Pilsen Auditorium. The female writer of the articles visited the Sokol Chicago Hall on the occasion of an entertainment given by the "Ynot Club," and the Pilsen Auditorium during an evening arranged by the "Moon Glide Club." We shall not dwell upon the qualities of the two clubs, as we are not acquainted with them. However we are concerned with the insinuations cast upon the two halls, as we consider them as our own. We are ready to concede the fact that much of the entertainment of our dance halls needs moderation, but we shall not admit that conditions are such as described in the articles. . . .

We take exception against similar attacks because they are indirectly aimed at our girls of whom it cannot be generally contended that they drink immoderately, permit improper familiarity to the men in their company, or conduct themselves publicly in a manner not fit for decent women. Our Czech girls frequent, as far as our knowledge goes, orderly entertainments only, which they can enjoy without detriment to their reputation. They are usually chaperoned by both parents, or at least by their mothers, who certainly are their best guardians. The girls from our middle-class and from the laboring strata do not need any one to control their behavior. Their bearing decidedly does not call for any of the diverse morals commissions, not to mention the supervision of the *Chicago American*. They have enough judgment to regulate their own deportment.

We have already admitted that there are exceptions. They are, however, scarce. They are to be looked for in clubs and club affairs, which are in no way connected with the owners of the places. Our halls should be stricken from the list of objectionables. More so, as there are many others available for sound criticism, particularly those of the so-called better American societies, some of which could be pointed at as the very hotbeds of sin, ill behavior, and scandalous revelry. These places are not even remotely considered for an entertainment by our girls, who would blush for shame and recoil on their threshold.

Are places such as these unknown to the *Chicago American?* Is that paper ignorant of their existence in some fashionable hotels within the [L]oop, where the indulgent closing hour initiated veritable orgies to which the attention of the police had to be called? How about the cabarets in some downtown hotels where the Merriam Commission uncovered debauchery that defies description? Does the *Chicago American* know nothing of the club rooms of the wealthy, the "creme of society," the unbridled carousals which remind one of the one time "Red Light District," where ladies in gorgeous attire imbibe until they sink into a drunken stupor and are then brought home by gentlemen in dress suits and patent leather pumps, equally paralyzed, and who are not necessarily their husbands[?] Were the *Chicago American* an honest sheet, it would expose these places before all others as those for which an institution like the morals court has been established. This court would, however, prove utterly inadequate if all that mire should be brought before it. Immorality and scandalous behavior are not rampant among the immigrant population, for that privilege has always been enjoyed by the upper and rich classes, simply because these latter have a monopoly on immunity.

After all, we would not worry about the whole [incident] if it were not for the probability that the *Chicago American,* after an aggression against one hall, will proceed against all of our own halls. Bearing this in mind we rise in protest in behalf of the Czech halls. We know too well how much sacrifice and toil was the price of the creation of our halls. We know equally as well, how much these localities have contributed to our national, economic and social life and do not, therefore, intend to silently stand aside and endure what a Pharisaic paper, foreign to our tongue, has to say about our places of assembly.

7. Emma Goldman Analyzes "The Traffic in Women," 1911

Our reformers have suddenly made a great discovery—the white slave traffic. The papers are full of these "unheard of conditions," and lawmakers are already planning a new set of laws to check the horror. . . .

To assume that the recent investigation of the white slave traffic (and, by the way, a very superficial investigation) has discovered anything new, is, to say the least, very foolish. Prostitution has been, and is, a widespread evil, yet mankind goes on its business, perfectly indifferent to the sufferings and distress of the victims of prostitution. As indifferent, indeed, as mankind has remained to our industrial system, or to economic prostitution. . . .

What is really the cause of the trade in women? Not merely white women, but yellow and black women as well. Exploitation, of course; the merciless Moloch of capitalism that fattens on underpaid labor, thus driving thousands of women and girls into prostitution. . . . [T]hese girls feel, "Why waste your life working for a few shillings a week in a scullery, eighteen hours a day?"

Naturally our reformers say nothing about this cause. They know it well enough, but it doesn't pay to say anything about it. It is much more profitable to play the Pharisee, to pretend an outraged morality, than to go to the bottom of things. . . .

Nowhere is woman treated according to the merit of her work, but rather as a sex. It is therefore almost inevitable that she should pay for her right to exist, to keep a position in whatever line, with sex favors. Thus it is merely a question of

Emma Goldman, "The Traffic in Women," in *Anarchism and Other Essays* (New York: Mother Earth Publishing Co., 1911), 183–200.

degree whether she sells herself to one man, in or out of marriage, or to many men. Whether our reformers admit it or not, the economic and social inferiority of woman is responsible for prostitution. . . .

It would be one-sided and extremely superficial to maintain that the economic factor is the only cause of prostitution. There are others no less important and vital. That, too, our reformers know, but dare discuss even less than the institution that saps the very life out of both men and women. I refer to the sex question, the very mention of which causes most people moral spasms.

It is a conceded fact that woman is being reared as a sex commodity, and yet she is kept in absolute ignorance of the meaning and importance of sex. Everything dealing with the subject is suppressed, and persons who attempt to bring light into this terrible darkness are persecuted and thrown into prison. Yet it is nevertheless true that so long as a girl is not to know how to take care of herself, not to know the function of the most important part of her life, we need not be surprised if she becomes an easy prey to prostitution, or to any other form of a relationship which degrades her to the position of an object for mere sex gratification.

It is due to this ignorance that the entire life and nature of the girl is thwarted and crippled. We have long ago taken it as a self-evident fact that the boy may follow the call of the wild; that is to say, that the boy may, as soon as his sex nature asserts itself, satisfy that nature; but our moralists are scandalized at the very thought that the nature of a girl should assert itself. . . .

Society considers the sex experiences of a man as attributes of his general development, while similar experiences in the life of a woman are looked upon as a terrible calamity, a loss of honor and of all that is good and noble in a human being. This double standard of morality has played no little part in the creation and perpetuation of prostitution. It involves the keeping of the young in absolute ignorance on sex matters, which alleged "innocence," together with an overwrought and stifled sex nature, helps to bring about a state of affairs that our Puritans are so anxious to avoid or prevent.

Not that the gratification of sex must needs lead to prostitution; it is the cruel, heartless, criminal persecution of those who dare divert from the beaten paths, which is responsible for it.

Girls, mere children, work in crowded, over-heated rooms ten to twelve hours daily at a machine, which tends to keep them in a constant over-excited sex state. Many of these girls have no home or comforts of any kind; therefore the street or some place of cheap amusement is the only means of forgetting their daily routine. This naturally brings them into close proximity with the other sex. It is hard to say which of the two factors brings the girl's over-sexed condition to a climax, but it is certainly the most natural thing that a climax should result. That is the first step toward prostitution. Nor is the girl to be held responsible for it. On the contrary, it is altogether the fault of society, the fault of our lack of understanding, of our lack of appreciation of life in the making; especially is it the criminal fault of our moralists, who condemn a girl for all eternity, because she has gone from the "path of virtue"; that is, because her first sex experience has taken place without the sanction of the Church.

The girl feels herself a complete outcast, with the doors of home and society closed in her face. Her entire training and tradition is such that the girl herself feels depraved and fallen, and therefore has no ground to stand upon, or any hold that will lift her up, instead of dragging her down. Thus society creates the victims that it afterwards vainly attempts to get rid of. The meanest, most depraved and decrepit man still considers himself too good to take as his wife the woman whose grace he was quite willing to buy, even though he might thereby save her from a life of horror. Nor can she turn to her own sister for help. In her stupidity the latter deems herself too pure and chaste, not realizing that her own position is in many respects even more deplorable than her sister's of the street. . . .

Much stress is laid on white slaves being imported into America. How would America ever retain her virtue if Europe did not help her out? I will not deny that this may be the case in some instances, any more than I will deny that there are emissaries of Germany and other countries luring economic slaves into America; but I absolutely deny that prostitution is recruited to any appreciable extent from Europe. It may be true that the majority of prostitutes in New York City are foreigners, but that is because the majority of the population is foreign. The moment we go to any other American city, to Chicago or the Middle West, we shall find that the number of foreign prostitutes is by far a minority.

Equally exaggerated is the belief that the majority of street girls in this city were engaged in this business before they came to America. Most of the girls speak excellent English, are Americanized in habits and appearance, —a thing absolutely impossible unless they had lived in this country many years. That is, they were driven into prostitution by American conditions, by the thoroughly American custom for excessive display of finery and clothes, which, of course, necessitates money, —money that cannot be earned in shops or factories.

In other words, there is no reason to believe that any set of men would go to the risk and expense of getting foreign products, when American conditions are overflooding the market with thousands of girls.

E S S A Y S

To what degree did working-class and immigrant women claim a degree of sexual agency? How did they understand their own sexuality, in light of middle-class moral interventions, their own communities' customs, and their everyday lives? Peggy Pascoe, of the University of Oregon, examines one of the worst forms of sexual exploitation for working women, forced prostitution, and considers the experiences of Chinese-American women "rescued" by white female reformers. Moral and sexual redemption came at a price: reformers imposed Anglo-American concepts of womanhood and supervised the marriages of the former prostitutes. As Pascoe shows, Chinese women could use the authority of the rescue missions for their own purposes, navigating between the sex/gender systems of their homeland and that of the American middle class. Kathy Peiss, of the University of Pennsylvania, shows how young working-class women in New York carved out a space of sexual and personal autonomy, despite the limits placed on them at home and work. Engaging in the "sexual economy"— exchanging sexual favors for theater tickets, meals, and the like—they denied they were prostitutes but asserted their respectability. As these articles show, middle-class standards of virtue and vice did not always reflect the experiences and perceptions of working-class women.

The Marriages of Mission-Educated Chinese-American Women

PEGGY PASCOE

As soon as Wong Ah So entered the United States in 1922, she was sold into prostitution. Her owner, a Chinese woman who moved her from one town to another, took most of her earnings, but Wong Ah So scraped up extra money to send to her impoverished family in Hong Kong. When the man who had helped smuggle her into the country demanded $1000 for his services, Wong Ah So, who was afraid of him, borrowed the money to pay him. Shortly afterwards, she developed an illness, apparently venereal disease, that required daily treatment and interfered with her work as a prostitute.

In February 1924, Protestant missionaries raided the residential hotel in Fresno, California, where Wong Ah So was staying. Wong Ah So was frightened. Her owner had tried to keep her away from missionaries by telling her that their leader, Donaldina Cameron, "was in the habit of draining blood from the arteries of newly 'captured' girls and drinking it to keep up her own vitality." But Wong Ah So was also tired, sick, and afraid that she could not repay her heavy debts. She agreed to enter Cameron's Presbyterian Mission Home in San Francisco. Wong Ah So would live in the Mission Home for only a little more than a year, but the course of the rest of her life would be changed by her contact with missionary women.

From the late nineteenth century to the present, accounts like that of Wong Ah So fed the white American taste for exoticism and formed a unique genre in the popular mythology of American race relations. Missionary women called them "rescue" stories and saw them as skirmishes in a righteous battle against sexual slavery. Newspaper reporters exploited the stories for sensational copy, attracting readers with provocative headlines such as "Slave Girls Taken in Raid on Chinese," or "Woman Tells of Traffic in Slave Girls." Anti-Chinese politicians relied on images of so-called "Chinese slave girls" to bolster their successful 1882 campaign to restrict the immigration of Chinese laborers.

In the rescue genre, sensational images of victimized Chinese women were accompanied by equally sensational portrayals of nefarious Chinese organizations—the tongs—that kidnapped, enslaved and exploited prostitutes. Because rescue stories suggested that every Chinese organization thrived on organized vice, they left scandalized readers ignorant of the distinction between the tongs that controlled prostitution and the Chinese family and district associations that had little connection to the trade. . . .

The alternatives available to Chinese immigrant women in American Chinatowns were conditioned by Victorian racial hierarchies, but they were also affected by the conflict between gender systems revealed in the contact between Chinese immigrant women and Protestant women reformers. Because rescue stories illuminate both race relations and gender systems, missionary records are an ideal source for

Peggy Pascoe, "Gender Systems in Conflict: The Marriage of Mission-Educated Chinese American Women, 1874–1939," *Journal of Social History* 22 (Summer 1989), 631–652. Reprinted by permission.

exploring the complexity of race *and* gender relations between dominant groups and minority groups in American society. To explore these issues, I will use the case files of the Presbyterian Mission Home that Wong Ah So entered in 1924 as a window on gender relations in San Francisco's Chinatown at the turn of the century.

Specifically, I want to do three things: first, describe the two different gender systems idealized in China and in nineteenth-century America; second, show how the immigrant context made Chinese women in San Francisco particularly vulnerable to exploitation yet, at the same time, put some of them in a particularly opportune position to challenge traditional male prerogatives; and finally, show how Chinese immigrant women used the conflict between traditional Chinese and Victorian American gender systems to shape one set of possibilities for a distinctive Chinese American culture.

Let's begin with the gender system of traditional China, the set of ideals Wong Ah So and many other immigrant women were raised to emulate. In traditional China, families provided the social glue of society, and families focused their energies on the importance of raising male heirs to carry on the lineage. For this reason, young girls were considered to be less important than young boys from birth. Especially—but not only—in impoverished families, young girls might be sold to pay debts or expected to demonstrate their filial piety by working for wages. Something like this happened to Wong Ah So when her mother bargained with a young man who told them that in San Francisco, Wong Ah So could make money to support her family as an entertainer at Chinese banquets. When the young man offered the mother $450 for her daughter, Wong Ah So went to California.

Although historians should be cautious in equating cultural ideals with individual behavior, there is little doubt that Wong Ah So understood and accepted her subordinate position in this traditional gender system. Even after she awoke from her dreams of fancy entertaining to the harsh reality of prostitution in immigrant California, Wong Ah So's letters to her mother in Hong Kong were framed in traditional terms. "Daughter is not angry with you," she wrote in one letter later found and saved by missionary women, "It seems to be just my fate." Dutifully reciting familiar stories of Chinese children renowned for their filial piety, she promised her mother that "after I have earned money by living this life of prostitution, I will return to China and become a Buddhist nun." "By accomplishing these two things," she ended rather hopefully, "I shall have attained all the requirements of complete filial piety."

The full weight of the gender system of traditional China descended on young women at the time of marriage. Matches were generally arranged by go-betweens, with little personal contact between prospective mates. In and of themselves, new brides held little status until they produced male heirs; until then, they were expected to serve their mothers-in-law. Whether mothers or daughters-in-law, women were expected to display female submission to male authority. Thus Wong Ah So knew by heart what she called "the three great obediences": "At home, a daughter should be obedient to her parents; after marriage, to her husband; after the death of her husband, to her son."

The subordination of young wives was ensured by a series of social sanctions. Wives who didn't produce male heirs might find their husbands taking concubines; there was a highly-stratified system of prostitution from which such concubines could be chosen. Furthermore, wives who didn't behave according to custom might find themselves divorced and sent back to their own families in disgrace. Even young wives' most forceful weapon of complaint—committing suicide to protest against bad treatment—brought social judgment on their in-laws only at the cost of their own lives.

Young women who adapted to the constraints of this traditional patriarchal system, however, could achieve significant social status later in life as mothers and mothers-in-law. As Wong Ah So noted, evidently trying to resign herself to her situation, "Now I may be somebody's daughter, but some day I may be somebody's mother." Wives who gave birth to sons could look forward to becoming mothers-in-law, a position of some authority within the patrilineal lineage.

By the late nineteenth century, when Chinese immigration to the United States was in full swing, the traditional system of patriarchal control was beginning to lose some of its power in China. In Kwangtung, the area from which most immigrants to America came, some young women who were able to find employment in the sericulture industry were mounting a "marriage resistance" movement and entering all-women's houses rather than living with parents or in-laws. Their relative freedom was based on a unique combination of economic circumstances that allowed them to support themselves outside of marriage.

It appears that most Chinese women who immigrated to America were more impoverished and less able to challenge the traditional ideals of marriage head-on than the marriage resisters of their native land. Yet when immigrant women reached the United States, they encountered a Victorian gender system which stood in some contrast to the traditional gender system of late nineteenth-century China. Victorian Americans held up an ideal some historians have called "companionate" marriage. According to these historians, companionate marriage differed from traditional marriage in significant respects. Companionate unions were based on attraction between spouses rather than parental arrangement and in them, at least according to the ideal, women were idealized as nurturant mothers and sexually pure moral guardians.

Yet, as feminist historians have pointed out, Victorian marriages also reflected an unequal arrangement of gender power. Companionate marriage may have differed from traditional marriage, but women who held to the Victorian ideal gained affection and moral influence at the cost of legal and economic powerlessness. Throughout the nineteenth century, middle-class American women had to fight for such basic rights as the chance to be considered legal guardians of their own children. Often deprived of formal control over their property, women were expected by society to be the economic dependents of men, a status that sharply limited their alternatives in and outside of marriage.

The ideal of companionate marriage was the rhetorical panacea put forth by the middle-class women who established the Presbyterian Mission Home Wong Ah So entered in San Francisco. Yet the Mission Home matrons who espoused companionate marriage were themselves single women devoted to professional careers in missionary work, women who had encountered in their own lives few of the daily restraints of Victorian marriage and who occupied a somewhat marginal place within the Victorian gender system. . . .

The cultural ideals of these two distinct gender systems clashed in American Chinatowns, where a unique pattern of immigration rendered Chinese immigrant women easily exploitable even as it held before them the promise of unprecedented opportunity. At the root of this unique social context was an extreme numerical imbalance between male immigrants (who formed the vast majority of the Chinese population in America) and the much smaller number of female immigrants. The number of Chinese women who traveled to the United States in the nineteenth century was so small that by 1882, when American exclusion legislation cut Chinese immigration drastically, the sex ratio in Chinese immigrant communities was already sharply skewed. In California, there were 22 Chinese men for every Chinese woman in 1890; in 1920, there were still 5 Chinese men for every Chinese woman.

This population imbalance created a demand for sexual services that sustained a thriving network of organized prostitution in Chinese immigrant communities. Only a few married Chinese women traveled to America, since respectable young wives were expected to remain with in-laws in China. Most of the female immigrants were young women who, like Wong Ah So, were placed into prostitution. Young women entered prostitution by a variety of means. Very few Chinese prostitutes were independent entrepreneurs. Many had been enticed into dubious marriages in China only to be sold into the trade on their arrival in America. Others had been purchased from their poverty-stricken parents; still others had been kidnapped by procurers and smuggled into American ports.

Compared to white American prostitutes of the same period, Chinese prostitutes were particularly powerless; in fact, many were kept in conditions that render some truth to the sensational stereotype of the "Chinese slave girl." Some were indentured, with few hopes of paying off their contracts; others were virtually enslaved. Most were under the control of tong leaders and their henchmen, many of whom operated with the collusion of white officials.

Thus, the skewed sex ratio of immigrant Chinatowns increased the vulnerability of Chinese immigrant woman to sexual exploitation. At the same time, however, the extreme sexual imbalance also offered unusual opportunities for those immigrant women who could find a way to take advantage of them. . . . [B]oth the skewed sex ratio and the absence of established in-laws created unique opportunities for immigrant prostitutes to marry in order to leave prostitution behind.

And here is where rescue homes founded by Protestant women came in. Rescue homes gave missionary women space and time to impose the Victorian gender system and its ideal of companionate marriage on Chinese immigrant women. Even the very term "rescue home" is a significant clue to their intentions. It conveyed the twin goals of Protestant women: on the one hand, they wanted to "rescue" Chinese women who had been sold or enticed into prostitution; on the other, they wanted to inculcate in all women their particular concept of the "Christian home." Protestant women believed that their institutions would separate women victims from the men who preyed on them, providing space for the supposedly natural virtues of Victorian "true womanhood"—purity and piety—to come to the surface. These Victorian ideals clashed with the more traditional gender system held by Chinese women. Nowhere was this conflict between gender systems more intense than in the Presbyterian Mission Home for Chinese women, founded in San Francisco in 1874 and in operation until 1939.

Support for Victorian female values was built into the institutional routine of the Presbyterian Mission Home. The Victorian conception of female purity, for example, was ensured by drawing strict boundaries between the rescue home and the surrounding community. . . . Mission Home residents were never allowed out-side the institution without escorts; in the early years, they were even hidden behind a screen at church services.

Further, the Home had trusted doorkeepers whose job it was to screen visitors —men in particular—and keep them away from the women within. Contact with people outside the Home was limited to those approved by the mission staff—schoolteachers, employers judged suitable for domestic servants, and young men of "good" character who had been scrutinized by staff members. Matrons read all incoming and outgoing mail and confiscated letters they thought would prove detrimental to the residents' journey toward true womanhood.

Victorian female piety was encouraged in the Mission Home by continual at-tempts to convert residents to Protestant Christianity. Morning and evening prayers, with more extended sessions on weekends, were the rule. . . .

Along with this emphasis on purity and piety came a routine of constant busy-ness, which was desired both as a means of training in domesticity and as a way of keeping rescue home residents from looking longingly at their old lives. The day began with 7 a.m. prayers, followed by breakfast, an hour of supervised housework, morning and afternoon school classes, dinner, a 7 p.m. prayer meeting, a study session, and then lights out. Each resident cleaned her own room and did her own laundry in addition to the shared household tasks. Pairs of women were assigned each day to special tasks—cooking the Chinese and American meals, perhaps, or caring for the few babies in residence at any one time, a favorite assignment. The staff depended on the most trusted residents to translate, for most missionaries did not speak Chinese. . . .

The capstone to all this training in purity, piety, and domesticity was the mar-riage of a rescue home resident. Missionary women believed that, by separating "degraded" women from their unsuitable liaisons with male "betrayers" and allow-ing them to regain their supposedly natural moral purity, Christian homes would be formed in which moral wives and mothers would preside, their womanhood respected and honored by kindly Protestant husbands. Accordingly, matrons kept count of the number of "Christian homes" formed by residents and considered them the surest measure of institutional success. They lavished praise on young married couples, orchestrated elaborate wedding celebrations, and published photographs accompanied by society-page-style descriptions of the ceremonies.

Given the relatively small population of Chinese immigrant women, the num-bers of these marriages are impressive. Mission Home workers claimed that by 1888, only 14 years after the establishment of the institution, 55 Home residents had been married; by 1901, they took credit for 160 such marriages. No comparable summary figures are available for the twentieth century, but, extrapolating from the average number of marriages recorded in occasional yearly statistics, I estimate that as many as 266 Chinese women married after residing in the Home in the period between 1874 and 1928. . . . [W]e can locate specific information on 114 marriages. These marriages can be divided into two groups—those of prostitutes marrying suitors chosen well before entering the Mission Home and those arranged directly by Mission Home officials.

For the first two decades of its existence, the Presbyterian Mission Home sur-vived by attracting women of the first group—Chinese prostitutes with suitors who exchanged prostitution for marriage by agreeing to submit to a concentrated mission-administered dose of the Victorian gender system. In the context of immigrant Chinatowns, marriage offered young women social respectability and a chance at financial security without the traditional period of apprenticeship to mothers-in-law, since so many in-laws remained in China. But, for the typical prostitute, the chance to marry was limited by the virtual slavery of the tong-controlled prostitution system. Tong leaders were reluctant to release prostitutes under any conditions, and when they did let women go, they demanded exorbitant fees (ranging from $300 to $3000) to offset their initial investment and expected loss of earnings. Women who ran away without paying these fees could expect to be tracked down by tong "highbinders" or enforcers.

Under these circumstances, running away from prostitution was no small feat. To achieve it, young women had to find a way to escape from their owners' control long enough to enter the Presbyterian Mission Home; in fact, rescue homes sometimes lived up to their names when mission workers accompanied by white policemen with hatchets in hand "rescued" young prostitutes directly from brothels. What prompted most prostitutes to take such a daring step was the hope of marriage—typically, they had made plans to marry young men who were unable or unwilling to buy out their contracts or purchase their persons.

The early pattern can be seen in a letter addressed to Mission Home workers in 1886 by a young man who asked missionaries to collect his fiancé. He wrote:

> I have the case of a prostitute named Ah—, to bring forward to your notice. . . . I wish to succor her, but fear for my life. I also wish to redeem her, and have not sufficient means for that purpose. I find it hard to rescue her from her state of bondage. I thought of running away with her, but dread her keepers and accomplices' violence to me if intercepted. Even if we are furnished with wings, it is difficult to fly. . . . This girl wishes to enter your school. Here I have few friends of my own surname, so I am powerless to rescue her here. For this reason I have instead written to you for aid. I beseech you, with pitying heart and ability, to save her from her present difficulties and sufferings. This accomplished, there will be happiness all round. . . .

In the years between 1874 and 1900, a steady stream of prostitutes with suitors approached the Home to obtain protection from the tongs so they could marry. Mission Home workers offered assistance only to women who agreed to reside in the institution for six months to a year. Loi Kum, who entered the Home in July 1879, was one of them. According to Mission workers, Loi Kum "ran away to escape a dissolute life" and appeared at their doorstep "accompanied by a friend, who proposes to make her his wife." By agreement with Mission officials, Loi Kum remained in the Home for several months. When her fiance returned to arrange for their marriage, the missionaries were reluctant to let her go. They put the young man off several times by requiring him to pay $72 for her board and to obtain a legal marriage license. Finally, however, the wedding took place on July 16, 1880, almost a year after Loi Kum had entered the institution. She and her husband left the Mission Home secure in the knowledge that they would have behind them the force of mission workers' access to police power and judicial authority should they be pursued by tong members.

Because missionaries harbored deep reservations about the young men who brought prostitutes to the Home, they did little to publicize these marriages. . . .

When they could, missionaries convinced women to break off their engagements with the men who accompanied them to the Home and choose mission-approved husbands instead. . . .

In the meantime, however, San Francisco Presbyterian women had expanded their mission and their rescue work to include neglected or abused children as well as betrothed prostitutes. Some children were brought to the Home by child protection authorities; others were left there by struggling immigrant parents who wanted an inexpensive refuge or an English education for their children. As these young girls grew into adulthood, they, too, were married, again with considerable intervention on the part of Mission Home workers. . . .

Perhaps the first such marriage was that of Ah Fah, held on Saturday, April 13, 1878. Ah Fah married Ng Noy, a Chinese Christian man employed as a servant. The service was conducted in Chinese by a Presbyterian missionary and attended by Mission Home workers as well as friends of the couple. One of the missionary guests wrote a lengthy account of the event. Displaying typical racial attitudes, she commented approvingly that "this organization of a home on Christian principles" was "the first step upwards from heathenism to civilization." On behalf of Protestant women, she wished the newly-married couple well, trusting, she said, that their "future housekeeping" would "indeed be a *home*-keeping."

To arrange for the marriages of long-term residents like Ah Fah, missionaries screened applicants chosen from the many Chinese immigrant men who approached the Mission Home looking for wives. Matrons quizzed applicants about their previous marital status, their religious convictions, and their financial prospects in the belief that, as they put it, "he who would win a member of the Mission Home family for his wife must present the very best credentials." Only those Chinese men who fit the white Protestant ideal of the Christian gentleman were allowed to write or call on Mission Home residents.

Chinese men had several motivations for seeking Mission Home brides. First, they were handicapped in finding wives by the skewed sex ratio of the Chinese immigrant community in San Francisco. Second, they had few other alternatives. Intermarriage was not a possibility for them, since Chinese immigrants were prohibited from marrying whites by California miscegenation laws. Bringing a bride from China was at least equally difficult. Few minor merchants had the financial resources to pay for the trip, and those who did found themselves at the mercy of unpredictable immigration officials. For these reasons, there was no shortage of suitors for Mission Home residents. Mission Home employee Tien Fu Wu found that she was approached by potential suitors even on a trip to Boston. "Everybody is after me for girls," she wrote to Donaldina Cameron back in San Francisco, jokingly adding, "I might as well open a Matrimony Bureau here in the east." Mission marriages, then, were sought out by Chinese immigrant men. They also represented a significant advance in social status for Mission Home women, many of whom had originally been destined for lives of prostitution, neglect, abuse, or hard-working poverty.

In fact, mission-arranged marriages placed immigrant women at a particular level of the emerging social structure of San Francisco's Chinatown. In contrast to the social structure in China, which was dominated by scholars and officials, the social structure in immigrant Chinatowns in America was dominated by merchants.

The wealthiest of these merchants tended to disdain immigrant women and had the resources to seek brides in China. A step below these wealthy merchants, however, stood a group of less prosperous merchants who were destined to become significant as growing immigrant communities came to depend on them for goods, services, and community leadership. It was these minor merchants, many of whom started with very little, who most actively sought—and accomplished—marriage with Presbyterian Mission Home residents. Although historians have largely ignored the immigrant marriages that were formed in this period (commonly referred to as the "bachelor" years of San Francisco's Chinatown), it is possible to argue that, by pairing promising Chinese merchants with young women inculcated with Victorian family ideology, mission-arranged marriages created a core of middle-class Protestant Chinese American families in many cities. . . .

Thus, for both groups of women—prostitutes with suitors and children raised in the institution—the Mission Home facilitated marriages. Whether the residents entered the Home specifically for this reason or came there for other reasons, whether they entered the Home voluntarily or involuntarily, mission marriages seem to have offered Chinese immigrant women something of value. . . .

In fact, the prospect of mission marriages proved so appealing that some already-married women came to the Mission Home in search of new husbands. Some of these women had, like Wong Ah So, been the victims of men who had deceived them into technical marriage ceremonies to smuggle them into the country. Others had been married quite legitimately according to Chinese custom but wanted to leave incompatible mates. One such woman wrote matron Donaldina Cameron in 1923 to ask her to "let me enter your Home and study English [because] I am going to divorce with my husband for the sake of free from repression." "I understand," she explained, "that you as a Superintendent of the Home, always give aid to those who suffer from ill-treatment at home."

Mission workers, who were horrified by the deceptions and conditioned by racial and cultural bias to believe that Chinese marriages weren't really marriages at all, did help many women secure annulments or divorces. In at least a handful of these cases, missionaries arranged for new husbands as well. Occasional facilitation of second marriages persisted despite the fact that it exposed the Mission Home to criticism from observers in the white community. One lawyer who participated in a divorce proceeding initiated by a Mission Home resident could not restrain his sarcasm. When the divorce was declared final, he commented acidly that "the cute little defendant is now at liberty to marry whosomever the good lord may direct across her path."

The Mission Home offered married women more than the chance to form new marriages—it also offered them a chance to jockey for position vis-à-vis their current husbands. In fact, workers at the Presbyterian Mission Home were repeatedly asked to intervene on behalf of unhappy Chinese immigrant wives. . . .

In domestic cases, several complaints loomed large. The most frequent was wife abuse. When unhappy wives complained of mistreatment at the hands of their husbands, they were granted temporary shelter in the Mission Home while missionaries, shocked at the ritualized complaints they heard, made it their business to shape unhappy marriages into the Victorian companionate mode. Because they believed that "the fault usually lies with the husband," missionaries almost always tried to ensure better treatment for the wife. One woman, Mrs. Tom She Been, entered the Home "badly bruised from a beating" at the hands of her husband. Her husband, a well-known Chinese doctor, apologized to the missionaries and asked his wife to return to him, but not until the secretary of the Chinese Legation offered to intercede on her behalf did the woman agree. Missionaries were not, of course, always successful in solving the problem. One young woman who twice sought help from the Mission Home and both times went back to her husband committed suicide in March 1924.

Other Chinese immigrant women approached the Home in order to gain leverage in polygamous marriages. One such woman, Mrs. Yung, requested help from the Mission Home after her husband took a concubine. Although concubinage was a recognized institution in China, Yung's own mother advised her to resist it. "I know," she wrote to her daughter in the Home, "how the second wife has brought all these accusations against you, causing your husband to maltreat you and act savagely. . . . You must make him send the concubine back to China. . . . It isn't right to acquire a concubine and especially this concubine." Mr. Yung, backed up by his father, apparently refused, but when Mrs. Yung complained to the Mission Home, Protestant women speedily arranged for the deportation of the concubine.

Still other Chinese immigrant women came to the Mission Home to flee from marriages arranged by their parents that were distasteful to them. The unsatisfied ex-resident who committed suicide was one of them. As word got around that Mission Home workers were hostile to arranged marriages, a number of young women found their way to the institution soon after their parents proposed unappealing matches. Bow Yoke, a young woman whose father had accepted $600 for agreeing to make her the second wife of a much older man, refused to go along with the plan. She fled to the Police Station, and then to the Mission Home, before it could be carried out. . . .

The possibility of Mission Home intervention offered Chinese immigrant women in any of these positions bargaining room to improve the terms of their marriages or their relations with relatives. In one quite typical case, a woman entered the Presbyterian Mission Home in 1925 and did not return to her husband until mission workers convinced him to sign an agreement stipulating that: 1) he would not use opium, 2) he would treat her with "kindness and consideration" and "provide for them as comfortable a home as his income will permit," 3) he would give her money to care for herself and her children, and 4) if she died he would give the children to the Mission Home or to their grandmother (rather than selling them). . . .

Most of the public—and some of the private—accounts of Mission Home marriages stressed how thoroughly Chinese immigrant women adopted the Victorian gender system and its correlate, the ideal of companionate marriage. One of the Mission Home women in Philadelphia, for example, described her marriage to Mission Home superintendent Donaldina Cameron in a letter written during a lengthy illness. "My husband has been nursing me day and night," she reported, "he even gave up his restaurant to another party to look after, so he can nurse me, altho, our restaurant is the largest one in town." She went on to say that "he treats me like a real Christian. I regret very much that Heaven doesn't give me longer time to be with him. Yet, I thank God and you [Cameron] that we have had one another for more than ten years. As husband and wife we are most satisfied."

As this example suggests, some mission marriages did mirror the companionate ideals of Victorianism, but I think it would be more correct to say that, faced with the conflict between two distinct gender systems, Chinese immigrant women sifted through the possibilities and fashioned their own end-product, one which reveals some of the weaknesses of the Victorian gender system for women. The argument must remain speculative here, because most of the sources come not from the women who entered the Mission Home, married, and remained in contact with missionaries, but from those who refused to enter the Home in the first place or who ran away after a short residence. Still, the Mission Home case files suggest just how selectively immigrant women responded to missionary overtures.

The files show, for example, the attitudes held by young prostitutes who refused to enter the Mission Home in the first place. Despite their sexual exploitation, young prostitutes were accustomed to receiving fine clothing and gifts of cash or jewelry from their customers or their owners. Unless they had chosen a particular husband or found themselves especially ill-treated by their owners, they were unlikely to trade these material advantages for the general promise of Victorian moral respectability and economic dependence on husbands. On one occasion in 1897, when the Mission Home accepted sixty prostitutes arrested in a government raid, the matron recorded that the women "shrieked and wailed beating the floor with their shoes" and "denounce[ed] the Home in no unmeasured terms." The matron removed the angriest prostitutes to another room, but even those remaining rejected her offer of "protection" and residence in the Home "with scorn and derision."

The disdain of these prostitutes was echoed by another group of Mission Home residents—young Chinese American women judged by American courts to be the victims of "immoral" men. Such young women were much more likely than abused children or unhappy wives to criticize the most coercive aspect of the Mission Home—the attempt to mold all women to fit the Victorian belief that women were "naturally" morally pure and pious. In 1924, for example, Rose Seen, an unhappy fourteen-year-old girl who longed to be reunited with her lover, Bill, a Chinese man who had been charged with contributing to her delinquency, was sent to the Presbyterian Mission Home. In a note addressed "to my dearest beloved husband," Seen pleaded with Bill "to find some easy job and go to work so just to make them think you are not lazy and go to church on Sunday so pretend that you were a Christian cause Miss Cameron does not allow the girls to marry a boy that doesn't go to work." When this plan failed (Mission Home women confiscated the note and reported Bill to his probation officer), Seen tried another tack. Remaining in the Home for more than a year, she and a fellow resident convinced Mission Home officials of their sincerity to the extent that they were entrusted with the funds of a student group. In December 1925, however, both young women ran away from the Home, taking the money and some jewelry, hoping to reunite with Bill and his friends.

By running away from the Mission Home, Rose Seen escaped the moral supervision of missionaries. Amy Wong, a married ex-resident, was not so lucky. When she came to the Mission Home asking for help in a marital dispute, Protestant women decided that she, not her husband, was in the wrong. They promptly suggested that she sign an agreement that echoed those they ordinarily presented to husbands. According to its terms, her husband would take her back if she gave up smoking, drinking, gambling, and attending the Chinese theater and if she agreed "not to be out later than ten o'clock at night without my husband's knowledge and consent, or in his company." Additionally, she was to attend church and part-time school regularly, and to spend the rest of her time working to earn money for further education. The Wong agreement is the only one of its kind among Mission Home sources, but the Victorian pattern of female purity and piety it sought to enforce was a common assumption on the part of Protestant women.

Yet, even though women like Rose Seen and Amy Wong eschewed the moral restrictiveness of Victorian culture, the clash between traditional and Victorian ideologies in immigrant Chinatowns rendered certain tenets of the traditional Chinese gender system particularly vulnerable. For Chinese women who had decided to marry, the traditional Chinese family ideals upheld by immigrant communities contrasted with important realities, including the relative absence of in-laws and the difficulty young men had in finding wives. In such a situation, Chinese immigrant women used the Home to help tip the balance between vulnerability and opportunity in immigrant Chinatowns—to facilitate forming marriages and to exert some control over relations within marriage itself.

Perhaps we can best understand this process by returning once again to the case of Wong Ah So, whose life so clearly reveals the connection between individual experience and shifts in the gender system of Chinese immigrant communities. After residing in the Mission Home for one year, Wong Ah So married an aspiring merchant who had established a foothold in Boise, Idaho. A few years later, Wong Ah So wrote a letter to missionary Donaldina Cameron at the Presbyterian Mission Home. She started out by displaying the gratitude expected by Mission Home workers. "Thank you," she wrote, "for rescuing me and saving my soul and wishing peace for me and arranging for my marriage." Wong Ah So had more than thank-you's on her mind, though: she had written to ask for help with her marriage. Her husband, she said, was treating her badly. Her complaints were three: first, her husband had joined the Hop Sing tong; second, he refused to educate his daughters (by a previous wife); and third, he was so unhappy that Wong Ah So did not provide him with children that he had threatened to go to China to find a concubine to have a son for him.

In this letter, it is possible to see not only a conflict between two gender systems but also to see how Wong Ah So's ideals had changed over the years since she left China behind. As a former prostitute who had suffered from illness, she may have been unable to have the son whose birth would earn her female authority in traditional culture; in any case, what she wanted now was an education for her step-daughters. As a result, she had come to question the traditional ideals her husband still held. To retain his power, her husband threatened to return to China to find a willing concubine, a step that would have reinforced Wong Ah So's vulnerability. To offset his power, Wong Ah So invoked the aid of Mission Home women, who, reading Wong Ah So's carefully-worded charges as an all-too-familiar indictment of "heathen" behavior, promptly sent a local Protestant woman to investigate.

Wong Ah So's case is especially revealing, but it was hardly unique. Because the Presbyterian Mission Home offered immigrant women a pathway to marriage in immigrant Chinatowns, its sources show in concentrated form the clash between traditional Chinese and Victorian gender systems. The clash itself, however, was a society-wide process. Many Chinese immigrant women in America, in or outside of Mission Homes, found themselves in a position to use the gap between gender systems to maneuver for specific protections for individual women. Their dreams were played out over and over again as immigrant Chinatowns transformed themselves into Chinese American communities in the early twentieth century.

Charity Girls and City Pleasures

KATHY PEISS

Uncovering the history of working-class sexuality has been a particularly intractable task for recent scholars. Diaries, letters, and memoirs, while a rich source for studies of bourgeois sexuality, offer few glimpses into working-class intimate life. We have had to turn to middle-class commentary and observations of working people, but these accounts often seem hopelessly moralistic and biased. The difficulty with such sources is not simply a question of tone or selectivity, but involves the very categories of analysis they employ. Reformers, social workers, and journalists viewed working-class women's sexuality through middle-class lenses, invoking sexual standards that set "respectability" against "promiscuity." When applied to unmarried women, these categories were constructed foremost around the biological fact of premarital virginity, and secondarily by such cultural indicators as manners, language, dress, and public interaction. Chastity was the measure of young women's respectability, and those who engaged in premarital intercourse, or, more importantly, dressed and acted as though they had, were classed as promiscuous women or prostitutes. Thus labor investigations of the late nineteenth century not only surveyed women's wages and working conditions, but delved into the issue of their sexual virtue, hoping to resolve scientifically the question of working women's respectability.

Nevertheless, some middle-class observers in city missions and settlements recognized that their standards did not always reflect those of working-class youth. As one University Settlement worker argued, "Many of the liberties which are taken by tenement boys and girls with one another, and which seem quite improper to the 'up-towner,' are, in fact, practically harmless." Working women's public behavior often seemed to fall between the traditional middle-class poles: they were not truly promiscuous in their actions, but neither were they models of decorum. A boarding-house matron, for example, puzzled over the behavior of Mary, a "good girl": "The other night she flirted with a man across the street," she explained. "It is true she dropped him when he offered to take her into a saloon. But she does go to picture shows and dance halls with 'pick up' men and boys." Similarly, a city missionary noted that tenement dwellers followed different rules of etiquette, with the observation: "Young women sometimes allow young men to address them and caress them in a manner which would offend well-bred people, and yet those girls

Kathy Peiss, " 'Charity Girls' and City Pleasures: Historical Notes on Working Class Sexuality, 1880–1920," in Ann Snitow et al., eds., *Powers of Desire: The Politics of Sexuality* (New York: Monthly Review Press, 1983), 74–87. Reprinted by permission of the author.

would indignantly resent any liberties which they consider dishonoring." These examples suggest that we must reach beyond the dichotomized analysis of many middle-class observers and draw out the cultural categories created and acted on by working women themselves. How was sexuality "handled" culturally? What manners, etiquette, and sexual style met with general approval? What constituted sexual respectability? Does the polarized framework of the middle class reflect the realities of working-class culture?

Embedded within the reports and surveys lie small pieces of information that illuminate the social and cultural construction of sexuality among a number of working-class women. My discussion focuses on one set of young, white working women in New York City in the years 1880 to 1920. Most of these women were single wage earners who toiled in the city's factories, shops, and department stores, while devoting their evenings to the lively entertainment of the streets, public dance halls, and other popular amusements. Born or educated in the United States, many adopted a cultural style meant to distance themselves from their immigrant roots and familial traditions. Such women dressed in the latest finery, negotiated city life with ease, and sought intrigue and adventure with male companions. For this group of working women, sexuality became a central dimension of their emergent culture, a dimension that is revealed in their daily life of work and leisure.

These New York working women frequented amusements in which familiarity and intermingling among strangers, not decorum, defined normal public behavior between the sexes. At movies and cheap theaters, crowds mingled during intermissions, shared picnic lunches, and commented volubly on performances. Strangers at Coney Island's amusement parks often involved each other in practical jokes and humorous escapades, while dance halls permitted close interaction between unfamiliar men and women. At one respectable Turnverein ball, for example, a vice investigator described closely the chaotic activity in the barroom between dances:

> Most of the younger couples were hugging and kissing, there was a general mingling of men and women at the different tables, almost everyone seemed to know one another and spoke to each other across the tables and joined couples at different tables, they were all singing and carrying on, they kept running around the room and acted like a mob of lunatics let lo[o]se.

As this observer suggests, an important aspect of social familiarity was the ease of sexual expression in language and behavior. Dances were advertised, for example, through the distribution of "pluggers," small printed cards announcing the particulars of the ball, along with snatches of popular songs or verse; the lyrics and pictures, noted one offended reformer, were often "so suggestive that they are absolutely indecent."

The heightened sexual awareness permeating many popular amusements may also be seen in working-class dancing styles. While waltzes and two-steps were common, working women's repertoire included "pivoting" and "tough dances." While pivoting was a wild, spinning dance that promoted a charged atmosphere of physical excitement, tough dances ranged from a slow shimmy, or shaking of the hips and shoulders, to boisterous animal imitations. Such tough dances as the grizzly bear, Charlie Chaplin wiggle, and the dip emphasized bodily contact and the suggestion of sexual intercourse. . . . In contrast, middle-class pleasure-goers accepted the animal dances only after the blatant sexuality had been tamed into refined movement. While cabaret owners enforced strict rules to discourage contact between strangers, managers of working-class dance halls usually winked at spieling, tough dancing, and unrestrained behavior.

Other forms of recreation frequented by working-class youth incorporated a free and easy sexuality into their attractions. Many social clubs and amusement societies permitted flirting, touching, and kissing games at their meetings. One East Side youth reported that "they have kissing all through pleasure time, and use slang language, while in some they don't behave nice between [sic] young ladies." Music halls and cheap vaudeville regularly worked sexual themes and suggestive humor into comedy routines and songs. At a Yiddish music hall popular with both men and women, one reformer found that "the songs are suggestive of everything but what is proper, the choruses are full of double meanings, and the jokes have broad and unmistakable hints of things indecent." Similarly, Coney Island's Steeplechase amusement park, favored by working-class excursionists, carefully marketed sexual titillation and romance in attractions that threw patrons into each other, sent skirts flying, and evoked instant intimacy among strangers.

In attending dance halls, social club entertainments, and amusement resorts, young women took part in a cultural milieu that expressed and affirmed heterosocial interactions. As reformer Belle Israels observed, "No amusement is complete in which 'he' is not a factor." A common custom involved "picking up" unknown men or women in amusement resorts or on the streets, an accepted means of gaining companionship for an evening's entertainment. Indeed, some amusement societies existed for this very purpose. One vice investigator, in his search for "loose" women, was advised by a waiter to "go first on a Sunday night to 'Hans'l & Gret'l Amusement Society' at the Lyceum 86th Str & III Ave, there the girls come and men pick them up." The waiter carefully stressed that these were respectable working women, not prostitutes. Nor was the pickup purely a male prerogative. "With the men they 'pick up,'" writer Hutchins Hapgood observed of East Side shop girls, "they will go to the theater, to late suppers, will be as jolly as they like."

The heterosocial orientation of these amusements made popularity a goal to be pursued through dancing ability, willingness to drink, and eye-catching finery. . . . Many women used clothing as a means of drawing attention to themselves, wearing high-heeled shoes, fancy dresses, costume jewelry, elaborate pompadours, and cosmetics. As one working woman sharply explained, "If you want to get any notion took of you, you gotta have some style about you." The clothing that such women wore no longer served as an emblem of respectability. "The way women dress today they all look like prostitutes," reported one rueful waiter to a dance hall investigator, "and the waiter can some times get in bad by going over and trying to put some one next to them, they may be respectable women and would jump on the waiter."

Underlying the relaxed sexual style and heterosocial interaction was the custom of "treating." Men often treated their female companions to drinks and refreshments, theater tickets, and other incidentals. Women might pay a dance hall's entrance fee or carfare out to an amusement park, but they relied on men's treats to see them through the evening's entertainment. Such treats were highly prized by young working women; as Belle Israels remarked, the announcement that "he treated" was "the acme of achievement in retailing experiences with the other sex."

Treating was not a one-way proposition, however, but entailed an exchange relationship. Financially unable to reciprocate in kind, women offered sexual favors of varying degrees, ranging from flirtatious companionship to sexual intercourse, in exchange for men's treats. "Pleasures don't cost girls so much as they do young men," asserted one saleswoman. "If they are agreeable they are invited out a good deal, and they are not allowed to pay anything." Reformer Lillian Betts concurred, observing that the working woman held herself responsible for failing to wangle men's invitations and believed that "it is not only her misfortune, but her fault; she should be more attractive." Gaining men's treats placed a high premium on allure and personality, and sometimes involved aggressive and frank "overtures to men whom they desire to attract," often with implicit sexual proposals. One investigator, commenting on women's dependency on men in their leisure time, aptly observed that "those who are unattractive, and those who have puritanic notions, fare but ill in the matter of enjoyments. On the other hand those who do become popular have to compromise with the best conventional usage."

Many of the sexual patterns acceptable in the world of leisure activity were mirrored in the workplace. Sexual harassment by employers, foremen, and fellow workers was a widespread practice in this period, and its form often paralleled the relationship of treating, particularly in service and sales jobs. Department store managers, for example, advised employees to round out their meager salaries by finding a "gentleman friend" to purchase clothing and pleasures. An angry saleswoman testified, for example, that "one of the employers has told me, on a $6.50 wage, he don't care where I get my clothes from as long as I have them, to be dressed to suit him." Waitresses knew that accepting the advances of male customers often brought good tips, and some used their opportunities to enter an active social life with men. "Most of the girls quite frankly admit making 'dates' with strange men," one investigator found. "These 'dates' are made with no thought on the part of the girl beyond getting the good time which she cannot afford herself."

In factories where men and women worked together, the sexual style that we have seen on the dance floor was often reproduced on the shop floor. Many factories lacked privacy in dressing facilities, and workers tolerated a degree of familiarity and roughhousing between men and women. One cigar maker observed that his workplace socialized the young into sexual behavior unrestrained by parental and community control. Another decried the tendency of young boys "of thirteen or fourteen casting an eye upon a 'mash.'" Even worse, he testified, were the

> many men who are . . . respected as working men, and who would not under any circumstances offer the slightest insult or disrespectful remark or glance to a female in the streets, but who, in the shops, will whoop and give expressions to "cat calls" and a peculiar noise made with their lips, which is supposed to be an endearing salutation.

In sexually segregated workplaces, sexual knowledge was probably transmitted among working women. A YWCA report in 1913 luridly asserted that "no girl is more 'knowing' than the wage-earner, for the 'older hands' initiate her early through the unwholesome story or innuendo." Evidence from factories, department stores, laundries, and restaurants substantiates the sexual consciousness of female workers. Women brought to the workplace tales of their evening adventures and gossip about dates and eligible men, recounting to their co-workers the triumphs of the latest ball or outing. Women's socialization into a new shop might involve a ritualistic exchange about "gentlemen friends." In one laundry, for example, an investigator repeatedly heard this conversation:

"Say, you got a feller?"
"Sure. Ain't you got one?"
"Sure."

Through the use of slang and "vulgar" language, heterosexual romance was expressed in a sexually explicit context. Among waitresses, for example, frank discussion of lovers and husbands during breaks was an integral part of the work day. One investigator found that "there was never any open violation of the proprieties but always the suggestive talk and behavior." Laundries, too, witnessed "a great deal of swearing among the women." A 1914 study of department store clerks found a similar style and content in everyday conversation: "While it is true that the general attitude toward men and sex relations was normal, all the investigators admitted a freedom of speech frequently verging upon the vulgar." . . .

In their workplaces and leisure activities, many working women discovered a milieu that tolerated, and at times encouraged, physical and verbal familiarity between men and women, and stressed the exchange of sexual favors for social and economic advantages. Such women probably received conflicting messages about the virtues of virginity, and necessarily mediated the parental, religious, and educational injunctions concerning chastity, and the "lessons" of urban life and labor. The choice made by some women to engage in a relaxed sexual style needs to be understood in terms of the larger relations of class and gender that structured their sexual culture.

Most single working-class women were wage-earners for a few years before marriage, contributing to the household income or supporting themselves. Sexual segmentation of the labor market placed women in semi-skilled, seasonal employment with high rates of turnover. Few women earned a "living wage," estimated to be $9.00 or $10.00 a week in 1910, and the wage differential between men and women was vast. Those who lived alone in furnished rooms or boarding houses consumed their earnings in rent, meals, and clothing. Many self-supporting women were forced to sacrifice an essential item in their weekly budgets, particularly food, in order to pay for amusements. Under such circumstances, treating became a viable option. "If my boy friend didn't take me out," asked one working woman, "how could I ever go out?" While many women accepted treats from "steadies," others had no qualms about receiving them from acquaintances or men they picked up at amusement places. . . . Financial resources were little better for the vast majority of women living with families and relatives. Most of them contributed all of their earnings to the family, receiving only small amounts of spending money, usually 25¢ to 50¢ a week, in return. This sum covered the costs of simple entertainments, but could not purchase higher priced amusements.

Moreover, the social and physical space of the tenement home and boarding house contributed to freer social and sexual practices. Working women living alone ran the gauntlet between landladies' suspicious stares and the knowing glances of male boarders. One furnished-room dweller attested to the pressure placed on young, single women: "Time and again when a male lodger meets a girl on the landing, his salutation usually ends with something like this: 'Won't you step into my place and have a glass of beer with me?'"

The tenement home, too, presented a problem to parents who wished to maintain control over their daughters' sexuality. Typical tenement apartments offered limited opportunities for family activities or chaperoned socializing. Courtship proved difficult in homes where families and boarders crowded into a few small rooms, and the "parlor" served as kitchen, dining room, and bedroom. Instead, many working-class daughters socialized on streetcorners, rendezvoused in cafes, and courted on trolley cars. As one settlement worker observed, "Boys and girls and young men and women of respectable families are almost obliged to carry on many of their friendships, and perhaps their lovemaking, on tenement stoops or on street corners." Another reformer found that girls whose parents forebade men's visits to the home managed to escape into the streets and dance halls to meet them. Such young women demanded greater independence in the realm of "personal life" in exchange for their financial contribution to the family. For some, this new freedom spilled over into their sexual practices.

The extent of the sexual culture described here is particularly difficult to establish, since the evidence is too meager to permit conclusions about specific groups of working women, their beliefs about sexuality, and their behavior. Scattered evidence does suggest a range of possible responses, the parameters within which most women would choose to act and define their behavior as socially acceptable. Within this range, there existed a subculture of working women who fully bought into the system of treating and sexual exchange, by trading sexual favors of varying degrees for gifts, treats, and a good time. These women were known in underworld slang as "charity girls," a term that differentiated them from prostitutes because they did not accept money in their sexual encounters with men. As vice reformer George Kneeland found, they "offer themselves to strangers, not for money, but for presents, attention, and pleasure, and most important, a yielding to sex desire." Only a thin line divided these women and "occasional prostitutes," women who slipped in and out of prostitution when unemployed or in need of extra income. Such behavior did not result in the stigma of the "fallen woman." Many working women apparently acted like Dottie: "When she needed a pair of shoes she had found it easy to 'earn' them in the way that other girls did." Dottie, the investigator reported, was now known as a respectable married woman.

Such women were frequent patrons of the city's dance halls. Vice investigators note a preponderant number of women at dances who clearly were not prostitutes, but were "game" and "lively"; these charity girls often comprised half or more of the dancers in a hall. One dance hall investigator distinguished them with the observation, "Some of the women . . . are out for the coin, but there is a lot that come in here that are charity." One waiter at La Kuenstler Klause, a restaurant with music and dancing, noted that "girls could be gotten here, but they don't go with men for money, only for good time." The investigator continued in his report, "Most of the girls are working girls, not prostitutes, they smoke cigarettes, drink liqueurs and dance dis.[orderly] dances, stay out late and stay with any man, that pick them up first." Meeting two women at a bar, another investigator remarked, "They are both supposed to be working girls but go out for a good time and go the limit."

Some women obviously relished the game of extracting treats from men. One vice investigator offered to take a Kitty Graham, who apparently worked both as a department store clerk and occasional prostitute, to the Central Opera House at 3 A.M.; he noted that "she was willing to go if I'd take a taxi; I finally coaxed her to come with me in a street car." Similarly, Frances Donovan observed waitresses "talking about their engagements which they had for the evening or for the night and quite frankly saying what they expected to get from this or that fellow in the line of money, amusement, or clothes." Working women's manipulation of treating is also suggested by this unguarded conversation overhead by a journalist at Coney Island:

> "What sort of a time did you have?"
> "Great. He blew in $5 on the blow-out."
> "You beat me again. My chump only spent $2.50."

These women had clearly accepted the full implications of the system of treating and the sexual culture surrounding it.

While this evidence points to the existence of charity girls—working women defined as respectable, but who engaged in sexual activity—it tells us little about their numbers, social background, working lives, or relationships to family and community. The vice reports indicate that they were generally young women, many of whom lived at home with their families. One man in a dance hall remarked, for example, that "he sometimes takes them to the hotels, but sometimes the girls won't go to [a] hotel to stay for the night, they are afraid of their mothers, so he gets away with it in the hallway." While community sanctions may have prevented such activity within the neighborhood, the growth of large public dance halls, cabarets, and metropolitan amusement resorts provided an anonymous space in which the subculture of treating could flourish.

The charity girl's activities form only one response in a wide spectrum of social and sexual behavior. Many young women defined themselves sharply against the freer sexuality of their pleasure-seeking sisters, associating "respectability" firmly with premarital chastity and circumspect behavior. One working woman carefully explained her adherence to propriety: "I never go out in the evenings except to my relatives because if I did, I should lose my reputation and that is all I have left." Similarly, shop girls guarded against sexual advances from co-workers and male customers by spurning the temptations of popular amusements. "I keep myself to myself," said one saleswoman. "I don't make friends in the stores very easily because you can't be sure what any one is like." Settlement workers also noted that women who freely attended "dubious resorts" or bore illegitimate children were often stigmatized by neighbors and workmates. Lillian Betts, for example, cites the case of working women who refused to labor until their employer dismissed a co-worker who had borne a baby out of wedlock. To Betts, however, their adherence to the standard of virginity seemed instrumental, and not a reflection of moral absolutism: "The hardness with which even the suggestion of looseness is treated in any group of working girls is simply an expression of self-preservation."

Other observers noted an ambivalence in the attitudes of young working women toward sexual relations. Social workers reported that the critical stance toward premarital pregnancy was "not always unmixed with a certain degree of admiration for the success with the other sex which the difficulty implies." According to this study, many women increasingly found premarital intercourse acceptable in particular situations: "'A girl can have many friends,' explained one of them, 'but when she gets a "steady," there's only one way to have him and to keep him; I mean to keep him long.'" Such women shared with charity girls the assumption that respectability was not predicated solely on chastity.

Perhaps few women were charity girls or occasional prostitutes, but many more must have been conscious of the need to negotiate sexual encounters in the workplace or in their leisure time. Women would have had to weigh their desire for social participation against traditional sanctions regarding sexual behavior, and charity girls offered to some a model for resolving this conflict. This process is exemplified in Clara Laughlin's report of an attractive but "proper" working woman who could not understand why men friends dropped her after a few dates. Finally she receives the worldly advice of a co-worker that social participation involves an exchange relationship: "Don't yeh know there ain't no feller goin' t'spend coin on yeh fer nothin'? Yeh gotta be a good Indian, Kid—we all gotta!"

For others, charity girls represented a yardstick against which they might measure their own ideas of respectability. The nuances of that measurement were expressed, for example, in a dialogue between a vice investigator and the hat girl at Semprini's dance hall. Answering his proposal for a date, the investigator noted, she "said she'd be glad to go out with me but told me there was nothing doing [i.e., sexually]. Said she didn't like to see a man spend money on her and then get disappointed." Commenting on the charity girls that frequented the dance hall, she remarked that "these women get her sick, she can't see why a woman should lay down for a man the first time they take her out. She said it wouldn't be so bad if they went out with the men 3 or 4 times and then went to bed with them but not the first time."

For this hat girl and other young working women, respectability was not defined by the strict measurement of chastity employed by many middle-class observers and reformers. Instead, they adopted a more instrumental and flexible approach to sexual behavior. Premarital sex *could* be labeled respectable in particular social contexts. Thus charity girls distinguished their sexual activity from prostitution, a less acceptable practice, because they did not receive money from men. Other women, who might view charity girls as promiscuous, were untroubled by premarital intimacy with a steady boyfriend.

This fluid definition of sexual respectability was embedded within the social relations of class and gender, as experienced by women in their daily round of work, leisure, and family life. Women's wage labor and the demands of the working-class household offered daughters few resources for entertainment. At the same time, new commercial amusements offered a tempting world of pleasure and companionship beyond parental control. Within this context, some young women sought to exchange sexual goods for access to that world and its seeming independence, choosing not to defer sexual relations until marriage. Their notions of legitimate premarital behavior contrast markedly with the dominant middle-class view, which placed female sexuality within a dichotomous and rigid framework. Whether a hazard at work, fun and adventure at night, or an opportunity to be exploited, sexual expression and intimacy comprised an integral part of these working women's lives.

FURTHER READING

Ruth M. Alexander, *"The Girl Problem": Female Sexual Delinquency in New York, 1900–1930* (1995).

Marlene D. Beckman, "The White Slave Traffic Act: Historical Impact of a Federal Crime Policy on Women," *Women & Politics* 4 (1984): 85–101.

Anne M. Butler, *Daughters of Joy, Sisters of Misery: Prostitutes in the American West, 1865–90* (1987).

Timothy J. Gilfoyle, *City of Eros: New York City, Prostitution, and the Commercialization of Sex, 1790–1920* (1992).

Marion Goldman, *Gold Diggers and Silver Miners: Prostitution and Social Life on the Comstock Lode* (1981).

Linda Gordon, *Heroes of Their Own Lives: The Politics and History of Family Violence, Boston 1880–1960* (1988).

Lucie Cheng Hirata, "Free, Indentured, Enslaved: Chinese Prostitutes in Nineteenth-Century America," *Signs* 5 (1979): 3–29.

Barbara Hobson, *Uneasy Virtue: The Politics of Prostitution and the American Reform Tradition* (1987).

Joan Hori, "Japanese Prostitution in Hawaii during the Immigration Period," in Nobuya Tsuchida, ed., *Asian and Pacific American Experiences: Women's Perspectives* (1982).

Helen Horowitz and Kathy Peiss, eds., *Love Across the Color Line: The Letters of Alice Hanley to Channing Lewis* (1996).

Yuji Ichioka, "Ameyuki-San: Japanese Prostitutes in Nineteenth-Century America," *Amerasia Journal* 4 (1977): 1–21.

Regina Kunzel, *Fallen Women, Problem Girls: Unmarried Mothers and the Professionalization of Social Work, 1890–1945* (1993).

David J. Langum, *Crossing over the Line: Legislating Morality and the Mann Act* (1994).

Elizabeth Lunbeck, "'A New Generation of Women': Progressive Psychiatrists and the Hypersexual Female," *Feminist Studies* 13 (1987): 513–539.

Randy McBee, *Dance Hall Days: Intimacy and Leisure among Working-Class Immigrants in the United States* (2000).

Joanne J. Meyerowitz, "Sexual Geography and Gender Economy: The Furnished Room Districts of Chicago, 1890–1930," *Gender & History* 2 (Autumn 1990): 274–296.

Kevin J. Mumford, *Interzones: Black/White Sex Districts in Chicago and New York in the Early Twentieth Century* (1997).

Mary Odem, *Delinquent Daughters: Protecting and Policing Adolescent Female Sexuality in the United States, 1885–1920* (1995).

Katherine M. B. Osburn, "'To Build Up the Morals of the Tribe': Southern Ute Women's Sexual Behavior and the Office of Indian Affairs, 1895–1932," *Journal of Women's History* 9 (1997): 10–27.

Peggy Pascoe, *Relations of Rescue: The Search for Female Moral Authority in the American West, 1874–1939* (1990).

George Peffer, "Forbidden Families: Emigration Experiences of Chinese Women under the Page Law, 1875–1882," *Journal of American Ethnic History* 6 (1986): 28–46.

Kathy Peiss, *Cheap Amusements: Working Women and Leisure in Turn-of-the-Century New York* (1986).

Ruth Rosen, *The Lost Sisterhood: Prostitution in America, 1900–1918* (1982).

Robert A. Trennert, "Victorian Morality and the Supervision of Indian Women Working in Phoenix, 1906–1930," *Journal of Social History* 22 (1988): 11–28.

Sharon R. Ullman, *Sex Seen: The Emergence of Modern Sexuality in America* (1997).

CHAPTER
9

The Politics of Reproduction

Women have always used methods of contraception and abortion to control the number and timing of children. In the nineteenth century, the birthrate fell dramatically, especially among white, middle-class women. Most states had made abortion a crime by the 1890s, and the Comstock Act drastically curbed the birth control information available to women. Still, women found ways around the law, although many suffered from unsafe contraceptives and unqualified abortion providers. In the 1910s, Margaret Sanger initiated a campaign to challenge the legal restrictions on birth control devices and information. When she was arrested for opening a birth control clinic in 1916, thousands rallied to her cause and a mass movement for reproductive rights was born.

The politics of the birth control movement have long been subject to debate: Was this a movement for women's bodily self-determination or an effort to exert social control? Feminists asserted a new, radical vision of sexual freedom. They claimed that divorcing sexuality from its reproductive consequences was necessary for women's emancipation. Others argued that birth control and smaller families would lead to greater economic security and mobility for working-class Americans. Although birth control advocates in the 1910s stressed these and other goals, the movement narrowed in the 1920s and 1930s. Population control and family planning, not women's freedom, increasingly became the aim.

Alarms about "race suicide" and the overpopulation of the "unfit" had been issued since the late nineteenth century, as white, educated women bore fewer children and the numbers of immigrants and people of color increased. By the 1920s—a period that witnessed immigration restriction and the revival of the Ku Klux Klan—eugenics gained a wide audience. Improving offspring and the population overall held different meanings to different people. Eugenic ideas filtered into public health programs for maternal and infant care, for example, and into efforts to encourage contraceptive use to time childbearing, in order to give each child greater health and educational benefits. But eugenics was most notorious as a form of social control. State-run sterilization programs targeted individuals with physical disabilities and the so-called feeble-minded, a sweeping category that disproportionately included sexually active young women, the poor, immigrants, and people of color. Why did feminist ideas disappear from the birth control movement in the 1920s? Why did eugenic ideas strike a chord among many birth control advocates? How did women themselves respond to the different arguments—sexual freedom, economic security, family planning, and "racial betterment"—that informed the birth control movement?

▐ D O C U M E N T S

Even before the rise of the birth control movement, fertility rates declined sharply. Although criminalized after 1867, abortion remained a means of fertility control widely used by women. In Document 1 Walter J. Hoffman, a doctor and ethnologist, described abortion as a common and apparently safe practice among Absaroka (Crow) and Dakota Indian women. A letter from farmer Eugene Caves (Document 2) to the Wisconsin state attorney in 1896, however, documented the dangers of illegal abortion and expressed the outrage of a community. Accurate and safe birth control was needed, Margaret Sanger explained in a 1917 legal brief (Document 3), to relieve the poverty of the working class and to gain greater freedom for women. Eugenic ideas, mentioned in Sanger's case for birth control, were widely accepted in the 1920s. The belief that social problems could be eradicated by preventing the "unfit" from reproducing may be seen in Document 4, a 1927 Supreme Court decision that upheld the sterilization of the "feeble minded" in Virginia. How did women themselves explain the need for birth control? Letters from poor, working-class, and rural women to Margaret Sanger presented a variety of compelling economic, health, and personal reasons (Document 5). And despite the threat eugenics posed to people of color, black women too sought birth control information in impressive numbers, according to Document 6, a 1929 report of a Baltimore birth control clinic.

1. Walter J. Hoffman Describes Childbirth and Abortion Among the Absaroka (Crow) and Dakota Indians, 1888

The Crow women believe that conception occurs within two weeks after the appearance of the *catamenia* [menses], [rather] than between the termination of that time and the appearance of the next menstrual discharge. They suckle their children until they are able to run about with safety, in the belief that conception does not occur during such nursing.

The number of abortions, among the Crows, is said to equal the number of births.

Marriage takes place early in life, often before puberty. The husband is not, according to their mode of thinking, permitted with propriety to have communication with the bride during the first two weeks of married life. Girls are taught by their mothers that first contact with a man is extremely painful, and therefore the husband is expected to wait until the fears of the bride are dispelled, by becoming more familiar with the idea of being married and its consequences. . . .

Among these Indians, abortion is brought about in two ways. First, a midwife or assistant, reaches around the abdomen of a pregnant woman, and by the utmost pressure endeavors to induce pains. This is only in advanced stages of pregnancy, and usually practised during childbirth. Second, in early pregnancy, a mixture is prepared by chopping up very fine the hair of a Black-tailed Deer's tail, which is mixed with the fat of a Bear's paw. The gastric irritation may, in such instances, induce uterine contraction sufficient to expel the foetus, as the desired result is brought about. . . .

Walter J. Hoffman, "Childbirth and Abortion Among the Absaroka (or Crow) and Dakota Indians (1888)," ed. and trans. Peter Bolz, *European Review of Native American Studies* 2, no. 1 (1988): 9–10. Reprinted by permission.

The adoption of modern modes of living is rapidly causing change of custom with regard to primitive methods, especially since every Indian Agency is supplied by a physician appointed by the government. Though, in so far as it pertains to many other forms of sickness, the Shaman is the personage who professes to exorcise the demons or evil spirits causing disease, and so long as this individual is permitted to practise his profession of sorcery and incantation, so long will some of the individual Indians, as well as some other tribes, continue to oppose the attempts at civilization.

2. Eugene Caves Reports a Death from Illegal Abortion in Rural Wisconsin, 1896

A Double Murder

Coloma, Wis[consin]
November 21, 1896

Wm. H. Mylrea
State Attorney
Madison, Wis.

Dear Sir:

On the first day of May 1893 We hired a girl fifteen years of age to do house work of but little or no experience by the name of Rosa Petrusky[.] being a bright girl [she] was learned to work and kept in our employ one year and eight months[.] our family thought a great deal of her. Some time in Mar. or Apr. 1895, She went to work for Mr. Pratt of Pine Grove, Wis. Has visited us four or five times on her way home and return. On Oct. 22 1896 she came into our house between 7 & 8 oclock P.M.[,] nearly crying when asked the cause [she] said she had been doing wrong. further questioning revealed that she was in the family way[,] that she had been taking something and expected to be sick that night and wanted my wife to take care of her. At first [she] refused to tell who brought her here, but finally stated Mr. Pratt[']s son took her to the train at Plainfield [and] had also met her at Coloma Sta[tion] with a Livery team. After questioning her she said she was three months along. she said about two weeks before she had taken something[,] not liquid or powder but pills, young Mr. Pratt got them for her[.] But *they* did her no good.

Also Young Pratt . . . took her along the road [al]most to Hancock and met a Dr. & the Dr. had done something to her, had probed her womb and she expected to be sick that night[. She] said it was this same young Pratt got her in that fix[. She] said the first time he ever did anything to her was July 21st/96, that they were out riding[,] said no one had ever touched her but him, that he first talked of sending her to Stevens Point to get rid of it, but decided to bring her here, telling her she would have better care here, that her expenses would be all paid and her wages would go on till she got back. He wanted her to write him and let him know how she was getting

Eugene Caves to Wm. H. Mylrea, State Attorney, November 21, 1896, Governor, Executive Department, Minor Charges and Complaints, 1880–1914, Series 82, box 1, State Historical Society of Wisconsin, Madison, Wis.

along. [She] said she did not know who the Dr. was they met in the road[,] that his face was covered up, had fur overcoat with collar turned up. My wife and I thought best to send her to her own home to her Mother. . . . [She] gave her Mother $2.00 and said *don[']t* tell Father so did not. . . . [On] Oct 25/96 . . . Young Pratt came to her house and took her away. . . . Next we knew, two weeks later news came to us that she had died, at a widow woman[']s . . . by the name of Mrs. Stoker. Her Parents went after the corpse, later in the day & . . . insisted upon having an inquest held. Complaint was made to a Justice at Plainfield [to] sen[d] for District Att[orne]y, and for him to bring a Dr. from Wautoma with him but he did not do it. . . . We believe he was paid by Pratt[']s friends. This widow Stoker has a Son living with her. . . . [They l]ive in a little old cottage and are very poor[.] She says the girl came there about 8 oclock Sunday evening. (On the same day she left her Father[']s.) No one knowing she was there until the following Tuesday P.M. A neighbor woman happening in there while at the door heard a terrible screaming and asked who's that[.] the old Lady replied, Oh & we got a sick girl here[,] and opened the bedroom door and the girl was lying on the floor. They helped her back on the bed. . . . The Neighbors say the girl refused to tell them her name or where her parents lived. On Wed. P.M. the Neighbor was called to go for a Dr. The young man [Mrs. Stoker's son] claims at first he did not know she was there until Wednesday. (He works away from home for a Brother of said Young Pratt[.]) A little later he tells me she was there when he came home from Church on Sunday evening, shook hands with her [and] called her Rosa, knew she was the girl that worked to Pratt[']s. That same Evening she told him her condition[,] that she was sick. Had taken 40 pills in 5 [?] days. . . .

Pratt[']s folks are farmers, and have considerable money, bought the coffin[,] sent a livery with the corpse, Had a man to try to settle with her Father. . . . Dis[tri]ct Att[orne]y does not try to make a case, her Father is poor. People are very indignant about it [and] want the guilty punished. . . .

Please Answer immediately

Yours Very Respectfully.

Eugene Caves
Coloma,
Waushara Co. Wis.

3. Margaret Sanger Argues "The Case for Birth Control," 1917

For centuries woman has gone forth with man to till the fields, to feed and clothe the nations. She has sacrificed her life to populate the earth. She has overdone her labors. She now steps forth and demands that women shall cease producing in ignorance. To do this she must have knowledge to control birth. This is the first immediate step she must take toward the goal of her freedom.

Margaret H. Sanger, *The Case for Birth Control: A Supplementary Brief and Statement of Facts* (New York: Modern Art Printing Co., 1917), 5–11.

Those who are opposed to this are simply those who do not know. Any one who like myself has worked among the people and found on one hand an ever-increasing population with its ever-increasing misery, poverty and ignorance, and on the other hand a stationary or decreasing population with its increasing wealth and higher standards of living, greater freedom, joy and happiness, cannot doubt that birth control is the livest issue of the day and one on which depends the future welfare of the race.

Before I attempt to refute the arguments against birth control, I should like to tell you something of the conditions I met with as a trained nurse and of the experience that convinced me of its necessity and led me to jeopardize my liberty in order to place this information in the hands of the women who need it.

My first clear impression of life was that large families and poverty went hand in hand. I was born and brought up in a glass factory town in the western part of New York State. I was one of eleven children—so I had some personal experience of the struggles and hardships a large family endures.

When I was seventeen years old my mother died from overwork and the strain of too frequent child bearing. I was left to care for the younger children and share the burdens of all. When I was old enough I entered a hospital to take up the profession of nursing.

In the hospital I found that seventy-five per cent. of the diseases of men and women are the result of ignorance of their sex functions. I found that every department of life was open to investigation and discussion except that shaded valley of sex. The explorer, scientist, inventor, may go forth in their various fields for investigation and return to lay the fruits of their discoveries at the feet of society. But woe to him who dares explore that forbidden realm of sex. No matter how pure the motive, no matter what miseries he sought to remove, slanders, persecutions and jail await him who dares bear the light of knowledge into that cave of darkness.

So great was the ignorance of the women and girls I met concerning their own bodies that I decided to specialize in woman's diseases and took up gynecological and obstetrical nursing.

A few years of this work brought me to a shocking discovery—that knowledge of the methods of controlling birth was accessible to the women of wealth while the working women were deliberately kept in ignorance of this knowledge!

I found that the women of the working class were as anxious to obtain this knowledge as their sisters of wealth, but that they were told that there are laws on the statute books against importing it to them. And the medical profession was most religious in obeying these laws when the patient was a poor woman.

I found that the women of the working class had emphatic views on the crime of bringing children into the world to die of hunger. They would rather risk their lives through abortion than give birth to little ones they could not feed and care for.

For the laws against imparting this knowledge force these women into the hands of the filthiest midwives and the quack abortionists—unless they bear unwanted children—with the consequence that the deaths from abortions are almost wholly among the working-class women.

No other country in the world has so large a number of abortions nor so large a number of deaths of women resulting therefrom as the United States of America. Our law makers close their virtuous eyes. A most conservative estimate is that there are 250,000 abortions performed in this country every year.

How often have I stood at the bedside of a woman in childbirth and seen the tears flow in gladness and heard the sigh of "Thank God" when told that her child was born dead! What can man know of the fear and dread of unwanted pregnancy? What can man know of the agony of carrying beneath one's heart a little life which tells the mother every instant that it cannot survive? Even were it born alive the chances are that it would perish within a year.

Do you know that three hundred thousand babies under one year of age die in the United States every year from poverty and neglect, while six hundred thousand parents remain in ignorance of how to prevent three hundred thousand more babies from coming into the world the next year to die of poverty and neglect?

I found from records concerning women of the underworld that eighty-five per cent. of them come from parents averaging nine living children. And that fifty per cent. of these are mentally defective.

We know, too, that among mentally defective parents the birth rate is four times as great as that of the normal parent. Is this not cause for alarm? Is it not time for our physicians, social workers and scientists to face this array of facts and stop quibbling about woman's morality? I say this because it is these same people who raise objection to birth control on the ground that it *may* cause women to be immoral. . . .

Is woman's health not to be considered? Is she to remain a producing machine? Is she to have time to think, to study, to care for herself? Man cannot travel to his goal alone. And until woman has knowledge to control birth she cannot get the time to think and develop. Until she has the time to think, neither the suffrage question nor the social question nor the labor question will interest her, and she will remain the drudge that she is and her husband the slave that he is just as long as they continue to supply the market with cheap labor.

Let me ask you: Has the State any more right to ravish a woman against her will by keeping her in ignorance than a man has through brute force? Has the State a better right to decide when she shall bear offspring?

Picture a woman with five or six little ones living on the average working man's wage of ten dollars a week. The mother is broken in health and spirit, a worn out shadow of the woman she once was. Where is the man or woman who would reproach me for trying to put into this woman's hands knowledge that will save her from giving birth to any more babies doomed to certain poverty and misery and perhaps to disease and death[?]

Am I to be classed as immoral because I advocate small families for the working class while Mr. [Theodore] Roosevelt can go up and down the length of the land shouting and urging these women to have large families and is neither arrested nor molested but considered by all society as highly moral?

But I ask you which is the more moral—to urge this class of women to have only those children she desires and can care for, or to delude her into breeding thoughtlessly[?] Which is America's definition of morality?

You will agree with me that a woman should be free.

Yet no adult woman who is ignorant of the means to prevent conception can call herself free.

No woman can call herself free who cannot choose the time to be a mother or not as she sees fit. This should be woman's first demand.

Our present laws force woman into one of two ways: Celibacy, with its nervous results, or abortion. All modern physicians testify that both these conditions are harmful; that celibacy is the cause of many nervous complaints, while abortion is a disgrace to a civilized community. Physicians claim that early marriage with knowledge to control birth would do away with both. For this would enable two young people to live and work together until such time as they could care for a family. I found that young people desire early marriage, and would marry early were it not for the dread of a large family to support. Why will not society countenance and advance this idea? Because it is still afraid of the untried and the unknown. . . .

My work has been to arouse interest in the subject of birth control in America, and in this, I feel that I have been successful. The work now before us is to crystallize and to organize this interest into action, not only for the repeal of the laws but for the establishment of free clinics in every large center of population in the country where scientific, individual information may be given every adult person who comes to ask it. . . .

Woman must be protected from incessant childbearing before she can actively participate in the social life. She must triumph over Nature's and Man's laws which have kept her in bondage. Just as man has triumphed over Nature by the use of electricity, shipbuilding, bridges, etc., so must woman triumph over the laws which have made her a childbearing machine.

4. The Supreme Court Upholds Forced Sterilization, 1927

The Virginia statute providing for the sexual sterilization of inmates of institutions supported by the State who shall be found to be afflicted with an hereditary form of insanity or imbecility, is within the power of the State under the Fourteenth Amendment. . . .

Mr. I. P. Whitehead for plaintiff [Carrie Buck].

The plaintiff in error contends that the operation of salpingectomy, as provided for in the Act of Assembly, is illegal in that it violates her constitutional right of bodily integrity and is therefore repugnant to the due process of law clause of the Fourteenth Amendment. In Munn v. Illinois, . . . this Court, in defining the meaning of "deprivation of life," said: "The inhibition against its deprivation extends to all those limbs and faculties by which life is enjoyed. The deprivation not only of life but whatever God has given to everyone with life . . . is protected by the provision in question." The operation of salpingectomy clearly comes within the definition. It is a surgical operation consisting of the opening of the abdominal cavity and the cutting of the Fallopian tubes with the result that sterility is produced. . . .

. . . The inherent right of mankind to go through life without mutilation of organs of generation needs no constitutional declaration. . . .

If this Act be a valid enactment, then the limits of the power of the State (which in the end is nothing more than the faction in control of the government) to

---

Buck v. Bell, 274 U.S. 200 (1927).

rid itself of those citizens deemed undesirable according to its standards, by means of surgical sterilization, have not been set. We will have "established in the State the science of medicine and a corresponding system of judicature." A reign of doctors will be inaugurated and in the name of science new classes will be added, even races may be brought within the scope of such regulation, and the worst forms of tyranny practiced. In the place of the constitutional government of the fathers we shall have set up Plato's Republic.

Mr. Aubrey E. Strode for defendant [Superintendent of the State Colony of Epileptics and Feeble Minded].

The act does not impose cruel and unusual punishment. A constitutional provision prohibiting the infliction of cruel and unusual punishment is directed against punishment of a barbarous character, involving torture, such as drawing and quartering the culprit, burning at the stake, cutting off the nose, ears or limbs, and the like, and such punishments as were regarded as cruel and unusual at the time the Constitution was adopted. . . .

. . . An exercise of the police power analogous to that of the statute here in question may be found in the compulsory vaccination statutes; for there, as here, a surgical operation is required for the protection of the individual and of society; and that requirement has been upheld when imposed upon school children only, those attending public institutions of learning, though not imposed upon the public as a whole. . . . The State may and does confine the feeble minded, thus depriving them of their liberty. When so confined they are by segregation prohibited from procreation—a further deprivation of liberty that goes unquestioned. The appellant is under the Virginia statues already by law prohibited from procreation. The precise question therefore is whether the State, in its judgment of what is best for appellant and for society, may through the medium of the operation provided for by the sterilization statute restore her to the liberty, freedom and happiness which thereafter she might safely be allowed to find outside of institutional walls. No legal reason appears why a person of full age and sound mind, and even though free from any disease making such operation advisable or necessary, may not by consent have the operation performed for the sole purpose of becoming sterile, thus voluntarily giving up the capacity to procreate. The operation therefore is not legally malum in se [evil in itself]. It can only be illegal when performed against the will or contrary to the interest of the patient. Who then is to consent or decide for this appellant whether it be best for her to have this operation? She cannot determine the matter for herself both because being not of full age her judgment is not to be accepted nor would it acquit the surgeon, and because she is further incapacitated by congenital mental defect. . . .

MR. JUSTICE HOLMES delivered the opinion of the Court. . . .

Carrie Buck is a feeble minded white woman who was committed to the State Colony above mentioned in due form. She is the daughter of a feeble minded mother in the same institution, and the mother of an illegitimate feeble minded child. She was eighteen years old at the time of the trial of her case in the Circuit Court, in the latter part of 1924. An Act of Virginia, approved March 20, 1924, recites that the health of the patient and the welfare of society may be promoted in certain cases by the sterilization of mental detectives, under careful safeguard, &c.; that the sterilization may be effected in males by vasectomy and in females by salpingectomy, without serious pain or substantial danger to life; that the Commonwealth is supporting in various institutions many defective persons who if now discharged would become a menace but if incapable of procreating might be discharged with safety and become self-supporting with benefit to themselves and to society; and that experience has shown that heredity plays an important part in the transmission of insanity, imbecility, &c. The statute then enacts that whenever the superintendent of certain institutions including the above named State Colony shall be of opinion that it is for the best interests of the patients and of society than an inmate under his care should be sexually sterilized, he may have the operation performed upon any patient afflicted with hereditary forms of insanity, imbecility, &c., on complying with the very careful provisions by which the act protects the patients from possible abuse....

... The judgment [of the Virginia Supreme Court of Appeals] finds ... that Carrie Buck "is the probable potential parent of socially inadequate offspring, likewise afflicted, that she may be sexually sterilized without detriment to her general health and that her welfare and that of society will be promoted by her sterilization," and thereupon makes the order. In view of the general declarations of the legislature and the specific findings of the Court, obviously we cannot say as matter of law that the grounds do not exist, and if they exist they justify the result. We have seen more than once that the public welfare may call upon the best citizens for their lives. It would be strange if it could not call upon those who already sap the strength of the State for these lesser sacrifices, often not felt to be such by those concerned, in order to prevent our being swamped with incompetence. It is better for all the world, if instead of waiting to execute degenerate offspring for crime, or to let them starve for their imbecility, society can prevent those who are manifestly unfit from continuing their kind. The principle that sustains compulsory vaccination is broad enough to cover cutting the Fallopian tubes. . . . Three generations of imbeciles are enough.

5. Women Write Margaret Sanger for Birth Control Advice, 1924, 1930, 1935, 1936

Lee Center, New York
April 21 1924

Dear Mrs. Sanger,

When I saw the ad in a magazine about birth control you can hardly imagine how happy I was. I thought that already I found what I have been looking for. But . . . although I learned a lot after purchasing the book, still I did not find out what I wanted to know. Then when I saw that probably you would tell me if I wrote to you as you put in your personal address[,] I thought to try my poor luck once more.

Client Letters to Margaret Sanger, April 21, 1924 (reel 2), February 9, 1930 (reel 6), November 12, 1935, March 11, 1936 (Reel 11), all in Series II (Subseries 1—Correspondence), Margaret Sanger Papers, Sophia Smith Collection, Smith College, Northampton, Mass. Reprinted by permission of Alexander Sanger, Executor of the Estate of Margaret Sanger.

I belong to one of the poor imported breed[,] as is expressed in your book[,] and belonged to a family of nine other luckless and loveless children. It seems no one wanted us[,] it was some scrap to get the poor learning I got, followed by hard work before and after school. I married when sixteen hardly old enough for breeding. Now I have to take a man's job on the farm[,] having children and working till your eyesight is blurred and back breaking. The only thing is the children have fresh air but no care can be given the poor things by me. . . . I tried a number of times the last year not to overbreed the world my self but you can't imagine how luckless I am. Every doctor I can afford will simply tell me nothing. Now I am at the end of the rope so I would be ever so much obliged to you for ever and ever if . . . you could write me and tell me in very simple words what to do as I may not understand it otherwise. . . . Just think about my poor neglected children lacking care and proper food and see if your heart won't prompt you to help me out.

A broken hearted mother . . .

Feb 9 1930
Bloomfield Ky

Dear Madam

Please give me some advise for i am in so much trouble and need help so bad[.] i have six dear little babys five girls and one boy. My husband has T.B. and epilipsy fits and is not able to work at all, the county feeds us and people gives us clothes[.] i have had to send four of my dear babys to a home for children because I had nothing to feed them. O it was so hard to give them up and still my husband wants me to run the risk of having more[.] i cant bear the thought of doing so I dont want to bring any more little ones here . . . this is breaking up our home[.] We live in a fuss all [the] time i am trying to do my duty but i don't think it is right to go on raising children when i know i have nothing to feed or clothe them on. . . .

From a mother in despair

Norman Okla.
Nov. 12, 1935

Dear Mrs. Sanger:

Have just finished reading your book "Happiness in Marriage." . . . I want to express my love and appreciation to and for a woman who is trying and accomplishing the good work you are doing for the young girls and women. May God bless you in your great undertaking. I have only one daughter who will be married in the Spring and I feel so helpless to give the right kind of advi[c]e to her. . . . I want her to be able to look after her health and I wish you would be so kind as to write me the things she should know. Understand me, I don't think a home is complete without children, but I must say right here I believe in birth control. I think it creates hate and divorce when a mother is so poor she can't have the necessary necessities of life. . . . My husband is a retired Methodist Minister and we don't agree on this one subject. Yet we never have hard words and are very happy. Will you please write me what is safe and the same time not injurious to health, a "safe" preventive from becoming pregnant until you can have a family. I have a young friend who uses Zep tabs or "Lanteen[.]" You understand her husband consulted a doctor yet some doctor[s] don't know and will not tell you one thing, if so the right preventive to use. . . . My daughter is a sincerely christian young lady and I sincerely don't want her to go into matrimony as green and unqualified as I am right now. I have been on the operating table ten times, I believe through abuse and ignorance. . . .

St. Louis, Mo.
March 11, 1936

My Dear Mrs. Sanger:

I hardly know just how to start this letter that I hope will bring me some advice that I can rely upon about "birth control." I am 20 years of age my husband 21. We have a darling baby girl that we love dearly, age 3 years. So you know that I was just 16 when we married, we loved each other dearly + still do. I have gone to many a doctor and ask him just what to do but the answer was, sleep in different beds, now how can a married couple do that when we want to be close to each other + help each other[,] so we can have a nice home to look forward to, something to show for our work. We have 3 rooms + bath, we heat with coal stoves[.] He makes $18.00 a week, that isn't much but we are happy that it is that much. We try to save a little in case he gets out of work. Living expenses are so high that we have a pretty hard time to make ends meet. . . .

I am so sick + nervous + always worried about getting pregnant. I have had one miscarriage since the baby came. It wasn't an or[din]ary one either. I brought it on by carrying ½ bushel baskets of coal to the second floor, worked hard, and took 24 5 gr. quinine capsules. They made me so sick I said I would never do it again. It brought it on [the miscarriage] so that is all that mattered. Now I take douches with vinegar, I have [done] that for so long that I now have a discharge. . . . But that constant worry is always on our mind of me getting in the family way again. We love babys + we would have another if we know we could support it properly. We would like to wait about 3 years or more but you never know when another one will pop up. We are afraid to have intimate moments always afraid that something will happen. One of us always try to get to bed + to sleep before the other gets to bed, Alway[s] afraid to show our love that is so strong.

When I read your story in True Confessions I was so happy that I sat right down + started this letter. I have never heard of one of these "Birth Control Clinic[s]." I would surely appreciate it if you would please tell me the nearest one to my house in St. Louis, Mo. I do hope that there is one in St. Louis. If there isn't, would you please tell [m]e a few facts about my female parts.

Perhaps you wonder why I don't ask my mother some of these questions. My mother has never told me the facts that a young girl should know. When I had my first menstru[a]l flow I didn't know what happened[.] I thought I was dying. I was almost crazy. When I ask her w[h]ere babys came from[,] Instead of telling me the best she could, she said that they came from the <u>river</u>. I have never forgiven her for that, because that one thing has caused me a lot of trouble. . . .

6. Women's Use of a Baltimore Birth Control Clinic, 1929

The Baltimore Committee on Contraceptive Advice has issued the first annual report of its Bureau for Contraceptive [A]dvice, founded November 1927.

Statistical Report

The statistical report prepared by Dr. Raymond Pearl presents some very interesting facts: Of the 168 patients advised, 29 or 17.3 per cent. were colored, and 139 or 82.7 per cent. were white. In 1925, the last year for which data are available, 14.7 per cent. of the total population of Baltimore was made up of negroes. It is thus seen that the attendance of negroes on the clinic is slightly higher than their representation in the general population. So far, then, as this first year's experience may be taken as indicative, it tells against the argument frequently made against Birth Control, to the effect that the economically less fortunate and less foresighted elements of the population would not avail themselves of contraceptive advice if it were freely offered.

The average age of the 168 women was 30.98 years, or just a week under 31 years. Half were under 30.8 years of age when they came to the Bureau. All the patients are married. The distribution of the lengths of time they had been married before they came to the Bureau demonstrates at once the fallacy of one of the arguments sometimes raised against the giving of contraceptive advice, to the effect that it is chiefly sought by the young as a means of escaping the moral responsibilities of marriage. One-half of the patients coming to the Bureau had been married more than 11.8 years when they came. The average duration of marriage of these 168 women was 12.3 years.

The average mother who came to the Bureau had been pregnant more than six times and had borne five or more (4.93 exactly) children before she came. But the average age of this group of 168 women was only thirty-one years, and, on the average they had been married only 12.3 years. Such reproductive rates are not conducive to either private or public health. A more perfect demonstration of the need for the Bureau for Contraceptive Advice, *as a health measure*, than this fact affords would be difficult to imagine.

The most widely heard criticism of Birth Control, from a social viewpoint, is that only the "upper" or "socially desirable" classes, whatever precisely these designations may mean, practice it. But among our patients the only groups which, in fact, could possibly be regarded as falling under the first of these designations are the "Professional men, managers and capitalists" on the one hand, and the "Public servants" on the other hand. But actually the three "Public servants" were one policeman, one fireman, and one coast guard. So we are left with only the 10 persons in the Professional class, or 6 per cent. of the total. The other 94 per cent. of the patients cannot justly be accused of belonging to the "upper classes," though they include a great many desirable citizens. This 94 per cent. earned their living as railwaymen, clerks, farmers, domestic servants, tradesmen, skilled, semi-skilled or unskilled laborers.

"The Baltimore Birth Control Clinic," *Birth Control Review* 13 (May 1929): 137. Reprinted by permission of Alexander Sanger, Executor of the Estate of Margaret Sanger.

Medical Report

The medical report is prepared by Dr. Whitridge Williams. The Bureau was founded with the unusual provision that only women sent by physicians would be advised. Since the poor who were to be its chief clients seldom have a family physician, special arrangements were made for patients sent by social service and other charitable workers. All cases accepted were such as came under the description for the cure or prevention of disease and the medical report shows the distribution of disease or predisposition to ill health.

The larger group of patients showed family medical indications, some of which are nervous diseases, tuberculosis, kidney, heart or thyroid trouble, syphilis, epilepsy and recent operations. A smaller group were suffering from too frequent pregnancies with complications, and a group of sixty from too frequent pregnancies "without complications". That the help given this latter group represented true preventive medicine is indicated by the number of children already brought into the world by some of these mothers, one of whom had 9 children in 12 years, others, 8 children in 10 years, 11 children in 13 years, 12 children in 14 years, 9 children in 9 years, 12 children in 16 years, 6 children in 6 years, 10 children in 15 years, 11 children in 14 years.

E S S A Y S

In this excerpt from *Woman's Body, Woman's Right,* Linda Gordon of New York University discusses the emergence of the birth control movement in the 1910s. Although identified especially with the leadership of Margaret Sanger, birth control was initially a product of grassroots activism. The movement gained strength, Gordon argues, not only from the genuine needs of women for contraceptives, but also from the ideas and politics of sex radicals, feminists, and socialists. This revolutionary movement did not prevail, however, and, as Molly Ladd-Taylor of York University shows, the politics of reproductive welfare became tied much more closely to eugenics after World War I. She compares two eugenic policies from the 1910s to the 1930s: efforts to improve maternal and infant health and the movement for compulsory sterilization. Public health programs for "better babies" had limited government and medical support, while compulsory sterilization was more successful. Ladd-Taylor shows how racial, class, and gender biases affected who was sterilized, but she also finds evidence that some women accepted eugenic sterilization as a form of contraceptive control.

Birth Control and Social Revolution

LINDA GORDON

The enthusiasm of the birth controllers in this period came from their conviction that birth control was an idea whose "time had come." They observed and sensed social changes that led to mass acceptance of contraception and demands for reproductive self-determination. The most immediate of these changes were the shrinking birth

Linda Gordon, "Birth Control and Social Revolution," in *Woman's Body, Woman's Right: A Social History of Birth Control in America* (New York: Penguin, 1977, © 1976), 189–190, 206–208, 212–216, 226–233. Used with permission of the author and the University of Illinois Press.

rate, smaller families, increased use of contraception, and increased public admission of the use of birth control. An example of the many signs that birth control was "here to stay" was the publicity given to two court cases in which women accused of theft were released by sympathetic judges in 1916. One in New York City and one in Cleveland, both defendants argued that they had stolen to feed their children; the first was given a suspended sentence and the second acquitted; both judges argued in their opinions, delivered from the bench, for spreading birth-control information among the poor.

Behind this attitude was an acceptance, even among birth-control opponents, of the fact that the practice was unstoppable. Public opinion spiraled: the more evidence of birth-control use became public, the more birth control became acceptable. A second factor, evident in the judges' opinions, was what we might call a neo-race-suicide view: the prosperous would use birth control anyway, so keeping it from the poor was socially destructive. A third and probably most important factor was a generally more positive attitude toward sex itself.

Some historians have argued that there was a "sexual revolution" in the early twentieth century. Whether these changes in sexual behavior and attitudes constituted a revolution or not, they created a new concept of birth control. Birth control now meant reproductive self-determination along with unlimited sexual indulgence. This new definition . . . understood sexual activity and reproduction as two separately justified human activities. Either might be considered immoral under certain circumstances, but they did not need to be connected. The eventual mass acceptance of this new morality required the conviction not only that sexual indulgence without the risk of pregnancy was a good thing, but also that fear of illegitimacy was not necessary to maintain an acceptable public morality. . . .

The movement that first coalesced around the slogan "birth control," a phrase invented by Margaret Sanger in 1915, was a force of people fighting for their own immediate needs, and because of this it had an intensely personal dimension for its participants. The fact that the birth controllers often stood to gain immediately in their personal lives from legalization of birth control did not narrow their vision but strengthened their commitment. They united their personal experience and emotional understanding with political thought and action. They created a politics based on women's shared experience which had the potential to unite masses of women. At the same time the birth controllers transcended women's immediate needs. They were not seeking incremental improvements in their sex lives or medical care; they did not view birth control as primarily a sexual or medical reform at all, but as a social issue with broad implications. They wanted to transform the nature of women's rights—indeed, of human rights—to include free sexual expression and reproductive self-determination.

In challenging the traditional limits of people's control over their own lives, they used birth control to make a revolutionary demand, not a reform proposal. They did not want just to limit their pregnancies; they wanted to change the world. They believed that birth control could alleviate much human misery and fundamentally alter social and political power relations, thereby creating greater sexual and class equality. In this they shared the voluntary-motherhood analysis—that involuntary motherhood was a major prop of women's subjection—and added a radical version of a Neo-Malthusian analysis—that overlarge families weakened the working class in its just struggle with the capitalist class. They also demanded sexual freedom.

The birth controllers were putting forward these demands at a time when American radicalism was at one of its peaks of strength and breadth. Indeed, the birth-control movement that began in 1914 was a part of a general explosion of resistance to economic and social exploitation. Joining that resistance, birth controllers appealed for support to the powerless, particularly to women and to working-class and poor people in general, because they believed that lack of control over reproduction helped perpetuate an undemocratic distribution of power.

Strategically their analysis tried to draw together the women's movement and the working-class movement. The leading birth controllers between 1914 and 1920 were both feminists and socialists and wanted to unite their respective goals and constituencies. Many of them came to the birth-control cause from multi-issue reform or revolutionary movements, ranging from the suffrage organizations to the IWW [Industrial Workers of the World]. Few were themselves working class, although some important leaders—Margaret Sanger is only one—had working-class origins. Their experience of the common oppression of women in sexual and reproductive matters convinced them that they could transcend their class differences and create a movement that would fight for the interests of the least privileged women.

They failed in this grand intention, but that does not mean that their analysis and strategy were completely wrong or that their experiences are useless to us today. Their belief that birth control could create a new freedom and dignity for women and a new right for all people was not wrong just because it was incompletely realized. . . .

The most notorious for her outspokenness on sexual questions was Emma Goldman. Goldman, more than any other person, fused into a single ideology the many currents that mingled in American sex radicalism. She had connections with European anarchism, syndicalism, and socialism; she knew and was influenced by American utopian anarchists and free lovers such as Moses Harman; she was also familiar with American feminism and with dissident doctors such as [William J.] Robinson. In 1900 she had attended the secret conference of Neo-Malthusians in Paris and had even smuggled some contraceptive devices into the United States. In New York Goldman was tremendously influential on other women radicals, as a role model and a practitioner of the new morality. One woman strongly influenced by Goldman was Margaret Sanger. . . .

Moving to New York City in 1911 and searching for something to do, Sanger's background as a nurse made it natural for her to take an interest in sex education. She began writing articles for the *New York Call.* At about the same time she was hired as an organizer for the Women's Commission of the Socialist party (with a small salary) and elected secretary of the Harlem Socialist Suffrage Society. In both capacities she began making speeches and was so enthusiastically received when she spoke on health and sex topics that she began to specialize in these areas. Questions and responses at the meetings and letters to the *Call* gave Sanger reinforcement and a sense of appreciation.

On the other hand, Sanger was disappointed in her more "orthodox" socialist organizing, working with striking laundry workers and trying to garner support for a legislative campaign for a wages-and-hours bill. She resigned as an organizer in January 1912. But her dissatisfaction with her Socialist-party work did not at first push her more deeply into sex-education activities; rather she was drawn, as were so many radical intellectuals at the time, toward the greater militancy of the IWW, with its direct-action tactics. When the strike of Lawrence, Massachusetts, textile workers, supported by the IWW, broke out in January 1912, Sanger became involved in support work for the strikers, which she continued until June 1912.

Sanger resumed her articles in the *Call* in November 1912 with a series, "What Every Girl Should Know." It was more daring than the first series, which had been called "What Every Mother Should Know" and had been designed to help mothers tell their children about sex and reproduction, largely through analogy to flowers and animals. The second series spoke more fully of human physiology, especially the female sexual and reproductive apparatus, and argued that the "procreative act" was something natural, clean, and healthful. But when Sanger turned to the problem of venereal disease, which had for decades been discussed in public only with euphemisms such as the "social problem" and "congenital taint," the Post Office could take no more. They declared the article unmailable under the Comstock law. The *Call* responded by printing the headline of the column—"What Every Girl Should Know"—and in a big, blank box underneath it, the words, "NOTHING, by order of the Post-Office Department." . . .

Up until this time, however, Sanger had not discussed birth control in writing. Her sex-education work was again interrupted by a more urgent demand for her services—the Paterson silk-workers' strike that began in February 1913. The workers asked the IWW for help, and Big Bill Haywood sent Sanger and Jessie Ashley (a socialist, feminist lawyer later to be active in birth control) to Paterson to organize picket lines. Sanger worked there until the strike's failure in the summer. She did not write anything further on sexual hygiene that year, and in October sailed for Europe with her husband and children. In Paris she began the first stage of her "research" into birth control—the sociological phase. Not yet interested in libraries and sexual theory, she spoke with her neighbors, with the French syndicalists that Bill Haywood (also then in Paris) introduced her to, with druggists, midwives, and doctors. She collected contraceptive formulas. She discovered that birth control was respectable, widely practiced, and almost traditional in France. Women told her that they had learned about contraception from their mothers. In fact, birth-control advocates in the United States such as William J. Robinson had been publishing articles about the low birth rate and widespread contraceptive use in France for years. Emma Goldman knew these facts about France. All this, however, was new to Sanger in 1913. For the rest of her life, birth control was to be her single, exclusive passion. . . .

But the reason she chose contraception rather than venereal disease or sex education was her recognition of the potential historical and political meaning of birth control. Most American socialists at this time, primarily oriented to class relations, saw birth control in Neo-Malthusian terms, that is, in terms of economics. They were concerned to help raise the standard of living of workers and thus increase their freedom to take political control over their own lives. Measured against this goal, birth control was at most an ameliorative reform. Seen in terms of sexual politics, however, birth control was revolutionary because it could free women entirely from the major burden that differentiated them from men, and made them dependent on men. Sanger did not originally have this perspective. Although female and concerned about women's rights, her political education had been a male-defined one. She gained this perspective in Europe from the sexual-liberation theorists like Havelock Ellis. Ellis literally tutored Sanger. His idealism about the potential beauty and expressiveness of human sexuality and his rage at the damage caused by sexual repression fired Sanger with a sense of the over-whelming importance, urgency, and profundity of the issue of birth control, a sense lacking in most other American radicals.

The entire future course of birth control in the United States was influenced by Sanger's European "education" on birth control. And yet the conviction, curiosity, and drive that led her to her research in Europe would almost certainly have led someone else there if Margaret Sanger had been diverted. Sanger's European trips took place in the midst of a flurry of activity for sexual change in the United States which began before Sanger's influence was great and which would in-evitably have led to a birth-control campaign before long. Sanger was stimulated by it and returned to shape it, but in all respects she was a part of a movement, not its inventor. . . .

Two kinds of political groups were primarily responsible for the birth-control agitation in 1915: women's Socialist-party groups and IWW locals. In many places people had been introduced by Emma Goldman to Sanger's pamphlet, Sanger's name, and sometimes *The Woman Rebel,* just as later Goldman was to raise money for Sanger's defense on her speaking tours. Elizabeth Gurley Flynn spoke about birth control in the Northwest and pledged local IWW and other anarchist support if Sanger would go on a speaking tour there. Socialists saw Sanger, or adopted her, as one of their own and flooded her with letters of support and, inevitably, advice. Eugene Debs was one of the first to write and promised her the support of a "pretty good-sized bunch of revolutionists." Goldman, in her motherly way, wanted to take Sanger under her wing, not only recommending a tactical plan for Sanger's trial but suggesting, "Hold out until I come back the 23rd of this month. Then go away with me for 2 weeks to Lakewood or some place . . . we'd both gain much and I would help you find yourself. . . ." Others like Kate Richards O'Hare, Rose Pastor Stokes, Georgia Kotsch, Caroline Nelson, Rockwell Kent, Alexander Berkman, William J. Robinson, Jessie Ashley, and many lesser-known socialist organizers sent her messages of support and spoke on her behalf. Liberals supported her too: for example, *The New Republic* published several editorials in her favor after March 1915. In May 1915 birth-control supporters held a large meeting at the New York Academy of Medicine, urging public birth-control clinics. Many liberals spoke there. But in March 1915, when a primarily liberal group organized the National Birth Control League (despite its name, the NBCL was never more than a New York City group), they would not support Sanger or any law-defying tactics. (They also excluded Goldman and other radicals.) To the end of 1915 at least, those who sup-ported Sanger and did local birth-control organizing everywhere except New York City were socialists.

In September 1915 William Sanger, Margaret's estranged husband, was tried for distributing her *Family Limitation* pamphlet. (He had been entrapped by a Post Office agent who requested a pamphlet.) Sanger was convicted in a dramatic trial in which he defended himself. The trial was dominated by radicals, who shouted at the judge until he ordered the police to clear the courtroom. Messages of support came from various parts of the country. From Portland, Oregon, a strong IWW city that was a veritable hotbed of birth-control fervor, came a handwritten petition:

1. A woman has the right to control her own body even to the extent of deciding when she will become a mother.
2. Unwelcome or unfit children ought not to be born into the world.
3. Motherhood is dignified and noble only when it is desired and a joy. . . .
4. Scientific knowledge of sex-physiology can never be classified as impure or obscene. Those who do so classify it, proclaim only the impurity of their own minds.

The first signer added after his name: "The industrial system which needs children as food for powder or factories may desire unlimited propagation, but the masses who suffer in poverty have no right to add sufferers to the already too many competing for bread." In these phrases were summarized fifty years of different birth-control arguments as they had reached the grass roots in the United States: women's rights, hereditarian social thought, social purity transformed by a faith in science and human dignity, and Neo-Malthusianism. It was such letters that made William Sanger believe his trial a great success, making "birth control a household word [*sic*]." The responses that flowed in to the Sangers showed that the concept of birth control, if not the term, was already widely known and supported. It was as if people had been waiting for leadership to ask them for help. . . .

[T]he grass-roots work in organizing for birth control was being done by radicals. In Cleveland (the first major city to organize a birth-control group, and a place where the birth-control campaign was later to be especially successful), workers' groups sponsored Sanger's tremendously successful speeches and led the birth-control movement. In St. Paul the Women's Socialist Club led the birth-control movement, and in Ann Arbor, Agnes Inglis, a socialist activist, organized a group. Even the relatively staid Massachusetts Birth Control League was led by socialists. In small towns as well as big cities socialists were organizing for birth control. And although Sanger varied her appeals to particular audiences, she made several sharp attacks on the conservatism of privileged groups. When the snobbish Chicago Women's Club cancelled her speaking engagement, she attacked it, saying she did not care to speak to a "sophisticated" audience anyway. "I want to talk to the women of the stock yards, the women of the factories—they are the victims of a system or lack of system that cries out for corrections. I am interested in birth control among working women chiefly."

In 1916 birth control in the United States was a radical movement and a large movement. Birth control as a political demand had demonstrated an ability to involve not only educated but also working-class women in a participatory social movement. [Labor activist] Elizabeth Gurley Flynn wrote to Sanger that she found everywhere in the country the "greatest possible interest" in birth control: ". . . one girl told me the women in the stockyards District [Chicago] kissed her hands when she distributed [Sanger's birth-control pamphlet]." In 1913 in Tampa, Florida, Flynn had visited a cigar factory with Spanish-speaking workers where the reader was reading aloud a pamphlet on birth control. Letters from women all over the country came pouring in not only to Sanger but also to others who were identified in newspapers as birth-control activists, letters asking for contraceptive information and thanking them for the fight they were making. Often they were fearful: "I nearly had nervous prostration after I had mailed you my letter asking for that 'information' . . ." Or: "Please send me one of your Papers on birth control, I have had seven children and cannot afford any more. Please don't give my name to the Papers." Usually they poured out the difficulties of their lives, with their most intimate sexual problems and most externally caused economic problems intermingled—as they indeed always are in real life. . . . Many of the letters expressed exasperation at the class injustice behind the fact that they were deprived of birth control information. "Tell me how it is the wealthier class of people can get information like that and those that really need it, can't?" And many others plunged immediately into political action. . . .

Not only was there a potentially large movement here, but its people were ready for action. What they wanted personally, the *minimum* demand, was to be given information in defiance of the law. Beyond that, women in many places quickly moved to a strategy that logically followed—opening illegal birth-control clinics to give that illegal information to others. There was a practical reason for this: the best contraceptive—a vaginal diaphragm—required a private fitting. Sanger was already convinced of the efficacy of "direct action." She gained support for this plan by what she learned on her national tour. In many ways that tour was as much a learning experience for Sanger as a teaching one. In Ann Arbor, Michigan, socialist Agnes Inglis had a de facto clinic functioning before Sanger returned to New York. In St. Paul socialist women announced plans for a clinic in June. Sanger herself dreamed of a "glorious 'chain' of clinics" throughout the country.

Returning to New York City in July 1916, Sanger organized a clinic of her own in the Brownsville section of Brooklyn. Brownsville was then a Jewish and Italian immigrant neighborhood, an extremely poor slum. Sanger worked with her sister Ethel Byrne, also a nurse, and Fania Mindell, whom Sanger had recruited in Chicago. The three women rented an apartment and gave out to every family in the district a handbill printed in English, Yiddish, and Italian. They were not prepared to fit women with contraceptives, but only to "give the principles of contraception, show a cervical pessary to the women, explain that if they had had two children they should have one size and if more a larger one." Women were lined up outside when the clinic opened on October 16. As many Catholics came as Jews. Sanger asked one Catholic woman what she would say to the priest at confession. "It's none of his business," she answered. "My husband has a weak heart and works only four days a week. He gets twelve dollars, and we can barely live on it now. We have enough children." Most of the neighbors were friendly and supportive. The baker gave them free doughnuts and the landlady brought them tea. By the end of nine days, the clinic had 464 case histories of women on file.

Then, inevitably, one of the patients turned out to be a policewoman. She seemed prosperous; Fania Mindell suspected her but did not turn her away. The next day she returned as Officer Margaret Whitehurst, arrested the three women, and confiscated all the equipment and case histories. Tried separately, Ethel Byrne was sentenced to thirty days on Blackwell's Island. Byrne immediately announced her intention to go on a hunger strike. (The hunger strikes of British suffragists were at this time an international symbol of feminist resistance.) Like the British suffragists, she was force-fed by tubes through the nose; the combination of her starvation and the brutality of the force-feeding left her so weakened she required a year to recuperate. . . . Sanger also was sentenced to thirty days but conducted herself cooperatively. . . .

Many activists were arrested and jailed for their birth-control activities—at least twenty besides Sanger on federal charges alone. . . .

Commitment to action was strong among these birth controllers. As socialists, most of them believed that working-class strength was the key to political progress, and thus they wanted above all to reach working-class people with their message and service. As feminists, they wanted to improve the position of women. They believed that the subjugation of women supported capitalism directly by creating profit, and indirectly by weakening the socialist movement: depriving it of half its potential constituency and allowing socialist men to cling to privileges that corrupted. All of them, even the non-Marxists, shared an interest in improving the lives of poor people in the present and did not try to fob them off with promises of postrevolutionary paradise. Their work in trying to reach working-class women was made more difficult by their own class origins. Most of the leadership of this movement was from professional, even capitalist, backgrounds. Their superior confidence and articulateness often made them better talkers than listeners. But their humanitarianism, their desire to eliminate material misery, was not a symptom of elitism. Indeed it was shared by those among them of "lower" origins—like Stokes, Goldman, Equi, and Sanger. It was also a conscious tactical choice, a rejection of the myth that greater misery makes workers more revolutionary.

Eugenics, Sterilization, and Social Welfare

MOLLY LADD-TAYLOR

The immense publicity accorded *The Bell Curve,* the recent invective on race, class, and intelligence by Charles Murray and the late Richard Herrnstein, marks a resurgence of the eugenic creed that mesmerized so many American scientists and reformers in the early twentieth century. Couched in supposedly scientific terms about genetically based differences in intelligence, *The Bell Curve* is actually a sweeping attack on what is left of the American welfare state. As such, it taps into American anxieties about welfare dependency, illegitimacy, and crime, as well as race.

Concern about the "quality" of the population in a period of social stress is nothing new in the United States. In the turbulent first decades of the twentieth century, like today, middle-class reformers responded to economic change, immigration, and a supposed decline in family life by looking for new ways to ensure a "better," more productive population. Compulsory sterilization and government-funded maternal and child health services, like legalized birth control, endeavored to "rationalize" reproduction by making childbearing more efficient and predictable and bringing it under human control. . . .

Molly Ladd-Taylor, "Saving Babies and Sterilizing Mothers: Eugenics and Welfare Politics in the Interwar United States," *Social Politics* 4 (Spring 1997): 137–153. Reprinted by permission of Oxford University Press, England.

Both infant health reform, which culminated in the 1920s with the passage and administration of the Sheppard-Towner Act, and eugenic sterilization were considered preventive health measures and justified in terms of race progress. As Progressive-Era reforms (though they did not achieve their biggest legislative successes until after the First World War), they also reflected the progressive enthusiasm for science and statistics. Health reformers utilized investigations of infant deaths to support their assertion that infant mortality was preventable, while proponents of sterilization invoked numerous studies, such as the famous one of the Jukes family, which "proved" that feeblemindedness, alcoholism, immorality, and epilepsy were hereditary—and thus preventable as well.

Supporters of both reforms also justified their causes in terms of efficiency and economy. Writers described the fight against infant mortality as a "business matter, with a return to society and the state that can be figured in actual dollars and cents." Compulsory sterilization was similarly portrayed as a bargain for taxpayers, who would otherwise have to pay for charity or the costs of institutionalizing the "unfit" and their children. Indeed, the association between sterilization and reducing welfare costs was undoubtedly one reason that sterilization programs achieved more lasting success in the United States than government- (i.e. taxpayer-) funded public health services.

A comparison between the "baby-saving" and sterilization movements highlights what I call the "welfare aspect" of eugenic sterilization in the United States. As many scholars have observed, sterilizations were frequently performed not for eugenic, but for social reasons, such as punishing criminals and cutting social welfare spending. Moreover, these sterilizations continued well into the 1970s, long after eugenic science had fallen into disrepute. Indeed, although compulsory sterilization in the United States is generally studied in the context of the history of science and medicine, it had as much to do with taxpayer stinginess, controlling women's sexuality, and political expediency as with eugenics or the "rationalization" of reproduction.

Although both can be characterized as progressive reforms, maternal and child health care and compulsory sterilization rested on very different ideas about the state's responsibility for social welfare. However, they possessed a similar gender ideology. Historian Atina Grossmann, writing on Germany, has remarked on the existence of what she calls a "'motherhood-eugenics' consensus that . . . transcended traditional left/right, socialist/conservative distinctions and emphasized the importance of protected motherhood and healthy offspring." In the United States, the "motherhood-eugenics" consensus is evident in the writings of scientists in the American Eugenics Society, in the views of feminist birth controllers like Margaret Sanger, and even in the affiliations of maternalist welfare reformers. For example, the left-leaning Children's Bureau chief Grace Abbott, a long-time resident of Hull House and an outspoken opponent of immigration restriction (a legislative priority of more conservative eugenicists), held an honorary post on the board of the American Eugenics Society for a short time during the 1920s. . . .

Still, as Grossmann emphasizes in her study of German sex reform, "eugenics" and "the importance of protected motherhood" could mean many different things. Thus, although advocates of maternal and child health reform and compulsory sterilization employed similar language about race betterment and healthy motherhood, they did so to very different ends. Health reformers such as Abbott drew on the rhetoric of virtuous motherhood to demand a welfare state that protected *all* mothers and children. Proponents of eugenic sterilization evoked the antithetical image of the irresponsible and sexually active "bad" mother, unfit to raise—or even bear—the nation's citizens, and warned of the dangers of charity. The image of the "good" mother provided the impetus for constructing a welfare system which protected women and children; unfortunately, the contrasting image of the "bad" mother, exemplified today in the icon of the black welfare recipient, has had the more lasting effect on American social politics.

The Sheppard-Towner Maternity and Infancy Protection Act of 1921 was arguably the closest the American government has come to the "rationalization" of reproduction. The first federal welfare measure in the United States, Sheppard-Towner aimed at reducing infant and maternal mortality by distributing matching funds to the states for prenatal and infant health education. Paid and volunteer health workers energetically promoted the need for medical care during pregnancy and childbirth and disseminated "scientific" childrearing advice that took for granted Anglo-American middle-class ideas about family life. In seven years of operation, Sheppard-Towner agents established thousands of permanent health clinics, distributed millions of pieces of literature, and visited three million homes. By 1929, when Sheppard-Towner funding was withdrawn, the federal Children's Bureau estimated that the government's childrearing advice had reached the mothers of half of all the babies born in the United States that year.

Many child health advocates considered their work part of the eugenics movement and described their campaign for "better babies" in the language of racial improvement. The American Association for the Study and Prevention of Infant Mortality included a section on eugenics, and the baby health contest that played such an important part in the campaign against infant mortality was invented by a eugenicist. University of Kansas physician Florence Brown Sherbon, the author of numerous books on child health and a contributing editor to *Eugenics,* the magazine of the American Eugenics Society, vigorously promoted both well-baby clinics and the more overtly eugenic Fitter Families Contests as tools for teaching good health habits and the value of a "clean" inheritance.

On balance, however, the campaign against infant mortality challenged eugenic principles more than it supported them. For one thing, the insistence that infant deaths could and should be prevented was based on the assumption that parent education and environmental reform could overcome minor genetic deficiencies. As Sherbon put it, a health examination "does not pretend to draw any more line between heredity and environment than is drawn by the stock judge when he judges and examines stock and takes into consideration the heredity, the feeding, and the care of the product." Public funding for child health care thus challenged the more orthodox eugenicist view that saw infant death as part of a natural order which allowed the fittest to survive—and considered high death rates among blacks and immigrants as evidence of their inferiority. In the words of Paul Popenoe and Roswell Johnson, authors of the popular textbook *Applied Eugenics,* baby-saving was not a "fundamental piece of race betterment," but a means of "race impairment" instead. Conceding that infant health services did keep babies alive, Popenoe and Johnson asserted that the gain was "temporary and illusory"; babies who lived to adulthood as a result of welfare work would undoubtedly transmit their weak constitutions to their offspring. They would grow up to be an economic burden on society.

. . . Popenoe and Johnson opposed social programs like mothers' pensions and the minimum wage, which, they feared, would benefit the mentally inferior.

The 1927 defeat of the Sheppard-Towner Act in the face of medical and right-wing opposition suggests that the U.S. government ultimately had limited interest in the "rationalization" of reproduction. Physicians objected that Sheppard-Towner was a step toward "state medicine," while right-wing organizations protested the federal government's health campaign as an invasion of privacy that threatened the sanctity of home and motherhood as well as states' rights. In spite of the bill's popularity among women and its apparent success at reducing infant mortality, Congress defeated efforts to renew Sheppard-Towner in 1927. Funding was extended for two more years but finally withdrawn in 1929. Infant mortality stopped being a national political issue after Sheppard-Towner was defeated—even though babies of color and the very poor continued to die in large numbers. This is largely because a substantial decline in infant mortality (especially among whites) and improvements in health care for those who could afford private physicians increased middle-class women's feeling of control over their own reproductive health—while immigration restriction reduced Anglo-American anxieties about the "quality" of the population. Although federal funding for maternal and child health was restored under Title V of the 1935 Social Security Act, public health services were run by the medical establishment and available only to the economically disadvantaged.

The Sheppard-Towner Act can be said to have "rationalized" reproduction in the United States by accelerating the medicalization of birth and child care among working-class and farm families and assimilating growing numbers of people into middle-class "American" norms. By making childbirth and infancy safer and improving health care, it also benefited individual mothers and babies. The evidence is overwhelming that ordinary mothers were grateful for the services. In contrast, the legalization of compulsory eugenic sterilization—a more extreme example of rationalized reproduction—placed the interests of race and nation clearly above those of the individual. Indeed, a substantial number of the more than 33,000 people legally sterilized by 1939 had the procedure done without their knowledge or against their will!

The American sterilization movement began with the enactment of the first law in Indiana in 1907, but at the end of the First World War it was foundering. Fifteen states had sterilization laws and more than 3,200 institutionalized people (mostly men) had been sterilized by 1921, but seven state laws were declared unconstitutional and most of the others were infrequently enforced. California was the notable exception; by 1921 nearly 80 percent of all compulsory sterilizations in the United States were performed in that one state.

The sterilization movement revived in the 1920s—just as progressive welfare reform was coming under attack by social spending conservatives and right-wing groups. The Supreme Court's famous decision *Buck v. Bell* (274 U.S. 200) upheld the constitutionality of eugenic sterilization in 1927—the same year that Congress defeated the bill renewing the Sheppard-Towner Act.

Support for sterilization paralleled the anti-immigrant, anti-welfare, and indeed anti-mother sentiment of the 1920s, a decade which saw not only a retreat from welfare spending and a restrictive immigration bill, but also a cultural shift in the womanly ideal from mother to flapper. Childrearing experts no longer described mothers in sentimental terms or even with approval; instead, they warned readers about the dangers of mother-love. The behaviorist John Watson even dedicated his bestselling advice book to the first mother to bring up a happy child!

Historians disagree on the degree of popular support for eugenic sterilization in the United States, but it is clear that it never received the active and broad-based support enjoyed by the infant health campaign in the 1910s and 1920s. . . . [M]ost compulsory sterilization laws were passed largely on the basis of the testimony and lobbying efforts of "experts" such as penologists and the superintendents of institutions for the insane and feebleminded. Women's club members, social workers, and physicians played a crucial lobbying role in a number of states, but they were usually not the leaders of the sterilization drive, as they were of the maternal and infant health campaign. . . .

The 1920s offered a favorable political climate, but the legislative success of the sterilization drive was more directly the result of a persistent eugenicist lobby and efforts to resolve the pressures of overcrowding in state institutions by releasing inmates into the community. In fact, the actual administration of sterilization policy over the years had as much to do with containing welfare costs and what historian James Trent calls "institutional population control" as with the prevention of hereditary defects. For instance, in Minnesota, a vigorous campaign by the state Eugenics Society succeeded in passing a law in 1925 that permitted the sterilization of feebleminded or insane persons who were committed as wards of the state. Yet the number of operations reached a peak during the mid 1930s—at the same time that relief rolls expanded because of the Depression. By 1941 nearly 1,700 legal sterilizations had been performed in Minnesota, and more than 38,000 in the nation as a whole.

Despite being convinced that most feeblemindedness was hereditary, Minnesota officials repeatedly rebuffed the efforts of eugenicists to broaden the state's sterilization law to include persons not under state guardianship and three-time felons. They chose instead to take a more cautious approach based on the social work principles of individual casework. . . . Minnesota officials rejected "wholesale sterilization" as impractical and inadvisable. Instead, they endorsed "selective sterilization" in individual cases. The "socio-economic justification of sterilization, that the feeble-minded parent cannot provide a stable and secure family life for his children," was paramount. Sterilization policy was as much about preventing child-*rearing* by the so-called feebleminded as it was about preventing child-*bearing*.

In Minnesota as elsewhere, the diagnosis of feeblemindedness—the main indication for compulsory sterilization for women—was based on behavior and economic status as well as the results of an IQ test. According to one definition circulated by state authorities, mentally "deficient" adults "lack common sense, foresight, are unable to resist ordinary temptations, act on impulse, and have little or no initiative. They have about the same desires as normals, including sexual, but lack ability to control them. They usually have poor homes." Today these traits are still used to describe the alleged behavior of an urban "underclass," but (*The Bell Curve* notwithstanding) they are more often attributed to the environment—and a "culture of poverty"—than to a biological defect.

The story of Carrie Buck, the eighteen-year-old white Virginia woman whose sterilization was upheld by the Supreme Court, illustrates the association between feeblemindedness, sexual deviance, and working-class status. We now know that Buck was not retarded but was an impoverished single mother who was institution-alized after becoming pregnant as a result of rape. An inmate of the Virginia Colony for Epileptics and Feebleminded, Buck was the "illegitimate" daughter of another inmate, as well as the unmarried mother of an allegedly feebleminded child. Harry Laughlin of the Eugenics Record Office provided the expert testi-mony. Using information supplied him by Colony officials—but not examining Carrie Buck, her mother, or her baby, Vivian, in person—Laughlin concluded that the Bucks belonged to the "shiftless, ignorant, and worthless class of anti-social whites of the South," and that their "feeblemindedness and moral delinquency" were due to inheritance and not the environment.

What sociologist Rosalind Petchesky has called the "two-sided character of eugenics as a means of social-sexual control" is further revealed in *Sterilization for Human Betterment,* a study by eugenicists Paul Popenoe and Ezra Gosney on ster-ilizations performed in California between 1909 and 1929. The California law pro-vided for the sterilization of anyone with a supposedly hereditary illness who was committed to a state hospital for the insane or feebleminded. During the period of the study, 6,255 sterilizations were performed in California, almost three times as many as in the rest of the nation. Women comprised 45 percent of all sterilized per-sons, but 61 percent of sterilizations among the feebleminded. There was a marked increase in the proportion of single women sterilized during the course of the 1920s and a slight increase in sterilizations among the foreign born.

Despite the claim of the study's authors that sterilization legislation did not dis-criminate against any racial or economic group, their research shows that judgments about who was feebleminded or insane—and therefore likely to be sterilized—were fraught with class and race bias. "Economically dependent" men and women were three times as likely to be sterilized as those who were more prosperous. Dispro-portionate numbers of unskilled laborers were sterilized because they were consid-ered insane, while the "higher ranks" of the population were rarely sterilized. And, although researcher Popenoe claimed that the number of sterilizations performed on the "Latin races" was in proportion to their numbers among the feebleminded, Latinos were more likely than whites to be considered feebleminded. Not surpris-ingly, native-born whites were underrepresented in the sterilized group.

The connection between "feeblemindedness" and the violation of established gender roles is also evident in the California study. Feebleminded men were de-scribed as unaggressive, "undersexed," unambitious, and unable to support them-selves. None of the men in Popenoe's study had been married before they were sterilized, and only three married after the operation. Possibly gay, these men clearly challenged traditional expectations of masculine sexual and social behavior. In con-trast to their male counterparts (and to proper feminine behavior), feebleminded women were considered "oversexed," uninhibited, and sexually aggressive. Seventy-five percent of those sterilized in California had been considered "sex delinquents" before the operation; the fact that only one woman out of twelve was sexually "delin-quent" afterwards was presented as evidence of the operation's success.

For sterilized women as for "normal" women, marriage was considered the pin-nacle of success. Although only 16 percent of the sterilized women in the study were known to have married after the operation, Popenoe boasted that two-thirds of their marriages were "successful." Yet "successful" marriages for sterilized women were judged differently from those of other women. While the "superior" woman was expected to remain at home with her family, the sterilized wife was supposed to work for pay outside the home. Despite prevailing ideas about a married woman's place in the home, wage-earning was considered a necessity for the sterilized wife: in addition to making a contribution to the family income, Popenoe explained, she would be kept busy and "out of mischief."

Similar conceptions of gender and sexuality are apparent in Minnesota's sterilization program. Most sterilized women in that state fell into two general categories: they were either sex "delinquents" (often unmarried mothers) who were committed as feebleminded through the court system, or they were older women with a number of children on welfare. For example, of the twenty-four women admitted in 1938 to the State School for the Feebleminded with the expectation that they would be sterilized and released, nine were unmarried mothers, nine were married but had families exhibiting "degrees of mental defect," and six were married but no longer living with their husbands. None of them fit conventional gender expectations.

Most historians of female delinquency and "feeblemindedness" see sterilization as part of an attempt by experts and parents to control young women's sexuality, and indeed this was an important factor in Minnesota's sterilization program. Among the first group of women released from the School for the Feebleminded and placed in a group home, for example, most of those institutionalized after the age of 14 had had "illegitimate sex experiences." Similarly, five out of seven women sterilized in September 1928 were described as promiscuous or sex delinquents. Four of them had a total of six "illegitimate" children, and four had venereal disease. Three of the seven had other family members in state institutions. The youngest, whose case history included no reference to sex, was "committed because of poor home conditions."

Yet a closer look at the case histories of feebleminded "sex delinquents" complicates the picture often drawn by historians—and proponents of sterilization—that highlights their sexual rebelliousness and agency. Some feebleminded women undoubtedly were resisting the norms of a repressive society, but others were victims of sexual assault and incest. For example, Mabel, "an attractive Indian girl" from Minnesota, was tormented by men who "not only made vile remarks to her but did things they would never do to a white girl." A particularly sad case was that of Lucille, a "feebleminded" mother of two illegitimate children, who was said to have "cohabited" with her father and brother. (The father served time in the state prison for incest.) Lucille, whose first child died when only one week old, was sent to the Minnesota School for the Feebleminded at the age of nineteen, when her second child was one year old. The head of the institution considered Lucille overly inclined to worry about her surviving child, but wrote that she was "quiet, well-mannered, and responds to kind treatment. Her delinquencies seem to have been beyond her control, and she has none of the tendencies toward prostitution." Lucille's unhappiness and "delinquencies" were attributed to feeblemindedness at the time, but today they would more likely be considered the result of sexual abuse and grief over the loss of her children.

Sexual behavior was considered an important indicator of feeblemindedness, but it was not the only one. On another list of five Minnesota women considered for sterilization and release in May 1933, not one was described in terms of sexual immorality or delinquency! Instead, four of the five—all of whom were between the ages of 18 and 25—were described mainly as having "feebleminded" mothers. . . . [I]t is worth noting that the case histories contained no reference to eugenicist concepts of family pedigree, or even to other "defective" family members. Instead, they were written in the environmentalist language of social work, emphasizing the negative impact of poverty and inadequate home conditions on children. Two of the women on the list were sisters whose father was deceased and whose mother was in an institution. Their family was described as having "no delinquent tendencies . . . just extreme poverty and mental backwardness." Evidence for the feeblemindedness of the mothers of two other girls was the fact that one had an illegitimate child and the other was receiving county aid. . . .

Scholars have recently begun to examine the impact of sterilization on the individuals most affected. They have documented the suffering of survivors (including the special anguish of those who did not know they had been sterilized), and they have uncovered considerable evidence of resistance to sterilization policies. Family members, for example, often tried to protect their loved ones from the operation. The steady stream of runaways from the institution where operations were performed, and the frequent breaking of rules (especially regarding socializing with men) are further evidence that sterilized and institutionalized women did not passively accept their lot.

Yet there is also surprising evidence that at least some women willingly accepted—and in some cases, even sought out—eugenic sterilization as a form of contraceptive control. According to historian Johanna Schoen, fully 17 percent of the petitions to the North Carolina Eugenics Board between 1960 and 1972 concerned women seeking sterilization for contraceptive purposes.

The likelihood that some women saw sterilization as a form of contraceptive control is supported by a survey of patient attitudes conducted by Popenoe. Despite his obvious bias and very small sample size (less than 5 percent of those sterilized in California), Popenoe's findings are suggestive. Eighty-one percent of the women who replied to the questionnaire reported satisfaction with the operation. No doubt many of those surveyed considered sterilization preferable to the alternative: long-term institutionalization. However, in the context of poverty, inadequate medical care, and the illegal status of birth control and abortion, it is possible that some women may have seen sterilization as a form of contraception or as a treatment for "female complaints." Take, for example, the following letter from a woman sterilized under the compulsory law:

> As a girl, even before my marriage, I was nervous, and had many headaches—and after my last baby was born it seemed I could hardly stand their baby naughtyness—it would make me so nervous. But since the operation they never affect me in that way. I enjoy their companionship and I never have headaches. It is wonderful to be so well.
>
> I do not know whether this is all due just to the operation or not, but I do know that I feel stronger physically and seem to be in perfect health mentally as well.

Similar statements are found in the survey of "volunteers" for surgical sterilization. Because of the potential for lawsuits over compulsory sterilizations, 75 percent of sterilizations performed in California (like almost all of those in Minnesota) were "voluntary"; that is, performed at the recommendation of social workers with written consent of relatives. A significant and (according to Popenoe) growing number of voluntary sterilizations were also done by private practitioners, almost always for health reasons. "Voluntary" sterilizations at state institutions were performed on three groups of women: (1) women whom social workers thought had too many children and thus imposed a burden on public charities; (2) "helpless," severely retarded women living at home who needed "protection" from men who might "take advantage" of them; and (3) "troublesome delinquents," often unmarried mothers, whose "antisocial" behavior meant that they needed close supervision if they were released into the community. Undoubtedly, members of the first group were most likely to see sterilization as a health measure. One woman wrote:

> After four serious operations (two cesareans [*sic*] and two curettements), almost losing my life during three of them, it is only natural, in spite of my love for children and my desire for a family, that I am glad the operation was performed. I have one little boy and I want to live to raise him. I feel that I could never go through another operation.

My point is not that compulsory sterilization is acceptable (even in cases where it is classed as "voluntary"), but that eugenicists' desire to control women's sexuality and prohibit the "degenerate" from having children may have converged with the interests of some impoverished women to control childbearing and improve their health. (The 1982 film *La Operacion* makes a similar point about forced sterilization in Puerto Rico.) In any case, much more research needs to be done on women's responses to sterilization.

The number of sterilizations performed in the United States increased in the 1930s, despite the declining support for eugenic ideas and negative publicity about the excesses of the Nazi sterilization program. Given the association between feeblemindedness and economic dependency, this should be no surprise. During the Depression, state institutions could not possibly accommodate the apparently growing numbers of feebleminded, and social workers wanted to limit the number of children on relief. Still, it is significant that sterilization was rarely mentioned in the public arena, even though its frequency was actually increasing. There was little public discussion on the "menace of the feebleminded"—or, outside of professional circles, of mental retardation at all.

During the Depression, proponents of sterilization talked more about preventing the feebleminded from placing a burden on taxpayers than about preventing the transmission of genetic defects. Young, unmarried women who were classed as bad mothers because of their poverty, youth, and sexual activity became the principal candidates for sterilization. The image of the overburdened "good" mother, once employed so effectively by maternalists campaigning for maternal and child health services and the expansion of the social welfare function of government, now figured little in public discussions on social spending. By the 1930s the "bad" or incompetent mother dependent on public charity loomed much larger in the politics of welfare and reproduction.

Today, images of good and bad motherhood still exercise a huge impact on social policy. Unmarried mothers are punished for their "selfish" sexuality. Some recent court rulings have required young mothers on welfare to use the birth control device Norplant, while the 1996 welfare law permits states to deny the mothers benefits if they do not work, go to school, or even—for those under 18—if they do not live at home. While "good" mothers (who are white and not on welfare) are applauded for staying home with their children, media images of black teenage mothers and welfare "queens" reinforce the all-too-common perceptions that the poor and unfit are having too many children. Once again, in a period of social stress, "science," along with powerful images of "bad" motherhood, is manipulated to control women's sexuality and cut welfare costs. As in the past, the results are sure to be tragic for many individuals, as well as for society.

FURTHER READING

Janet Farrell Brodie, *Contraception and Abortion in Nineteenth-Century America* (1994).

Adelaida R. Del Castillo, "Sterilization: An Overview," in Magdalena Mora and Adelaida R. Del Castillo, eds., *Mexican Women in the United States* (1980), 65–70.

DNA Learning Center, Cold Spring Harbor Laboratory, *Image Archive on the American Eugenics Movement* [http:vector.cshl.org/eugenics/].

Nancy Gallagher, *Breeding Better Vermonters: The Eugenics Project in the Green Mountain State* (1999).

Joan M. Jensen, "The Death of Rosa: Sexuality in Rural America," *Agricultural History* 67 (Fall 1993): 1–12.

———, "The Evolution of Margaret Sanger's *Family Limitation* Pamphlet, 1914–1921," *Signs* 6 (1981): 548–567.

Edward J. Larson, *Sex, Race, and Science: Eugenics in the Deep South* (1995).

Carole McCann, *Birth Control Politics in the United States, 1916–1945* (1994).

Ellen Messer and Kathryn E. May, *Back Rooms: An Oral History of the Illegal Abortion Era* (1988).

James Mohr, *Abortion in America* (1978).

Leslie Reagan, *When Abortion Was a Crime* (1997).

James Reed, *From Private Vice to Public Virtue: The Birth Control Movement and American Society Since 1830* (1978).

Phillip Reilly, *The Surgical Solution: A History of Involuntary Sterilization in the United States* (1991).

Jessie M. Rodrique, "The Black Community and the Birth Control Movement," in Kathy Peiss and Christina Simmons, eds., *Passion and Power* (1989), 138–154.

Loretta Ross, "Afro-American Women and Abortion, 1800–1970," in Stanlie M. James and Abena P. A. Busia, eds., *Theorizing Black Feminisms* (1993), 141–159.

Richard A. Soloway, "The 'Perfect Contraceptive': Eugenics and Birth Control Research in Britain and America in the Interwar Years," *Journal of Contemporary History* 30 (1995): 637–664.

Andrea Tone, "Contraceptive Consumers: Gender and the Political Economy of Birth Control in the 1930s," *Journal of Social History* (Spring 1996): 485–506.

———, *Devices and Desires: A History f Contraceptives in America* (2001).

Amy Vogel, "Regulating Degeneracy: Eugenic Sterilization in Iowa, 1911–1977," *Annals of Iowa* 5 (1995): 119–143.

Susan Cotts Watkins and Angela D. Danzi, "Women's Gossip and Social Change: Childbirth and Fertility Control among Italian and Jewish Women in the United States, 1920–1940," *Gender and Society* 9 (August 1995): 469–490.

CHAPTER
10

Heterosexual Norms and Homosexual Identities in Popular Culture

*Today most Americans understand sexual attraction largely in binary terms—
as in gay and straight—but this way of thinking is a relatively recent development.
A concept of homosexual identity emerged in the late nineteenth century, as a new
medical framework for understanding sexuality formed and urban same-sex subcultures developed. Initially, neurologists, psychologists, and physicians singled out
"inverts"—those who exhibited the gender characteristics of the other sex—and
labeled their physiological and psychological traits an abnormal and innate identity. But Sigmund Freud and sexologist Havelock Ellis, among others, fostered the
modern concept of sexuality when they separated homosexual desire from gender
inversion. In Freud's terms, the* sexual object *to which one was attracted was
distinct from the* sexual aim, *the type of sexual encounter or role one preferred.*

*In many ways, the medical model was an effort to make sense of visible changes
in everyday life and culture. Gay men fashioned homosexual identities as they gravi-
tated to large cities, lived in rooming houses and apartments, and found each other
in saloons, dance halls, public parks, and the streets. Lesbians too carved out distinct
spaces for social life, including working-class bars, bohemian salons, and house
parties. By the 1920s and 1930s, a "gay world," with its own language and style,
had become part of the urban scene, flourishing despite police crackdowns during
the Depression. Drag balls and "pansy parades"—led by working-class gay men—
even found a heterosexual audience that enjoyed the cross-dressing, flamboyant
performances, and encounter with a sexual "other."*

*If homosexuality is a historical phenomenon, what about heterosexuality? In the
view of some historians, heterosexuality was "invented" in response to a homosexual
identity that had become more visible and widespread. Popular commercial culture
of the 1920s and 1930s—from magazines and advertising to movies and songs—
self-consciously articulated heterosexual norms as an aspect of the more liberal sexual mores of the period. The images of heterosexuality in popular culture were not
uniform, however, nor were they perceived identically by men and women. Although*

337

the homosexual/heterosexual binarism became the governing framework of American sexuality, gender, class, race, and ethnicity continued to shape how sexual orientation and desires were understood and expressed.

DOCUMENTS

A popular culture that embraced heterosexuality flowered in the years between the World Wars. In the 1920s, images of "flaming youth" filled the silver screen and magazines. Sexually uninhibited young people dated, drank (illegally under Prohibition), parked, petted, and necked. In Document 1, a male student from the Philippines described his shock at first witnessing the manners and morals of American women in Los Angeles. Phyllis Blanchard and Carlyn Manasses, in their 1930 survey *New Girls for Old*, excerpted in Document 2, indicated that this culture often confused and troubled young women, who needed to steer between new sexual pressures, an older morality, and their own sense of self. In Document 3, Henry James Forman's *Our Movie-Made Children* emphasized the powerful—and in his view negative—influence of movies on sexual desire and identity. When assessing the delinquent girls he quotes, consider his selection of evidence and imagine the limited possibilities of their lives. Responding to concerns about promiscuity and youthful delinquency, movie producers and distributors agreed to enforce a Production Code (Document 4) that put strict limits on sexual depictions. Originally written in 1930 and revised several times, the Production Code remained in effect until 1967; this version appeared in 1934.

Under the radar of most "straight" Americans, a homosexual culture also flourished in this period. In Document 5, Mabel Hampton described black lesbian social life in Harlem in the 1920s, while La Forest Potter's account of a drag ball (Document 6)—part of his "study in sexual abnormalities"—vibrantly conveyed the ongoing importance and pleasure of gender inversion in gay culture in the 1930s.

1. A Filipino's Impressions of America in the 1920s

I have been shocked with some of the things that I saw here for the first time. Most of all was the girls in their bathing suits. I first saw an American lady in her bathing suit in the boat where I rode. Then I went to the beach for the first time. I have seen girls and boys (young people) in their bathing suits, catching each other, and playing without any delicacy on the part of the girls. Some of the girls were almost naked. This freedom and enjoyment of the young people has not yet been comprehended by our people at home [in the Philippines]. The girls are so delicate that they are very careful not to expose their legs especially before young men.

Again, in the movie, I have seen young people (lovers and sweethearts) who sit together and have the arms of the young men around the necks of the young women. Their actions shocked me very much. Those actions might be done in their

Social Science Institute, Fisk University, *Orientals and Their Cultural Adjustment: Interviews, Life Histories and Social Adjustment Experiences of Chinese and Japanese . . . in the United States*, Social Science Source Documents, no. 4 (Nashville: Fisk University, 1946), 132–134. Published by permission of Fisk University.

private rooms. Even in the street and in the street cars, the intimacy between lovers is too much for the public.

The freedom of young women is beyond my comprehension. Some ladies are let by their parents to go anywhere. They do as they please. They are free to go out with their boy friends, even late at night. They go out riding even at nights. I have been staying in a house where there was a lady. A boy friend comes to visit even late at night, and when the friend comes the parents leave her in the living room with him and the girl and the boy stay alone together. Such freedom has never yet been given to the girls at home. They are carefully watched for who knows what will happen, for they, the young people, are in their impulsive and sensitive nature!

I was talking with a lady friend about the freedom of young girls in this country and about their love affairs, and she said that a girl might go out riding in the machine with a boy whom she meets the first time in the street. She said that most of the American girls when the boys take them out to a show or riding, give those boys a good time, that is, by kissing and all sorts of happy good time, because if not the boys would not take them out again for the next time. When the girls get together, they talked of what they did to the boys and how they gave them a good time. These statements were a great surprise to me. Surely the moral life is degrading. She also said that these young people make love for the time being. They are engaged for the time being without any thought of getting married afterwards. The young people at home never do this. When they make love and are engaged, they are sure that they will marry. In the newspapers we read about the effects of this free love making. Marriage is very cheap because divorce is easily taken. Love stories, suggestions for young people about love affairs, are read in the press. One time I read, "A young beautiful lady who is supporting a father wants a husband." Love is even advertised! Almost all of the movies are full of love stories. I believe that all of these read in the newspapers and seen in the movies have a great moral effect upon the lives of the young people.

I observe that the independence of women in this country is too much. The center of life here is the individual, while at home the family is the center. I don't see any conflict of these young people with their parents in this country. I believe in the freedom of the young people to think for themselves, to act for themselves. But oftentimes the young people do not do just the right thing because of inexperience in life or because of their acting upon their impulse at the moment. The individual freedom must not go so far as to disregard the opinions, advice, and suggestions of older people.

2. Young Women Discuss Petting, 1930

The girl who has been brought up to believe that petting, smoking and drinking are wrong, but sees one or all of these things done by many of her friends, is doubtful as to what course she shall pursue. Shall she cleave to parental ideals or transfer her allegiance to her own age-group? The following letters from a newspaper advice column indicate how puzzling this question may become.

Phyllis Blanchard and Carlyn Manasses, *New Girls for Old* (New York: Macaulay Co., 1930), 62–66, 69–71.

I've had a feeling that I never intended going out with everyone who cared to take me out, or I never wanted to be kissed by anyone except the one I would some day marry. . . . When I entered high school the rest of my girl friends went out with different boys, but I refused. . . . Now in the office the girls are the same as the ones I knew in high school. They do not think it is wrong to smoke and pet. I myself would never think of doing either, but I want you to understand that I would not look down on those girls, for all they do is their own personal affair.

Sometimes I get the blues so badly that if anyone were there I would do what the rest of my friends do, but, thank goodness, there is something that seems to hold me back. . . . Am I doing right, or have I been in a trance for twenty-one years?

My girl friend and I don't pet, smoke or drink. The fellows go out with me once. Is it because I don't pet? I hate to kiss any fellows. Why is it? My girl friends do. . . . My girl friends have boy friends, but not me. Where can I find one? . . . I am only eighteen. Shall I wait, or shall I go out and pet every fellow I know? What shall I do?

I am not popular. Is it because I won't neck and pet? When the boys ask me for dates I very seldom go, but if I do it ends up by the person I am with being slapped. Then we don't speak for months at a time. I have told these boys again and again I don't care to be necked. Still they insist on having the same thing over every time we go out. The crowd I go with all say I am a "flat tire" because I won't neck. . . . Please tell me what to do.

I am almost seventeen and I am in my last year of high school. I do not smoke or drink, and I simply cannot stand a young man pawing me or necking, particularly if I don't care a whole lot for him. I have dates fairly regularly, but not very many with the same boy. Do you suppose it is because I won't neck? Do you think all boys expect that privilege if they take you out? . . . Which would you do—sit at home or have dates and be necked?

I should like to meet some of these girls who say how popular they are, but they don't smoke or drink. How they do it is beyond me. I am seventeen and have been going with boys since I was thirteen. I am considered attractive, yet I have to smoke, drink, etc., to secure dates. The boys I go with go to college, and I have yet to find one who does not want a girl to pet the first time he meets her. They take you to the fraternity houses, when we all know it isn't proper. Still, the girls go rather than be called poor sports. Many of the boys have apartments. . . . The first thing they do is call up the bootlegger and get gin, etc. to make highballs then put the radio on and dance. Of course petting is a side line to all this. . . . Believe me after you have finished drinking you aren't fit to go home to your parents. But what are we going to do if we want to have a good time? Certainly, if you don't have a good time when you are young you won't get it when you get older.

Which is the better way, I ask you, to behave and stay home or to misbehave and have a great time? . . .

That these girls should sufficiently need the help of another person to seek the impersonal advice of the newspaper columnist is an indication of how impossible they find it to settle the conflicts aroused by the clash between the old and new manners. . . . [W]e sent out questionnaires to a group of college and working girls, inquiring as to their attitudes on these various subjects. Altogether we received 252 replies, from girls and young women between the ages of fifteen and twenty-six, nearly three-fourths being between eighteen and twenty-three years old. With the exception of a few young married women, the replies were about equally divided between the school and working groups.

Surprisingly enough, the replies indicated considerable disapproval of petting, for only twenty-three per cent of the girls accepted this as a routine part of their relationships with boys, and only eighteen per cent thought it necessary to insure popularity. . . .

Although only one-fifth (approximately) of the girls who answered our questionnaires expressed a complete acceptance of petting as characteristic of modern behavior, this will undoubtedly be an occasion of concern to older people who are unwilling to go so far. Many parents think that petting is wrong, in itself; other object to it principally because they fear that it will lead to other things. They fear that petting will so stimulate the girl, sexually, that she will experience a desire for intercourse too ardent to be denied. They do not understand what we have already mentioned, that for many girls and boys petting becomes an end in itself, to some extent a substitute for more advanced sexual activities, bringing about relief of physical tension in many instances without the need of carrying it over into intercourse. . . .

. . . [V]ery many girls draw a distinct line between the exploratory activities of the petting party and complete yielding of sexual favors to men. In the group of girls who answered our questionnaires, for instance, although twenty-three per cent placed no restrictions upon petting, only seven per cent were willing to permit themselves indulgence in extra-marital intercourse. Ninety-two per cent definitely classed extra-marital sex relations as immoral or unwise. . . .

When we sum up the reasons given for objecting to extra-marital sex relations there seems to be a combination of ethical and practical considerations. More than half of the girls would fear to cause their parents grief, to contract venereal disease, to be troubled later by feelings of regret, or to find themselves pregnant. Thus, however emancipated intellectually the modern girl may be, she apparently realizes that social customs are still too powerful for the individual to defy them without risking personal happiness. . . .

Nevertheless, many of the girls have advanced in their thinking so far beyond their early training as to draw a distinct line between promiscuity and premarital intercourse with the man they expect to marry. "Where one's love is deep and one's motives high, marriage is a mere form that does not deeply matter." "I have lost my virginity to the man I love and expect to marry." "I disapprove of promiscuous relations on moral grounds; not, however, between a man and woman in love." These are typical remarks. The code which the girls have worked out for themselves declares that sexual intercourse without marriage can safely be indulged in when it is a prelude to the more permanent arrangement of matrimony. Promiscuity is clearly differentiated, and largely condemned as "cheap" and "common."

3. Henry James Forman Considers the Movies' Influence on Sexual Behavior, 1933

In a state training-school for delinquent girls, one hundred and twenty-one of 252, virtually half, declare that they "felt like having a man make love to them" after they had seen a passionate love picture. In the cases of these girls, . . . the distance

---

Henry James Forman, *Our Movie Made Children* (New York: Macmillan, 1933), 222–226, is reprinted by permission of the Payne Fund, Inc., Cleveland, Ohio.

between feelings of passionate love and sexual behavior is small. As one inmate, sixteen years old, admits with singular lucidity: "When I was on the outside I went to the movies almost every night, but only about twice in two months to a dance. I don't like dances as well as I do movies. A movie would get me so passionate after it was over that I just had to have relief. You know what I mean."

A contemporary of hers gives an even more graphic description of her thrills and stirrings under the impact of sex movies:

> When I see movies that excite me I always want to go home and do the same things that I saw them do. Pictures where a fellow kisses a girl and holds her a long time is what gets me excited, and I just want to do that myself . . . Passionate love pictures do stir me up. Some and most times I go out from a movie and stay out late with a fellow. Sometimes never think of coming in until two-thirty in the morning. . . . One night I went to a movie with a fellow of mine who drives a very chic little sport roadster. In the movie he sat with his arms around me, and every time the fellow would kiss the girl, he would look at me lovingly and squeeze my hand; after the movie we went to my girl friend's house and got her and her fellow. Then we all went for a moonlight spooning ride and had sexual relations.

"Movies," declares a seventeen-year-old delinquent, "taught me a lot pertaining to men: They have taught me how to kiss, how a girl should appear in the presence of her beau, how I should go about loving a fellow, how to do hot dances, how to court, etc. A fellow is expected to take his girl to the movies, dances, skating parties, etc., and according to modern times he is expected to take her to a place, whatever the circumstances may be, and to make passionate love to her, and she is expected to show him a good time as he shows her."

The case above is of a girl who probably ought never to see any movies, and least of all such movies as those whence she gleaned her principles. Nevertheless, all movies are open wide, alike to moron and philosopher and to all that come between, with all the sanction and seeming approval that a broad and general publicity carries. The results are—the results.

Girls, of course, differ in temperament and physical constitution. All these who are here testifying were in a state institution expiating sexual delinquency. At least twenty-five per cent of them acknowledge engaging in sexual relations after becoming aroused at a movie. That they were possessed of a propensity to sexual experience is entirely likely. Nevertheless it appears quite clear that motion pictures were a direct contributing influence and incitement. Those who admitted it are, as we see from their statements, exceedingly frank—perhaps merely more frank than their reticent sisters. What, for example, could be more open and explicit than this account of a seventeen-year-old girl?

> I like to see men and women fall in love in the movies and go out on parties, etc. I also like to see them kiss, drink, smoke and make love to each other. It makes me get all stirred up in a passionate way. Love pictures, wild west pictures, murder cases are the pictures I like best, because I like to love, myself, and I know others want to do the same. After I see them I go out and make love and go on wild parties and only do worse. Movies teach me how to treat my men and fool them. When I see a wild west picture, especially when I see a cowboy falling in love with a girl and running away with her and when they go out riding with her it makes me want to be out in the West—Colorado— with someone I could live around with and have relations with. When I saw the picture, "All [Quiet] on the Western Front," I was so thrilled and excited I could hardly realize

I was seeing the picture. It seems as though it was myself and the boy I was sitting with. I have always wanted to have the experience and thrill of being held in the arms of some masculine man and being loved . . . Love pictures are my favorites. They teach me how to love and kiss. Oh! How thrilled I am when I see a real passionate movie! I watch every little detail, of how she's dressed, and her make-up, and also her hair. They are my favorite pictures. The most exciting pictures are passionate plays. I get excited most when they are kissing and loving and having experiences I wish I could have. When I see these movies I leave the movies most always immediately and go out to some roadhouse or an apartment with my man and get my wants satisfied. Especially when I get all stirred up and my passion rises. I feel as if I never want my man to leave me, as if I can't live without him. I have a feeling that can't be expressed with words but with actions.

. . . [T]his delinquent girl, notwithstanding a certain muddle-headedness, is probably not unique—to her sex pictures have brought a new freedom and a new stimulus, as well, perhaps, as some of the muddle-headedness. In a way, she has always existed. But the movies have brought a stream of suggestions and patterns within easy reach of such large numbers of her that they amount to a school, with the addition of public sanction—a sanction expressed by universal attendance and wide-flung advertising, by bright lights, vivid posters and press advertisements.

4. The Motion Picture Production Code Sets Sexual Standards, 1934

General Principles

1. No picture shall be produced which will lower the moral standards of those who see it. Hence the sympathy of the audience shall never be thrown to the side of crime, wrong-doing, evil or sin.

2. Correct standards of life, subject only to the requirements of drama and entertainment, shall be presented.

3. Law, natural or human, shall not be ridiculed, nor shall sympathy be created for its violation.

Particular Applications

Sex   The sanctity of the institution of marriage and the home shall be upheld. Pictures shall not infer that low forms of sex relationship are the accepted or common thing.

1. **Adultery and Illicit Sex,** sometimes necessary plot material, must not be explicitly treated or justified, or presented attractively.
2. **Scenes of Passion**
   a. These should not be introduced except where they are definitely essential to the plot.
   b. Excessive and lustful kissing, lustful embraces, suggestive postures and gestures are not to be shown.

Motion Picture Producers and Distributors of America, Inc., *A Code to Govern the Making of Motion and Talking Pictures* (n.p.: MPPDA, 1934), 6–9, 17.

c. In general, passion should be treated in such manner as not to stimulate the lower and baser emotions.

3. **Seduction or Rape**
   a. These should never be more than suggested, and then only when essential for the plot. They must never be shown by explicit method.
   b. They are never the proper subject for comedy.

4. **Sex perversion** or any inference to it is forbidden.

5. **White slavery** shall not be treated.

6. **Miscegenation** (sex relationship between the white and black races) is forbidden.

7. **Sex hygiene** and venereal diseases are not proper subjects for theatrical motion pictures.

8. Scenes of **actual child birth,** in fact or in silhouette, are never to be presented.

9. **Children's sex organs** are never to be exposed.

Obscenity   Obscenity in word, gesture, reference, song, joke, or by suggestion (even when likely to be understood only by part of the audience) is forbidden.

Costume

1. **Complete nudity** is never permitted. This includes nudity in fact or in silhouette, or any licentious notice thereof by other characters in the pictures.
2. **Undressing scenes** should be avoided, and never used save where essential to the plot.
3. **Indecent or undue exposure** is forbidden.
4. **Dancing costumes** intended to permit undue exposure or indecent movements in the dance are forbidden.

Dances

1. Dances suggesting or representing sexual actions or indecent passion are forbidden.
2. Dances which emphasize indecent movements are to be regarded as obscene.

Locations   The treatment of bedrooms must be governed by good taste and delicacy.

Sex   Out of regard for the sanctity of marriage and the home, the triangle, that is, the love of a third party for one already married, needs careful handling. The treatment should not throw sympathy against marriage as an institution.

   Scenes of passion must be treated with an honest acknowledgment of human nature and its normal reactions. Many scenes cannot be presented without arousing dangerous emotions on the part of the immature, the young or the criminal classes.

   Even within the limits of **pure love,** certain facts have been universally regarded by lawmakers as outside the limits of safe presentation.

   In the case of **impure love,** the love which society has always regarded as wrong and which has been banned by divine law, the following are important:

1. Impure love must **not** be presented as **attractive and beautiful.**
2. It must **not** be the subject of **comedy or farce,** or treated as material **for laughter.**

3. It must **not** be presented in such a way as **to arouse passion** or **morbid curiosity** on the part of the audience.
4. It must **not** be made to seem **right and permissible.**
5. In general, it must **not** be **detailed** in method and manner.

5. Black Entertainer Mabel Hampton Recalls Lesbian Life in the 1920s and 1930s

Hampton: In 1920, I was about seventeen years old. I lived at 120 West 22nd Street. I had rooms there. A girlfriend of mine was livin' in that house. They lived next door and they got me three rooms there on the ground floor and there was a bedroom, a living room, and a big kitchen. I don't think I paid them more than two dollars a week for that apartment. And I stayed there till I met Lillian [Lillian Foster, who lived with Ms. Hampton from 1932 until her death in 1978]. I went away with people, and I worked and I went away but I always kept a room or something, then I'd come back. Then I went in the show.

Next door, this girl, they were all lesbians, she had four rooms in the basement and she gave parties all the time. And sometimes we would have pay parties. We'd buy up all the food—chicken and different vegetables and salads and things, potato salad, and I'd chip in with them you know 'cause I'd bring my girlfriends in, you know. We also went to rent parties—where you go in and you pay a couple of dollars. You buy your drinks and meet other women and dance and have fun. But with our house, we just give it for our close friends. Sometimes there would be twelve or fourteen women there. We'd have pig feet, chitlins. And sometimes it was corn. In the wintertime it was black-eyed peas and all that stuff.

Most of the women wore suits. Very seldom did any of them have slacks or anything like that because they had to come through the street. Of course, if they were in a car, they wore the slacks. And most of them had short hair. And most of them was good-lookin' women too. There was singles and couples because the girls just come and bring—the bulldykers used to come and bring their women with them, you know. And you wasn't supposed to jive with them, you know. You wasn't supposed to look over there at all. They danced up a breeze. They did the Charleston, they did a little bit of everything. They were all colored women. Sometimes we ran into someone who had a white woman with them. But me, I'd venture out with any of them. I just had a ball. I had a couple of white girls from downtown in the Village and tell them about it and they would come up. We got along fine. Then at that time I was acting in the Cherry Lane Theater [in Greenwich Village]. I didn't have to go to bars because I would go to the women's houses. Like Jackie Mables would have a big party and all the girls from the show would go—she had all the women there.

Interviewer: What were some words you called yourselves?

Hampton: Bulldykers and ladylovers, stud and butch, and the other ladies, "This is my friend, my wife." Most we heard "stud" when we went to a big party like on 110 Street. Now there was a woman that knew me very well, and I used to go

---

up to her house. At her house, we had a marriage between two women. That was around 1938. Anyhow, she called us, "Mabel, you know Florence, she's getting married. Yes, she's going down, her and her friend and her mamma is going down to get the marriage certificate and the Reverend Monroe will marry them." So that's how I knew he was gay. He was a faggot. He was at 114th Street and St. Nicholas Avenue. He was a fine guy. So naturally we dressed fine, you know, and there must have been about thirty-five people there. In their house. The girls had on tuxes—white neckties and everything. I had on a white suit. My hair was long. I had the girl fix my hair. She rolled it up and I put water in it and waved it. And Lillian always looked like a fashion plate. So we went to this party and the guests started arriving, all women, no men outside of the minister. And, of course, the girl who was marrying, her mother gave her away. The wife had a veil—a wedding dress and white shoes and the brides-maids had different dresses on with flowers and the music was playing. The groom had on white pants. They passed downtown at City Hall! That girl looked so much like a fellow you couldn't tell her apart—just like some of them do today. She was the splitting image and didn't have to change her voice. The went down there, had a blood test and everything and got it and brought it back and gave it to the minister. The service was just like the regular. "Do you take this woman to be your lawfully married . . . ? Do you take this man to be your lawfully wedded husband?" There were so many people and I was so far back. I could hear her sayin', "Yes." One of the girls was twenty-five and the other was thirty. And then after, Reverend Monroe said, "Now kiss the bride," and he knew they were women. He knew because he was gay hisself. And that's all he went in for—was to marry men and women.

You know, in a small town you wouldn't have a chance to get around and meet people. Now in New York, you met them all over the place: from the theater to the hospital to anything. I even went one night to a political meeting and I met two women there. I knew they were gay. I knew it. Yes, New York is a good place to be a lesbian. You learns so much and you see so much.

Interviewer: How did women help each other through the hard times?

Hampton: Well, they worked together. They worked. They lived together and they worked. When someone got sick the friend would come and help them—bring food, bring money and help them out 'cause all of us had a little piece of money. Nobody was broke then. I never felt lonely because I was too busy working.

6. Dr. La Forest Potter Describes a Drag Ball, 1933

It is stated, on the authority of one who has frequently attended the "Mardi Gras" festival at New Orleans, and the "Rose Pageant" held in Pasadena, California, that, not infrequently, the most beautifully decorated floats, the most gorgeous costumes, the loveliest gowns are worn by urnings [homosexuals] of the effeminate type.

At all the festivals I have mentioned the "bars are down." All restrictions concerning the wearing of women's clothes by men or the wearing of men's clothes by women are withdrawn. In fact, there is the greatest possible tolerance shown for

La Forest Potter, *Strange Loves: A Study in Sexual Abnormalities* (New York: Robert Dodsley, 1933), 184, 186–189.

almost anything—short of murder—just as during the old Greek Bacchanalia or the Roman Lupercalia and Saturnalia.

Under ordinary circumstances, in most American cities, the "fairy"—with plucked eyebrows, rouged lips, powdered face, and marcelled, blondined hair—who attempts to walk the streets, attired in woman's costume, is practically certain of arrest and severe punishment. . . .

In addition to the pageants, however, there are still other festivities at which the ban against *transvestism*—or the wearing of the clothes and "make-up" of the opposite sex—is permiss[i]ble.

These are the famous "Drag Balls," held in many of our principal cities, on the average of once a year. The men, dressed in the clothes of women, are called "drags."

In New York City there are at least two outstanding Drag Balls yearly—one held at Webster Hall, in Greenwich Village, the other in the Manhattan Casino, up in Harlem. Of late years this place has had "the run."

The Drag Ball is really a great masquerade party, at which many of the men who attend wear the fancy dress costumes of women. Substantial prizes are offered for the most striking and original costumes. And it may here be said that many costumes worn by the men are really superb creations.

These balls offer a meeting place for the "drags" at which those of the intermediate world may dance with one another to their heart's content, while thousands of normal men and women, seeking a novel thrill, look on and applaud.

Among those who come to stimulate jaded senses are society people, lights of the literary and theatrical world, prize-fight promoters, "racket" chiefs and their "gun molls," clubmen, show-girls and financiers, gangsters and hoodlums. They fill the balconies to the bursting point, and peer down upon the motley throng that surges and sways to the blood-boiling rhythm of a Negro band.

Hundreds and hundreds of Negroes also—of every shade of black and brown—from the octoroon, hardly to be distinguished from a strikingly lovely brunette Caucasian girl, to the burly blackamoor, of pure Ethiopian type—are crowded, cheek by jowl, into sense-maddening proximity. For the Harlem Drag Ball is a "mixed" affair, attended by whites and blacks alike.

On the floor of the hall, in every conceivable sort of fancy dress, men quaver and palpitate in each other's embrace. Many of the "effeminates" are elaborately coiffured, in the powdered head dresses of the period of Madame Pompadour. They wear the billowy, ballooning skirt of that picturesque pre-guillotine era.

Others affect the platinum blond hair, made popular by one of our motion picture actresses a few years ago. Still others wear the long, tight-fitting gowns which were a recent vogue, and which fit the figure like a seal skin coat fits the seal that owns it.

Still others wear the long, trailing skirts and the constricting corsets of the 1880's—yards of elaborately furbelowed material, frou-frouing behind them, when space permits. At other times they carry the impending contraption draped over their left arm.

The grace and the assuredness with which the men wear these costumes proclaim long weeks of practice in the art and science of handling what must always seem to normal men strange and often burdensome draperies.

Nevertheless, the homosexuals, in some instances, seem to have out-womened the women themselves in these sex-twisted efforts. . . .

The crowds, who come to "get a kick" out of all this, fill the boxes, pack the aisles, jam the stairways—perhaps violating fundamental Fire Department rulings, just as the "pansies," in their one-night-a-year freedom under police protection, violate the stupid Penal Code of the State of New York.

Finally the dancing floor is cleared by the police for the chief event of the evening. It is the big "kick" for which most of the spectators have come—the "parade of the fairies," with a prize of two hundred dollars to be awarded to the "fairy" who displays the loveliest and most artistic costume.

A long elevated platform is erected in the center of the hall. Everyone who has not already secured a point of vantage surges to the narrow aisle between the solid banks of human flesh—an aisle kept open by the muscular minions of the law themselves.

The "fairies" now come forward in Indian file. They mount the platform and walk slowly across to the other side—as "bathing beauties" and "style manikins" walk in the news reels.

The "pansies" halt every few steps in their slow course, to strike a pose, twirl a fan, kick a train, or perform some other incredibly feminine action.

☐ E S S A Y S

In his essay, "The Invention of Heterosexuality," Jonathan Ned Katz, independent historian and archivist of the gay past, argues that heterosexuality needs to be understood not as a timeless and natural phenomenon, but rather as a historical development that emerged in conjunction with the modern conception of homosexuality. He highlights the important role of science and popular culture in creating and reinforcing the heterosexual/homosexual binary. In contrast, George Chauncey, Jr., focuses on the way gay men asserted their sexual identities in an urban commercial culture and claimed public space despite municipal efforts to police "deviant" behavior. Chauncey, a University of Chicago historian and author of the pioneering study *Gay New York,* shows how gay men made Times Square their own, creating a flourishing "gay world" within America's premier entertainment district. Taken together, these two essays suggest that the popular culture of the 1920s and 1930s articulated heterosexual norms and gay identities not as simple binaries but in complex and overlapping ways that were also differentiated by gender, class, and other social distinctions.

The Invention of Heterosexuality

JONATHAN NED KATZ

Heterosexuality is old as procreation, ancient as the lust of Eve and Adam. That first lady and gentleman, we assume, perceived themselves, behaved, and felt just like today's heterosexuals. We suppose that heterosexuality is unchanging, universal, essential: ahistorical.

Jonathan Ned Katz, "The Invention of Heterosexuality," *Socialist Review* 20 (January–March 1990): 6–20, 28–30. "The Invention of Heterosexuality" is condensed from the original, published in *Socialist Review.* Copyright © 1990 by Jonathan Ned Katz. Reprinted by permission of the author.

Contrary to that common sense conjecture, the concept of heterosexuality is only one particular historical way of perceiving, categorizing, and imagining the social relations of the sexes. Not ancient at all, the idea of heterosexuality is a modern invention, dating to the late nineteenth century. The heterosexual belief, with its metaphysical claim to eternity, has a particular, pivotal place in the social universe of the late nineteenth and twentieth centuries that it did not inhabit earlier. This essay traces the historical process by which the heterosexual idea was created as ahistorical and taken-for-granted.

. . . [T]his essay focuses on the history of heterosexuality (and a complementary homosexuality) as words and ideas—as ideology recorded in a variety of sources, medical journals and books, works on sexual theory, sexual and gender advice literature, sexual surveys, dictionaries, a play, a movie, a Broadway show song, fiction, and *The New York Times*. . . . [It] argues that the rise of the hetero notion is associated with the development of a historically-specific heterosexual identity, role, psychology, behavior, and institution. Since heterosexuality didn't exist, it had to be invented.

Considering the popularity of the heterosexual idea, one imagines that tracing the notion's history would have tempted many eager scholar-beavers. The importance of analyzing the dominant term of the dominant sexual ideology seems obvious. But heterosexuality has been the idea whose time has not come. The role of the universal heterosexual hypothesis as prop to the dominant mode of sexual organization has determined its not-so-benign scholarly neglect.

By not studying the heterosexual idea in history, analysts of sex, gay and straight, have continued to privilege the "normal" and "natural" at the expense of the "abnormal" and "unnatural." Such privileging of the norm accedes to its domination, protecting it from questions. By making the normal the object of a thoroughgoing historical study we simultaneously pursue a pure truth and a sex-radical and subversive goal: we upset basic preconceptions. We discover that the heterosexual, the normal, and the natural have a history of changing definitions. Studying the history of the term challenges its power.

Contrary to our usual assumption, past Americans and other peoples named, perceived, and socially organized the bodies, lusts, and intercourse of the sexes in ways radically different from the way we do. If we care to understand this vast past sexual diversity, we need to stop promiscuously projecting our own hetero and homo arrangement. Though lip-service is often paid to the distorting, ethnocentric effect of such conceptual imperialism, the category heterosexuality continues to be applied uncritically as a universal analytical tool. Recognizing the time-bound and culturally-specific character of the heterosexual category can help us begin to work toward a thoroughly historical view of sex. . . .

Though this article contests the universality of a heterosexual identity, experience, and behavior, the legitimacy of that identification, emotion, and activity are certainly not in question. The social construction of heterosexuality and homosexuality implies nothing at all about their reality, profundity, and importance. The value of any eros is independent of its origin.

This is an exploratory first pass at an historically-specific heterosexual history— a call for a complete rethinking and total historicization of heterosexuality, and for new research based on that radical reviewing. So, come with me on a journey into the sexual past to observe and ponder the invention of heterosexuality.

In the early nineteenth-century United States, from about 1820 to 1860, the hetero-sexual did not exist. Middle-class white Americans idealized a True Womanhood, True Manhood, and True Love, all characterized by "purity"—the freedom from sensuality. Presented mainly in literary and religious texts, this True Love was a fine romance with no lascivious kisses. This ideal contrasts strikingly with late-nineteenth and twentieth century American incitements to a hetero sex.

Early Victorian True Love was only realized within the mode of proper procrea-tion, marriage, the legal organization for producing a new set of correctly gendered women and men. Proper womanhood, manhood, and progeny—not a normal male-female eros—was the main product of this mode of engendering and of human reproduction.

The actors in this sexual economy were identified as manly men and womanly women and as procreators, not specifically as erotic beings or heterosexuals. Eros did not constitute the core of a heterosexual identity that inhered, democratically, in both men and women. True Women were defined by their distance from lust. True Men, though thought to live closer to carnality, and in less control of it, aspired to the same freedom from concupiscence.

Legitimate natural desire was for procreation and a proper manhood or woman-hood; no heteroerotic desire was thought to be directed exclusively and naturally toward the other sex; lust in men was roving. The human body was thought of as a means towards procreation and production; penis and vagina were instruments of reproduction, not of pleasure. Human energy, thought of as a closed and severely limited system, was to be used in producing children and in work, not wasted in libidinous pleasures. . . .

Heterosexuality and "homosexuality" did not appear out of the blue in the 1890s. These two eroticisms were in the making from the 1860s on. In late Victorian America and in Germany, from about 1860 to 1892, our modern idea of an eroti-cized universe began to develop, and the experience of a heterolust began to be widely documented and named. . . .

. . . [I]n Germany, in a letter of May 6, 1868 to [Karl Heinrich] Ulrichs, [an] early sodomy-law reformer, Karl Maria Kertbeny, is first known to have *privately* used two new terms coined by him: "heterosexuality" and "homosexuality"—the debut of the modern lingo! Kertbeny's "Heterosexualität" referred to a strong lust drive toward "opposite sex" intercourse (associated with numbers of morally reprehen-sible acts). It had the same sense as another of his new terms, "Normalsexualität." Kertbeny's term homosexual was first used *publicly* in an 1869 appeal for sodomy-law reform. His term heterosexual was first used publicly in Germany, in 1880, in a defense of homosexuality published as the work of "Dr. M". Kertbeny's coinage of the term heterosexual in the service of homosexual emancipation is—considering the term's later use—one of sex history's grand ironies.

Heterosexual next made its public appearance in 1889, in the fourth German edition of Dr. Richard Krafft-Ebing's *Psychopathia Sexualis,* where it was distin-guished from homosexual. The homosexual emancipationist's word homosexual was appropriated by Krafft-Ebing and other late Victorian German medical men (and later, by American doctors) as these Dr. Frankensteins' way of naming, condemning, and asserting their own right to regulate a group of homoerotic creatures just then emerging into sight in the bars, dance halls, and streets of their countries' larger cities.

But naming and specifying the sex deviant simultaneously delimited a sex norm—the new heterosexuality. The medical moralists' interest in a few powerless perverts would help to ensure the conformity of the majority to a new sex ethic, one that was congruent with the pursuit of consumer happiness and capitalist profit.

In the late nineteenth-century United States, several social factors converged to cause the eroticizing of consciousness, behavior, emotion, and identity that became typical of the twentieth-century Western middle class. The transformation of the family from producer to consumer unit resulted in a change in family members' relation to their own bodies; from being an instrument primarily of work, the human body was integrated into a new economy, and began more commonly to be perceived as a means of consumption and pleasure. . . .

The growth of a consumer economy also fostered a new pleasure ethic. This imperative challenged the early Victorian work ethic, finally helping to usher in a major transformation of values. While the early Victorian work ethic had touted the value of economic production, that era's procreation ethic had extolled the virtues of human reproduction. In contrast, the late Victorian economic ethic hawked the pleasures of consuming, while its sex ethic praised an erotic pleasure principle for men and even for women.

In the late nineteenth century, the erotic became the raw material for a new consumer culture. Newspapers, books, plays, and films touching on sex, "normal" and "abnormal," became available for a price. Restaurants, bars, and baths opened, catering to sexual consumers with cash. Late Victorian entrepreneurs of desire incited the proliferation of a new eroticism, a commoditized culture of pleasure.

In these same years, the rise in power and prestige of medical doctors allowed these upwardly mobile professionals to prescribe a healthy new sexuality. Medical men, in the name of science, defined a new ideal of male-female relationships that included, in women as well as men, an essential, necessary, normal eroticism. . . .

. . . The earliest-known American use of the word "heterosexual" occurs in a medical journal article by Dr. James G. Kiernan of Chicago, read before the city's medical society on March 7, 1892 and published that May[, one of the] portentous dates in sexual history. But Dr. Kiernan's heterosexuals were definitely not exemplars of normality. Heterosexuals, said Kiernan, were defined by a mental condition, "psychical hermaphroditism." Its symptoms were "inclinations to both sexes." These heterodox sexuals also betrayed inclinations "to abnormal methods of gratification," that is, techniques to insure pleasure without procreation. Dr. Kiernan's heterogeneous sexuals did demonstrate "traces of the normal sexual appetite" (a touch of procreative desire). Kiernan's normal sexuals were implicitly defined by a monolithic other-sex inclination and procreative aim. Significantly, they still lacked a name.

Dr. Kiernan's article of 1892 also included one of the earliest known uses of the word homosexual in American English. Kiernan defined "Pure homosexuals" as persons whose "general mental state is that of the opposite sex." Kiernan thus defined homosexuals by their deviance from a gender norm. His heterosexuals displayed a double deviance from both gender and procreative norms.

Though Kiernan used the new words heterosexual and homosexual, an old procreative standard and a new gender norm coexisted uneasily in his thought. His word heterosexual defined a mixed person and compound urge, abnormal because they wantonly included procreative and non-procreative objectives, as well as same-sex and different-sex attractions.

That same year, 1892, Dr. Krafft-Ebing's influential *Psychopathia Sexualis* was first translated and published in the United States. But Kiernan and Krafft-Ebing by no means agreed on the definition of the heterosexual. In Krafft-Ebing's book, "hetero-sexual" was used unambiguously in the modern sense to refer to an erotic feeling for a different sex. "Homo-sexual" refered unambiguously to an erotic feeling for a "same sex." In Krafft-Ebing's volume, unlike Kiernan's article, hetero-sexual and homosexual were clearly distinguished from a third category, a "psycho-sexual hermaphroditism," defined by impulses toward both sexes.

Krafft-Ebing hypothesized an inborn "sexual instinct" for relations with the "opposite sex," the inherent "purpose" of which was to foster procreation. Krafft-Ebing's erotic drive was still a reproductive instinct. But the doctor's clear focus on a different-sex versus same-sex sexuality constituted a historic, epochal move from an absolute procreative standard of normality toward a new norm. His definition of heterosexuality as other-sex attraction provided the basis for a revolutionary, modern break with a centuries-old procreative standard.

It is difficult to overstress the importance of that new way of categorizing. The German's mode of labeling was radical in referring to the biological sex, masculinity or femininity, and the pleasure of actors (along with the procreant purpose of acts). Krafft-Ebing's heterosexual offered the modern world a new norm that came to dominate our idea of the sexual universe, helping to change it from a mode of human reproduction and engendering to a mode of pleasure. . . .

Despite the clarity of Krafft-Ebing's heterosexual/homosexual distinction, Dr. Kiernan was not the only American medical writer to have difficulty understanding the hetero/homo pair as a normal/pervert duo. Perceived as ambivalent procreator, the heterosexual did not at first exemplify the quintessence of the normal. . . . The hetero, as person of mixed, procreative and nonprocreative, disposition, still stood with the nonprocreative homo as abnormal characters in the late nineteenth-century pantheon of sexual perverts.

. . . As late as 1901, *Dorland's Medical Dictionary,* published in Philadelphia, still defined "Heterosexuality" as "Abnormal or perverted appetite toward the opposite sex."

Only gradually did doctors agree that heterosexual referred to a normal, "other sex" eros. This new standard-model heterosex provided the pivotal term for the modern regularization of eros that paralleled similar attempts to standardize masculinity and femininity, intelligence, and manufacturing. The idea of heterosexuality as the master sex from which all others deviated was (like the idea of the master race) deeply authoritarian. The doctors' normalization of a sex that was hetero proclaimed a new heterosexual separatism—an erotic apartheid that forcefully segregated the sex normals from the sex perverts. The new, strict boundaries made the emerging erotic world less polymorphous—safer for sex normals. However, the idea of such

creatures as heterosexuals and homosexuals emerged from the narrow world of medicine to become a commonly accepted notion only in the early twentieth century. In
1901, in the comprehensive *Oxford English Dictionary,* "heterosexual" and "homosexual" had not yet made it.

. . . Starting among pleasure-affirming urban working-class youths, southern blacks,
and Greenwich-Village bohemians as defensive subculture, heterosex soon triumphed
as dominant culture.

In its earliest version, the twentieth-century heterosexual imperative usually
continued to associate heterosexuality with a supposed human "need," "drive," or
"instinct" for propagation, a procreant urge linked inexorably with carnal lust as it
had not been earlier. In the early twentieth century, the falling birth rate, rising
divorce rate, and "war of the sexes" of the middle class were matters of increasing
public concern. Giving vent to heteroerotic emotions was thus praised as enhanc-
ing baby-making capacity, marital intimacy, and family stability. (Only many years
later, in the mid-1960s, would heteroeroticism be distinguished completely, in
practice and theory, from procreativity and male-female pleasure sex justified in its
own name.)

The first part of the new sex norm—hetero—referred to a basic gender divergence. The "oppositeness" of the sexes was alleged to be the basis for a universal,
normal, erotic attraction between males and females. The stress on the sexes'
"oppositeness," which harked back to the early nineteenth century, by no means
simply registered biological differences of females and males. The early twentieth-
century focus on physiological and gender dimorphism reflected the deep anxieties
of men about the shifting work, social roles, and power of men over women, and
about the ideals of womanhood and manhood. That gender anxiety is documented,
for example, in 1897, in *The New York Times'* publication of the Reverend Charles
Parkhurst's diatribe against female "andromaniacs," the preacher's derogatory,
scientific-sounding name for women who tried to "minimize distinctions by which
manhood and womanhood are differentiated." The stress on gender difference was
a conservative response to the changing social-sexual division of activity and feeling which gave rise to the independent "New Woman" of the 1880s and eroticized
"Flapper" of the 1920s.

The second part of the new hetero norm referred positively to sexuality. That
novel upbeat focus on the hedonistic possibilities of male-female conjunctions also
reflected a social transformation—a revaluing of pleasure and procreation, consumption and work in commercial, capitalist society. The democratic attribution of
a normal lust to human females (as well as males) served to authorize women's
enjoyment of their own bodies and began to undermine the early Victorian idea of
the pure True Woman—a sex-affirmative action still part of women's struggle. The
twentieth-century Erotic Woman also undercut nineteenth-century feminist assertion of women's moral superiority, cast suspicions of lust on women's passionate
romantic friendships with women, and asserted the presence of a menacing female
monster, "the lesbian."

A major medical manufacturer of the heterosexual mystique was Dr. Havelock
Ellis, whose multi-volume *Studies in the Psychology of Sex* began to be published
in Philadelphia in 1901. The other early, major hetero-mystique maker was Dr.

Sigmund Freud, whose *Three Contributions to the [Theory of Sex]* was first published in New York in 1910.

In this work, Freud presented heterosex as a familial imposition upon an originally roving eros. Freud's 1910 version of the normal developmental process involved fantasies of incest and parent and sibling murder—high melodrama, to say
the least. Despite its deeply troubled origins, heterosexuality was finally defined
by Freud's arbitrary, authoritarian assertion as "maturity." Homosex was similarly
defined as the "fixated," "immature" resolution of the same family sex play. In the
name of Freud and popular psychology, heterosexuality would be proclaimed
throughout the land as, simply, perfection.

In conscious opposition to Freud, Ellis claimed that heterosexuality and homosexuality were inborn; he nervously rejected the idea that the species might depend
for its continued reproduction on such an open-ended intrafamily war and fallible
developmental process as that proposed by Freud. Despite their argument over the
physiological versus family origins of heterosex, both doctors were major publicists
of the different-sex erotic among a "progressive" public.

From about 1900 on through the 1920s, a mixed bag of novelists, playwrights,
sex educators, and profit-seeking publishers and play producers struggled to establish the legal right to discuss and distribute a new commodity, the explicit (for its
time) heterosexual drama, novel, and advice book. The writers included James
Branch Cabell, Theodore Dreiser, F. Scott Fitzgerald, Elinor Glyn, James Joyce,
D. H. Lawrence, and sex educators like Mary Ware Dennett.

In the perspective of heterosexual history, this early twentieth century struggle
for the more explicit depiction of an "opposite-sex" eros appears in a curious new
light. Ironically, we find sex-conservatives, the social-purity advocates of censorship and repression, fighting against the depiction not just of sexual perversity but
also of the new normal heterosexuality. . . .

Before 1930 in the United States, heterosexuality was still fighting an uphill
battle. As late as 1929, a federal court in Brooklyn found Mary Ware Dennett, author of a 21-page sex education pamphlet for young people, guilty of mailing this
obscene essay. Dennett's pamphlet criticized other sex-education materials for not
including a "frank, unashamed declaration that the climax of sex emotion is an un-
surpassed joy, something which rightly belongs to every normal human being"
after they fell in love and married. If it seemed "distasteful" that the sex organs
were "so near . . . our 'sewerage system,'" Dennett assured America's youth that
this offensive positioning of parts was probably protective ("At any rate, there they
are, and our duty is . . . to take mighty good care of them."). The word heterosexual
did not appear.

In 1930, in *The New York Times,* heterosexuality first became a love that dared
to speak its name. On April 30th of that year, the word "heterosexual" is first known
to have appeared in *The New York Times Book Review.* There, a critic described the
subject of André Gide's *The Immoralist* proceeding "from a heterosexual liaison
to a homosexual one." The ability to slip between sexual categories was referred to
casually as a rather unremarkable aspect of human possibility. This is also the first
known reference by *The Times* to the new hetero/homo duo.

The following month the second reference to the hetero/homo dyad appeared in
The New York Times Book Review, in a comment on Floyd Dell's *Love in the Machine*

Age. This work revealed a prominent antipuritan of the 1930s using the dire threat of homosexuality as his rationale for greater heterosexual freedom. *The Times* quoted Dell's warning that current abnormal social conditions kept the young dependent on their parents, causing "infantilism, prostitution and homosexuality." Also quoted was Dell's attack on the "inculcation of purity" that "breeds distrust of the opposite sex." Young people, Dell said, should be "permitted to develop normally to heterosexual adulthood." "But," *The Times* reviewer emphasized, "such a state already exists, here and now." And so it did. Heterosexuality, a new gender-sex category, had been distributed from the narrow, rarified realm of a few doctors to become a nationally, even internationally cited aspect of middle-class life.

In 1933, in an English novel published in the United States, the colloquial abbreviation "hetero" is first known to have made its published appearance. In Eileen A. Robertson's *Ordinary Families* a character declared: "The odd thing about me is that . . . I should be so purely 'hetero' in spite of lack of opportunity." Quote marks around that 'hetero' suggest the newness of the colloquialism. But the slang usage suggests that people were now on quite familiar terms with the hetero on both sides of the Atlantic.

By December 1940, when the risque musical *Pal Joey* opened on Broadway, a song titled "Zip" satirized the striptease artist Gypsy Rose Lee, who was quoted: "I don't like a deep contralto, Or a man whose voice is alto, Zip, I'm a heterosexual." That lyric registered the historically new, self-conscious, public proclamation of a heterosexual identity. . . .

Our brief survey of the heterosexual idea suggests a new hypothesis. Rather than naming a conjunction old as Eve and Adam, heterosexual designates a word and concept, a norm and role, an individual and group identity, a behavior and feeling, and a peculiar sexual-political institution particular to the late nineteenth and twentieth centuries.

Because much stress has been placed here on heterosexuality as word and concept, it seems important to affirm that heterosexuality (and homosexuality) came into existence before it was named and thought about. The formulation of the heterosexual idea did not create a heterosexual experience or behavior; to suggest otherwise would be to ascribe determining power to labels and concepts. But the titling and envisioning of heterosexuality did play an important role in consolidating the construction of the heterosexual's social existence. Before the wide use of the word heterosexual, I suggest, women and men did not mutually lust with the same profound, sure sense of normalcy that followed the distribution of "heterosexual" as universal sanctifier.

According to this proposal, women and men make their own sexual histories. But they do not produce their sex lives just as they please. They make their sexualities within a particular mode of organization given by the past and altered by their changing desire, their present power and activity, and their vision of a better world. . . .

. . . Heterosexual history can help us see the place of values and judgments in the construction of our own and others' pleasures, and to see how our erotic tastes— our aesthetics of the flesh—are socially institutionalized through the struggle of individuals and classes.

The study of heterosexuality in time will also help us to recognize the *vast historical diversity of sexual emotions and behaviors*—a variety that challenges the monolithic heterosexual hypothesis. . . . Only when we stop assuming an invariable essence of heterosexuality will we begin the research to reveal the full variety of sexual emotions and behaviors.

. . . To understand the subtle history of heterosexuality we need to look carefully at correlations between (1) society's organization of eros and pleasure; (2) its mode of engendering persons as feminine or masculine (its making of women and men); (3) its ordering of human reproduction; and (4) its dominant political economy. . . .

A historical view locates heterosexuality and homosexuality in time, helping us distance ourselves from them. This distancing can help us formulate new questions that clarify our long-range sexual-political goals: what has been and is the social function of sexual categorizing? Whose interests have been served by the division of the world into heterosexual and homosexual? Do we dare not draw a line between those two erotic species? Is some sexual naming socially necessary? Would human freedom be enhanced if the sex-biology of our partners in lust was of no particular concern, and had no name? In what kind of society could we all more freely explore our desire and our flesh?

Gay Men's Strategies of Everyday Resistance

GEORGE CHAUNCEY, JR.

"Forty-second Street was *it,* when I was a teenager," recalled Sebastian ("Sy") Risicato, referring to the days in the late 1930s when he still lived with his parents in the Bronx but was beginning to explore New York's gay world. "Forty-second Street then was our stamping ground," he continued:

> Closet queens, gay queens, black, white, whatever, carrying on in men's rooms, and in theaters. There was a Bickford's [cafeteria] there all night, and a big cafeteria right there on 42nd Street, one of those bright cafeterias where johns used to sit looking for the young queens. Lots of queens, everybody was painted and all, but they weren't crazy queens: drugs weren't big then. Forty-second Street was like heaven—not heaven, [but] it was a joy to go there! And the sailors at the Port Authority, and the soldiers, and the bars. . . . During the war all the soldiers and sailors used to go to the "crossroads" and you'd pick them up—Forty-second Street and Times Square—and you'd take them out to the furnished rooms in the neighborhood: furnished rooms, and dumpy little hotels and Eighth Avenue rooms, which you'd rent for the night. There were a lot of gays living in that area, [too,] oh yes, people from out of town, and the boys whose fathers had pushed them out, with the tweezed eyebrows and beards. . . . You'd go down to Forty-second Street and feel like, *here's where I belong.*

Forty-second Street was almost heaven in the 1930s for the self-described "painted queens" and "street fairies" like Sy Risicato who were forced to escape the hostility of their own neighborhoods and families in order to forge a community

---

George Chauncey, Jr., "Gay Men's Strategies of Everyday Resistance," in William R. Taylor, ed., *Inventing Times Square* (New York: Russell Sage, 1991), 315–328, 417–420. © 1991 Russell Sage Foundation, New York, New York. Reprinted by permission.

of their own. The world they built in the furnished rooms, cafeterias, theaters, and streets of Times Square offered them enormous support and guidance in their rejection of the particular forms of masculinity and heterosexuality prescribed by the dominant culture. By the 1930s they had made Times Square one of the most important centers of gay life—particularly white, working-class gay male life—in the city. But the heaven such men created seemed hellish to many of the other people who knew the Square. Risicato's coterie was a notable part of the "undesirable" element regularly implicated in the "decline" of the theater district by more respectable New Yorkers, who mobilized a variety of policing agencies and strategies to eradicate their presence from the Square. They also appalled many other gay men who frequented the theater district, particularly middle-class men more conventional in their behavior, who regarded the "fairies" as undesirable representatives of the homosexual world. These men constructed their own, more carefully hidden gay world in the theater district; but they, too, had to contend with the agencies of moral policing.

Ironically, the world gay men created in the 1920s and 1930s has remained even more invisible to historians than it was to contemporaries; most historians who have bothered to consider the matter have assumed that gay men remained isolated from each other and helplessly subject to the self-hatred preached by the dominant culture. This [essay] proposes an alternative view of gay life in these years. It examines the manner in which gay men, like other criminalized and marginalized peoples, constructed spheres of relative cultural autonomy in the interstices of an amusement district governed by hostile powers. It analyzes the stratagems different groups of gay men developed to appropriate certain commercial institutions and public spaces as their own and their complex relationship to the district's commercial entrepreneurs and moral guardians. A battery of laws criminalized gay men's association with each other and their cultural styles as well as their narrowly "sexual" behavior. Their social marginalization gave the police even broader informal authority to harass them and threatened anyone discovered to be homosexual with loss of livelihood and social respect. But the culture of the theater district, the weakness of the policers themselves, and the informal bargains struck between the policers and the policed—often with the mediation of certain commercial entrepreneurs, including those of the criminal underworld—enabled gay men to claim much more space for themselves than those obstacles implied.

Thus, while this [essay] surveys the ways in which the agents of the dominant cultural order sought to police the presence of gay men in the Square, it focuses on the informal strategies gay men developed to resist that policing on an everyday basis in the decades before the emergence of a gay political movement. Analyzing the emergence of a gay world in Times Square illuminates the character of urban gay male culture in the interwar years more generally, since gay men visiting the district were forced to draw on the same panoply of survival strategies they had developed in other settings as well. . . .

. . . Times Square was not so much the site of "anonymous," furtive encounters between strangers (although there were plenty of those) as the site of an organized, multilayered, and self-conscious subculture, or, to use gay men's own term, a "gay world," with its own meeting places, argot, folklore, and norms of behavior. Rather than focusing on the supposed "anonymity" of Times Square, then, it will prove more productive to analyze the ways in which people manipulated the spatial and cultural complexity of the city to constitute the Square as their *neighborhood,* where some of them worked or lived, and many others joined them to build a community.

Indeed, a gay enclave developed in Times Square in part because so many gay men lived and worked in the area. The theater and the district's other amusement industries attracted large numbers of gay workers, who got jobs as waiters and performers in restaurants and clubs, as busboys in hotels, and as chorus boys, actors, stagehands, costume designers, publicity people, and the like in the theater industry proper. Although gay men hardly enjoyed unalloyed acceptance in such work environments, the theatrical milieu offered them more tolerance than most workplaces. As one man who had been a theatrical writer in the mid-teens observed, "the New York theatrical world [of that era was] . . . a sort of special world . . . with its own standards of fellowship [and] sexual morals." Homosexuality, along with other unconventional sexual behavior, was judged by unusually tolerant standards by people who were themselves often marginalized because of the unconventional lives they led as theater workers. Some men could be openly gay among their coworkers, while many others were at least unlikely to suffer serious retribution if their homosexuality were discovered. The eccentricity attributed to theater people and "artistic types" in general provided a cover to many men who adopted widely recognized gay styles in their dress and demeanor.

Moreover, many men working in the amusement district lived there as well, and they were joined by other gay men who appreciated the advantages of the transient housing the district offered. Times Square and, to the west of Eighth Avenue, Hell's Kitchen together comprised one of the major centers of housing for single adults in the city. In many respects the area constituted a prototypical furnished room district, the sort of neighborhood dominated by a nonfamily population in which . . . unconventional sexual behavior was likely to face relatively little community opposition. The district was crowded with rooming houses, theatrical boardinghouses, and small residential and transient hotels serving theater workers, as well as most of the city's elegant bachelor apartments. The housing varied in quality and social status, but most of it shared certain qualities useful to gay men as well as to transient theater workers. Most of the rooms were cheap, they were minimally supervised, and the fact that they were usually furnished and hired by the week made them easy to leave if an occupant got a job on the road—or needed to "disappear" because of legal troubles.

Middle-class men tended to live to the north and east of the Square in the West Forties and Fifties, where many of the city's fashionable apartment hotels designed for affluent bachelors were clustered, and where many of the elegant old row houses between Fifth and Sixth avenues had been converted into rooming houses as the intrusion of commerce resulted in the departure of their original residents. Another, poorer group of men lived to the west of the Square in the tenements of Hell's Kitchen and the large number of cheap hotels and rooming houses to be found west of Seventh Avenue and Broadway. . . . Groups of theater and restaurant workers were joined by gay teenagers forced out of their natal homes by hostile parents (as Risicato recalled), gay migrants from small towns and the outer boroughs, hustlers, gay bartenders, and men who had more conventional jobs elsewhere in the city but who valued the privacy, convenience, and tolerance such housing offered. The district also included numerous transient hotels and rooming houses where male (or heterosexual) couples who met in a bar or on the street could rent a room for an hour.

The men who lived and worked in the district formed the core of a social world—or several social worlds, really—in which men who both lived and worked elsewhere could participate. Times Square served as the primary social center for many such nonresidents, the place where they met their friends, built their strongest social ties, "let their hair down" (once a camp expression for being openly gay), and constructed public identities quite different from those they maintained at work and elsewhere in the straight world. They built a gay world for themselves on the basis of the ties they developed in the commercial institutions which entrepreneurs had developed to serve the needs of the theater workers rooming in the district and the tourists who flocked there.

Gay men mixed unobtrusively with other customers at most of the district's restaurants, but a few places attracted a predominantly gay patronage and developed a muted gay ambiance. Louis' Restaurant on West Forty-ninth Street, for instance, became well known to gay men and lesbians as a rendezvous for several years in the early 1920s, and even came to the attention of private anti-vice investigators in 1925 as a "hangout for fairies and lady lovers [lesbians]." But the people who met there were sufficiently guarded in their behavior—at least in the main public dining rooms—that outsiders were unlikely to suspect they were gay. A sedate 1925 restaurant guide even recommended Louis' to its readers, describing it, clearly without apprehending the full significance of its observation, as "one of the institutions of the neighborhood."

Such restaurants had existed before the 1920s, but, ironically, they proliferated and became more secure during Prohibition. Prohibition had been enacted in part to control public sociability—and in particular to destroy the immigrant, working-class male culture of the saloon, which seemed so threatening to middle-class and rural Americans. But in cities such as New York, Prohibition had resulted instead in the expansion of the sexual underworld and had undermined the ability of the police and anti-vice societies to control it. . . . [T]he popular opposition to enforcement, the proliferation of speakeasies, and the systematic use of payoffs and development of criminal syndicates to protect those speakeasies all served to protect gay clubs as well as straight. It became easier during Prohibition for establishments where gay men gathered, such as Louis', to survive, because they stood out less. All speakeasies—not just gay speakeasies—had to bribe the authorities and warn their customers to be prepared to hide what they were doing at a moment's notice.

Prohibition also changed the character of the Square in ways which led to the increased visibility of a group of gay men different from those who patronized Louis'. It drove many of the district's elegant restaurants, cabarets, and roof gardens out of business, and they were replaced by cheap cafeterias and restaurants whose profits depended on a high turnover rate rather than on a high liquor-based profit margin. Moreover, by the end of the twenties the decline of the district's theater industry, due to the collapse of the national theatrical road circuits as well as the rise of the movies, forced growing numbers of theaters to convert into movie houses, often of the cheaper sort. Both factors combined to transform the Square in the 1920s and early 1930s, in the eyes of many contemporaries, from a distinguished theater district to a "tawdry" amusement district, a development only hastened by the onset of the Depression.

It was in this context that the flamboyant gay men known as fairies began to play a more prominent role in the culture and reputation of the Square. . . .

The Square already had something of a reputation for fairies in the early 1920s (one 1924 account bemoaned the number of "impudent sissies that clutter Times Square"). But as the Square became more of a "tawdry" amusement park, visiting it became more of a theatrical experience in itself, and "fairies" increasingly became part of the spectacle of the Square, part of the exotica clubgoers and tourists expected and even hoped to see there. Thus, when *Vanity Fair's* "intimate guide to New York after dark" noted in 1931 that the tourist could see "anything" on Broadway at night, it included "pansies" among the sights along with the more predictable "song writers, college boys, . . . big shots, [and] bootleggers." A New York tabloid added that "The latest gag about 2 A.M. is to have your picture taken with one or two pansies on Times Square. The queens hang out there for the novel racket."

If the highly flamboyant, working-class street fairies who gathered at Bryant Park represented one extreme of gay self-presentation, the highly circumspect middle-class men and women who met at restaurants like Louis' represented another. But the self-described fairies—not the "normal"-looking men at Louis'—constituted the dominant public image of the male homosexual during this period; as a character representing the author in a 1933 gay novel complained, "*we're all*," to the "normal man, . . . like the street corner 'fairy' of Times Square—rouged, lisping, mincing." This distressed many of the more conventional men, who felt the fairy drew unwanted and unflattering attention to the gay world. Ironically, though, it was the very brilliance of the fairies that diverted attention from those other, more guarded men, and thus helped to keep them safely in the shadows. The presence of the fairies facilitated the process by which such middle-class men constructed their own, more carefully hidden, gay world in the theater district.

Different groups of men, then, adopted different strategies for negotiating their presence in the city, and the divisions within the gay world of Times Square became even more complex as the district continued to reel from the impact of Prohibition, the declining fortunes of the theater industry, and the onset of the Depression. The effect of these changes is best seen in the changing organization of the district's street culture. . . .

The Square, already an important center of female prostitution, became one of the city's most significant centers of male prostitution in the 1920s. Initially, two distinct groups of male prostitutes, whose interactions with customers were construed in entirely different ways, worked the Times Square area. Well-dressed, "mannered," and gay-identified hustlers serving a middle-class, gay-identified clientele generally met their customers as the latter walked home from the theater. . . . Although a regular part of the Times Square scene, neither the hustlers nor their customers attracted much attention since neither conformed to the era's dominant stereotypes of homosexuals. During the 1920s, though, a second group of prostitutes, much more easily recognized by outsiders, came to dominate Forty-second Street itself between Fifth and Eighth avenues: effeminate (but not transvestite)

"fairy prostitutes" who sold sexual services to other gay men and to men who identified themselves as "normal," including the Italians and Greeks living to the west
of the Square in Hell's Kitchen, as well as tourists from afar. The self-presentation
of the prostitutes operating on the two streets thus differed markedly, as did the
self-conception of their customers, and their proximity highlights the degree to
which Times Square was the site of multiple sexual systems, each with its own cultural dynamics, semiotic codes, and territories.

The transformation of Forty-second Street during the late 1920s and early
1930s had enormous repercussions for the street's gay scene, and resulted in a
new group of hustlers coming to dominate it. Forty-second Street was the site of
the oldest theaters in the Times Square district, and the city's elite had regarded it
as a distinguished address early in the century. By 1931, however, it had effectively become a working-class male domain. The conversion of two prominent
theaters into burlesque houses in 1931 had both signified and contributed to the
masculinization of the street: not only the strippers inside but the large quasi-
pornographic billboards and barkers announcing the shows on the streets outside
contributed to the image of the street as a male domain, threatening to women.
The masculinization of the street was confirmed by the conversion of the remaining theaters to a "grind" policy of showing male-oriented action films on a continuous basis and the opening of several men's bars and restaurants that catered to
the increasing numbers of sailors, servicemen, and unemployed and transient men
who frequented the street.

As the gender and class character of Forty-second Street changed, it became a
major locus of a new kind of "rough" hustler and of interactions between straight-
identified servicemen and homosexuals. As the Depression deepened, growing
numbers of young men—many of them migrants from the economically devastated
cities of Pennsylvania, Massachusetts, New York, and the industrial South, and ome
of them servicemen—began to support themselves or supplement their income by
hustling. Not gay-identified themselves, many became prostitutes for the same reason some women did: the work was available and supplied a needed income. "In the
Depression the Square swarmed with boys," recalled one man who began patronizing their services in 1933. "Poverty put them there." The hustlers, aggressively masculine in their self-presentation and usually called "rough trade" by gay men, took
over Forty-second Street between Seventh and Eighth avenues, forcing the "fairy"
prostitutes to move east of Sixth Avenue, to Bryant Park. . . .

The precise locus of the hustlers' and other gay men's activity on Forty-second
Street shifted several times over the course of the 1930s. . . . The hustler street scene
followed the bars from Sixth to Eighth Avenue and from the north to the south side
of Forty-second Street in part because the bars attracted customers and offered
shelter from the elements, but also because the streets and bars functioned as ex-
tensions of each other. Each site had particular advantages and posed particular
dangers in men's constant territorial struggles with policing agents, as the men
subject to that policing well knew. The purchase of a beer at a bar legitimized behavior involved in cruising which might have appeared more suspicious on the
streets, including a man's simply standing about aimlessly or striking up conversations with strangers. But while the police periodically tried to "clean up" the streets

by chasing hustlers and other undesirable loiterers away, they could not permanently close the streets in the way they could close a bar. Moreover, in a heavily trafficked, nonresidential area such as Forty-second Street, no one had the same interest in controlling pedestrians' behavior on behalf of the police that a bar owner who was threatened with the loss of his license had in controlling his customers. Thus, while the police might harass men on the street simply for standing about with no apparent purpose, bars might evict them simply for touching, and plainclothesmen might arrest them for homosexual solicitation in either locale. . . .

The numerous cheap cafeterias, Automats, and lunchrooms that crowded the Times Square district were perhaps the safest commercial spaces available to poorer gay men. The Automats seem to have become even more secure with the onset of the Depression, when they developed a reputation, due to their cheap prices and lack of supervision, for being a refuge for the unemployed and luckless. . . .

Automats were particularly famous for their lack of inhibition, but even the large cafeterias in the Childs chain could become astonishingly open. This was particularly true late in the evening, after the dinner hour, when managers tolerated a wide range of customers and behavior in order to generate trade. Indeed, several cafeterias seem to have premised their late-night operations on the assumption that by allowing homosexuals to gather on their premises they would be able to attract sightseers out to see a late-night "fairy hangout." Gay men seized on the opportunities this portended and quickly spread the word about which restaurants and cafeterias would let them gather without guarding their behavior; moreover, the campy antics of the more flamboyant among them became part of the draw for other customers. One gay man who lived in the city in the late 1920s recalled that the Childs restaurant in the Paramount Building was regularly "taken over" by "hundreds" of gay men after midnight. Even if his recollection exaggerates the situation, it suggests his sense of the extent to which gay men felt comfortable there; in any case, *Vanity Fair's* 1931 guide to New York informed its readers that the Paramount Childs was particularly interesting because it "features a dash of lavender."

Well-established chains such as Childs usually had sufficient clout to prevent police raids, although raids did occasionally occur when either the police or the private anti-vice societies thought gay patrons had become too uproarious, or the management feared that the authorities were about to reach that conclusion. In February 1927, for instance, after gay men had been congregating at the Forty-second Street Liggett's drugstore for some time, the management, perhaps sensing a temporary hardening of police attitudes or simply fearing for its reputation, suddenly called on the police to drive the men from its premises, which led to a raid and the arrest of enough men to fill two police vans.

After the repeal of Prohibition in 1933 gay bars quickly became the most important centers of gay male sociability in the city, but they also became the most sharply contested. The legalization of bars made them more numerous, more accessible, and easier to find—for gay men as well as straight. But it also subjected them to the authority of the newly created State Liquor Authority (SLA), which quickly proved to be a much more effective agent in the enforcement of state regulations than the Prohibition era's Volstead agents had been. From its inception, the SLA threatened to revoke the liquor license of any bar that served homosexuals, whose very presence, it ruled, made a bar "disorderly." In the three decades following Repeal its agents and the police investigated and closed hundreds of bars in New York that served gay men or lesbians, sometimes through administrative action, sometimes through raids that resulted in the arrest of the staff and, in some cases, even the patrons. . . .

During such crackdowns, some straight bars in "suspicious" neighborhoods such as Times Square or the Village sought to protect themselves by posting signs over the bar reading "If You Are Gay, Please Stay Away" or "It is Against the Law to Serve Homosexuals—Do Not Ask Us to Break the Law." At other bars, the bartenders were simply instructed to eject anyone who appeared to be gay, or, if they had not suspected them initially, to refuse to serve them any more drinks once they did.

Gay bars that continued to serve gay patrons during crackdowns sought to protect themselves by hiring floormen who made sure that men did not touch each other or engage in campy, or otherwise "obvious," behavior, which might draw the attention of the authorities by marking the bar's patrons as gay. State policies thus had the effect of turning bar managers into agents of SLA policy enforcement. They also exacerbated the class and cultural cleavages already dividing the gay world: since the presence of "obvious" homosexuals or "fairies" in a bar invited the wrath of the SLA and the police, most bars refused to serve them, and other gay men were encouraged in their hostility toward them.

The number of bars serving homosexuals—and particularly those serving *exclusively* homosexuals—proliferated in the 1930s and 1940s, but most of them were short-lived, and gay men were forced to move constantly from place to place, dependent on the gay grapevine to inform them of where the new meeting places were. When the SLA launched a campaign against bars serving homosexuals as part of its effort to "clean up the city" in the months before the 1939 World's Fair opened, it quickly discovered just how effective that grapevine could be. After closing several bars in the area patronized by homosexuals, including the Consolidated Bar and Grill on West Forty-first Street, the Alvin on West Forty-second, and more distant bars that were part of the same circuit, the Authority's investigators discovered that many of the patrons of those bars had simply converged on the Times Square Bar & Grill on West Forty-second Street and turned it into their new rendezvous. In late October an SLA investigator, sent to the bar after a police report that "about thirty . . . fairys [sic] and fags" had been seen there, noted that several of the gay men he had previously seen at the other bars were "now congregating" there, along with a large number of soldiers. The owner himself, who sought to cooperate with the police in ridding his bar of homosexuals once he realized their presence threatened his liquor license, insisted that "we never looked for . . . this kind of business. . . . [The police] close some places; [the fairies] come over here. . . . It was the neighborhood—[the fairies] know what places . . . are [open to them]. The word passes so fast. They knew [when a bar] is a degenerate place."

Although many men continued to go to gay bars despite the risks, some stopped patronizing them during crackdowns for fear of being caught in a raid, which might result in their being arrested or at least being forced to divulge their names and places of employment, which carried the threat of further penalties if the police contacted their landlords or employers. Nonetheless, they found other places to meet their friends and to continue their participation in gay society. Private parties

were especially important at such times, but so, too, were commercial establishments not known for their gay patronage. Not only were the police less likely to
raid such places, but a man's homosexuality would not necessarily be revealed if
he happened to be seen there by a straight associate. Some men of moderate means
joined the fairies in the restaurants and cafeterias in the area, which, because they
operated without liquor licenses, continued to be relatively safe even after Repeal,
but men of greater wealth and social status had access to more secure venues, whose
very respectability offered them protection against the dangers of being arrested or
recognized as homosexual. Several of the elegant nightclubs that opened to the
north and east of the Square in the late twenties and thirties tolerated or even welcomed such men, so long as they remained discreet.

A somewhat more varied group of men frequented the highly respectable businessmen's bars found in many hotels, such as the Oak Room at the Plaza and the
King Cole Room at the St. Regis, whose respectability and political clout offered
them protection, and where well-dressed men drinking by themselves or with a few
male friends would hardly draw attention.

The longest-lived and most famous such bar in the Times Square area (although
not the most elegant one) was the Astor Hotel bar at the corner of Seventh Avenue
and Forty-fifth Street. Although it had served as a gay meeting place since the
1910s, it became particularly well known during the Second World War, when it
developed a national reputation among gay servicemen as a place to meet civilians
when passing through New York. Gay men's use of the bar was carefully orchestrated—in both its spatial and cultural dimensions—to protect both their identities
and its license. Gay men gathered on only one side of the oval bar, where the management allowed them to congregate so long as they did not become too "obvious."
As one man who frequented the Astor during the war recalled, "the management
would cut us down a little bit when it felt we were getting a little too obvious. . . . If
you got a little too buddy, or too cruisey . . . too aggressive, they'd say cut it out,
men, why don't you go somewhere else? You had to be more subtle." Men on the
other side of the bar, he added, were allowed to "do anything they wanted; they
could put *their* arms around each other, *they* could touch, because it was very obvious that they were butch."

Gay men had to be "subtle" so that the straight men all around them—including
the occasional strangers who unknowingly sat down on the gay side of the bar—
would not realize they were surrounded by "queers." Gay men used the same codes
they had developed in other contexts to alert each other to their identities: wearing
certain clothes fashionable among gay men but not stereotypically associated with
them, introducing certain topics of conversation, or casually using code words well
known within the gay world but unremarkable to those outside it ("gay" itself was
such a word in the 1930s and 1940s). Using such codes, men could carry on extensive and highly informative conversations whose real significance would remain
unintelligible to the people around them.

Two other examples will illustrate gay men's ability to covertly but surely
appropriate public spaces for their own purposes, even in the context of the post-
Prohibition clampdown. For, on a much larger scale than at the Astor, gay men
regularly gathered en masse at the performances of entertainers who . . . assumed

special significance in gay culture. Whether or not the other members of the audience noticed them, *they* were aware of their numbers in the audience and often shared in the collective excitement of transforming such a public gathering into a "gay space," no matter how covertly. Judy Garland's concerts would take on this character in later years; Beatrice Lillie's concerts were among the most famous such events within the gay world in the early 1930s. "The Palace was just packed with queers, for weeks at a time, when Lillie performed," remembered one man who had been in the audience; one of her signature songs, "There Are Fairies at the Bottom of My Garden," was a camp classic in the gay world, and twenty years later Lillie noted that she still "always" got requests for it from her audience.

The Metropolitan Opera, on Broadway at Fortieth Street, was another "standard meeting place," according to the same man, and another man whimsically recalled that "since there were no known instances of police raids on [such distinguished] cultural events, all stops were pulled out as far as costume and grooming. The hairdos and outlandish clothes many gays wore were not to be equaled until the punk rock era." The cultural significance of such events had always been determined as much by the audience as by the stage; but as their role in gay culture suggests, such events were the site of multiple audiences and productive of multiple cultural meanings, many of them obscure to the class that nominally dominated them.

Far from being confined to marginalized locales, then, gay men claimed some of the most conventional of cultural spaces as their own. Such were the politics of public space in much of Times Square. Gay men and straight men often used the same sites in entirely different ways, with the latter not suspecting the presence of the "queers" in their midst, in part because the "queers" did not look or behave like the "fairies" they saw at Bryant Park. Thus the Astor maintained its public reputation as an eminently respectable Times Square rendezvous, while its reputation as a gay rendezvous and pickup bar assumed legendary proportions in the gay world; and on certain nights the Metropolitan Opera became the "biggest bar in town."

Still, gay men's use of the Square was a hard-won and unstable victory, which required them to engage in constant territorial struggles with the agents of the dominant cultural order. Different groups of men adopted different strategies of everyday resistance to the dominant order, different strategies for staking out and defining their worlds, and those differences often brought them into conflict. Nonetheless, even those men who chose to remain most hidden from the dominant culture were not hidden from each other. Gay men became part of the spectacle of Times Square, but they also transformed it into a haven.

FURTHER READING

Beth L. Bailey, *From Front Porch to Back Seat: Courtship in Twentieth-Century America* (1988).

George Chauncey, Jr., *Gay New York* (1994).

George F. Custen, "Too Darn Hot: Hollywood, Popular Media and the Construction of Sexuality in the Life of Cole Porter," *Radical History Review* 59 (1994): 142–171.

Angela Y. Davis, *Blues Legacies and Black Feminism* (1998).

Karen Dubinsky, *The Second Greatest Disappointment: Honeymooning and Tourism at Niagara Falls* (1999).

John D'Emilio, "Capitalism and Gay Identity," in Ann Snitow et al., eds., *The Powers of Desire* (1983), 100–106.

Lewis Erenberg, *Steppin' Out: New York Nightlife and the Transformation of American Culture, 1890–1930* (1981).

Lillian Faderman, *Odd Girls and Twilight Lovers: A History of Lesbian Life in Twentieth-Century America* (1991).

Paula Fass, *The Damned and the Beautiful: American Youth in the 1920s* (1977).

Estelle Freedman, "Uncontrolled Desires: The Response to the Sexual Psychopath, 1920–1960," *Journal of American History* 74 (1987): 83–106.

Eric Garber, "A Spectacle in Color: The Lesbian and Gay Subculture of Jazz Age Harlem," in Martin Duberman et al., eds., *Hidden from History* (1989), 318–331.

Leigh Gilmore, "Obscenity, Modernity, Identity: Legalizing *The Well of Loneliness* and *Nightwood*," *Journal of the History of Sexuality* 4 (1994): 603–624.

Pamela Haag, "In Search of 'The Real Thing': Ideologies of Love, Modern Romance, and Women's Sexual Subjectivity in the United States, 1920–1940," *Journal of the History of Sexuality* 2 (1992): 547–577.

Marybeth Hamilton, *"When I'm Bad, I'm Better": Mae West, Sex, and American Entertainment* (1996).

Sherrie A. Inness, "Who's Afraid of Stephen Gordon? The Lesbian in the United States Popular Imagination of the 1920s," *NWSA Journal* 4 (1992): 303–320.

Margaret D. Jacobs, "Making Savages of Us All: White Women, Pueblo Indians, and the Controversy over Indian Dances in the 1920s," *Frontiers* 17 (1996): 178–209.

Jonathan Ned Katz, *The Invention of Heterosexuality* (1995).

Peter Laipson, "'Kiss Without Shame, for She Desires It': Sexual Foreplay in American Marital Advice Literature, 1900–1925," *Journal of Social History* (1996): 507–525.

Valerie Matsumodo, "Desperately Seeking 'Deirdre': Gender Roles, Multicultural Relations, and Nisei Women Writers of the 1930s," *Frontiers* 12, no. 1 (1991): 19–32.

Elaine Tyler May, *Great Expectations: Marriage and Divorce in Post-Victorian America* (1980).

Lary May, *Screening Out the Past* (1980).

Vicki L. Ruiz, "The Flapper and the Chaperone: Cultural Constructions of Identity and Heterosexual Politics among Adolescent Mexican American Women, 1920–1950," in Sherrie A. Inness, ed., *Delinquents and Debutantes* (1998), 199–226.

Christina Simmons, "Modern Sexuality and the Myth of Victorian Repression," in Kathy Peiss and Christina Simmons, eds., *Passion and Power: Sexuality in History* (1989), 157–177.

Jennifer Terry, *An American Obsession: Science, Medicine, and Homosexuality in Modern Society* (1999).

Kevin White, *The First Sexual Revolution: The Emergence of Male Heterosexuality in Modern America* (1993).

C H A P T E R
11

Open Secrets in
Cold War America

In 1948 and again in 1953, Alfred Kinsey shocked Americans when he reported that they had sex—lots of it, and in many different configurations. With massive quantities of data, the Kinsey reports documented the wide gap between what Americans did and what they said. In the post–World War II years, many Americans—not only married couples but single heterosexuals, gay men, and lesbians—welcomed a wide range of sexual interactions and private erotic gestures.

Public discussion of sexuality was another matter. On the one hand, sex was to take place behind closed doors. On television, where the nuclear family reigned supreme, mom and dad slept in twin beds—an image that still predominates in our view of the 1950s. On the other hand, anxieties about "normal" marital heterosexuality were pervasive. Psychologists, national leaders, and editorialists all warned that sexual "deviance" threatened American families and freedom. The "homosexual menace" extended from comic books to the State Department. The real threat, however, was felt by those who did deviate from sexual norms, such as the many gay men and lesbians expelled from teaching jobs, government employment, and military positions.

How should we make sense of the contradictions between private behavior and public values? Some have characterized the history of sexuality in the 1950s in terms of containment—a domestic version of America's Cold War policy to stop the spread of Soviet Communism. What may be most striking about this time, however, is the sheer volume of information disseminated about homosexuality, transsexualism, masturbation, premarital intercourse, and other forms of "deviancy," all in the name of restraining their influence. Were the efforts to channel erotic life toward marital heterosexual norms successful? How did people respond to reports about homosexuals in government service or Christine Jorgensen's very public "sex-change" operation? We need to look closely at the way government and news media represented sexuality in these reports. We also need to consider the variety of responses. If many kept their desires "closeted," the new visibility of nonmarital sexualities may have had the opposite effect on others. Exposing "deviant" sexual practices placed them within the realm of imagination—and from there, to the realm of action—opening up new possibilities for sexual identities and communities.

▌D O C U M E N T S

Biologist Alfred Kinsey began his career investigating wasps and ended it as the leading sex researcher of the twentieth century. The Kinsey Reports (1948 and 1953), excerpted in Document 1, remain crucial sources for understanding Americans' sexual behavior. Densely packed with statistical information about virtually every sexual practice, they gave Americans a picture of themselves that offended many and delighted others, as women's letters to the editors of *Life* and *Look* indicate in Document 2. Kinsey used the authority of science to attack what he saw as the pieties of the postwar period—its conventional sexual morality and judgments based on concepts of sexual "normality" and "deviance." News coverage of Christine Jorgensen—whose "sex change" operation made headlines in 1952—illustrated these ideas well. Trying to explain transgendered identity to the public, male reporters at first saw Christine as a desirable "glamour girl"; within four months, however, they concluded that in fact she was no woman, only a transvestite and castrated male (Document 3).

The concern with the "truth" of Christine Jorgensen is echoed in the efforts to expose homosexuals as hazards to youth, society, and the state. In 1950, the U.S. Senate issued its report on the employment of homosexuals in the government (Document 4). Nor were superheroes Batman, Robin, and Wonder Woman free from charges of "perverting" the heterosexual development of children, as psychiatrist Fredric Wertham warned in 1953 (Document 5). What impact did these messages have? In her diary, excerpted in Document 6, poet and writer Marge McDonald discussed how the social condemnation of homosexuality affected her entrance into "gay life" in Columbus, Ohio, in 1955. In Document 7, Del Martin addressed the problems of fear, exposure, and concealment as she argued for a lesbian political organization, the Daughters of Bilitis, in 1956.

1. Alfred Kinsey Reports on Americans' Sexual Behavior, 1948–1953

Sexual Behavior in the Human Male

For some time now there has been an increasing awareness among many people of the desirability of obtaining data about sex which would represent an accumulation of scientific fact completely divorced from questions of moral value and social custom. Practicing physicians find thousands of their patients in need of such objective data. Psychiatrists and analysts find that a majority of their patients need help in resolving sexual conflicts that have arisen in their lives. An increasing number of persons would like to bring an educated intelligence into the consideration of such matters as sexual adjustments in marriage, the sexual guidance of children, the pre-marital sexual adjustments of youth, sex education, sexual activities which are in conflict with the mores, and problems confronting persons who are interested

Alfred C. Kinsey, Wardell B. Pomeroy, and Clyde E. Martin, *Sexual Behavior in the Human Male* (Philadelphia: W. B. Saunders, 1948), 3, 7, 347, 610–611, 616–617, 623. Reprinted by permission of The Kinsey Institute for Research in Sex, Gender, and Reproduction, Inc.
Alfred C. Kinsey, *Sexual Behavior in the Human Female* (Philadelphia: Saunders, 1953), 285–287, 298–299, 453–454, 467–469. Reprinted by permission of The Kinsey Institute for Research in Sex, Gender, and Reproduction, Inc.

in the social control of behavior through religion, custom, and the forces of the law. Before it is possible to think scientifically on any of these matters, more needs to be known about the actual behavior of people, and about the inter-relationships of that behavior with the biologic and social aspects of their histories. . . .

All kinds of persons and all aspects of human sexual behavior are being included in this survey. No preconception of what is rare or what is common, what is moral or socially significant, or what is normal and what is abnormal has entered into the choice of the histories or into the selection of the items recorded on them. Such limitations of the material would have interfered with the determination of the fact. Nothing has done more to block the free investigation of sexual behavior than the almost universal acceptance, even among scientists, of certain aspects of that behavior as normal, and of other aspects of that behavior as abnormal. The similarity of distinctions between the terms normal and abnormal, and the terms right and wrong, amply demonstrates the philosophic, religious, and cultural origins of these concepts, and the ready acceptance of those distinctions among scientific men may provide the basis for one of the severest criticisms which subsequent generations can make of the scientific quality of nineteenth century and early twentieth century scientists. This is first of all a report on what people do, which raises no question of what they should do, or what kinds of people do it. It is the story of the sexual behavior of the American male, as we find him. It is not, in the usual sense, a study of the normal male or of normal behavior, any more than it is a study of abnormal males, or of abnormal behavior. It is an unfettered investigation of all types of sexual activity, as found among all kinds of males. . . .

[Among men,] [p]re-martial intercourse may be had either with companions or with prostitutes. In every social level coitus with girls who are not prostitutes is more frequent. In younger age groups there is a 10 to 1 or still higher difference in favor of the non-prostitutes. In older age groups, males of the lower educational level who are not yet married turn to prostitutes more often than they did when they were younger; but non-prostitutes still provide a larger part of the coitus. At the college level, contacts with companions exceed the prostitute relations by some factor which lies between 20 and 100 in every age group, including the older groups.

Pre-marital intercourse, whatever its source, is more abundant in the grade school and high school levels, and less common at the college level. Even in the period between adolescence and 15 the active incidence includes nearly half (48% and 43%) of the lower educational groups, but only 10 per cent of the boys who will ultimately go to college. In the later teens, 85 per cent of the grade school group and 75 per cent of the high school group is having pre-marital intercourse, while the figure for the college group is still only 42 per cent. . . .

The frequency figures show still greater differences between educational levels. In the age period between 16 and 20, the grade school group has 7 times as much pre-marital coitus as the college group. There is not much drop in the differential even in the older age groups. The mother who is afraid to send her boy away to college for fear that he will be morally corrupted there, is evidently unaware of the histories of the boys who stay at home. . . .

In the total male population, single and married, between adolescence and old age, 24 per cent of the total outlet [orgasms] is derived from solitary sources (masturbation and nocturnal emissions), 69.4 per cent is derived from heterosexual sources (petting and coitus), and 6.3 per cent of the total number of orgasms is derived from homosexual contacts. It is not more than 0.3 per cent of the outlet which is derived from relations with animals of other species.

Homosexual contacts account, therefore, for a rather small but still significant portion of the total outlet of the human male. The significance of the homosexual is, furthermore, much greater than the frequencies of outlet may indicate, because a considerable portion of the population, perhaps the major portion of the male population, has at least some homosexual experience between adolescence and old age. In addition, about 60 per cent of the pre-adolescent boys engage in homosexual activities, and there is an additional group of adult males who avoid overt contacts but who are quite aware of their potentialities for reacting to other males. . . .

Until the extent of any type of human behavior is adequately known, it is difficult to assess its significance, either to the individuals who are involved or to society as a whole; and until the extent of the homosexual is known, it is practically impossible to understand its biologic or social origins. It is one thing if we are dealing with a type of activity that is unusual, without precedent among other animals, and restricted to peculiar types of individuals within the human population. It is another thing if the phenomenon proves to be a fundamental part, not only of human sexuality, but of mammalian patterns as a whole. . . .

. . . [T]here is only about half of the male population whose sexual behavior is exclusively heterosexual, and there are only a few percent who are exclusively homosexual. Any restriction of the term homosexuality to individuals who are exclusively so demands, logically, that the term heterosexual be applied only to those individuals who are exclusively heterosexual; and this makes no allowance for the nearly half of the population which has had sexual contacts with, or reacted psychically to, individuals of their own as well as of the opposite sex. Actually, of course, one must learn to recognize every combination of heterosexuality and homosexuality in the histories of various individuals.

It would encourage clearer thinking on these matters if persons were not characterized as heterosexual or homosexual, but as individuals who have had certain amounts of heterosexual experience and certain amounts of homosexual experience. Instead of using these terms as substantives which stand for persons, or even as adjectives to describe persons, they may better be used to describe the nature of the overt sexual relations, or of the stimuli to which an individual erotically responds. . . .

In these terms (of physical contact to the point of orgasm), the data in the present study indicate that at least 37 per cent of the male population has some homosexual experience between the beginning of adolescence and old age. This is more than one male in three of the persons that one may meet as he passes along a city street. Among the males who remain unmarried until the age of 35, almost exactly 50 per cent have homosexual experience between the beginning of adolescence and that age. Some of these persons have but a single experience, and some of them have much more or even a lifetime of experience; but all of them have at least some experience to the point of orgasm. . . .

[1948]

Sexual Behavior in the Human Female

There are curiously mixed attitudes in our own country concerning coitus. Religious and legal codes, the psychologic and social sciences, psychiatric and other clinical theory, and public attitudes in general, agree in extolling heterosexual coitus as the most desirable, the most mature, and the socially most acceptable type of sexual activity. Simultaneously, however, the religious and legal codes and much clinical theory condemn such activity when it occurs outside of marriage and thereby, to a greater extent than most persons ordinarily comprehend, negate all of these claims concerning the desirability of coitus. Such conflicting appraisals of similar if not identical acts often constitute a source of considerable disturbance in the psycho-sexual development of American youth. These disturbances may have far-reaching effects upon subsequent adjustments in marriage. Our case histories show that this disapproval of heterosexual coitus and of nearly every other type of heterosexual activity before marriage is often an important factor in the development of homo-sexual activity.

Because of this public condemnation of pre-marital coitus, one might believe that such contacts would be rare among American females and males. But this is only the overt culture, the things that people openly profess to believe and to do. . . .

Nearly 50 per cent of the females in our sample had had coitus before they were married. A considerable portion of the pre-marital coitus had been had in the year or two immediately preceding marriage, with a portion of it confined to the fiancé in a period just before marriage. Consequently the incidences had depended upon the age of marriage. The females who married at earlier ages had had pre-marital coitus when they were younger; the females who married at later ages had not begun coitus until much later. There is an obvious correlation between the two phenomena and it is a question whether early experience in coitus leads to early marriage, or whether the possibility of a forthcoming marriage leads, as it certainly does in some cases, to an acceptance of coitus just before marriage. . . .

In contrast to the limited importance of the female's educational and parental home backgrounds, the decade in which she was born shows a marked influence on the incidences and frequencies of her premarital coitus.

Among the females in the sample who were born before 1900, less than half as many had had pre-marital coitus as among the females born in any subsequent decade. For instance, among those who were still unmarried by age twenty-five, 14 per cent of the older generation had had coitus, and 36 per cent of those born in the next decade. This increase in the incidence of pre-marital coitus, and the similar increase in the incidence of pre-marital petting, constitute the greatest changes which we have found between the patterns of sexual behavior in the older and younger generations of American females.

As in the case of pre-marital petting, practically all of this increase had oc-curred in the generation that was born in the first decade of the present century and, therefore, in the generation which had had most of its pre-marital experience in the late teens and in the 1920's following the first World War. The later generations appear to have accepted the new pattern and maintained or extended it. . . .

Homosexual activity among the females in the sample had been largely con-fined to the single females and, to a lesser extent, to previously married females who had been widowed, separated, or divorced. Both the incidences and frequencies were distinctly low among the married females. Thus, while the accumulative incidences of homosexual contacts had reached 19 per cent in the total sample by age forty, they were 24 per cent for the females who had never been married by that age, 3 per cent for the married females, and 9 per cent for the previously married females. The age at which the females had married seemed to have had no effect on the pre-marital incidences of homosexual activity, even though we found that the pre-marital heterosexual activities (petting and pre-marital coitus) had been stepped up in anticipation of an approaching marriage. The chief effect of marriage had been to stop the homosexual activities, thereby lowering the active incidences and frequencies in the sample of married females. . . .

The higher frequency of orgasm in the homosexual contacts [than in marital coitus] may have depended in part upon the considerable psychologic stimulation provided by such relationships, but there is reason for believing that it may also have depended on the fact that two individuals of the same sex are likely to understand the anatomy and the physiologic responses and psychology of their own sex better than they understand that of the opposite sex. Most males are likely to approach females as they, the males, would like to be approached by a sexual partner. They are likely to begin by providing immediate genital stimulation. They are inclined to utilize a variety of psychologic stimuli which may mean little to most females. Females in their heterosexual relationships are actually more likely to prefer techniques which are closer to those which are commonly utilized in homosexual relationships. They would prefer a considerable amount of generalized emotional stimulation before there is any specific sexual contact. They usually want physical stimulation of the whole body before there is any specifically genital contact. They may especially want stimulation of the clitoris and the labia minora, and stimulation which, after it has once begun, is followed through to orgasm without the interruptions which males, depending to a greater degree than most females do upon psychologic stimuli, often introduce into their heterosexual relationships.

It is, of course, quite possible for males to learn enough about female sexual responses to make their heterosexual contacts as effective as females make most homosexual contacts. With the additional possibilities which a union of male and female genitalia may offer in a heterosexual contact, and with public opinion and the mores encouraging heterosexual contacts and disapproving of homosexual contacts, relationships between females and males will seem, to most persons, to be more satisfactory than homosexual relationships can ever be. Heterosexual relationships could, however, become more satisfactory if they more often utilized the sort of knowledge which most homosexual females have of female sexual anatomy and female psychology. . . .

That there are individuals who react psychologically to both females and males, and who have overt sexual relations with both females and males in the course of their lives, or in any single period of their lives, is a fact of which many persons are unaware; and many of those who are academically aware of it still fail to comprehend the realities of the situation. It is a characteristic of the human mind that it tries to dichotomize in its classification of phenomena. Things either are so, or they are not so. Sexual behavior is either normal or abnormal, socially acceptable or unacceptable, heterosexual or homosexual; and many persons do not want to believe that there are gradations in these matters from one to the other extreme.

In regard to sexual behavior it has been possible to maintain this dichotomy only by placing all persons who are exclusively heterosexual in a heterosexual category, and all persons who have any amount of experience with their own sex, even including those with the slightest experience, in a homosexual category. The group that is identified in the public mind as heterosexual is the group which, as far as public knowledge goes, has never had any homosexual experience. But the group that is commonly identified as homosexual includes not only those who are known or believed to be exclusively homosexual, but also those who are known to have had any homosexual experience at all. Legal penalties, public disapproval, and ostracism are likely to be leveled against a person who has had limited homosexual experience as quickly as they are leveled against those who have had exclusive experience. It would be as reasonable to rate all individuals heterosexual if they have any heterosexual experience, and irrespective of the amount of homosexual experience which they may be having. The attempt to maintain a simple dichotomy on these matters exposes the traditional biases which are likely to enter whenever the heterosexual or homosexual classification of an individual is involved.

[1953]

2. Women Write *Life* and *Look* About the Kinsey Report, 1953

I am surprised that LOOK . . . would stoop . . . to publishing *For Women Only—What Every Woman Should Know About Kinsey* . . . , knowing it would go into homes where thousands of young people might read it with resultant misgivings about their own parents' premarital relationships. . . . There are a lot of women . . . throughout the United States . . . who have always known how to sublimate the primary sex urge . . . to higher mental, moral and spiritual urges and interests. As one who spent nearly a quarter of a century working directly with the youth of America . . . I want to go on record as saying that irregular sex practices and relationships were one of our least frequent problems . . . .

I resent the implications that the findings of Dr. Kinsey . . . are in any sense scientific. Any sampling of 5,940 women of the barroom, dance hall type . . . cannot represent the mental, moral or spiritual integrity of American womanhood.

I read the article on Dr. Kinsey's report with disgust. He takes a so-called survey of a few American women with bad morals and sets them up as an example of typical American womanhood.

A kiss on both cheeks for Dr. Kinsey from this median female guppy! It is a great refreshment to find a real scientist spitting so accurately in Dr. Freud's late eye. This wishful thinking and vicarious eroticism of psychiatrists (male) in presupposing and

Letters to the Editor on the Kinsey Report: *Look* 17 (October 20, 1953): 121; *Life*, September 14, 1953, 17–18. Reprinted by permission.

encouraging ravening sexuality in women may now, at last, come to an inglorious end. . . . It should by now be sufficiently demonstrated that women will engage in activities they do not particularly enjoy, and which are frowned on by convention, just to escape a status combining the features of household utensil and plaster saint.

As one of Dr. Kinsey's interviewed "samples," I stick up for him and his book. The questions are so skillfully organized, interestingly presented and tactfully asked that it would be harder to lie than to come out with the simple truth. Why would a woman offer to give her history if she were prepared to hold back the true facts?

Whatever is said in praise or blame, the book presents a picture of female sexual activity as it is. No amount of protesting is going to change it.

3. *Time* Covers the Transformation of Transsexual Christine Jorgensen, 1952–1953

The Great Transformation

The New York *Daily News,* which covers sexy, sensational stories with a flair that no other tabloid can match, last week broke a story that surprised even hardened *News* readers. Splashed across Page One was a banner headline: EX-G.I. BECOMES BLONDE BEAUTY. Said the story: "A Bronx youth, who served two years in the Army during the war and was honorably discharged, has been transformed by the wizardry of medical science into a beautiful woman." Under the banner were pictures of George W. Jorgensen, 26, the George who "is no more," and Christine, "the new woman" he became after "five major operations, a minor operation and almost 2,000 [hormone] injections" in a Copenhagen hospital.

The paper was tipped to its exclusive by a letter that *News* Reporter Ben White received from a friend who is a laboratory technician in Copenhagen. White tracked down the parents of George and/or Christine in New York City, talked them into giving him the full story, together with pictures of Christine in a low-cut dress and a letter from her breaking the news to the folks at home. Wrote she: "I am still the same old Brud, but my dears, nature made a mistake, which I have had corrected and now I am your daughter." Wire services and other papers pounced on the *News* exclusive, phoned Copenhagen directly and sent dozens of correspondents converging on Christine's room in the hospital, where she is awaiting a final operation.

Needlework or Ball Games. "Lying in a hospital bed," said an A.P. dispatch from Copenhagen, "her long yellow hair curling on a pillow, [she] widened her grey-blue eyes and lifted her hands in a surprised, frightened gesture." One newsman got into her hospital room using a bouquet of flowers as a pass key. Others bombarded her with such questions as "Do you sleep in a nightgown or pajamas?" "Will you ever be a mother?" "Do you still have to shave?" "Are your interests male or female? I mean are you interested in, say, needlework, rather than a ball game?"

"The Great Transformation," *Time,* December 15, 1952, 58–59; "The Case of Christine," *Time,* April 20, 1953, 82–84. Reprinted by permission.

The *News* added its own fillip from its correspondent in Copenhagen who cabled: "Chris now is a girl I could have fallen in love with had I met her under different circumstances." At Bentwaters Air Force Base in England, reporters found a U.S. Air Force sergeant who said he had dated Christine six months ago. When they asked him for details, he obligingly observed: "She's got a personality that's hard to beat, and the best body of any girl I ever met." Many an editor and reporter found himself in the same fix as father Jorgensen, who blurted out amidst all the uproar: "This business is very confusing. I'll be in the middle of a conversation and I'll say 'he' when I mean 'she.'"

[15 December 1952]

The Case of Christine

For a while, having achieved notoriety, she was Manhattan's No. 1 glamour girl. A blonde with a fair leg and a fetching smile, she seemed to be everywhere that was anywhere, with everybody who was anybody. Columnist Leonard Lyons introduced her to a gaggle of celebrities. Broadway Star Yul Brynner and she grinned at each other over a couple of highballs at El Morocco. She appeared in Madison Square Garden at a charity rally sponsored by Walter Winchell, on half a dozen television programs, and was photographed in a soft *tailleur* for the Easter Parade.

Last week came the revelation that Christine Jorgensen was no girl at all, only an altered male.

This was no surprise to U.S. psychiatrists . . . or to careful readers of Jorgensen's own story in the Hearst newspapers. Jorgensen, a onetime G.I. named George, told how he "was in . . . affections more like a woman than a man"; how two years ago, at 24, he had heard of a doctor in Denmark who might help him live like the woman he wanted to be; how the Danish doctors had diagnosed him as a transvestite, treated him for a year with female hormones, then operated on him to remove "the evidence of masculinity."

Jorgensen acknowledged in his article that his organs had been normal in the first place. But many readers jumped to the conclusion that his was one of the not uncommon cases of pseudohermaphroditism (organs of one sex so malformed or concealed as to be mistaken for those of the other), or one of the rare cases of true hermaphroditism (possessing the gonads of both sexes). In either instance the operations would have left Jorgensen a girl, or a reasonable facsimile thereof.

The New York *Post* put the facts on the line. Reporter Alvin Davis, who flew to Denmark to interview Jorgensen's doctors, established two main points: 1) Jorgensen's case was not one of hermaphroditism or pseudohermaphroditism; 2) in an attempt to accommodate his urge to transvestitism, his Danish doctors had simply amputated penis and testes, left him a male castrate. The disclosure kicked up a storm of discussion around questions of medical practice.

Can transvestites be cured? In relatively mild cases of transvestitism, involving patients who actually want to be normal, U.S. doctors agree that psychiatric treatment, sometimes accompanied by hormones of the patient's own sex, often effect real cures. But in some cases of transvestitism, as in severe cases of homosexuality, cures are exceptional at best. . . .

Can a male transvestite possibly lead a relatively happy life as a "woman"?
Absolutely not, say most U.S. psychiatrists. The castration many of them crave
may give them the temporary illusion of womanhood, but it can be nothing more
than an illusion, and when it disappears, the disappointment and frustration are
likely to make their last state worse than their first.

With this the Danish doctors flatly disagree. Jorgensen may well be in for much
suffering, they admit, but if so, the publicity given to the operation will be to blame.
If Jorgensen had been able to slide quietly into society and be accepted as a woman,
the prognosis would be much more favorable.

[April 20, 1953]

4. The U.S. Senate Investigates "Sex Perverts" in Government, 1950

In the opinion of this subcommittee h[o]mosexuals and other sex perverts are not
proper persons to be employed in Government for two reasons; first, they are generally unsuitable, and second, they constitute security risks.

Overt acts of sex perversion, including acts of homosexuality, constitute a
crime under our Federal, State, and municipal statutes and persons who commit
such acts are law violators. Aside from the criminality and immorality involved in
sex perversion such behavior is so contrary to the normal accepted standards of
social behavior that persons who engage in such activity are looked upon as out-
casts by society generally. The social stigma attached to sex perversion is so great
that many perverts go to great lengths to conceal their perverted tendencies. This
situation is evidenced by the fact that perverts are frequently victimized by black-
mailers who threaten to expose their sexual deviations. . . .

Most of the authorities agree and our investigation has shown that the presence
of a sex pervert in a Government agency tends to have a corrosive influence upon
his fellow employees. These perverts will frequently attempt to entice normal individuals to engage in perverted practices. This is particularly true in the case of
young and impressionable people who might come under the influence of a pervert. Government officials have the responsibility of keeping this type of corrosive
influence out of the agencies under their control. It is particularly important that the
thousands of young men and women who are brought into Federal jobs not be subjected to that type of influence while in the service of the Government. One homosexual can pollute a Government office.

Another point to be considered in determining whether a sex pervert is suitable for Government employment is his tendency to gather other perverts about
him. Eminent psychiatrists have informed the subcommittee that the homosexual is
likely to seek his own kind because the pressures of society are such that he feels
uncomfortable unless he is with his own kind. Due to this situation the homosexual
tends to surround himself with other homosexuals, not only in his social, but in
his business life. Under these circumstances if a homosexual attains a position in

U.S. Senate, *Employment of Homosexuals and Other Sex Perverts in Government*, Senate Document
No. 241, 81st Cong., 2nd Sess. (Washington, D.C.: Government Printing Office, 1950), 3–10.

Government where he can influence the hiring of personnel, it is almost inevitable that he will attempt to place other homosexuals in Government jobs.

The conclusion of the subcommittee that a homosexual or other sex pervert is a security risk is not based upon mere conjecture. That conclusion is predicated upon a careful review of the opinions of those best qualified to consider matters of security in Government, namely, the intelligence agencies of the Government. Testimony on this phase of the inquiry was taken from representatives of the Federal Bureau of Investigation, the Central Intelligence Agency, and the intelligence services of the Army, Navy and Air Force. All of these agencies are in complete agreement that sex perverts in Government constitute security risks.

The lack of emotional stability which is found in most sex perverts and the weakness of their moral fiber, makes them susceptible to the blandishments of the foreign espionage agent. It is the experience of intelligence experts that perverts are vulnerable to interrogation by a skilled questioner and they seldom refuse to talk about themselves. Furthermore, most perverts tend to congregate at the same restaurants, night clubs, and bars, which places can be identified with comparative ease in any community, making it possible for a recruiting agent to develop clandestine relationships which can be used for espionage purposes. . . .

Other cases have been brought to the attention of the subcommittee where Nazi and Communist agents have attempted to obtain information from employees of our Government by threatening to expose their abnormal sex activities. It is an accepted fact among intelligence agencies that espionage organizations the world over consider sex perverts who are in possession of or have access to confidential material to be prime targets where pressure can be exerted. In virtually every case despite protestations by the perverts that they would never succumb to blackmail, invariably they express considerable concern over the fact that their condition might become known to their friends, associates, or the public at large. The present danger of this security problem is well illustrated by the following excerpt from the testimony of D. Milton Ladd, Assistant to the Director of the Federal Bureau of Investigation, who appeared before this subcommittee in executive session:

> The Communists, without principles or scruples, have a program of seeking out weaknesses of leaders in Government and industry. In fact, the FBI has in its possession information of unquestionable reliability that orders have been issued by high Russian intelligence officials to their agents to secure details of the private lives of Government officials, their weaknesses, their associates, and in fact every bit of information regarding them, hoping to find a chink in their armor and a weakness upon which they might capitalize at the appropriate time. . . .

The subcommittee has attempted to arrive at some idea as to the extent of sex perversion among Government employees by obtaining information from the personnel records of all Government agencies and the police records in the District of Columbia. . . .

An individual check of the Federal agencies revealed that since January 1, 1947, the armed services and civilian agencies of Government have handled 4,954 cases involving charges of homosexuality or other types of sex perversion. It will be noted that the bulk of these cases are in the armed services as is indicated by the fact that 4,380 of the known cases in Government involved military personnel and

574 involved civilian employees. However, in considering these statistics it is pointed out that the incidence of homosexuality and other forms of sex perversion is usually higher in military organizations or other groups where large numbers of men (or women) live and work in close confinement and are restricted in their normal social contacts. Furthermore it must be borne in mind in relation to the larger numerical figures of the military departments that the armed services are numerically several times larger than any civilian agency of government. Another important consideration in drawing conclusions from these statistics is the fact that the military services, unlike most other Government agencies, traditionally have been aggressive in ferreting out and removing sex perverts from their ranks and this is bound to make for a larger number of known cases in the services. . . . [O]f the total 4,380 military removals since January 1, 1947, 470 persons have been separated as the result of general court martial and 3,910 have been separated by means other than general court martial. . . .

An examination of the statistical data gathered from the civilian agencies of Government indicates that from January 1, 1947 through October 31, 1950, 574 cases have been handled in these agencies. Of that number 207 have been dismissed from the Government service and 213 have resigned. In 85 cases it was determined by the employing agency that the facts did not substantiate the charges and the persons involved were retained. . . .

It is significant to note that it was about April 1 of this year that the employment of sex perverts in Government was given widespread publicity as the result of preliminary studies by the Senate Appropriations Subcommittee. Shortly after that time records of persons arrested in the District of Columbia on charges of sex perversion were made available to the various Government agencies and since that time there has been a marked increase in the number of cases handled by the Government departments. . . .

[T]he military establishments over a period of years have followed a rather uniform and constant pattern in ferreting out and removing these persons from the services while most of the civilian agencies of Government have taken action in the majority of cases only in the past few months. . . .

. . . Under present procedures all applicants for Government positions are screened by the Civil Service Commission soon after their appointment. While these applicants are not subject to a so-called full field investigation, their fingerprints are checked against the files of the FBI to determine whether they have a prior arrest record, and other name checks are also made. As a result of this screening process, the Civil Service Commission is notified in the event the applicant has a police record of sex perversion; and, if such a record does exist, further investigation is conducted to determine the complete facts. A spot check of the records of the Civil Service Commission indicates that between January 1, 1947, and August 1, 1950, approximately 1,700 applicants for Federal positions were denied employment because they had a record of homosexuality or other sex perversion.

Furthermore, in most of the sensitive agencies of the Government, including the Atomic Energy Commission, the State Department, and the FBI, all applicants are subjected to a full field investigation. Needless to say, this type of investigation should eliminate most sex perverts and other undesirables from positions in these agencies. However, it must be borne in mind that as a practical matter even the most elaborate and costly system of investigating applicants for Government positions will not prevent some sex perverts from finding their way into the Government service. . . .

There also appears to have been a tendency in many Government agencies to adopt a head-in-the-sand attitude toward the problem of sex perversion. Some agencies tried to avoid the problem either by making no real effort to investigate charges of homosexuality or by failing to take firm and positive steps to get known perverts out of Government and keep them out. In other cases some agencies did get rid of perverts, but in an apparent effort to conceal the fact that they had such persons in their employ, they eased out these perverts by one means or another in as quiet a manner as possible and circumvented the established rules with respect to the removal or dismissal of unsuitable personnel from Government positions.

5. Psychiatrist Fredric Wertham "Outs"
Batman and Robin, 1953

Comic books, like other books, can be read at different levels, with different people getting out of them different things. That does not depend only on differences in age; it is affected also by more subtle factors of constitution, experience, inclination and unconscious susceptibilities. . . .

Many adolescents go through periods of vague fears that they might be homosexual. Such fears may become a source of great mental anguish and these boys usually have no one in whom they feel they can confide. In a number of cases I have found this sequence of events: At an early age these boys become addicted to the homoerotically tinged type of comic book. During and after comic-book reading they indulged in fantasies which became severely repressed. Life experiences, either those drawing their attention to the great taboo on homosexuality or just the opposite—experiences providing any kind of temptation—raise feelings of doubt, guilt, shame and sexual malorientation. . . .

Several years ago a California psychiatrist pointed out that the Batman stories are psychologically homosexual. Our researches confirm this entirely. Only someone ignorant of the fundamentals of psychiatry and of the psychopathology of sex can fail to realize a subtle atmosphere of homoerotism which pervades the adventures of the mature "Batman" and his young friend "Robin." . . .

In the Batman type of comic book such a relationship is depicted to children before they can even read. Batman and Robin, the "dynamic duo," also known as the "daring duo," go into action in their special uniforms. They constantly rescue each other from violent attacks by an unending number of enemies. The feeling is conveyed that we men must stick together because there are so many villainous creatures who have to be exterminated. They lurk not only under every bed but also behind every star in the sky. Either Batman or his young boy friend or both are captured, threatened with every imaginable weapon, almost blown to bits, almost

Fredric Wertham, *Seduction of the Innocent* (New York: Rinehard & Co., 1953), 188–193. Reprinted by permission.

crushed to death, almost annihilated. Sometimes Batman ends up in bed injured and young Robin is shown sitting next to him. At home they lead an idyllic life. They are Bruce Wayne and "Dick" Grayson. Bruce Wayne is described as a "socialite" and the official relationship is that Dick is Bruce's ward. They live in sumptuous quarters, with beautiful flowers in large vases, and have a butler, Alfred. Batman is sometimes shown in a dressing gown. As they sit by the fireplace the young boy sometimes worries about his partner: "Something's wrong with Bruce. He hasn't been himself these past few days." It is like a wish dream of two homosexuals living together. Sometimes they are shown on a couch, Bruce reclining and Dick sitting next to him, jacket off, collar open, and his hand on his friend's arm. Like the girls in other stories, Robin is sometimes held captive by the villains and Batman has to give in or "Robin gets killed."

Robin is a handsome ephebic boy, usually shown in his uniform with bare legs. He is buoyant with energy and devoted to nothing on earth or in interplanetary space as much as to Bruce Wayne. He often stands with his legs spread, the genital region discreetly evident.

In these stories there are practically no decent, attractive, successful women. A typical female character is the Catwoman, who is vicious and uses a whip. The atmosphere is homosexual and anti-feminine. If the girl is good-looking she is undoubtedly the villainess. If she is after Bruce Wayne, she will have no chance against Dick. For instance, Bruce and Dick go out one evening in dinner clothes, dressed exactly alike. The attractive girl makes up to Bruce while in successive pictures young Dick looks on smiling, sure of Bruce. Violence is not lacking in these stories. You are shown Batman and Robin standing in a room with a whole row of corpses on the floor. . . .

In many adolescents the homoerotic, anti-feminist trend unconsciously aroused or fostered by these stories is demonstrable. We have inquired about Batman from overt homosexuals treated at the [Quaker Emergency Service] Readjustment Center, to find out what they thought the influence of these Batman stories was on children and adolescents. A number of them knew these stories very well and spoke of them as their favorite reading. The reply of one intelligent, educated young homosexual was typical: "I don't think that they would do any harm sexually. But they probably would ruin their morals."

One young homosexual during psychotherapy brought us a copy of *Detective Comics,* with a Batman story. He pointed out a picture of "The Home of Bruce and Dick," a house beautifully landscaped, warmly lighted and showing the devoted pair side by side, looking out a picture window. When he was eight this boy had realized from fantasies about comic-book pictures that he was aroused by men. At the age of ten or eleven, "I found my liking, my sexual desires, in comic books. I think I put myself in the position of Robin. I did want to have relations with Batman. The only suggestion of homosexuality may be that they seem to be so close to each other. I remember the first time I came across the page mentioning the 'secret bat cave.' The thought of Batman and Robin living together and possibly having sex relations came to my mind. You can almost connect yourself with the people. I was put in the position of the rescued rather than the rescuer. I felt I'd like to be loved by someone like Batman or Superman." . . .

The Lesbian counterpart of Batman may be found in the stories of Wonder Woman and Black Cat. The homosexual connotation of the Wonder Woman type of story is psychologically unmistakable. The *Psychiatric Quarterly* deplored in an editorial the "appearance of an eminent child therapist as the implied endorser of a series . . . which portrays extremely sadistic hatred of all males in a framework which is plainly Lesbian."

For boys, Wonder Woman is a frightening image. For girls she is a morbid ideal. Where Batman is anti-feminine, the attractive Wonder Woman and her counterparts are definitely anti-masculine. Wonder Woman has her own female following. They are all continuously being threatened, captured, almost put to death. There is a great deal of mutual rescuing, the same type of rescue fantasies as in Batman. Her followers are the "Holliday girls," i.e. the holiday girls, the gay party girls, the gay girls. Wonder Woman refers to them as "my girls." Their attitude about death and murder is a mixture of the callousness of crime comics with the coyness of sweet little girls.

6. Marge McDonald Enters the Lesbian Community of Columbus, Ohio, 1955

[T]en o'clock found me driving around the block near the Town Grill [the name of the bar], trying to summon up enough nerve to go in by myself.

Finally, having whipped up my courage, I walked in and took a seat among the girls at the bar. I was a wreck. My elbows were shaking even though I had them propped up on the bar. I was too frightened to look at anybody. I stared straight in front of me. A cute girl with brown hair and warm eyes came up and took my order for a beer after I proved I was twenty-one (I was twenty-three at the time).

I had sat there for a while when the girl on my left turned and said something about the weather. I mumbled some stupid reply about being so nervous I could hardly talk. I mentally kicked myself for not having started a conversation. I had sat there for what seemed like an hour but probably wasn't when a pretty blonde walked up to me and said in a warm friendly voice, "I hope you don't think I am being fresh, but I have noticed that you are new here and that no one has been talking to you. They think you are a policewoman. I'm JoAnne and I want you to feel free to walk up and say 'Hi' to me anytime you see me." I managed a weak smile and said I would. I sat there, my brain jumping from one thought to another so fast my head was swimming. But through it all came the hope that they would accept me and like me and the fear that they wouldn't. I sat there looking at a boyish-looking girl behind the bar in slacks and a man's shirt. She had short dark brown hair and wore no lipstick. She attracted me that first night more than anyone. After 11:30, the crowd started thinning out and soon there were only a few left at the bar.

The woman on my left finally started a conversation and we talked about everything—books, music. After talking awhile, she had managed to draw out the

"From the Diary of Marge McDonald," in Joan Nestle, ed., *The Persistent Desire: A Butch-Femme Reader* (Boston: Alyson Publications, 1992), 124–127. Reprinted by permission of the Lesbian Herstory Archives.

pertinent facts that I was a homosexual but that I had never been around my own kind before.

Her name was Lynn and we sat and talked until closing, twelve A.M. on Saturday. They locked the door and still we sat there. She kept playing "Ebbtide" on the juke-box and talking about her life in the navy. She said that if she had known what she was in the navy, she would have been court-martialed.

At about 12:45, we left. I insisted on giving her a lift home. She lived in the North End in a trailer, and on the way, I learned a lot of things that left me very surprised. I had supposed that you just met a girl and fell in love. I found out that the more masculine girls were called "butch" and the feminine girls were "femme." A "homosexual" was a "gay" person. A so-called normal person was a "straight" person. Well, I thought, Margie, you are in the "gay" life now!

Lynn warned me that it was no bed of roses and I agreed to that. I could realize that society would condemn me, people would shrink from me as if I were a leper, but I also realized that there would be the happiness of being around my own kind to make up for it. I decided that the happiness would outweigh the sorrow and that the "gay" life was for me.

When we arrived at the trailer, she invited me in for coffee. I accepted eagerly, glad of the chance to talk and be alone with a gay person. Lynn was obviously butch. She wore men's jeans, a t-shirt, and she walked like a boy. I asked how you could tell the difference between a femme and a butch and was told that a butch is the aggressor when making love. I decided I was butch, but she said she thought I was a femme. She soon drew my story out of me.

I found myself telling her of my father, who had died when I was five. I had a wonderful aunt, Dora, who because she could not have children sort of adopted me. . . . She centered her world around me, but because she was very religious, I . . . hurt her deeply. I like to smoke, wear slacks, drink, and had my hair cut very short. She was brokenhearted about it.

I told Lynn how on New Year's Eve of 1949, I married a boy I had known for seven months. I thought I loved him; I didn't like it at home. I guess I thought being loved by him was better than not being loved at all. I had had crushes on girls when I was in my early teens. I thought it was just a stage I was going through and that I had outgrown it, until I developed a crush on a girl at work while my husband was in Las Vegas in the air force.

I spent the next six months going to a psychiatrist. He told me that when you put a person who is a child emotionally into a world full of adults and expect this person to act like an adult, it is too much for them and they retreat into a world of their own. He thought he had cured me of being a homosexual. I had an affair with a man just to prove to myself it was over.

On Thanksgiving, 1954, I went up to my husband's sister's house for dinner. Their mother and I were very good friends and when we were alone, she told me about her girlfriend and how beautiful their love had been. She told me that she had loved *me* for a long time. She said all of this without knowing I was a lesbian, just because I was easy to talk to. I was very surprised and began thinking about loving women again. Her daughter was in New York and I went up every night to keep her from becoming too lonely.

After a few weeks, I admitted that I had always been attracted to women. I decided then that I might as well stop fighting my true feelings and be happy. I stopped dating men and began the search for my own kind. I would drive around the city, feeling so lonely, thinking of all the people like me in this city, yet I couldn't find them. I knew the Blue Feather was for men and that it was listed in the white pages of the telephone book but not in the yellow pages, so I started going through the white pages, writing down the names of every bar that wasn't listed in the yellow pages and investigating them. I was only through the B's when I found the Townie.

Five o'clock found us sitting side by side on the couch still talking. We thought we should get some sleep, so Lynn decided to be my pillow. She held me in her arms. My face was against her breast. I wasn't sleepy though, so we continued to talk all the while. I was so happy to be so close to a woman. I lifted my face and she kissed me. My first kiss from a woman! I could never describe my feelings, so I won't even try.

It is sufficient to say that as long as I live, I shall never forget that moment—or the kiss.

7. Del Martin Explains Why Lesbians Need the Daughters of Bilitis, 1956

Since 1950 there has been a nationwide movement to bring understanding to and about the homosexual minority.

Most of the organizations dedicated to this purpose stem from the Mattachine Foundation which was founded in Los Angeles at that time. Members of these organizations—The Mattachine Society, One, and National Association for Sexual Research—are predominantly male, although there are a few hard working women among their ranks.

The Daughters of Bilitis is a women's organization resolved to add the feminine voice and viewpoint to a mutual problem. While women may not have so much difficulty with law enforcement, their problems are none the less real—family, sometimes children, employment, social acceptance.

However, the Lesbian is a very elusive creature. She burrows underground in her fear of identification. She is cautious in her associations. Current modes in hair style and casual attire have enabled her to camouflage her existence. She claims she does not need help. And she will not risk her tight little fist of security to aid those who do.

But surely the ground work has been well laid in the past 5½ years. Homosexuality is not the dirty word it used to be. More and more people, professional and lay, are becoming aware of its meaning and implications. There is no longer so much "risk" in becoming associated with [it].

And why not "belong"? Many heterosexuals do. Membership is open to anyone who is interested in the minority problems of the sexual variant and does not necessarily indicate one's own sex preference.

Del Martin, "President's Message," *The Ladder* 1 (October 1956): 6–7. Reprinted by permission of Ayer Company Publishers.

Women have taken a beating through the centuries. It has been only in this 20th, through the courageous crusade of the Suffragettes and the influx of women into the business world, that woman has become an independent entity, an individual with the right to vote and the right to a job and economic security. But it took women with foresight and determination to attain this heritage which is now ours.

And what will be the lot of the future Lesbian? Fear? Scorn? This need not be—IF lethargy is su[p]planted by an energized constructive program, if cowardice gives way to the solidarity of a cooperative front, if the "let Georgia do it" attitude is replaced by the realization of individual responsibility in thwarting the evils of ignorance, superstition, prejudice, and bigotry.

Nothing was ever accomplished by hiding in a dark corner. Why not discard the hermitage for the heritage that awaits any red-blooded American woman who dares to claim it?

▉ E S S A Y S

In the ideology of the Cold War, guarding the nation from communism went hand in hand with strong families, "normal" heterosexuality, and strictly separated gender roles. According to many historians, government agencies, academic experts, and the mass media sought to connect private behavior, public order, and national security. How did these ideas affect sexual beliefs and behavior in the 1950s? David Harley Serlin, of the National Library of Medicine, considers the notion of the "closet"—the culture of secrecy, confession, and exposure—to be a defining attribute of sexuality in the Cold War. Examining media responses to Christine Jorgensen, the first American to undergo a "sex change" operation, Serlin finds that the shifting definitions of Jorgensen's sexual orientation and gender identity mirrored Cold War anxieties over national security. Jeffrey Escoffier, an independent scholar, looks at this era through a different lens. He discusses how the act of reading in the 1950s and early 1960s— especially reading sociological studies about homosexuality—shaped his own coming out. These works framed homosexuality as a *social* issue and presented a "gay world" to closeted men. Popular sociology, psychology, and literature placed homosexuals within a strictly defined, conformist discourse, he argues, but it also enabled them to see the possibilities of living life *as* gay men.

Christine Jorgensen and the Cold War Closet

DAVID HARLEY SERLIN

[T]his essay will examine the early case history of Christine (née George) Jorgensen, a Bronx-bred ex-GI who, in the winter of 1952, was the first American man to undergo a "sex change" operation, achieving international status as a woman. . . . [T]he dual effects of Jorgensen's surgical transformation and her bizarre rise to stardom on the American cultural imagination hardly seems consonant with the historical

This material is an edited version of "Christine Jorgensen and the Cold War Closet," by David Harley Serlin, in *Radical History Review* 62 (1995): 137–165. Copyright 1995, MARHO: The Radical Historians' Association. All rights reserved. Reprinted by permission of Duke University Press.

moment that nourished McCarthyism. . . . But Jorgensen's biography—or the elements of her biography as they were revealed to popular audiences—forces us to reconsider the ways in which the political economy of the Cold War exploited ideas about sexual orientation and gender identity to promote and disseminate American nationalism and domestic security.

Although this essay will not presume to tell her entire life story, the earliest moments of Christine Jorgensen's rise to stardom are worth recounting if only because there is a great deal of ambiguity and inaccuracy surrounding her intertwined surgical and sexual histories. . . . What current professionals in the field of sex reassignment surgery consider to be the definitive (some would say defining) operation for transsexuals—vaginoplasty for male-to-females, and phalloplasty for female-to-males—was beyond the scope of even those medical experts in Denmark in whom Jorgensen had entrusted her faith. The best that contemporary physicians could offer Jorgensen in 1952, the year in which she experienced the bulk of her "conversion," was electrolysis, hormone injections, and removal of the penis and testicles. In the earliest media spectacles that accompanied her return from Copenhagen—the place where she had, ostensibly, "changed her sex"—Jorgensen merely assumed her new position as a full-fledged American woman. Jorgensen was able to maintain her charade of female authenticity for almost six months, during which time she was known internationally as "the most talked-about girl in the world." But when medical experts were called upon to define, in layperson's terms, exactly what steps had been taken to transform Jorgensen from one gender to another, they instead announced the bitter truth about Jorgensen's inauthentic anatomy. In April 1953, newspapers outed her as "an altered male," and Jorgensen supporters around the world were outraged to discover that Christine was not a "real" woman. Within a few months, Jorgensen's social significance had shifted from that of "glamour girl" and scientific miracle to medical oddity and psychological subject.

According to a 1968 radio interview that she gave to promote her newly published autobiography, Jorgensen did not become an anatomically correct transsexual—that is, did not have a surgically constructed vagina—until 1954, almost two years after her first appearance in the media. But by the time she underwent that last and final operation in her transformation from George to Christine, Jorgensen's public identity and reputation had already dramatically shifted. The real *case* of Christine Jorgensen demonstrates how and why the various media and scientific communities welcomed and celebrated her, and why they ultimately lashed out against her within six months of her initial appearance. . . . Between December 1952 and April 1953, the American media diffused and refracted the image of Christine Jorgensen through a variety of cultural conventions such as fashion photography, "behind the scenes" reportage, and the reprinting of personal letters that Jorgensen had sent to her parents and a Marine stationed in Britain who was known shortly thereafter as Jorgensen's boyfriend. These discursive traits and provocative references had the unprecedented effect of normalizing Jorgensen rather than alienating her and thus secured her reputation as a sterling example of what constituted a "real American woman."

. . . Christine Jorgensen's early success rested almost entirely on her ability to remain inside the closet of sexual ambiguity and to constitute herself as a shining symbol of American nationalism. But immediately after her "fall from grace," the popular media expunged Jorgensen's biography of any positive, romantic, or nation-alistic attributes it had acquired just months earlier. Jorgensen's status as a sexually ambiguous eunuch was not only treated with homophobic disdain, but also was folded surreptitiously into the rhetoric of anti-Americanism, so that she was marked as someone who had forsaken her natural biological duty and had, in effect, con-verted to the other side. Within six months of her initial appearance, Jorgensen was transformed into a pariah of sexual deviance. . . .

On 1 December 1952, the *New York Daily News* ran an exclusive headline across its masthead: "EX-GI BECOMES BLONDE BEAUTY." Beneath the 72-point block capital letters . . . was the shadowy profile shot of what seemed to be an attractive young woman who looked something like Marilyn Monroe. Facing the right side of the front page, with her nose crinkled and her eyes opened slightly, she seemed frozen, like a mannequin—or, perhaps more fittingly, like a[n] introverted celebrity caught off-guard by an invasive paparazzi. Beneath the grainy photograph read the caption: "George Jorgensen, Jr., son of a Bronx carpenter, served in the Army for two years and was given an honorable discharge in 1946. Now George is no more. After six operations, Jorgensen's sex has been changed and today she is a striking woman, working as a photographer in Denmark. Parents were informed of the big change in a letter Christine (that's her new name) sent to them recently." Inside the front page, the reader was treated to "before" and "after" photographs of both George and Christine, including one narrow vertical shot of Jorgensen as a leggy bombshell, similar in style and pose to the type that George's Army buddies (or George himself, prophetically perhaps) may have displayed, in locker doors or on barracks walls, of Betty Gable or Rita Hayworth. The *Daily News* reprinted the complete text of the letter written by Christine to her parents, George, Sr., and Florence Jorgensen. . . . In it, Christine described the pain and secrecy involved in her decision to leave for Denmark and undergo two years' worth of operations and hormone injections.

The *Daily News* first presented Jorgensen's story in a form that resembled fa-miliar feature articles of local and national interest that were common to the media of the late 1940s and early 1950s. The *Daily News* prided itself on being the first newspaper to break the story—indeed, the "story" of how Jorgensen's story was captured became a corollary tale to the earliest accounts of her celebrated trans-formation. According to the legend, which was reproduced in syndicated versions of Christine's story, *News* reporter Ben White heard about Jorgensen from a friend working at Rigs Hospital in Copenhagen, where Christine had been recuperating for several months following her surgery. Within a few days of White's initial inter-view and cover story, the location of Jorgensen's hospital room became public knowledge and the subsequent site of an international media circus. When major weeklies such as *Time, Life,* and *Newsweek* seized upon the Jorgensen story, they did not fail to reiterate White's professional account of how he "got" his news. . . .

But Jorgensen was, of course, no mere feature article in a newspaper tabloid story—and repeatedly the *News* announced and identified her as a former GI who had served honorably in World War II. This may have been due to the fact that the Korean War was already in full swing, so that the residual effects of the "soldier's story"—especially the feature story of the soldier returning home after many years abroad—had never really disappeared from the cultural imagination. But it may also have been because, in many ways, Jorgensen exuded all the insecurities of the conventional (and heterosexual) soldier's story. From the very outset, the newspaper constructed Christine as a celebrity news "item" firmly ensconced in the tradition of military reportage. . . . The *New York Times* followed the *News*'s lead with a dismissive, satiric presentation of Jorgensen that was echoed in its headline, "Bronx 'Boy' is Now a Girl: Danish Treatments Change Sex of Former Army Clerk." . . . When she returned from Copenhagen in February 1953, however, a *New York Times* headline announced "Miss Jorgensen Returns from Copenhagen: Ex-GI Back 'Happy to be Home,'" which made explicit the connection between Jorgensen's arrival back in the United States and the soldier's return home from war. *Newsweek* announced Christine's arrival at New York International Airport in an article called "Homecoming." According to the article, Christine was busily writing her memoirs for William Randolph Hearst's *American Weekly* in a plush suite at the Carlyle Hotel; she intended her life story to provide spiritual and emotional guidance for those suffering in what she called "the no-man's land of sex," which must rank as the ultimate civilian appropriation of military jargon. . . .

But to what degree, if at all, did these journalistic conventions change to accommodate a soldier who had been transformed into the opposite sex? Major periodicals tended to represent Jorgensen within the familiar discursive strategies of wartime reportage—not to mention the hyperbolic language of tabloid journalism—in order to legitimate Jorgensen's putative "realness" and "humanness." Photographs and feature articles made certain that the distinctions between Jorgensen's dual identities of ex-GI and aspiring starlet were highly negotiable, if not collapsed outright. According to a *News* article, "The Girl Who Used to Be a Boy Isn't Quite Ready for Dates," Christine was "a former GI who became a beautiful blonde with silken hair," a tendentious statement that allowed the reporter to endow the present Christine with erotic qualities ("silken hair") that she never could have possessed (or that he never could have openly acknowledged) in her "former" life as a soldier. Jorgensen's wistful, campy response—"I'm womanly enough to be glad that it is such nice blonde hair"—suggested that she knew only too well what it was like to avoid an explicit statement about another man's hair. None of these emphatic commentaries on her female authenticity seemed to conflict awkwardly with her military identity; indeed, even Christine's parents framed the discussion of their (new) daughter's transformation in terms of military service. In a *Daily News* piece, "Folks Proud of GI Who Became Blonde Beauty," father George declared that "[She] deserves an award higher than the Congressional Medal of Honor. She volunteered to undergo this guinea pig treatment for herself and to help others." Florence Jorgensen expressed the delight and frustration similar to that of many army mothers when she explained that, "You send a person over [to Europe] and you have a completely different person coming back." When a reporter asked if Jorgensen had enjoyed his service in the Army, Florence replied, "Who likes the Army? She was very brave. And she is a beautiful girl, believe me." . . .

The media's emphasis on Jorgensen's prior military identity seemed to commingle strangely with her new, postwar sexual identity and thus connected her not only to the genre of wartime reportage, but also to images of innocence and vulnerability that such journalism hoped to instill in its consumers. In a bizarre twist on the standard military hospital scene, *Time's* initial Jorgensen story, "The Great Transformation," described her "[l]ying in a hospital bed, her long yellow hair curling on a pillow . . . Christine widened her grey-blue eyes and lifted her hands in a surprised frightened gesture," which made her sound like a cross between a wounded fawn and a soldier recuperating after a bloody battle. . . . Jorgensen's surgical transformation may have seemed like the logical outcome of military service: it aligned her with the ways in which enfeebled soldiers were feminized, however temporarily, by their physical or mental inactivity. It was as if, by way of her conversion from agile manhood to fragile womanhood, Jorgensen stood symbolically for the vulnerable American male body besieged by a foreign power.

Jorgensen's reputation as a man who had become a woman was secured, not denied, because of these military embellishments on her identity. They ensured that she could be included within the bounds of the heterosexual imagination. Given the extent to which the news media embraced her as a "real" woman, Jorgensen's military associations co-existed peacefully with her so-called femininity. Several days after her initial appearance, the *Daily News* featured an article "Christine's GI Beau Pops Up: Boy, Wotta Gal!" which identified Jorgensen's boyfriend as Air Force Staff Sergeant Bill Calhoun. . . . Calhoun met Jorgensen while on a weekend pass from a U.S. Air Force base in Bentwater, England: "I was on leave in Copenhagen this Spring [of 1952] with nothing much to do. I saw this good looking blonde in a park. She looked like an American, and I decided to ask her." After she took him on a brief guided tour through the city, Calhoun had to depart, but the two agreed to exchange letters throughout the summer. In September, Calhoun returned to Copenhagen on an extended six-day pass to spend time with Christine "on the continent"; he remarked later that "I can honestly say that it was the best time of my life." Interestingly, Calhoun claimed that it was not until that December, when Jorgensen's surgical transformation was announced publicly, that he discovered his girlfriend's special *je ne sais quoi.* According to Calhoun, a friend brought the matter to his attention after noticing that a picture of "the sergeant's blonde pinup girl" resembled a woman featured in an issue of *Stars & Stripes,* the U.S. military's overseas newspaper. Although Calhoun admitted that finding out the truth about Christine was like "a trip to the moon," he defended her honor as well as his own integrity: "When I met her she was a girl and, as far as I'm concerned, she's a girl now. She's got a personality that's hard to beat, the best looks, best clothes, best features, and best body of any girl I ever met . . . I consider it a very intimate friendship." The *News* explained that "[Calhoun's] feelings for Christine have not changed but . . . he had 'taken a ribbing from boys on the base'—good naturedly."

. . . For immediate consumption, the story was framed as a military romance, in the purest sense of the phrase. A tale of the handsome young soldier who, on leave, discovered the girl of his dreams—the American girl . . . in whose honor Calhoun had vowed to defend and protect his country in the first place. Their story became so entrenched in both the romantic rituals of courtship and the generic conventions of military journalism that there was nothing that could be coded as "different" or "illicit" about their relationship. Indeed, quite to the contrary, the news of their relationship was so utterly banal that Bill's friends' mockery was presented as nothing more than the gentle derision that any heterosexual male might receive (and expect) from his peers.

Yet this is precisely what remains so intriguing about this episode: the fact that this conflation of Jorgensen's multiple identities seems to have provoked little or no discomfort in the military itself. Perhaps this was because the news media's focus on her new "female" status—. . . that she truly had become a "woman"—began to subsume all other aspects of her biography. In an article entitled "'I Could Have Gone for the He-She Girl,' Says Reporter," *Daily News* writer Paul Ifverson admitted to his readers that "Chris is now a girl I could have fallen in love with had I met her under different circumstances." Despite the fact that doctors were still trying to "help Christine adjust her still masculine mentality and to become truly feminine," Ifverson had no qualms about commenting on the "beautiful, emotional, feminine hands" of "the chic, obviously American girl." . . . [I]t was the attention Ifverson paid to Jorgensen's putative femininity that legitimated his infatuation and diffused the homoerotic tensions of his description. And it was the exact same attention Bill Calhoun paid to "the best looks, best personality, best features, and best body" of Jorgensen that sanctioned their publicly celebrated romance. A romance that, under "different circumstances" (i.e., that of an open, same-sex couple), would have surely branded Calhoun a homosexual and forced him to leave the Air Force via courtmartial or dishonorable discharge. . . .

While Jorgensen was not, anatomically speaking, a woman—this was not known publicly—her identity could be affirmed culturally as the material apotheosis of postwar popular culture. . . . [T]he *Daily News*'s [headline] . . .—"Ex-GI Becomes Blonde Beauty"—satisfied the binary terms on which American postwar culture understood gender and helped to explain what those terms actually meant to begin with. The ubiquitous, recurring [theme] of "Americanism" throughout her early case history not only served to temper Jorgensen's sexual ambiguity, but also became part of the inviolable bulwark of domestic, nationalistic propaganda that could be used to justify why wars were waged and why men's lives were lost in the first place.

. . . Clearly, the media's attention upon her "naturally" female character traits gave a conceptual framework for the physical and even, perhaps, the philosophical dilemmas posed by her new identity. Such attention also served to assuage the confusion voiced by some of the more disconcerted members of the press, who were unable to imagine Jorgensen's transformation. . . . During her first interview from her Copenhagen hospital room, *Time* reported that Christine was forced to field questions, such as "Do you sleep in a nightgown or pajamas?" "Do you still have to shave?" "Are your interests male or female? I mean, are you interested in, say, needlework, rather than a ball game?" As one reporter observed, albeit in a slightly more hostile tone, Jorgensen "lit a cigarette like a girl, husked 'Hello' and tossed off a Bloody Mary like a guy, then opened her fur coat. Jane Russell has nothing to worry about." In this sense, Jorgensen's external features were the most vigorously contested aspect of her personality. . . .

But far from being manufactured passively by news agencies or journalistic conventions, Jorgensen herself played an extremely important part in the production and dissemination of her own identity. . . . Jorgensen herself was amazingly good at how she dressed and what she said in public. After her return from Copenhagen, the *New York Times* noted that, "wearing a loose fitting nutria coat and carrying a mink cape over one arm, the blonde woman declared: 'I'm happy to be home. What American woman wouldn't be?'" In this passage, Jorgensen's poised gesture, expensive and tasteful ensemble, and quick wit—all of which seem endowed with a self-consciously, campy gay flourish— . . . served as a kind of physical rhetoric that allowed her to sit comfortably within the parameters of the heterosexual imagination. We cannot reasonably dispute Jorgensen's authority as a "woman" in these passages because she knew exactly how to present herself, both verbally and somatically, to "pass" according to the presumed cultural terms of American womanhood. . . . The *Daily News* reported that Jorgensen was "[d]ressed in a sophisticated tailored black suit . . . Christine used pearls as the only jewelry to relieve the severe black of her costume. A pearl cluster adorned the side of her black hat and another cluster her high-collared blouse. Pearl earclips added the final, brightening touch . . . [She was] manifestly pleased at the attention bestowed on her feminine charm."

If the dominant culture seemed to scrutinize Jorgensen unceasingly, it was because her behavior self-consciously confused or collapsed those social gestures and mannerisms that, in the 1950s, were thought to reveal the outward signs or movements of masculinity and femininity. Comments such as "I am very happy to be a woman" and "I'm just a natural girl" were strategies of self-promotion through which Christine intended to challenge and parody the assumptions that people brought, often cynically, to her new life. . . . Her clothes, gestures, and physical presence became, in a way, openly dramatized "events" that were buttressed ultimately by the media's perpetual retelling or re-enactment of the myths and secrets that surrounded her life story. Jorgensen's newly constructed persona also functioned as a public disavowal of her former male identity, of her former life as a soldier, and of whatever physical or psychological male attributes with which she still felt burdened. Whether intended or not, Jorgensen's self-generated female virtues and her self-styled conception of vampish, womanly wiles distanced her not only from the dangerous and subversive sexual implications of her surgery, but also from her unglamorous, unsexy former life as the son of a Bronx carpenter.

But clothing and mannerisms were only part of Jorgensen's strategy to authenticate herself as a legitimate woman. . . . Although she may have performed a convincing and coherent gender identity through her external appearance, it was on the question of Christine's soul that, for all intents and purposes, the jury was still hung. The letter that Jorgensen wrote to her parents in the summer of 1952 . . . speaks . . . to many of the questions of authenticity and performativity raised by Jorgensen's public displays and announcements.

At first glance, the letter bears an unfaltering resemblance to what is now called, in popular parlance, a "coming out" letter: that is, it is a claim, defense, or partial explanation for her struggle with, and triumph over, her sexual identity. "Right from the beginning," Jorgensen announced, "I realized that I was working toward the release of myself from a life I knew would always be foreign to me. Just how does a child tell its parents such a story as this?" But given the delicacy, poignancy, and emotional investment that one would normally expect from such a life-altering document, the narrative content of Jorgensen's letter is anything but private or domestic. Nothing in the letter strikes one as terribly colloquial or inaccessible in the way intimate family correspondence often is; that is, no editorial annotations are necessary to preserve Christine's original meaning. "Sometimes a child is born and to all outward appearances seems to be of a certain sex. During childhood, nothing is noticed; but at the time of puberty, where the sex hormones come into action, the chemistry of the body seems to take an opposite turn and chemically the child is not of the supposed sex, but rather of the opposite sex. . . . I was one of those people. . . . It was not an easy fact to face but only for the happiness it brought me I should not have had the strength to go through these two years. . . . I am still the same old Brud, but, my dears, nature made a mistake which I have had corrected and now I am your daughter."

The public quality of Jorgensen's prose—honest, familiar, linear, reassuring— was more than simply calculated to mitigate the confusion and anxieties produced presumably by her physical appearance. The letter's goal was to locate and seize the voice of reason and the language of confession. . . . Jorgensen's letter invoked this generic language and tone precisely because she herself expected—and rightly so—that this was what her readers, parents and tabloids alike, would want to hear in a description of a postoperative "sex change" recipient. . . .

In these and other passages, Christine demonstrated her obvious compulsion to explain herself and choose a singular life from the enigmatic haze of her formerly ambiguous gender identity. . . . She wrote, "Life is a strange affair and seems to be stranger as we experience more of it . . . [we] strive through science to answer the great question of 'Why'—Why did it happen, where did something go wrong, and, last but not least, what can we do to prevent it and cure it if it has already happened." . . . Jorgensen's prose in these passages took on an almost spiritual dimension: representing her surgery as a type of religious conversion, Christine could describe her struggle as a triumph of spirit over flesh, wherein she chose to alter, through the miracle of modern science, the poor hand she had been dealt in life. One might even say that Jorgensen's decision to rename herself "Christine," and not "Georgette," "Georgia," or "Georgina," functioned, like self-conscious performances of her femininity, as a kind of resurrection. . . .

Whatever other qualities it possessed, transparent or otherwise, Jorgensen's writing here was without doubt a work of confession, of explanation, revelation, and personal transformation. . . . [H]er "confession" of innocence and her presumption of authenticity . . . seemed to replicate the rhetoric of other confessional tracts popularized during the immediate postwar period, especially during the rise of the House Committee on Un-American Activities (HUAC) and the onset of domestic anti-Communist propaganda. . . .

. . . Her physical conversion to a new body did not simply emulate the act of confession, but *was* the very act of confession: the creation of the authentic private body and authentic public identity that she had so eagerly sought from the very beginning. The surgery—like the letters she sent home, or like the perpetual exhibition of her femininity—was the material proof of Jorgensen's redemption for her former life as a man.

On 20 April 1953, *Time* ran a lengthy article entitled "The Case of Christine":

> For a while, having achieved notoriety, she was Manhattan's No. 1 glamour girl. . . . Last week came the revelation that Christine Jorgensen was no girl at all, only an altered male.

Within several days of *Time*'s announcement, the media descended upon the Jorgensen case and exposed her secret to an extremely disenchanted and visibly offended

American popular audience. Her "secret"—the fact that she had not undergone "real" surgical conversion from one sex to the other—made her physical and rhetorical performances more than patently unreal: they betrayed her as nothing more than an unmitigated sham. But had Jorgensen really betrayed the public's trust and confidence? Had she blatantly lied to them or misled them? Or was she merely caught within the ideological nets of the Cold War[?] . . .

After April, references to her former military life and professions of her female authenticity began to vanish and were replaced by the sober opprobrium of rational science. A May 1953 *Newsweek* confirmed that "[l]atest medical testimony seems to indicate that the now celebrated Christine Jorgensen is not a hermaphrodite, not a pseudohermaphrodite, and not a female. The former George Jorgensen is a castrated male." The interesting continuum of biologically coded gender identities provided by the article (and the pragmatic reiteration of her given male name) not only suggested the degree to which Jorgensen had previously avoided scientific scrutiny, but also demonstrated how control over the word "testimony" had shifted ultimately from Jorgensen to that of the medical profession. As a legitimate woman, even as a legitimate hermaphrodite who had found ways to valorize her new identity and gain public acceptance, Jorgensen's personal narrative had inspired the cultural imagination with the kind of warm, familial comfort that seemed anathema to the cold vernacular of surgery or psychiatry. But as an exposed, illegitimate woman—and perhaps, more importantly, an illegitimate *man*—Christine's secret had betrayed more than just the trust and goodwill of the American public. Later references to Jorgensen labeled her a "fugitive" who had been "emasculated" to "suit his inclinations," and descriptions of Jorgensen were based, as *Time* related, on "more pity than facts."

Although Jorgensen's spectacular status as "the most talked about girl in the world" disappeared, what did *not* disappear, as a consequence of her public exposure, was her status as a medical exhibit. During the spring of 1953, she was offered a contract with a prominent Las Vegas casino to perform in a supper club-cabaret at a weekly salary of $12,000. Her act consisted of singing show tunes, narrating a photographic slide show of her two years spent in Copenhagen, and doing what [British writer] Quentin Crisp remembers as "jaunty little dance numbers, although she couldn't sing or dance to save her life." The cabaret show culminated with Jorgensen parading around on stage dressed in a Wonder Woman costume and knee-high boots while holding ignited sparklers. Although one is tempted to read her performance as Wonder Woman, the all-American comic book heroine who assisted the Allied Forces during World War II, as a reference to her former military identity, the performance also demonstrates that Jorgensen could only earn her salary after 1953 by playing exaggerated cartoon roles that highlighted her as a cultural and medical oddity. . . . Jorgensen's career move to Las Vegas seems, in retrospect, the only possible option suited to her new public persona as a performing freak. For better or worse, she became a refugee trapped forever in the cultural "no-man's land" between risqué entertainment and high kitsch.

By June, Jorgensen jokes had become positively *de rigueur:* comedy routines, among other forms, were the most visible public manifestations of animosities directed at Christine. A summer 1953 broadcast of the *Jack Benny Show* included a sketch in which Benny and Bob Hope, dressed as jungle explorers, capture a tiger that when reversed is revealed to be a leopard. . . . Hope, taking full advantage of the immediacy provided by early live television, remarked to an especially anxious Benny that the tiger "must have gone to a veterinarian in Denmark. . . . He had his paw on his hip when I shot him. . . . Look, his claws have been manicured." . . . Hope's reiteration of "he" and "him" . . . [and] improvised line about "manicured claws" demonstrated the logical progression of intolerance subsequent to Jorgensen's eviction from the closet of female authenticity—"he" was nothing more than a limp-wristed sissy who indulged in female activities of vanity and external decoration. . . .

. . . Not only did such sketches transform her into the butt of jokes about gay behavior (she was certainly not the first, nor would she be the last), but they implicitly demoted her to the level of transvestite/homosexual/deviant, a suspect and criminal category that denied her any of the privileges of womanhood—however socially circumscribed in 1953—to which she so conspicuously aspired. After her exposure, Christine Jorgensen did not cease to be a novelty; on the contrary, the media shaped her social identity to conform to the demonized status of other homosexuals, who were ceaselessly identified throughout the 1950s as a scourge against American family values, national security, and the moral hygiene of the body politic.

. . . The very act of outing Jorgensen, as it were, served the same impulses for Cold War culture as had the act of praising her female authority and feminine wiles six months earlier. When Jorgensen had been identified as a "real" woman, it would have been unthinkable for media pundits to put her under any kind of scrutiny. Considering the decorum of 1950s public culture, which dictated what was proper or improper to discuss in the public sphere, to question Jorgensen's female authenticity openly would have been an inappropriate social transgression far too "indelicate" for a lady of Jorgensen's glamorous stature to endure. But when medical experts intervened to demystify the tenets of Jorgensen's putative "womanhood" for popular audiences, they exposed her as an "altered male"—and, later, a "morbid" transvestite. . . .

[But what,] after all, had been *discovered* and consequently *exposed* by the Jorgensen case? The dangerous duplicity of a homosexual transvestite who wanted to be known only as a woman? Or the embarrassed homoerotic imagination of American postwar culture that invested Jorgensen with utopian dreams and domestic fantasies that she could never fulfill?

Popular Sociology, Reading, and Coming Out

JEFFREY ESCOFFIER

In the fall of 1960, I drove to my first day of college with a young man with whom I was in love. Although I had already had a couple of homosexual affairs in high school, I had not yet identified myself as a homosexual. I was worried that I was queer, but I thought (perhaps hoped is more accurate), "Who knows? Maybe I'm bisexual." I had as yet no knowledge of the gay world. I knew that there were

Jeffrey Escoffier, "Homosexuality and the Sociological Imagination: Hegemonic Discourses, the Circulation of Ideas, and the Process of Reading in the 1950s and 1960s," *American Homo: Community and Perversity* (Berkeley: University of California Press, 1998), 79–98, 244–248. Copyright © 1998 The Regents of the University of California. Reprinted by permission of the University of California Press.

cruising spots and bars, but I was not very brave and had not had any casual sexual encounters. My homosexual feelings were about love; homosexual sex seemed like only a pleasant, but also anxiety-producing, by-product of these profound feelings for other males. How did I eventually figure out that I was homosexual, find a way out of my closet, and enter the social world of other homosexuals?

It took almost ten years before I entered and joined the gay world fully. Before this happened, I embarked on a rather prolix process of learning to identify myself as homosexual. I started this process by reading, by searching through the available discourse for the knowledge I needed. Eventually, by adopting positive representations and rejecting homophobic ones, I identified myself as a homosexual. There were no maps to guide an earnest young homosexual through the quagmire of discourses dominated by medical and psychiatric theories. Only now, some thirty years later, do I begin to see the patterns that the discourses formed as I try to understand the role that the popular sociological books on homosexuality played.

During the early 1960s, I read my way through the literature on homosexuality. Meanwhile, notions that homosexuals had a social world of their own, even a community, circulated through the hodgepodge of discourses regulating interpretations of homosexuality, whether popular, psychological, legal, or literary. This "discovery" of the homosexual subculture was increasingly accompanied by the idea that homosexuality was a benign variation of sexual behavior. Thus, three very different sources influenced my socialization into "the homosexual role" (as sociologist Mary McIntosh called it): the hegemonic discourses on homosexuality, new ideas about homosexual identity and community, and my own rather idiosyncratic reading.

One of the most important developments for lesbians and gay men in the 1950s and 1960s was the increasing appearance of public representations that revealed the social dimension of gay life. For homosexual women and men living relatively isolated lives, discovering that the gay world had an enduring pattern of symbolic interaction and social interrelations was no inconsequential event. Lesbians or gay men had to find a way out of their individual isolation into such a social world, even if they only did so through their intellects or imaginations at first.

For this reason, discourses such as those in popular sociology books and articles had all the more significance. These were homosexualizing discourses; they provided new categories and interpretations of social knowledge about gay life, as well as new categories of self-interpretation and presentation of an individual's identity. . . .

It is almost impossible to know what effect the popular sociology literature had on homosexuals themselves—there were no surveys and no one collected readership statistics or sales figures to tell us who or how many people read these books. Because I was a young man coming to terms with my homosexuality at that time, I will use myself as a piece of evidence in gauging the significance of this small body of publications.

During the 1950s, the sway of conformity in American society demonstrated the power of the social. The ideology of conformism constructed everyday social life in postwar America. The emerging homosexual identity depended on this experience of conformism, which both denied homosexuality and yet, at the same time, created the conditions that made it possible. . . .

In the year of Stonewall, the psychiatric discourse on homosexuality was hegemonic. Three years later, Allen Young noted how few books about homosexuality were available in the average bookstore or public library. Of those few, virtually all had been written by "six shrinks" whom Young placed "in the ranks of the worst of war criminals." . . . In contrast, "The only pro-gay book of the 1950s, Donald Cory's *The Homosexual in America,* was published by a tiny publishing house and was generally unavailable." Young starkly juxtaposed the powerful but repressive and antihomosexual psychoanalytic literature to the more affirmative, though still somewhat ambivalent, literature of popular sociology about the homosexual community. . . .

    . . . In two ways, these writers refashioned homosexuality as a social phenomenon, rather than a purely psychological or individual one. First, they defined homosexuality as a *social problem,* ambiguously framing it either as an issue of homosexuals' social adjustment or as a matter of eliminating prejudice against homosexuals. Second, these writers publicly recognized the existence of a homosexual social world. . . .

    Immediately after World War II, homosexuality emerged in Americans' public consciousness with surprising vigor. The controversy in 1948, after Alfred Kinsey reported widespread incidence of homosexual experience, firmly established homosexuality as a public issue. In the early 1950s, Senator McCarthy reinforced this with his highly publicized witch-hunt to fire homosexuals, as well as communists, from government employment. These two events alone probably made homosexuality an issue in American public life more than any other source.

    Not only did Kinsey publish his report at the end of the 1940s, but many fictional works about homosexuality appeared at that time as well. Most such fiction was published in only the last two years of that decade—1948 and 1949. Homosexuality's threat to the postwar social order, as well as the plight of homosexuals, was extensively examined in novels, plays, and popular magazines. In his comparative study of the writers from the two world wars, John Aldridge argued that post–World War II writers (such as John Horne Burns, Gore Vidal, Paul Bowles, Norman Mailer, Truman Capote, and Merle Miller) had to compensate for Hemingway's and Fitzgerald's exhaustion of the modernist tradition by developing "new subject matter which [had] not been fully exploited in the past and which, therefore, still [had] emotive power. They . . . made two important discoveries in this area—homosexuality and racial conflict."

    Images of the gay social world also began to surface in the mass media. Three of the more notable examples were: the famous gay bar scene in the popular 1962 Hollywood movie *Advise and Consent,* which was the first representation of gay life in movies since the Production Code was adopted in the 1930s; the 1964 *Life* magazine article called "Homosexuality in America"; and the 1969 *Esquire* article titled "The New Homosexual."

    Nevertheless, throughout the 1950s and early 1960s, the literary and popular sociology discourses on homosexuality were overshadowed by psychoanalysis, which remained the hegemonic discourse. The Kinsey reports, for example, had almost no impact on psychoanalytic discussions. In fact, the psychoanalytic profession's writing on male homosexuality throughout the 1950s and early 1960s took on an ever more moralistic tone and tended increasingly to reflect conventional social values.

The political hysteria of McCarthyism exacerbated the postwar demand for a return to an idealized version of prewar American life. The political turmoil and anxieties of the late 1940s and early 1950s provoked reactions on a number of fronts, including Hollywood film noir, which depicted postwar anxieties about how returning war veterans could fit into American life; the theater of Arthur Miller and Tennessee Williams; and the outpouring of publications by intellectuals on the psychological pressures of conformism and the problem of alienation.

Critical writing on the psychological and sociological consequences of conformism served as an important bridge to the discovery of the gay social world. Postwar conformism emphasized the norm and stigmatized the deviant—for instance, the homosexual. In this period, an academic literature on the sociology of deviance also emerged. Initially, deviance was interpreted as resulting from psychological maladjustment.

One man forcefully and articulately opposed this understanding of deviance, however. Psychoanalyst Robert Lindner was best known as the author of a book-length case history called *Rebel without a Cause: The Story of a Criminal Psychopath* (the movie of the same name shares little more than the title itself). In a series of essays first published in 1956 as *Must You Conform?* Lindner explored the issues of rebellious youth, political dissent, educational theory, and homosexuality.

Lindner saw homosexuality as a "solution to the conflict between the urgency of the sexual instincts and repressive efforts brought to bear upon sexual expression by the reigning sex morality." He concluded then, "The condition is . . . a reaction of non-conformity, a rebellion of the personality that seeks to find—and discovers—a way in which to obtain expression for the confined erotic drives. . . . It seems that the issue of sexual conformity is raised more acutely and at an earlier period than it is with heterosexuals."

Although Lindner promoted rebellion against conformity and criticized prejudice against homosexuals, he also claimed, "The proposal that homosexuality is directly related to sex-conformance pressure offers the hope that it can be eradicated." He believed that "homosexuality is the source of immense quantities of unhappiness and frustration of individuals and a chronically irritating generator of intrahuman hostility." . . .

Lindner devoted his life to combating one of the dominant myths of the 1950s and early 1960s—that nonconformity and mental illness are synonymous. Clearly, however, he was unable to disentangle himself from the psychoanalytic interpretation of homosexuality long enough to endorse unequivocally the homosexual revolt against the socially constructed ethos of conformity. Nor could he support the emergence of the homosexual social world. . . .

The ambivalence underlying the critique of conformism provided no useful way for most homosexuals to grapple with their identities. Given this ambivalence, it seemed impossible either to acknowledge their homosexuality actively, thereby suffering the rejection of a conformist society, or to view themselves as unhappy and frustrated rebels who should give up such a hopelessly negative form of revolt.

In discussing homosexuality, neither the critical discourse on conformity and alienation nor mainstream journalism and the mass media could escape the powerful psychological and cultural norms that dominated American social life in this period. In addition, acknowledging homosexuality as a social problem did not immediately provide the symbolic capital necessary to banish the stigmatizing norms of mainstream American culture. Only exploring the existing social life of homosexuals could provide public categories of social knowledge about this everyday reality.

During the 1950s and 1960s, popular sociology books frequently made the bestseller list. *The Lonely Crowd* (1950) by David Reisman, *The Organization Man* by William Whyte (1956), C. Wright Mills's *The Power Elite* (1956), Robert Lindner's *Must You Conform?* (1956), Vance Packard's *The Hidden Persuaders* (1957), Paul Goodman's *Growing up Absurd* (1960)—these books, which were all profoundly critical of the status quo and conformism, had tremendous influence on the American politics and culture of the period. They all grew out of a deep sense of frustration and were motivated by the possibility of social change. All of them recognized the growing desire for social reform in American life. Homosexuality was ripe for popular sociology. From 1951 through 1968, the year before the Stonewall riots, almost a dozen books were published that portrayed the social world of the homosexual. Addressed to the general public, these popular sociology books explored homosexuality as a *social* problem—"perhaps *the most serious undiscussed problem* in the United States today," in the words of Martin Hoffman, author of *The Gay World*. . . .

Throughout this period, psychological works, which often treated homosexuality as an individualized pathological form of sexual behavior, remained the most influential nonfiction genre that addressed homosexuality for a general audience. The new popular sociology approach marked a growing awareness that homosexual communities existed in American cities. Among the popular sociology authors, both Donald Cory and Martin Hoffman knew that the existence and development of a gay social world implied something new and important about homosexuality.

Although two of the popular sociology books explored lesbian life, this discourse was preoccupied primarily with male homosexuality. The emphasis on male homosexuality reflected a widespread preoccupation in U.S. society with its implications for masculinity. An obsession with effeminacy and its significance in gay male life pervades all the books that address male homosexuality. These authors commonly viewed homosexual desires as a threat to a man's masculinity. . . . It is certain, though, that effeminacy, camp humor, and drag were prominent aspects of gay life in the 1950s and early 1960s. We also know that fear of effeminacy prohibited many men from acknowledging their homosexuality and entering the gay social world.

The first work to reveal the social world of homosexuals came, naturally enough, from within the homosexual community itself. Donald Webster Cory, the pseudonymous alter ego of Edward Sagarin (who later, ironically, became an extremely homophobic critic of gay liberation), published the first exploration of homosexual society in 1951. Between 1951 and 1964, Cory and his occasional collaborator John P. LeRoy published the four most thorough and sophisticated books about homosexual life to predate Stonewall. Cory's books covered the full range of gay life—relationships, the social origins of homophobia, the role of gay bars, the significance of the gay contribution to culture, and a critique of the psychological theory of homosexuality. Cory's books probably never reached a very large public because they were all published by small presses, although at least one, *The Lesbian in America,* was reprinted as a mass-market paperback by MacFadden Books in 1965.

It would be interesting to know what concrete social situation existed in 1951 that enabled Donald Webster Cory to write and publish *The Homosexual in America*—the first work of American popular sociology on homosexuality. . . . Cory's book, an ambitious defense of the homosexual way of life, derives its strength from his fundamental belief that homosexual patterns of behavior are socially constructed. Moreover, Cory quite self-consciously views the existence of a gay social world as the necessary foundation of homosexuals' happiness. In his concluding chapter, he directly addresses his fellow homosexuals. "Do not fear the group life of the gay world," is one of his most ardent pleas. "In the gay life," he urges us, "you can be yourself and form friendships with those who know what you are and who accept you and love you. . . . The group life is not a thing of shame, a den of iniquity. It is a circle of protection, a necessary part of a minority society."

But even such a profoundly sociological approach could not escape the hegemony of psychiatric discourse. In *The Homosexual in America,* Cory engages in a dialogue with mainstream American society and confronts its homophobia (a word not yet at his disposal). Although he addresses his fellow gay men (and to a much lesser extent lesbians), he devotes considerable energy to challenging the discourse of psychiatry. Over and over again, Cory takes on notions about homosexuals that derive from psychiatry—the causes of homosexuality, whether it is possible to cure homosexuals, whether sublimation allows people to avoid a homosexual way of life—and offers many strong and cogent criticisms of the psychiatric arguments.

If Cory displays any ambivalence, it is in the way he dismisses certain aspects of gay life that he finds negative. His discussion of effeminacy overlooks the cultural centrality of camp, and he dismisses as a stereotype the importance of queens in the gay life of the 1940 and 1950s. He glosses over the significance of alcoholism. There is no discussion at all of potentially embarrassing topics, such as sexually transmitted diseases or public sex in restrooms. The major tragedy of gay life is, in Cory's view, the need for concealment. He interprets many of the psychological characteristics and social patterns of gay life as resulting from the stigma and the need for secrecy.

In the middle of this twenty-year publishing arc, Jess Stern produced *The Sixth Man* (on male homosexuality) and *The Grapevine* (on lesbians). They were published by Doubleday, one of the largest American publishing houses at that time. They also both appeared in mass-market paperback form. A former reporter for the *New York Daily News* and an editor of *Newsweek,* Jess Stern claimed that his study of male homosexuals, *The Sixth Man,* "is as unbiased a report . . . as a disinterested reporter could make it." Despite his stated intention to adopt a neutral journalistic approach, however, Stern's books displayed ambivalence, hypocrisy, and contempt toward homosexuals.

With a false liberalism, he set out to report on "the everyday aspects of the homosexual's world—his social adjustment to himself, his job, his friends, and his family—but even more importantly, perhaps, the non-homosexual's problem with him." Homosexuality, in Stern's view, was a tragedy for homosexuals and society. The homosexual world, he wrote, was "a glittering make-believe world—at times tragic, sometimes ludicrous, even comical." The dire aspect of gay life was so apparent to him that he announced, "I had yet to meet a truly happy homosexual." This very idea of tragedy encapsulated the moralistic liberal's patronizing expression of sympathy and contempt.

. . . Virtually every chapter recounted the negative impact of homosexuality on American life. Stern devoted several chapters to the role of homosexuals in the fashion industry. These were the most vicious chapters in the book. He believed that homosexuals had an overwhelmingly bad influence on the fashion industry; in his view, they promoted fashion models who were beautiful but too thin and flat-chested, all because homosexuals hated women and wanted them to look like boys. Other chapters examined the impact of homosexuals on the entertainment, white-collar, and fitness industries, as well as the marriages of closeted gay men to unsuspecting women. Everywhere, from his perspective, the presence of homosexuals undermined the norms of gender roles and sexual decency because homosexuals were secretive and vindictive.

Stern was not always able to shape his material to reflect his gloomy, conspiratorial vision, however. Occasionally, he encountered a gay person who was not ambivalent about being a homosexual, but he attempted to use such examples to demonstrate homosexuals' antisocial ethos. At one point, he interviewed a "typical American college boy" whom he found it difficult to believe was gay: "His face looked out alertly, a slight smile playing on sensitive lips. His hair a crewcut, his eyes clear. . . ." His conversation with the college boy, Frank, could almost be a dialogue between a young gay militant of the 1990s with a tough-minded liberal from the 1950s.

> "I'm quite happy being a homosexual. I don't want to be anything else."
> He seemed amused. "You remind me of my father," he said.
> I pointed out that I had understood he actually was not a confirmed homosexual, and could go either way. "You certainly don't look the part," I said.
> "You mean," he said almost mockingly, "I have a chance."
> He seemed to be enjoying himself. "If instead of trying to help us, people would just leave us alone, there would be no problem. . . ."
> "If everybody felt like you," I said, "it might be the end of the human race."
> "And what would be so horrible about that?" he asked with an engaging grin. "After all, if everything we read is true, we're on the verge of destruction any day, anyway."
> "Don't you feel there's a certain morality involved?"
> "I don't see how I'm being immoral by being with somebody who wants to be with me. There's no force or coercion, and I am not picking on small children."
> . . . "Don't you ever wonder whether you're kidding yourself?"
> His eyes went blank. "I don't understand."

"Actually, haven't you chosen a way of life which is wrong, for purely selfish reasons, and are now trying to justify it philosophically?"

He smiled almost pityingly. "Why should I have to justify it at all?"

This young college student prefigured a new generation of homosexual men who were more and more visible in the books and magazine of the 1960s.

One of the most important contributions to the new discourse that built on the discovery of the social was Hendrik Ruitenbeek's anthology *The Problem of Homosexuality in Modern Society,* which Dutton published as a widely available quality paperback original. It captured perfectly the period's ambivalent mix of psychoanalysis and sociology. Ruitenbeek's anthology republished a series of classic psychoanalytic essays by Sandor Ferenczi, Abram Kardiner, and Clara Thompson on the theory of homosexuality. It also included Freud's famous and very positive statement, "Letter to an American Mother" about her son's homosexuality, Simone de Beauvoir's chapter from *The Second Sex* called "The Lesbian," and Evelyn Hooker's pathbreaking article on the psychologically well-adjusted homosexual. . . . Although Ruitenbeek's anthology had a more intellectual tone than any of the other popular sociology books, it was widely available in paperback. . . .

Popular sociology represented the discovery by both homosexuals and nonhomosexuals of an image of the gay social world—an imagined community. Both kinds of people read these books and articles "to find themselves" through a process of either identification or counteridentification. They read these works to sort out their relation to the imagined homosexual world of American society in the 1950s and 1960s. In many of these works, particularly those by authors who were not openly homosexual, even those that represented themselves as sympathetic, homosexuals' lives were presented as tortured and unfulfilled, at the very least because of social oppression.

Reading such an ambivalent discourse generated "misrecognitions" for the individual undergoing a process of homosexual identity formation. There were several different types of gay readers. Many, probably most, of the male homosexuals who were already familiar with the gay social world had found it by going to bars, by cruising parks and toilets, and through friends. The vast majority of homosexuals, however, were isolated and asocial members of the homosexual minority—they were in the closet. These closeted gay men used the popular sociology, literary, and psychoanalytic discourses to name themselves, describe themselves, judge themselves—and, by these means, to homosexualize themselves.

By the time I graduated from college in 1964, I was twenty-one years old. I had come to see myself as homosexual—"queer," as I often thought with a vacillating mixture of acceptance and self-contempt. I had still had no experience of the homosexual world itself, although I did have a number of homosexual affairs in college. I had put together my own representation of the homosexual world primarily from fictional works and books such as Hendrik Ruitenbeek's anthology.

During college, my main strategy of "consciousness raising" (or as we might say now, identity formation) was reading. For a young college student who had little contact (or even initially, little idea of how to have contact) with other homosexual men or the gay community, this was an essential way of learning about homosexuality. As [literary theorist] Roland Barthes observed, "Reading is steeped in Desire (or Disgust)."

Later, during summer vacations, I supplemented my reading by cruising in Washington Square Park. Reading and cruising are not such dissimilar techniques. Both require one to "read" signs and to construct a discourse that opens one to a knowledge of homosexualities and a long process of reconstruction of one's sense of self. Responding to or identifying with cultural themes and figures has helped people significantly to crystallize homosexual identities; for men, it has worked to take an interest in opera, female popular singers, or art, or even to have a strong disinterest in sports. . . . In this process of reading, as Barthes suggests, one rediscovers one's desires, fantasies, and even one's imagined place in society.

"My own private discourse" began when I had my first homosexual affair during the summer after my sophomore year of high school. Richie and I decided that we weren't fags as long as we didn't kiss—although we fucked and sucked. Did I really believe that I wasn't a fag if we didn't kiss? I don't think so, but I thought my agreeing with that statement would reassure Richie.

I have no memory of what led me to James Baldwin's *Giovanni's Room*. It was sometime later, after Richie and I had stopped seeing one another. It may have been an accident that I discovered it at the main library on Staten Island. *Giovanni's Room* was the most explicit rendering of homosexual love I had ever encountered. My vivid memory of some scenes dates from my first reading. In *Giovanni's Room,* Baldwin recounted the main character David's first homosexual affair as an adolescent. This affair was a transfigurative experience of love, but David says it also opened up a "cavern . . . in my mind, black, full of rumor, suggestion. . . . I could have cried, cried for shame and terror, cried for not understanding how this could have happened to me." After repeated flights from homosexual relationships, David becomes involved with a woman, Hella, only to fall in love once more with a man, Giovanni. Although Baldwin offered a positive portrait of homosexual love, it was doomed to fail, largely because the gay social world—haunted by the desperate search for sex—could not sustain it.

I began to look for other books that would help me understand myself. Soon I found *Advertisements for Myself* by Norman Mailer. It contained two essays—"The White Negro" and "The Homosexual Villain"—that gave me license to think more adventurously about my homosexuality.

"The Homosexual Villain" was a modest and candid piece that Mailer wrote for the homosexual rights magazine *One*. In the essay, Mailer examined the way he had characterized several villains in his novels as homosexuals. What particularly impressed me was his laudatory discussion of Donald Webster Cory's *The Homosexual in America*. "I can think of few books," Mailer wrote, "which cut so radically at my prejudices and altered my ideas so profoundly." Mailer realized that he had been closing himself off from understanding a very large part of life. He also acknowledged that Cory's book had helped him to realize that his anxieties about "latent homosexuality" had disappeared when he accepted homosexuals: "Close friendships with homosexuals had become possible without sexual desire or even sexual nuance—at least no more sexual nuance than is present in all human relations."

The other essay, "The White Negro," became my credo, my political manifesto. The essay was full of foolish, even repugnant things, but it also enunciated a philosophy of risk and psychological growth. It synthesized existentialism, the liberatory potential of jazz and black culture, sexual radicalism, and the violence of the psychopath. How often I would examine myself and strive to be one of those with the "knowledge that what is happening at each instant of the electric present is . . . good or bad for their cause, their love, their action, their need," and recognize that I was "moving through each moment of life forward into growth or backward into death."

"The White Negro" was a direct descendant of Robert Lindner's *Rebel without a Cause* (which Mailer quoted at length), for the white Negro was the hipster, the psychopath, the American existentialist. Where Lindner had been unwilling to endorse homosexuality as rebellion against conformity, however, Mailer wholeheartedly included homosexuality as one form of sexual radicalism. Mailer's discussions in these two essays—of the sexual radicalism of black culture, and of homosexuality—contributed to my growing consciousness of homosexuality's social implications.

Norman Mailer's vision of the pivotal role of black culture and its sexual radicalism encouraged me to look to the black experience for lessons relevant to my situation as a homosexual. This was further reinforced when I discovered, through Leslie Fiedler's *Love and Death in the American Novel,* the homoerotic tradition in American literature that paired a white man with a man of color—for example, Ishmael and Queequeg, Huck Finn and Jim. Fiedler's book was rather homophobic (which I was quite aware of at the time). . . . I was grateful, nevertheless, that he had identified homoerotic themes in American fiction. . . .

Exploring the homoerotic tradition in American literature provided a counterpoint to my other reading about black civil rights and black cultural politics, which allowed me to think through and politicize homosexual issues. Baldwin's homosexuality, and then the publication in 1962 of the essays that later made up *The Fire Next Time,* made him the perfect guide into my new homosexual "identity politics" (as it later came to be called). My awareness of the politics of identity was soon reinforced when "black power" emerged.

In those years, Baldwin explored the tragedy of difference, of divisions created by power and violence, of "definitions" of black and white, male and female, that we cannot transcend. In the novels and essays I read in this period, Baldwin seemed to explore the possibility of love and the difference that love might make in America's racial conflicts and in our sexual lives. He reached for "a region where there were no definitions of any kind, neither of color nor of male and female."

Although Baldwin rejected any relationship to "the gay community," he did believe that homosexuality was a legitimate form of love. Baldwin was deeply ambivalent about homosexuality, yet for me his ambivalence was productive. He helped me situate my thinking about it in light of the most important social issues of the day. Coming to terms with homosexuality was part of my relationship to politics and society. Baldwin's vision of love, Mailer's sexual politics, and the homoerotic current of American literature encouraged me to enter into relationships with black men, which I pursued, off and on, for fifteen years. Through my identification with Baldwin and my new sexual experiences, I began to think of myself as part of a minority—and the struggles of African Americans seemed linked to my own. . . .

At some point as a homosexual reader, I began to accept my task as a historical actor. My intellectual development found no outlet until I moved to New York City after graduating in 1964 and began acquiring more sexual experience. During the Summer of Love in 1967, I first walked hand-in-hand with a man on the Lower East Side and publicly socialized with other gay people. I vividly remember reading the July 3, 1969, issue of the *Village Voice* with its account of the Stonewall riots. In the following months, I began to come out to my friends. When I moved to Philadelphia in 1970, I went as an openly gay man and was active in the gay movement there. I had finally entered the gay social world.

FURTHER READING

David Allyn, "Private Acts/Public Policy: Alfred Kinsey, the American Law Institute and the Privatization of American Sexual Morality," *Journal of American Studies* 30 (1996): 405–428.

Beth Bailey and David Farber, *The First Strange Place: The Alchemy of Race and Sex in World War II Hawaii* (1992).

Brett Beemyn, ed., *Creating a Place for Ourselves: Lesbian, Gay, and Bisexual Community Histories* (1997).

Allan Bérubé, *Coming Out Under Fire: Gay Men and Women in World War II* (1990).

John D'Emilio, "Homophobia and the Trajectory of Postwar American Radicalism: The Career of Bayard Rustin," *Radical History Review* 62 (1994): 80–103.

————, "The Homosexual Menace," in Kathy Peiss and Christina Simmons, eds., *Passion and Power* (1989), 226–240.

————, *Sexual Politics, Sexual Communities: The Making of a Homosexual Minority in the United States, 1940–1970*, 2nd ed. (1998).

Rachel Devlin, "Female Juvenile Delinquency and the Problem of Sexual Authority in America, 1945–1965," in Sherrie A. Inness, ed., *Delinquents and Debutantes* (1998), 83–106.

John Howard, *Men Like That: A Southern Queer History* (1999).

Bernice L. Hausman, "Demanding Subjectivity: Transsexualism, Medicine, and the Technologies of Gender," *Journal of the History of Sexuality* 3 (1992): 270–302.

David K. Johnson, "'Homosexual Citizens': Washington's Gay Community Confronts the Civil Service," *Washington History* (Fall/Winter 1994–1995): 45–63, 93–96.

James H. Jones, *Alfred C. Kinsey: A Public/Private Life* (1997).

Janet Kahn and Patricia A. Gozemba, "In and Around the Lighthouse: Working-Class Lesbian Bar Culture in the 1950s and 1960s," in Susan Reverby and Dorothy O. Helley, eds., *Gendered Domains* (1993), 90–106.

Elizabeth Lapovsky Kennedy and Madeleine D. Davis, *Boots of Leather, Slippers of Gold: The History of a Lesbian Community* (1993).

Regina Kunzel, "Pulp Fictions and Problem Girls: Reading and Rewriting Single Pregnancy in the Postwar United States," *American Historical Review* 100 (1995): 1465–1487.

Matthew Lasar, "The Triumph of the Visual: Stages and Cycles in the Pornography Controversy from the McCarthy Era to the Present," *Journal of Policy History* 7 (1995): 181–207.

Elaine Tyler May, *Homeward Bound: American Families in the Cold War Era* (1988).

Leisa D. Meyer, *Creating GI Jane: Sexuality and Power in the Women's Army Corps During World War II* (1996).

Richard Meyer, "Rock Hudson's Body," in Diana Fuss, ed., *Inside/Out* (1991), 259–288.

Joanne Meyerowitz, "Women, Cheesecake, and Borderline Material: Responses to Girlie Pictures in the Mid-Twentieth-Century U.S.," *Journal of Women's History* 8 (Fall 1996): 9–35.

Joan Nestle, "Butch-Fem Relationships: Sexual Courage in the 1950s," *Heresies* 4 (1981): 21–24.

Esther Newton, *Cherry Grove, Fire Island: Sixty Years in America's First Gay and Lesbian Town* (1993).

Donna Penn, "The Meanings of Lesbianism in Postwar America," *Gender & History* 3 (Summer 1991): 190–203.

Geoffrey S. Smith, "National Security and Personal Isolation: Sex, Gender, and Disease in the Cold War United States," *International History Review* 14 (1992): 221–240.

Rickie Solinger, *"Wake Up Little Susie": Single Pregnancy and Race before Roe v. Wade* (1992).

CHAPTER
12

Sexual Revolution(s)

What was the sexual revolution? Its signs were widespread throughout the 1960s and into the 1970s. Single women increasingly embraced premarital sex, as witnessed in the immediate popularity of the birth control pill and the skyrocketing numbers of illegal abortions. By the late 1960s, colleges were ending "in loco parentis" rules and eliminating single-sex dorms. The Supreme Court struck down laws prohibiting interracial marriages. Sexual speech became more public. The courts ruled against anti-obscenity laws; such X-rated films as "Deep Throat" and "I am Curious (Yellow)" were box office hits, and Alex Comfort's The Joy of Sex *and other "how-to" manuals climbed the bestseller list. Sexual experimentation took many forms, from public nudity and "love ins" to group sex and spouse swapping. These examples suggest that the 1960s and early 1970s were indeed a time of startling discontinuity and a watershed in the social, political, and personal meaning of sexuality to Americans.*

Taking a longer perspective raises important historical questions. How "revolutionary" was this period? Many of these explosive changes had, in fact, been building since 1920: the increase in premarital sexual activity, use of contraceptives, an emphasis on sexual satisfaction in marriage, the emergence of gay and lesbian communities. Female nudity and sexual imagery had been gradually moving "above ground," from World War II "pin ups" to the publication of Playboy *in 1953. An evolution in attitudes and behavior formed the backdrop for the sexual revolution of the 1960s.*

Whose revolution was this? The sexual revolution took on many distinct meanings. Some groups, like the Sexual Freedom League, envisioned sexual liberation as a route to social revolution: erotic pleasure would liberate Americans from monotonous work, consumerism, and hypocrisy. By the late 1960s, however, the nascent feminist movement viewed the sexual revolution as a form of male domination and began to imagine a nonpatriarchal female sexuality. For gay men and many lesbians, the sexual revolution led to a political movement to liberate homosexuals from invisibility and pathologizing definitions. Although feminist and gay organizations remain significant players on the stage of sexual politics, ironically it may have been commercial interests—from "adult entertainment" to mainstream advertising—that gained the most from the sexual revolution.

■ D O C U M E N T S

As these documents show, the sexual revolution brought erotic life into public view
and debate. Yet Americans perceived the sexual revolution from many different vantage points. In his memoir, *The Motion of Light in Water* (Document 1), renowned
African-American author Samuel Delany described anonymous sex with men in the
early 1960s. In Document 2, David Mura wrote of "the internment of desire" as a
young Asian-American man masturbating to *Playboy* and fantasizing about white
women. In Document 3, part of a longer essay on Chicanas in film, Rosa Linda
Fregoso, now a professor at the University of California, Davis, recalled the sexually
savvy and streetwise *pachucas*, "the girls my mother warned me about." *Pachucas*
predated the sexual revolution, but in the 1960s came to symbolize the possibilities
of Chicana female sexual assertion. For Mildred and Richard Loving and other interracial couples, the Supreme Court's ruling against "anti-miscegenation" laws in 1967
(Document 4) gave them freedom to love and marry across the color line. By the late
1960s some women began to re-evaluate the sexual revolution and respond collectively to women's specific needs. An underground abortion service called "Jane"
served many Chicago women before the legalization of abortion in 1974, as a former
member recollected in Document 5. Anselma Dell-Olio spoke for many feminists
when she asserted in Document 6 that "the sexual revolution wasn't our war" and
demanded women's sexual liberation. In a similar vein, Carl Wittman issued "A Gay
Manifesto" (Document 7) that censured heterosexism and called for a sweeping
vision of gay liberation.

1. Samuel Delany Describes Communal Public Sex in New York in the Early 1960s

I woke, late, hot, alert, slid out of bed, and turned on the light. What time, I wondered, could it be? I didn't feel at all like going back to sleep, so I dressed in my
jeans, sneakers, rolled up my shirt-sleeves, and went outside. The street was far
cooler than the apartment. Slurred here and there with dark water, already mostly
dry, the sidewalk was empty. It was probably after eleven, if not midnight. I crossed
to go down the alley and head over through the Village, making for the waterfront.

By Christopher Street, I realized it was even later than I'd thought. Clocks
glimpsed through the dark windows of this liquor store and that dry cleaner had
confirmed it was after three.

At one, at two, the activity among the trucks tended to fall off—except for
weekends. And even then, there was always some change of tenor.

Sometimes to walk between the vans and cabs was to amble from single sexual
encounter—with five, twelve, forty minutes between—to single sexual encounter.
At other times to step between the waist-high tires and make your way between the
smooth or ribbed walls was to invade a space at a libidinal saturation impossible to

Samuel R. Delany, *The Motion of Light in Water: Sex and Science Fiction Writing in the East Village,
1957–1965* (New York: Arbor House, 1988), 129–130. Copyright © 1988 by Samuel R. Delany. Reprinted
by permission of the Author and Henry Morrison, Inc., his agents.

describe to someone who has not known it. Any number of pornographic film-makers, gay and straight, have tried to portray something like it—now for homosexuality, now for heterosexuality—and failed because what they were trying to show was wild, abandoned, beyond the edge of control, whereas the actuality of such a situation, with thirty-five, fifty, a hundred all-but-strangers is hugely ordered, highly social, attentive, silent, and grounded in a certain care, if not community. At those times, within those van-walled alleys, now between the trucks, now in the back of the open loaders, cock passed from mouth to mouth to hand to ass to mouth without ever breaking contact with other flesh for more than seconds; mouth, hand, ass passed over whatever you held out to them, sans interstice; when one cock left, finding a replacement—mouth, rectum, another cock—required moving only the head, the hip, the hand no more than an inch, three inches.

That evening, because it was late, because it was not the weekend, as I crossed under the highway, I expected to find the former. But because activity always increased just before dawn, because the rain had kept people in at the night's start, the latter is what I stepped into.

It was engrossing; it was exhausting; it was reassuring; and it was very human. At one point I heard someone saying to one guy who, I guess, got overexcited, "Okay, okay—calm down now. Relax for a moment. Just take it easy." And later, when I emerged into a small opening, I saw, sitting on the back of one van, a tall black guy, in jeans and a red T-shirt, about thirty, whom I'd seen there every night I'd ever come, but who never seemed to do anything, fanning himself with a folded newspaper and looking very pleased.

I vaulted up into the van and was caught by two guys ("You okay there?") steadying me, one of whom, I realized as I moved forward between him and someone else, was naked.

Later, pausing for minutes, I stood at the great beam along the edge of the water. Beyond the covered dock to the south, the sky was getting light. Looking to the west, I saw the black had taken a cobalt glaze. The water shook and shimmered with the cobalt reflection.

A little way down stood a white guy in his late twenties, early thirties. He wore workman's greens, short sleeves rolled up over muscular arms. He had one workshoe up on the weathered ten-by-ten that ran the concrete edging. He looked like a driver from one of the trucks. He saw me looking at him and beckoned me over. I walked down the few feet between us, and he squatted, then sat on the blackened wood, put one hand on my hip, and, with very thick fingers, tugged my fly open. He moved forward, and I took his head, his ears against my palms. His brown hair was pulling away from his temples and thinning over a coming bald spot.

He grinned up, then went down.

Looking over his head at the water, I felt very good and very tired. Running across the stretch of dawn river just below us, two nets, one of shadow, one of light, on the wrinkling and raveling blue interlaced, interpenetrated, pulled endlessly one out of the other.

It seemed for a moment that both would become one, or would reveal themselves to be two aspects, differently lighted, of a complex singularity . . .

2. David Mura Reflects on "The Internment of Desire" in the Mid-1960s

It was in eighth grade, sometime in the fall, a gray day, in late October, when I discovered my sexuality. This time period was the last I was ever to get in trouble at school for conduct. Through my grade school years, I was constantly being reprimanded for talking in school. Although I did well scholastically I always seemed to be mouthing off, making wisecracks. Given my more quiet nature as an adult, it's hard for me to convince friends now how absolutely obnoxious I could get then.

Were my actions in school a result of the strictness of my home life? My father had a second-generation immigrant's fierceness, and he still kept to some of the strictness of Japanese culture and schooling. I was not to be frivolous or to misbehave like other kids; I was constantly being admonished to "buckle down," and on my report cards my father would constantly write—in a second-generation sense of the formalities of English—"I have talked to David and he has assured me his deportment will improve." In essence, what he meant was: "I have spanked, I have beaten David, and have told him that more of the same will be coming if he doesn't shape up." Somehow, as evidenced by the F in deportment I was to get in science class that fall, these beatings never helped. But all this was about to change.

I am lying in bed. My room, on the second floor of our bi-level, is dark. My mother has gone to the store. I cross the hall to my parents' room, which looks so much like the bedrooms of my friends' parents. There's a dresser in Swedish modern, two mirrors at each end; a nightstand on both sides of the bed. A green quilted bedspread. Everything is neat, uncluttered, though not as neat and uncluttered as my parents' bedroom in later years (my mother's sense of aesthetic seemed gradually through the years to become more upper-class, cleaner, sparer, a yoking of her economic aspirations and her Japanese heritage).

I don't remember if I looked in the nightstands, though I know I did later. Instead, I slide open their closet. (It is a scene I've described often before, in poems, letters for my therapist, prose jottings.) The hangers all face one way, as do the shoes, lined precisely in a row. There's a gold quilted garment bag, about two feet wide. I slip my hands inside and—I don't know even now how I knew it was there, though my therapist, years later, remarked that news travels unconsciously in families, does not need the directness of speech—I pull it out. A *Playboy*. June 1964.

On the cover is a woman in white tights, curled inside a moon. Quickly, I open to the foldout. I have seen *Playboys* before, in my friend Terry Hoffberg's basement, in the locker room once at school. Each time I felt fascinated by them, drawn to them, at the same time, of course, feeling their forbidden nature, the sense of trespassing on something I can't name. But this is the first time I have seen one alone. The woman inside, Donna, is a blond, a UCLA coed; her breasts seem enormous. Though only eighteen, she seems frightfully older. Overwhelming, imposing in her beauty. (Years later, discovering her picture while in an X-rated secondhand bookstore, I feel disappointed; her body seems a bit bloated, chubby, her hairstyle crude, carrying the cardboard pompadoured chignons of an out-of-fashion era: the economy and fashion of desire.)

I sit down on my parents' bed. My penis is hard. I keep staring. I pull down my pants and look at my penis, fascinated by how big it is. I look at the glossy picture. How she leans on the edge of a red folding screen, over which a red blanket is draped, so that her body seems to be emerging from the act of undressing. She doesn't stare at the camera, it is me she's staring at. The curves of her breast, the dark brown of the nipples, float off the page, both attached to her body and detached, constituting a vision, a realm of their own. I make a game of pulling my foreskin tighter, trying to make my penis grew bigger. It too seems somehow detached, to take on a force of its own.

I look at the blue vein on the back of the shaft, the way it rises, can be seen through the skin. I feel this pleasure shooting through my body, a trembling I cannot control. A wave washes over me, another, a rending of my body from my consciousness, my consciousness from my surroundings, this instant from the continuum of time.

The moment I ejaculate I'm startled, overcome, staring at what shoots out of me, seeing, sensing that this is what explains the morning sheets, wet, sticky, cold. At the same time I feel I've done something wrong, something which should be kept secret; though I don't think I had any sense of invading my father's privacy, I know somehow I'm trespassing. But whatever frightened or guilty feelings arise, there also arises an urge to feel this pleasure again, to look at the pictures again, to experience this explosion inside. I bend down and wipe up the milk-white pool on the floor. I repeat the ritual. My secret life has begun.

Adolescence is when we learn the power of secrets and lies, when we learn to create a life apart from our parents. Through this act I had marked out an existence, a world of my own. But with this creation I felt no sense of power, because I had not created that existence, that world. It seemed to erupt from me or, in another sense, it created me. Certainly, it seems now impossible to talk of my life, of who I am, without the story of my sexual desires.

My discovery of sexuality was, I suppose, no different from that of many American adolescents. But the fervor with which I subsequently went back to this discovery, the endless, compulsive repetition of that act, marked me as different, though at the time I had no way of knowing this. I simply put the magazine back in my parents' closet, and again and again, waited for a chance to steal back, to take another look. In between I contented myself with the darkness under my covers, each morning when I woke up, each night when I went to bed. Two, four, six times a day. In a way my father's *Playboy* was like a stash of alcohol an adolescent alcoholic has discovered, only I didn't need that stash. All I needed was to be alone, behind a closed door.

Only now does it occur to me to think of how my father perceived these *Playboys*, why he bought them or what my mother thought. Did he too masturbate over them? Did my mother object to them and, if she did, did she voice this objection? How did he reconcile these pictures with his increasing participation during those years in our Episcopalian church?

All of these seem the expected questions an American son might ask in such a situation. But there is an added element here. My father was a Japanese American in a generation where Japanese Americans almost always married inside their race. I remember reading a journal my father kept when he was twenty-four and living in Chicago, working at a country club. In the clubhouse kitchen one night, he and a few of the other Nisei boys are talking about women. The line that sticks out in my memory went like this: "Mas has gone out with white girls, and he says it wasn't that bad." I'm surprised at this remark that dating white girls wasn't significantly different, and at the same time, I wonder if he could have expressed what those differences were. His awareness of the color line was not the same as mine. From adolescence on, I felt that my inability to attract girls had something to do with my race. And yet I was only attracted to white girls and was sure I would eventually end up with one.

I try to imagine my father staring at the foldout of Miss June, the UCLA coed, try to imagine what are the connections through which he yokes his sexuality to hers. He is sitting on the toilet, in a washroom of blue walls and blue tile and blue porcelain. I can see him there, a magazine on his lap, but when I try to imagine him staring at that image I feel pained, that unbearable pain when we see the pain of a parent, yearning for what he or she cannot have. He puts down the magazine. She, the girl, the woman, is too far away. Beyond his world. Perhaps this explains why, in a few years, I find no more of these magazines in his closet.

It is I who keep the images from *Playboy,* in my briefcase, my closet, in my head. The images there, the beautiful white bodies, are not too far away for me to dream of, though they seem beyond my touching. In this, their presence in my life as images seems appropriate: the images are there before me, but what they portray is not. Somehow, in my coming back to them again and again, I am completing a path into America that my father started, but I am going beyond my father, into the pull and frustrations of desires he never quite permitted himself, though, for a brief period, these images, these *Playboy*s, were part of his life too.

3. Rosa Linda Fregoso Recalls Her Sexual Education in "Homegirls, *Cholas,* and *Pachucas* in Cinema," 1995

Where I grew up in South Texas, *pachucas* were the objects of parental scorn. As a young Catholic-school girl, I was both fearful of and fascinated by *pachucas.* They went to public schools, hung out mostly at corner stores, smoked cigarettes, wore lots of make-up, were loud in public and quick to start a fight. My first lesson in sex education came from a *pachuca* named Mary Ester.

With peroxide-orange hair, big, light-brown eyes circled by Maybelline black eye-liner, eyebrows shaped and painted like wings, reddish-orange lips, and a teased beehive hairdo that my mother said was a nest for cockroaches, Mary Ester was a *guera* (light-skinned girl) who lived across the street from my gramma's house in Corpus Christi. I once heard she was my Tio's *movida* (lover). Yet what I remember most about Mary Ester was how she disturbed my childhood innocence, teaching

Rosa Linda Fregoso, "Home Girls, *Cholas,* and *Pachucas* in Cinema: Taking Over the Public Sphere," *California History* 74 (Fall 1995): 317–319. Reprinted by permission of the California Historical Society.

me the meaning of that popular lyric, "Let me tell you about the birds and the bees." One day I was walking down the street with her when Mary Ester asked me about the due date for my mother's baby. "What baby?" I responded. "The one in her stomach, *mensa* (dummy). That's why she's so fat. . . . Don't you know anything about the birds and the bees?" I didn't, except that they were somehow related to "a thing called love." Several hours later I stood in the middle of my gramma's dark, enclosed kitchen, before the tribunal of my mother, gramma, and Tio Pepe. I was proud of my sudden deconstruction of that song about the birds and the bees. And with the bright-eyed innocence of a nine-year-old girl, I shared that new knowledge with these family members, whose judgmental looks shamed me. I was silenced and punished immediately for knowing where babies come from. Yet I never forgot Mary Ester's casual frankness, nor her role in unlocking my sexual curiosity. I was always fascinated by that *pachuca* masquerade she wore in public, by how she had made her face into her canvas. She died several years later of a drug overdose.

Another *pachuca* named Gloria taught me the meaning of female solidarity. When I was fifteen years old, gang-banging was spreading throughout Corpus. Gang-banging referred to group rape: a group of guys getting a girl high on drugs, driving her to the beach, then raping and abandoning her. One Saturday night, I was hanging around the Carousel dancehall, stoned on "reds," walking from car to car, smoking, drinking, and listening to music. Gloria and a friend were there as well. Gloria did not like me. I could tell by the way she glared at me. I was friends with her ex-boyfriend, one of two brothers I knew who were *pachuco* drug dealers. That Saturday night one of the brothers invited me to go cruising: "Maybe the beach," he said. Right before I entered that tan Chevrolet station wagon, Gloria drove up and yelled, "Get in the car. I'm gonna take you for a ride." I don't know what stirred inside me, but without hesitating or protesting, I followed Gloria's command. She took me home and on the way told me that the guys, including my friends the two brothers, were "preparing a gang-banging" with me as their victim. I knew she was right. The hurt and terror I felt drove me away from my Carousel hangout. I even quit doing drugs. And all that summer I wondered why Gloria had intervened to save me. What I didn't understand then was Gloria's gift to me: a *pachuca's* sense of female solidarity.

In some Chicano *familias,* mothers warn their daughters about lesbians. In mine, I was cautioned about *pachucas—por ser muchachas corrientes y calle-jeras* (cheap, street-roaming girls). They fought like guys and would stand up to anybody's provocation. And, most of all, the street was their turf. Indeed, the street constitutes the social geography of urban space, the arena where *pachucas* apprehend public life. But the streets are also contested semiotic terrains within the public sphere, functioning, in the words of philosopher Nancy Fraser, as "culturally specific rhetorical lenses that filter and alter the utterances they frame." In the eyes of parents, the streets are sites of danger, where young girls become *pachucas* and *callejeras* (street-roamers). For *pachucas,* the street is an arena where they appropriate public space. Refusing to stay in the place assigned to them by Chicano society, *pachucas* are trespassers in public spaces, violating the boundaries of femininity.

In my childhood, *pachucas* were often viewed by adults as transgressive girls who disturbed private and public patriarchy, *la familia,* and the Catholic church.

They threatened the foundations of *la familia*'s gendered structure by speaking and acting in the public sphere. Mary Ester disrupted my family's acquiescence to the Church's moral prohibitions regarding sexuality. In public, she spoke openly about her sexual knowledge. And, on the streets of Corpus Christi as well, Gloria subverted patriarchal misogyny. She had intervened to stop men from inflicting their powerful violence and privilege on my body. In public spaces, both of these young women exhibited this mastery over and resistance to the sanctimony of patriarchal culture and religion.

I now understand the reason for parental scorn. In their appropriation of the public sphere, *pachucas* set a "bad" example. Most importantly, in their rebellion, *pachucas* failed to do what the Chicano family demands of girls and women. They rejected and challenged parental norms by refusing to stay inside the home. Their provocative language and dress style served to further refute *la familia's* authority. Boldly displaying their sexuality, *pachucas* refused to be confined by domesticity. The *pachuca* is therefore the body that marks the limits of *la familia* and is also the one who introduces disorder into its essentially patriarchal project.

4. The Supreme Court Rules on Interracial Marriage, 1967

Mr. Chief Justice WARREN delivered the opinion of the Court.

This case presents a constitutional question never addressed by this Court: whether a statutory scheme adopted by the State of Virginia to prevent marriages between persons solely on the basis of racial classifications violates the Equal Protection and Due Process Clauses of the Fourteenth Amendment. For reasons which seem to us to reflect the central meaning of those constitutional commands, we conclude that these statutes cannot stand consistently with the Fourteenth Amendment.

In June 1958, two residents of Virginia, Mildred Jeter, a Negro woman, and Richard Loving, a white man, were married in the District of Columbia pursuant to its laws. Shortly after their marriage, the Lovings returned to Virginia and established their marital abode in Caroline County. At the October Term, 1958, of the Circuit Court of Caroline County, a grand jury issued an indictment charging the Lovings with violating Virginia's ban on interracial marriages. On January 6, 1959, the Lovings pleaded guilty to the charge and were sentenced to one year in jail; however, the trial judge suspended the sentence for a period of 25 years on the condition that the Lovings leave the State and not return to Virginia together for 25 years. He stated in an opinion that:

> Almighty God created the races white, black, yellow, malay and red, and he placed them on separate continents. And but for the interference with his arrangement there would be no cause for such marriages. The fact that he separated the races shows that he did not intend for the races to mix. . . .

Loving et Ux. v. Virginia, 388 U.S. 1 (1967).

The two statutes under which appellants were convicted and sentenced are part of a comprehensive statutory scheme aimed at prohibiting and punishing interracial marriages. The Lovings were convicted of violating §20-58 of the Virginia Code:

> *Leaving State to evade law.* — If any white person and colored person shall go out of this State, for the purpose of being married, and with the intention of returning, and be married out of it, and afterwards return to and reside in it, cohabiting as man and wife, they shall be punished as provided in §20-59, and the marriage shall be governed by the same law as if it had been solemnized in this State. The fact of their cohabitation here as man and wife shall be evidence of their marriage.

Section 20-59, which defines the penalty for miscegenation, provides:

> *Punishment for marriage.* — If any white person intermarry with a colored person, or any colored person intermarry with a white person, he shall be guilty of a felony and shall be punished by confinement in the penitentiary for not less than one nor more than five years.

Other central provisions in the Virginia statutory scheme are §20-57, which automatically voids all marriages between "a white person and a colored person" without any judicial proceeding, and §§20-54 and 1-14 which, respectively, define "white persons" and "colored persons and Indians" for purposes of the statutory prohibitions. The Lovings have never disputed in the course of this litigation that Mrs. Loving is a "colored person" or that Mr. Loving is a "white person" within the meanings given those terms by the Virginia statutes.

Virginia is now one of 16 States which prohibit and punish marriages on the basis of racial classifications. Penalties for miscegenation arose as an incident to slavery and have been common in Virginia since the colonial period. The present statutory scheme dates from the adoption of the Racial Integrity Act of 1924, passed during the period of extreme nativism which followed the end of the First World War. The central features of this Act, and current Virginia law, are the absolute prohibition of a "white person" marrying other than another "white person," a prohibition against issuing marriage licenses until the issuing official is satisfied that the applicants' statements as to their race are correct, certificates of "racial composition" to be kept by both local and state registrars, and the carrying forward of earlier prohibitions against racial intermarriage. . . .

There is patently no legitimate overriding purpose independent of invidious racial discrimination which justifies this classification. The fact that Virginia prohibits only interracial marriages involving white persons demonstrates that the racial classifications must stand on their own justification, as measures designed to maintain White Supremacy. We have consistently denied the constitutionality of measures which restrict the rights of citizens on account of race. There can be no doubt that restricting the freedom to marry solely because of racial classifications violates the central meaning of the Equal Protection Clause. . . .

Marriage is one of the "basic civil rights of man," fundamental to our very existence and survival. . . . To deny this fundamental freedom on so unsupportable a basis as the racial classifications embodied in these statutes, classifications so directly subversive of the principle of equality at the heart of the Fourteenth Amendment, is surely to deprive all the State's citizens of liberty without due process of law. The Fourteenth Amendment requires that the freedom of choice to marry not be restricted by invidious racial discriminations. Under our Constitution, the freedom to marry, or not marry, a person of another race resides with the individual and cannot be infringed by the State.

These convictions must be reversed.

It is so ordered.

5. A Memoir of "Jane," an Illegal Abortion Service from 1969 to 1973

In the '60s women began to break their isolation and speak publicly about their abortions. Across the country, women and men organized counseling and referral services to help women negotiate the frightening and sometimes dangerous world of illegal abortions. In Chicago, a group of women formed an abortion counseling and referral service called "Jane." They picked the name Jane because they thought that women would be more comfortable calling someone by a name, and Jane was an every woman's name. When a woman called, a woman from Jane provided the counseling, then they would turn over her name and number to the doctor and they wouldn't hear from the woman again until after her abortion.

The women in the group were not satisfied with this arrangement. They realized that they needed to have more control and that they needed to get the price down. Once we were able to watch the abortions, we decided to learn to do abortions so we could charge a lot less money. Soon women in the group began to be involved with giving shots, inserting specula, doing all the preparatory steps to a D&C. At around the same time it became clear to the group that the doctor that we were working with was not in fact a real doctor. This discovery prompted a crisis for many women in the group. About half of the group members left at this point. At that same meeting, one woman said, "Well, if he can do it and he's not a doctor, then we can do it too."

Within six months women within the group were doing everything. We were able to lower our price to $100.00 or what a woman could afford. The average payment we received was $40.00 for an abortion. Here is how it worked: a woman would call a phone number with a message tape attached—everyone has answering machines now, nobody had them then—our message always said "This is Jane from women's liberation, if you need assistance please leave your name and phone number and someone will call you back." One of the group members called women back. She took some basic information—name, address, age, number of previous pregnancies, any health problems—told them briefly what was going to happen, and then told women a counselor would be in touch. That information was put on 3X5 cards and brought to meetings and the cards were passed around. If there were too many for that group then there were a few Jane members who took them home and called other members begging, "This one's easy, you can take this one." A woman would

"Just Call 'Jane,'" *The Fight for Reproductive Freedom: A Newsletter for Student Activists* 4, no. 2 (Winter 1990): 1–2, 4, 6. Reprinted by permission of Civil Liberties and Public Policy Program, Hampshire College, Amherst, MA.

get a call from her counselor who arranged a time when they could meet, usually at the counselor's home. Sometimes we counseled women individually, sometimes in small groups, depending on how many people needed counseling that week.

The night before a woman was scheduled for her abortion she would be called with a phone number and the address of the front, which was an apartment or a house that belonged to one of us or one of our friends. The front was a gathering place. It was one of the few steps we took to be conscious of security. . . .

From the front, women were driven in carloads, usually about five women at a time, to another apartment or house that belonged to one of us or one of our friends where the abortions took place. Each woman went to a bedroom—we did abortions on regular beds—and was asked to take her clothes off from the waist down. There was always a woman from the service sitting with her, holding her hand, and talking with her throughout the whole procedure. The person doing the procedure also talked with the woman about her life, her kids, school, whatever. Women sang during their abortions, they cried during their abortions, they laughed during their abortions, all kinds of interactions happened in an incredibly intimate way with women who were basically strangers. After the abortion, she was given two boxes of pills, one for bleeding and one as preventative for infections and a list of do's and don'ts for the next month then taken back to the front. Each counselor kept in touch with the women she counseled for up to two weeks, as a way to monitor their recoveries. One of our biggest problems was that we had little medical backup and so monitoring people was a very big issue for us and it was the thing that made us most nervous. From 1969, which was the inception of Jane, to when we folded in the spring of 1973, we estimate that we performed over 11,000 abortions.

Let me tell you a little about the kinds of women who came to Jane. In the earliest days, when we were working with the abortionist the original price he charged was $600.00. The kind of women who could afford those abortions was limited— college students, women from the suburbs, housewives from all over the city. A lot of women were left out. Our first negotiation with the abortionist was to get the price down. The first deal he cut with us was that he would do some free abortions and then he began to lower the price. Over the years that we worked with this particular person he eventually became a salaried employee, and at that point no woman was ever turned away. So we snuck in all kinds of women. As the price gradually lowered, until finally it was whatever you had with a maximum of $100, the demographics really changed, and almost all the women we saw were poor. In 1970, New York legalized abortion. So, women with money could get on a plane and fly to New York[,] get an abortion and fly back the same day. That left women who had no money at all, and a lot of very young women in Chicago. The women who came to Jane ranged in age from 13 to their 50's, from every racial group, and every economic status. Jane cut across all of those lines that divide women from each other, as does the whole issue of abortion. By the last year . . . of Jane we saw about 70% . . . women of color[,] most of whom were living on a subsistence wage or welfare with very poor health care available. Many women had never used birth control, and never had a gynecological exam. A lot of the women already had several children and had experienced birth control failures with every method known at the time. We estimate that there were about 120 women who were involved in Jane at one time or another with no more than twenty really active members at any one time.

I will tell you how I came to Jane and then I will tell you a little bit about how other people came to Jane. I moved to Chicago in the fall of 1971, and right after I moved there, my best friend got pregnant on an I.U.D. We went to one of the free clinics. In the 60's and early 70's there were many free health centers. . . . My friend took a pregnancy test and found out she was pregnant. She had no money, she had just graduated from college and was really upset. A woman who was working there said to her, "Don't worry, call this number, they can help you." So she had an abortion with Jane. Afterwards, she told me about this, and she was high from it. She was so excited that I couldn't believe that she had just had an illegal abortion. She took me to meet her counselor who was an interesting woman with two kids and lived in our neighborhood. A week later there was a training session for new counselors . . .

When I left New York in the fall of 1971, I knew I wanted to be directly and actively involved in this new women's movement. I was looking for the booth to sign up and this was the booth I found. I wasn't really interested in abortion as an issue, since I had come from a state where abortion was legal. There were many women who came to Jane directly from their abortion experiences, either with Jane or someplace else. There were a number of women who came because of a political commitment. There were women who were looking for something to do. We ranged in age from 19 to 50, with the bulk of women between the ages of 20 and 30. We were mostly white, though there were always [a] few women of color in the group. We had vast political differences, there were women who were really active in NOW, there were suburban school teachers and there were many of us who might be termed sort of radical hippie feminists. All of us were driven by our commitment and even more so by the challenges working with this organization presented us.

The service was much more than the 11,000 abortions we performed. One of the members said to me that the pain of abortion is unchanging, the context is everything. . . . We wanted each woman to have control over her life and over this abortion experience. We saw ourselves as working with women, not on them or for them. We told each woman from the beginning that what she was involved with was illegal, and that we were trusting her with our lives just as she was trusting us with her life. By including her, we equalized power between women providing abortions and the women who came to the service. About 70% of the women working in Jane had abortions with Jane. . . . We never saw anyone as a client or a patient; we didn't use drapes, we didn't wear uniforms. By not using drapes, we didn't separate ourselves physically from any woman so our working with her was very physical. We often rubbed women's legs, or held them if they got shaky.

I have been talking about women's choices and decisions; there were some things we didn't give people a choice about, for instance, we didn't give a choice not to know. To give an example, in 1971 women from the self-help movement in California did a self-help with women from the service. Immediately we bought mirrors so that we could show women their cervixes during the abortions. In the beginning, we would ask women, whether they wanted to see their cervixes. After a time we just said, "Here, look at your cervix." We tried to share knowledge because knowledge is strength and enables people to take charge of their lives.

Clearly, most of us lived fairly law abiding lives, and had never seen ourselves in conflict with the law. When your life, your identity and what you need to survive is in conflict with what society dictates, it can be a real opportunity to see the world in a new way, and to understand how power works. . . .

We worked three days a week, doing about one hundred abortions, then counseled women at night in our homes. We also ran around to buy sheets and equipment. For many of us, it was more than full time work. Everyone in this group was encouraged to go beyond what they thought they could do in terms of competence, taking responsibility, leadership because of the necessity of our work. That challenge transformed us individually. We were pushed through some kind of hidden, invisible wall. We became women we didn't expect to become, who we loved becoming.

6. Feminist Anselma Dell'Olio Argues That "The Sexual Revolution Wasn't Our War," 1971

The Women's Liberation Movement caught men off guard. They thought women had *already* been liberated by the Sexual Revolution.

According to most men, a liberated woman was one who put out sexually at the drop of a suggestive comment, who didn't demand marriage, and who "took care of herself" in terms of contraceptives. As far as men were concerned, that's all the liberation any woman needed. The bonus of bra-lessness and economically independent women simply fueled the misconception that the Women's Liberation Movement was in some way a continuation of the Sexual Revolution, also known as the More-Free-Sex-For-Us Revolution.

In truth, women had been liberated only from the right to say "no" to sexual intercourse with men. Kinsey in the fifties, and Masters and Johnson in the sixties, contributed scientific ammunition for the Sexual Revolution which freed women from Victorian morality. This gift relieved us of centuries of moral and social pressure which had dictated that no *nice* woman would ever "go all the way" with a man until marriage.

But it destroyed the sanctuary of maidenhood, pressuring us to give our bodies without respite from late adolescence to old age, or until our desirability as sex objects waned. For the first time, we were shorn of all protection (patronizing as it may have been, and selective in terms of class privilege) and openly exhorted to prostitute ourselves in the name of the New Morality.

We have come to see that the so-called Sexual Revolution is merely a link in the chain of abuse laid on women throughout patriarchal history. While purporting to restructure the unequal basis for sexual relationships between men and women, our munificent male liberators were in fact continuing their control of female sexuality.

With the advent of the new feminism, women finally began to ask, "What's in it for us?" And the answer is simple. We've been sold out. The Sexual Revolution was a battle fought by men for the great good of mankind. Womankind was left holding the double standard. We're supposed to give but what do we get? Kinsey's *Sexual Behavior in the Human Female* offered a priceless handbook for the Revolution in

Anselma Dell'Olio, "The Sexual Revolution Wasn't Our War," in Francine Klagsbrun, ed., *The First Ms. Reader* (New York: Warner Books, 1973), 124–130. Reprinted by permission.

its findings that 1) women could and did enjoy sex after all, 2) there is no such thing as a frigid woman, only inept men, 3) virginity in women was no longer considered important or particularly desirable by most men, and 4) women and men were now equals in bed and equally free to screw their bottoms off for the sheer fun of it.

What the popularizers of Kinsey's findings neglected to emphasize would have provided the seeds for a *real* revolution in the bedroom. We still remained ignorant about the difference between orgasm and ejaculation, about the speed-of-response differential between male and female orgasm, about the fallacy of the vaginal-clitoral orgasm dichotomy, about women's multi-orgasmic nature, and so on. Because of this deliberate or unconscious *excising* of Kinsey, and later Masters and Johnson, we have managed to survive into the seventies with the double standard intact, alive and well in the minds of average American males. And many females as well.

The new freedom of the Sexual Revolution was at best a failure, at worst a hoax—because it never caused significant changes in the social attitudes and behavior of men to correspond with this New Morality being forced upon women. There has been no real revolution in the bedroom. For this crucial reason, the Sexual Revolution and the Women's Movement are polar opposites in philosophy, goals and spirit.

The real point is that there are not many women—liberated, unliberated, feminist or otherwise—who are sleeping around for the sheer pleasure of it. The Achilles' heel of the Sexual Revolution is persistent male ignorance of the female orgasm. . . .

If pleasure is rarely the reward, women's continued willingness to have intercourse doesn't make sense. Why, then, are we doing it?

The truth is we are often pressured into it, and not only by the litany of the Sexual Revolution. It may be the need for affection and attention. Or the desire to please; the need for approval. It's no news to any of us that men can have intercourse with women they are totally disinterested in as human beings. For many women sex fails to bring physical satisfaction, and depersonalized sex denies women even the side benefits of communication and approval.

What the Sexual Revolution should have taught us is that *need* shouldn't be confused with *love;* that men and women can neither give nor receive love until we stop confusing it with a need for security and approval. The Women's Movement is trying to teach that lesson. Love is not getting high on fantasies of romance, the perfect lover, absolute happiness and sexual ecstasy. Love is based on two-way communication and respect, and that only exists between equals.

When feminists are critical of romance, there is often a panicked reaction: "But you can't possibly want to get rid of love?"

No, we don't want to negate the emotion. We want a better definition. We want to get rid of the sick and hoary old illusions which women have pursued relentlessly at the price of our humanity. What is called love now is so clearly exploitative and unsatisfactory that it should make us suspicious that men want to preserve it at all costs. What is called love now is vital to the oppression of women. . . .

Therefore, a sexually liberated woman without a feminist consciousness is nothing more than a new variety of prostitute for the Sexual Revolution. If we don't sell ourselves for money in the street or security in the suburbs, we sell ourselves in exchange for some measure of approval and (we hope) lasting affection. . . .

There are many women who have decided to challenge the hypocrisy of the Sexual Revolution by refusing to tolerate this double-standard nonsense and becoming at least as sexually liberated as men are. They soon find out that, emotional problems aside (and they are not insignificant), the physical obstacles are close to insurmountable. The physical price a woman stands to pay for sexual nonchalance is staggering. A woman's chances of getting pregnant are still good (meaning bad), and those chances get better (meaning worse) as the frequency of, and number of partners for, intercourse increases.

The Pill is hazardous, and other forms of contraception are a drag, a distraction and a nuisance, not to mention being failure-prone. Tampering with women's vastly more complex reproductive system is all right with men, but vasectomy, still the most practical, inexpensive method of birth control which can be performed in minutes in a doctor's office, is not; at least, not with most men. The virility-fertility connection is sacrosanct. And there you have the clearest evidence of why feminists view the Sexual Revolution as one more male ego-trip. What kind of Sexual Revolution is it when, in the year 1971, the possibility of a practical male contraceptive still goes largely unresearched and unpublished?

7. Carl Wittman Issues a Gay Manifesto, 1969–1970

San Francisco is a refugee camp for homosexuals. We have fled here from every part of the nation, and like refugees elsewhere, we came not because it is so great here, but because it was so bad there. By the tens of thousands, we fled small towns where to be ourselves would endanger our jobs and any hope of a decent life; we have fled from blackmailing cops, from families who disowned or "tolerated" us; we have been drummed out of the armed services, thrown out of schools, fired from jobs, beaten by punks and policemen.

And we have formed a ghetto, out of self-protection. It is a ghetto rather than a free territory because it is still theirs. Straight cops patrol us, straight legislators govern us. Straight employers keep us in line, straight money exploits us. We have pretended everything is OK, because we haven't been able to see how to change it—we've been afraid.

In the past year there has been an awakening of gay liberation ideas and energy. How it began we don't know; maybe we were inspired by black people and their freedom movement; we learned how to stop pretending from the hip revolution. Amerika in all its ugliness has surfaced with the war and our national leaders. And we are revulsed by the quality of our ghetto life.

Where once there was frustration, alienation, and cynicism, there are new characteristics among us. We are full of love for each other and are showing it; we are full of anger at what has been done to us. And as we recall all the self-censorship and repression for so many years, a reservoir of tears pours out of our eyes. And we are euphoric, high, with the initial flourish of a movement.

We want to make ourselves clear: our first job is to free ourselves; that means clearing our heads of the garbage that's been poured into them. This article is an attempt at raising a number of issues and presenting some ideas to replace the old ones. It is primarily for ourselves, a starting point of discussion. If straight people of good will find it useful in understanding what liberation is about, so much the better.

It should also be clear that these are the views of one person, and are determined not only by my homosexuality, but my being white, male, middle class. It is my individual consciousness. Our group consciousness will evolve as we get ourselves together—we are only at the beginning.

I. On Orientation

1. *What homosexuality is:* Nature leaves undefined the object of sexual desire. The gender of that object is imposed socially. Humans originally made homosexuality taboo because they needed every bit of energy to produce and raise children: survival of species was a priority. With overpopulation and technological change, that taboo continued only to exploit us and enslave us.

As kids we refused to capitulate to demands that we ignore our feelings toward each other. Somewhere we found the strength to resist being indoctrinated, and we should count that among our assets. We have to realize that our loving each other is a good thing, not an unfortunate thing, and that we have a lot to teach straights about sex, love, strength, and resistance.

Homosexuality is *not* a lot of things. It is not a makeshift in the absence of the opposite sex; it is not hatred or rejection of the opposite sex; it is not genetic; it is not the result of broken homes except inasmuch as we could see the sham of American marriage. *Homosexuality is the capacity to love someone of the same sex.*

2. *Bisexuality:* Bisexuality is good; it is the capacity to love people of either sex. The reason so few of us are bisexual is because society made such a big stink about homosexuality that we got forced into seeing ourselves as either straight or non-straight. Also, many gays got turned off to the ways men are supposed to act with women and vice-versa, which is pretty fucked-up. Gays will begin to turn on to women when 1) it's something that we do because we want to, and not because we should, and 2) when women's liberation changes the nature of heterosexual relationships.

We continue to call ourselves homosexual, not bisexual, even if we do make it with the opposite sex also, because saying "Oh, I'm Bi" is a cop out for a gay. We get told it's OK to sleep with guys as long as we sleep with women, too, and that's still putting homosexuality down. We'll be gay until everyone has forgotten that it's an issue. Then we'll begin to be complete.

3. *Heterosexuality:* Exclusive heterosexuality is fucked up. It reflects a few people of the same sex, it's anti-homosexual, and it is fraught with frustration. Heterosexual sex is fucked up, too; ask women's liberation about what straight guys are like in bed. Sex is aggression for the male chauvinist; sex is obligation for traditional woman. And among the young, the modern, the hip, it's only a subtle version of the same. For us to become heterosexual in the sense that our straight brothers and sisters are is not a cure, it is a disease.

II. On Women

1. *Lesbianism:* It's been a male-dominated society for too long, and that has warped both men and women. So gay women are going to see things differently from gay men; they are going to feel put down as women, too. Their liberation is tied up with both gay liberation and women's liberation.

This paper speaks from the gay male viewpoint. And although some of the ideas in it may be equally relevant to gay women, it would be arrogant to presume this to be a manifesto for lesbians. . . .

2. *Male Chauvinism:* All men are infected with male chauvinism—we were brought up that way. It means we assume that women play subordinate roles and are less human than ourselves. (At an early gay liberation meeting one guy said, "Why don't we invite women's liberation—they can bring sandwiches and coffee.") It is no wonder that so few gay women have become active in our groups.

Male chauvinism, however, is not central to us. We can junk it much more easily than straight men can. For we understand oppression. We have largely opted out of a system which oppresses women daily—our egos are not built on putting women down and having them build us up. Also, living in a mostly male world we have become used to playing different roles, doing our own shit-work. And finally, we have a common enemy: the big male chauvinists are also the big anti-gays.

But we need to purge male chauvinism, both in behavior and in thought among us. Chick equals nigger equals queer. Think it over.

3. *Women's liberation:* They are assuming their equality and dignity and in doing so are challenging the same things we are: the roles, the exploitation of minorities by capitalism, the arrogant smugness of straight white male middle-class Amerika. They are our sisters in struggle.

Problems and differences will become clearer when we begin to work together. One major problem is our own male chauvinism. Another is uptightness and hostility to homosexuality that many women have—that is the straight in them. A third problem is differing views on sex: sex for them has meant oppression, while for us it has been a symbol of our freedom. We must come to know and understand each other's style, jargon and humor.

III. On Roles

1. *Mimicry of straight society:* We are children of straight society. We still think straight: that is part of our oppression. One of the worst of straight concepts is inequality. Straight (also white, English, male, capitalist) thinking views things in terms of order and comparison. A is before B, B is after A; one is below two is below three; there is no room for equality. This idea gets extended to male/female, on top/on bottom, spouse/not spouse, heterosexual/homosexual; boss/worker, white/black and rich/poor. Our social institutions cause and reflect this verbal hierarchy. This is Amerika.

We've lived in these institutions all our lives. Naturally we mimic the roles. For too long we mimicked these roles to protect ourselves—a survival mechanism. Now we are becoming free enough to shed the roles which we've picked up from the institutions which have imprisoned us.

"Stop mimicking straights, stop censoring ourselves."

2. *Marriage:* Marriage is a prime example of a straight institution fraught with role playing. Traditional marriage is a rotten, oppressive institution. Those of us who have been in heterosexual marriages too often have blamed our gayness on the breakup of the marriage. No. They broke up because marriage is a contract which smothers both people, denies needs, and places impossible demands on both people. And we had the strength, again, to refuse to capitulate to the roles which were demanded of us. . . .

3. *Alternatives to Marriage:* People want to get married for lots of good reasons, although marriage won't often meet those needs or desires. We're all looking for security, a flow of love, and a feeling of belonging and being needed. . . .

We have to define for ourselves a new pluralistic, role free social structure for ourselves. It must contain both the freedom and physical space for people to live alone, live together for a while, live together for a long time, either as couples or in larger numbers; and the ability to flow easily from one of these states to another as our needs change.

Liberation for gay people is defining for ourselves how and with whom we live, instead of measuring our relationship in comparison to straight ones, with straight values.

4. *Gay "stereotypes":* The straights' image of the gay world is defined largely by those of us who have violated straight roles. There is a tendency among "homophile" groups to deplore gays who play visible roles—the queens and the nellies. As liberated gays, we must take a clear stand. 1. Gays who stand out have become our first martyrs. They came out and withstood disapproval before the rest of us did. 2. If they have suffered from being open, it is straight society whom we must indict, not the queen.

5. *Closet queens:* This ph[r]ase is becoming analogous to "Uncle Tom." To pretend to be straight sexually, or to pretend to be straight socially, is probably the most harmful pattern of behavior in the ghetto. The married guy who makes it on the side secretly; the guy who will go to bed once but who won't develop any gay relationships; the pretender at work or school who changes the gender of the friend he's talking about; the guy who'll suck cock in the bushes but who won't go to bed.

If we are liberated we are open with our sexuality. Closet queenery must end. *Come out.*

But: In saying come out, we have to have our heads clear about a few things: 1) closet queens are our brothers, and must be defended against attacks by straight people; 2) the fear of coming out is not paranoia; the stakes are high: loss of family ties, loss of job, loss of straight friends—these are all reminders that the oppression is not just in our heads. It's real. Each of us must make the steps toward openness at our own speed and on our own impulses. Being open is the foundation of freedom: it has to be built solidly. 3) "Closet queen" is a broad term covering a multitude of forms of defense, self-hatred, lack of strength, and habit. We are all closet queens in some ways, and all of us had to come out—very few of us were "flagrant" at the age of seven! We must afford our brothers and sisters the same patience we afforded ourselves. And while their closet queenery is part of our oppression, it's more a part of theirs. They alone can decide when and how.

E S S A Y S

The research of Alfred Kinsey and others documented a shift in sexual practices after 1920: despite varying degrees of public moralizing, American men and especially women engaged increasingly in nonmarital sex. Many historians have concluded, in fact, that the twentieth century witnessed a long-term process of sexual liberalization. If that is the case, what made the 1960s a "sexual revolution"? Independent historian and writer David Allyn highlights the Sexual Freedom League to characterize this era. Active in major cities and on college campuses, it merrily ridiculed middle-class hypocrisy and prudery, promoted frank sexual language and nudity, and fought legal restrictions on sex commerce, pornography, and birth control. Although short-lived and largely ineffective, it was the leading edge of the "hippie" counterculture and articulated the developing view that sex freedom was a political issue. That view, Marc Stein of York University writes, was central to homosexual activism in Philadelphia in the 1960s, where lesbians and gay men formed alliances based on sexuality as well as gender. Throughout the 1960s, they debated the problem of self-definition and strategies of representation: While a number promoted an image of clean-cut respectability to counter demeaning stereotypes, others claimed a place in the sexual revolution and made gay sex an explicit part of a gay political identity.

Fomenting a Sexual Revolution

DAVID ALLYN

August is a cold month in San Francisco. The city has its real summer in September and October. But in August 1965, two young men and two young women tentatively stripped off their clothes and staged a nude "wade-in" off a San Francisco city beach. Imitating civil rights protesters in the South, the four self-proclaimed sexual-freedom fighters disobeyed local laws and customs to make a point about personal liberty. Jefferson Poland, the twenty-three-year-old leader of the group, believed anti-nudity ordinances were a denial of basic civil liberties and, worse, led to sexual repression in society. The founder of the New York League for Sexual Freedom, which by 1965 had evolved into the "national" Sexual Freedom League, Jeff Poland knew that a nude wade-in would capture the attention of the media. He forgot that in August, temperatures in San Francisco often dipped below 60 degrees. The week before the protest, he organized a handful of supporters, mostly North Beach beat-niks, and alerted the local press. On the morning of the appointed day, Poland, wearing a swimsuit and a flower behind his ear, arrived with his three friends at the municipal beach known as Aquatic Park. Before cheering crowds and several cam-eramen, the four would-be protesters entered the icy ocean water and three of them disrobed (the fourth got scared at the last minute). A nineteen-year-old anarchist supporter stood on the shore and waved a banner asking, "Why Be Ashamed Of Your Body?" Other supporters formed a picket line on the beach and chanted, "Sex is clean! Law's obscene!" Reporters, unimpressed with the skinny-dipping stunt but eager for a good story, urged the nude swimmers to return to the shore in order to get arrested. Soon enough they were cited for violating San Francisco's municipal code regulating swimming attire. The two women received suspended sentences and six months' probation. Poland was required to spend five weekends in jail. . . . The story made the national news.

Jefferson Poland was one of the first hippies. He was wearing flowers in his hair well before the rest of his generation. He was a beatnik who, several years before it would become a trend, dropped the pretensions of urbane ultrasophistication for the back-to-nature simplicity of Rousseauian romanticism, a long-haired kid who saw the power of combining utopian social protest with over-the-top theatrics while the majority of male college students were still wearing jackets and ties to class.

Born in Indiana in 1942, just before the beginning of the postwar baby boom, Poland was the son of working-class parents. His father was a machinist in an automobile manufacturing plant, his mother a pink-collar worker. As a boy he often wet his bed. His father, determined to "cure" him of this habit, would come into his bedroom every morning and check to see if the bed was wet. If it was, he would tell Jeff to strip and then whipped the naked boy with a belt. Eventually Jeff told his mother about his father's beatings, and mother and son fled to Houston, Texas. They remained on the move. Jefferson attended over twenty schools before going to college. As a result, he perpetually felt like a "newcomer," an exceptionally creative outsider who "retreated into books" and "hardly knew anyone except" his mother.

Jefferson eventually left his mother's home and began hitchhiking his way to California. On one occasion he had sex with a man who gave him a ride; he enjoyed the experience, but also felt an intense sense of shame. He became an itinerant student, drifting in and out of schools, searching for meaning and purpose. By the time he was eighteen, he was having sex with women. He began to question sexual mores, and as an undergraduate at San Francisco State University turned to popular authors like Philip Wylie and Albert Ellis to make sense of his own sexual tastes and the assumptions of American society. Their texts piqued Poland's interest in erotic freedom, but he felt frustrated by the fact that "sexual liberation seemed to exist mainly in books."

Like other young beatniks, Poland moved into a group house to save rent. His roommates were two young women, both of them self-proclaimed anarchists. They taught Poland about "free love," a doctrine of anarchism since the movement began in the early 1900s. . . . By the 1960s, anarchism was all but dead in America, but the idea that monogamy and jealousy were outdated and ought to be abolished had survived among intellectuals and bohemians. Poland was quickly converted to the cause.

Many of the left-wing dissidents of the early sixties congregated at Poland's group house. One was former University of Illinois biology professor Leo Koch, who was famous among radicals for being fired from his teaching position because of a letter he'd written to the student newspaper in defense of premarital sex. Koch had tried to sue the university and, having lost in the lower courts, was still awaiting a decision by the Supreme Court.

Poland, deeply impressed by Koch's sense of conviction and willingness to challenge moral authority, decided to dedicate himself to the cause of sexual freedom.

When comedian Lenny Bruce was arrested on obscenity charges in San Francisco in 1961, Poland participated in protests on Bruce's behalf. At San Francisco State, Poland ran for student office on a platform promising the sale of contraceptives in the school bookstore. Poland lost the election but not his interest in politics.

In the summer of 1963, Poland, like hundreds of other college students, joined the civil rights movement as a volunteer. He endured the summer heat to register voters in Louisiana, where he learned about the growing student movement. In the fall, he moved to New York City in search of work. Two days after the assassination of John F. Kennedy in November 1963, Poland again met Leo Koch. Koch was well connected in Manhattan, and he introduced Poland to the writers of the New York Beat scene. Poland met Allen Ginsberg, who had returned to New York after several years in San Francisco; Diane Di Prima, one of the few women in the Beat community of poets; Ed Sanders, editor of a Beat journal named *Fuck You: A Magazine of the Arts;* and Tuli Kupferberg, a pacifist and songwriter. Poland also met avant-garde actors, directors, and playwrights like Judith Malina and Julian Beck, the founders of the Living Theater, an experimental troupe that used nudity to challenge conventional morality.

In January 1964, the Supreme Court announced that it would not review Koch's case against the University of Illinois. In response, Poland and Koch decided to form a group to challenge American sexual laws and values. They took the name the League for Sexual Freedom, mistakenly believing it to have been the name of an earlier organization formed in Germany. . . . Such literary luminaries as Beck, Ginsberg, Di Prima, Sanders, Peter Orlovsky, and Paul Krassner were founding members. But Poland, Kupferberg, and a young activist named Randy Wicker were the real leaders of the League.

Tuli Kupferberg, a so-called "red diaper baby" because he was the son of Communist Party members, was an anarchist and a sexual radical in his own right. Like other anarchists, Kupferberg rejected monogamy as an outdated, bourgeois notion. He and his wife had an agreement that both were free to sleep with other people. In the midsixties, he and Ed Sanders formed a folk-rock band, the Fugs, named after Norman Mailer's euphemism in his war novel *The Naked and the Dead* (1948). Their songs were silly yet provocative, with titles like "Group Grope," "Boobs a Lot," "Kill for Peace," "What Are You Doing After the Orgy?" and "Dirty Old Man." The Fugs appealed to fellow bohemians and the growing number of baby boomers who were seeking alternatives to the sappy lyrics and melodies of pop music.

As soon as Kupferberg and Poland met, they became close friends, sharing as they did an interest in sexual freedom. Kupferberg was a devotee of Wilhelm Reich, the renegade psychoanalyst who believed that sex and politics were deeply linked. Reich had been one of Freud's leading disciples during the early years of psychoanalysis; unlike Freud, however, Reich was a socialist who thought it imperative to combine political activism and sexual theory. Sexual repression, Reich argued, was the cornerstone of totalitarianism, so in order to liberate people politically it was necessary to liberate them sexually first. But Reich was eventually expelled from the Communist Party, rejected by Freud, and ultimately forced into exile by the Nazis. In 1939, he fled to the United States, where he acquired a small but influential group of followers, all of whom subscribed to his notion that sexual repression caused serious psychological damage. In line with his teachings,

Reichian analysts taught their patients how to achieve maximum pleasure through intercourse and thereby experience the full release of all pent-up energies. Reich died in 1957 and his library was destroyed by the federal government, but thirty-one Reichian analysts continued to practice his techniques, and his ideas infused the writings of many important intellectuals of the sixties. Kupferberg spent time in Reichian therapy, and Reich's ideas underscored Kupferberg's own beliefs about sexual freedom.

Randy Wicker, the third leading figure in the Sexual Freedom League, was no stranger to sexual politics when he met Jefferson Poland and Tuli Kupferberg in the early sixties. Wicker had been involved for several years with the Mattachine Society, the gay rights organization founded in the fifties in New York by Rudi Gernreich and his friend Harry Hay. In 1962, Wicker had successfully persuaded a New York radio station to allow gay men to speak on the air about their own lives, a first for American radio. In addition, he convinced reporters to write stories on homosexual life for the *Village Voice,* the *New York Post,* and *Harpers.* But when a female friend needed an abortion and could not find a doctor willing to perform the operation (she ended up taking quinine, having a miscarriage, and spending several years in Bellevue mental hospital), Wicker realized that sexual freedom meant more than gay rights. . . .

At first, the New York League members merely engaged in discussion. At weekly gatherings in Greenwich Village, Poland, Kupferberg, Wicker, and others would meet to debate the meaning of "sexual freedom." The discussions often dwelled on hypothetical situations, lending an abstract, intellectual dimension to the organization's endeavor. They argued the moral merits of prostitution, pedophilia, bestiality (the group decided bestiality was okay if an animal failed to resist), and other controversial sex practices. Wicker recalls that one of the liveliest discussions involved the legitimacy of public masturbation. The group members decided that there was nothing wrong with it so long as a man did not actually hit someone with his semen during ejaculation, which would be a violation of the other person's rights. There were fewer than a dozen core members of the group, but every so often prominent figures in New York's avant-garde would join in the discussions.

Occasionally, group members would stand on the streets of Manhattan and pass out fliers about sexual freedom. To jaded urban passersby, League members were a mere curiosity. In April 1964, League members held a speak-out at Columbia University, hoping that college students would rally to their cause. Poland and his fellow activists demanded "respect for sexual freedom as a fundamental civil liberty," and called for the decriminalization of interracial marriage, fellatio, cunnilingus, anal intercourse, bestiality, and transvestism. They also attacked censorship laws, laws against public nudity, laws against contraception and abortion, college parietal rules, statutory rape laws, and strict divorce laws. They called for the freedom of "homosexuals and other harmless deviates" from police persecution and for the legalization of prostitution "under conditions which will reduce VD and protect the welfare of prostitutes."

League members were as concerned about sexual equality as they were about sexual freedom. "Each person," they announced, "should be free to choose his or her activities and roles without being forced by social pressure or law to conform to rigid masculine and feminine stereotypes."

Taking their cue from the burgeoning civil rights movement, the League members staged a series of demonstrations, some more successful than others. An early protest targeted the New York City district attorney's office after city police arrested filmmaker Jonas Mekas in March 1964 on obscenity charges for showing an underground film called *Flaming Creatures,* which contained close-up images of breasts and genitals, men in drag, and suggestions of masturbation, oral sex, and gang rape. Then when comedian Lenny Bruce was again arrested on obscenity charges in April, Allen Ginsberg and other members of the League organized a committee to fight for his release. Ginsberg issued a press release with the signatures of dozens of important intellectuals. The League also organized a protest in front of the New York Public Library in an effort to bring attention to the library's policy of segregating sex books. On August 23, 1964, the League sponsored a demonstration outside the Women's House of Detention, where a majority of inmates were prostitutes. Jeff Poland, who picketed in front of the building carrying an American flag, attracted the attention of some reporters by calling for the total decriminalization of prostitution. Then, on September 19, Poland and Wicker sponsored the first public demonstration for homosexual rights in New York City. Together they protested the military's policy of investigating and outing "suspected homosexuals" by picketing the city's Armed Forces Induction Center. In October, when Walter Jenkins, an assistant to Lyndon Johnson, was forced to resign over allegations of engaging in homosexual activity in a public rest room, the League adopted a statement in his defense. . . . But none of these activities attracted much public notice or galvanized a genuine political movement.

Despite its initial ineffectiveness, the New York League for Sexual Freedom foreshadowed the rise of the hippie counterculture and the radicalism of the late sixties. It brought together a coalition of intellectuals, artists, other bohemians, and sexual minorities opposed to the regulation and zoning of sex. Still, keeping the coalition together was not easy. Wicker wrote to Poland in frustration, "Give up on the homosexuals. . . . Gay kids, by and large, are a bunch of mentally stunted, genitally fixated squares whose sexual interest extends no farther than their next trick's big cock." The League eventually dissolved, and Jefferson Poland moved back to San Francisco.

When Poland arrived in San Francisco in the spring of 1965, students at UC Berkeley were embroiled in a controversy over the politics of profanity. The "filthy speech movement" (so called because it grew out of the "Free Speech movement," which had involved a series of campus protests a few months earlier against university rules about political activism on university property) was forcing nearly everyone in California to reexamine their views about morality and censorship.

In March 1965, a twenty-eight-year-old Berkeley beatnik named John Thomson was arrested by campus police for holding up a protest sign bearing the word *fuck.* The next day four students protested Thomson's arrest. They set up a table with a placard reading "Fuck Fund" and read aloud the final passage from D. H. Lawrence's *Lady Chatterley's Lover,* including lines like "My soul softly flaps in the little pentecost flame with you, like the peace of fucking. We fucked a flame into being. Even the flowers are fucked into being between the sun and the earth. But it's a delicate thing, and takes patience and the long pause." Lawrence's novel, highly regarded among students of English literature, had been granted constitutional protection by a federal court in 1959. Nonetheless, the four students were also arrested.

The campus was divided over the arrests. A senior prelaw student filed a suit against the four students for obscenity. The student newspaper called for the protesters' expulsion. Tensions escalated when a college fraternity distributed "I Like Pussy" buttons as part of an organized contest. One male student was so offended by the buttons, he filed a complaint against the fraternity. When the university investigated the incident, the fraternity brothers argued that "Pussy" referred to Pussy Galore, a character in the James Bond film *Goldfinger*, and that the buttons had been approved by the dean's office before they were distributed. The fraternity quickly distanced itself from the filthy speech movement, however, "a movement we deplore." In general, there was little support for the use of profanity; even the leaders of the original Free Speech movement wanted nothing to do with the issue. They resented the arrested students for trivializing the issue of free speech. . . .

Nonetheless, the controversy expanded rapidly. The California Assembly called for the expulsion of the four students who had been arrested. Clark Kerr, president of the university, appeared to be losing his control of the campus and, in a dramatic move, offered his resignation, which was subsequently declined by the faculty. After winning a vote of confidence from the faculty, Kerr suspended, but did not expel, the students who had been arrested. The *Spider,* a campus magazine of political satire, carried an article about the controversy titled "To Kill a Fucking-word," a play on the title of Harper Lee's 1960 novel about racial prejudice, *To Kill a Mockingbird.* Kerr banned the issue. Once again the campus fell into an uproar. Enraged protesters, among them avant-garde filmmaker Kenneth Anger, distributed fliers in support of the student press. As one professor wrote to another,

> This poor ambiguous little word almost toppled the government of the university; it called a thousand professors from class, laboratory, library and study; it seriously troubled the main elective officials of the state; it exhausted the lino-typists of the metropolitan newspapers who set the letters to the editor. The students who used the word did not intend to have this effect: they wanted to show that the adult world was composed of hypocrites. To their amazement and chagrin, they were successful!

Despite the desires of the Free Speech activists, the controversy over "filthy speech" could not be ignored.

Jefferson Poland was not directly involved in the filthy speech movement, but he was certainly inspired by the publicity it generated. In August 1965, as the filthy speech controversy finally dissipated, Poland organized the nude wade-in, thereby taking the entire issue of candor one step further. Like generations of nudists before him, Poland believed that there was nothing obscene about the naked body. Laws against nakedness, Poland felt, produced unhealthy attitudes and a cultural obsession with sex. According to the Bible, nudists pointed out, God ordered Isaiah to go naked for three years, while King David danced naked in the town square.

Newspaper and magazine reports of his August wade-in gave Poland a national spotlight. He renamed his group, calling it the Sexual Freedom League, . . . and invited interested members across the country to form regional chapters.

By now college campuses were bulging with baby boomers. Student populations were larger than they had ever been. These young people knew about the pill;

they had read *Playboy* and Helen Gurley Brown in high school. As one sex educator wrote approvingly, "A very real freedom now exists for adolescent couples and for youth in mixed groups to speak openly and frankly about sexual matters." Like Poland many of them had no patience with their parents' hypocrisy: their willingness, for instance, to accept nudity in a titillating magazine like *Playboy* but not on the beaches of San Francisco. Within a year after the wade-in, sexual freedom groups had formed at Stanford, UC Berkeley, UCLA, and the University of Texas. Stanford's Sexual Freedom Forum issued a Statement of Principles, which read: "We view sexual rights as a proper extension of individual civil liberties. We prefer open honest acceptance of varying personal sexual practices to the massive hypocrisy of many parts of our society. . . . The private sexual activities of consenting adults are sacrosanct." A photo in the *San Francisco Chronicle* showed a handsome young man and two attractive "coeds" handing out leaflets on the college campus. The members of the Stanford Sexual Freedom Forum managed to collect 450 student signatures supporting the distribution of contraception to unmarried women. Students then voted in favor of the measure, 1,866 to 853. The director of Stanford's health service derided the Forum's efforts as "a tragically crude and simplistic approach to an enormously complex and sensitive issue." But as students began selling buttons with the slogan "Make Love, Not War," the link between sexual freedom and student activism was cemented. The slogan expressed the commonly held view that sexual liberation would lead to a decrease in social tensions. "Our capacity for violence," wrote Jefferson Poland and Sam Sloan in *The Sex Marchers,* "is a spill-over, a natural consequence of our repressed sexuality, our caged libidos." As a pithy response to the escalating war in Vietnam, the slogan quickly captured the media's attention.

At the University of Texas in Austin, the Student League for Responsible Sexual Freedom counted fifteen members in 1966, who opposed limiting the sale of contraceptives on campus to married women and sought the decriminalization of homosexuality and the repeal of laws against sodomy. Texas state senator Grady Hazelwood threatened that he would "never vote another appropriation for the University" if the group were not abolished. The day after Hazelwood's threat, the university banned the group from campus. . . . Across the country, Sexual Freedom League chapters took on a variety of issues. At the University of Florida, the school chapter of the Sexual Freedom League vocally opposed miscegenation laws. Members of the Berkeley Campus Sexual Freedom Forum were inspired by this effort and in November 1966 declared in their Resolution on Race and Gender as Sexual Restrictions "each of us must make special efforts to overcome these barriers and find lovers of different races." As the Sexual Freedom League grew, so did the idea that a sexually liberated society would be less exploitative, less tempted by mass-market pornography, suggestive advertising, and other forms of commercialized titillation. When a representative of *Playboy* came to Iowa's Grinnell College to speak in 1965, students, male and female, protested what they perceived as *Playboy*'s pseudo-liberated philosophy by coming to the talk naked.

Like many countercultural groups in the midsixties, the Sexual Freedom League never garnered broad popular appeal. Most college students were too busy experimenting with drugs and sex, listening to the new music, campaigning for civil rights, and marching against the war in Vietnam to devote time and energy to protesting social attitudes about the body. Few saw any real need to demand changes in the law.

Though it was still technically illegal to sell or display birth control in some states, students had easy access to condoms, diaphragms, and the pill, so most felt like the sexual revolution was a fait accompli. Many sexually oriented materials could still not be printed or published, but students had little reason to care. Even though a large number of baby boomers had grown up in households where sex was never mentioned or certain sexual activities were explicitly denounced, by the midsixties college students could generally set their own moral standards. They had the money to do as they pleased.

Moreover, premarital sex was a fact on college campuses, and administrators knew they could never punish one student for having sex without punishing hundreds, if not thousands. As a Yale University dean told a reporter in 1966, "We are not interested in the private lives of students as long as they remain private." Ruth Darling, an assistant dean at Cornell, agreed: "We don't ask what they do and don't want to know." In 1965, the Group for the Advancement of Psychiatry, representing 260 psychiatrists, published a report on parietal rules and campus sexual behavior. The report, *Sex and the College Student,* advised administrators to ignore private sexual behavior. "The student's privacy requires respect; sexual activity privately practiced with appropriate attention to the sensitivities of other people should not be the direct concern of the administration." Though controversial, the report had a strong influence on academics and administrators.

Following this advice from the psychiatric experts, college administrators in the midsixties essentially adopted a "don't ask, don't tell" policy on premarital sex. But such a policy could work only if students agreed to draw a sharp line between their private and public lives, keeping their sexual activity secret. The members of the Sexual Freedom League had already shown their unwillingness to pretend that sex was purely a private matter. So long as there were laws regulating speech, dress, and consensual sexual behavior, sex would never be purely private. As far as Sexual Freedom League members were concerned, they were not making sex public, they were merely acknowledging its already public dimension.

Relatively speaking, the Sexual Freedom League was a minuscule movement that was never able to mobilize a significant number of supporters. Few Americans even knew that it existed, and the organization failed to achieve notable political or legal change. But the stories of failed experiments can tell us something about our social structures and cultural values. The Sexual Freedom League failed in part because its founders refused to focus exclusively on the needs of any one particular interest group. Had the League represented solely the interests of gays or women or prostitutes or pornographers or straight males, it would surely have had a larger impact on society than it did. But by attempting to fight sexual repression on every front, the leaders of the SFL never managed to attract a core constituency of supporters. Straights, gays, feminists, free-speech activists, pornographers, sex workers, and the like failed to see the utility of joining a coalition-based movement. Even people who are comfortable with their own sexual desires tend to be squeamish about the desires of others that they do not share.

The Sexual Freedom League also failed because its founders believed they could use political activism to change deep-seated cultural attitudes. Poland did not appreciate the extent of American ambivalence about sexuality. It would take far more than protests or demonstrations to force Americans to recognize the hypocrisy of celebrating American liberty and individualism while prohibiting freedom of sexual self-expression. Moreover, the leaders of the SFL had no vision of the society they were working toward. Without a clear blueprint for the future, they had no hope of ever enlisting major support from college students and other young adults, who already enjoyed unprecedented freedom to have premarital sex. Finally, compared to the serious issues involved in the civil rights movement and the nascent antiwar movement, the mission of the SFL could only seem trivial.

By the beginning of 1966, Jefferson Poland had faded from the national scene. He remained a colorful figure in the Bay Area counterculture (going so far as to change his name legally to Jefferson Fuck and then Jefferson Clitlick), but the increasingly dramatic events of the sixties overshadowed Poland's modest efforts to effect social change. Across the country, thousands of students joined protests against the Vietnam War and thousands more let their hair grow long and began calling themselves "freaks," and later, "hippies." . . . As the ranks of the hippies grew, Jefferson Poland and his fellow Sexual Freedom Leaguers believed bourgeois morality to be on the brink of collapse. The gates of Eden were to be reopened at last.

Sex Politics in the City of Sisterly and Brotherly Loves

MARC STEIN

On Monday evening, 22 August 1960, sixteen law enforcement officers and one postal inspector in the well-to-do Main Line suburb of Radnor descended on one of the first meetings held in the Philadelphia area to discuss forming a local "homophile" political organization. In what one newspaper called "the biggest raid of its kind in township history," eighty four people were rounded up, transported to police headquarters, and arrested on charges related to the showing of "allegedly objectionable films." According to Jack Adair, whose family owned the estate where the meeting was held, "almost all" of those arrested were men, and most were middle class and white. Officials spent several hours identifying and interrogating those arrested and examining the movies seized. By Tuesday morning, eighty two of those arrested had been released on condition that they later appear as witnesses. As the long night of the Radnor raid ended, bail was set for Adair and "Albert J. de Dion," the chairman of the New York Area Council of the Mattachine Society, the first sustained homophile organization in the United States.

According to Adair, the films shown contained "no graphic sex scenes," and "not even touching or hand holding." Barbara Gittings, who lived in Philadelphia and in 1958 helped found the New York chapter of the national lesbian organization, the Daughters of Bilitis (DOB), was not present at the raid but remembers hearing that the films were "not porn," "nor were they even skin flicks." . . . The homophile magazine *ONE* reported that the movies included *Fireworks,* hastening

This material is an edited version of "Sex Politics in the City of Sisterly and Brotherly Loves," by Marc Stein, in *Radical History Review* 59 (1994): 60–92. Copyright 1994, MARHO: The Radical Historians' Organization. All rights reserved. Reprinted by permission of Duke University Press.

to add that this was "a film about homosexuality which had previously been cleared by the courts." . . .

Whether the films were scientific documentaries, male physique movies, avant garde underground works, pornographic films, or some combination thereof, the police and post office evidently decided that obscenity charges would not hold up in court. Pennsylvania's film obscenity law had been declared unconstitutional just days before the raid. With no film obscenity or censorship laws on the books in Pennsylvania, all remaining charges were eventually dropped.

Discussing the Radnor raid, Gittings argues that despite the final outcome, the events of 1960 demonstrate that "the real power of the police is the power to arrest." Ironically, Adair remembers that one of the reasons the meeting was held in the suburbs was that this was thought to be safer than the city. . . . With the Radnor raid, Philadelphia's suburbs earned the distinction of being the site of the first police raid of a lesbian-gay political meeting in the United States.

Several months after the raid, a group of Philadelphia-area residents met with Mattachine Public Relations Director Curtis Dewees to establish a local chapter (MSP), elect officers, and plan activities for the 150 people whose names appeared on an initial mailing list. The first issue of the *Mattachine Philadelphia Newsletter* appeared in March 1961, described the Radnor raid, and made efforts to address the fears that the police action undoubtedly inspired: "There is no reason to believe it need ever occur again. This was the first time the police have ever disrupted any Mattachine meeting, and we have confidence it will be the last. To those of you still hiding in the bushes, up in the hay loft, under beds, and behind locked doors, we would like to shout . . . 'COME OUT! COME OUT! WHEREVER YOU ARE!!' "

The story of the Radnor raid introduces several of the most important themes of lesbian-gay politics in the 1960s. Time and time again, police repression and postal surveillance would constrain lesbian-gay political organizing. Mainstream media would continue to choose when and how to report on lesbian-gay news, while lesbian-gay political organizations would develop media specifically addressed to their imagined communities. Lesbians and gay men would continue their efforts to carve out protected spheres of activity in their urban and suburban neighborhoods. Political activists would continue to debate strategies for cultivating respectability. And lesbian-gay historical memory would again and again be influenced by desires to reclaim a sexually respectable past.

Inspired by the efforts of other "minority" political groups, the work of homo-phile organizations in other cities, and daily struggles to survive and thrive, a small number of Philadelphia lesbians and gay men came to believe that forming politi-cal organizations might be the best way to address the problems their communities faced. In the 1950s, Philadelphians had faced controversies over homosexuality without benefit of organized lesbian-gay action. The Catholic Church had mounted an anti-gay campaign against naming the Delaware River's new bridge in honor of Walt Whitman. [Police Inspector Frank] Rizzo had mobilized anti-gay sentiment in widely publicized coffeehouse raids. And street violence had begun to surround the drag queen parades that marched through Center City every Halloween night.

Working in political organizations was only one of many options lesbians and gay men had for improving the quality of their lives, and the specific political work engaged in by these organizations required making choices among a variety of competing projects. Activists made decisions about alliances and tactics, and they also selected their targets from among the social institutions that most oppressed lesbians and gay men—the state, religion, science and medicine, the family, business, education, and the media. Nothing about this process was inevitable. As it turned out, the very acts of forming these organizations—meeting in private homes and public places, renting offices, publishing and distributing literature, sponsoring public events, advertising in local newspapers, and engaging in public demonstrations—forced Philadelphians to re-negotiate the conditions of lesbian and gay life in their city. A "late beginning" relative to Los Angeles, San Francisco, and New York marked the Radnor meeting and the subsequent history of lesbian-gay activism in Philadelphia in the 1960s. Harry Hay and a small group of gay leftists in Los Angeles had found the Mattachine Society in 1951. Del Martin and Phyllis Lyon had established the lesbian-focused Daughters of Bilitis (DOB) as a women's organization in San Francisco in 1955. . . . By the time of the Radnor raid, the male-dominated Mattachine had embraced what [historian] John D'Emilio describes as a conservative and assimilationist "retreat to respectability." The DOB, which strongly defended the need for a "separate and distinct women's organization" within the homophile movement, was equally respectable and joined Mattachine in developing small chapters around the country.

Although Philadelphia's lesbian-gay organizational politics were initially inspired by developments elsewhere, within a few years Philadelphians struck out in new directions. In fact, in the years between 1963 and 1969, Philadelphia supplied much of the leadership for the most militant female and male wings of the national homophile movement. Philadelphia's lesbian-gay politics in the 1960s also differed markedly from those of many other cities in that many of its most dynamic groups brought together lesbians and gay men in the same organizations.

Whether sex-mixed or not, Philadelphia's most distinctive contributions to the national homophile movement in the 1960s were rooted in two political formations not always emphasized in previous scholarship—one, a militant, sexual liberationist, and misogynist gay male politics; the other, a militant lesbian politics closely allied with gay male counterparts. . . . Somewhat paradoxically, Philadelphia was at the center of both of these tendencies.

Political relations between lesbians and gay men in Philadelphia were sometimes cooperative, sometimes ridden with conflict, but they were frequently based on conceptions of lesbian-gay community that differed from those of activists in other cities and nonactivists in Philadelphia. . . . Most lesbian and gay male activists would come to think of themselves as both members of the same community and members of sex-specific communities. But the balance between these two senses of community changed dramatically over time. . . . In the end, the conditions of life for lesbians and gay men in Philadelphia would be set not only in ongoing negotiations with straight society, and not only in ongoing negotiations between lesbians and gay men within their own communities, but in the ways that these two processes were intricately linked.

The period from 1960 through early 1965 was marked by a high degree of cooperation between lesbians and gay men in Philadelphia's political organizations, as members of both communities joined together first in a Mattachine chapter and then in the Janus Society (JS). Mae Polikoff was MSP's and then Janus's first president. According to "Mark Kendall," who joined MSP and served as Janus vice president, about equal numbers of women and men attended meetings in 1962–1963.

. . . MSP at this time was not all-white, but it was more white than Philadelphia's population as a whole. Philadelphia may have been distinctive in organizing lesbians and gay men together, but it was typical in failing to organize successfully beyond the European-American community. Lesbians and gay men of color, and white lesbian[s] and Latinos/as in Philadelphia certainly engaged in political activity, but for the most part they did not work within homophile groups in the early 1960s. This would change in the mid to late sixties when African-American writer Adrian Stanford's poem "Remembrance of Rittenhouse Square" appeared in *ONE* magazine, when Japanese-American human rights activist Kyoshi Kuromiya took part in homophile movement demonstrations, and when Cuban emigré Ada Bello became a local DOB leader. In the early 1970s, African-American lesbian-feminist Anita Cornwell would start writing for the lesbian press and local lesbians and gay men of color would take the lead in gay liberation.

MSP and Janus's mixed-sex organizing in part reflected the community experiences that its members brought to the organization. For example "Joan Fraser" explained that as a teenager she "fell in with a set of gay boys" and "When lesbians came along and I met them I was sort of set up for them." . . .

. . . Gittings, although affiliated with DOB and not MSP or Janus, also had forged bonds with gay men that affected her sense of identity and community. In the 1950s, Gittings dressed as a boy, hitchhiked to New York, and frequented the gay bars there, until she found out about the existence of bars in Philadelphia, where she came to be known as "Sonny."

Asked about relations between gay men and lesbians during these years, Gittings recently explained, "I didn't know any lesbians. Or practically none. Mostly [it was] gay men I was socializing with." The bonds Gittings felt with gay men increased after she witnessed a violent attack by Marines on a gay male friend named Pinky outside a Philadelphia bar.

Looking back on her early years, Gittings remembers "no trouble at all, being my own person, as a girl, as a female, when I was growing up. But the one problem I really did have was coming to terms with being gay. . . . I am very strongly gay-identified. I am not, what some lesbians call themselves, a woman-identified woman." . . .

If mixed-sex organizing in part reflected experiences prior to movement activity, lesbian and gay encounters within MSP and the JS also affected future developments. Adair doesn't remember conflicts in these groups. "Kendall" recalls that in this period he "didn't see any real problems" between the men and women and thought there was a "feeling of cooperation." . . .

Marge McCann also thinks that lesbians and gay men in the early Janus "got along" and doesn't think there was a lot of conflict. She remembers that she and her lover "Joan Fraser" "hung out with the men and with the women." . . . McCann argues that being "brought into activism in a mixed-gender organization" influenced her greatly. "[I]f my first organization had been DOB, my philosophy as a growing activist would have been shaped by that. Instead it was shaped by Mattachine and Janus."

Lack of conflict does not necessarily imply lack of discrimination. Later on, McCann could look back and identify sexism within the early Janus. "There wasn't a women's movement yet so there wasn't anything to have a conflict about. We knew our place." McCann remembers "that we were always the coffee makers . . . typing things in triplicate. . . . I mean there was a clear set of . . . chores for women." On the other hand, she doesn't think that there was more inequality in the homophile movement than in other movements. Moreover, "there were so few of us that I think there was more opportunity for a woman to be in a leadership position."

In late 1962, *Greater Philadelphia Magazine* published Gaeton Fonzi's groundbreaking article, "The Furtive Fraternity," which highlighted the central role that lesbian-gay cooperation played in the homophile movement's strategies of respectability. Although the piece focused almost exclusively on gay men's lives (and for its title used a distinctly male term), one section focused on mixed-sex political organizing. Janus's membership was said to be about 25 percent female, but four of the seven activists interviewed on the subject of political organizing were women. . . .

The Janus members' comments reveal a great deal about the assumptions that underlay early Philadelphia homophile activism. Fonzi explained that "the primary point they were all eager to get across was that the majority of homosexuals are, in everything but their sexual inclinations, no different than anyone else." But their words also suggest that in many ways the lesbians and gay men interviewed thought of themselves as not different from each other. Responding to the "fallacy" that sexual coercion led to lesbian-gay identity, Jane argued not in female terms but in male ones: "This idea of the old sex deviate preying on the young boy and turning him into a homosexual is ridiculous." . . . Describing why they didn't want their full names to be used in the article, Marge, Mel, and Joan all explained the social and occupational dangers they might face.

The female and male Janus members also took pains to downplay the sexual aspects of their lives and to criticize the "swishy type of homosexual who brought contempt and derision on the majority of homosexuals." "The Janus Society," they said, "urged all homosexuals to adopt a behavior code which would be beyond criticism and which would eliminate many of the barriers to integration with the heterosexual world." Paradoxically, although these lesbian and gay activists identified closely with each other because of the shared problems and possibilities presented by their sexual orientations, they [believed] that their mutual cause would be advanced if their communities adhered to conventional sex and gender norms that distinguished clearly between women and men. Lesbian-gay political community was being built on the ground of female-male difference.

The election of a gay man to lead Janus changed the terms of lesbian-gay cooperation. Having defeated McCann in 1963, Clark Polak began to dominate the organization. Cooperation, however, did not disappear immediately, shifting instead to a fragile division of labor. While Polak took control locally, "Fraser" and McCann became leading national activists as Janus delegates to the regional federation, East Coast Homophile Organizations (ECHO). . . .

A second division of labor appeared in Janus's early publications. While a gay man became the editor of Janus's newsletter, "Fraser" edited a woman's page. When Polak began pouring his energies into the organization's monthly *DRUM* magazine, "Barbara Harris" became the editor of the new monthly newsletter distributed to Janus members only. "Fraser" contributed articles and a "Woman's Way" advice column to *DRUM*. . . .

An aggressive championing of respectability marked many of Janus's activities in these years. Janus sponsored discussion groups, social events, and a lecture series that drew as many as four hundred people at a time to some of the city's major hotels. The group regularly sent out speakers, some of whom were interviewed on radio programs. Janus opened an office from which it provided legal, medical, and psychological referrals. Much of Janus's work involved engaging in critical dialogue with the media, the psychotherapeutic professions, law enforcement officials, and politicians. Among the group's most important activities were its work for the revision of Pennsylvania's sodomy law; against the exclusion of homosexuals from the military and federal employment; and against discrimination in public accommodations.

This strategy continued to rely on a joint lesbian-gay effort to conform to dominant sex-gender conventions. For example, *Confidential* magazine reported that delegates at the 1963 ECHO conference "looked more like grey-flannel business men than obvious limp-wristers." *Confidential* writer Ken Travis wrote that "deadly respectability was the keynote" and that "everyone was conservatively dressed" with the men in "Ivy League fashion," the women in "dresses or suits," and no "swishing" and no "bottled-in-blond men, limp wrists or lisping" permitted. In fact, according to Travis, "A couple of local queens who sashayed up to one session were told politely but firmly to go home and come back only if they were properly dressed and behaved."

If Travis is to believed, this effort to cloak themselves in signs of respectability was not always successful, as he noticed that "a high proportion of the women had very short haircuts." That cultivating respectability was a strategy is suggested in a story told by one hotel elevator operator. "I took a couple of women up to their rooms," he said, "but when they came down, they were men!" . . .

The combination of lesbian respectability and gay male respectability simultaneously strengthened the activists' strategy and made worse the exclusions that this strategy required. Working with gay men, lesbians could gain the public visibility more often afforded gay men and could make use of greater male access to sociocultural resources. In the company of lesbians, gay men could hope to shed their images as sexually predatory perverts who were not in any ways "domesticated" by "female influence." Both lesbians and gay men could use heterosocial visibility to keep the sexual aspects of their homosexualities invisible. As an accommodationist strategy for both groups, otherwise unconventional activists could be seen as conforming to heterosocial sex-gender conventions. Because sex between lesbians and gay men was presumed rare, this strategy could also work subversively by challenging expectations that female-male relations were necessarily sexual and that homosexuality was linked to hatred or fear of the "other" sex. One cost of this strategy was the exclusion of gender crossers; another was the acceptance of conventional sex-gender and heterosocial norms. To the extent that such norms were central to the oppression of lesbians and gay men, these strategies of respectability were necessarily limited.

If lesbian-gay cooperation was part of a consciously devised strategy of cultivating respectability, it also both expressed and contributed to shared senses of community. Although lesbians and gay men were also developing sex-separate identities, in those spheres of activity in which they mixed, lesbians and gay men often identified with and played important roles for one another. At times, activists discussed quite openly their efforts to build unity. One Janus discussion focused on the question "Can Homosexual Men and Women Get Along Together?" and another asked "Should Male Homosexuals Marry Female Homosexuals?" . . .

Even in such discussions of lesbian-gay male difference, what is striking is the effort to build a sense of community that would encompass lesbians and gay men. This was spearheaded by lesbians. Gay men rarely spoke about such differences, discussing homosexuality in sex-neutral terms that in fact ignored or downplayed lesbian-gay differences. In those Janus activities controlled more by men, men's interests dominated. To the extent that the work of political organizations reflected more broadly and deeply based community developments, the period from late 1960 through early 1965 illustrated the promise of lesbian-gay cooperation. . . .

Relations between Philadelphia's lesbian and gay activists were never free from tension. But conflict reached new heights and took new forms in 1965. D'Emilio describes this period as one of renewed militancy in the national movement, as radicals pressed more insistently for social change through direct action. One of the most important projects of militants was the annual July 4th demonstrations at Philadelphia's Independence Hall (1965–1969). And two of the most nationally important homophile publications were led by militant Philadelphians: Polak, who edited *DRUM* (1964–1969), and Gittings, who edited the national DOB publication, *The Ladder: A Lesbian Review* (1963–1966). . . .

The first break in lesbian-gay organizational cooperation can be seen in the 1965 decision to kick Janus out of ECHO, the regional coalition, and to welcome instead a new MSP founded by "Fraser" and McCann. The main source of conflict was Janus's magazine *DRUM*. One of the main activities of the early homophile movement was producing periodicals that offered more positive portrayals of homosexuality than had been previously available. Scholars have identified *Mattachine Review, ONE,* and *The Ladder* as the premier homophile publications of the 1950s and early 1960s. With circulations in the hundreds and low thousands, these magazines reached a small national community with their careful efforts to promote respectability and alliances with professionals.

When Polak placed an advertisement for his new publication in the 1964 ECHO conference program, homophile activists around the country were undoubtedly shocked. "*DRUM* presents news for 'queers,' and fiction for 'perverts,'" the ad explained. "Photo essays for 'fairies' and laughs for 'faggots.'" *DRUM* combined male physique photography (including nude shots beginning with the December 1965 issue), the raw, risque, and campy comic strip "Harry Chess," and hard-hitting news, features, parodies, editorials, and reviews. In promoting a radical and entertaining vision of sexual liberation, *DRUM* challenged the carefully constructed image of respectability cultivated by much of the homophile movement.

The first issue of *DRUM* appeared in October 1964. Polak explained the magazine's title by quoting Thoreau: "If a man does not keep pace with his companions, perhaps it is because he hears a different drummer." From the start, Polak knew that he was establishing a new genre of lesbian-gay periodicals. *"DRUM* is a new concept in magazine publishing," he wrote. "To our knowledge, a balance of top level photography, fiction, news and humor directed specifically to the male homosexual has never before been attempted."

DRUM's advertisements sought to appeal to potential readers by placing the magazine within discourses of both sexual and homosexual liberation. The approach to queers, perverts, fairies, and faggots was preceded by the statement that:

> DRUM stands against the common belief that sexual drives may be dismissed like a stray dog—with a shout and a kick. Or that they can be sermonized away or replaced by a veil of beauty. Or that if one does enough gymnastics or knitting, there won't be enough time to think about sex. DRUM stands for a realistic approach to sexuality in general and homosexuality in particular. DRUM stands for sex in perspective, sex with insight, and, above all, sex with humor.

In weaving these two discourses together, this advertisement worked to liberate gay men sexually and ally the homosexual cause with the broader sexual liberation movement.

In fact, Polak wrote in 1965 that *DRUM*'s objective was a "gay *Playboy,* with the news coverage of *Time.*" He continued, "By putting 'sex' back into 'homosexuality', by producing a magazine geared to the homosexual as an individual who is something other than an abused, ever-sinned-against outcast, by approaching our goals with a light and sometimes audacious view, and by being unequivocally (sic) pro-homosexual, we will continue to rock the boat." These pro-sex and pro-gay messages were specifically not aimed at a "general audience." In 1966, *DRUM*'s contents page began including a statement that the magazine was "published by male homosexuals for the information and entertainment of other male homosexuals." . . .

DRUM quickly became the largest circulation homophile publication in the United States, larger than all other homophile publications combined. Despite this fact, *DRUM* has been largely ignored by historians. Occupying an anomalous position as a hybrid of physique photography and homophile movement magazines, *DRUM* failed to fall neatly into one category or the other. Like the movies shown the night of the Radnor raid, *DRUM* has also been forgotten in part because it presents problems for those concerned about nonrespectable historical evidence.

While tens of thousands of readers embraced *DRUM*'s unique blending of sexual liberation and homophile activism, lesbian and gay male homophile leaders around the country lined up solidly against the magazine. Nearly every activist critic of *DRUM* rejected not the existence of the magazine but its explicit and open relationship to homophile politics. . . . MSNY's Dick Leitsch wrote "I don't object to titillating pictures being published; I only reject the right of someone claiming to be a part of this movement doing it." . . . Drawing a clear line between politics and entertainment, Leitsch concluded that "If we're in business to entertain, then let's go whole hog and provide drag shows, muscle movies, gay bars, dances and orgies!"

The most comprehensive and public (if indirect) attack on *DRUM* came from one of the most militant homophile organizations on the East Cost. An editorial penned by the Mattachine Society of Washington (MSW) and appearing in *Eastern Mattachine Magazine* announced that in the future, no MSW material would be sent to publications that featured physique photos. "The policy," the editorial explained, "is viewed as the only concrete means which the MSW has to place itself against the rising tide of 'combination' magazines which contain both articles of serious homophile interest and photographs of naked teenage boys in provocative poses. These magazines, which may sometimes have the best of intentions, can easily bolster the public's erroneous image of the homosexual as a child-molesting sex fiend." . . . What Polak had identified as a highly successful strategy for promoting homophile activism, MSW and other homophile groups saw as their movement's greatest danger.

And *DRUM* did pose risks for the homophile movement. Beginning in 1964, Polak, Janus, and *DRUM* were targeted by customs, post office, and federal, state, and local law enforcement officials. Government agencies conducted an ongoing campaign of surveillance against not only Janus activists in Philadelphia, but also readers of *DRUM* around the country. Richard Schlegel, the founder of a Janus chapter in Harrisburg, lost his high-level job as the Pennsylvania Department of Highways's Director of Finance in 1965 after the results of postal monitoring of his mail were revealed to his superiors. . . .

. . . Polak was not the only editor of a national homophile publication experimenting with photographs in 1964. Barbara Gittings and Kay Lahusen began using photo covers for *The Ladder* in the same year. Although the photographs that were used in *The Ladder* were highly respectable, Lahusen was "enthusiastic" about the idea of nude photographs in the magazine. For his part, Polak selected what he considered "artistic" and "aesthetic" photos over those more "sexual" and "erotic." In another interesting parallel, both publications first featured photographic images of African Americans in 1966. Juxtaposing these developments in *The Ladder* and *DRUM*, it seems clear that both the lesbian and gay movements had reached a stage in which lesbian-gay identities were being "embodied" in some of their most visible representations. Lesbian and gay bodies had for a long time been marked as diseased and disfigured, and these photographic innovations can be seen as an effort to challenge these visions. The human body had become a crucial site for representing positive lesbian and gay identities.

But comparing the photos used in *The Ladder* and *DRUM* also offers an opportunity to explore lesbian-gay differences as well. *DRUM* used paid models; *The Ladder* relied on unpaid volunteers. *DRUM*'s photographic subjects were easily recognizable; *The Ladder* featured shots that usually concealed the subjects' individual identities. *DRUM*'s subjects were nearly or fully nude, while *The Ladder's* were more fully clothed. Most importantly, *DRUM*'s photographs were rejected by the homophile movement; *The Ladder*'s were celebrated.

Lesbian activists from Philadelphia figured centrally in the isolation of Janus, *DRUM,* and Polak from much of the homophile movement in 1965. Their actions, however, belie any attempt to interpret this rejection as a simple conflict between lesbians and gay men, between militants and accommodationists, or between sexual liberationists and sexual respectables. Although opposed to Polak, Philadelphia's leading lesbian activists generally supported working closely with gay men. And while they continued to defend sexually respectable strategies, these women were militant supporters of direct action tactics. As earlier strategies of heterosocial respectability were abandoned by those who favored Polak's sexual liberationism or DOB's sex-separatism, Philadelphia's lesbian activists became more militant about their commitments to work with gay men, cultivate respectability, and improve the conditions of lesbian-gay life.

On 6 February 1965, ECHO unanimously voted to accept the new MSP led by "Fraser" and McCann and to expel Janus. Responding to Polak's request for an explanation, "Fraser" drafted a formal letter that articulated the strategy of respectability that remained a mainstay even among ECHO militants:

> [C]ontroversial, unconventional, and unusual ideas and positions have far higher probability of being listened to and accepted, if presented within the framework of, and clothed with the symbols of acceptability, conventionality, and respectability (in the listener's terms, not in the speakers'), as arbitrary as we grant most of those symbols to be. . . .

No sooner had Philadelphia lesbians and Washington and New York gay men formed an alliance of militant respectability against Polak than conflicts with DOB lesbians tore ECHO apart. On 5 June 1965, ECHO accepted Frank Kameny's proposal, against the wishes of the DOB-NY delegates, to sponsor picketing demonstrations on 26 June at the Civil Service Building in Washington, D.C. and on July 4th at Independence Hall. Reaction was swift, and, within days, DOB withdrew from ECHO. Philadelphia lesbians tried to use their positions as both women and militants to force DOB's hand. Descending on a DOB-NY meeting on 11 July, lesbian militants pushed through a resolution proposed by McCann encouraging the national DOB to support ECHO's demonstrations. Unlike Mattachine, however, DOB remained a centralized national organization, and in the end, the East Coast militant lesbians lost out. Within a short time, McCann was no longer a national DOB officer and Gittings, who actively supported the militant position, was removed as editor of *The Ladder.* . . .

While "Fraser" and McCann's decision to break with Janus was very much a product of lesbian-gay conflict, they were not opposed to working closely with gay men, which they underlined by choosing to adopt the Mattachine name and resisting pressure to affiliate with DOB. National DOB leader Del Martin hoped "Fraser" and McCann would start a DOB-Philadelphia chapter: "[C]reating another Mattachine Society will not endear you to the San Francisco group here." DOB was an "important cog in the homophile movement," Martin argued, "since the organizations lean heavily toward the male orientation and neither understand nor pretend to deal with the problems of the female." . . .

. . . McCann's response to Martin defined the dominant lesbian activist position in Philadelphia in this period:

> First, I should assure you that MSP will not be one of those homophile groups which ignores the existence of the Lesbian. For one thing, we are. For another, I think that all too few Lesbians feel any real "kinship" with male homosexuals, feeling rather that "those nasty boys" deserve whatever they get in the courts and in public opinion. I, for one, do not feel that way. We may not get into legal predicaments as often, but we, too, have to hide, most of the time, our real natures, from society, family, employers, etc. Yes, some of the problems of the Lesbian are unique, and so are some of the problems

that male homosexuals have. However, the Janus Society here does not represent either the Lesbian *or* the male homosexual, and there is work to be done. . . .

Despite their "unique" problems, McCann imagined lesbians and gay men sharing identities, communities, and politics.

. . . Objecting to DOB opposition to picketing, "Fraser" stressed the common identity she felt with gay men and not with certain kinds of feminists: "To those ardent feminists in the movement who see no reason why we women should 'stick out our necks' so the men can cruise in freedom, let me remind you that women in government are subject to the same pressures as men and lose their jobs just as quickly."

. . . The first picket in Washington, she continued, "was composed of conservatively dressed people carrying signs." "I mention all of this to allay the fears of those who visualize us as wild-eyed, dungareed radicals." In their defense of picketing, many militants focused on the respectability of activist clothing, which depended upon visible distinctions between female and male dress. The "Rules for Picketing" used for the July 4th demonstration included requirements for "conservative and conventional dress," which meant suits, white shirts, and ties for men; and dresses for women. Lesbian-gay political militancy, too, was being built on the ground of female-male difference.

How did Polak respond to these developments? Although isolated by the homophile movement, Polak was the leader of one of the most active gay organizations in the country, the most widely read homophile publication, and an increasingly successful pornography business he ran under the name Trojan Book Service. Polak supported the turn to direct action, and even organized a sit-in at Dewey's restaurant in Philadelphia in April-May 1965, just before the first July 4th demonstration. While ECHO insisted on respectable dress in its demonstrations, the Dewey's sit-in was organized to defend the rights of "masculine" women, "feminine" men, and those lesbians and gay men who didn't "appear to be heterosexual," many of whom had been denied service at the restaurant. But if many of his activities defied the politics of respectability, Polak also poured his profits into highly respectable legal battles.

In mid 1965, the Janus newsletter announced that Polak would resign as Janus president and become its executive director. A short time later, plans were announced to divide Janus into three components, the Janus Trust, *DRUM* Publishing Company, and the Homosexual Law Reform Society (HLRS). Some had hopes that "Barbara Harris," who was the Janus newsletter editor, membership chair, and lecture series moderator, would emerge as the new leader of Janus. . . .

. . . Dick Leitsch wrote[,] "You are quite an attractive and sensible spokesman for the Society. Perhaps a woman's touch in *DRUM* would make it less faggot orientated and more community minded." Apparently Leitsch thought that a feminine lesbian leader would help Janus appeal to straight audiences: "We aren't going to interest anybody but gay boys as long as we cater to them, and as long as we present only male homosexuals to the public. This is why I was so glad to see that you are a non-stereotype." . . .

For reasons that are unclear, Janus remained fully under Polak's control, but he increasingly focused attention on HLRS. One HLRS case was won in the New Jersey Supreme Court in 1967 and established the right of "well-behaved" lesbians and gay men to congregate in bars. A second case, *Boutilier,* challenged anti-gay immigration law, emphasizing the good behavior of the litigant, but was lost 6–3 in the U.S. Supreme Court in 1967. . . . If some activists believed in respectability as an expression of their identities and aspirations, Polak used respectability selectively, aiming carefully tailored messages to specific audiences.

Polak also responded with a direct attack on the homophile movement. These attacks only increased after more respectable activists took objection to the arrangements Polak made for a national homophile conference to be held in 1966 at a physique photography studio in Kansas City owned by Troy Saxon, a.k.a. Stu "Pinky" Rosenbloom. . . . Polak struck out again at a national conference: "Anti-homosexuality is rampant within the organizations and the concern is for the 'good' homosexuals—which I call Aunt Maryism. . . . Your publications, besides being often illiterate and poorly edited, are also reeking with anti-homosexuality, groveling obsequeousness (sic) and seem almost designed to maintain the homosexual's position of inferiority."

But if Polak was increasingly alienated from the homophile movement, he maintained a large following among *DRUM*'s readers, and he emphatically articulated broad visions of sexual liberation. In one article, for example, Polak assailed the "anti-sexualism" of laws and attitudes on "abortion, birth control, obscenity, prostitution, adulter (sic), fornication, and cohabitation." And he wrote in *DRUM* "Sex cannot be 'dirty' because it cannot be 'pure.' It cannot 'enoble' one any more than it can 'debase.' It is not, under some circumstances, 'good' and under others, 'bad.' You in no way change it by calling a 'cock' a 'penis,' or a 'vagina' a 'cunt.'"

Be that as it may, Polak had a much easier time talking about cocks than cunts. It is not precisely true that Polak failed to consider lesbians at all in his political work. But the grounds he imagined for alliances between lesbians and gay men were as based in sex differences as the [views of] respectable militants and the old guard homophiles. Polak wrote that "Interest in visual sexual stimulation is a peculiarly masculine trait as women almost never achieve the same kind of arousal from photographs or artistic representations. Lesbians, for instance, are no more concerned with the *Playboy* fold out than straight women are with *TM* [*Tomorrow's Man*]."

In a 1966 interview, Polak again turned to the theme of lesbian-gay and female-male sexual differences:

> . . . Males and females, regardless of their sexual orientations, are males and females first. When a male is walking down the street—with either his girlfriend or his boyfriend—he's eyeing everyone who appeals to him. In the heterosexual and lesbian situations, the female's non-concern with a variety of sexual partners acts as a stabilizing influence.

Polak here linked gay men with straight men and lesbians with straight women, establishing grounds for same-sex bonds and identifications.

But Polak's vision of sexual differences also created grounds for lesbian-gay alliances: . . . "[T]he male homosexual attitude toward promiscuity is quite properly different from the heterosexual attitude because heterosexuality includes women." Because women are less concerned with sex, Polak argued, a balance is required in heterosexuality "in which males tone done their sexual interest and females increase their sexual interest." Homosexual men, on the other hand, were free to have more sexual partners while homosexual women "tend to be far less promiscuous." What lesbians and gay men had in common, then, was that both were more true to their "real" sexes than straights.

Had Polak built the JS around this idea, with as much attention to lesbians as gay men, Philadelphia might have produced a separate and equal path for lesbian and gay activism. But Polak's vision functioned more as an excuse to ignore lesbians than as a model for equality and cooperation. If strategies of sexual respectability were limited because of the ways they failed to challenge conventional sex-gender norms, strategies of gay male sexual liberation were limited because of the ways they failed to challenge conventional sexual norms.

The end of 1966 brought to a conclusion two years of intense conflicts in the national homophile movement, conflicts in which Philadelphians played central roles. Lesbian and gay Philadelphians would draw on their experiences of coopera-tion and conflict in the coming years. A DOB chapter would be established in 1967, only to dissolve into the sex-mixed Homophile Action League in 1968. Clark Polak, *DRUM,* and Trojan Book Service would face increasing harassment by law enforcement, post office, and customs officials. Obscenity convictions would play a role in Polak's decision to leave Philadelphia in the early 1970s. And lesbian and gay life in Philadelphia would be transformed by the twin revolutions of Stonewall in 1969, and the rise of lesbian-feminism in the early 1970s.

The history of lesbian-gay activism in Philadelphia in the 1960s suggests that when scholars look beyond New York, San Francisco, Los Angeles, and Washington, they will need to transform their views of the pre-Stonewall political movements of lesbians and gay men. Activists formed not only exclusively lesbian chapters of the DOB and predominantly gay male Mattachine chapters in the pre-Stonewall era. In Philadelphia, lesbians and gay men worked together in organizations such as Mattachine and Janus and lesbians led both Mattachine chapters. Also, as the his-tory of Clark Polak and *DRUM* demonstrate, sexual liberation was adopted by the gay political movement well before the 1970s. The Janus Society stood at the center of a "sex war" in the 1960s that predated and in some ways prefigured the more widely discussed "sex wars" of the 1970s. Finally, lesbian political history in Phila-delphia suggests the need to consider more seriously the place of militant activist lesbians who worked and identified closely with gay men.

FURTHER READING

Ninia Baehr, "Woman Controlled Abortion: The Self-Help Movement," *Abortion without Apology* (1990).

Beth Bailey, *Sex in the Heartland* (1999).

———, "Sexual Revolution(s)," in David Farber, ed., *The Sixties* (1994), 235–259.

John D'Emilio, *Sexual Politics, Sexual Communities: The Making of a Homosexual Minority in the United States, 1940–1970* (1983).

Martin B. Duberman, *Stonewall* (1993).

Alice Echols, *Daring to Be Bad: Radical Feminism in America, 1967–1975* (1989).

Barbara Ehrenreich, *The Hearts of Men: American Dreams and the Flight from Commitment* (1983).

Sara Evans, *Personal Politics* (1979).

David Garrow, *Liberty and Sexuality: The Right to Privacy and the Making of Roe v. Wade* (1994).

Terence Kissack, "Freaking Fag Revolutionaries: New York's Gay Liberation Front, 1969–1971," *Radical History Review* 62 (1995): 104–134.

Matthew Lasar, "The Triumph of the Visual: Stages and Cycles in the Pornography Controversy from the McCarthy Era to the Present," *Journal of Policy History* 7 (1995): 181–207.

Eric Marcus, *Making History: The Struggle for Gay and Lesbian Equal Rights, 1945–1990, An Oral History* (1992).

Ruth Rosen, *The World Split Open: How the Modern Women's Movement Changed America* (2000).

Alix Kates Shulman, "Sex and Power: Sexual Bases of Radical Feminism," in Catharine Stimpson and Ethel Person, eds., *Women: Sex and Sexuality* (1980), 21–35.

Daniel Scott Smith, "The Dating of the American Sexual Revolution: Evidence and Interpretation," in Michael Gordon, *The American Family in Social-Historical Perspective* (1978), 321–335.

Marc Stein, *City of Sisterly and Brotherly Loves : Lesbian and Gay Philadelphia, 1945–1972* (2000).

Verta Taylor and Leila J. Rupp, "Women's Culture and Lesbian Feminist Activism: A Reconsideration of Cultural Feminism," *Signs* 19 (1993): 32–61.

Jeffrey Weeks, "An Unfinished Revolution: Sexuality in the 20th Century," in Victoria Harwood et al., eds., *Pleasure Principles* (1993), 1–19.

C H A P T E R
13

Sexually Transmitted
Diseases

Syphilis and AIDS differ in their epidemiology and in the development of medical treatments, but their social and political histories reveal striking similarities. Twentieth-century Americans have oscillated in their response to diseases transmitted mainly through sexual contact: Are they primarily medical or moral problems? Do they justify state restrictions on individual liberty? Responses to sexually transmitted diseases (STDs) have been shaped by their identification with outcast or disadvantaged groups—prostitutes, African Americans, homosexual men—already stereotyped as sexually promiscuous, diseased, and immoral. In the early twentieth century, syphilis and gonorrhea were termed "the wages of sin." Decades later, AIDS was called by some a divine judgment against homosexuality; that was never a universal view, but the notion that AIDS is a "gay disease" persists in public opinion. Fears of epidemic infection and mass death commingle with moral convictions—as well as confusion, ignorance, and shame—about sexuality.

How did social attitudes about sexuality and disease affect the public health response? Again, a historical comparison between syphilis and AIDS is instructive. Considered an epidemic in the early 1900s, syphilis was treated—not always successfully—with painful injections of arsenic compounds until World War II, when penicillin was introduced as a reliable cure. Mobilization for World War I had set the stage for large-scale public health education and state intervention. The large number of draftees with syphilis alarmed government officials and resulted in an educational campaign at army bases, factories, and recreational facilities; in addition, many prostitutes submitted to compulsory inspections and were sometimes imprisoned. In the 1930s, anti-syphilis campaigns used newspaper publicity and widespread testing—including a test before receiving a marriage license. State-sponsored efforts to detect, treat, and prevent the disease took different forms, depending on the population targeted. The Tuskegee syphilis study reveals how black Americans were singled out for horrifying mistreatment. How could those who funded and conducted this research have viewed their ethical obligations, the role of the state, and civil liberties?

The AIDS crisis emerged in the 1980s under very different circumstances. A forceful political movement for gay rights made demands upon the state and scientific community for research, treatment, and prevention programs. Yet many of the earlier ethical and political questions remain: In what ways should the state intervene in sexual behavior? What is the moral dimension to the disease, if any? In the face of an epidemic, how should privacy rights and civil liberties be protected?

The history of sexually transmitted diseases is not only academic. Historical memory—the collective understanding of the past—has profoundly shaped responses to AIDS by the groups who have been disproportionately affected. The history of bathhouses, parks, and public restrooms—as places of policing and sexual freedom—informs the defense of civil liberties mounted by a number of gay political groups. Even more significant, the legacies of racism and betrayal embodied in the forty-year Tuskegee study have caused many African Americans to distrust public health programs to stop the spread of AIDS. Tragically, blacks are now nearly ten times more likely than whites to contract this disease.

◼ D O C U M E N T S

Public health campaigns to fight sexually transmitted diseases have often reflected larger social prejudices and reinforced sexual and racial stereotypes. In Document 1, Eunice Rivers, a black public health nurse, offered a close-up view of the rural black patients and the doctors involved in the Tuskegee syphilis study. How did she justify the study and her own role in it? In 1997, President Bill Clinton apologized on behalf of the nation to the survivors of the Tuskegee study—sixty-five years after it began, twenty-five years after it ended (Document 2). What is the significance of this formal public apology? Unlike earlier epidemics of sexually transmitted diseases, AIDS sparked an organized and often effective grassroots response. People with AIDS (PWAs) fought to define themselves, the nature of the disease, and their rights to treatment, privacy, and sexuality, as exemplified by the Denver Principles (Document 3) issued in 1983. In a private journal (Document 4), Robert Garcia wrote of his own AIDS-related illnesses and impending death. This gay man of color and activist with the AIDS Coalition to Unleash Power (ACT UP) revealed both his terror and his strength; he died in 1993 at age thirty-one. Municipal officials offered a different picture of gay men and the "promiscuity" that led to AIDS in a 1995 inspection report and court affidavit (Document 5); they documented the ongoing efforts by the New York City Department of Health to regulate and close gay theaters. A 1998 news article from the *Cleveland Plain Dealer* (Document 6) suggested several reasons—the memory of the Tuskegee study, religious values, and the belief that AIDS is a "white" and "gay" disease—for the inadequate response to AIDS in black communities. At the same time, it pointed out innovative efforts—from church vigils to beauty parlor teaching—to educate African Americans about the disease.

1. Nurse Eunice Rivers Describes the Tuskegee Syphilis Study, 1953

One of the longest continued medical surveys ever conducted is the study of untreated syphilis in the male Negro. This study was begun by the Public Health Service in the fall of 1932 in Macon County, Ala., a rural area in the eastern part of the State, and is now entering its twenty-second year. . . .

Eunice Rivers et al., "Twenty Years of Followup Experience in a Long-Range Medical Study," *Public Health Reports* 68 (April 1953): 391–395.

In beginning the study, schedules of the blood-drawing clinics throughout the county were announced through every available source, including churches, schools, and community stores. The people responded willingly, and 600 patients were selected for the study—400 who had syphilis and, for controls, 200 who did not. The patients who had syphilis were all in the latent stage; any acute cases requiring treatment were carefully screened out for standard therapy.

At Tuskegee, each of the 600 patients initially was given a complete physical examination, including chest X-rays and electrocardiograms. Careful histories were taken and blood tests were repeated. Thereafter, each of the patients was followed up with an annual blood test and, whenever the Public Health Service physicians came to Tuskegee, physical examinations were repeated.

There have been four surveys: in 1932, 1938, 1948, and 1952. Between surveys contact with the patients was maintained through the local county health department and an especially assigned public health nurse, whose chief duties were those of followup worker on this project. The nurse also participated in a generalized public health nursing program, which gave her broad contact with the families of the patients and demonstrated that she was interested in other aspects of their welfare as well as in the project. The nurse was a native of the county, who had lived near her patients all her life, and was thoroughly familiar with their local ideas and customs.

A most important phase of the study was to follow as many patients as possible to postmortem examination, in order to determine the prevalence and severity of the syphilitic disease process. Cooperation of patients with this plan was sought by offering burial assistance . . . on condition that permission be granted for autopsy. For the majority of these poor farmers such financial aid was a real boon, and often it was the only "insurance" they could hope for. The Federal Government offered physical examinations and incidental medication, such as tonics and analgesics, but was unable to provide financial assistance on a continuous basis. The Milbank Memorial Fund burial assistance made it possible to obtain a higher percentage of permissions for postmortem examinations than otherwise would have been granted.

Transportation to the hospital for X-rays and physical examination was furnished by the nurse. Her car was too small to bring in more than two patients at one trip; therefore two men were scheduled for examination in the morning, and two for the afternoon. During the early years of the study, when the county was strictly a rural one, the roads were very poor, some being impassible during the rainy season. Very often, the patients spent hours helping to get the car out of a mudhole. Now, with modern conveniences (telephones, electricity, cars, and good roads) the nurse's problems are fewer than in the early days.

Having a complete physical examination by a doctor in a hospital was a new experience for most of the men. Some were skeptical; others were frightened and left without an examination. Those who were brave enough to remain were very pleased. Only one objection occurred frequently: the "back shot," never again! There are those who, today, unjustifiably attribute current complaints (backaches, headaches, nervousness) to those spinal punctures.

The patients have been followed through the years by the same nurse but by different doctors. Some doctors were liked by all the patients; others were liked by only a few. The chief factor in this was the length of time doctor and patients had to get to know each other. If the doctor's visit to the area was brief, he might not have time to learn and to understand the habits of the patients. Likewise, the patients did not have an opportunity to understand the doctor. Because of their confidence in the nurse, the patients often expressed their opinion about the doctor privately to her. She tried always to assure them that the doctor was a busy person, interested in many things, but that they really were first on his program.

It is very important for the followup worker to understand both patient and doctor, because she must bridge the gap between the two. The doctors were concerned primarily with obtaining the most efficient and thorough medical examination possible for the group of 600 men. While they tried to give each patient the personal interest he deserved, this was not always possible due to the pressure of time. Occasionally the patient was annoyed because the doctor did not pay attention to his particular complaint. He may have believed that his favorite home remedy was more potent than the doctor's prescription, and decided to let the whole thing go. It then became the task of the nurse to convince him that the examinations were beneficial. If she failed, she might find that in the future he not only neglected to answer her letters but managed to be away from home whenever she called. Sometimes the doctor grumbled because of the seemingly poor cooperation and slowness of some of the patients; often the nurse helped in these situations simply by bridging the language barrier and by explaining to the men what the doctor wanted.

Sometimes the nurse assisted the physician by warning him beforehand about the eccentricities of the patients he was scheduled to see during the day. For example, there was the lethargic patient with early cancer of the lip who needed strong language and grim predictions to persuade him to seek medical attention. On the other hand, there was the hypochondriac who overheard the doctor mention the 45° angle of rotation of his body during the X-ray examination; the next day, the entire county was buzzing with gossip about their remarkable friend who was still alive, "walking around with his heart tilted at a 45° angle."

Following a group of patients in a specialized field over a period of years becomes monotonous to patient and nurse, and both could lose interest easily. For the patients, the yearly visits by the "Government doctor," with free medicines, revived their interest. The annual blood tests and the surveys were always scheduled at "slack" times, between fall harvest and spring planting. The patients congregated in groups at churches and at crossroads to meet the nurse's car in the morning. As the newness of the project wore off and fears of being hurt were relieved, the gatherings became more social. The examination became an opportunity for men from different and often isolated parts of the county to meet and exchange news. Later the nurse's small car was replaced with a large, new, Government station wagon. The ride to and from the hospital in this vehicle with the Government emblem on the front door, chauffeured by the nurse, was a mark of distinction for many of the men who enjoyed waving to their neighbors as they drove by. They knew that they could get their pills and "spring tonic" from the nurse whenever they needed them between surveys, but they looked forward happily to having the Government doctor take their blood pressure and listen to their hearts. Those men who were advised about their diets were especially delighted even though they would not adhere to the restrictions.

Because of the low educational status of the majority of the patients, it was impossible to appeal to them from a purely scientific approach. Therefore, various methods were used to maintain and stimulate their interest. Free medicines, burial assistance or insurance (the project being referred to as "Miss Rivers' Lodge"), free hot meals on the days of examination, transportation to and from the hospital, and an opportunity to stop in town on the return trip to shop or visit with their friends on the streets all helped. In spite of these attractions, there were some who refused their examinations because they were not sick and did not see that they were being benefited. Nothing provoked some of the patients more than for a doctor to tell them that they were not as healthy as they felt. This attitude sometimes appeared to the examining physician as rank ingratitude for a thorough medical workup which would cost anyone else a large amount of money if sought at personal expense. At these times the nurse reminded the doctor of the gap between his education and health attitudes and those of the patients.

When a patient asks the nurse for help because he is a "Government patient" and she explains there are no funds for this, he may point out that he needs assistance while he is living, not after he is dead. Whenever the nurse heard this complaint, she knew that there was danger of a lost patient. She appealed to him from an unselfish standpoint: What the burial assistance would mean to his family, to pay funeral expenses or to purchase clothes for his orphaned children. Even though a large number wished they might derive more benefits from being "Government patients," most of them answered the call to meet the doctor, some willingly, others after much persuasion.

The study group was composed of farmers who owned their homes, renters who were considered permanent residents and day laborers on farms and in sawmills. The laborers were the hardest to follow. Some of the resident farmers traveled to other sections seeking work after their own crops had been harvested, but they came back when it was time to start planting. An effort was made continually through relatives to keep informed of the patients' most recent addresses, and this information regularly has been placed in their records. During the 20 years of the study, 520 of the original 600 men have been followed consistently if living, or to autopsy. It is possible that some of the 80 now considered lost will at some time return to the county or write the nurse from distant places for medical advice.

The excellent care given these patients was important in creating in the family a favorable attitude which eventually would lead to permission to perform an autopsy. Even in a friendly atmosphere, however, it was difficult for the nurse to approach the family, especially in the early years of the project, because she herself was uneasy about autopsies. She was pleasantly surprised to receive fine response from the families of the patients—only one refusal in 20 years and 145 autopsies obtained. Finally, the nurse realized that she and not the relatives had been hesitant and squeamish.

Sometimes the family asked questions concerning the autopsy, but offered no objections when they were assured that the body would not be harmed. If the patient had been ill for a long time and had not been able to secure any relief from his symptoms, they were anxious to know the reason. If he had died suddenly, they were anxious for some explanation. They also feared that some member of the family might have the same malady, and that information learned from the autopsy might aid them. Now, after many years, all of the patients are aware of the autopsies. When a member of "Miss Rivers' Lodge" passes, his surviving colleagues often will remind the family that the doctor wants "to look at his heart." Autopsies today are a routine; neither nurse nor family objects.

One cannot work with a group of people over a long period of time without becoming attached to them. This has been the experience of the nurse. She has had an opportunity to know them personally. She has come to understand some of their problems and how these account for some of their peculiar reactions. The ties are stronger than simply those of patient and nurse. There is a feeling of complete confidence in what the nurse advises. Some of them bring problems beyond her province, concerning building, insurance, and other things about which she can give no specific advice. She directs them always to the best available sources of guidance. Realizing that they do depend upon her and give her their trust, she has to keep an open mind and must be careful always not to criticize, but to help in the most ethical way to see that they get the best care.

2. President Bill Clinton Apologizes for the Tuskegee Syphilis Study, 1997

The eight men who are survivors of the syphilis study at Tuskegee are a living link to a time not so very long ago that many Americans would prefer not to remember, but we dare not forget. It was a time when our nation failed to live up to its ideals, when our nation broke the trust with our people that is the very foundation of our democracy. It is not only in remembering that shameful past that we can make amends and repair our nation, but it is in remembering that past that we can build a better present and a better future. And without remembering it, we cannot make amends and we cannot go forward.

So today America does remember the hundreds of men used in research without their knowledge and consent. We remember them and their family members. Men who were poor and African American, without resources and with few alternatives, they believed they had found hope when they were offered free medical care by the United States Public Health Service. They were betrayed.

Medical people are supposed to help when we need care, but even once a cure was discovered, they were denied help, and they were lied to by their government. Our government is supposed to protect the rights of its citizens; their rights were trampled upon. Forty years, hundreds of men betrayed, along with their wives and children, along with the community in Macon County, Alabama, the City of Tuskegee, the fine university there, and the larger African American community.

The United States government did something that was wrong—deeply, profoundly, morally wrong. It was an outrage to our commitment to integrity and equality for all our citizens.

To the survivors, to the wives and family members, the children and the grandchildren, I say what you know: No power on Earth can give you back the lives lost, the pain suffered, the years of internal torment and anguish. What was done cannot

"Remarks by the President in Apology for Study Done in Tuskegee," Office of the Press Secretary, the White House, May 16, 1997.

be undone. But we can end the silence. We can stop turning our heads away. We can look at you in the eye and finally say on behalf of the American people, what the United States government did was shameful, and I am sorry.

The American people are sorry—for the loss, for the years of hurt. You did nothing wrong, but you were grievously wronged. I apologize and I am sorry that this apology has been so long in coming.

To Macon County, to Tuskegee, to the doctors who have been wrongly associated with the events there, you have our apology, as well. To our African American citizens, I am sorry that your federal government orchestrated a study so clearly racist. That can never be allowed to happen again. It is against everything our country stands for and what we must stand against is what it was.

So let us resolve to hold forever in our hearts and minds the memory of a time not long ago in Macon County, Alabama, so that we can always see how adrift we can become when the rights of any citizens are neglected, ignored and betrayed. And let us resolve here and now to move forward together.

The legacy of the study at Tuskegee has reached far and deep, in ways that hurt our progress and divide our nation. We cannot be one America when a whole segment of our nation has no trust in America. An apology is the first step, and we take it with a commitment to rebuild that broken trust. We can begin by making sure there is never again another episode like this one. We need to do more to ensure that medical research practices are sound and ethical, and that researchers work more closely with communities. . . .

We face a challenge in our time. Science and technology are rapidly changing our lives with the promise of making us much healthier, much more productive and more prosperous. But with these changes we must work harder to see that as we advance we don't leave behind our conscience. No ground is gained and, indeed, much is lost if we lose our moral bearings in the name of progress.

The people who ran the study at Tuskegee diminished the stature of man by abandoning the most basic ethical precepts. They forgot their pledge to heal and repair. They had the power to heal the survivors and all the others and they did not. Today, all we can do is apologize. But you have the power, for only you—Mr. [Herman] Shaw [survivor], the others who are here, the family members who are with us in Tuskegee—only you have the power to forgive. Your presence here shows us that you have chosen a better path than your government did so long ago. You have not withheld the power to forgive. I hope today and tomorrow every American will remember your lesson and live by it.

3. The Denver Principles to Empower People with AIDS, 1983

We condemn attempts to label us as "victims," a term which implies defeat, and we are only occasionally "patients," a term which implies passivity, helplessness, and dependence upon the care of others. We are "People With AIDS."

Statement of the Advisory Committee of the People with AIDS, The Denver Principles (1983), document posted on web site of ACT-UP New York [http://www.actupny.org/documents/Denver.html].

Recommendations for all People

1. Support us in our struggle against those who would fire us from our jobs, evict us from our homes, refuse to touch us or separate us from our loved ones, our community or our peers, since available evidence does not support the view that AIDS can be spread by casual, social contact.
2. Not scapegoat people with AIDS, blame us for the epidemic or generalize about our lifestyles.

Recommendations for People with AIDS

1. Form caucuses to choose their own representatives, to deal with the media, to choose their own agenda and to plan their own strategies.
2. Be involved at every level of decision-making and specifically serve on the boards of directors of provider organizations.
3. Be included in all AIDS forums with equal credibility as other participants, to share their own experiences and knowledge.
4. Substitute low-risk sexual behaviors for those which could endanger themselves or their partners; we feel people with AIDS have an ethical responsibility to inform their potential sexual partners of their health status.

Rights of People with AIDS

1. To as full and satisfying sexual and emotional lives as anyone else.
2. To quality medical treatment and quality social service provision without discrimination of any form including sexual orientation, gender, diagnosis, economic status or race.
3. To full explanations of all medical procedures and risks, to choose or refuse their treatment modalities, to refuse to participate in research without jeopardizing their treatment and to make informed decisions about their lives.
4. To privacy, to confidentiality of medical records, to human respect and to choose who their significant others are.
5. To die—and to LIVE—in dignity.

4. ACT UP Activist Robert Garcia Faces AIDS, 1991

The first thing is—fuck all the bullshit. No more time for it. Time to live on homo-reality time. This is who I am. . . .

POW psychological profiles fit how one confronting AIDS feels. Suddenly surrounded by those who we have been suspicious of in the past. Government, medical, mental establishments—legal[,] suddenly my life is dependent on their conventions & codes of conduct. . . .

I want to live to be old enough to have a mid-life crisis and a old-life crisis and a post-senile life crisis[.] Goddammit!   [January? 1991]

Robert Garcia Journal, box 1, folder 4 (1991), Robert Garcia Papers, Collection #7574, Human Sexuality Collection, Division of Rare and Manuscript Collections, Cornell University Library.

[T]ook AZT for the first time. Talk about breaking denial.   [February 7, 1991]

> The scratching of the pen as it
>   moves along the page
> Is an act of rebellion
> An act of being
> An act of wishing to continue an existence
> Just as no one writes in a vacuum
> So no one writes to an unspecified audience
> Once the commotion of writing stops,
> The future audience is born.

I am other because there is no other of me. I am not another version of you or yours. I am different. And wish to remain so. It is that desire that creates the friction that we call a life. Experiences, actions, memories, all revolve around the notion of uniqueness[,] not, as many would have it[,] around normalcy.

> EXOR[C]ISE/EXERCISE THE DEMON
> SHATTERING DREAMS OF DEATH
> STALKING, HAUNTING ME
> JUST THE LINGERING TASTE OF
> HORROR REMAINS WHEN I RISE
> LEFT TO FEEL WHAT MY PSYCHE
> HAS JUST EXPERIENCED
> THIS ECHOING, DYING SENSE OF
> UTTER DOOM LEAVES ME WEAK,
> HELPLESS, IMMOBILE, A FOOL.
> I CRY. CONTINUOUSLY, I CRY.
> EVEN NOW
> I AM ITS PREY.
> IT HAS TAKEN AWAY MY
>   ARMOR MY SHIELD
> BUT I HADN'T REALIZED
>   HOW STRONG I HAD BECOME
> THEY HAVE TAKEN AWAY MY SECURITY BLANKET
> NOW NO PROTECTION FROM THE COLD
> WHO WILL KEEP ME
>   SAFE
> I HAVE NEEDS OF SECURITY JUST LIKE
>   ANYONE ELSE.
> DO YOU UNDERSTAND HOW UPFRONT
> FIRST LINE—OUT I HAVE BEEN
> AT WHAT COST I ASK
> DON'T YOU DARE DENY ME MY RIGHT TO
>   EXISTENCE
> I MAY BE DAMAGED GOODS BUT
>   BEAUTY REMAINS.

[February 1991]

5. Policing Public Sex in a Gay Theater, 1995

New York City Department of Health Inspection Report

Report of a Facility Inspected for Prohibited Sexual Activity Under Subpart 24-2.2 of the New York State Sanitary Code:

1. Name of Facility: _____ Hollywood _____
2. Address of Facility: _____ Broadway & 47th St, Manhattan _____
[. . . .]
5. Date of Inspection: _____ 5-3-95 _____
6. Time Inspection Commenced: ____ 7 PM _____
7. Time Inspection Completed: _____ 9 PM _____
8. Was this inspection announced?   Yes ( )   No (X)
9. How many incidents of prohibited sexual activity were observed? ____2____
    How many persons were observed participating in these incidents? ____4____
    How many incidents of fellatio occurred? _____2_____
    How many participants? _____4_____
    How many incidents of anal intercourse? ____0____
    How many participants? _____0_____
    How many incidents of vaginal sex? _____0_____
    How many participants? _____0_____
10. Approximately how many patrons were in the facility during your
    inspection? _____40_____
A. Facility's Education Efforts
[. . . .]
14. Were there public service announcements warning against
    prohibited sexual activities on the premises?   Yes ( )   No (X)
[. . . .]
E. Prohibited Sexual Activities:
28. Under what circumstances did the prohibited sexual activity that you observed
    take place? For each activity that you mentioned in item number 9, state in
    which part of the facility the act occurred, and provide specific information
    concerning the appearance and physical characteristics of the patron who
    performed it, such as their manner of dress, height, weight, race and apparent
    age. State whether a condom was used or not used, if it was possible to observe
    this. State the distance in feet between you and each act of prohibited sex that
    you mention. Describe the lighting conditions under which each act occurred.
    Use additional sheets if necessary.

    1. Fellatio in the "gay theatre." A while male mid 60's, gray hair, glasses, in a
    blue raincoat was having fellatio performed by another white male, also in
    his 60's with grey hair and wearing glasses, and a blue blazer. No condom
    was used. I was sitting behind these men some 10 ft. away.

New York public documents as reproduced in Dangerous Bedfellows, *Policing Public Sex: Queer Politics and the Future of AIDS Activism* (Boston: South End Press, 1996), 308–309, 312–315.

2. Fellatio in the "gay theatre." A black male, mid-30's, wearing a leather jacket with glasses was performing fellatio on a white male, mid-30s, bald, wearing white tank-top t-shirt and jeans. No condom was used. I saw this act while standing in the aisle. I was about 15 ft. away.

<u>Expenses</u>

Admission Fee:	$6.00
Other (Please itemize)	$ [. . . .]
	Total: $6.00

[Signed by inspector]
Date and Time Signed: 5-3-95 10 PM

SUPREME COURT OF THE STATE OF NEW YORK
COUNTY OF NEW YORK
————————————————X
THE CITY OF NEW YORK and THE NEW YORK
CITY DEPARTMENT OF HEALTH,   <u>AFFIRMATION</u>
                                 Plaintiffs,

           -against-
777-779 EIGHT AVENUE CORP. d/b/a
HOLLYWOOD TWINS, [and others],
                                 Defendants.
————————————————X

   BENJAMIN A. MOJICA, M.D., M.P.H., a physician authorized by law to practice medicine in the State of New York, affirms the following under penalties of perjury . . . :

   1. I am an Acting Commissioner of the New York City Department of Health ("DOH"), one of the plaintiffs herein. This affirmation is submitted in support of plaintiffs' motion for a preliminary injunction and for a temporary closing and re-straining order against the premises known as the Hollywood Twin Theater where high risk sexual activities have been repeatedly observed by inspectors from DOH. The facts herein are based on DOH records and my personal knowledge.

   2. This action is being brought as part of the City's continuing effort to control the spread of human immunodeficiency virus ("HIV") which has been identified as the cause of AIDS (Acquired Immune Deficiency Syndrome). Since the beginning of the HIV/AIDS epidemic, over 74,000 cases have been reported in New York City. Over 50,000 adults, or 67%, are known to have died of the disease. AIDS is the leading cause of death among adults aged 25 to 44 in New York City. There are now approximately 1000 new cases of AIDS reported in New York City every month. There is currently no curative treatment for AIDS or HIV infection.

   3. The New York State Public Health Council has determined that three of the major risk behaviors associated with the transmission of the virus are anal inter-course, fellatio and vaginal intercourse. The Council also has determined that var-ious establishments which make facilities available for the purpose of engaging in

such acts contribute to the propagation and spread of HIV. The State Sanitary Code therefore declares that facilities in which such activities take place "shall constitute a threat to the public health" and are prohibited, and may be closed by local health officers as constituting a "public nuisance."

4. The City has inspected and will continue to inspect establishments where high risk sexual activity is or may be occurring. These inspections are directed at activities which constitute a public health nuisance and danger. Following investigations by City employees, the City has obtained court orders closing eleven other facilities, including seven theaters, where high risk sexual activities have been observed.

5. The annexed affidavits of two inspectors establish that exactly the type of sexual activities which have been prohibited in commercial establishments by the State due to the high risk of transmitting the AIDS virus were observed at least 85 times within the past four months at the Hollywood Twin Theater. The behaviors observed also constitute high risk activities for the transmission of sexually transmitted diseases (or "STDs"), such as syphilis and gonorrhea.

6. The DOH has attempted to eliminate the high risk sexual activity at the Hollywood Twin Theater in a less restrictive way by informing the theater of the existence of the dangerous conditions, asking for the management's voluntary compliance with State and City law, and advising that closure might be necessary if the management failed to improve those conditions.

7. The DOH has inspected the Hollywood Twin on a periodic basis. During visits in March and April, inspectors observed several acts of fellatio.

8. Therefore, by letter dated April 13, 1995, I wrote to the theater explaining that DOH inspectors had observed instances of high risk sexual activity at the Hollywood Twin Theater, and insisting that the management take immediate action to solve the problem, or be subject to closure. My letter stated: . . .

> You are hereby notified that this Department has reason to believe that your establishment has facilitated legally prohibited sexual activities on your premises. Specifically, acts of fellatio have been observed in various parts of your establishment. You are further notified that inspections of your facility are being conducted on a continuing basis.
>
> Nothing short of immediate cessation of the prohibited sexual activities in your theater is acceptable. Unless you eliminate such activities at once, we will seek a court order closing your premises.

[. . . .]

9. The Department did not receive a response to the letter. In 35 visits to the Hollywood Twin Theater between April 13 and August 5, 1995 inspectors observed at least 85 incidents of prohibited sexual activity engaged in by the patrons of the Hollywood Twin.

10. Given the degree of high risk sexual activity regularly observed at the Hollywood Twin Theater, the management's failure to monitor effectively not only encourages the activity to continue, but draws people to the theater for the precise purpose of engaging in this activity. It appears that patrons are paying an admission fee to enter the theater so that they may engage in public, largely anonymous, high risk sexual activity, not to watch movies. Defendants are operating a facility the effect of which is to spread disease.

[. . . .]

13. In sum, the City is seeking to close down this establishment because of the serious health risks it presents, as defined by State law, and because it is clear that less restrictive measures have not succeeded in eliminating the high risk sexual activities in the theater.

14. In seeking this relief, the City is taking a prudent and necessary measure to protect public health. It is important that, in addition to necessary health education, appropriate enforcement measures be taken to address the AIDS crisis in New York City and limit the ongoing transmission of this deadly virus.

15. In light of the severity of the AIDS epidemic, the operation of a premises such as the Hollywood Twin Theater warrants not only the issuance of a closing order but the imposition of severe penalties so that these defendants and others similarly situated will be deterred from facilitating a public health nuisance in their establishments.

WHEREFORE, it is respectfully requested that the Court grant plaintiffs' request for a temporary closing order, a temporary restraining order, preliminary injunctive relief and such other relief as the Court may deem just and proper.

Dated: New York, New York
    August 8, 1995

BENJAMIN A. MOJICA

6. Cleveland's Black Community Responds to AIDS, 1998

Blacks in Greater Cleveland and nationwide have been hit so hard by AIDS that some advocates say it is time for blacks to take the lead in dealing with the epidemic.

Denial about the AIDS risk of needle drug use and unprotected sex, mistrust of a white-dominated medical system, and the misconception that AIDS is only a white, gay disease are in part to blame for the disproportionately high number of cases among blacks. In Cuyahoga County, for example, blacks make up a quarter of the population, yet accounted for more than half of the 719 AIDS cases diagnosed between 1994 and 1996.

Because of those obstacles, some black leaders and AIDS educators now say the responsibility for slowing the spread of human immunodeficiency virus among blacks must fall to the black community. Activists are attacking the problem in the streets and from the pulpit, two of the most direct routes to reach those who are at risk. But they contend that not enough is being done locally or nationally.

"The black community as a whole, led by the churches, is in a state of denial," said Akida Sababu, director of the Jeffrey D. Heard HIV/AIDS Counseling & Outreach Center. . . . The Heard Center serves all people, but its emphasis is on education and prevention among blacks. "Here we are 18 years into the epidemic and they still equate it as a gay disease," said Sababu, who is black. "The black community won't step up to the plate and take responsibility when it comes to this disease. That is one of the biggest reasons we blacks are falling through the gap."

Part of the problem for black churches—which are a strong moral force in the community—is trying to balance compassion for AIDS victims and concern for those at risk with the belief that casual sex and drug use that can lead to the disease cannot be condoned.

Although there is not universal agreement on the point, the Rev. Marvin McMickle is convinced black churches have a major role to play in stopping the spread of AIDS and HIV. "The church needs to talk about behavioral issues and not be afraid to include the topics of casual sex and drug use more openly," said McMickle, pastor of Antioch Baptist Church, a prominent black church on Cleveland's East Side. "Many people are so busy moralizing on the issue that it is not treated as a medical emergency," he said. "I don't want to discount people for treating it as a moral issue, but . . . when do we start teaching people to stay healthy, and when do we start dealing with the issues of safe sex and illicit drug use?"

Blacks make up 13 percent of the U.S. population, yet account for about 57 percent of all new infections with HIV, the virus that causes AIDS, according to the U.S. Centers for Disease Control and Prevention. Among blacks 13 to 24, the infection rate is even higher: 63 percent of the new infections, based on data collected from 25 states between January 1994 and June 1997. And while the death rate from AIDS is dropping overall, the disease remains the No. 1 killer of blacks ages 25 to 44, both nationally and in Cuyahoga County, according to the Ohio Department of Health.

"The black community needs a wake-up call in a language people can understand and from within the community," said Stephen Sroka, an AIDS educator for the Cleveland public schools and an assistant professor at Case Western Reserve University's School of Medicine.

Earl Pike, director of education for the AIDS Taskforce of Greater Cleveland, whose clientele is 70 percent black, said he encounters blacks who know the dangers, but do not change behaviors that put them at risk for AIDS because of mistrust of the medical community or because they face more pressing problems, such as poverty and violence. "When people walk outside their door and see these things, they are more immediate than this abstract thing called AIDS," he said.

As Sababu spent one recent evening distributing condoms and talking to homeless people about HIV, he encountered a homeless black man on Superior Ave. near 17th St., who admitted he engages in unprotected sex and intravenous drug use. "He said, 'I want to be honest with you. What happens is I get high, I drink and I smoke crack and I throw caution to the wind.' This is sad, but it is so typical," Sababu said.

Denial is compounded by a belief by some blacks that AIDS is a manufactured disease unleashed by the government to wipe out the black population. That suspicion has roots in the notorious Tuskegee Syphilis Study, in which the U.S. Public Health Service withheld treatment for decades from 399 black men without their knowledge in order to study the effects of syphilis.

"One of the barriers which is . . . fairly widespread is the belief that AIDS was created to wipe out certain groups of people," Pike said. "In light of the history of public health in this country and the Tuskegee experiment, it makes perfect sense to believe this. "But . . . even if AIDS was a created disease, you still must practice safer sex. Even if a group of bigots got together in the 1970s and created the virus, we know now how to stop it."

Another widely held belief in the black community is that AIDS is strictly a gay white man's disease, so heterosexual blacks don't have to worry about it, no matter what other risky behaviors they might undertake. "Dealing with homosexuality is such a difficult subject in the black community," Sroka said. "The shame and guilt is much greater there."

But AIDS education from the pulpit that does not deal with the immorality of homosexuality is wrong, said the Rev. Sterling Glover of Cleveland's Emmanuel Baptist Church. In other words, preaching safe sex among gays may be a good preventive strategy, but it's not acceptable religious philosophy.

"The teaching of the scriptures we go by is that we deplore any kind of contact between same sexes," Glover said. "If that is the cause of [AIDS], my thing is, regardless of what, we have to deal with the person. At the same time, we can't relax our vigilance for the moral code given to us by God."

McMickle said one way to stop the denial and misconceptions is for pastors to talk from the pulpit about the need for lifestyle changes. Last March, Antioch was among several churches that hosted prayer vigils for the National Black Church Week of Prayer For Healing AIDS, a program sponsored locally by the Jeffrey D. Heard Center. In addition to prayer, there were display tables with information about HIV and AIDS, as well as workshops.

Preachers also must begin to leave their pulpits and go into the streets to talk to people about the disease, Sroka said, because many people who are at risk for HIV do not attend church.

Some of that street-level education and assistance is being done by organizations such as the Jeffery D. Heard Center and Stopping AIDS Is My Mission, an organization operated by the AIDS Taskforce of Greater Cleveland that targets adolescents, especially minority youths. "Education now is more subtle and side-door than before," said Pike of the AIDS Taskforce. "We educate hair stylists and they teach their clients. We take the message to gyms, basketball leagues and places other than gay bars." SAMM sends teenagers to do education and prevention work on the streets and in the Cleveland schools to talk to the mostly black student population between the ages of 13 and 18.

Sababu said that despite some reluctance to accept the message, agencies should continue to do outreach in the black community using graphic messages that show examples of what happens to people when they are stricken with AIDS.

Although they are controversial, programs that allow drug addicts to exchange used needles for clean ones are needed in the black community, Sroka said, but those programs often meet opposition because of the belief that they encourage drug use.

Pike would like to see more minority AIDS educators because they are better able to deliver the prevention message to minority communities. At the AIDS Taskforce, two-thirds of the educators are minorities.

AIDS education should be geared to youngsters as early as elementary school, before risky behavior begins, said Sroka, who talks to teachers, students and parents in the Cleveland School District. By junior high and high school, it is often too late because many teenagers have already become involved with sex and drugs.

"Advertisers know how to get through to youth with a clear, consistent repetitive message," Sroka said. "AIDS educators have to learn how to do that."

E S S A Y S

These case studies examine public health responses to sexually transmitted disease, focusing on the process of decision making, the cultural assumptions of those involved, and the social and moral implications resulting from their actions. Allan M. Brandt of Harvard University, a leading social and medical historian, wrote this article on the Tuskegee syphilis study in 1978, only six years after the federal government ended the forty-year study and issued an investigative report. Asking probing questions and using primary sources, Brandt documents how racism—including stereotypes of black sexuality—led doctors and health officials who had the public trust to lie and violate their responsibility to treat the disease. Even when the study finally ended, the government failed to face up to the full ethical implications of the research it had sponsored. Ronald Bayer of Columbia University, a medical ethicist and historian of public health, examines the controversy over closing San Francisco's bathhouses as an AIDS-prevention measure in 1983 and 1984. Unlike the Tuskegee study, grassroots opposition arose immediately and produced political conflict. Bayer traces the political decisions that led to regulation, exploring the tensions between individual claims to liberty and privacy and the state's claims to intervene for the public good. Importantly, he reveals the disagreements *within* groups—whether gay activists, doctors, or public health officials—as well as between them.

The Tuskegee Syphilis Study

ALLAN M. BRANDT

In 1932 the U.S. Public Health Service (USPHS) initiated an experiment in Macon County, Alabama, to determine the natural course of untreated, latent syphilis in black males. The test comprised 400 syphilitic men, as well as 200 uninfected men who served as controls. The first published report of the study appeared in 1936 with subsequent papers issued every four to six years, through the 1960s. When penicillin became widely available by the early 1950s as the preferred treatment for syphilis, the men did not receive therapy. In fact on several occasions, the USPHS actually sought to prevent treatment. Moreover, a committee at the federally operated Center for Disease Control decided in 1969 that the study should be continued. Only in 1972, when accounts of the study first appeared in the national press, did the Department of Health, Education and Welfare halt the experiment. At that time seventy-four of the test subjects were still alive; at least twenty-eight, but perhaps more than 100, had died directly from advanced syphilitic lesions. In August 1972, HEW appointed an investigatory panel which issued a report the following year. The panel found the study to have been "ethically unjustified," and argued that penicillin should have been provided to the men.

This article attempts to place the Tuskegee Study in a historical context and to assess its ethical implications. Despite the media attention which the study received, the HEW *Final Report,* and the criticism expressed by several professional organizations, the experiment has been largely misunderstood. The most basic questions

---

Allan M. Brandt, "Racism and Research: The Case of the Tuskegee Syphilis Study," *Hastings Center Report* 8, no. 6 (1978): 21–29. Reproduced by permission. © The Hastings Center.

of *how* the study was undertaken in the first place and *why* it continued for forty years were never addressed by the HEW investigation. Moreover, the panel misconstrued the nature of the experiment, failing to consult important documents available at the National Archives which bear significantly on its ethical assessment. Only by examining the specific ways in which values are engaged in scientific research can the study be understood.

A brief review of the prevailing scientific thought regarding race and heredity in the early twentieth century is fundamental for an understanding of the Tuskegee Study. By the turn of the century, Darwinism had provided a new rationale for American racism. Essentially primitive peoples, it was argued, could not be assimilated into a complex, white civilization. Scientists speculated that in the struggle for survival the Negro in America was doomed. Particularly prone to disease, vice, and crime, black Americans could not be helped by education or philanthropy. Social Darwinists analyzed census data to predict the virtual extinction of the Negro in the twentieth century, for they believed the Negro race in America was in the throes of a degenerative evolutionary process.

The medical profession supported these findings of late nineteenth- and early twentieth-century anthropologists, ethnologists, and biologists. Physicians studying the effects of emancipation on health concluded almost universally that freedom had caused the mental, moral, and physical deterioration of the black population. They substantiated this argument by citing examples in the comparative anatomy of the black and white races. As Dr. W. T. English wrote: "A careful inspection reveals the body of the negro a mass of minor defects and imperfections from the crown of the head to the soles of the feet. . . ." Cranial structures, wide nasal apertures, receding chins, projecting jaws, all typed the Negro as the lowest species in the Darwinian hierarchy.

Interest in racial differences centered on the sexual nature of blacks. The Negro, doctors explained, possessed an excessive sexual desire, which threatened the very foundations of white society. As one physician noted in the *Journal of the American Medical Association,* "The negro springs from a southern race, and as such his sexual appetite is strong; all of his environments stimulate this appetite, and as a general rule his emotional type of religion certainly does not decrease it." Doctors reported a complete lack of morality on the part of blacks:

> Virtue in the negro race is like angels' visits—few and far between. In a practice of sixteen years I have never examined a virgin negro over fourteen years of age.

A particularly ominous feature of this overzealous sexuality, doctors argued, was the black males' desire for white women. "A perversion from which most races are exempt," wrote Dr. English, "prompts the negro's inclination towards white women, whereas other races incline towards females of their own." Though English estimated the "gray matter of the negro brain" to be at least a thousand years behind that of the white races, his genital organs were overdeveloped. As Dr. William Lee Howard noted:

> The attacks on defenseless white women are evidences of racial instincts that are about as amenable to ethical culture as is the inherent odor of the race. . . . When education will reduce the size of the negro's penis as well as bring about the sensitiveness of the

terminal fibers which exist in the Caucasian, then it will also be able to prevent the African's birthright to sexual madness and excess.

One southern medical journal proposed "Castration Instead of Lynching," as retribution for black sexual crimes. "An impressive trial by a ghost-like kuklux klan [sic] and a 'ghost' physician or surgeon to perform the operation would make it an event the 'patient' would never forget," noted the editorial.

According to these physicians, lust and immorality, unstable families, and reversion to barbaric tendencies made blacks especially prone to venereal diseases. One doctor estimated that over 50 percent of all Negroes over the age of twenty-five were syphilitic. Virtually free of disease as slaves, they were now overwhelmed by it, according to informed medical opinion. Moreover, doctors believed that treatment for venereal disease among blacks was impossible, particularly because in its latent stage the symptoms of syphilis become quiescent. As Dr. Thomas W. Murrell wrote:

> They come for treatment at the beginning and at the end. When there are visible manifestations or when harried by pain, they readily come, for as a race they are not averse to physic; but tell them not, though they look well and feel well, that they are still diseased. Here ignorance rates science a fool. . . .

Even the best educated black, according to Murrell, could not be convinced to seek treatment for syphilis. Venereal disease, according to some doctors, threatened the future of the race. The medical profession attributed the low birth rate among blacks to the high prevalence of venereal disease which caused stillbirths and miscarriages. Moreover, the high rates of syphilis were thought to lead to increased insanity and crime. One doctor writing at the turn of the century estimated that the number of insane Negroes had increased thirteen-fold since the end of the Civil War. Dr. Murrell's conclusion echoed the most informed anthropological and ethnological data:

> So the scourge sweeps among them. Those that are treated are only half cured, and the effort to assimilate a complex civilization driving their diseased minds until the results are criminal records. Perhaps here, in conjunction with tuberculosis, will be the end of the negro problem. Disease will accomplish what man cannot do.

This particular configuration of ideas formed the core of medical opinion concerning blacks, sex, and disease in the early twentieth century. Doctors generally discounted socioeconomic explanations of the state of black health, arguing that better medical care could not alter the evolutionary scheme. These assumptions provide the backdrop for examining the Tuskegee Syphilis Study.

In 1929, under a grant from the Julius Rosenwald Fund, the USPHS conducted studies in the rural South to determine the prevalence of syphilis among blacks and explore the possibilities for mass treatment. The USPHS found Macon County, Alabama, in which the town of Tuskegee is located, to have the highest syphilis rate of the six counties surveyed. The Rosenwald Study concluded that mass treatment could be successfully implemented among rural blacks. Although it is doubtful that the necessary funds would have been allocated even in the best economic conditions, after the economy collapsed in 1929, the findings were ignored. It is, however, ironic that the Tuskegee Study came to be based on findings of the Rosenwald Study that demonstrated the possibilities of mass treatment.

Three years later, in 1932, Dr. Taliaferro Clark, Chief of the USPHS Venereal Disease Division and author of the Rosenwald Study report, decided that conditions in Macon County merited renewed attention. Clark believed the high prevalence of syphilis offered an "unusual opportunity" for observation. From its inception, the USPHS regarded the Tuskegee Study as a classic "study in nature," rather than an experiment. As long as syphilis was so prevalent in Macon and most of the blacks went untreated throughout life, it seemed only natural to Clark that it would be valuable to observe the consequences. He described it as a "ready-made situation." Surgeon General H. S. Cumming wrote to R. R. Moton, Director of the Tuskegee Institute:

> The recent syphilis control demonstration carried out in Macon County, with the financial assistance of the Julius Rosenwald Fund, revealed the presence of an unusually high rate in this county and, what is more remarkable, the fact that 99 per cent of this group was entirely without previous treatment. This combination, together with the expected cooperation of your hospital, offers an unparalleled opportunity for carrying on this piece of scientific research which probably cannot be duplicated anywhere else in the world.

Although no formal protocol appears to have been written, several letters of Clark and Cumming suggest what the USPHS hoped to find. Clark indicated that it would be important to see how disease affected the daily lives of the men:

> The results of these studies of case records suggest the desirability of making a further study of the effect of untreated syphilis on the human economy among people now living and engaged in their daily pursuits.

It also seems that the USPHS believed the experiment might demonstrate that antisyphilitic treatment was unnecessary. As Cumming noted: "It is expected the results of this study may have a marked bearing on the treatment, or conversely the nonnecessity of treatment, of cases of latent syphilis."

The immediate source of Cumming's hypothesis appears to have been the famous Oslo Study of untreated syphilis. Between 1890 and 1910, Professor C. Boeck, the chief of the Oslo Venereal Clinic, withheld treatment from almost two thousand patients infected with syphilis. He was convinced that therapies then available, primarily mercurial ointment, were of no value. When arsenic therapy became widely available by 1910, after Paul Ehrlich's historic discovery of "606," the study was abandoned. E. Bruusgaard, Boeck's successor, conducted a follow-up study of 473 of the untreated patients from 1925 to 1927. He found that 27.9 percent of these patients had undergone a "spontaneous cure," and now manifested no symptoms of the disease. Moreover, he estimated that as many as 70 percent of all syphilitics went through life without inconvenience from the disease. His study, however, clearly acknowledged the dangers of untreated syphilis for the remaining 30 percent.

Thus every major textbook of syphilis at the time of the Tuskegee Study's inception strongly advocated treating syphilis even in its latent stages, which follow the initial inflammatory reaction. In discussing the Oslo Study, Dr. J. E. Moore, one of the nation's leading venereologists wrote, "This summary of Bruusgaard's study is by no means intended to suggest that syphilis be allowed to pass untreated." If a complete cure could not be effected, at least the most devastating effects of the disease could be avoided. Although the standard therapies of the time, arsenical compounds and bismuth injection, involved certain dangers because of their toxicity, the alternatives were much worse. As the Oslo Study had shown, untreated syphilis could lead to cardiovascular disease, insanity, and premature death. . . . "Another compelling reason for treatment," noted Moore, "exists in the fact that every patient with latent syphilis may be, and perhaps is, infectious for others." In 1932, the year in which the Tuskegee Study began, the USPHS sponsored and published a paper by Moore and six other syphilis experts that strongly argued for treating latent syphilis.

The Oslo Study, therefore, could not have provided justification for the USPHS to undertake a study that did not entail treatment. Rather, the suppositions that conditions in Tuskegee existed "naturally" and that the men would not be treated anyway provided the experiment's rationale. In turn, these two assumptions rested on the prevailing medical attitudes concerning blacks, sex, and disease. For example, Clark explained the prevalence of venereal disease in Macon County by emphasizing promiscuity among blacks:

> This state of affairs is due to the paucity of doctors, rather low intelligence of the Negro population in this section, depressed economic conditions, and the very common promiscuous sex relations of this population group which not only contribute to the spread of syphilis but also contribute to the prevailing indifference with regard to treatment.

In fact, Moore, who had written so persuasively in favor of treating latent syphilis, suggested that existing knowledge did not apply to Negroes. Although he had called the Oslo Study "a never-to-be-repeated human experiment," he served as an expert consultant to the Tuskegee Study:

> I think that such a study as you have contemplated would be of immense value. It will be necessary of course in the consideration of the results to evaluate the special factors introduced by a selection of the material from negro males. Syphilis in the negro is in many respects almost a different disease from syphilis in the white.

Dr. O. C. Wenger, chief of the federally operated venereal disease clinic at Hot Springs, Arkansas, praised Moore's judgment, adding, "This study will emphasize those differences." On another occasion he advised Clark, "We must remember we are dealing with a group of people who are illiterate, have no conception of time, and whose personal history is always indefinite."

The doctors who devised and directed the Tuskegee Study accepted the mainstream assumptions regarding blacks and venereal disease. The premise that blacks, promiscuous and lustful, would not seek or continue treatment, shaped the study. A test of untreated syphilis seemed "natural" because the USPHS presumed the men would never be treated; the Tuskegee Study made that a self-fulfilling prophecy.

Clark sent Dr. Raymond Vonderlehr to Tuskegee in September 1932 to assemble a sample of men with latent syphilis for the experiment. The basic design of the study called for the selection of syphilitic black males between the ages of twenty-five and sixty, a thorough physical examination including x-rays, and finally, a spinal tap to determine the incidence of neuro-syphilis. They had no intention of providing any treatment for the infected men. The USPHS originally scheduled the whole experiment to last six months; it seemed to be both a simple and inexpensive project.

The task of collecting the sample, however, proved to be more difficult than the USPHS had supposed. Vonderlehr canvassed the largely illiterate, poverty-stricken population of sharecroppers and tenant farmers in search of test subjects. If his circulars requested only men over twenty-five to attend his clinics, none would appear, suspecting he was conducting draft physicals. Therefore, he was forced to test large numbers of women and men who did not fit the experiment's specifications. This involved considerable expense since the USPHS had promised the Macon County Board of Health that it would treat those who were infected, but not included in the study. Clark wrote to Vonderlehr about the situation: "It never once occurred to me that we would be called upon to treat a large part of the county as return for the privilege of making this study. . . . I am anxious to keep the expenditures for treatment down to the lowest possible point because it is the one item of expenditure in connection with the study most difficult to defend despite our knowledge of the need therefor." Vonderlehr responded: "If we could find from 100 to 200 cases . . . we would not have to do another Wassermann on useless individuals . . ."

Significantly, the attempt to develop the sample contradicted the prediction the USPHS had made initially regarding the prevalence of the disease in Macon County. Overall rates of syphilis fell well below expectations; as opposed to the USPHS projection of 35 percent, 20 percent of those tested were actually diseased. Moreover, those who had sought and received previous treatment far exceeded the expectations of the USPHS. Clark noted in a letter to Vonderlehr:

> I find your report of March 6th quite interesting but regret the necessity for Wassermanning [sic] . . . such a large number of individuals in order to uncover this relatively limited number of untreated cases.

Further difficulties arose in enlisting the subjects to participate in the experiment, to be "Wassermanned," and to return for a subsequent series of examinations. Vonderlehr found that only the offer of treatment elicited the cooperation of the men. They were told they were ill and were promised free care. Offered therapy, they became willing subjects. The USPHS did not tell the men that they were participants in an experiment; on the contrary, the subjects believed they were being treated for "bad blood"—the rural South's colloquialism for syphilis. They thought they were participating in a public health demonstration similar to the one that had been conducted by the Julius Rosenwald Fund in Tuskegee several years earlier. In the end, the men were so eager for medical care that the number of defaulters in the experiment proved to be insignificant.

To preserve the subjects' interest, Vonderlehr gave most of the men mercurial ointment, a noneffective drug, while some of the younger men apparently received inadequate dosages of neoarsphenamine. This required Vonderlehr to write frequently to Clark requesting supplies. He feared the experiment would fail if the men were not offered treatment.

> It is desirable and essential if the study is to be a success to maintain the interest of each of the cases examined by me through to the time when the spinal puncture can be completed. Expenditure of several hundred dollars for drugs for these men would be well

worth while if their interest and cooperation would be maintained in so doing. . . . It is my desire to keep the main purpose of the work from the negroes in the county and continue their interest in treatment. That is what the vast majority wants and the examination seems relatively unimportant to them in comparison. It would probably cause the entire experiment to collapse if the clinics were stopped before the work is completed.

On another occasion he explained:

Dozens of patients have been sent away without treatment during the past two weeks and it would have been impossible to continue without the free distribution of drugs because of the unfavorable impression made on the negro.

The readiness of the test subjects to participate of course contradicted the notion that blacks would not seek or continue therapy.

The final procedure of the experiment was to be a spinal tap to test for evidence of neuro-syphilis. The USPHS presented this purely diagnostic exam, which often entails considerable pain and complications, to the men as a "special treatment." Clark explained to Moore:

We have not yet commenced the spinal punctures. This operation will be deferred to the last in order not to unduly disturb our field work by any adverse reports by the patients subjected to spinal puncture because of some disagreeable sensations following this procedure. These negroes are very ignorant and easily influenced by things that would be of minor significance in a more intelligent group.

The letter to the subjects announcing the spinal tap read:

Some time ago you were given a thorough examination and since that time we hope you have gotten a great deal of treatment for bad blood. You will now be given your last chance to get a second examination. This examination is a very special one and after it is finished you will be given a special treatment if it is believed you are in a condition to stand it. . . .

REMEMBER THIS IS YOUR LAST CHANCE FOR SPECIAL FREE TREATMENT. BE SURE TO MEET THE NURSE.

. . . [T]he men participated in the study under the guise of treatment.

Despite the fact that their assumption regarding prevalence and black attitudes toward treatment had proved wrong, the USPHS decided in the summer of 1933 to continue the study. Once again, it seemed only "natural" to pursue the research since the sample already existed, and with a depressed economy, the cost of treatment appeared prohibitive—although there is no indication it was ever considered. Vonderlehr first suggested extending the study in letters to Clark and Wenger:

At the end of this project we shall have a considerable number of cases presenting various complications of syphilis, who have received only mercury and may still be considered untreated in the modern sense of therapy. Should these cases be followed over a period of from five to ten years many interesting facts could be learned regarding the course and complications of untreated syphilis.

"As I see it," responded Wenger, "we have no further interest in these patients *until they die.*" Apparently, the physicians engaged in the experiment believed that only autopsies could scientifically confirm the findings of the study. . . .

Bringing the men to autopsy required the USPHS to devise a further series of deceptions and inducements. Wenger warned Vonderlehr that the men must not realize that they would be autopsied:

> There is one danger in the latter plan and that is if the colored population become aware that accepting free hospital care means a post-mortem, every darkey will leave Macon County and it will hurt [Dr. Eugene] Dibble's hospital.

"Naturally," responded Vonderlehr, "it is not my intention to let it be generally known that the main object of the present activities is the bringing of the men to necropsy." The subjects' trust in the USPHS made the plan viable. The USPHS gave Dr. Dibble, the Director of the Tuskegee Institute Hospital, an interim appointment to the Public Health Service. As Wenger noted:

> One thing is certain. The only way we are gong to get post-mortems is to have the demise take place in Dibble's hospital and when these colored folks are told that Doctor Dibble is now a Government doctor too they will have more confidence.

After the USPHS approved the continuation of the experiment in 1933, Vonderlehr decided that it would be necessary to select a group of healthy, uninfected men to serve as controls. Vonderlehr, who had succeeded Clark as Chief of the Venereal Disease Division, sent Dr. J. R. Heller to Tuskegee to gather the control group. Heller distributed drugs (noneffective) to these men, which suggests that they also believed they were undergoing treatment. Control subjects who became syphilitic were simply transferred to the test group—a strikingly inept violation of standard research procedure.

The USPHS offered several inducements to maintain contact and to procure the continued cooperation of the men. Eunice Rivers, a black nurse, was hired to follow their health and to secure approval for autopsies. She gave the men noneffective medicines—"spring tonic" and aspirin—as well as transportation and hot meals on the days of their examinations. More important, Nurse Rivers provided continuity to the project over the entire forty-year period. By supplying "medicinals," the USPHS was able to continue to deceive the participants, who believed that they were receiving therapy from the government doctors. Deceit was integral to the study. When the test subjects complained about spinal taps one doctor wrote:

> They simply do not like spinal punctures. A few of those who were tapped are enthusiastic over the results but to most, the suggestion causes violent shaking of the head; others claim they were robbed of their procreative powers (regardless of the fact that I claim it stimulates them).

Letters to the subjects announcing an impending USPHS visit to Tuskegee explained: "[The doctor] wants to make a special examination to find out how you have been feeling and whether the treatment has improved your health." In fact, after the first six months of the study, the USPHS had furnished no treatment whatsoever.

Finally, because it proved difficult to persuade the men to come to the hospital when they became severely ill, the USPHS promised to cover their burial expenses. The Milbank Memorial Fund provided approximately $50 per man for this purpose beginning in 1935. This was a particularly strong inducement as funeral rites constituted an important component of the cultural life of rural blacks. One report of the study concluded, "Without this suasion it would, we believe, have been impossible to secure the cooperation of the group and their families."

Reports of the study's findings, which appeared regularly in the medical press beginning in 1936, consistently cited the ravages of untreated syphilis. The first paper, read at the 1936 American Medical Association annual meeting, found "that syphilis in this period [latency] tends to greatly increase the frequency of manifestations of cardiovascular disease." Only 16 percent of the subjects gave no sign of morbidity as opposed to 61 percent of the controls. Ten years later, a report noted coldly, "The fact that nearly twice as large a proportion of the syphilitic individuals as of the control group has died is a very striking one." Life expectancy, concluded the doctors, is reduced by about 20 percent.

A 1955 article found that slightly more than 30 percent of the test group autopsied had died *directly* from advanced syphilitic lesions of either the cardiovascular or the central nervous system. . . . In 1950, Dr. Wenger had concluded, "We now know, where we could only surmise before, that we have contributed to their ailments and shortened their lives." As black physician Vernal Cave, a member of the HEW panel, later wrote, "They proved a point, then proved a point, then proved a point."

During the forty years of the experiment the USPHS had sought on several occasions to ensure that the subjects did not receive treatment from other sources. To this end, Vonderlehr met with groups of local black doctors in 1934, to ask their cooperation in not treating the men. Lists of subjects were distributed to Macon County physicians along with letters requesting them to refer these men back to the USPHS if they sought care. The USPHS warned the Alabama Health Department not to treat the test subjects when they took a mobile VD unit into Tuskegee in the early 1940s. In 1941, the Army drafted several subjects and told them to begin antisyphilitic treatment immediately. The USPHS supplied the draft board with a list of 256 names they desired to have excluded from treatment, and the board complied.

In spite of these efforts, by the early 1950s many of the men had secured some treatment on their own. By 1952, almost 30 percent of the test subjects had received some penicillin, although only 7.5 percent had received what could be considered adequate doses. Vonderlehr wrote to one of the participating physicians, "I hope that the availability of antibiotics has not interfered too much with this project." A report published in 1955 considered whether the treatment that some of the men had obtained had "defeated" the study. The article attempted to explain the relatively low exposure to penicillin in an age of antibiotics, suggesting as a reason: "the stoicism of these men as a group; they still regard hospitals and medicines with suspicion and prefer an occasional dose of time-honored herbs or tonics to modern drugs." The authors failed to note that the men believed they already were under the care of the government doctors and thus saw no need to seek treatment elsewhere. Any treatment which the men might have received, concluded the report, had been insufficient to compromise the experiment.

When the USPHS evaluated the status of the study in the 1960s they continued to rationalize the racial aspects of the experiment. For example, the minutes of a 1965 meeting at the Center for Disease Control recorded:

> Racial issue was mentioned briefly. Will not affect the study. Any questions can be handled by saying these people were at the point that therapy would no longer help them. They are getting better medical care than they would under any other circumstances.

A group of physicians met again at the CDC in 1969 to decide whether or not to terminate the study. Although one doctor argued that the study should be stopped and the men treated, the consensus was to continue. Dr. J. Lawton Smith remarked, "You will never have another study like this; take advantage of it." A memo prepared by Dr. James B. Lucas, Assistant Chief of the Venereal Diseases Branch, stated: "Nothing learned will prevent, find, or cure a single case of infectious syphilis or bring us closer to our basic mission of controlling venereal disease in the United States." He concluded, however, that the study should be continued "along its present lines." When the first accounts of the experiment appeared in the national press in July 1972, data were still being collected and autopsies performed.

HEW finally formed the Tuskegee Syphilis Study Ad Hoc Advisory Panel on August 28, 1972, in response to criticism that the press descriptions of the experiment had triggered. The panel, composed of nine members, five of them black, concentrated on two issues. First, was the study justified in 1932 and had the men given their informed consent? Second, should penicillin have been provided when it became available in the early 1950s? The panel was also charged with determining if the study should be terminated and assessing current policies regarding experimentation with human subjects. The group issued their report in June 1973.

By focusing on the issues of penicillin therapy and informed consent, the *Final Report* and the investigation betrayed a basic misunderstanding of the experiment's purposes and design. The HEW report implied that the failure to provide penicillin constituted the study's major ethical misjudgment; implicit was the assumption that no adequate therapy existed prior to penicillin. Nonetheless medical authorities firmly believed in the efficacy of arsenotherapy for treating syphilis at the time of the experiment's inception in 1932. The panel further failed to recognize that the entire study had been predicated on nontreatment. Provision of effective medication would have violated the rationale of the experiment—to study the natural course of the disease until death. On several occasions, in fact, the USPHS had prevented the men from receiving proper treatment. Indeed, there is no evidence that the USPHS ever considered providing penicillin.

The other focus of the *Final Report*—informed consent—also served to obscure the historical facts of the experiment. In light of the deceptions and exploitations which the experiment perpetrated, it is an understatement to declare, as the *Report* did, that the experiment was "ethically unjustified," because it failed to obtain informed consent from the subjects. The *Final Report*'s statement, "Submitting voluntarily is not informed consent," indicated that the panel believed that the men had volunteered *for the experiment*. The records in the National Archives make clear that the men did not submit voluntarily to an experiment; they were told and they believed that they were getting free treatment from expert government doctors for a serious disease. The failure of the HEW *Final Report* to expose this critical fact—that the USPHS lied to the subjects—calls into question the thoroughness and credibility of their investigation.

Failure to place the study in a historical context also made it impossible for the investigation to deal with the essentially racist nature of the experiment. The panel treated the study as an aberration, well-intentioned but misguided. Moreover, concern that the *Final Report* might be viewed as a critique of human experimentation in general seems to have severely limited the scope of the inquiry. . . . The *Report* assures us that a better designed experiment could have been justified:

> It is possible that a scientific study in 1932 of untreated syphilis, properly conceived with a clear protocol and conducted with suitable subjects who fully understood the implications of their involvement, might have been justified in the pre-penicillin era. This is especially true when one considers the uncertain nature of the results of treatment of late latent syphilis and the highly toxic nature of therapeutic agents then available.

This statement is questionable in view of the proven dangers of untreated syphilis known in 1932.

Since the publication of the HEW *Final Report,* a defense of the Tuskegee Study has emerged. These arguments . . . center on the limited knowledge of effective therapy for latent syphilis when the experiment began. . . . Others have suggested that the men were fortunate to have been spared the highly toxic treatments of the earlier period. Moreover, even these contemporary defenses assume that the men never would have been treated anyway. . . . Several doctors who participated in the study continued to justify the experiment. Dr. J. R. Heller, who on one occasion had referred to the test subjects as the "Ethiopian population," told reporters in 1972:

> I don't see why they should be shocked or horrified. There was no racial side to this. It just happened to be in a black community. I feel this was a perfectly straightforward study, perfectly ethical, with controls. Part of our mission as physicians is to find out what happens to individuals with disease and without disease.

These apologies, as well as the HEW *Final Report,* ignore many of the essential ethical issues which the study poses. The Tuskegee Study reveals the persistence of beliefs within the medical profession about the nature of blacks, sex, and disease— beliefs that had tragic repercussions long after their alleged "scientific" bases were known to be incorrect. Most strikingly, the entire health of a community was jeopardized by leaving a communicable disease untreated. There can be little doubt that the Tuskegee researchers regarded their subjects as less than human. As a result, the ethical canons of experimenting on human subjects were completely disregarded.

The study also raises significant questions about professional self-regulation and scientific bureaucracy. Once the USPHS decided to extend the experiment in the summer of 1933, it was unlikely that the test would be halted short of the men's deaths. The experiment was widely reported for forty years without evoking any significant protest within the medical community. Nor did any bureaucratic mechanism exist within the government for the periodic reassessment of the Tuskegee experiment's ethics and scientific value. The USPHS sent physicians to Tuskegee every several years to check on the study's progress, but never subjected the morality or usefulness of the experiment to serious scrutiny. Only the press accounts of 1972 finally punctured the continued rationalizations of the USPHS and brought the study to an end. Even the HEW investigation was compromised by fear that it would be considered a threat to future human experimentation.

In retrospect the Tuskegee Study revealed more about the pathology of racism than it did about the pathology of syphilis; more about the nature of scientific inquiry than the nature of the disease process. The injustice committed by the experiment went well beyond the facts outlined in the press and the HEW *Final Report.*

The degree of deception and damages have been seriously underestimated. As this history of the study suggests, the notion that science is a value-free discipline must be rejected. The need for greater vigilance in assessing the specific ways in which social values and attitudes affect professional behavior is clearly indicated.

AIDS and the Bathhouse Controversy

RONALD BAYER

In the course of th[e] struggle [for civil rights and social toleration], and working against the legacy of fear, the defense of privacy became a central feature of gay political ideology. . . . Since the state had criminalized homosexuality it was only natural that gay political groups would adopt as part of their strategic posture the civil libertarian's suspicion of government.

What a bitter irony, then, that the very survival of gay men during the AIDS epidemic would require a strategy that would subject their most intimate behaviors to close scrutiny and necessitate calls by public health officials and gay leaders alike for the radical transformation of sexual conduct. Historically rooted antagonisms to the agencies of government would have to be confronted and overcome if effective interventions were to be developed.

For public health officials, whose legacy of anti-venereal disease campaigns included periodic sweeps of red-light districts and closure of houses of prostitution and whose control of epidemics had historically relied upon coercive state power, the ultimate challenge was to develop a language and practice of public health that would encourage the participation, rather than the resistance, of gay men. They would have to press for changed sexual behavior without appearing to don the robes of moralism. Collaborative relationships with gay organizations would have to be built without antagonizing conservative social forces that would consider such efforts a public sanction of immorality. Finally, it would, at times, be necessary to exercise public health authority in opposition to the most articulate forces in the gay community.

These challenges would present themselves dramatically . . . in San Francisco . . . in the furious and deeply divisive debate over gay bathhouses. Commercial enterprises that permitted and facilitated multiple and often anonymous sexual encounters, the baths had emerged in the 1970's as a singular expression of bold gay sexuality. That they existed so openly was evidence of a changed sociopolitical climate of sexuality, at least in the most cosmopolitan American cities. Their fate would be brought into question by the AIDS epidemic, when the demands of public health confronted the claims of an inviolate domain of privacy. . . .

In the first year of the AIDS epidemic, as the number of new cases continued to mount, case control studies undertaken by epidemiologists began to identify what was believed to be a subset of homosexual men who were more likely to be at risk

Reprinted and edited with the permission of The Free Press, a Division of Simon & Schuster, Inc., from *Private Acts, Social Consequences: AIDS and the Politics of Public Health* by Ronald Bayer (New York: Free Press, 1989), 20–22, 29–53. Copyright © 1989 by Ronald Bayer.

for developing Kaposi's sarcoma and the other opportunistic infections associated with immunosuppression. These men were more likely to have had many anonymous sexual partners, to have had a history of a variety of sexually transmitted diseases, and to have engaged in sexual practices that increased the risk of exposure to small amounts of blood and feces. Early on, the director of the Centers for Disease Control noted that "the most important variable was that AIDS patients had more male sexual partners than the controls, an average of sixty per year for patients compared to twenty-five per year for the controls."

As each new report documented the outcropping of the pattern of lethal opportunistic infections and Kaposi's sarcoma among gay and bisexual men, concern mounted in gay communities across the country, but especially on the East and West coasts. The suggestion that there might be a link between sexual lifestyle and the likelihood of falling victim to the disorders reported by the CDC in its accounts of the unfolding epidemic forced some gay commentators to ask disturbing questions about the pattern of sexual behavior that seemed responsible for the still inexplicable and fatal diseases. But concern and rising anxiety were, even in the first months of the epidemic, balanced by efforts to contain the panic that could be socially and psychologically disruptive to gay men and that, it was feared, might spark a wave of antigay outbursts from those who would be threatened by the "gay cancer," first called "gay-related immune deficiency." . . .

As the public health dimensions of the AIDS epidemic increasingly took center stage, the limitations of . . . perspectives that were focused solely on the decisions of gay men as private individuals were to become ever more apparent. This was the context within which the question of the gay bathhouse was to become the subject of an acrimonious controversy that would divide the gay community and force a confrontation over privacy, sexual behavior, and limits of state intervention in the name of public health. . . . Randy Shilts, the gay San Francisco *Chronicle* reporter who was to emerge as a strong antagonist of the bathhouses, the sexual culture they fostered, and the timidity of gay political leaders in confronting the public health implications of the continued operation of such establishments, was sharper and more blunt when he wrote in the *New York Native,* "By the mid 1970s promiscuity was less a lifestyle than an article of faith. . . . Before long an entire subculture and business network emerged catering to drugged out alcoholic gay men with penchants for kinky promiscuous sexual acts." And so in cities across America bathhouses opened their doors, "unprecedented in that they were businesses created solely for the purpose of quick multiple sexual acts, often accomplished without speaking so much as one word." Because of the visceral antagonism to anything that resembled the moralism that had made of homosexuality itself a despised form of love, none of this was ever questioned.

But in the face of the AIDS epidemic and with wide-scale recognition that promiscuity posed a grave health hazard to the gay community, the bathhouse could no longer avoid scrutiny. For some the solution was to mandate the posting of warnings in the bathhouses. . . .

Despite the occasional public suggestion that the gay community might have to collaborate with pubic health officials in regulating the bathhouses or in limiting the activity permitted to occur within them, the dominant ideological voice projected by the gay press was antistatist. . . . Indeed, despite the language of community that filled the columns of the gay press, a radical, almost asocial individualism inspired much of the early rhetoric about the bathhouse. In 1983, Lawrence Mass, often a voice of sober reflection in the unfolding AIDS crisis, thus wrote in the *New York Native:* "What we decide to do about these health hazards will depend on how we decide to deal with them as individuals. . . .The issue is not where we have sex, but with whom and with how many. If the baths were to be closed or transformed, it should be because the market has changed, not because of vigilante impulsivity."

The specter of an intrusive paternalistic state haunted Mass's vision. Closing the baths could inevitably lead to "laws that would eliminate opportunities to have casual sex." Such restrictions might in turn be just one small step from legislation that would control smoking, alcohol consumption, and homosexuality itself. As his rhetorical pitch rose, Mass concluded, "To demand that the bathhouses be shut down would probably do little to limit the spread of the disease, but could significantly hasten the no-longer creeping pace of fascism against minorities in this country." . . .

The arguments about the public health benefits that might follow from regulating or closing the baths and about the rights of those who chose to engage in high-risk sexual activity in commercial establishments were to appear again and again in the public debate over the next year. But the abstract discussion of principles and epidemiological judgments took on concrete form in San Francisco, where, beginning in mid-1983, the gay community, the city government, and the public health authorities . . . [became] embroiled in a fifteen-month confrontation over how to respond to the bathhouses in the face of the AIDS epidemic.

Two years after the onset of the AIDS epidemic, in mid-1983, little had changed in the operation of the San Francisco bathhouses. Despairing of the possibility that the proprietors would ever undertake modifications that would affect their commercial interests and impatient with those who had failed to grasp the significance of the epidemic, some gay activists believed it time to move beyond voluntarism and to engage the power of the state to foster changes in the sex establishments. And so they began to urge the director of the city's Department of Health, Mervyn Silverman, to use his authority to elicit the agreement of bathhouse owners to post warnings about unsafe sexual practices. Others believed that warnings were not enough. In the summer of 1983 Mayor Dianne Feinstein made it clear to Silverman that she wanted him to shut the bathhouses. A demand for dramatic action was to come from at least one politically prominent gay figure, Larry Littlejohn, a veteran of the early years of the gay liberation movement and a leader in the struggle of the early 1970s to eliminate homosexuality from American psychiatry's classification of mental diseases.

In his response to Littlejohn, Silverman demonstrated a remarkable caution that was to make him the target of the mayor's ire and win for him the admiration of most politically vocal elements in the gay community. Alone among public health figures across the country, Silverman was to be forced in this period to confront openly the cross-pressures of those who viewed the bathhouses as dangerous to the public health and those who saw them as important because of their potential role in educating the sexually active about the risks to which they were exposing themselves and their symbolic significance in the struggle for the defense of the freedom of the gay community. In a letter to Littlejohn written in mid-May, Silverman seemed utterly opposed to any moves that would entail coercive intervention. Closure was unjustified on public health grounds, would be politically unacceptable, and would represent an unwarranted restriction of civil liberties. Though he was aware that AIDS was a sexually transmitted disease and was cognizant of the activities that took place within the baths, he refused to term them a threat to the public health. "Because the facilities of most bathhouses do not present a public health hazard I feel it would be inappropriate and in fact illegal for me to close down all bathhouses and other such places that are used for anonymous and multiple sex contacts." Furthermore, such a move would entail a political insult, an insult to the "intelligence of many of our citizens." Finally, closure would represent an "invasion of . . . privacy." Rather than undertaking such repressive measures, Silverman stressed the importance of educating the gay community about the risks of AIDS and suggested therefore the "voluntary" posting of warnings in the bathhouses. . . .

The threat of bathhouse closure was further underscored by Pat Norman, the coordinator of gay and lesbian services at the health department and an activist in the city's lesbian community. Closure, she said, would be a "largely meaningless gesture" from a public health perspective. Norman viewed the pressure on the gay community to shut the baths as a political price being demanded by a hostile society—a ransom to prove the moral worthiness of those at risk for AIDS, a demonstration that the funds requested for research and medical care would be well spent. "Has the debate shifted from the containment of the disease to the containment of a people?"

As the controversy continued to fester in San Francisco, no visible public health official appeared willing to adopt publicly the position being pressed by Larry Littlejohn and privately by some physicians concerned by the spreading epidemic. . . . Edward Brandt, Jr., the assistant secretary of health and the federal official most responsible for national policy on AIDS, deferred to local authorities. "There are few issues more volatile than human sexuality and privacy. They are not issues for the [Department of Health and Human Services]. It is important that the gay community and public health officials clear that [discussion up] and fast." . . . In language reflecting the public timidity of the period, [James Curran, head of the AIDS Activity Office, at the Centers for Disease Control said,] "I [don't] see a role for government in legislating sexual behavior or legislating change." . . .

With no public support for closing the baths by the nation's health officials and with apparently only isolated individuals within the gay community calling for closure, Silverman continued to stress throughout the first three months of 1984 that any action directed against the bathhouses would have to come from gay organizations. Extremely sensitive to how a misstep on his part might disrupt the effective working relationship he believed he had developed with gay groups and which he felt was critical to his overall strategy for containing the AIDS epidemic, he refused to take steps "that might make me look good to a lot of straight people in the community." The lessons of history were clear to San Francisco's chief health official: government was not an effective agent for getting people to change their sexual behavior.

By mid-March of 1984 Larry Littlejohn, frustrated by his inability to press the Department of Public Health to take aggressive measures against San Francisco's bathhouses and despairing of his ability to mobilize the leadership of the city's gay community behind such a move, decided upon a dramatic course—one that would fundamentally alter the nature of the bathhouse debate. Littlejohn planned to launch a petition campaign that would place an initiative on the November ballot requiring the city's Board of Supervisors to prohibit sexual activity in the baths. Justifying this move with its obvious risks of stirring local and national antihomosexual sentiments, Littlejohn cited the empirical evidence of failure of the city's modest educational efforts to modify the behavior of those who attended the bathhouses. Health promotion campaigns had failed to solve the problem of drug abuse and drunk driving, had not succeeded in gaining compliance from drivers to wear seat belts, had not prevented unwanted pregnancies. "We must not fool ourselves. There are no educational programs that will effectively change high risk for AIDS sex habits of bathhouse patrons to safe sex." . . .

Aware that he would be charged with calling upon the state to violate the realm of privacy in a way that was anathema to the political outlook of the organized gay community, Littlejohn drew a sharp distinction between public settings and the home. "If people want to continue dangerous sex activities in the privacy of their homes—so be it, that is their right. They are foolish to do so. However, bathhouses are public places. They are licensed by the city; they are the proper subject of public policy considerations." There were for Littlejohn "no real civil liberties issue[s] here." For those who might accuse him of a betrayal of the cause of gay liberation, he asserted the preeminence of saving gay lives. "I care more for my gay brothers. I care enough to speak out even if that should make me unpopular with some persons."

When Littlejohn's plans were made public at the end of March the pace of debate intensified. Mervyn Silverman met with several gay physicians who spoke to him about the medical consequences of failing to close the bathhouses. The director of health underscored his concern that any action to be taken on the bathhouses have the support of the gay community. Without such support he could not move despite the threat of Littlejohn's efforts. And so a small group of prominent gay individuals met to plan the mobilization of that support. Motivated by the dread of an electoral battle over the baths, the fear that the gay community's major achievements would be lost in the process, as well as by the toll being taken by AIDS, all but two of those attending the session agreed to sign a letter to Silverman calling upon him to close the baths. In addition to lending their own support to a move on Silverman's behalf, each of the participants agreed to seek the support of others—in all approximately one hundred prominent figures in the gay community were targeted for this effort.

But the enthusiasm of those who believed they could organize broad-scale gay community backing for closure—a condition set by Silverman—was not shared by others. Not only did they fail to generate additional signatures, but their effort generated significant political and professional opposition. The National Gay Task Force issued a statement that, though warning of the risks associated with "anonymous sex with multiple partners," expressed unalterable opposition to state intervention. "NGTF feels most strongly that personal behavior should not be regulated by the state, which historically has been an instrument of our oppression. Furthermore, state closure of such establishments would be largely symbolic, a largely symbolic gesture that would provide a false sense of security that the AIDS epidemic had somehow been contained." . . .

In San Francisco itself resistance was reflected at a meeting of gay leaders on the evening of March 29. At that session, it became clear to Silverman that given his requirement of gay community support he would be unable to act. And so on March 30 Silverman appeared before a planned press conference and announced that he would need more time to formulate the health department's policy.

Even for some who had signed the original letter calling for closure, there was a sense of relief that so dramatic a move had not been forced in three days as the result of the announcement of Littlejohn's effort. Frank Robinson, a writer who had signed the call, stated, "I'm personally pleased that there is more time for more input, for more discussion on the subject." He hoped that bathhouse owners would, in the time available, "board up the glory holes . . . close the orgy rooms, turn on the lights," provide a condom to every customer, and a copy of the safe sex education pamphlet "Let's Talk." But he also urged the gay community to acknowledge that "the biggest threat to the gay community is not that some people want to close the bathhouses. The biggest threat is a hideous, disfiguring, terminal disease called AIDS." Alluding to the March 29 meeting, at which it became clear to Silverman that he could not expect broad-scale support from the gay community for closure, Robinson lamented, "At Thursday's meeting . . . there were 172 ghosts who were not heard from, but if they could have spoken I think they would have reminded us of the terribly bitter fact that many of us seem to have forgotten. AIDS is something we give to each other."

Very different was the tone of an editorial that appeared in a gay newspaper, the *Bay Area Reporter (BAR)*. Listing the names of the sixteen individuals, including the "traitor extraordinaire," Larry Littlejohn, who supported closure, the *BAR* equated each of these individuals to Marshal Pétain [French collaborator with the Nazis]. "The people would have given away our right to assemble, our right to do with our own bodies what we choose, the few gains we have made in the past 25 years. These sixteen would have killed the movement—gladly handing it all over to forces that have beaten us down since time immemorial."

In the period immediately following the March 30 press conference, Silverman was praised by civil liberties and gay rights groups for his restraint, his unwillingness to capitulate to political pressure from pro-closure forces, his determination to assert the primacy of what they considered the requirements of public health over expediency, and his respect for the critically important values of civil liberties. . . .

But despite pressures to refrain from action, the forces set in motion by Larry Littlejohn's initiative, the insistent pressure of Mayor Dianne Feinstein, the persistent though often private warnings of many gay physicians associated with the treatment of AIDS patients, and Silverman's own changing perception of what was required to confront the AIDS crisis in San Francisco made it certain that the aborted announcement of March 30 would not end with a complete about-face. Action against the baths was inevitable.

In the face of such pressures, Silverman was warned by the city attorney's office that closure solely on health grounds would not withstand legal challenge.

This, of course, was Silverman's nightmare: to take the fateful step of closing the bathhouses as a way of reinforcing the message about the risks of unsafe sexual activity and to have such a move overruled by the courts. The result would be a deep fissure between the health department and the gay community, as well as a confused public message about the dangers of high-risk sex.

This was the context within which Silverman convened a meeting of local, state, and federal health experts to discuss the future of the bathhouses. . . . Instead of closing the baths, the group settled on a regulatory approach. "There should be no sex between individuals in public facilities which would lead to the spread of AIDS." The decision to prohibit all sex between individuals at the bathhouses was fateful because of its rejection of the distinction between safe, possibly safe, and unsafe sex so central to the educational efforts being undertaken by both the city and gay health organizations. In explaining that decision, Silverman said, "There was no way, really, that we could inspect to see if someone was wearing a condom, if they had put it on correctly—talk about infringement—that would have been incredible."

Six days later Silverman addressed the press. Flanked by gay physicians, he reported the unanimous conclusion of his advisory panel that "all sexual activity between individuals be eliminated in pubic facilities in San Francisco where the transmission of AIDS is likely to occur." While he underscored the role his action would have on the course of the AIDS epidemic, he stressed that his move was only part of a much broader program of education. Among the most visible gay physicians supporting Silverman's move were Don Abrams and Marcus Conant. Both were haunted by visions of their dying patients, and by the toll being taken by AIDS. Abrams viewed the bathhouse as uniquely contributing to an environment within which the disease could spread. Dismissing the objections of physicians who opposed this course, he noted that many were psychiatrists who had never seen "what AIDS does to its victims. . . . We're talking about life and death." Conant was moved by the knowledge that some of his own patients continued to attend the baths. "They have no moral problem with it. Clearly, any public health measure ever taken limits people's civil liberties. . . . A year ago I opposed bathhouse closure because I felt gay men would stop going out of fear." They had not. . . .

To those who had struggled to protect the bathhouse from state control, Silverman's decision represented a grave defeat with critical implications for the privacy rights of gay men, not only in San Francisco but across the nation. What made the decision all the more troubling was that its potential impact on halting the spread of AIDS was not at all certain. The health department's decision seemed, despite the effort to provide medical and epidemiological justifications, important primarily because of its symbolic value. But the costs to privacy would be anything but symbolic.

The issues were sharply cast by Thomas Stoddard, legislative director of the New York Civil Liberties Union, who was to become the executive director of the gay Lambda Legal Defense and Education Fund. . . . "There are two principles at stake here: the right of sexual privacy and the right of gay people to the equal protection of the laws." Acknowledging that the bathhouse might indeed promote conduct implicated in the spread of AIDS, he nevertheless underscored his opposition to state interference. "To admit that we confront a problem of grave significance, disease related sexual conduct at public bathhouses is not the same issue as whether government should be the means by which we solve the problem. That is, it seems to me, a fundamental precept of civil liberties. . . . Civil libertarians are naturally distrustful of government. . . . Therefore, they turn to the state only when there is no real alternative." Action on the part of the gay community, picket lines outside the bathhouses, would be an acceptable method of pressing the bathhouses to change. The specter of sodomy statutes haunted Stoddard's communication. "With the history [of sodomy laws] and with consensual sodomy still a crime in nearly half the states, it hardly seems appropriate to invite the state to regulate private sexual conduct when now it does not." For Stoddard the issues went beyond San Francisco. "Let me also state that I have an ulterior motive in writing this letter. San Francisco is being watched by those in New York, Illinois, by those in Texas, and by those in every other part of the country. If San Francisco—the mecca of gay culture—chooses to close down or regulate public bathhouses, it will give incentive to other cities . . . and in those places, I can virtually assure you, the actions taken will be far harder to keep within reasonable limits. . . . San Francisco will have given succor and encouragement to bigots and homophobes throughout the country to regulate, restrict and punish gay people." . . .

By May the lines of ideological conflict were sharply drawn. Civil liberties groups and gay rights and gay medical organizations saw in the anticipated regulations an unwarranted intrusion upon constitutionally protected privacy rights. Those supporting regulations saw in them a legitimate and rational exercise of the public health authority of the state. . . . In the confrontation and controversy that were to fester over the next six months, these diametrically opposed perspectives would be played out in a complex series of bureaucratic encounters. Framing the entire imbroglio was the open and lingering clash between Mayor Dianne Feinstein, who in both private and public settings accused the health department of dragging its feet on the bathhouse issue, and Mervyn Silverman, who saw himself as trying to chart a judicious and effective course, one that would have an impact on the course of the AIDS epidemic in San Francisco, one that would not alienate the gay community.

In the face of repeated challenges to the public health justification for his proposed course of action, yet a new and more serious threat to Silverman's goal of regulating the bathhouses was to emerge in the summer of 1984, this time from an utterly unexpected source, the Centers for Disease Control. . . . [T]he epidemiological relationship between AIDS and bathhouse attendance—the very foundation of the public health case for regulation or closure—was brought into question. Although an earlier national case control study had showed evidence of such a relationship, [CDC senior research sociologist William] Darrow found no such association in his just-completed examination of data derived from the San Francisco Clinic cohort study. "Although numbers of partners and AIDS are significantly related, and men who go to bathhouses tend to have greater numbers of partners, bathhouse attendance [itself] is *not* significantly associated with AIDS."

. . . Silverman and Dean Echenberg, his deputy for communicable diseases, were furious and indeed would expend some effort to force a modification of the letter's conclusions by protesting to Darrow's superiors at the CDC. Ultimately, they were successful in wresting a new analysis, with conclusions that were more compatible with the effort to justify the regulation of the bathhouses. But that was not to be for three months. In the summer of 1984 they had to confront the inevitable political consequences of the new CDC findings as gay leaders seized upon the Darrow letter in an effort to force a retreat.

Silverman resisted such pressure and continued to bridle under the bureaucratic restraints that had thwarted his plans to regulate the baths. To break the stalemate, he once again called together the advisory group that had urged the regulation of bathhouse activity. But this time consensus eluded the group. Five supported closure of the commercial establishments at the earliest possible moment; five sought to give the gay community additional time to develop an effective strategy for dealing with bathhouse behavior. Faced with this failure, Silverman chose to do what he had resisted doing for more than a year. He decided to close the baths. . . .

Following the city attorney's advice, Silverman authorized the surveillance of the bathhouses and sex clubs. What made the reports of the city's investigators remarkable was not only the vivid detail with which they described—often in the clumsy language of those unprepared to describe sexual encounters among men, frequently involving more than two individuals—the results of their surveillance, but the fact that they would become part of the public record as affidavits in the city's case against the bathhouses. Some of what was described, acts of mutual masturbation, for example, did not involve "high-risk sex." Some did.

One investigator described darkened hallways in which groups of men would gather "and masturbate themselves or someone else." Then he provided a graphic picture of multiple sexual encounters, and an orgy involving fellatio. "At approximately 10 P.M. two white males knelt on their knees in a darkened hallway next to the orgy room and committed fellatio on a tall white male wearing a black cowboy hat and vest. They would alternate. One would suck the penis while the other would lick the testicles and inner thigh areas. This activity attracted approximately five or six other males to the area to watch and participate. The two men who were doing the fellatio to the cowboy would periodically switch and begin sucking other erect penises that were nearby. The male wearing the cowboy hat ejaculated in the mouth of the small dark man. . . . It appeared the sperm was swallowed."

This report and those prepared by the other investigators achieved the desired impact. Whatever the actual tabulation of safe, unsafe, and possibly safe sex acts observed might have revealed, the descriptions portrayed the existence of activity that would serve to shock the sensibilities of the conventional and disturb those concerned with the transmission of a deadly disease.

With evidence in hand to buttress the decision he had already made, Silverman moved directly against fourteen sex establishments, declaring them public nuisances. Involved were six baths, four gay sex clubs, two gay movie theaters, and two gay bookstores. On October 9 Silverman issued the following announcement: "The places that I have ordered closed today have continued in the face of this epidemic to provide an environment that encourages and facilitates multiple unsafe sexual contacts, which are an important contributory factor in the spread of this deadly disease. When activities are proven to be dangerous to the public and continue to take place in commercial settings, the Health Department has the duty to intercede and halt the operation of such establishments."

Thus did Silverman reject the claims of those who sought to protect the bathhouse by the invocation of the principles governing the state's relationship to private sexual behavior between consenting adults. The very commercial nature of the establishments involved removed, for him, the protective mantle and provided the warrant for intervention. Responding to those who he knew would charge that his actions represented a profound assault on the interests of gay men, and a reversal of the social and legal advances attained by San Francisco's homosexual community, Silverman ended his statement by declaring, "Make no mistake about it. These fourteen establishments are not fostering gay liberation. They are fostering disease and death." Gone were the concerns about privacy that had been so prominently featured in Silverman's responses to Larry Littlejohn when the health department first had been pressed to move against the baths. Having obtained what he believed was the political support of important elements in the gay community for closure, he could discard the rhetoric of individual liberty. . . .

Despite the protracted debate over the bathhouses, the city's move produced a very modest public demonstration attended by only three hundred protestors. Though they were few, their anger was manifest. Banners read "Keep the City Out of Our Sex Lives," "Personal Rights vs. Public Hysteria," "Closure Feeds Bigotry," "Self-Control Not State Control." Randy Stallings, chair of the rally, declared, "What you are seeing in this city in 1984 is an attack on gay male sexuality and that has nothing to do with the worst tragedy we have ever faced. While they attack our sexuality and our rights to assemble, people are dying of AIDS." Jim Geary, director of the Shanti Project, which provided psychological and social support to AIDS patients, went further. "The closure does not save gay lives—but gives license to antigay violence and suffocates our sexual and emotional nature. We are being portrayed as uncontrollable animals without a conscience."

Ultimately Silverman's decision transformed the political struggle that had been waged for more than a year into a legal confrontation to be fought out in the courts. . . . [T]he city sought a grant of authority to exercise great discretion in the pursuit of the public health. . . . [T]he city asserted, "The right to operate a business in a manner contributing to the spread of a fatal disease cannot be deemed 'fundamental' or 'implicit in the concept of ordered liberty,' so as to be included in the right of personal privacy." . . .

Silverman's declaration, appended to the city's brief, provided the public health rationale for the city attorney's legal strategy. . . . "As a public health officer, I consider it my duty to fashion and implement public policies designed to . . . bring to an end [the operations of] commercial enterprises that involve exploitation for profit of an *individual's willingness* to engage in potentially lethal forms of recreation." Stressing the public setting within which such behavior occurred—with dire consequences for the spread of "virulent disease" and losses to the community measured in the cost of providing care and in the premature death of those who might otherwise have been expected to contribute to the public well-being—he asserted, "Altering sexual activity is a matter of individual privacy; when that sexual activity takes place in a commercial setting, this government has the prerogative and duty to intercede." . . .

Perhaps most remarkable in the city's well-prepared case was the failure to obtain a clear declaration of support for closure from any nationally known epidemiologist involved in the study of AIDS and the patterns of sexual behavior among gay men. . . .

The case presented by the bathhouse owners challenged the city's case on both empirical and constitutional grounds. . . .

Citing statements made by Silverman when he was resisting pressure to close the baths, the defendants stressed that even the city's chief public health officer had grave doubts about the impact of such a move on the spread of the AIDS epidemic. "The simple fact . . . is that closure of a few locations will simply move bath patrons elsewhere." Both the CDC's data . . . and the city's own research findings were used to demonstrate that closure would do little to control the spread of AIDS. Furthermore, the city's assertion that the baths were the venue of demonstrably unsafe sexual activity was rejected. While denouncing the reliance upon the city's investigators to obtain evidence about bathhouse behavior as "government snooping in the extreme," the defendants argued that a close examination of their reports failed to substantiate the city's claims. "The evidence reveals that over the course of at least eight visits . . . and untold hours of surveillance . . . the total number of unsafe sex incidents equaled two from one premise and three from another."

But such empirical challenges were preliminary to the central constitutional arguments upon which the defendants chose to rest their case. It was here that the radical distinction between those who sought to define a broad realm of privacy and those who defined the bathhouse as public space, appropriately subject to public regulation, was most sharply drawn. But unlike those who had argued that bathhouse intervention would ineluctably lead to control over the bedroom, . . . the proprietors argued that there was no conceptual distinction between the bathhouse and the bedroom. The commercial nature of the establishments, so central to the city's case, was deemed legally irrelevant. "There is simply no legal basis to distinguish the right to engage in consensual sexual activity in defendants' premises from the right to engage in consensual sexual activity in hotels or private homes. [There is] no difference between someone who rents a cubicle in a bathhouse and someone who makes a mortgage payment on his house." . . .

To buttress their case, the bathhouse owners included declarations from epidemiologists, public health officials, physicians associated with the care of AIDS patients and the defense of gay rights, as well as a social historian. The centerpiece of the defense came from Alan R. Kristal, director of the Office of Epidemiological Surveillance for the New York City Health Department. Based upon estimates of the number of gay men still patronizing San Francisco's bathhouses, he sought to demonstrate that closure would have virtually no impact on the AIDS epidemic. The maximum overall reduction in AIDS cases from bathhouse closure would be less that 1/4 of 1 percent. Could such an impact provide the basis for rational, not to speak of constitutional, public health policy? For Kristal, the answer was clear. "No public health official would institute a public health intervention based upon such a tiny expected benefit, and I know of no comparable *public* health crisis where similar intervention was attempted based on such a tiny expected benefit." . . .

Finally, the case against closure was set in the context of the long history of attacks on gay institutions. Among the declarations provided by the defense was a lengthy social history of the baths by Allan Bérubé. Unlike those who sought to portray the baths solely as reservoirs of infection, Bérubé saw their emergence and survival as "an integral part of gay political history." In the face of stigmatization and persecution the "bathhouses represent a major success [of gay people] in a century-long political struggle to overcome isolation and develop a sense of community and pride in their sexuality, to gain their right to sexual privacy, to win the right to associate with each other in public and to create 'safety zones' where gay men could be sexual and affectionate with each other with a minimal threat of violence, blackmail, loss of employment, arrest, imprisonment, and humiliation." For the general public the closure of the baths might simply be viewed as a public health measure involving a minor restriction in the face of an epidemic. For the gay community, argued Bérubé, such an effort would evoke the memory of the long and bitter history of bathhouse raids. Appealing to the prudence of those charged with protecting the public health, he warned that closure would foster mistrust of government and a lack of compliance with government health programs.

On November 28, Judge Roy Wonder issued his long-awaited order. The city's move for closure was rejected. Instead, the court ordered bathhouse owners to hire monitors to prohibit "high-risk" sexual activity, as defined by the private San Francisco AIDS Foundation. The ruling also prohibited proprietors from renting or operating "any and all private rooms." The doors to the individual video cubicles, booths, or rooms were to be removed. Thus to the question of whether the closed booth represented private and protected space, the judge responded by eliminating the possibility of retreating behind the closed door. Finally, acknowledging the argument that the bathhouses could serve as centers for safe sex education, Judge Wonder mandated that they undertake such programs.

Wonder's order, which came close to Silverman's initial April proposals for regulation, was denounced in the press, by those involved in the litigation, and by San Francisco's mayor. The San Francisco *Examiner* termed the decision "the epitome of judicial folly" and called upon the Board of Supervisors to enact an emergency decree closing the establishments. The San Francisco *Chronicle,* in an editorial entitled "Putting Spies in Sex Clubs," declared, "The order defies common sense. It is something like selling tickets to a swimming pool and forbidding anyone to get wet." Mayor Feinstein, long a bitter opponent of the bathhouses, and a critic of what she had viewed as Silverman's vacillation, remarked, "Most importantly, the ruling allows the continued exposure . . . to AIDS." Thomas Steel, attorney for the bathhouses, asserted that the orders entailed a judicially mandated invasion of privacy. Silverman, who acknowledged the order as being close to his own earlier regulatory proposals, was primarily concerned with how the new rules could be enforced. Modifications in the judicial order made one month later conceded to the city on all matters that were deemed critical from Silverman's perspective.

And so nine months after Mervyn Silverman had first proposed the regulation of bathhouse behavior, with the unanimous support of his expert panel, such regulations were in place as a result of a court-ordered modification of a move to close the establishments. Commenting on the extraordinarily complex and lengthy political process that had produced this final outcome and the tentativeness with which he had made his first moves, Silverman stressed that his concern for preserving an open and collaborative relationship with the gay community had been a critical factor. "If it had been a heterosexual disease, I'd have closed them immediately." Though his restraint has been denounced as the reflection of timidity and fecklessness, Silverman had, in fact, been constrained by his understanding of the political and social context within which he had been pressed to respond to AIDS and the specter of political isolation from those he sought to influence. He had thus charted a prudent, if modest, course. From the perspective of public health, if he had erred, it was because he had relied initially on the language of the rights of privacy to justify his refusal to move against the baths. Having asserted that principle rather than pragmatic concerns limited the course available to him, he had lost an early opportunity to engage in a forthright public debate over the role of his department in shaping the culture of sexual behavior in the context of the AIDS epidemic.

FURTHER READING

Dennis Altman, *AIDS in the Mind of America* (1986).

Virginia Berridge and Philip Strong, *AIDS and Contemporary History* (1993).

Allan M. Brandt, "AIDS and Metaphor: Toward the Social Meaning of Epidemic Disease," *Social Research* 55 (1988): 413–432.

———, "AIDS in Historical Perspective: Four Lessons from the History of Sexually Transmitted Disease," *American Journal of Public Health* 78 (April 1988).

———, *No Magic Bullet: A Social History of Venereal Disease in the United States Since 1880* (1987).

Dangerous Bedfellows, *Policing Public Sex* (1996).

Douglas Crimp, "Portraits of People with AIDS," in Domna Stanton, ed., *Discourses of Sexuality* (1992), 362–388.

———, ed., *AIDS: Cultural Analysis, Cultural Activism* (1988).

Steven Epstein, *Impure Science: AIDS, Activism, and the Politics of Knowledge* (1996).

Elizabeth Fee, "Sin versus Science: Venereal Disease in Twentieth-Century Baltimore," in Kathy Peiss and Christina Simmons, eds., *Passion and Power* (1989), 178–198.

Elizabeth Fee and Daniel M. Fox, eds., *AIDS: The Burdens of History* (1988).

———, eds., *AIDS: The Making of a Chronic Disease* (1992).

Douglas A. Feldman and Julia Wang Miller, *The AIDS Crisis: A Documentary History* (1998).

B. Michael Hunter, ed., *Sojourner: Black Gay Voices in the Age of AIDS* (1993).

James H. Jones, *Bad Blood: The Tuskegee Syphilis Experiment* (1981).

Cindy Patton, *Inventing AIDS* (1990).

Suzanne Poirier, *Chicago's War on Syphilis, 1937–1940* (1995).

Susan M. Reverby, ed., *Tuskegee's Truths: Rethinking the Tuskegee Syphilis Study* (2000).

Richard Rodriguez, "Late Victorians, San Francisco, AIDS and the Homosexual Stereotype," *Harper's*, October 1990, 57–66.

Randy Shilts, *And the Band Played On* (1988).

CHAPTER
14

Sexual Identities, Family Matters, and Border Crossings in Contemporary America

The role of sexuality in defining personal relationships has undergone significant changes in recent decades, as Americans debated and revised their notions of family, kinship, and affinity. A growing number of gay men and lesbians have exchanged commitment vows, raised children, and sought the right to marry. Beginning in the 1980s, some cities, universities, and businesses granted domestic partnership rights. Such measures remain highly controversial, with conservatives mounting political opposition based upon religious and cultural beliefs about the family. At the present time, the legislative record is mixed. Although the Hawaii Supreme Court opened the door to gay marriages in 1993, the state legislature slammed it shut by passing a constitutional amendment restricting marriage to heterosexual couples. In contrast, Vermont passed a civil unions law in 2000, granting most of the benefits of marriage to gay men and lesbians.

Beliefs about the "traditional" family—nuclear, heterosexual, based on "blood" and biology—have been challenged in other ways as well: through the use of new reproductive technologies and surrogate motherhood, by the growing numbers of single parents, and by the creation of "blended families" through divorce and re-marriage. These reflect new attitudes toward sexuality and morality. Complicating this picture further is the profound change in the American population resulting from global migrations. Not since the early twentieth century has there been such a large percentage of immigrants and their children in the United States. As was true earlier in American history, conflicts over sexual cultures rooted in national differences and ethnic traditions continue to shape sexual identities and choices deeply.

The implications of these cultural and social transformations for the lived experience and politics of sexuality remain to be seen. Will sexual subcultures—from the Filipino custom of mail marriages to the gay liberationist group Sex Panic—flourish? Or will cultural "margins" disappear into the mainstream? What will sexual encounters, marriage, and family mean in the future? Even as sharp lines have been drawn in political controversies and public scandals, a more nuanced and complex conversation about sexual matters is taking place in Americans' everyday lives. As those exchanges continue, this seems a period marked less by assimilation than by border crossings, where sexual categories are blurred, allegiances unpredictable, and identities fluid.

◖ D O C U M E N T S

What is a family, and do lesbian and gay Americans have a place in it? This question was at the heart of the Sharon Kowalski case, which pitted Kowalski's "blood" family against her life partner, as legal scholar-activist Nan D. Hunter explained in Document 1. In Document 2, journalist Andrew Sullivan claimed the right of homosexuals to marry and form families. In contrast, the members of Sex Panic, as reported in the *New York Times,* vigorously oppose gay assimilation into the mainstream and argue that promiscuous sex is central to gay male identity (Document 3). Debates over sexuality and family take on a different coloration in many immigrant communities. In Document 4, Roberto Ordonez noted how the old practice of "mail order brides" has been modernized by new global technologies; such marriages contain many risks for Filipinas, but can be a route of economic mobility and family formation. M. Evelina Galang, in an excerpt from "Deflowering the Sampaguita" (Document 5), wrote evocatively of Filipina-American daughters who routinely cross cultural borders; she suggested the inner struggle to understand one's sexuality, navigate the expectations of family and community, and create an identity in a complex social world.

1. Nan D. Hunter Defines the Family in the Sharon Kowalski Case, 1991

In the effort to end second-class citizenship for lesbian and gay Americans, no obstacle has proved tougher to surmount than the cluster of issues surrounding "the family." For the past twenty years, the concept of family has functioned as a giant cultural screen. Projected onto it, contests over race, gender, sexuality and a range of other "domestic" issues from crime to taxes constantly create and recreate a newly identified zone of social combat, the politics of the family. Activists of all persuasions eagerly seek to enter the discursive field, ever-ready to debate and discuss: Who counts as a family? Which "family values" are the authentic ones? Is there a place in the family for queers? As battles are won and lost in this cultural war, progressives and conservatives agree on at least one thing—the family is highly politicized terrain.

For lesbians and gays, these debates have dramatic real-life consequences, probably more so than with any other legal issue. Relationship questions touch almost every person's life at some point, in a way that military issues, for example, do not. Further, the unequal treatment is blatant, de jure and universal, as compared with the employment arena, where discrimination may be more subtle and variable. No state allows a lesbian or gay couple to marry. No state recognizes (although

Nan D. Hunter, "Nan D. Hunter Defines the Family in the Sharon Kowalski Case, 1991" originally titled "Sexual Dissent and the Family: The Sharon Kowalski Case." Reprinted with permission from the October 7, 1991 issue of *The Nation* (406–411).

sixteen counties and cities do) domestic partnership systems under which unmarried couples (gay or straight) can become eligible for certain benefits usually available only to spouses. The fundamental inequity is that, barring mental incompetence or consanguinity, virtually any straight couple has the option to marry and thus establish a next-of-kin relationship that the state will enforce. No lesbian or gay couple can. Under the law, two women or two men are forever strangers, regardless of their relationship.

One result is that every lesbian or gay man's nightmare is to be cut off from one's primary other, physically incapacitated, stranded, unable to make contact, without legal recourse. It is a nightmare that could not happen to a married couple. But it did happen to two Minnesota women, Sharon Kowalski and Karen Thompson, in a remarkable case that has been threading its way through the courts for six years.

Sharon Kowalski, notwithstanding the Minnesota State District Court's characterization of her as a "child of divorce," is an adult with both a committed life partner and parents who bitterly refuse to acknowledge either her lesbianism or her lover. Kowalski is a former physical education teacher and amateur athlete, whose Minnesota women's high school shot-put record still stands. In 1983, she was living with her lover, Thompson, in the home they had jointly purchased in St. Cloud. Both women were deeply closeted; they exchanged rings with each other but told virtually no one of their relationship. That November, Kowalski suffered devastating injuries in a car accident, which left her unable to speak or walk, with arms deformed and with major brain damage, including seriously impaired short-term memory.

After the accident, both Thompson and Kowalski's father petitioned to be appointed Sharon's guardian; initially, an agreement was entered that the father would become guardian on the condition that Thompson retain equal rights to visit and consult with doctors. By the summer of 1985, after growing hostilities, the father refused to continue the arrangement and persuaded a local court that Thompson's visits caused Kowalski to feel depressed. One doctor hired by the father wrote a letter stating that Kowalski was in danger of sexual abuse. Within twenty-four hours after being named sole guardian, the father cut off all contact between Thompson and Kowalski, including mail. By this time, Kowalski had been moved to a nursing home near the small town where she grew up in the Iron Range, a rural mining area in northern Minnesota.

Surely one reason the Kowalski case is so compelling is that for millions of parents, learning that one's son is gay or daughter is lesbian would be *their* worst nightmare. That is all the more true in small-town America, among people who are religiously observant and whose expectations for a daughter are primarily marriage and motherhood. "The good Lord put us here for reproduction, not that kind of way," Donald Kowalski told the *Los Angeles Times* in 1988. "It's just not a normal life style. The Bible will tell you that." Karen Thompson, he told other reporters, was "an animal" and was lying about his daughter's life. "I've never seen anything that would make me believe" that she is lesbian, he said to *The New York Times* in 1989. How much less painful it must be to explain a lesbian daughter's life as seduction, rather than to experience it as betrayal.

. . . Thompson's stubborn struggle to "bring Sharon home" . . . entered a new stage. In late 1988 a different judge, sitting in Duluth, ordered Kowalski moved to a new facility for medical evaluation. Soon thereafter, based on staff recommendations from the second nursing facility, the court ordered that Thompson be allowed to visit. The two women saw each other again in the spring of 1989, after three and a half years of forced separation. . . . Kowalski, who can communicate by typing on a special keyboard, . . . said that she wants to live in "St. Cloud with Karen."

. . . In May 1990, citing a heart condition for which he had been hospitalized, Donald Kowalski resigned as his daughter's guardian. This resignation set the stage for Thompson to file a renewed petition for appointment as guardian, which she did. But in an April 1991 ruling, Minnesota State District Court Judge Robert Campbell selected as guardian Karen Tomberlin—a friend of both Kowalski and her parents, who supported Tomberlin's request. On the surface, the court sought balance. The judge characterized the Kowalski parents and Karen Thompson as the "two wings" of Sharon Kowalski's family. He repeatedly asserted that both must have ample access to visitation with Kowalski. He described Tomberlin as a neutral third party who would not exclude either side. But the biggest single reason behind the decision, the one that he characterized as "instrumental," seemed to be the judge's anger at Thompson for ever telling Kowalski's parents (in a private letter), and then the world at large, that she and Kowalski were lovers.

The court condemned Thompson's revelation of her own relationship as the "outing" of Sharon Kowalski. Thompson did write the letter to Kowalski's parents without telling Kowalski (who was at the time just emerging from a three-month coma after the accident) and did build on her own an active political organization around the case, composed chiefly of disability and lesbian and gay rights groups. Of course, for most of that period, she could not have consulted Kowalski because the two were cut off from each other.

In truth, though, the judge's concern seemed to be more for the outing of Kowalski's parents. He describes the Kowalskis as "outraged and hurt by the public invasion of Sharon's privacy and their privacy," and he blames this outing for the bitterness between Thompson and the parents. Had Thompson simply kept this to herself, the court implies, none of these nasty facts would ever have had to be discussed. But then Thompson would never have been able to maintain her relationship with her lover. . . .

The conflict in the Kowalski case illustrates one of the prime contradictions underlying all the cases seeking legal protection for lesbian and gay couples. This culture is deeply invested with a notion of the ideal family as not only a zone of privacy and a structure of authority (preferably male in the conservative view) but also as a barrier against unlicensed sexuality. Even many leftists and progressives, who actively contest male authority and at least some of the assumptions behind privacy, are queasy about constructing a family politics with queer sex on the inside rather than the outside. . . .

A debate continues within the lesbian and gay community about whether [the] effort [to legalize gay marriage] is assimilationist and conservatizing and whether same-sex marriage would simply constitute the newest form of boundary. Much of that debate, however, simply assumes that the social meaning of marriage is unchanging and timeless. If same-sex couples could marry, the profoundly gendered structure at the heart of marriage would be radically disrupted. Who *would* be the "husband" in a marriage of two men, or the "wife" in a marriage of two women? And either way—if there can be no such thing as a female husband or a male wife, as the right wing argues with contempt; or if indeed in some sense there *can* be, as lesbian and gay couples reconfigure these roles on their own terms—the absolute conflation of gender with role is shattered. What would be the impact on hetero-sexual marriage?

The law's changes to protect sexual dissent within the family will occur at dif-ferent speeds in different places, which might not be so bad. Family law has always been a province primarily of state rather than federal regulation and often has varied from state to state; grounds for divorce, for example, used to differ dramati-cally depending on geography. What seems likely to occur in the next wave of fam-ily cases is the same kind of variability in the legal definition of the family itself. Those very discrepancies may help to denaturalize concepts like "marriage" and "parent" and expose the utter contingency of the sexual conventions that, in part, construct the family.

2. Andrew Sullivan Makes a Conservative Case for Gay Marriage, 1989

[In July 1989,] in New York, a court ruled that a gay lover had the right to stay in his deceased partner's rent-control apartment because the lover qualified as a member of the deceased's family. The ruling deftly annoyed almost everybody. Conservatives saw judicial activism in favor of gay rent control: three reasons to be appalled. Chastened liberals[,] . . . while endorsing the recognition of gay relation-ships, also worried about the abuse of already stretched entitlements that the ruling threatened. What neither side quite contemplated is that they both might be right, and that the way to tackle the issue of unconventional relationships in conventional society is to try something both more radical and more conservative than putting courts in the business of deciding what is and is not a family. That alternative is the legalization of civil gay marriage.

The New York rent-control case did not go anywhere near that far, which is the problem. The rent-control regulations merely stipulated that a "family" member had the right to remain in the apartment. The judge ruled that to all intents and purposes a gay lover is part of his lover's family, inasmuch as a "family" merely means an interwoven social life, emotional commitment, and some level of finan-cial interdependence.

It's [a] principle now well established around the country. Several cities have "domestic partnership" laws, which allow relationships that do not fit into the cate-gory of heterosexual marriage to be registered with the city and qualify for benefits that up till now have been reserved for straight married couples. . . . In these cities, a variety of interpersonal arrangements qualify for health insurance, bereavement leave, insurance, annuity and pension rights, housing rights (such as rent-control

Andrew Sullivan, "Here Comes the Groom: A (Conservative) Case for Gay Marriage," *The New Republic* 201 (August 28, 1989): 20–22. Reprinted by permission of *The New Republic*.

apartments), adoption and inheritance rights. Eventually, according to gay lobby groups, the aim is to include federal income tax and veterans' benefits as well. . . .

. . . [T]he concept of domestic partnership chips away at the prestige of traditional relationships and undermines the priority we give them. This priority is not necessarily a product of heterosexism. Consider heterosexual couples. Society has good reason to extend legal advantages to heterosexuals who choose the formal sanction of marriage over simply living together. They make a deeper commitment to one another and to society; in exchange, society extends certain benefits to them. Marriage provides an anchor, if an arbitrary and weak one, in the chaos of sex and relationships to which we are all prone. It provides a mechanism for emotional stability, economic security, and the healthy rearing of the next generation. We rig the law in its favor not because we disparage all forms of relationship other than the nuclear family, but because we recognize that not to promote marriage would be to ask too much of human virtue. In the context of the weakened family's effect upon the poor, it might also invite social disintegration. One of the worst products of the New Right's "family values" campaign is that its extremism and hatred of diversity has disguised this more measured and more convincing case for the importance of the marital bond.

The concept of domestic partnership ignores these concerns, indeed directly attacks them. This is a pity, since one of its most important objectives—providing some civil recognition for gay relationships—is a noble cause and one completely compatible with the defense of the family. But the way to go about it is not to undermine straight marriage; it is to legalize old-style marriage for gays.

The gay movement has ducked this issue primarily out of fear of division. Much of the gay leadership clings to notions of gay life as essentially outsider, antibourgeois, radical. Marriage, for them, is co-optation into straight society. For the Stonewall generation, it is hard to see how this vision of conflict will ever fundamentally change. But for many other gays—my guess, a majority—while they don't deny the importance of rebellion 20 years ago and are grateful for what was done, there's now the sense of a new opportunity. A need to rebel has quietly ceded to a desire to belong. To be gay and to be bourgeois no longer seems such an absurd proposition. Certainly since AIDS, to be gay and to be responsible has become a necessity. . . .

Legalizing gay marriage would offer homosexuals the same deal society now offers heterosexuals: general social approval and specific legal advantages in exchange for a deeper and harder-to-extract-yourself-from commitment to another human being. Like straight marriage, it would foster social cohesion, emotional security, and economic prudence. Since there's no reason gays should not be allowed to adopt or be foster parents, it could also help nurture children. And its introduction would not be some sort of radical break with social custom. As it has become more acceptable for gay people to acknowledge their loves publicly, more and more have committed themselves to one another for life in full view of their families and their friends. A law institutionalizing gay marriage would merely reinforce a healthy social trend. It would also, in the wake of AIDS, qualify as a genuine public health measure. Those conservatives who deplore promiscuity among some homosexuals should be among the first to support it. . . .

Of course, some would claim that any legal recognition of homosexuality is a de facto attack upon heterosexuality. But even the most hardened conservatives recognize that gays are a permanent minority and aren't likely to go away. Since persecution is not an option in a civilized society, why not coax gays into traditional values rather than rail incoherently against them?

There's a less elaborate argument for gay marriage: it's good for gays. It provides role models for young gay people who, after the exhilaration of coming out, can easily lapse into short-term relationships and insecurity with no tangible goal in sight. My own guess is that most gays would embrace such a goal with as much (if not more) commitment as straights. Even in our society as it is, many lesbian relationships are virtual textbook cases of monogamous commitment. Legal gay marriage could also help bridge the gulf often found between gays and their parents. It could bring the essence of gay life—a gay couple—into the heart of the traditional straight family in a way the family can most understand and the gay offspring can most easily acknowledge. It could do as much to heal the gay-straight rift as any amount of gay rights legislation.

If these arguments sound socially conservative, that's no accident. It's one of the richest ironies of our society's blind spot toward gays that essentially conservative social goals should have the appearance of being so radical. But gay marriage is not a radical step. It avoids the mess of domestic partnership; it is humane; it is conservative in the best sense of the word.

3. Sex Panic Opposes Gay Assimilation, 1997

One night last May, a handful of New York City's best-known gay journalists, artists and academics called together some friends to bemoan what they viewed as a backlash against the sexual practices of homosexuals. The turnout surprised them: five dozen people jammed into an overheated room.

They swapped stories of police crackdowns on sex in public restrooms and closings of gay discos and pubs. And they complained about new books taking aim at what remains, even in the AIDS era, a central feature of gay urban life: sex clubs, bathhouses and weekend-long drug parties where men may have intercourse with a dozen partners a night.

"It sounds like a traditional sex panic," someone declared, borrowing a term historians use to describe a wave of societal prudishness. Thus the group adopted a name: Sex Panic.

Gay activist groups are hardly in short supply. What makes Sex Panic different are its enemies: three of the nation's most prominent gay authors, Gabriel Rotello, Michaelangelo Signorile and Larry Kramer. All sound alarms about the homosexual culture of sexual freedom, warning that its promiscuous pursuit by a core of gay men threatens to perpetuate epidemic AIDS.

As viruses go, H.I.V. is fragile and difficult to transmit. But in the late 70's and early 80's, Mr. Rotello writes[,] . . . H.I.V. found a home in the homosexual fast lane. As their movement for sexual liberation took hold, gay men changed sex partners as often as some people changed clothes. But the very behavior favored by

Sheryl Gay Stolberg, "Gay Culture Weighs Sense and Sexuality," *New York Times*, November 23, 1997, 4:1, 6. Copyright © 1997 by the New York Times Co. Reprinted by permission.

them—anal intercourse—was particularly conducive to the spread of AIDS. Gay men began dying.

When scientists learned that latex condoms blocked H.I.V., public health officials and AIDS activists created a "safe sex" strategy. But what Mr. Rotello calls "the condom code"—the idea that the number of partners doesn't matter, so long as you always use a condom—hasn't stamped out H.I.V., mainly because not everyone follows it. Now, two decades into the epidemic, bathhouses and unsafe sex are coming back.

"The whole culture has to change," Mr. Kramer said in an interview. "We have created a culture that in fact murdered us, killed us. What you can't help but think, if you've got any brains, is don't people ever learn anything?"

Such remarks have won him few fans at Sex Panic. "A culture doesn't kill people," retorted Kendall Thomas, a law professor at Columbia University and a founder of Sex Panic. "The virus kills people."

The volleying has deeply divided the gay intelligentsia. For the first time since the publication in 1987 of "And The Band Played On" by Randy Shilts, there is open debate among homosexuals about promiscuity's role in AIDS. For many of them, it is a terrifying discussion, one they fear could fan the flames of discrimination as it becomes public by focusing on their behavior as a cause of the epidemic. "It is something a lot of people are really afraid to speak up about," Mr. Signorile said.

A Question of Assimilation

How this argument is settled will have broad implications for all of America as the financial, social and emotional toll of AIDS continues. While death rates have been declining, studies show that men who have sex with men still account for the majority of AIDS cases, and that a young gay man has as much as a 50 percent chance of acquiring H.I.V. by middle age.

But the debate is about more than public health; it is about what it means to be homosexual. As some homosexuals press for same-sex marriage, adoption and other forms of societal acceptance, welcoming President Clinton's address this month to a gay and lesbian civil rights group (the first by a sitting President), others protest assimilation.

On one side are those like Mr. Kramer, who are beseeching homosexuals to adopt a culture rooted as much in art, literature and relationships as in "what's between our legs and what we do with it."

On the other are those like Mr. Thomas and Michael Warner, an English professor at Rutgers University and a founder of Sex Panic, who argue that promiscuous sex is the essence of gay liberation, and that any attempt to fight AIDS by changing the culture is doomed.

"It is an absurd fantasy to expect gay men to live without a sexual culture when we have almost nothing else that brings us together," Mr. Warner said.

The debate occurs against a backdrop of evidence that homosexuals are returning to what they call "bare-back sex," anal intercourse without condoms. In a survey of 205 gay men in Miami's South Beach, Dr. William W. Darrow, a public health professor at Florida International University, found that 45 percent had unprotected anal sex in the past year. . . .

The reasons aren't fully understood. Mr. Signorile blames the social scene; . . . he attacks the "circuit," a national series of weekend-long bashes laden with drugs.

"What we are seeing," he said in an interview, "is a kind of live-and-let-live intense party scene that is very similar to the same scene that contributed to the AIDS epidemic exploding in the 1970's."

Invincible Youth

The myth of invincible youth is also a factor; a generation of young men has now grown up amid AIDS. Some men have simply grown weary of wearing condoms. And there is evidence that the life-saving promise of protease inhibitors is backfiring; as drugs extend the lives of AIDS patients, more people take risks. . . .

. . . [A]s the number of partners goes up, use of condoms goes down, said Ron Stall, a behavioral scientist at the Center for AIDS Prevention Studies at the University of San Francisco. He fears that if gay men continue to have unsafe sex in the age of protease inhibitors, drug-resistant strains of H.I.V. will spread. "We have then yielded the epidemiological nightmare," he said.

To Sex Panic, this sounds like an alarmist pretext for restricting gay civil rights. Promiscuity and safe sex can coexist, its members argue. And while it may be difficult for heterosexuals to understand anonymous sex with multiple partners, to many homosexuals it is a cornerstone of liberation. Homosexuals had been discriminated against for the way they had sex; liberation meant having as much sex as possible, as publicly as possible.

"We want to reinsert sexual liberation back in our movement," said Tony Valenzuela, an actor in gay pornographic films who organized Sex Panic's first national conference, held in San Diego this month. "For those of us who like anonymous sex, there is something very erotic," he said, adding that safe sex is standard in gay porn. "The important thing is that it can be healthy."

The debate is only likely to intensify. "In the end," Dr. Stall said, "it is a cultural fight as much as an epidemiological fight. What is the future of gay culture going to be like?"

4. The Risks of Mail Marriage, 1996

The trial of an American in Washington State for the death by shooting of his Filipina wife and her two friends in a courthouse in Seattle March 1 last year while appearing as protagonists in a messy divorce contest highlights yet again the problems confronting so-called "mail-order brides" and the dilemma in convincing Filipino women to avoid getting married through mail or computer wife-ordering services. Timothy C. Blackwell, a computer technician, met Susana Remerata, a comely Filipina restaurant management graduate, via a catalogue called Asian Encounters, one of several dozen such publications that feature Asian women. The women, whose photos peer out from the catalogue's pages, were supposed to be looking for "pen pals," but the men knew they were hunting for husbands.

Roberto C. Ordonez, "Mail Marriage Very Risky," *Filipino Reporter*, May 31–June 6, 1996, 21, 27. Reprinted by permission.

At any rate, following some exchanges of letters and pictures and other information, the two got married barely a week after they met personally when Blackwell went to the Philippines. That marriage lasted only two weeks. Susana fled from Blackwell claiming she was being abused. Last year Susana and the two Filipinas were shot at point-blank range by Blackwell in a courthouse where a divorce proceeding involving him and his estranged wife was set to be heard. Blackwell, 48, now faces three murder charges for killing Susana, 23, and her two friends, Phoebe Dizon, 46, and Veronica Laureta Johnson, 42. A manslaughter charge has been added after an eight-month old fetus in Susana's womb died as a result of the shooting. Blackwell brought the divorce case against Susana claiming that she was not attentive to his needs and that he had suspected that he was "duped" in an immigration "con" game. He was asking that she pay him $20,000, the amount he had spent in pursuing their love affair. His lawyer argued that Blackwell suffered a "mental snap" after learning that his wife became pregnant by a Filipino after she had left him. Susana, however, in her counter suit insisted that she had been a victim of physical and sexual brutality by Blackwell since arriving in the U.S. She added that, at one time, he nearly choked her to death. She fled from him in fear of her life.

Recently the Philippines passed a law banning all types of mail-order bride schemes. The law provides stiff penalties for violators. Passing such a law is one thing. How to stop this kind of operation, which through the years has been turned into a highly profitable industry, is another. Yearly, no less than 20,000 Filipinas leave the country as fiancées of foreigners. Most come to America, but many thousands more also find their way to France, Great Britain, Germany, the Scandinavian and Benelux countries, and Asian countries like Japan, Korea, Taiwan, Thailand, and Singapore, and the Middle East. There are many reasons why these Filipinas seek ways to leave the safety and warmth of the country, even by marrying foreigners whose past many of them are not even aware of. Foremost among these reasons, of course, is the dire economic condition back home. Their perception of despair and hopelessness, and the lack of a bright future to bank on prompts them to seek greener pastures, so to speak. The Western influence is also one of the factors. But since it's difficult to seek employment due to cumbersome requirements, and likewise when one does not possess skills, their only means is to turn to the mail-order bride industry.

Women advocates in the U.S. are trying to hammer out laws that would ban any form of advertisement that entices men to correspond with women for romantic intentions or otherwise. There are . . . others who want simply to outlaw outright any business that has to do with pairing men with women. But these moves may seem difficult to pursue given the penchant of courts to protect First Amendment rights. Then, too, from the catalogue or magazine operation, the mail order bride industry has been transformed into a highly technical computerized undertaking. Women's photos, vital statistics and related information are all over cyberspace. And so they say that as long as there are lonely men and there are women searching for what they believe are better opportunities or the perception that they can improve their status in life, they would find ways to get in touch with one another. Who is to stop them? And who is to blame?

Instead of finger pointing, Filipino advocates and organizations overseas should try to allot part of their time to assist Filipinas who leave the country as a postal bride or somesuch. Support groups may be set up in the countries of destination among those who are already residing or working there. This is an area of concern that should interest groups like the Lions, Jaycees, professional, religious, and other civic organizations to pool resources and set up some sort of support groups. But most important, there should be a massive information and education campaign starting right in the Philippines to acquaint Filipinas seeking foreign husbands on what could happen to them or what they may expect, just in case. Women should be advised to demand a background check of their husbands to be, for instance. New York City requires several hours of counselling for those intending to get married. Why not a special seminar for the Filipina who is plunging into a marital relationship with someone she met via the postal service? . . . In the U.S., . . . it takes three years following the marriage for the alien spouse to be eligible for citizenship. In the meantime, it is not uncommon for a woman to feel that her continued stay here lies in the hands of her husband. The woman becomes powerless and insecure. She tends to submit meekly even to a point when she becomes what appears to a man as a willing or uncomplaining victim of verbal, physical, or even sexual assault. The fact that they spent money to go to the Philippines to claim their brides, marry them, put up a wedding party, and bring them to the U.S. would let most men believe that the women, like chattel or a piece of property, are owned by them and, therefore, in their complete control. They may do as they want to with them, even turn them into punching bags.

Recently, Pres. Clinton signed into law a bill that gives a woman the right to pursue her citizenship on her own if she is a victim of spousal or domestic abuse. But as I have said before, there are thousands and thousands of mail order brides, on the other hand, who are living comfortably, raising their children and building good families in many parts of the world, including the United States. There are thousands, too, who are living in obscurity, fear, and horror, refraining from making contacts with their compatriots precisely because of the bad connotation given to mail-order brides or due to lack of information or just out of plain ignorance. They should be encouraged to report their arrival in any country and subsequent whereabouts to the nearest Philippine embassy or consulate. They must be enticed to socialize or even find ways to improve themselves by acquiring some skills. They ought to be persuaded to come out in the open when they are being abused.

5. M. Evelina Galang Evokes "Deflowering the Sampaguita," 1997

With a group of your best Pinay friends, and their boyfriends, pile into a van and take over a local dance club. Dance less than a breath apart. Crowd the floor like a cluster of rich red grapes, threaded together by a single vine. You have colored your mouth burgundy, teased your hair, and decorated your neck, your ears, your skinny brown arms with gold and copper bangles. You have stretched a cotton shirt, scoop

M. Evelina Galang, "Deflowering the Sampaguita," in Maria P. P. Root, ed., *Filipino Americans: Transformation and Identity* (Thousand Oaks, Calif.: Sage Publications, 1997), 225–229. Reprinted by permission.

necked and slightly swollen at the breast, around your body. Your pants hang low, slide across your hips, just about reveal your belly. You and your friends are beautiful flowers, fragrant, sweet, ripe. You draw your boyfriends close. They hover just above you. Gaze into your eyes. Run their strong hands along your waist, torso, and thigh. Dance holding hands. Move together. To the beat. Closer and closer. Close your eyes, and he wraps his arms around you. Taken.

It is as though you move to that drum, that tribal gong. Your hips and legs move and sway, knees bend and pose, like a mountain princess crossing the river—head up, eye to eye. The drumming brings you closer, the bells chiming in the distance dispel reality. It is the Kulintang, dense rhythmic drumming. And even though you were never a Mindanao Princess, even if you never took a folk dance lesson in your life, the pressure of the heels, down on the linoleum floor; the way you hold your back up straight, tall and proud; the way you cast your spell, hypnotic and full as the golden moon; the way you float right out of consciousness is something that comes easy, part of your blood, indeed, part of your human condition.

Amid the confusion, of what to say, to think, to feel, you lose yourself someplace in the middle of a kiss. Feel stars bursting inside you, oceans washing up against your hips, water welling and brimming just below your pelvis, and before you can swim your way back to your senses, he is deep inside you. You not only let him in, you invite him. "Right this way," you whisper. Become part of this wave, this delightful tumult. Know nothing, only that you hope this feeling never stops. This is right. This is natural. This is your intuitive self, honest and true. You let go.

In the aftermath gloom sets in, chaos begins. Picture your mother and father, sitting in a pew before God and all the heavens. Think, better to die than ever let them know. Better to keep things a secret. Wonder how something this beautiful can be that wicked? Are you going to hell?

The very first time, when you knew little of love, when hormones controlled the sky and moon, he came and you said to yourself, "Is that all?" Like a tailor with a needle, he slipped in and out and in and out of you and you thought, so? And still, you couldn't help yourself, you opened up. Again and again. For years, you switched boys, lovers, men. You learned about give and take and generosity. Sewing turned into surfing, riding a wave high, wild, free, and dangerous. Instead of "Is that all," you thought, "Please, let's don't ever stop." You learned the difference between fucking and making love. You preferred the latter and saved your body for men you loved. The act became a gift you shared with lovers.

And when a baby grows, ripe and free, fills your baby fat belly with baby. You confess. Are sent away. You have a baby. You do one of two things: You give her away, like a door prize on Philippine Independence Day, or you bring her home and she becomes your baby sister. Your baby is not your baby. Your mommy no longer looks at you as if she were your mommy. Your daddy stops speaking. Be grateful, they tell you, you are lucky this is all.

Other girls from your First Holy Communion didn't get this far. Never got to see their babies. Sleeping was easier for them, dying was less disgraceful than bearing a child. There was no stopping the chaos in their bodies, no one to talk to, and there the fight died. And who could blame them, really? All that confusion bottled up inside, all that and a child smaller than each teenage girl, just as sweet and innocent as the child mother, in search of someone to love, to talk to, to cry to—all that bursting out of their still boylike bodies. Who could blame them for silencing the conflict of their hearts?

Or maybe you are one of the many who marry after all. Three months pregnant, 20 years young, loving your high school sweetheart. Nobody knows, just you and your boyfriend, your parents and his. No one tells. You bear your child, you bear many, and nobody is wiser. Not a word spoken. When your daughter and son grow, when their bodies change and their voices drift away from childhood, you begin the practice of silent disapproval, you continue the cycle. You insist on impossible chastity. You attempt to keep the Sampaguita in bloom, fresh, young, never acknowledging the nature of things.

You live your life like a spy. Secret agent 99, complete with double life. Another you. The doctor daughter, the lawyer daughter, the wife daughter, the well-behaved and decent daughter. You cook, you serve, you lead the family prayers. And when you leave your parents, you slow your walk. You sway. Smile out of the corner of your eye. Whisper. Charmer you, you seduce unknowingly. Walk into your cousin's office and kiss her boss on top of his balding head. Do it without thinking twice. Do it because you are young and you know that everyone will think it's cute. Do it because you know this and a thousand other traditionally unacceptable gestures are things you and only you can get away with. When your *ate* tells you to stop it, cut it out, and "Don't go kissing my boss on the crest of his balding head," say, "But he's so delicious." Your mother, who knows you better than you think, who secretly knows, maybe even remembers what it's like to be this young, this beautiful, this brimming with sex appeal and truly powerful, says, "You've got to learn to control yourself, *hija,* even if he is delicious."

Sex stimulates you like a drug. Empowers you in new ways. Teaches you about walking around slinky and smooth, as if in constant dance, constant seduction. Teaches you that men want to do your bidding when you smile just so, or look away just when. Sex and being sexy charms you, and you like it. You can't help it. And when you try, when you let your two selves battle out right and wrong, marry love and lust, there is nothing but turmoil, and your lover wonders why he can never do anything right. "You are a walking contradiction," he tells you.

Because there is the family. Think. What if they found out. This prospect haunts you like ghosts in an old hotel. Pops up when you least expect, in the breath you take just after you've been together. Taps you on the shoulder as you answer the telephone. Think if on top of defiling your body, you made a baby too. Run away, first choice. Suicide, second. No, suicide first, run away after the failed suicide. You would rather die. You would rather float away in a stream, clear and fresh and cold. Take me away, you think. Take me far away, where Mom and Dad will never have to see me. Never have to be embarrassed because of me. Ultimately, you worry their worry is what others will say, will think.

Wild and fresh, little white star with fragrant petals, once planted, once in bloom you are left clinging to the vine that is the family you were born to. Face up to the sun, stretching out, reaching, but never breaking free, you are tangled in two worlds—wanting and not wanting. Speaking and silent at once. Filipina girl, American born and of two cultures, Western like MTV, tropical as the Sampaguita, you are left alone to figure out the rest. Because no one dares to tell you that when you make love to your lover, your husband, your boyfriend; when you date one another and flirt; and when he leans over for that first kiss, first moment of intimacy, sinking into you long and slow; it is your first holy communion all over again. Spirit floating high in the sky and then, for an instant, for one breath, you are one.

E S S A Y S

The perception that the family is natural and biological—its members related by "blood"—reinforces its role as a powerful arbiter of normative heterosexuality; in this view, lesbians and gay men—by virtue of their nonreproductive sexuality—are outside the family circle. As anthropologist Kath Weston of Brandeis University writes, historically homosexuals accepted the equation that "straight is to gay as family is to not-family." In the 1980s, however, a new discourse on the gay family emerged. Weston examines the "families we choose," formed through nonbiological bonds of affinity and commitment, and identifies specific historical changes—in the beliefs, social relations, and politics of gay and lesbian Americans—that fostered these new family forms. Tomás Almaguer of San Francisco State University suggests that for Chicano men, the question of sexual identity and family is more complex, because the U.S. and Mexico construct homosexuality and the family in distinct ways. In Mexico and Chicano communities, men who have sex with men are divided into "active" and "passive" categories based on sex acts. Almaguer argues that white, middle-class concepts of gay identity have been less prevalent among Chicanos; for those men, to "choose" a gay identity or a gay family means to embrace American bourgeois values.

Gay Families as the "Families We Choose"

KATH WESTON

Lesbian and gay San Francisco during the 1980s offered a fascinating opportunity to learn something about how ideologies arise and change as people lock in conflict, work toward reconciliation, reorganize relationships, establish or break ties, and agree to disagree. In an apartment on Valencia Street, a young lesbian reassured her gay friend that his parents would get over their initially negative reaction if he told them he was gay. On Polk Street, a 16-year-old searched for a place to spend the night because he had already come out to his parents and now he had nowhere to go. While two lovers were busy organizing an anniversary party that would bring blood relations together with their gay families, a woman on the other side of the city reported to work as usual because she feared losing her job if her employer should discover that she was mourning the passing of her partner, who had died the night before. For every lesbian considering parenthood, several friends worried about the changes children would introduce into peer relationships. For every eight or nine people who spoke with excitement about building families of friends, one or two rejected gay families as an oppressive accommodation to a heterosexual society.

From *Families We Choose: Lesbians, Gays, and Kinship,* by Kath Weston. © 1991 Kath Weston. Reprinted by permission of the publisher (New York: Columbia University Press, 1991), excerpted from pp. 21–23, 25, 27, 108–113, 118, 120–123, 127–133, 135–136.

Although not always codified or clear, the discourse on gay families that emerged during the 1980s challenged many cultural representations and common practices that have effectively denied lesbians and gay men access to kinship. In earlier decades gay people had also fought custody battles, brought partners home to meet their parents, filed suit against discriminatory insurance policies, and struggled to maintain ties with adoptive or blood relations. What set this new discourse apart was its emphasis on the kinship character of the ties gay people had forged to close friends and lovers, its demand that those ties receive social and legal recognition, and its separation of parenting and family formation from heterosexual relations. For the first time, gay men and lesbians systematically laid claim to families of their own. . . .

For years, and in an amazing variety of contexts, claiming a lesbian or gay identity has been portrayed as a rejection of "the family" and a departure from kinship. . . . Two presuppositions lend a dubious credence to [media] imagery: the belief that gay men and lesbians do not have children or establish lasting relationships, and the belief that they invariably alienate adoptive and blood kin once their sexual identities become known. By presenting "the family" as a unitary object, these depictions also imply that everyone participates in identical sorts of kinship relations and subscribes to one universally agreed-upon definition of family. . . .

It is but a short step from positioning lesbians and gay men somewhere beyond "the family"—unencumbered by relations of kinship, responsibility, or affection— to portraying them as a menace to family and society. . . . Proposition 6 (the Briggs initiative), which appeared on the ballot in California in 1978, was defeated only after a massive organizing campaign that mobilized lesbians and gay men in record numbers. The text of the initiative, which would have barred gay and lesbian teachers (along with heterosexual teachers who advocated homosexuality) from the public schools, was phrased as a defense of "the family":

> One of the most fundamental interests of the State is the establishment and preservation of the family unit. Consistent with this interest is the State's duty to protect its impressionable youth from influences which are antithetical to this vital interest.

Other anti-gay legislative initiative campaigns adopted the slogans "save the family" and "save the children" as their rallying cries. . . .

Some lesbians and gay men in the Bay Area had embraced the popular equation of their sexual identities with the renunciation of access to kinship, particularly when first coming out. "My image of gay life was very lonely, very weird, no family," Rafael Ortiz recollected. "I assumed that my family was gone now—that's it." After Bob Korkowski began to call himself gay, he wrote a series of poems in which an orphan was the central character. Bob said the poetry expressed his fear of "having to give up my family because I was queer." When I spoke with Rona Bren after she had been home with the flu, she told me that whenever she was sick, she relived old fears. That day she had remembered her mother's grim prediction: "You'll be a lesbian and you'll be alone the rest of your life. Even a dog shouldn't be alone." . . .

At the height of gay liberation, activists had attempted to develop alternatives to "the family," whereas by the 1980s many lesbians and gay men were struggling to legitimate gay families as a form of kinship. When Armistead Maupin spoke at a gathering on Castro Street to welcome home two gay men who had been held hostage in the Middle East, partners who had stood with arms around one another upon their release, he congratulated them not only for their safe return, but also as representatives of a new kind of family. Gay or chosen families might incorporate friends, lovers, or children, in any combination. Organized through ideologies of love, choice, and creation, gay families have been defined through a contrast with what many gay men and lesbians in the Bay Area called "straight," "biological," or "blood" family. If families we choose were the families lesbians and gay men created for themselves, straight family represented the families in which most had grown to adulthood. . . .

The families I saw gay men and lesbians creating in the Bay Area tended to have extremely fluid boundaries, not unlike kinship organizations among sectors of the African-American, American Indian, and white working class. . . . Listen for a moment to Toni Williams' account of the people she called kin:

> In my family, all of us kids are godparents to each others' kids, okay? See we're very connected that way. But when I go to have a kid, I'm not gonna have my sisters as godparents. I'm gonna have people that are around me, that are gay. That are straight. I don't have that many straight friends, but certainly I would integrate them in my life. They would help me. They would babysit my child, or . . . like my kitty, I'm not calling up my family and saying, "Hey, Mom, can you watch my cat?" No, I call on my inner family—my community, or whatever—to help me with my life.
>
> So there's definitely a family. And you're building it; it keeps getting bigger and bigger. Next thing you know, you have hundreds of people as your family. Me personally, I might not have a hundred, because I'm more of a loner. I don't have a lot of friends, nor do I *want* that many friends, either. But I see [my lover] as having many, many family members involved in what's going on.

What Toni portrayed was an ego-centered calculus of relations that pictured family members as a cluster surrounding a single individual, rather than taking couples or groups as units of affiliation. This meant that even the most nuclear of couples would construct theoretically distinguishable families, although an area of overlapping membership generally developed. At the same time, chosen families were not restricted to person-to-person ties. Individuals occasionally added entire groups with preexisting, multiplex connections among members. In one such case, a woman reported incorporating a "circle" of her new lover's gay family into her own kinship universe. . . .

Obituaries provide a relatively overlooked, if somber, source of information about notions of kinship. Death notices in the *Bay Area Reporter* (a weekly newspaper distributed in bars and other gay establishments) were sometimes written by lovers, and included references to friends, former lovers, blood or adoptive relatives (usually denominated as "father," "sister," etc.), "community members" present at a death or assisting during an illness, and occasionally coworkers. While I was conducting fieldwork, the *San Francisco Chronicle,* a major citywide daily, instituted a policy of refusing to list gay lovers as survivors, citing complaints from relatives who could lay claim to genealogical or adoptive ties to the deceased. Although the *Chronicle*'s decision denied recognition to gay families, it also testified to the growing impact of a discourse that refused to cede kinship to relations organized through procreation.

By opening the door to the creation of families different in kind and composition, choice assigned kinship to the realm of free will and inclination. . . . People often presented gay families as a foray into uncharted territory, where the lack of cultural guideposts to mark the journey engendered fear and exhilaration. Indeed, there was a utopian cast to the way many lesbians and gay men talked about the families they were fashioning. Jennifer Bauman maintained that as a gay person, "you're already on the edge, so you've got more room to be whatever you want to be. And to create. There's more space on the edge." What to do with all that "space"? "I create my own traditions," she replied. . . .

Despite the ideological characterization of gay families as freely chosen, in practice the particular choices made yielded families that were far from randomly selected, much less demographically representative. When I asked people who said they had gay families to list the individuals they included under that rubric, their lists were primarily, though not exclusively, composed of other lesbians and gay men. Not surprisingly, the majority of people listed tended to come from the same gender, class, race, and age cohort as the respondent.

Both men and women consistently counted lovers as family, often placing their partners at the head of a list of relatives. A few believed a lover, or a lover plus children, would be essential in order to have gay family, but the vast majority felt that all gay men and lesbians, including those who are single, can create families of their own. The partner of someone already considered family might or might not be included as kin. "Yeah, they're part of the family, but they're like in-laws," laughed one man. "You know, you love them, and yet there isn't that same closeness." . . .

A lover's biological or adoptive relatives might or might not be classified as kin, contingent upon their "rejecting" or "accepting" attitudes. Gina Pellegrini, for example, found refuge at a lover's house after her parents kicked her out of her own home as an adolescent. She was out to her lover's mother before her own parents, and still considered this woman family. . . . After years of listening to her father attack homosexuality, remembered Roberta Osabe, "My girlfriend Debi and my father shot pool together. And she whipped his ass! . . . That was his way, I think, of trying to make amends." Jerry Freitag and his partner Kurt had made a point of introducing their parents to one another. "My mother and his mother talk on the phone every once in a while and write letters and stuff. Like my grandmother just died. Kurt's mother was one of the first people to call my mom." For Charlyne Harris, however, calling her ex-lover's mother "family" would have been out of the question. "Her mother didn't like me. Number one, she didn't want her to be *in* a lesbian relationship; number two, she knew that I was black. So I didn't have a lot of good things to say about her mother. . . . Pam told me, 'She can't even say your name!'"

In addition to friendships and relationships with lovers or ex-lovers, chosen family might also embrace ties to children or people who shared a residence. *Gay Community News* published a series of letters from gay male prisoners who had united to form "the Del-Ray Family" (only to be separated by the warden). Back in San Francisco, Rose Ellis told me about the apartment she had shared with several friends. One woman in particular, she said, was "like a big sister to me." When this woman died of cancer, the household split up, and "that kind of broke the family thing." In other circumstances, however, hardship drew people together across household lines. Groups organized to assist individuals who were chronically or terminally ill often incorporated love and persisted through time, characteristics some participants took as signs of kinship. Occasionally a person could catch a glimpse of potential family relationships in the making. When I met Harold Sanders he was making plans to live with someone to prepare for the possibility that he might require physical assistance as he moved into his seventies. Harold explained that he would rather choose that person in advance than be forced to settle for "just anyone" in an emergency. . . .

Like their heterosexual counterparts, most gay men and lesbians insisted that family members are people who are "there for you," people you can count on emotionally and materially. "They take care of me," said one man, "I take care of them." . . . [T]he "middle class" in the United States tends to share affective support but not material resources within friendships. In the Bay Area, however, lesbians and gay men from all classes and class backgrounds regularly rendered both sorts of assistance to one another. Many considered this an important way of demarcating friend from family. Diane Kunin, a writer, described family as people who will care for you when you're sick, get you out of jail, help you fix a flat tire, or drive you to the airport. Edith Motzko, who worked as a carpenter, said of a woman she had known ten years, "There's nothing in the world that [she] would ask of me that I wouldn't do for her." Louise Romero joked that a gay friend "only calls me when he wants something: he wants to borrow the truck 'cause he's moving. So I guess that's family!" . . .

. . . [D]iscussions of gay families pictured kinship as an *extension* of friendship, rather than viewing the two as competitors or assimilating friendships to biogenetic relationships regarded as somehow more fundamental. It was not unusual for a gay man or lesbian to speak of another as family in one breath and friend in the next. Yet the solidarity implicit in such statements has not always been a taken-for-granted feature of gay lives. . . . [R]ecognition of the possibility of establishing nonerotic ties among homosexuals constituted a key historical development that paved the way for the emergence of lesbian and gay "community"—and . . . for the later appearance of the ideological opposition between biological family and families we choose. . . .

The years following World War II—a watershed period for many groups in the United States—witnessed an unprecedented elaboration of nonerotic solidarities among homosexuals. During the 1950s and 1960s, gay men adapted kinship terminology to the task of distinguishing sexual from nonsexual relationships. At that time the rhetoric of brothers, sisters, and friends applied primarily to nonerotic relationships. In the film version of *The Boys in the Band,* one character quips, "If they're not lovers, they're sisters." . . .

The contrast between the sexual and the nonsexual was drawn only to be blurred in later years after the possibility of nonerotic ties among gay people became firmly established. By the 1970s both gay men and lesbians had begun to picture friends and lovers as two ends of a single continuum rather than as oppositional categories. "We women been waiting all our lives for our sisters to be our lovers," announced the lyrics of the song *Gay and Proud.* The contribution of lesbian-feminism toward codifying this notion of a continuum is evident in Adrienne Rich's work on "compulsory heterosexuality." Carroll Smith-Rosenberg's classic article on relations between women in the nineteenth-century United States was also widely read in women's studies classes and cited to buttress the contention that sexual and sisterly relations were semantically separable but overlapping in practice—with little regard for efforts to distinguish precisely these relationships during the intervening decades.

The realignment that linked erotic to nonerotic relations through the device of a continuum was not confined to political activists. As San Francisco moved into the 1980s, "friend" seemed to be overtaking "roommate" in popularity as a euphemistic reference to a lover in situations where lesbians and gay men elected not to reveal their sexual identities. . . . A similar continuity was implicit in coming-out stories narrated by women who had first claimed a lesbian identity during the 1970s. One said coming out was epitomized for her by the realization that "oh, wow, then I get to keep all my girlfriends!" Elaine Scavone explained with a laugh, "All of a sudden I felt I could be myself. I could be the way I really want to be with women: I could touch them, I could make friends, I could make my girlfriends and I could go home and kiss them." Although women were sometimes said to be more likely to come out by falling in love with a friend and men through an encounter instrumentally focused on sex, both men and women featured early attractions to friends in their coming-out stories. . . .

In retrospect, this shift from contrast to continuum laid the ground for the rise of a family-centered discourse that bridged the erotic and the nonerotic, bringing lovers together with friends under a single construct. But the historical development of friendship ties among persons whose shared "sexual" identity was initially defined solely through their sexuality turned out to be merely an introductory episode in a more lengthy tale of community formation.

Among lesbians and gay men the term "community" (like coming out) has become as multifaceted in meaning as it is ubiquitous. In context, community can refer to the historical appearance of gay institutions, the totality of self-defined lesbians and gay men, or unity and harmony predicated upon a common sexual identity. Older gay people generally considered the term an anachronism when applied to the period before the late 1960s, since "community" came into popular usage only with the rise of a gay movement. . . .

. . . During the 1970s the concept of community came to embody practical wisdom emerging from the bars, friendship networks, and a spate of new gay organizations: the knowledge that lesbians and gay men, joining together on the basis of a sexual identity, could create enduring social ties. In the process, sexuality was reconstituted as a ground of common experience rather than a quintessentially personal domain.

From its inception, activists pressed the community concept into the service of an identity politics that cast gays in the part of an ethnic minority and a subculture. Lesbians and gay men represent a constant 10 percent of the population, they contended, a veritable multitude prepared to claim its own distinct history, culture, and institutions. The basis for these arguments was, of course, laid earlier with the recognition that homosexuals could unite through bonds of friendship as well as sex, and elaborated through analogies with identity-based movements organized along racial lines. . . .

In extending homosexuality beyond the sexual, the notion of identity-based community opened new possibilities for using kinship terminology to imagine lesbians and gay men as members of a unified totality. Identity provided the linking concept that lent power to analogies between gay and consanguineal relations. Wasn't this what families in the United States were all about: identity and likeness mediated by the symbolism of blood ties?

Yet the application of kinship terminology to gay community differed from the subsequent discourse on gay families in that it described *all* lesbians and gay men as kin: no "choice" determined familial relationships. To claim a lesbian or gay identity was sufficient to claim kinship to any and every other gay person. Some people hoped community would replace alienated biological ties, appealing not to chosen families but to the collectivity: "If I could gain acceptance in the community of lesbians, I would have, I hoped, the loving family I missed." In gay bars across the nation, this was the era of circle dances to the popular music hit, *We Are Family* . . . .

By the late 1970s, signs of disenchantment with the unity implicit in the concept of community began to appear: a popular critique of the look-alike styles of "Castro [San Francisco gay neighborhood] clones"; a resurgence of butch/fem relations among lesbians that flew in the face of feminist prescriptions for androgyny; and a heated debate about sadomasochism (s/m), pedophilia, and other marginalized sexualities. Though some dissenters insisted upon their right to be included in the larger collectivity of lesbians and gay men, others did not experience themselves as community members, much less as agents in community formation. "I was just me, in a gay world," explained Kevin Jones.

During the same period, lesbians and gays of color critiqued the simplistic assumption that mutual understanding would flow from a shared identity. Along with Jewish lesbians and gay men, they drew attention to the racism and anti-Semitism pervading gay communities, and exposed the illusory character of any quest for an encompassing commonality in the face of the crosscutting allegiances produced by an identity politics. Predictably, this recognition of differences, while important and overdue, tended to undermine meanings of harmony and equality carried by "community." Accompanying the positive explorations of what it meant to be black and gay or lesbian and Latina was widespread disillusionment with the failure to attain the unity implicit in the ideal of *communitas*. . . .

During the 1980s, categories of identity remained integral to the process of making and breaking social ties among lesbians and gay men. Most gay bars and social or political organizations in San Francisco were segregated by gender. Some of the community institutions that lesbians associated with gay men maintained a nominal lesbian presence. A gay theater, for example, included scripts with lesbian characters in its annual repertoire, and the number of women in attendance grew from two or three to a third of the audience when lesbian plays were performed. Yet the most visible gay institutions, businesses, and pubic rituals (such as Halloween on Castro Street) remained male-owned and male-organized. Even the exceptions seemed to prove the rule. After a crafts fair in the gay South of Market area, the *Bay Area Reporter* published a picture of two women kissing, over the caption, "It wasn't all men at the Folsom Street Fair either."

When gay groups in southern California suggested adding a lambda to the rainbow flag supposed to represent all gay people, lesbians denounced the addition as a noninclusive male symbol. At a benefit for the Gay Games sponsored by the Sisters of Perpetual Indulgence (a group of gay men in nun drag), lesbians cheered the women's softball game and martial arts demonstration, but some voiced impatience with "all the boys parading around in their outfits." Disagreements periodically erupted concerning the proportion of men's to women's coverage in newspapers that attempted to serve "the community" as a whole. It was not uncommon for lesbians and gay men to stereotype one another, building on constructions of identity and difference in the wider culture. . . .

Like other differences, divisions between lesbians and gay men are not absolute, but socially, historically, and interpretively constructed. After a women's musical troupe was asked to play for a gay male swimsuit contest, group members voiced positions ranging from "support our gay brothers," to "porn is porn," to "who cares, let's take the money!" Several lesbians cited their work with AIDS organizations as an experience that had helped them "feel connected" to gay men. . . .

Class differences traced out lines of division within as well as between the men's and women's "communities." Many lesbians attributed the visibility of gay male institutions to the fact that men in general have greater access to money than women. Gay vacation spots at the nearby Russian River proved too expensive for many lesbians (as well as working-class and unemployed gay men), who tended to stay at campgrounds rather than resorts if they visited the area. Popular categories opposed "bikers" to "professionals" and "bar gays" (presumably working-class) to "politicals" (stereotyped as "middle class"). . . .

Individuals who had purposefully sought employment in gay businesses reported their surprise at finding the gay employer-employee relationship as marked by conflict and difference as any other. In a dispute between the lesbian owner of an apartment building and one of her lesbian tenants, both sides seemed perplexed to discover that their shared sexual identity could not resolve the issue at hand. . . . While merchants encouraged people to "buy gay" and pointed with pride to the proliferation of shops that had made it theoretically possible to live without ever leaving the Castro, only a very small segment of lesbians and gay men could have afforded to do so, even if they were so inclined.

Anyone who visits a variety of lesbian and gay households in the Bay Area will come away with an impression of generational depth. Gay organizations and establishments, however, tended to serve a relatively narrow middle age range. Bowling, for instance, is a sport that many people in the United States pursue into their older years. But gay league nights at bowling alleys across the city found the lanes filled with teams predominantly composed of men in their twenties and thirties. Young lesbians and gay men came to San Francisco expecting to find acceptance and gay mecca but instead experienced trouble getting into bars and often ended up feeling peripheral to "the community." . . . For their part, older people mentioned ageist door policies at bars, and complained about feeling "other" when surrounded by younger faces at community events.

Racially discriminatory treatment at gay organizations, white beauty standards, ethnic divisions in the crowds at different bars, and racist door policies were other frequently cited reasons for questioning the community concept. Kevin Jones, an African-American man, said that when he first came to San Francisco,

> I thought that if I was white, it would be a lot different then. Because it seemed like it was hard for me to talk to people in bars. But it didn't seem like other people were having a hard time talking to each other. It almost seemed like they *knew* each other. And if they didn't know each other, they were gonna go up and talk to each other and meet. But I'd go to the bars, and I could sit there and watch pool, and nobody would ever talk to me. And I couldn't understand that. And I thought, "If I was white, I bet you I would know a lot more of these people."

Something more is involved here than racial identity as a ground for difference and discrimination, or ethnicity as an obstacle to the easy interaction implicit in notions of community. Most people of color claimed membership in communities defined in terms of racial identity, attachments that predated coming out as a lesbian or gay man. . . .

For some, sexual identity had become a minimal defining feature, all "we" have in common. . . . "I knew that I didn't fit into the Castro any more than I fit into my family," another man insisted. Whether that sense of difference was based on categorical understandings of self (mediated by race, age, class, gender) or on tensions between the individual and the social, the result has been a generalized rejection of the unity and above all the sameness implicit in the concept of gay community.

In contrast, the family-centered discourse emerging during this period did not assume identity (in the sense of sameness) based upon sexuality alone. Lesbians and gay men who claimed membership in multiple communities but felt at home in none joined with those who had strategically repositioned themselves outside community in transferring the language of kinship from collective to interpersonal relations. While familial ideologies assumed new prominence in the United States at large during the 1980s, among gay men and lesbians the historical legacy of community-building and subsequent struggles to comprehend relations of difference mediated a shift in focus from friendship to kinship. Meanwhile the possibility of being rejected by blood relatives for a lesbian or gay identity shaped the specific meanings carried by "family" in gay contexts, undermining the permanence culturally attributed to blood ties while highlighting categories of choice and love.

Defined in opposition to biological family, the concept of families we choose proved attractive in part because it reintroduced agency and a subjective sense of making culture into lesbian and gay social organization. The institutionalized gay community of the 1970s, with its shops and bars and associations, by the 1980s could appear as something prefabricated, an entity over and above individuals into which they might or might not fit. Most understood gay families to be customized, individual creations that need not deny conflict or difference. Family also supplied the face-to-face relationships and concrete knowledge of persons promised by the romantic imagery of small-town community. As a successor to nonerotic ties elaborated in terms of community or friendship, chosen families introduced something rather novel into kinship relations in the United States by grouping friends together with lovers and children within a single cultural domain.

Chicano Men, A Cartography of Homosexual Identity and Behavior

TOMÁS ALMAGUER

The sexual behavior and sexual identity of Chicano male homosexuals is principally shaped by two distinct sexual systems, each of which attaches different significance and meaning to homosexuality. Both the European-American and Mexican/Latin-American systems have their own unique ensemble of sexual meanings, categories for sexual actors, and scripts that circumscribe sexual behavior. Each system also maps the human body in different ways by placing different values on homosexual erotic zones. The primary socialization of Chicanos into Mexican/Latin-American cultural norms, combined with their simultaneous socialization into the dominant European-American culture, largely structures how they negotiate sexual identity questions and confer meaning to homosexual behavior during adolescence and adulthood. Chicano men who embrace a "gay" identity (based on the European-American sexual system) must reconcile this sexual identity with their primary socialization into a Latino culture that does not recognize such a construction: there is no cultural equivalent to the modern "gay man" in the Mexican/Latin-American sexual system.

How does socialization into these different sexual systems shape the crystallization of their sexual identities and the meaning they give to their homosexuality? Why does only a segment of homosexually active Chicano men identify as "gay"? Do these men primarily consider themselves *Chicano* gay men (who retain primary emphasis on their ethnicity) or *gay* Chicanos (who place primary emphasis on their sexual preference)? How do Chicano homosexuals structure their sexual conduct, especially the sexual roles and relationships into which they enter? Are they structured along lines of power/dominance firmly rooted in a patriarchal Mexican culture that privileges men over women and the masculine over the feminine? Or do they reflect the ostensibly more egalitarian sexual norms and practices of the European-American sexual system? . . .

We know little about how Chicano men negotiate and contest a modern gay identity with aspects of Chicano culture drawing upon more Mexican/Latin-American configurations of sexual meaning. . . .

. . . Since the Mexican/Chicano population in the U.S. shares basic features of these Latin cultural patterns, it is instructive to examine this sexual system closely and to explore its impact on the sexuality of homosexual Chicano men and women.

The rules that define and stigmatize homosexuality in Mexican culture operate under a logic and a discursive practice different from those of the bourgeois sexual system that shaped the emergence of contemporary gay/lesbian identity in the U.S. Each sexual system confers meaning to homosexuality by giving different weight to the two fundamental features of human sexuality that Freud delineated in the

Tomás Almaguer, "Chicano Men, Homosexuality, and Conflicting Cultures," *Differences* 3.2 (Summer 1991): 75–100. An earlier and different version of this essay appeared in *Differences* 3.2. Reprinted by permission of Indiana University Press.

Three Essays on the Theory of Sexuality: sexual object choice and sexual aim. The structured meaning of homosexuality in the European-American context rests on the sexual object-choice one makes—i.e., the biological sex of the person toward whom sexual activity is directed. The Mexican/Latin-American sexual system, on the other hand, confers meaning to homosexual practices according to sexual aim— i.e., the act one wants to perform with another person (of either biological sex).

The contemporary bourgeois sexual system in the U.S. divides the sexual landscape according to discrete sexual categories and personages defined in terms of sexual preference or object choice: same sex (homosexual), opposite sex (heterosexual), or both (bisexual). Historically, this formulation has carried with it a blanket condemnation of all same-sex behavior. Because it is non-procreative and at odds with a rigid, compulsory heterosexual norm, homosexuality traditionally has been seen as either 1) a sinful transgression against the word of God, 2) a congenital disorder wracking the body, or 3) a psychological pathology gripping the mind. . . .

Unlike the European-American system, the Mexican/Latin-American sexual system is based on a configuration of gender/sex/power that is articulated along the active/passive axis and organized through the scripted sexual role one plays. It highlights sexual aim—the act one wants to perform with the person toward whom sexual activity is directed—and gives only secondary importance to the person's gender or biological sex. According to [anthropologist Roger] Lancaster, "it renders certain organs and roles 'active,' other body passages and roles 'passive,' and assigns honor/shame and status/stigma accordingly." . . . In the Mexican/Latin-American context there is no cultural equivalent to the modern gay man. Instead of discrete sexual personages differentiated according to sexual preference, we have categories of people defined in terms of the role they play in the homosexual act. The Latin homosexual world is divided into *activos* and *pasivos* (as in Mexico and Brazil) and *machistas* and *cochóns* (in Nicaragua).

Although stigma accompanies homosexual practices in Latin culture, it does not equally adhere to both partners. It is primarily the anal-passive individual (the *cochón* or *pasivo*) who is stigmatized for playing the subservient, feminine role. His partner (the *activo* or *machista*) typically "is not stigmatized at all and, moreover, no clear category exists in the popular language to classify him. For all intents and purposes, he is just a normal . . . male." In fact, Lancaster argues that the active party in a homosexual drama often gains status among his peers in precisely the same way that one derives status from seducing many women. This cultural construction confers an inordinate amount of meaning to the anal orifice and to anal penetration. This is in sharp contrast to the way homosexuality is viewed in the U.S., where the oral orifice structures the meaning of homosexuality in the popular imagination. In this regard, Lancaster suggests that the lexicon of male insult in each context clearly reflects this basic difference in cultural meaning associated with oral/anal sites. The most common derisive term used to refer to homosexuals in the U.S. is "cocksucker." Conversely, most Latin American epithets for homosexuals convey the stigma associated with their being anally penetrated. . . .

Therefore, it is anal passivity alone that is stigmatized and that defines the subordinate status of homosexuals in Latin culture. The stigma conferred to the passive role is fundamentally inscribed in gender-coded terms. . . . This equation makes homosexuals such as the *pasivo* and *cochón* into feminized men; biological males, but not truly men. . . .

Psychoanalyst Marvin Goldwert argues that this patriarchal cultural equation has special resonance for Mexicans and remains deeply embedded in the Mexican psyche. He claims that it has symbolic roots in cultural myths surrounding the Spanish conquest of Mexico in the sixteenth century. This colonial drama unfolded with the Spanish conquistadores playing the role of active, masculine intruders who raped the passive, feminine Indian civilization. . . .

Mexican men often find a tenuous assurance of their masculinity and virility in aggressive manliness and through a rigid gender role socialization that ruthlessly represses their own femininity. Psychoanalyst Santiago Ramirez identifies the Mexican family as the procrustean bedrock upon which this psychic structuring lies. From early childhood, the young Mexican male develops an ambivalence toward women, who are less valued than men in patriarchal Mexican society. This fundamental disdain for that which is feminine later gives way to an outpouring of resentment and humiliation onto one's wife or mistress and women in general. . . .

This cultural and psychic structure has particular significance for men who engage in homosexual behavior. [Octavio] Paz notes that the active/male and passive/female construction in Mexican culture has direct significance for the way Mexicans view male homosexuality. According to him, "masculine homosexuality is regarded with a certain indulgence insofar as the active agent is concerned. The passive agent is an abject, degraded being. Masculine homosexuality is tolerated, then, on condition that it consists in violating a passive agent." Aggressive, active, and penetrating sexual activity, therefore, becomes the true marker of the Mexican man's tenuous masculinity. It is attained by the negation of all that is feminine within him and by the sexual subjugation of women. But this valorization of hyper-masculinity can also be derived by penetrating passive, anal-receptive men as well.

Some of the most insightful ethnographic research on homosexuality in Mexico has been conducted by anthropologist J. M. Carrier. Like other Latin American specialists exploring this issue, Carrier argues that homosexuality is construed very differently in the U.S. and in Mexico. In the U.S., even one adult homosexual act or acknowledgment of homosexual desire may threaten a man's gender identity and throw open to question his sexual identity as well. In sharp contrast, a Mexican man's masculine gender and heterosexual identity are not threatened by a homosexual act as long as he plays the inserter's role. Only the male who plays the passive sexual role and exhibits feminine gender characteristics is considered to be truly homosexual and is, therefore, stigmatized. This "bisexual" option, an exemption from stigma for the "masculine" homosexual, can be seen as part of the ensemble of gender privileges and sexual prerogatives accorded Mexican men. Thus it is primarily the passive, effeminate homosexual man who becomes the object of derision and societal contempt in Mexico. . . .

Carrier's research suggests that homosexuality in Mexico is rigidly circumscribed by the prominent role the family plays in structuring homosexual activity. Whereas in the U.S., at least among most European-Americans, the role of the family as a regulator of the lives of gay men and lesbians has progressively declined, in

Mexico the family remains a crucial institution that defines both gender and sexual relations between men and women. The Mexican family remains a bastion of patriarchal privilege for men and a major impediment to women's autonomy outside the private world of the home.

The constraints of family life often prevent homosexual Mexican men from securing unrestricted freedom to stay out late at night, to move out of their family's home before marriage, or to take an apartment with a male lover. Thus their opportunities to make homosexual contacts in other than anonymous locations, such as the balconies of movie theaters or certain parks, are severely constrained. This situation creates an atmosphere of social interdiction which may explain why homosexuality in Mexico is typically shrouded in silence. The concealment, suppression, or prevention of any open acknowledgment of homosexual activity underscores the stringency of cultural dictates surrounding gender and sexual norms within Mexican family life. Unlike the generally more egalitarian, permissive family life of white middle-class gay men and lesbians in the U.S., the Mexican family appears to play a far more important and restrictive role in structuring homosexual behavior among Mexican men. . . .

. . . Carrier's research on mestizo homosexual men in Guadalajara found that the majority of the feminine, passive homosexual males become sexually active prior to puberty; many as young as from the ages of six to nine. Most of their homosexual contacts are with postpubescent cousins, uncles, or neighbors. They may occur quite frequently and extend over a long period or be infrequent and relatively short-lived in duration. These early experiences are generally followed by continued homosexual encounters into adolescence and adulthood. Only a segment of the homosexually active youth, however, develop a preference for the anal receptive, *pasivo* sexual role, and thus come to define their individual sense of gender in a decidedly feminine direction. . . .

In sum, it appears that the major difference between bisexually-active men in Mexico and bisexual males in the U.S. is that the former are not stigmatized because they exclusively play the active, masculine, inserter role. Unlike in the North American context, "one drop of homosexuality" does not, ipso facto, make a Mexican male a *joto* or a *maricón*. As Carrier's research clearly documents, none of the active inserter participants in homosexual encounters ever considers himself a "homosexual" or to be "gay." What may be called the "bisexual escape hatch" functions to insure that the tenuous masculinity of Mexican men is not compromised through the homosexual act; they remain men, *hombres,* even though they participate in this sexual behavior. Moreover, the Mexican sexual system actually militates against the construction of discernible, discrete "bisexual" or "gay" sexual identities because these identities are shaped by and draw upon a different sexual system and foreign discursive practices. One does not, in other words, become "gay" or "lesbian" identified in Mexico because its sexual system precludes such an identity formation in the first place. These "bourgeois" sexual categories are simply not relevant or germane to the way gender and sexual meanings are conferred in Mexican society.

Given the contours of the Mexican sexual system, and the central role the Mexican family plays in structuring homosexual behavior, it is not surprising that North

American sexual categories, identities, and identity-based social movements have only recently made their appearance in Mexico. . . . For example, there existed as late as 1980 only a very small and submerged gay scene in large cities such as Mexico City, Guadalajara, and Acapulco. There are no distinct "gay neighborhoods" to speak of, and only a few gay bars and discos. Those Mexican men who define their sexual identity as "gay" have clearly adopted North American homosexual patterns, such as incorporating both passive and active sexual roles into their homosexual behavior. This more recent incarnation of the "modern Mexican homosexual" is widely considered to be based on North American sexual scripts, and the "foreign" nature of such sexual practices has caused the men who adopt them to be commonly referred to as *internacionales*. . . .

The emergence of the modern gay identity in the U.S. and its recent appearance in Mexico have implications for Chicano men that have not been fully explored. What is apparent, however, is that Chicanos, as well as other racial minorities, do not negotiate the acceptance of a gay identity in exactly the same way white American men do. The ambivalence of Chicanos vis-à-vis a gay sexual identity and their attendant uneasiness with white gay/lesbian culture do not necessarily reflect a denial of homosexuality. Rather, I would argue, the slow pace at which this identity formation has taken root among Chicanos is attributable to cultural and structural factors which differentiate the experiences of the white and non-white populations in the U.S.

Aside from the crucial differences discussed above in the way homosexuality is culturally constructed in the Mexican/Latin-American and European- or Anglo-American sexual systems, a number of other structural factors also militate against the emergence of a modern gay identity among Chicano men. In this regard, the progressive loosening of familial constraints among white, middle-class homosexual men and women at the end of the nineteenth century, and its acceleration in the post–World War II period, structurally positioned the white gay and lesbian population to redefine their primary self-identity in terms of their homosexuality. The shift from a family-based economy to a fully developed wage labor system at the end of the nineteenth century dramatically freed European-American men and women from the previously confining social and economic world of the family. It allowed both white men and the white "new woman" of the period to transgress the stifling gender roles that previously bound them to a compulsory heterosexual norm. Extricating the nuclear family from its traditional role as a primary unit of production enabled homosexually inclined individuals to forge a new sexual identity and to develop a culture and community that were not previously possible. Moreover, the tremendous urban migration ignited (or precipitated) by World War II accelerated this process by drawing thousands of homosexuals into urban settings where the possibilities for same-sex intimacy were greater.

It is very apparent, however, that the gay identity and communities that emerged were overwhelmingly white, middle class, and male-centered. Leading figures of the first homophile organizations in the U.S., such as the Mattachine Society, and key individuals shaping the newly emergent gay culture were primarily drawn from this segment of the homosexual population. Moreover, the new communities founded in the post-war period were largely populated by white men who had the resources and talents needed to create "gilded" gay ghettos. This fact has given the contemporary gay community—despite its undeniable diversity—a largely white, middle class, and male form. In other words, the unique class and racial advantages of white gay men provided the foundation upon which they could boldly carve out the new gay identity. Their collective position in the social structure empowered them with the skills and talents needed to create new gay institutions, communities, and a unique sexual subculture.

Despite the intense hostility that, as gay men, they faced during that period, nevertheless, as white gay men, they were in the best position to risk the social ostracism that this process engendered. They were *relatively* better situated than other homosexuals to endure the hazards unleashed by their transgression of gender conventions and traditional heterosexual norms. The diminished importance of ethnic identity among these individuals, due principally to the homogenizing and integrating impact of the dominant racial categories which defined them foremost as white, undoubtedly also facilitated the emergence of gay identity among them. As members of the privileged racial group—and thus no longer viewing themselves primarily as Irish, Italian, Jewish, Catholic, etc.—these middle-class men and women arguably no longer depended solely on their respective cultural groups and families as a line of defense against the dominant group. Although they may have continued to experience intense cultural dissonance leaving behind their ethnicity and their traditional family-based roles, they were now in a position to dare to make such a move.

Chicanos, on the other hand, have never occupied the social space where a gay or lesbian identity can readily become a primary basis of self-identity. This is due, in part, to their structural position at the subordinate ends of both the class and racial hierarchies, and in a context where ethnicity remains a primary basis of group identity and survival. Moreover, Chicano family life requires allegiance to patriarchal gender relations and to a system of sexual meanings that directly militate against the emergence of this alternative basis of self-identity. Furthermore, factors such as gender, geographical settlement, age, nativity, language usage, and degree of cultural assimilation further prevent, or at least complicate, the acceptance of a gay or lesbian identity by Chicanos or Chicanas respectively. They are not as free as individuals situated elsewhere in the social structure to redefine their sexual identity in ways that contravene the imperatives of minority family life and its traditional gender expectations. How they come to define their sexual identities as gay, straight, bisexual or, in Mexican/Latin-American terms, as an *activo, pasivo,* or *macho marica,* therefore, is not a straightforward or unmediated process. . . .

. . . [O]ne unpublished study on homosexual Latino/Chicano men was conducted by Hector Carrillo and Horacio Maiorana in the spring of 1989. As part of their ongoing work on AIDS within the San Francisco Bay Area Latino community, these researchers developed a typology capturing the different points in a continuum differentiating the sexual identity of these men. Their preliminary typology is useful in that it delineates the way homosexual Chicanos/Latinos integrate elements of both the North American and Mexican sexual systems into their sexual behavior.

The first two categories of individuals, according to Carrillo and Maiorana, are: 1) Working class Latino men who have adopted an effeminate gender persona and usually play the passive role in homosexual encounters (many of them are drag queens who frequent the Latino gay bars in the Mission District of San Francisco); and 2) Latino men who consider themselves heterosexual or bisexual, but who furtively have sex with other men. They are also primarily working class and often frequent Latino gay bars in search of discrete sexual encounters. They tend to retain a strong Latino or Chicano ethnic identity and structure their sexuality according to the Mexican sexual system. Although Carrillo and Maiorana do not discuss the issue, it seems likely that these men would primarily seek out other Latino men, rather than European-Americans, as potential partners in their culturally-circumscribed homosexual behavior.

I would also suggest from personal observations that these two categories of individuals occasionally enter into sexual relationships with middle class Latinos and European-American men. In so doing, these working class Latino men often become the object of the middle class Latino's or the white man's colonial desires. In one expression of this class-coded lust, the effeminate *pasivo* becomes the boyish, feminized object of the middle class man's colonial desire. In another, the masculine Mexican/Chicano *activo* becomes the embodiment of a potent ethnic masculinity that titillates the middle class man who thus enters into a passive sexual role.

Unlike the first two categories of homosexually active Latino men, the other three have integrated several features of the North American sexual system into their sexual behavior. They are more likely to be assimilated into the dominant European-American culture of the U.S. and to come from middle class backgrounds. They include 3) Latino men who openly consider themselves gay and participate in the emergent gay Latino subculture in the Mission district; 4) Latino men who consider themselves gay but do not participate in the Latino gay subculture, preferring to maintain a primary identity as Latino and only secondarily a gay one; and, finally, 5) Latino men who are fully assimilated into the white San Francisco gay male community in the Castro District and retain only a marginal Latino identity.

In contrast to the former two categories, Latino men in the latter three categories are more likely to seek European-American sexual partners and exhibit greater difficulty in reconciling their Latino cultural backgrounds with their gay lifestyle. In my impressionistic observations, these men do not exclusively engage in homosexual behavior that is hierarchically differentiated along the gender-coded lines of the Mexican sexual system. They are more likely to integrate both active and passive sexual roles into their sexuality and to enter into relationships in which the more egalitarian norms of the North American sexual system prevail. . . .

. . . [W]e may seek clues about the social world of Chicano gay men in the perceptive writings of Chicana lesbians. . . . More than any other lesbian writer's, the extraordinary work of Cherríe Moraga articulates a lucid and complex analysis of the predicament that the middle class Chicana lesbian and Chicano gay man face in this society. . . .

An essential point of departure in assessing Cherríe Moraga's work is an appreciation of the way Chicano family life severely constrains the Chicana's ability to define her life outside of its stifling gender and sexual prescriptions. As a number of

Chicana feminist scholars have clearly documented, Chicano family life remains rigidly structured along patriarchal lines that privilege men over women and children. Any violation of these norms is undertaken at great personal risk because Chicanos draw upon the family to resist racism and the ravages of class inequality. Chicano men and women are drawn together in the face of these onslaughts and are closely bound into a family structure that exaggerates unequal gender roles and suppresses sexual non-conformity. Therefore, any deviation from the sacred link binding husband, wife, and child not only threatens the very existence of *la familia* but also potentially undermines the mainstay of resistance to Anglo racism and class exploitation. "The family, then, becomes all the more ardently protected by oppressed people and the sanctity of this institution is infused like blood into the veins of the Chicano. At all costs, la familia must be preserved," writes Moraga. Thus, "we fight back . . . with our families—with our women pregnant, and our men as indispensable heads. We believe the more severely we protect the sex roles within the family, the stronger we will be as a unit in opposition to the anglo threat."

These cultural prescriptions do not, however, curb the sexually non-conforming behavior of certain Chicanos. As in the case of Mexican homosexual men in Mexico, there exists a modicum of freedom for the Chicano homosexual who retains masculine gender identity while secretly engaging in the active homosexual role. Moraga has perceptively noted that the Latin cultural norm inflects the sexual behavior of homosexual Chicanos: "Male homosexuality has always been a 'tolerated' aspect of Mexican/Chicano society, as long as it remains 'fringe.' . . . But lesbianism, in any form, and male homosexuality which openly avows both the sexual and the emotional elements of the bond, challenge the very foundation of la familia." The openly effeminate Chicano gay man's rejection of heterosexuality is typically seen as a fundamental betrayal of Chicano patriarchal cultural norms. . . .

The constraints that Chicano family life imposed on Moraga herself are candidly discussed in her provocative autobiographical essays "La Guera" and "A Long Line of Vendidas" in *Loving in the War Years*. In recounting her childhood in Southern California, Moraga describes how she was routinely required to make her brother's bed, iron his shirts, lend him money, and even serve him cold drinks when his friends came to visit their home. The privileged position of men in the Chicano family places women in a secondary, subordinate status. She resentfully acknowledges that "to this day in my mother's home, my brother and father are waited on, including by me." Chicano men have always thought of themselves as superior to Chicanas, she asserts in unambiguous terms: "I have never met any kind of Latino who . . . did not subscribe to the basic belief that men are better." The insidiousness of the patriarchal ideology permeating Chicano family life even shapes the way a mother defines her relationships with her children: "The daughter must constantly earn the mother's love, prove her fidelity to her. The son—he gets her love for free."

Moraga realized early in life that she would find it virtually impossible to attain any meaningful autonomy in that cultural context. It was only in the Anglo world that freedom from oppressive gender and sexual strictures was remotely possible. In order to secure this latitude, she made a necessary choice: to embrace the white world and reject crucial aspects of her Chicana upbringing. In painfully honest terms, she states:

> I gradually became anglocized because I thought it was the only option available to me toward gaining autonomy as a person without being sexually stigmatized. . . . I instinctively made choices which I thought would allow me greater freedom of movement in the future. This meant resisting sex roles as much as I could safely manage and that was far easier in an anglo context than in a Chicano one.

Born to a Chicana mother and an Anglo father, Moraga discovered that being fair-complexioned facilitated her integration into the Anglo social world and contributed immensely to her academic achievement. . . . Consequently her life in Southern California during the 1950s and 1960s is described as one in which she "identified with and aspired toward white values." In the process, she "rode the wave of that Southern California privilege as far as conscience would let me."

The price initially exacted by anglicization was estrangement from family and a partial loss of the nurturing and love she found therein. In reflecting on this experience, Moraga acknowledges that "I have had to confront that much of what I value about being Chicana, about my family, has been subverted by anglo culture and my cooperation with it. . . . I realized the major reason for my total alienation from and fear of my classmates was rooted in class and culture." She poignantly concedes that, in the process, "I had disavowed the language I knew best—ignored the words and rhythms that were closest to me. The sounds of my mother and aunts gossiping—half in English, half in Spanish—while drinking cerveza in the kitchen." What she gained, on the other hand, was the greater autonomy that her middle class white classmates had in defining their emergent sexuality and in circumventing burdensome gender prescriptions. Her movement into the white world, however, was viewed by Chicanos as a great betrayal. By gaining control of her life, Moraga became one of a "long line of vendidas," traitors or "sell-outs," as self-determined women are seen in the sexist cultural fantasy of patriarchal Chicano society. This is the accusation that "hangs above the heads and beats in the hearts of most Chicanas, seeking to develop our own autonomous sense of ourselves, particularly our sexuality."

. . . In order to claim the identity of a Chicana lesbian, Moraga had to take "a radical stand in direct contradiction to, and in violation of, the women [sic] I was raised to be"; and yet she also drew upon themes and images of her Mexican Catholic background. Of its impact on her sexuality Moraga writes:

> I always knew that I felt the greatest emotional ties with women, but suddenly I was beginning to consciously identify those feeling as sexual. The more potent my dreams and fantasies became and the more I sensed my own exploding sexual power, the more I *retreated* from my body's messages and into the region of religion. By giving definition and meaning to my desires, religion became the discipline to control my sexuality. Sexual fantasy and rebellion became "impure thoughts" and "sinful acts." . . .

A crucial dimension of the dissonance Moraga experienced in accepting her lesbian sexuality and reconciling the Anglo and Chicano worlds was the conscious awareness that her sexual desires reflected a deeply felt love for her mother. "In contrast to the seeming lack of feelings I had for my father," she writes, "my long-ings for my mother and fear of her dying were the most passionate feelings that had ever lived inside of my young heart." These feelings led her to the realization that both the affective and sexual dimensions of her lesbianism were indelibly shaped by the love for her mother. "When I finally lifted the lid on my lesbianism, a profound connection with mother awakened in me," she recalls. "Yes, this is why I love women. This woman is my mother. There is no love as strong as this, refusing my separation, never settling for a secret that would split us off, always at the last minute, like now, pushing me to [the] brink of revelation, speaking the truth."

Moraga's experience is certainly only one expression of the diverse ways in which Chicana lesbians come to define their sense of gender and experience their homo-sexuality. But her odyssey reflects and articulates the tortuous and painful path traveled by working class Chicanas (and Chicanos) who embrace the middle class Anglo world and its sexual system in order to secure, ironically, the "right to pas-sion expressed in our own cultural tongue and movements." It is apparent from her powerful autobiographical writings, however, how much her adult sexuality was also inevitably shaped by the gender and sexual messages imparted through the Chicano family.

How this complex process of integrating, reconciling, and contesting various features of both Anglo and Chicano cultural life are experienced by Chicano gay men, has yet to be fully explored. . . . [I]t is likely that Chicano gay men incorporate and contest crucial features of the Mexican/Latin-American sexual system into their intimate sexual behavior. Despite having accepted a "modern" sexual identity, they are not immune to the hierarchical, gender-coded system of sexual meanings that is part and parcel of this discursive practice.

◖ *F U R T H E R   R E A D I N G*

Norma Alarcon, Ana Castillo, and Cherríe Moraga, *The Sexuality of Latinas* (1993).
Gloria Anzaldua, *Borderlands/La Frontera: The New Mestiza* (1987).
Allan Bérubé and Jeffrey Escoffier, "Queer Nation," *Outlook* 11 (Winter 1991): 12–13.
Alexander Chee, "A Queer Nationalism," *Outlook* 11 (Winter 1991): 15–23.
Lisa Duggan and Nan D. Hunter, *Sex Wars: Sexual Dissent and Political Culture* (1995).
Lillian Faderman, "The Return of Butch and Femme: A Phenomenon in Lesbian Sexuality of the 1980s and 1990s," *Journal of the History of Sexuality* (1992): 578–596.
Trisha Franzen, "Differences and Identities: Feminism and the Albuquerque Lesbian Com-munity," *Signs* 18 (Summer 1993): 891–906.
Faye D. Ginsburg, *Contested Lives: The Abortion Debate in an American Community* (1989).
Janice M. Irvine, ed., *Sexual Cultures and the Construction of Adolescent Identities* (1994).
JeeYeun Lee, "Toward a Queer Korean American Diasporic History," in David L. Eng and Alice Y. Hom, eds., *Q & A: Queer in Asian America* (1998), 185–209.
Russell Leong, ed., *Asian American Sexualities* (1996).
Ellen Lewin, *Lesbian Mothers: Accounts of Gender in American Culture* (1993).
———, *Recognizing Ourselves: Ceremonies of Lesbian and Gay Commitment* (1998).
———, ed., *Inventing Lesbian Cultures in America* (1996).

Kristin Luker, *Dubious Conceptions: The Politics of Teenage Pregnancy* (1996).
Cherríe Moraga, *Loving in the War Years* (1983).
Sarah Schulman, *My American History: Lesbian and Gay Life During the Reagan/Bush Years* (1994).
Suzanne Sherman, ed., *Lesbian and Gay Marriage* (1992).
Barbara Smith, ed., *Home Girls* (1983).
Sharon Thompson, *Going All the Way: Teenage Girls' Tales of Sex, Romance, and Pregnancy* (1995).
Kath Weston, *Render Me, Gender Me* (1996).

Major Problems in American History Series
Titles Currently Available

Allitt, *Major Problems in American Religious History,* 2000 (ISBN 0-395-96419-9)

Boris/Lichtenstein, *Major Problems in the History of American Workers,* 1991
(ISBN 0-669-19925-7)

Brown, *Major Problems in the Era of the American Revolution, 1760–1791,* 2nd ed., 2000
(ISBN 0-395-90344-0)

Chambers/Piehler, *Major Problems in American Military History,* 1999
(ISBN 0-669-33538-X)

Chan/Olin, *Major Problems in California History,* 1997 (ISBN 0-669-27588-3)

Chudacoff, *Major Problems in American Urban History,* 1994 (ISBN 0-669-24376-0)

Escott/Goldfield/McMillen/Turner, *Major Problems in the History of the American
South,* 2nd ed., 1999
Volume I: *The Old South* (ISBN 0-395-87139-5)
Volume II: *The New South* (ISBN 0-395-87140-9)

Fink, *Major Problems in the Gilded Age and the Progressive Era,* 2nd ed., 2001
(ISBN 0-618-04255-5)

Gjerde, *Major Problems in American Immigration and Ethnic History,* 1998
(ISBN 0-395-81532-0)

Gjerde/Cobbs Hoffman, *Major Problems in American History,* 2002
Volume I: *To 1877* (ISBN 0-618-06133-9)
Volume II: *Since 1865* (ISBN 0-618-06134-7)

Gordon, *Major Problems in American History, 1920–1945,* 1999 (ISBN 0-395-87074-7)

Griffith, *Major Problems in American History Since 1945,* 2nd ed., 2001
(ISBN 0-395-86850-5)

Hall, *Major Problems in American Constitutional History,* 1992
Volume I: *From the Colonial Era Through Reconstruction* (ISBN 0-669-21209-1)
Volume II: *From 1870 to the Present* (ISBN 0-669-21210-5)

Haynes/Wintz, *Major Problems in Texas History,* 2002 (ISBN 0-395-85833-X)

Holt/Barkley Brown, *Major Problems in African American History,* 2000
Volume I: *From Slavery to Freedom, 1619–1877* (ISBN 0-669-24991-2)
Volume II: *From Freedom to "Freedom Now," 1865–1990s* (ISBN 0-669-46293-4)

Hurtado/Iverson, *Major Problems in American Indian History,* 2nd ed., 2001
(ISBN 0-618-06854-6)

Kupperman, *Major Problems in American Colonial History,* 2nd ed., 2000
(ISBN 0-395-93676-4)

Kurashige/Yang Murray, *Major Problems in Asian American History,* 2002
(ISBN: 0-618-07734-0)

McMahon, *Major Problems in the History of the Vietnam War,* 2nd ed., 1995
(ISBN 0-669-35252-7)

Merchant, *Major Problems in American Environmental History,* 1993
(ISBN 0-669-24993-9)

Merrill/Paterson, *Major Problems in American Foreign Relations,* 5th ed., 2000
Volume I: *To 1920* (ISBN 0-395-93884-8)
Volume II: *Since 1914* (ISBN 0-395-93885-6)

Milner/Butler/Lewis, *Major Problems in the History of the American West,* 2nd ed., 1997
(ISBN 0-669-41580-4)

Norton/Alexander, *Major Problems in American Women's History,* 2nd ed., 1996
(ISBN 0-669-35390-6)

Major Problems in American History Series
Titles Currently Available

Peiss, *Major Problems in the History of American Sexuality,* 2002
(ISBN 0-395-90384-X)

Perman, *Major Problems in the Civil War and Reconstruction,* 2nd ed., 1998
(ISBN 0-395-86849-1)

Riess, *Major Problems in American Sport History,* 1997 (ISBN 0-669-35380-9)

Smith/Clancey, *Major Problems in the History of American Technology,* 1998
(ISBN 0-669-35472-4)

Vargas, *Major Problems in Mexican American History,* 1999 (ISBN 0-395-84555-6)

Warner/Tighe, *Major Problems in the History of American Medicine and Public Health,*
2001 (ISBN 0-395-95435-5)

Wilentz, *Major Problems in the Early Republic, 1787–1848,* 1992 (ISBN 0-669-24332-9)